ROUTLEDGE HANDBOOK ON THE UN AND DEVELOPMENT

International commissions, academics, practitioners, and the media have long been critical of the UN's development efforts as disjointed and not fit for purpose; yet the organization has been an essential contributor to progress and peacebuilding.

This handbook explores the activities of the UN development system (UNDS), the largest operational pillar of the organization and arguably the arena in which its ideational endeavors have made the biggest contribution to thinking and standards. Contributions focus on the role of the UNDS in sustainable social, economic, and environmental development, describing how the UNDS interacts with the other major functions of the UN system, and exploring how it performs operationally in the context of the 2030 development agenda focused on the 17 Sustainable Development Goals (SDGs).

The volume is divided into three sections:

- Realizing the SDGs: opportunities and challenges;
- Resources, partnerships, and management; and
- Imagining the future of the UN in development.

Composed of chapters by knowledgeable and authoritative UN experts, this book provides cutting-edge and up-to-date research on the strengths and weaknesses of the UNDS, with each chapter focusing on different operational and ideational aspects.

Stephen Browne is Co-Director of the Future of the UN Development System (FUNDS); Senior Fellow of the Ralph Bunche Institute for International Studies, The Graduate Center, The City University of New York; visiting lecturer at the Graduate Institute, Geneva; and former Deputy Executive Director of the International Trade Centre, Geneva.

Thomas G. Weiss is Presidential Professor of Political Science and Director Emeritus of the Ralph Bunche Institute for International Studies at The City University of New York's Graduate Center; he is also Co-Chair, Cultural Heritage at Risk Project, J. Paul Getty Trust; Distinguished Fellow, Global Governance, The Chicago Council on Global Affairs; and Eminent Scholar, Kyung Hee University, Korea.

ROUTLEDGE HANDBOOK ON THE UN AND DEVELOPMENT

Edited by
Stephen Browne and
Thomas G. Weiss

Routledge
Taylor & Francis Group

LONDON AND NEW YORK

First published 2021
by Routledge
2 Park Square, Milton Park, Abingdon, Oxon OX14 4RN

and by Routledge
52 Vanderbilt Avenue, New York, NY 10017

Routledge is an imprint of the Taylor & Francis Group, an informa business

British Library Cataloguing-in-Publication Data
A catalogue record for this book is available from the British Library

Library of Congress Cataloging-in-Publication Data
Names: Weiss, Thomas G. (Thomas George), 1946- editor. | Browne, Stephen, editor.
Title: Routledge handbook on the UN and development / edited by Stephen Browne and Thomas G. Weiss.
Description: Abingdon, Oxon ; New York, NY : Routledge, 2020. | Includes bibliographical references and index.
Identifiers: LCCN 2020008373 (print) | LCCN 2020008374 (ebook) | ISBN 9780367186852 (hardback) | ISBN 9780429197680 (ebook)
Subjects: LCSH: United Nations–Economic assistance. | United Nations–Management. | Sustainable Development Goals. | Economic development–International cooperation. | Sustainable development–International cooperation. | International organization.
Classification: LCC HC60 .R687 2020 (print) | LCC HC60 (ebook) | DDC 338.91–dc23
LC record available at https://lccn.loc.gov/2020008373
LC ebook record available at https://lccn.loc.gov/2020008374

ISBN: 978-0-367-18685-2 (hbk)
ISBN: 978-0-429-19768-0 (ebk)

Typeset in Bembo
by Wearset Ltd, Boldon, Tyne and Wear

CONTENTS

List of illustrations   *viii*
About the contributors   *x*
Preface and acknowledgments   *xv*
List of abbreviations   *xvii*

Introduction: development, the largest of four UN functions   1
Stephen Browne and Thomas G. Weiss

PART I
Realizing the SDGs: opportunities and challenges   7

1 The UN development system: origins, structure, status   9
   Stephen Browne and Thomas G. Weiss

2 The UN and development: objectives and governance   32
   José Antonio Ocampo

3 Emerging powers, a declining West, and multilateralism   43
   Kishore Mahbubani

4 Environment and development in the UN   56
   Maria Ivanova

5 Gender equality and the United Nations   68
   Saraswathi Menon

6 Human rights and sustainable development: together at last?   80
   Natalie Samarasinghe

7 Sustaining peace and the 2030 development agenda   96
   Sigrid Gruener and Henrik Hammargren

8 Sustaining peace: changing architecture and priorities for UN
   peacebuilding   109
   Gert Rosenthal

9 What does "leave no one behind" mean for humanitarians?   121
   Peter J. Hoffman

10 Migration and development in the UN global compacts   135
    Nicholas R. Micinski

PART II
Resources, partnerships, and management   **149**

11 Funding the UN: support or constraint?   151
    Max-Otto Baumann and Silke Weinlich

12 Private finance and partnerships at the UN   165
    Barbara Adams

13 The "Third UN": civil society and the world organization   184
    Roberto Bissio

14 The UN and the World Bank: collaboration toward stronger global
    governance?   198
    Richard Jolly

15 The WTO, the UN, and the future of global development   210
    Rorden Wilkinson

16 UN accountability: from frameworks to evidence and results   221
    Richard Golding

17 Toward better knowledge management in the UN   235
    Steve Glovinsky

PART III
Imagining the future of the UN in development   **247**

18 Change in the UN development system: theory and practice   249
    John Hendra and Ingrid FitzGerald

Contents

19 Looking to the UN's future   263
    Carsten Staur

20 Reforming the UN and governing the globe   274
    Georgios Kostakos

21 Reflections: prospects for the UN development system   286
    Stephen Browne and Thomas G. Weiss

    Index   *293*

ILLUSTRATIONS

Figures

1.1	UN development system, existing structure	14
3.1	China has become Africa's biggest economic partner	49
3.2	Evolution of regional and country shares of global GDP	51
3.3	Percentage share of world GDP (PPP terms), 1980–2050	51
4.1	Framework for environmental action of the Stockholm Action Plan	57
9.1	Humanitarian aid, 1989–2018 (in $ millions)	127
11.1	Real change over time of funding for UN-OAD, 2002–2017	152
11.2	Multilateral assistance channels of OECD-DAC countries, core and earmarked, 2013 and 2017 (in 2017 constant US$)	155
11.3	Contributions to UNDS	156
12.1	Main groups of funding sources, 2017	175
12.2	Non-state revenue for six UN organizations, 2017	176
16.1	UN accountability framework	222
16.2	Proposed parameters for a Funding Compact	231
17.1	Knowledge management strategies in the UN system, 2007–2020	238

Boxes

1.1	UNDS alphabet soup	13
1.2	Millennium Development Goals	23
1.3	Sustainable Development Goals	24
9.1	Standards and governance for and by the humanitarian sector and donors	122
10.1	Migration in the SDGs	141
10.2	Development in the Global Compact for Migration (GCM)	143
12.1	Appeal to individual giving	172
12.2	Excerpts from UN, *Financing for Development: Progress and Prospects 2018* (New York, 2018)	180
13.1	Escazú agreement: a regional attempt to expand civic space	192
13.2	Recommendations of the UN High Commissioner on Human Rights for the effective engagement of civil society	194

Tables

1.1 Main UN global, ad hoc conferences   21
6.1 The core international human rights instruments   84
12.1 Common set of exclusionary criteria   179

CONTRIBUTORS

The editors

Stephen Browne is Co-Director of the Future of the UN Development System (FUNDS) and Senior Fellow of the Ralph Bunche Institute for International Studies, The Graduate Center, The City University of New York, visiting lecturer at the Graduate Institute, Geneva and former Deputy Executive Director of the International Trade Centre, Geneva. He is the author of several books on development and the UN, including *UN Reform: 75 Years of Challenge and Change* (2019), *Sustainable Development Goals: Seven Decades of UN Goal-setting* (2017), and *The United Nations Development Programme and System* (2011), and co-editor with Thomas G. Weiss of *Post-2015 UN Development: Making Change Happen?* (2014).

Thomas G. Weiss is Presidential Professor of Political Science and Director Emeritus of the Ralph Bunche Institute for International Studies at The City University of New York's Graduate Center; he is also Co-Chair, Cultural Heritage at Risk Project, J. Paul Getty Trust; Distinguished Fellow, Global Governance, The Chicago Council on Global Affairs; and Eminent Scholar, Kyung Hee University, Korea. Previously, he was President of the International Studies Association and its 2016 Distinguished IO Scholar; Andrew Carnegie Fellow; and research director of the International Commission on Intervention and State Sovereignty. His most recent single-authored books include *Would the World Be Better without the UN?* (2018); *What's Wrong with the United Nations and How to Fix It* (2016); *Humanitarian Intervention: Ideas in Action* (2016); *Governing the World? Addressing "Problems without Passports"* (2014); *Global Governance: Why? What? Whither?* (2013); and *Humanitarian Business* (2013).

The contributors

Barbara Adams is President of Global Policy Forum and an adjunct professor at the New School University in New York City focusing on partnership, development, and governance. Trained as an economist, her experience has many facets—as a researcher, teacher, and policy advocate in addition to a long tenure as a UN official. She has authored and co-authored many articles, reports, studies, and books. She is a regular contributor to the Global Policy Watch briefings series that include analyses of partnerships and business sector engagement with the United Nations.

Max-Otto Baumann is Senior Researcher at the German Development Institute/Deutsches Institut für Entwicklungspolitik (DIE), a think tank for global development and international cooperation. Since 2015 he has been a member of the research program on inter- and transnational cooperation. His PhD is from Heidelberg University on the responsibility to protect. He follows the UNDS reform process with a focus on governance, coordination, funding, effectiveness, and North–South relations. In 2016, he was a personal assistant to Klaus Töpfer in his capacity as co-chair of ECOSOC's Independent Team of Advisors.

Roberto Bissio is Executive Director of the Third World Institute, Uruguay, and coordinates the secretariat of Social Watch. He serves as adviser to the Enhancing ICANN Accountability Process. Previously, he was a member of UNDP's Civil Society Advisory Group and has served on the board of the Women's Environment and Development Organization and the Montreal International Forum. As a journalist and columnist, he has written extensively about a range of development issues.

Ingrid FitzGerald has served as the Technical Adviser, Gender and Human Rights, with UNFPA's Asia-Pacific Regional Office, leading its work on gender equality and human rights, gender-based violence, and harmful practices. Previously she served as Special Adviser to the Senior UN Coordinator, "Fit for Purpose," for the 2030 Agenda for Sustainable Development, and as Special Adviser to the UN Women's Deputy Executive Director for Policy and Programme. She was Policy Specialist and Gender Adviser to the UNCT in Vietnam, Gender Adviser to the Cambodian Development Resource Institute, and UNIFEM technical adviser in Cambodia.

Steve Glovinsky is an international development consultant specializing in development and change—how the process of development succeeds or fails in producing positive, sustainable impact. He has four decades of experience in the UN system, primarily with UNDP, as a technical specialist and designer of development programs and projects for some 40 governments and multinational organizations. He was responsible for several initiatives, including introducing knowledge-sharing networks in UNDP, India, and elsewhere.

Richard Golding is a former senior PwC Consulting partner and chartered accountant, where he was its Global Relationship Partner from 2005 to 2012 for the United Nations system, The Global Fund to Fight Aids, Tuberculosis & Malaria, and other multilateral organizations. He is now an independent management consultant on international governance and risk management; a board member for ILRI, one of the largest international agricultural research centers of the CGIAR system; expert adviser to the Board of Unitaid; and part-time Finance Director of The New Humanitarian, providing not-for-profit journalism from the heart of crises.

Sigrid Gruener is Director of Programmes Building and Sustaining Peace, Dag Hammarskjöld Foundation with a focus on peacebuilding, security, and development goals. Prior to joining the Foundation, she worked as a practitioner, trainer, and researcher in the field of development, peacebuilding, and conflict transformation for International Solutions Group, Relief International, and Columbia University's Center for International Conflict Resolution. Her MA in International Affairs is from Columbia University's School of International and Public Affairs.

Henrik Hammargren is Executive Director of the Dag Hammarskjöld Foundation; he spent 25 years in managerial and policy analyst roles, advising bi- and multilateral development cooperation, and serving in the Swedish government and the OECD. With emphases on humanitarian aid, peacebuilding, and support to democracy and human rights, his field experiences were in Eastern, Southern, and Northern Africa and South East Asia. Appointments have included the Chairmanship of the Financing and Aid Architecture of the OECD/DACs Network on Conflict and Fragility (INCAF) and work on developing peace- and state-building goals and compacts for improved aid delivery in fragile states within the International Dialogue on Peacebuilding and State-Building. Hammargren introduced Good Humanitarian Donorship (GHD) at the OECD/DAC.

John Hendra is former UN assistant secretary-general who contributed to major UN change initiatives, including support for the MDGs (now SDGs); establishing UN Women; and the "Delivering as One" Initiative in Vietnam. He headed the UNDG's efforts to help the UNDS become more "fit for purpose" for the 2030 Agenda. In that context, he helped prepare the Secretary-General's two seminal reform reports and substantively supported the intergovernmental negotiations on the repositioning of the UNDS. Previously he served as deputy executive director at UN Women (2011–2014) and as UN Resident Coordinator and UNDP Resident Representative in Vietnam, Tanzania, and Latvia. Hendra earned an MA in Development Studies from the University of Toronto and was a Yale World Fellow. He has published numerous articles on UNDS reform, SDG financing, gender equality, and development effectiveness.

Peter J. Hoffman is Assistant Professor of International Affairs in the Julien J. Studley Graduate Programs in International Affairs at The New School, coordinator for the International Affairs program's Master of Science degree, and faculty supervisor for United Nations Summer Study. He is the author, with Thomas G. Weiss, of *Sword and Salve: Confronting New Wars and Humanitarian Crises* (2006) and of *Humanitarianism, War, and Politics: Solferino to Syria and Beyond* (2017).

Maria Ivanova is Associate Professor of Global Governance at the John W. McCormack Graduate School of Policy and Global Studies at the University of Massachusetts Boston and director of the Center for Governance and Sustainability. She is a member of the Scientific Advisory Board of the UN Secretary-General and a board member of the UN University Institute for the Advanced Study of Sustainability (UNU-IAS); in 2015, she was awarded an Andrew Carnegie fellowship.

Richard Jolly is Honorary Professor and Research Associate of the Institute of Development Studies, University of Sussex. He was UNICEF's Deputy Executive Director (1982–1995), Principal Coordinator and co-author of UNDP's widely acclaimed *Human Development Report* (1996–2000), and co-director of the UN Intellectual History Project (2000–2010). He has written many articles and books on development, including most recently (with Louis Emmerij and Thomas G. Weiss) *UN Ideas That Changed the World* (2009) and *UNICEF: Global Governance That Works* (2014). In 2001, he was knighted for services to the UN and international development.

Georgios Kostakos is Executive Director of the Foundation for Global Governance and Sustainability (FOGGS) based in Brussels. He previously served as Senior Adviser and Acting Deputy Executive Secretary of the UN Secretary-General's High-Level Panel on Global Sustainability, as well as in other positions at UN headquarters in New York, UN field missions, the Hellenic Foundation for European and Foreign Policy, and the University of Athens, and as an external consultant to the European Commission.

Kishore Mahbubani is Distinguished Fellow at the Asia Research Institute, National University of Singapore, where he was the founding Dean of the Lee Kuan Yew School of Public Policy and Professor of Practice (2004–2017). A former permanent representative of Singapore to the UN in New York, he is the author most recently of *The Great Convergence: Asia, the West, and the Logic of One World* (2013), *Has the West Lost It?* (2018), and *Has China Won?* (2020).

Saraswathi Menon was formerly director of the Policy Division of UN Women and director of the UN Development Programme's Evaluation Office. She was a member of the UN Secretary-General's Advisory Group of Experts on Review of Peacebuilding Architecture in 2015.

Nicholas R. Micinski is the ISA James N. Rosenau Postdoctoral Fellow 2019–2020, and a visiting researcher at the Center for the Study of Europe, Boston University, and Royal Holloway, University of London. His research focuses on international cooperation on migration. Previously, he was a research associate at the EU Studies Center in the Ralph Bunche Institute for International Studies and a research associate at FUNDS. He received his MA, MPhil, and PhD from the Graduate Center at The City University of New York, and his BA from Michigan State University.

José Antonio Ocampo is Professor and Member of the Committee on Global Thought at Columbia University, and Chair of the United Nations Committee for Development Policy. He was formerly UN Under-Secretary-General of Economic and Social Affairs, Executive Secretary of the Economic Commission for Latin America and the Caribbean, Minister of Finance and Agriculture, and Director of the National Planning Department of Colombia. His most recent book (with Luis Bértola) is *The Economic Development of Latin America Since Independence* (2012).

Gert Rosenthal is the former permanent representative of Guatemala to the United Nations and foreign minister; earlier he was the executive secretary of the Economic Commission for Latin America and the Caribbean. He is the author, most recently, of *Inside the United Nations: Multilateral Diplomacy Up Close* (2017).

Natalie Samarasinghe is deputy to the Special Adviser on the Preparations for the Commemoration of the 75th Anniversary of the United Nations. She previously served as senior speechwriter to the President of the 73rd Session of the General Assembly while on sabbatical as Executive Director of the United Nations Association-UK, where she led initiatives such as the 1 for 7 Billion campaign that secured changes to the Secretary-General selection process; she co-founded the Together First project on global governance reform. In 2018, the Global Challenges Foundation awarded Samarasinghe for a proposal to open up UN decision-making and delivery to external stakeholders. Previously she worked in local government and the private sector; she has degrees from the University of Oxford and the London School of Economics and Politics.

Carsten Staur is Ambassador of Denmark to the OECD and UNESCO in Paris. Previously he was Ambassador and Permanent Representative of Denmark to the United Nations in New York (2007–2013) and Geneva (2013–2018); State Secretary for Development Cooperation (2001–2007); Under-Secretary (1998–2001); and Ambassador to Israel (1996–1998).

Silke Weinlich is Senior Researcher at the German Development Institute/Deutsches Institut für Entwicklungspolitik (DIE), Bonn, a think tank for global development and international cooperation. She leads a research and policy advice project on the UN development system and its reform needs within the research program on inter- and transnational cooperation. She holds a PhD in political science from Bremen University. Over the last 15 years, she has followed UN reform processes in various policy fields ranging from peacekeeping and peacebuilding to sustainable development. Her current research interests include the reform of the UNDS and broader questions of global governance, multilateral development cooperation, and South–South cooperation.

Rorden Wilkinson is Pro-Vice-Chancellor for Education and the Student Experience and Professor of International Political Economy at the University of New South Wales, Sydney, Australia. His recent books include *What's Wrong with the WTO and How to Fix It* (2014) and *What's the Point of International Relations?* (2017). He and Thomas G. Weiss co-authored *Rethinking Global Governance* (2019) and co-edit the Routledge "Global Institutions Series."

PREFACE AND ACKNOWLEDGMENTS

In the more than three-quarters of a century since its establishment in 1945, the United Nations Organization and the system of universal agencies that form part of the UN system have been central to international relations. This Handbook focuses in particular on the activities related to the world organization's efforts over that time to foster economic and social development, the largest operational pillar of the world organization and arguably the arena in which its ideational endeavors have made the biggest contribution to thinking and standards.

It is the final product in our collaboration since 2010 in a research and advocacy effort, the "Future UN Development System" Project (FUNDS). This volume and our work would not have been possible without generous support from the governments of Sweden, Switzerland, Norway, and Denmark; we are truly grateful. The record of the global surveys, books, articles, and briefing papers is available at www.futureun.org/en. It has been gratifying that the UNDS has taken seriously and considered some of the ideas and recommendations arising from FUNDS.

We were pleased when Rob Sorsby of Taylor & Francis asked us in 2018 about the possibility of pulling together our work. We called upon many colleagues who had contributed to FUNDS but also had to recruit others for topics that had previously not been part of our efforts. Our task was to situate the UNDS's role in helping to realize international achievements that, by the standards of earlier centuries, should be considered unprecedented. While the bitter realities of world politics and perceived conflicts in national economic interests have influenced behavior and prospects over the last 75 years, nonetheless the vision and ambitions of the early years and founding pioneers have never been entirely lost. In documenting the past and looking to the future, we asked contributors to help formulate thoughts about what the project's website aspires to find: "The UN We Want, for the World We Want." The time horizon in looking toward the future is between now and the centennial in 2045—far enough from the present moment to think expansively about desirable change but not so far as to be science fiction.

One of the more agreeable tasks in writing a book is thanking the people who helped along the way. We begin with our partners at the Dag Hammarskjöld Foundation; Henrik Hammargren and Sigrid Gruener not only contributed a chapter to the volume but also co-sponsored the quality-control meeting in Uppsala, Sweden, in November 2019. All the contributors benefited immeasurably from collegial comments at that gathering; the improved content of all chapters is the result. We are thankful for their vote of confidence and contributions as well as for their assigning of Johanna Mårtnendal who handled the logistics impeccably.

The next round of appreciation goes to the contributors themselves whose analyses and prose grace these pages. We contacted what readers will agree is a world-class team. They have all either written extensively on the topic of their essays or been active practitioners in a related field—indeed, the vast majority have done both. Clearly, this Handbook reflects their collective wisdom.

It is no exaggeration to state that we could not have successfully completed a project of this magnitude and complexity without solid staff support. The lion's share of the staff work for the 10 years of FUNDS was accomplished at the Ralph Bunche Institute for International Studies of The Graduate Center of The City University of New York. For this Handbook, we are thankful that Giovanna Kuele, an advanced PhD candidate, helped keep the trains running on time.

The chapters here are independent examinations of the pluses and minuses of many aspects of the UNDS. We speak for all the contributors in specifying that the group consists of critical multilateralists. We have professional voices, who see the need to enhance, not reduce, international cooperation to solve the litany of challenges to human survival with dignity. At the same time, none is a card-carrying member of the UN fan club. The editors and authors do not speak for the United Nations or components of the UNDS. The pages of this book represent our informed thinking, no more and (we hope) no less.

To all who helped make these pages appear, our humble expression of gratitude seems inadequate.

S.B. and T.G.W

Geneva and New York

March 2020

ABBREVIATIONS

3Ts	three types of transfers [in migration and development]
AAAA	Addis Ababa Action Agenda
ACABQ	Advisory Committee on Administrative and Budgetary Questions
ACC	Administrative Committee on Coordination
ACP	African, Caribbean, and Pacific Group of States
AGE	Advisory Group of Experts
AIIB	Asian Infrastructure Investment Bank
ALNAP	Active Learning Network for Accountability and Performance
ASEAN	Association of Southeast Asian Nations
AU	African Union
BCSD	Business Council for Sustainable Development
BCUN	Business Council for the United Nations
BDP	Bureau for Development Policy
BRI	Belt and Road Initiative
BRICS	Brazil, Russia, India, China, and South Africa (Group of)
BWIs	Bretton Woods Institutions
CBD	Convention on Biological Diversity
CEB	Chief Executives Board for Coordination
CEDAW	Convention on the Elimination of all forms of Discrimination Against Women
CEO	chief executive officer
CERD	Committee on the Elimination of Racial Discrimination
CERF	Central Emergency Revolving Fund
CFS	Committee on World Food Security
CHR	Commission on Human Rights
CIA	Central Intelligence Agency (United States)
CONGO	Conference of Non-Governmental Organizations in Consultative Relationship with the United Nations
COP	Conference of the Parties
CPD	Commission on Population and Development
CRRF	Comprehensive Refugee Response Framework
CSD	Commission on Sustainable Development
CSO	civil society organization

CSR	corporate social responsibility
CSW	Commission on the Status of Women
CTC	Centre for Transnational Corporations
DAC	Development Assistance Committee [of the OECD]
DA'ESH	al-Dawla al-Islamiya (also known as ISIL or ISIS)
DaO	Delivering as One
DAW	Division for the Advancement of Women
DCO	Development Coordination Office
DESA	Department of Economic and Social Affairs
DHA	Department of Humanitarian Affairs
DHF	Dag Hammarskjöld Foundation
DIE	Deutsches Institut für Entwicklungspolitik (German Development Institute)
DOCO	Development Operations Coordination Office
DOS	Department of Operational Support
DPA	Department of Political Affairs
DPI	Department of Public Information
DPKO	Department of Peacekeeping Operations
DPO	Department of Peace Operations
DPPA	Department of Political and Peacebuilding Affairs
DRC	Democratic Republic of the Congo
EBFs	extra-budgetary funds
ECA	Economic Commission for Africa
ECE	Economic Commission for Europe
ECLAC	Economic Commission for Latin America and the Caribbean
ECOSOC	Economic and Social Council
EEC	European Economic Community
EFO	Economic and Financial Organization
EOSG	Executive Office of the Secretary-General
EPTA	Expanded Programme of Technical Assistance
ERC	Emergency Relief Coordinator
ERM	Enterprise-wide Risk Management
ESCAP	Economic and Social Commission for Asia and the Pacific
ESCWA	Economic and Social Commission for Western Asia
EU	European Union
FAO	Food and Agriculture Organization
FCV	fragility, conflict, and violence
FDI	foreign direct investment
FENSA	Framework for Engagement with Non-State Actors
FFD	Financing for Development
FOGGS	Foundation for Global Governance and Sustainability
FOGS	Functioning of the GATT System
FOWTO	Functioning of the WTO System
FUNDS	Future UN Development System Project
G-7	Group of Seven
G-8	Group of Eight
G-20	Group of 20
G-77	Group of 77
GAD	gender and development
GATT	General Agreement on Tariffs and Trade
GCIM	Global Commission on International Migration

GDP	gross domestic product
GEAR	Gender Equality Architecture Reform
GFMD	Global Forum on Migration and Development
GHGs	greenhouse gases
GMG	Global Migration Group
GNI	gross national income
GNP	gross national product
GWOT	Global War on Terrorism
HDI	Human Development Index
HDR	Human Development Report
HIV/AIDS	human immunodeficiency virus/acquired immune deficiency syndrome
HLP	High-Level Panel
HLPF	High-Level Political Forum
HRC	Human Rights Council
IAEA	International Atomic Energy Agency
IASC	Inter-Agency Standing Committee
IATI	International Aid Transparency Initiative
IBRD	International Bank for Reconstruction and Development [World Bank]
ICA	international commodity agreement
ICANN	Internet Corporation for Assigned Names and Numbers
ICAO	International Civil Aviation Organization
ICJ	International Court of Justice
ICPD	International Conference on Population and Development
ICRC	International Committee of the Red Cross
iCSO	integrated Civil Society Organizations
IDA	International Development Association
IDP	internally displaced person
IFAD	International Fund for Agricultural Development
IFRC	International Federation of Red Cross and Red Crescent Societies
IGO	intergovernmental organization
IHL	international humanitarian law
IIA	Institute of Internal Auditors
ILC	International Law Commission
ILO	International Labour Organization
ILOAT	Administrative Tribunal of the International Labour Organization
IMF	International Monetary Fund
IMFC	International Monetary and Financial Committee
IMO	International Maritime Organization
INF	Intermediate-Range Nuclear Forces Treaty
INGO	International Nongovernmental Organization
INSTRAW	International Research and Training Institute for the Advancement of Women
IO	international organization
IOM	International Organization for Migration
IPBES	Intergovernmental Science-Policy Platform on Biodiversity and Ecosystem Services
IPCC	Intergovernmental Panel on Climate Change
IPF	indicative planning figure
IPRs	intellectual property rights
IPSAS	International Public Sector Accounting Standards
ISIL	Islamic State of Iraq and the Levant (also known as DA'ESH and ISIS)

ISIS	Islamic State in Iraq and Syria (also known as DA'ESH and ISIL)
ISO	International Organization for Standardization
IT	information technology
ITA	Independent Team of Advisors
ITC	International Trade Centre
ITO	International Trade Organization
ITU	International Telecommunications Union
JIU	Joint Inspection Unit
JSC	Joint Steering Committee to Advance Humanitarian and Development Collaboration
KGB	Committee for State Security
KM	knowledge management
LDC	least developed country
LGBT	lesbian, gay, bi-sexual, and transgender
LIC	low-income country
LNOB	Leave No One Behind
MCO	multi-country office
M–D	migration–development [nexus]
MDG	Millennium Development Goal
MIC	middle-income country
MOPAN	Multilateral Organization Performance Assessment Network
MPTFO	Multi-Partner Trust Fund Office
MSF	Médecins Sans Frontières [Doctors without Borders]
NAM	Non-Aligned Movement
NATO	North Atlantic Treaty Organization
NGLS	Non-Governmental Liaison Service
NGO	nongovernmental organization
NIEO	New International Economic Order
OAD	operational activities for development
OAS	Organization of American States
OAU	Organization of African Unity
OBOR	One Belt and One Road initiative
OCHA	Office for the Coordination of Humanitarian Affairs
ODA	official development assistance
ODI	Overseas Development Institute
OECD	Organisation for Economic Co-operation and Development
OEEC	Organisation for European Economic Co-operation
OHCHR	Office of the High Commissioner for Human Rights
OIOS	Office of Internal Oversight Services
OPEC	Organization of Petroleum Exporting Countries
OPEX	operational and executive personnel
OPS	Office of Project Services
OR	other resources
ORE	other resources emergency
ORR	other resources regular
OSAGI	Office of the Special Adviser on Gender Issues
OUP	Oxford University Press
Oxfam	Oxford Committee for Famine Relief
P-5	five permanent members of the Security Council
PAHO	Pan American Health Organization

PBC	Peacebuilding Commission
PBF	Peacebuilding Fund
PBSO	Peacebuilding Support Office
PEA	political economic analysis
PIKMD	Public Information and Knowledge Management Division
PPP	purchasing power parity
PrepCom	Preparatory Committee
PRSPs	poverty reduction strategy papers
QCPR	Quadrennial Comprehensive Policy Review
R2P	responsibility to protect
RC	resident coordinator
RCP	regional consultative process
RR	resident representative
SBAA	Standard Basic Assistance Agreement
SCO	Shanghai Cooperation Organisation
SDG	Sustainable Development Goal
SDR	Special Drawing Right
SEA	sexual exploitation and abuse
SGBV	sexual and gender-based violence
SIDS	small island developing states
SOP	standard operating procedure
SRSG	special representative of the Secretary-General
TA	technical assistance
TAN	transnational advocacy network
TAP	Transparency, Accountability, and Participation Network
TB	tuberculosis
TNC	transnational corporation
ToC	theory of change
TRIPS	Trade-Related Aspects of Intellectual Property Rights
UDHR	Universal Declaration of Human Rights
UK	United Kingdom of Great Britain and Northern Ireland
UN	United Nations
UNAIDS	United Nations Joint Programme for AIDS
UNCDF	United Nations Capital Development Fund
UNCED	United Nations Conference on Environment and Development
UNCHE	United Nations Conference on the Human Environment
UNCHS	United Nations Centre for Human Settlements [Habitat]
UNCIO	United Nations Conference on International Organization
UNCLOS	United Nations Conference on the Law of the Sea
UNCT	United Nations country team
UNCTAD	United Nations Conference on Trade and Development
UNCTC	United Nations Centre on Transnational Corporations
UNDAF	United Nations Development Assistance Framework
UNDCO	United Nations Development Coordination Office
UNDEF	United Nations Democracy Fund
UNDG	United Nations Development Group
UNDP	United Nations Development Programme
UNDS	United Nations Development System
UNEF	United Nations Emergency Force
UNEG	United Nations Evaluation Group

UNEP	United Nations Environment Programme
UNESCO	United Nations Educational, Scientific and Cultural Organization
UNF	United Nations Foundation
UNFCC	United Nations Framework Convention on Climate Change
UNFIP	United Nations Office for International Partnerships
UNFPA	United Nations Population Fund
UNGC	United Nations Global Compact
UNHCR	[Office of the] United Nations High Commissioner for Refugees
UNICEF	United Nations Children's Fund
UNIDO	United Nations Industrial Development Organization
UNIFEM	United Nations Development Fund for Women
UNIHP	United Nations Intellectual History Project
UNITAR	United Nations Institute for Training and Research
UNODC	United Nations Office of Drugs and Crime
UNOP	United Nations Office for Partnerships
UNOPS	United Nations Office for Project Services
UN-RIAS	United Nations Representatives of Internal Audit Services
UNRRA	United Nations Relief and Rehabilitation Administration
UNRWA	United Nations Relief and Works Agency for Palestine Refugees in the Near East
UNSC	United Nations Statistical Commission
UNSDCF	United Nations Sustainable Development Cooperation Framework
UNSDG	United Nations Sustainable Development Group
UNSO	United Nations Statistical Office
UNU	United Nations University
UNWTO	United Nations World Tourism Organization
UPR	universal periodic review
UPU	Universal Postal Union
US	United States of America
USSR	Union of Soviet Socialist Republics
VNR	voluntary national review
WEF	World Economic Forum
WFP	World Food Programme
WHO	World Health Organization
WHS	World Humanitarian Summit
WID	women in development
WIPO	World Intellectual Property Organization
WMO	World Meteorological Organization
WTO	World Trade Organization
WWI/II	World War I/II

INTRODUCTION

Development, the largest of four UN functions

Stephen Browne and Thomas G. Weiss

The UN development system (UNDS) is a loose configuration of more than 30 largely self-governing organizations, five training and research institutes (including the UN University with more than a dozen of its own academic centers), five functional commissions, five regional economic commissions, and other entities of the United Nations Organization proper. The exact number of the main entities—depending on who is counting and how—is illustrative of the complexity of the system. Headquarters are located in 16 different cities; the total number of field offices numbers more than 1,400 in some 150 countries—and both numbers continue to grow.

The focus for this Handbook is on this dispersed, complex, and often dysfunctional development "family," whose collective expenditures constitute the largest of the four main functions (or pillars) of the UN system's operational and ideational activities—the others are international peace and security; human rights; and humanitarian action. This volume should guide the neophyte and seasoned veteran alike. The UNDS often works side by side with the UN's humanitarian machinery, which is like the UNDS in being mainly field-based. However, most of the humanitarian work is the responsibility of specialist relief organizations, principally the Office of the UN High Commissioner for Refugees (UNHCR), the World Food Programme (WFP), the International Organization for Migration (IOM, part of the UN since 2015), and the UN Relief and Works Agency for Palestine Refugees in the Near East (UNRWA). Some development organizations are also engaged in humanitarian work, especially the UN Children's Fund (UNICEF). Because of the growing volume of funding available for humanitarian action, other formerly development-only organizations are moving in the direction of becoming operational in the humanitarian arena as well.

As this Handbook makes clear, while the four UN pillars (or functions) are defined by different organizational entities with their own governance arrangements and separate staffing and funding, some of the most important work of the UN—and its comparative advantage, in our view—results from operating across its separate pillars. While this book focuses on the work of the UN system in the name of development—which now is often called "sustainable development"—it necessarily also describes how the UNDS interacts with the other major functions of the UN system.

In designing the contents for this volume, we necessarily had to make difficult and subjective judgments about what was essential, and what was less so. Authoritative analysts have written all the chapters; they have solid academic credentials, although many may have also spent large parts of their careers within an international secretariat. Short biographical sketches are in "About the contributors." The UN is distinct from other bureaucracies, but it is also similar in having a vocabulary that makes use of an "alphabet soup" of acronyms; a lengthy guide to key ones for this book appears before this Introduction.

Each chapter has endnotes with numerous citations to key primary and secondary sources. In addition, each chapter concludes with the author's recommended short list of recent published material under "Additional Reading."

Some crucial considerations

The reader may wish to keep in mind seven themes, most of which arise in many chapters or are lurking behind them. One, hinted at earlier, is that the so-called system is a misnomer. Robert Jackson a half-century ago began his 1969 *Capacity Study*'s evaluation of the UNDS by describing it as "becoming slower and more unwieldy like some prehistoric monster."[1] His co-author, and former under-secretary-general Margaret Joan Anstee, lamented that it remained "the 'Bible' of UN reform because its precepts are lauded by everyone but put into effect by no one."[2]

So, decentralization is a built-in element of the UN's structure. From the outset, the UNDS reflected a functionalist logic that recommended the location of specialized topics in specialized, and hence separate, organizational entities. The priorities of funders and the logic of bureaucratic competition have led to fragmentation and a lack of synergy that many contributors lament. Few would dispute that the UN has failed to perform at a level expected of the world organization; that it is "punching below its weight."[3] As one analyst bluntly summarized: "There is no point in mincing words: the UN is a structural monstrosity."[4] It would be foolish to ignore this result, or to exaggerate it. The chapters explain but do not justify fragmentation. They spell out how the system could be made to function better.

Two, this book appears three-quarters of a century into the experiment of the UNDS. That system has grown and evolved substantially. The founding fathers (only a few mothers) would be stunned by many of the institutions and global problems that confront humanity today. Environment and women, for instance, were not visible on the agenda in the early years. However, the UN Environment Programme (UNEP) began in 1972 after the UN Stockholm Conference on the Human Environment, and virtually every member of the UNDS has an environmental section. UN Women became operational in 2010 with the fusion of four smaller entities that had grown up over the years, especially after the first UN Conference on Women in 1976; moreover, ideas and activities now from peace operations to education emphasize the importance of women, girls, and gender. So, the UNDS has not been static but has evolved continually over its history.

Three, this book is about "development" writ large even if the focus is more narrowly on the mechanisms of the UNDS. This orientation means that necessarily some UN-related entities that are separate from the world organization intrude in these pages. Most important for any discussion of development are the World Bank and the International Monetary Fund (IMF); these international financial institutions (IFIs), also called the Bretton Woods institutions (BWIs) because they resulted from the wartime conference at a conference center with that name in New Hampshire, are de jure but not de facto part of the UN. The World Trade Organization (WTO), which is separate from the UN, also is essential to the discussion.

Four, in a related but broader sense, the issues of peace and security, human rights, humanitarian action, and sustainable development are increasingly hard to keep in distinct analytical categories for two reasons. The first is that the UN's peacebuilding mandate in war-torn, transitional, and fragile states has become the world organization's primary operational activity; this task necessarily brings together the UNDS's development expertise along with its security, humanitarian, and human rights capacities. Indeed, the wide range of UN capabilities is a comparative advantage.

The second and most crucial reason for the purposes of this collection of essays is that the 2015 agreement about a universal 2030 Agenda based on the 17 Sustainable Development Goals (SDGs) dominates intergovernmental conversations. While goal-setting is a long-standing asset on the UN's balance sheet, this latest set is far more ambitious and universal. These goals and 169 targets provide a leitmotif across the chapters because they permeate the UNDS in a way that previous goals and targets did not. This laundry list is long, albeit overlooking or shortchanging some essential topics. There is virtually nothing that is not on the UNDS agenda; as Ramesh Thakur has written, "The UN also became the principal international forum for collaborative action in the shared pursuit of the three goals of state-building, nation-building and economic development."[5]

Five, and in a related way, a clear success story of UN history is as the midwife of decolonization; its 193 member states, and counting, are almost four times the 50 present at the April–June 1945 meeting in San Francisco that led to the signing of the UN Charter. Beginning in the late 1940s and gaining speed during the 1950s and 1960s, former colonies formed two coalitions through which they articulated their security and economic interests vis-à-vis the major powers—the Non-Aligned Movement (NAM) and the Group of 77 (G-77). In addition to the East–West rivalry that maintained frigid temperatures during the Cold War, another rigid dichotomy was superimposed on the world map: the North–South divide.

While the East–West split disappeared with the collapse of the Berlin Wall and the implosion of the Soviet Union, the division of the world into rhetorically warring camps representing the North (developed countries) and Global South (developing countries that earlier were called the "Third World") has survived despite its unreality and, dare we say it, irrationality in a globalizing world. Many parts of the UN system, even the most "technical" of organizations such as the World Health Organization (WHO) or the Universal Postal Union (UPU), organize conversations around the simplistic and anachronistic division between the supposedly uniformly affluent North and poor Global South. Seemingly the only way to structure international debates is to organize a joust between the industrialized West (or "North" in UN discourse) and the proverbial "Rest"; this reality is reflected in both the history and current reality of the UNDS.

Six, the discussions about the UNDS and the UN itself go beyond what is typically in many minds about what constitutes the world organization. In one of the early classic textbooks, Inis Claude dubbed member states the "First UN," and he called the executive heads of UN organizations and secretariats the "Second UN." His two-fold distinction, between the world organization as an intergovernmental arena and as an actor,[6] provided the lenses through which analysts of the UN traditionally have peered. However, the in-depth interviews for the United Nations Intellectual History Project (UNIHP) pointed to another dimension. In order to explain the origins and refinement of UN ideas or of the application in operations, additional inputs came from outside the First UN of governments and the Second UN of international civil servants.[7] Throughout these pages too, the Third UN of experts, commissions, think tanks, operational and advocacy nongovernmental organizations (NGOs), the media, and the for-profit sector represents, at many moments, the essential components of "UN" efforts.[8] In the future, "partnerships" have become the favored approach to issues within the United Nations, and so various members of the Third UN undoubtedly will be an even more essential component.

Seven, one issue that reappears throughout many chapters is leadership. The quality of UN leaders, especially but certainly not only the secretary-general, has been the determining factor in the performance, and indeed the relevance, of the world body. Improved leadership at all levels is also central to the origins and outcomes of many recommendations about the future of the UN development system. To state the obvious, people matter: at the top, the middle, and the bottom of the UNDS's organizations. An essential ingredient in many UN successes and failures, of both ideas and operations, consists of initiatives by individuals. The future certainly will require courageous, competent, and charismatic thinkers and doers.

About this book

The Handbook starts with Part I: "Realizing the SDGs: opportunities and challenges." It begins with our own Chapter 1, "The UN development system: origins, structure, status." This first chapter provides an overview of the topic and is essential to understanding the other chapters—key background information is not repeated in individual chapters. While specialists may wish to pick and choose among the remaining chapters, this first one is a prerequisite for better comprehension of how more specific topics fit into three-quarters of a century of UN efforts to foster development. Also essential is Chapter 2, which is José Antonio Ocampo's overview of "The UN and development: objectives and governance." His chapter provides the basis to make a judgment about a basic question that reappears in many subsequent chapters, namely "can the world realize the SDGs?" Chapter 3 completes the initial overview with a provocative partial snapshot of the current tumultuous moment in world politics. Kishore Mahbubani examines some of the most recent sea changes since the UN's founding, namely "Emerging powers, a declining West, and multilateralism."

The two sides of the coin of this first part's subtitle, "Opportunities and challenges," are immediately evident in Chapter 4. Maria Ivanova synthesizes the world body's efforts to address what more and more individuals and governments view as the existential threat of climate change within the overall framework of "Environment and development in the UN." Saraswathi Menon's Chapter 5 follows, "Gender equality and the United Nations." She analyzes the struggle over three-quarters of a century to foster efforts across the UNDS to transform the way that the world organization approaches the challenge and opportunity of gender. Natalie Samarasinghe's Chapter 6 focuses on perhaps the most contested item in the UN's portfolio, "Human rights and sustainable development." Her subtitle suggests a hopeful direction, or unrealized opportunity: "Together at last?"

The next two chapters focus on the pressing topic of "Sustaining peace," another growth industry for the United Nations, which arguably is becoming its main operational orientation. Chapter 7 is "Sustaining peace and the 2030 development agenda." Sigrid Gruener and Henrik Hammargren examine the evolution of the concept and institutional elements as the focus of the importance of UN efforts at realizing the SDGs in fragile countries emerging from armed conflicts or still nurturing war-torn societies. Gert Rosenthal's Chapter 8 follows, "Sustaining peace: changing architecture and priorities for UN peacebuilding." He examines the crucial institutional challenges facing the UN system if it is truly to take advantage of its possible comparative operational advantage in this arena.

The final two chapters in Part I focus on the links between the UNDS and the increasing humanitarian needs of people on the move (refugees, internally displaced persons, and economic migrants) as well as those who may not have moved but are caught in the cross-hairs of violence. In Chapter 9, Peter J. Hoffman examines the puzzling reality of UN efforts in one part of the development arena, namely how to deal with the growth of suffering in countries where development is not even on the agenda: "What does 'leave no one behind' mean for humanitarians?" Yet another acute challenge for the UNDS results from "Migration and development in the UN global compacts," with which Nicholas R. Micinski grapples in Chapter 10.

Part II of this Handbook ambitiously aims to analyze the concrete issues often overlooked even by many specialists exploring the substance of the UN's contribution to development, namely the bread-and-butter issues of "Resources, partnerships, and management." The first two essays examine the crucially important topic of resources. In Chapter 11, Max-Otto Baumann and Silke Weinlich examine the changing patterns of government support, particularly of the growing percentage of tied contributions, for the UNDS in "Funding the UN: support or constraint?" Barbara Adams's Chapter 12 probes an alternative source of support for development that entails other constraints and costs, namely "Private finance and partnerships at the UN."

While development was a principle in the UN Charter and has been a growing and now dominant agenda item, the 2015 agreement on the pursuit of the SDGs has set an ambitious and universal global agenda for all member states and the components of the UNDS for the period ending in 2030. Hence, gauging the problems and prospects for delivering the SDGs relies on a wide range of partners. One of the important changes over time has been the growth in advocacy and operational capacities, which Roberto Bissio details in Chapter 13, "The 'Third UN': civil society and the world organization." The Washington-based international financial institutions (IFIs) are de jure but not de facto part of the UNDS, and Richard Jolly's Chapter 14 probes whether the differences could be bridged for the SDGs. His "The UN and the World Bank" asks "Collaboration toward stronger global governance?" Rorden Wilkinson's Chapter 15 examines another related partner that is outside of the UNDS. He addresses a challenge that has become even greater in the age of new nationalisms, namely "The WTO, the UN, and the future of global development."

The next two chapters examine underlying issues to determine whether we will interpret the end of the path to 2030 as a success or failure. A growing concern of individuals, the media, and member states is the value for money represented by the UNDS, which is analyzed by Richard Golding in Chapter 16, "UN accountability: from frameworks to evidence and results." Chapter 17 explores a low-cost but high-payoff approach used widely in business but haltingly in the UNDS. Steve Glovinsky's "Toward better knowledge management in the UN" examines the potential for this approach through several case studies of success and failure. Both of these chapters are pertinent for improved performance. The vast bulk of expenditures within the UNDS are for personnel; the international civil service is an experiment that began with the League of Nations and its principles require reinforcement.

Part III closes the Handbook by "Imagining the future of the UN in development." Much of the debate about world politics as well as the United Nations revolves around "continuity and change."[9] Chapter 18 examines the efforts at reform that have continued virtually since the ink dried on the signatures of the UN Charter in June 1945. John Hendra and Ingrid FitzGerald probe "Change in the UN development system" by examining what their subtitle contrasts as "Theory and practice." The perennial problem of resource mobilization will not be less important tomorrow than today; Carsten Staur's Chapter 19 puts forward a seasoned multilateral ambassador's ongoing struggle from a sympathetic donor's perspective in "Looking to the UN's future." There follows an alternative parsing of the impact of geopolitics on the current state of multilateralism, the forward-looking and future-oriented analysis by Georgios Kostakos in Chapter 20, "Reforming the UN and governing the globe."

Finally, the Handbook's concluding Chapter 21 contains our "Reflections." It represents our admittedly inadequate effort as editors to synthesize what we have learned from our colleagues' essays as well as from our substantial combined experience as practitioners and observers of the world organization. "Prospects for the UN development system" revisits many of the themes mentioned earlier. In addition, an existential question is obvious for friends and foes of the UN alike: With new nationalisms on the rise and multilateralism of all stripes under siege, is the UNDS still required?

This handbook was in press when the WHO declared the COVID-19 virus a pandemic. In the aftermath of a global economic meltdown comparable to the Great Depression and hundreds of thousands of deaths worldwide, the case for enhanced cooperation across the UN system would seem to be obvious. However, US president Donald Trump's reaction was to threaten the withdrawal of funding from WHO while other nationalist leaders could not see the ramifications of the crisis beyond their own borders. The inability of the United Nations to deal with structural issues has been thrown into sharp relief during this crisis, making the analyses in the following pages even more pertinent.

This volume began as a research contribution for the UN's 75th anniversary in 2020. However, if the answer to that question is "yes"—and we believe that it is—the UN development system certainly will be a dramatically different institution for the 100th anniversary.

NOTES

1 United Nations, *A Capacity Study of the United Nations Development System* (Geneva: UN, 1969), volume I, UN document DP/5, iii.
2 Margaret J. Anstee, "UN Reform: Top of the Agenda for the Next SG?" *FUNDS Briefing #25*, 4 December 2014.
3 Bruce Jenks and Bruce D. Jones, *Punching Below Its Weight: The UN Development System at a Crossroads* (New York: Center for International Cooperation, 2012).
4 Jussi M. Hanhimäki, *The United Nations: A Very Short Introduction* (Oxford: Oxford University Press, 2008), 1. See also Stephen Browne and Thomas G. Weiss, "Is the UN Development System Becoming Irrelevant?" *Development Dialogue Paper no. 4 (December 2013)*, Dag Hammarskjöld Foundation.
5 Ramesh Thakur, "Global Justice and National Interests: How R2P Reconciles the Two Agendas on Atrocity Crimes," *Global Responsibility to Protect* 11, no. 4 (2019): 428.
6 Inis L. Claude Jr., *Swords into Plowshares: The Problems and Prospects of International Organization* (New York: Random House, 1956); and "Peace and Security: Prospective Roles for the Two United Nations," *Global Governance* 2, no. 3 (1996): 289–298.
7 Thomas G. Weiss, Tatiana Carayannis, Richard Jolly, and Louis Emmerij, *UN Voices: The Struggle for Development and Social Justice* (Bloomington, IN: Indiana University Press, 2005). For the capstone book, see Richard Jolly, Louis Emmerij, and Thomas G. Weiss, *UN Ideas That Changed the World* (Bloomington, IN: Indiana University Press, 2009).
8 Thomas G. Weiss, Tatiana Carayannis, and Richard Jolly, "The 'Third' United Nations," *Global Governance* 15, no. 2 (2009): 123–142. See also Tatiana Carayannis and Thomas G. Weiss, *The "Third" United Nations: How Knowledge Brokers Help the UN Think* (Oxford: Oxford University Press, forthcoming).
9 See Thomas G. Weiss and Sam Daws, "The United Nations: Continuity and Change," *The Oxford Handbook on the United Nations*, ed. Weiss and Daws (Oxford: Oxford University Press, 2018), 2nd edn, 3–40; and Thomas G. Weiss and Rorden Wilkinson, "Change and Continuity in Global Governance," *Ethics & International Affairs* 29, no. 4 (2015): 391–395 and 397–406.

PART I

Realizing the SDGs

Opportunities and challenges

1

THE UN DEVELOPMENT SYSTEM

Origins, structure, status

Stephen Browne and Thomas G. Weiss

This first chapter describes where the complex "family" of UN development organizations came from, how it has evolved, and the different functions that it performs. Ideas and operations, the UN's two main outputs, appear throughout and provide the background for the subsequent pages in this Handbook.

The first new organizations

The League of Nations was dissolved in 1946, overlapping the creation of the UN by one year. At the final session of the League's Assembly, one of its founders and ardent defenders, Lord Robert Cecil, uttered his memorable sound bite: "The League of Nations is dead; long live the United Nations."[1] It is striking how many of the supposedly discredited ideas associated with the defunct League reappeared.[2] Leland Goodrich, a member of the US delegation, explained:

> Quite clearly there was a hesitancy in many quarters to call attention to the continuity of the old League and the new United Nations for fear of arousing latent hostilities or creating doubts which might seriously jeopardize the birth and early success of the new organization.[3]

In the development domain especially, the UN could trace its pedigree to the League, which had been preoccupied with the importance of economic, social, and financial cooperation from the 1930s.[4] The influential 1939 report from the former Australian prime minister Stanley Bruce[5] proposed the creation of a Central Committee for Economic and Social Questions, anticipating the creation a few years later of the UN's Economic and Social Council (ECOSOC). The League committee was never created as envisaged, but the Economic and Financial Organization (EFO) continued to discuss the virtues of an "ECOSOC" even after the EFO migrated from its Geneva base to the Institute of Advanced Study at Princeton University. Its new home reflected the continuing interest of the United States in this aspect of the League's work, even though it was not a member. The interest would translate subsequently into a firm US commitment to development in the UN.

The EFO reflected thinking from David Mitrany, a historian and political theorist who had worked for the League and who had written about the "functionalist" approach to international relations.[6] He maintained that international cooperation should concentrate on issues that unite people, keeping the technical separate from the political. Functionalism could be the basis of solutions to international problems faced by the post-war world and also the building blocks for more ambitious multilateralism, or "peace by pieces."

US president Franklin D. Roosevelt himself took a cooperative functionalist approach in calling for international conferences among countries of the new world organization, building upon the "Declaration by United Nations," signed in Washington, DC by 26 (later 44) Allies on 1 January 1942. These conferences led to the establishment of the first of the new agencies. In May 1943, a meeting in Hot Springs, Virginia on cooperation in food security and nutrition led to the creation of the UN's Food and Agriculture Organization (FAO). Later in the same year, the UN Relief and Rehabilitation Agency (UNRRA) was set up to meet the immediate humanitarian needs resulting from the war. The following year saw the convening of the UN Monetary and Financial Conference in Bretton Woods, New Hampshire, which conceived the creation of the International Bank for Reconstruction and Development (IBRD, later the World Bank), the International Monetary Fund (IMF), and the International Trade Organization (ITO). The IBRD and IMF became "specialized agencies" of the UN in name only; they were physically, ideologically, financially, and organizationally distanced from the system. The need for an international organization with the full UN membership governing world trade grew with time. However, the ITO was stillborn because of opposition from the US Congress, which thereby compromised the original vision of the UK's John Maynard Keynes for a triumvirate of economic governance organizations. In its place was a 1948 UN treaty, the General Agreement on Tariffs and Trade (GATT), which was mainly focused on facilitating industrial trade among developed countries; only much later, in 1995, was the World Trade Organization (WTO) born.

More conferences followed, concluding with agreements to establish the International Civil Aviation Organization (ICAO) and the UN Educational, Scientific and Cultural Organization (UNESCO), which opened their doors in 1946 and 1947, respectively, followed in 1948 by the World Health Organization (WHO). These creations were not the first of the UN's specialized agencies. The Treaty of Versailles had created the International Labour Organization (ILO) in 1919. When it met in Philadelphia in 1944, the United States supported its inclusion in the UN as long as its autonomy was preserved.

In the summer of 1944 at a conference in Dumbarton Oaks, Washington, DC, the United States, United Kingdom, Soviet Union, and Republic of China deliberated for seven weeks in order to agree on the design of the future UN. These so-called Washington conversations, chaired by the United States, agreed to several key features of the future world organization, including the principle of the veto for the permanent members of the future Security Council and to the establishment of ECOSOC. The latter's role was to prove crucial for the future UN development system (UNDS). The League's proposed Central Committee was to have had powers to "direct and supervise" the organizations under its aegis. But the authority of the future ECOSOC was watered down substantially. The UN's formal Charter Article 62 was agreed at San Francisco in 1945; it called for the specialized agencies to be "brought into relationship" with the UN; it defined ECOSOC as an intergovernmental body that may only "coordinate the activities of the specialized agencies through consultation."

This formulation had profound implications for an already structurally inchoate UNDS. On the positive side, the UN specialized agencies would enjoy the status and independence for their secretariats to attract the best specialists in their respective fields. On the negative side, their relative autonomy and the absence of an authoritative central overseer with financial leverage encouraged an ever-growing dispersion of interests and proliferation of overlapping mandates and operational duplication. From the UN's earliest days, the need for coordination of the growing development family was evident. One of the first senior appointments to the secretariat was the assistant secretary-general for coordination, Robert Jackson. He received a 1948 letter from the first director-general of FAO and future Nobel laureate, Lord Boyd Orr: "I earnestly hope that you will be able to do what I have been clamouring for in the last two years—bring the heads of the specialized agencies together, and try to get a coordinated drive."[7] Subsequently, the proposals for ECOSOC's reform and the need for an authoritative head of development have permeated the UNDS's history, concerns that all chapters in this book address.

Constant growth

Besides the ILO, other pre-existing international organizations were inducted into the UN family. Its oldest member is the International Telecommunication Union (ITU), founded under a slightly different name and for different technologies in 1865. The Universal Postal Union (UPU) was set up in 1874. In addition to the new post-war creations—FAO, UNESCO, ICAO, and WHO—a succession of additional specialized agencies came into being: the World Meteorological Organization (WMO, 1951), the International Atomic Energy Agency (IAEA, 1957), the International Maritime Organization (IMO, 1958), the World Intellectual Property Organization (WIPO, 1970), the International Fund for Agricultural Development (IFAD, 1977), the UN Industrial Development Organization (UNIDO, 1985), and the most recent of all, the UN World Tourism Organization (UNWTO, 2003). The World Intellectual Property Organization (WIPO), the UN Industrial Development Organization (UNIDO), and the UN World Tourism Organization (UNWTO) existed in slightly different forms before becoming specialized agencies.

Under the auspices of the secretary-general and the UN secretariat, a steady accretion of additional "funds and programs" responded to emerging needs and donor preferences. The early priorities were for humanitarian relief. UNRRA concluded operations in 1947; some of its resources were distributed to the UN International Children's Emergency Fund (now the UN Children's Fund, better known by the original acronym, UNICEF), which came into being in 1946.[8] The United Nations Relief and Works Agency for Palestine Refugees in the Near East (UNRWA) followed in 1949, the UN High Commission for Refugees (UNHCR) in 1951, and the World Food Programme (WFP) in 1963—initially as a joint venture between the UN and FAO. UNWRA, UNHCR, and WFP came to form the core of the UN's humanitarian action, jealously guarding their separate relief mandates. In 2016, the International Organization for Migration (IOM) became part of the UN family. UNICEF is something of a hybrid. Established initially as a relief organization on a temporary basis, it soon took on additional development responsibilities on behalf of children and women and, with the largest field network of all, it has also played a central role in the UNDS.[9]

Most of the new funds and programs had a developmental vocation. Two UN funds for development assistance were established in the 1950s: the Expanded Programme of Technical Assistance (EPTA, 1950) and the Special Fund (1958), which merged in 1965 to form the UN Development Programme (UNDP). Other funds and programs included the UN Conference on Trade and Development (UNCTAD) and the International Trade Centre (ITC) (both 1964), the UN Fund for Population Activities (UNFPA, 1969), the UN Environment Programme (UNEP, 1972), the UN Human Settlements Programme (UN Habitat, 1978), the UN Joint Programme for AIDS (UNAIDS, 1996), the Office for Drugs and Crime (UNODC, 1997), and the UN Entity for Gender Equality and the Empowerment of Women (UN Women, 2010).

All depended on voluntary funding; in most cases, richer member states authorized such in response to perceptions of emerging global needs. A sense of altruism drove the creation of the humanitarian agencies. In the development arena, there were more specific concerns. The creation of UNFPA was motivated by a desire on the part of some developed countries to roll back global population growth. UNEP was the product of rising environmental concerns following the first global UN conference in Stockholm on the subject in 1972; UN Habitat a response to rapid urban development and growing slums; UNAIDS to the growing HIV and AIDS pandemic; and UNODC, a continuation of the war against drugs and crime. The advent of UN Women in 2010 was, like UNDP and UNODC, the result of a merger; in this case, of four pre-existing entities. Combining UN organizations was a welcome but virtually unprecedented rollback from a continuing pattern of proliferation in the UNDS; duplication and competition remain the dominant characteristic.

The impetus for the creation of two organizations of the UNDS came mainly from developing countries. Early on, UNIDO began as a UN program within the secretariat and later was transformed into a specialized agency at the behest of the Global South seeking support for their manufacturing aspirations. Its protracted genesis was controversial for many developed countries; in recent years, they have withdrawn, purportedly harboring ideological misgivings about the role of a public sector organization in promoting industrialization.[10] With the failure of the ITO after Bretton Woods, UNCTAD and ITC helped to fill the absence of a trade negotiating forum for commodity producers, a need that became especially acute as evidence grew of the tendency for their terms of trade to deteriorate in the long term. UNIDO and UNCTAD, in particular, reflected the widely disparate views on most policy issues throughout the UNDS; the central cleavage was between industrialized countries of the North and developing countries of the Global South about how best to accelerate development.

Five other organizations of the family were inspired by emerging country interests: the five regional commissions. In response to a request by Poland, the Economic Commission for Europe (UNECE) began in Geneva in 1947, and was intended as a mechanism to facilitate the post-war reconstruction of Europe. The following year, the United States launched the Marshall Plan and invited the European countries to come up with their own plans for disbursing the considerable sums proposed as aid for reconstruction. Instead of the UNECE, however, the European governments created the Organization for European Economic Co-operation (OEEC) in Paris. The decision effectively weakened the UNECE, which continued as a forum for research and exchange among the wider European region.[11] Two more regional commissions were created: the Economic Commission for Asia and the Far East (ECAFE, later ESCAP, the Economic and Social Commission for Asia and the Pacific) in 1949 and the Economic Commission for Latin America (ECLA, later ECLAC with the addition of "and the Caribbean") in 1948. Both cases reflected an expectation that they could become conduits for regional aid, but funding on the necessary scale never materialized. Then, on the principle of not-three-without-five, UN regional commissions were duly set up in Africa (ECA, 1958) and West Asia (ESCWA, 1974). They have acted as forums for ideas and exchange, and later took on the implementation of technical assistance projects, but the five commissions have constantly sought clearer roles within the larger UN family. They have overlapping interests with the regional structures of other UN organizations[12] and coexist in their regions with many other more focused regional and sub-regional intergovernmental bodies and banks. A simplified organigram of the UNDS is shown in Figure 1.1, and a list of acronyms figures in Box 1.1.

Box 1.1 UNDS alphabet soup

		Seat (start–up year)
Special funds and programs		
UNDP	UN Development Programme	New York (1966)
UNICEF	UN Children's Fund	New York (1946)
WFP	World Food Programme	Rome (1963)
UNFPA	UN Population Fund	New York (1969)
UNCTAD	UN Conference on Trade and Development	Geneva (1964)
ITC	International Trade Centre	Geneva (1964)
UNEP	UN Environment Programme	Nairobi (1972)
UN Habitat	Human Settlements	Nairobi (1978)
UNAIDS	UN Joint Programme on HIV and AIDS	Geneva (1996)
UNEGEEW	UN Women	New York (2010)
UN Secretariat		
UNDESA	UN Department of Economic and Social Affairs	New York (1945)
UNODC	UN Office of Drugs and Crime	Vienna (1997)*
UNOPS	UN Office of Project Services	Copenhagen (1973)
Regional commissions		
ECA	Economic Commission for Africa	Addis Ababa (1958)
ECE	Economic Commission for Europe	Geneva (1947)
ECLAC	Economic Commission for Latin America and Caribbean	Santiago (1948)
ESCAP	Economic and Social Commission for Asia and Pacific	Bangkok (1949)
ESCWA	Economic and Social Commission for W. Asia	Beirut (1974)
Specialized agencies		
ILO	International Labour Organization	Geneva (1919)
FAO	Food and Agriculture Organization of the UN	Rome (1945)
UNESCO	UN Educational, Scientific and Cultural Organization	Paris (1945)
WHO	World Health Organization	Geneva (1948)*
UNIDO	UN Industrial Development Organization	Vienna (1985)#
IFAD	International Fund for Agricultural Development	Rome (1977)
UNWTO	UN World Tourism Organization	Madrid (2003)*#
ICAO	International Civil Aviation Organization	Montreal (1945)
IMO	International Maritime Organization	London (1958)*
ITU	International Telecommunication Union	Geneva (1865)*
UPU	Universal Postal Union	Berne (1874)
WMO	World Meteorological Organization	Geneva (1951)
WIPO	World Intellectual Property Organization	Geneva (1970)*
IAEA	International Atomic Energy Agency	Vienna (1957)

Training and research organizations

UNITAR	Training and research
UNICRI	Crime and justice research
UNIDIR	Disarmament research
UNRISD	Social development
UNU	UN University

Functional commissions

Sustainable development
Narcotic drugs
Crime prevention
Science and technology
Status of women
Population and development
Social development
Statistics

\# date of joining UN as specialized agency
* different name/status prior to UN

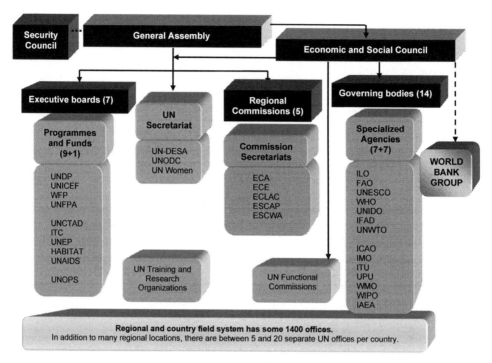

Figure 1.1 UN development system, existing structure.

The UN approach to "development"

The elaborate organizational infrastructure that became the UNDS was created in the name of international cooperation. Charter Article 1 stated that one of the purposes of the UN was "to achieve international cooperation in solving international problems of an economic, social, cultural ... character." In Charter Chapter IX, "International Economic and Social Cooperation," the UN would promote "conditions of economic and social progress and development." While the creation of the UN was driven by the post-war necessity to maintain peace and security, the operational *Zeitgeist* of the new organization increasingly became international cooperation, especially after the Cold War paralyzed the Security Council.

The notions of international cooperation begat the epistemological bases of the specialized agencies and the funds and programs that followed. Promoting these "conditions of economic and social progress" was the technical logic driving the UNDS. Augmented by the later addition of the environment, for which the word "sustainable" is the established surrogate, the UN development agenda reflects a tri-sectoral approach. The 2030 Agenda, which states agreed in 2015, is the latest example and itself defines the current scope of UN development aspirations.

For the sake of analytical clarity, this section parses the economic, social, and environmental components of development. First, however, it is useful to keep in mind that such categories are fluid. While the notion of "development" has long dominated UNDS discourse and practice, the term means different things to different people at different moments; it has also been contested on many levels. The historical evolution of the UN's development work has taken place in the context of changing theories of development as well as clashes between the views of developing and developed countries. UNCTAD's former secretary-general Kenneth Dadzie thought that the world organization's work could most usefully be examined across four phases, which also reflected the evolution of economic thought since World War II.[13] They were: 1945–1962, national state capitalism; 1962–1981, international affirmative action; 1981–1989, return to neoliberalism; and 1989–today, globalization and sustainable development.[14]

Economic development

In the early days of the UN, development was equated with economic progress. The term economic development was already of long date, at least since Schumpeter in the early part of the century,[15] but it was being conceived as a transitive process, rather than an intransitive concept. Economies in a state of "under-development" could be transformed with the appropriate stimuli.[16] The UN Secretariat produced several reports on economic development, and the UN General Assembly passed key resolutions 198 (III) and 200 (III) on the subject. More creative thinking was to come from the UN over the next few years from experts in and around the UN based mainly in New York, Geneva, and Santiago.[17]

Two themes, in particular, dominated debates. First, capital was pre-eminent: its investment would help to redress the imbalance between the developed and "under-developed" worlds by fueling economic growth through industrialization.[18] There was some irony in the insistence by the UN specialists on the primacy of capital and their urging of the new World Bank to provide concessional loans, about which it was initially reluctant. After the Bank's International Development Association (IDA) was created in 1959 to disburse "soft loans," the Bank became the largest provider of aid almost overnight, accompanied by a heftier voice in multilateral policy space based on its financial clout. There was no more distinctive example of money talking. From the 1960s, the UN and the World Bank became implacable development rivals for the attention of the Global South, made sharper by the Bank's own expanding programs of technical assistance.

Second, UN pioneering thinkers emphasized another prominent theme, the crisis of unequal exchange in international trade. Developing countries, principally raw material and commodity exporters, were facing growing difficulties in closing their external payments gaps—and meeting one of the fundamental prerequisites for lending by the Bretton Woods institutions (BWIs). Over the long run, their export prices fell, or rose more slowly than the prices of their industrial imports. The GATT held relatively modest benefits for developing countries; but it recognized the importance of the terms–of–trade argument.[19] Developing countries faced protectionism. For instance, the GATT's 1962 Multi-Fiber Arrangement imposed quantitative restrictions on imports of cotton textiles, which were the foundation of infant manufacturing sectors. The earlier formation of the European Economic Community (EEC) and its common agriculture policy erected high barriers to the import of some primary commodities from developing countries. Even while global trade was expanding rapidly, developing countries were losing ground. Between 1950 and 1962, their share shrank from 32 to 21 percent. In 1962, their collective trade deficit was estimated to be $2.3 billion for trade in goods and $3.3 billion for services, and the gap was continuing to widen.[20]

These concerns led directly to the creation of UNCTAD, as a forum for the negotiation of more favorable trade terms, and a fairer global economic balance. UNCTAD's early success was the Generalized System of Preferences (GSP) in 1968, allowing preferential access of developing country exports of manufactures to developed countries on a non-reciprocal basis. It was a step forward, even though the GSP largely reflected US and EEC rules and exemptions. UNCTAD sought to ameliorate conditions for developing countries on two other fronts. Its call for more sources of liquidity led to the establishment of the IMF's Special Drawing Rights (SDRs) in 1967. Its commodity policy, designed to limit the deterioration in terms of trade through the creation of managed buffer stocks, was initially less successful. Developed countries were circumspect about these International Commodity Agreements (ICAs) that, despite their own protectionist measures, entailed undue market interference.

The 1970s gave a boost to ICAs. The decade saw a collapse in the prices of many commodities along with the spectacular demonstration of the power of cartels with the restriction in the production of oil by the Organization of Petroleum Exporting Countries (OPEC). Oil prices rose fourfold in 1973–1974 and by almost the same in 1979–1980. OPEC's success swelled the ambitions of developing countries to alter the balance of benefits from growth in the world economy.

A General Assembly special session the following year agreed—over the reluctance of many industrialized countries—a "new international economic order." The NIEO proved a high water-mark for debates about restructuring the global economy, and some benefits resulted. ICAs were established for seven commodities initially and discussions began on establishing a Common Fund for Commodities (CFC) to finance stocks, but it was not until 1989 that governments agreed to establish the CFC in Amsterdam. Another important upshot of new-found OPEC wealth was an increase in Arab development assistance which, among other consequences, led in 1977 to the UN's International Fund for Agricultural Development (IFAD), which represented a welcome departure from the UN's almost exclusive reliance on developed country funding.[21]

The NIEO debate receded quickly after 1974; by the 1980s, the governments of the most powerful developed countries (notably, the United States, Germany, and United Kingdom) actively pursued a neoliberal agenda, labeled "the Washington consensus."[22] Structural adjustment was the approved economic medicine administered to the poorest developing countries, although these programs caused hardship in some because of cuts in public spending. The UN was no longer the locus for economic and financial debates. When the Asian financial crisis boiled over in the late 1990s, and during the global financial meltdown a decade later, industrialized countries steered discussions away from the UN, including ECOSOC, which had originally been established for the express purpose of addressing such global challenges. In the 2000s, the search for solutions went outside of the UN's universal membership to the smaller Group of 20 (G-20).

The endgame for trade came in 1995, when the WTO absorbed the GATT and expanded the global trade agenda to include the primary sector, which was of particular interest to developing countries. With its rapidly growing membership from the Global South, the WTO is formally outside the UNDS but has become the main international trade forum, supplanting UNCTAD, which became mainly a research organization with a small program of technical assistance.

Social development

If the UN became progressively marginalized in the economic realm, it remained active in thinking about the quality of growth and development. The ILO had long been venerated as the proponent of full employment and helped to refine the economic debate by proposing that growth be more people-centered. Its earlier "basic needs approach"[23] focused on ensuring welfare as one of the fruits of economic growth, including the provision of food, education, health, and shelter. The approach inspired discussion on "another development,"[24] which gave priority to the eradication of poverty, a theme not adopted until the 1990s by the World Bank. The ILO's work helped to link the economics of growth to the later conception of human development.

Other organizations in the UNDS were the sources of a substantial body of thinking and advocacy on aspects of social development. UNICEF was awarded the Nobel Peace Prize in 1965 as an early exponent of child and maternal protection. Both the ECA and UNESCO undertook research on the roles of women in development from the 1960s. The International Research and Training Institute for the Advancement of Women (INSTRAW) was established in 1980 in Santo Domingo, Dominican Republic,[25] and the UN Secretariat's Statistics Division has been producing data in *The World's Women* every five years.[26] The rights of women have been championed through research and advocacy by UNICEF, UNFPA, and, since 2010, UN Women; many other UN organizations have programs on gender in development.

The UN has always given priority to children and education, especially at primary level. UNICEF has invariably attached importance to the well-being and rights of children in every country, North and South, and produces the annual *State of the World's Children*. In 1989, at UNICEF's instigation, the General Assembly approved the Convention of the Rights of the Child, which has been more widely ratified than any other treaty. UNESCO, as its name suggests, was established as the principal UN education agency and is another key source of data through its annual monitoring reports. UNICEF, UNESCO, UNFPA, and ILO have all helped to establish education as a basic right, set standards and goals, and develop policy guidelines.[27]

UNESCO is also an agency of science and culture and was initially associated with many renowned idealistic thinkers. In the domain of culture, it is still best known for its designation of World Heritage Sites. But in the 1970s, encouraged by the Non–Aligned Movement (NAM, a forum of some 130 developing countries), UNESCO became critical of the Western media and of negative portrayals of events in the Global South, calling for more state control over information. The result was the proposed New World Information and Communication Order (NWICO), which incited two of the earliest UNESCO champions, the United States and United Kingdom, to withdraw from the organization.[28] Both countries subsequently rejoined, but Washington again withdrew in 2019 when UNESCO agreed to admit Palestine as a member.

With education, the health domain is regularly judged the most relevant and effective sector of UN activity.[29] The main standard-bearer is WHO, which is acknowledged as the global authority for health norms and at the forefront of campaigns against pandemics. In 1981, it defined "health for all by 2000" as a combination of nutrition, hygiene, and education norms, leading to the adoption by the General Assembly in resolution 36/43 of a global strategy in the same year. WHO combined with UNICEF and FAO to form the Committee on World Food Security (CFS) in 1974, as a policy advisory body on the production and means of access to food and the Standing Committee on Nutrition (SCN), which make periodic assessments of global nutritional performance.

Population and demography have also been a focus of UN thinking and research. Over the UN's 75-year history, the world population has more than tripled to some 7.5 billion people, which reflects better medical care, falling infant and child mortality, and rising life expectancy. The population aged over 60 has grown to 900 million.[30] The subject has always courted controversy. Earlier environmentalists used Malthusian arguments about the dangers of over-population to draw attention to problems of the carrying capacity of the planet, but dire predictions of mass famine have not materialized. More controversial have been measures of population control. Methods of birth control have proved to be relatively ineffective (as compared with female access to education) and religious dogma has often clashed with human rights in UN debates. Humane methods of control are consistent with the rights of families to choose the numbers of their offspring, but references to "reproductive health" have often been opposed by the Holy See, speaking for Catholics worldwide, by some Islamic states, and by the US government during periods of Republican Party ascendancy. UNFPA has often been a victim of these onslaughts; Washington, for example, withdrew all voluntary funding in 2017—about a quarter of the budget—on the unsubstantiated grounds that the organization supports programs of abortion.

Information and research on population are key functions of the UN Population Division (part of DESA), which is the most authoritative reference on demographic data. This role began with its publication of global population size, growth, and projections in the 1950s and has continued to the present day.

Environment and sustainability

Environmental considerations have become the most recent addition to the prevailing UN framework of ideational and operational roles. Early thinking can be traced to the 1970s when several developed countries became preoccupied with the health and sustainability of the human environment and natural resources. In 1971, a group of UN experts met in Founex, a Swiss village near Geneva, to draw up plans for a global conference, needing to convince some skeptical minds in developing countries about the compatibility of sound environmental management and development.[31] The 1972 Stockholm conference led to the establishment of UNEP and many national ministries of the environment. Ten years later, the UN passed the Convention of the Law of the Sea (UNCLOS), which established geographical jurisdictions over marine resources and drew up guidelines for their protection. In 1987, a report was published by the World Commission on Environment and Development, *Our Common Future*, which advocated "sustainable development" as a means of meeting the needs of the present without compromising the capacity to meet the needs of the future.[32]

By the 1980s, a sense of alarm was beginning to color environmental considerations. Scientists found evidence of ozone depletion over the North and South poles, which threatened humans and livestock through exposure to excessive ultraviolet radiation from the sun. The cause was determined to be the use of organic halogen compounds called chlorofluorocarbons (CFCs) used in refrigeration and cooling systems that had drifted into the upper atmosphere. In 1985, the UN's Vienna Convention on ozone-depleting substances (ODSs) led to the Montreal Protocol, which committed signatories to phasing out CFCs and their replacements with more benign alternatives. These agreements were successful in reducing the emission of ODSs and enhanced the credibility of the UN as a forum for addressing environmental crises.

In 1988, UNEP and WMO established the Intergovernmental Panel on Climate Change (IPCC), a high-profile collaboration between the UN and the scientific community. The IPCC assesses the causes and impact of climate change, publishing reports based on available scientific research worldwide. In its second campaign to prevent irreversible damage to the planet, the UN drew up the Framework Convention on Climate Change (UNFCCC), which negotiated the Kyoto Protocol in 1997. This agreement was the first to commit industrialized countries on a voluntary basis to reductions in the emissions of carbon dioxide and other so-called greenhouse gases (GHGs), factors in global warming. With the global economy so dependent on hydrocarbons, however, many member states have been slow to take action to reduce emissions. Nevertheless, successive IPCC reports have added to the urgency, and the damaging consequences of global warming have come to be more clearly perceived, inciting civil society to demand governments to act. A heightened sense of crisis at the 21st session of the UNFCCC Conference of the Parties in Paris in 2015, and again in 2018, led to a stronger voluntary commitment by governments to emissions reductions.

Other existential threats to the planet have been a UNDS concern. The UN's Convention on Biological Diversity (CBD) dates from 1993 and emerged from the second Earth Summit of the previous year. In 2012, the UN again brought science to bear on the problem supporting the creation of the Intergovernmental Science-Policy Platform on Biodiversity and Ecosystem Services (IPBES). In 2019, the latest assessment of biodiversity by IPBES determined that up to 1 million different species of animals and plants were at risk of extinction as a result of human action.[33]

Compliance is the largest item missing from the UN's toolbox and perhaps the most substantial gap in the contemporary architecture of global governance.[34] While it has no power to enforce its recommendations on saving the planet, the UN's work in the environmental domain reveals the best of the world body as a multilateral forum that incorporates the complexity of actors. In particular, the "three UNs" are fully in play and essential to understanding the dynamics of ideas and norms.[35] The Second UN of secretariats facilitates international agreements among the First UN of member states and urges action based on expert analysis. Involving the Third UN of civil society organizations in negotiations gives added weight to its recommendations and provides support and legitimacy to their advocacy. The "Earth Summit" (also called "Rio+20") in 2012 was used to launch the debate on the 2030 UN development agenda and guaranteed that considerations of sustainability were fully reflected in the resulting goals.

Human development: an integrating framework

The respective interests of the constituent organizations of the UNDS have influenced the three-fold sectoral framing of the UN's development agenda—economic, social, and environmental—while helping to reinforce the technical nature of the development pillar. In parallel, a genuinely new paradigm emerged from within the UNDS in the 1990s. UNDP was the main operational arm of the system, defined mainly by the totality of its myriad activities, but lacking a cohesive substantive focus. In 1989, the UNDP's administrator, William H. Draper, sought a stronger and more specific identity for the organization. In this quest, he hired the influential Pakistani economist Mahbub ul Haq, who had worked in the World Bank and had impressed Draper with his vision for new thinking on the human condition. There were intellectual antecedents in the UN for a more people-centered approach to development. The ILO had highlighted the importance of meeting basic needs and in the 1980s, UNICEF and ECA had published research on development with a "human face,"[36] partly as a riposte to the World Bank's structural adjustment programs that stressed neoliberal solutions. Ul Haq attracted other thinkers to the task, including most notably future Nobel laureate Amartya Sen who had pioneered the concept of the agency of the individual and of human freedom.[37]

In 1990, the first *Human Development Report* outlined the elements of what would become a new paradigm. At the center were the concerns of each individual, and development progress was to be measured by advances in human capabilities and the expansion of individual choices, which were both inherent and externally determined. Development advanced, in other words, when people from the poorest upwards gained choices and control over their destinies and those of their families. The paradigm was holistic and integrating because it encompassed all aspects of existence, bringing together considerations of needs satisfaction, individual rights, and security.[38] Ul Haq described human development as follows:

The basic purpose of development is to enlarge people's choices. In principle, these choices can be infinite and can change over time. People often value achievements that do not show up at all, or not immediately, in income and growth figures: greater access to knowledge, better nutrition and health services, more secure livelihoods, security against crime and physical violence, satisfying leisure hours, political and cultural freedoms and a sense of participation in community activities. The objective of development is to create an enabling environment for people to enjoy long, healthy and creative lives.[39]

Since 1990, UNDP has published *Human Development Reports* (HDRs) annually, each elaborating different aspects of the new approach. UNDP began to brand itself as the sustainable human development organization. The reports became the most widely read of UN research products, assisted by well-orchestrated launch campaigns and published in the early years by one of the world's best academic publishers, Oxford University Press. Each used a rough surrogate for measuring human development by combining income per capita, education, and longevity. These reports, together with the refinement of various human development indicators and indices (HDIs), broke new ground for the UN. They directly compared country performances, with the clear implication that governments themselves bore the main responsibility for progress or stagnation.

For the UNDS, the real significance of the paradigm was that it crossed the rigid boundaries of development, human rights, and human security, each of which was contained in an institutionally separate pillar of UN activity. Human development was also more closely attuned than tri-sectoral "sustainable development" to the original spirit of the UN Charter whose preamble referred to "fundamental human rights ... the dignity and worth of the human person" and the promotion of "social progress and better standards of life in larger freedom." Yet the UNDS essentially shunned the new approach. In 1995, five years after the appearance of the paradigm, the UN held two major development conferences: in Copenhagen on social development and in Beijing on women in development—see the listing in Table 1.1.[40] The outcome report of the first, the *Declaration on Social Development*, agreed to "place people at the centre of development"[41] but failed to mention human development in any of its 134 pages. For the Beijing conference, UNDP had prepared a special HDR on the role of women in development—each annual installment chose a different focus. However, the final document contained just two references to human development. Although publishing regional and country HDRs in addition to the global version, the concept has neither been mainstreamed nor given a clear operational mandate for UNDP staff. Human development was gradually downplayed, eventually disappearing even from the home page of the UNDP website. The unifying paradigm therefore came and went, leaving the top-down technical approach to development to prevail in the UNDS.

UN goals and global conferences

In order to be implemented, an agenda requires specific objectives, or goals, to provide a concrete means of assessing progress. UN goal-setting began in earnest in the 1960s with the declaration of the first UN Development Decade, a proposal inspired not by the UN secretariat, but by then US president John F. Kennedy. Over 10 years, the declaration established the goal of 5 percent real annual average economic growth for developing countries and an expansion of their commodity exports. It also called for an increase by the end of the decade in the transfer of financial resources from North to South, including foreign direct investment, amounting to 1 percent of the combined

Table 1.1 Main UN global, ad hoc conferences[1]

Decade	Year	Conferences
2010s (8)	2016	Human Settlements 3, Humanitarian Relief
	2015	Climate Change, Sustainable Development Goals, Financing for Development 3
	2012	Sustainable Development 4
	2011	LDCs 4
	2010	Millennium Development Goals 3
2000s (16)	2009	Racism 4
	2008	Financing for Development 2
	2005	Millennium Development Goals 2, Information Society 2, Women 5
	2004	Small Islands 2
	2003	Information Society 1
	2002	Financing for Development 1, Sustainable Development 3, Ageing 2, Children 2
	2001	LDCs 3, HIV/AIDS, Racism 3
	2000	Millennium Summit—Millennium Development Goals 1, Education 2
1990s (12)		
	1996	Food 2, Human Settlements 2
	1995	Women 4, Social Development
	1994	Population 5, Small Islands 1
	1993	Human Rights 2
	1992	Sustainable Development 2, Nutrition
	1990	Education 1, Children 1, LDCs 2
1980s (7)		
	1985	Women 3
	1984	Population 4
	1983	Racism 2
	1982	Ageing 1
	1981	LDCs 1, Renewable Energy
	1980	Women 2
1970s (10)	1979	Science and Technology
	1978	Primary Health Care, Racism 1
	1977	Water, Desertification
	1976	Human Settlements 1
	1975	Women 1
	1974	Food, Population 3
	1972	Sustainable Development 1
1960s (2)	1968	Human Rights 1
	1965	Population 2 (second population conference)
1950s (1)	1954	Population 1

Note
1 Stephen Browne, *Sustainable Development Goals and UN Goal-Setting* (London: Routledge, 2017). The list excludes the 14 UNCTAD conferences.

national income of developed countries. It was typical of contemporary thinking to link economic growth to flows of external finance; the relationship has continued to underpin thinking about development in the UN. When the decade ended, the growth target had been achieved when averaged out across all developing countries, but the financial target had fallen short. The target was then refined to 0.7 percent of developed country income in the form of official development assistance (ODA). This target continues as a measure of donor generosity:

After much discussion and background analysis, the UN's Second Development Decade began in 1970, raising the annual economic growth target to 6 percent. The ODA ratio began at 0.36 percent, and thus the aim was to double it. By the end of the decade, the average growth rate was above 5 percent but below the target. The Group of 77 (G-77) developing countries blamed the poor growth performance of many poorer countries on insufficient ODA, which had only attained 0.38 percent, on average.[42] The decade had unfolded against the backdrop of the heated debate on the NIEO, and many interpreted the ODA "shortfall" as a failure of developed countries to respect their international obligations.

During the Third and Fourth Development Decades, further declines occurred in the growth performances of developing countries and in the aid ratio. However, it was only the beginning of UN goal-setting. For instance, in 1982 UNICEF adopted and then promoted and supported worldwide a goal for reducing child mortality by 1990. Goals became a central feature of the growing number of global, ad hoc conferences that the UN convened on different development concerns (see Table 1.1).

Actions toward this goal were widely achieved and led to the first Global Summit held in the UN in September 1990 attended by 71 heads of state and a total of 159 countries.[43] Earlier in 1990, UNESCO, UNICEF, UNDP, and the World Bank had co-sponsored a major conference in Thailand on education; its declaration called for the attainment of universal primary education and halving the adult illiteracy rate by 2000. The declaration of the World Summit for Children added more goals, to be achieved by 2000, including reductions in under-5 and maternal mortality rates and universal access to safe drinking water and sanitation.[44] As important as the goals themselves was the resolve of UNICEF and UNESCO to begin monitoring progress toward them. Embarrassment, or naming and shaming, is an important measure, along with political and public mobilization and direct support.

Governments attended an even larger world summit in 2000 to mark the turn of the millennium. Many observers interpret it as a turning point for the UN's development cause. The summit came at the end of the Fourth Development Decade, which had been particularly unfavorable for the poorest countries. Their indebtedness, particularly to the BWIs, had risen; moreover, ODA had declined. A civil society campaign urged debt cancelation. The World Bank and IMF were obliged to devise a new set of short-term conditionalities (the "poverty reduction strategy papers," PRSPs) to enable the most indebted countries to be bailed out with bilateral assistance. In parallel, however, the UN established a set of goals with a more realistic timeframe than the short-term adjustments required by the PRSPs. The Millennium Development Goals (MDGs) are listed in Box 1.2; they consolidated those that various UN global conferences had agreed in the 1990s; they used 1990 as the base with goals to be achieved over a quarter-century, by 2015. The outcome document, the Millennium Declaration, was a comprehensive declaration of intent, signed by the then unprecedented number of 149 heads of state and government, covering all aspects of UN responsibilities across its operational pillars—international peace and security; human rights; humanitarian action; and sustainable development. Embedded within were the seven MDGs that reflected the basic human needs of poverty reduction, health, and education, with an oblique nod to environment. An eighth MDG on partnerships was added later to acknowledge the responsibilities of the industrialized countries in respect of trade, aid, and other measures.

Box 1.2 Millennium Development Goals

Goal 1: Eradicate extreme poverty and hunger

Goal 2: Achieve universal primary education

Goal 3: Promote gender equality and empower women

Goal 4: Reduce child mortality

Goal 5: Improve maternal health

Goal 6: Combat HIV/AIDS, malaria, and other diseases

Goal 7: Ensure environmental sustainability

Goal 8: Develop a global partnership for development

This MDG agenda was slow to get off the ground. The UN Secretariat initially treated the Millennium Declaration as if mere declamation were sufficient. A roadmap was promised in 2001, but at first there was no concerted campaign to publicize the effort. The UN's funds and programs, as the main sources of the goals, were on board and took responsibility for extracting the MDGs from the Millennium Declaration. However, there was virtual indifference among most specialized agencies—again, the "S" in UNDS was missing. Meanwhile, donors were more enthusiastic about and fully committed to the Washington Consensus and the PRSPs.

Nonetheless, the MDGs gradually gained prominence. In 2002 at the UN's first Financing for Development meeting in Monterrey, Mexico, a bargain emerged whereby developing countries would seek to meet the first seven MDGs, while the developed countries would ease trade restrictions and provide more ODA (MDG 8). The bargain did not stick, but some countries directed their attention to meeting the goals, and donor countries responded selectively with more assistance, particularly in the health domain (MDGs 4, 5, and 6), where external inputs seemingly had the greatest impact. With cooperation from the UN, but outside the UNDS, the Global Fund for AIDS, Tuberculosis and Malaria (GF) and the Global Alliance for Vaccinations and Immunization (GAVI) began operations in 2000. Aid to combat infectious diseases rose quickly over the first decade, from $11 billion in 2002 to $28 billion in 2012.[45]

The UN Secretariat began to monitor progress, and the largest UN summit to date met in 2005 to review the first five years' performance; a declaration resulted that was even more comprehensive than in 2000, emphasizing human security and human rights.[46] A high-level meeting in New York in 2010 reviewed additional progress on the MDGs. By 2015, the UN judged that many of the main targets had been met by a number of developing countries, particularly in health; the main shortcoming was gender parity in education. Aid and trade conditions had improved, and some of the poorest countries had enjoyed faster growth in GDP driven by more buoyant commodity exports.

By the time the search for a new long-term post-2015 agenda had begun, the UN's prominence in development goal-setting was firmly established. Building on the relative success of the MDGs, the Earth Summit in Rio in 2012 launched the next set of follow-on goals. Given the context, environmental considerations logically figured prominently, and "sustainability" dominated discourse. Hence, the conference called for a set of "Sustainable" Development Goals (SDGs), which "should address and incorporate in a balanced way *all three dimensions* of sustainable development and their interlinkages."[47] Conceptually, a third sector (environment) formally figured in the new global agenda.

The agenda also reflected a different watershed, disappointing in that the UN Secretariat (or Second UN) largely abandoned its earlier style and played a passive conceptualizing role; the task of formulating the new agenda passed to the First UN of governments. A high-level panel chaired by three serving heads of government reported in 2013, endorsing the Rio recommendations for goals that were "action-oriented, concise and easy to communicate, limited in number, aspirational, global in nature and universally applicable to all countries" (para. 247). An open-ended debate, in which civil society organizations participated, lasted two years. The principle of universality had the advantage of allowing widespread consultations, but the unambiguous language of the previous 15-year declarations, along with admonitions about conciseness, disappeared. The high-level panel proposed 12 illustrative goals and 54 targets, but member states eventually agreed 17 goals (see Box 1.3) with 169 "targets" (many of which were more in the nature of explanatory paragraphs). Following their endorsement in 2015, the UN Statistical Commission worked to identify measurable indicators, finding over 220.

Box 1.3 Sustainable Development Goals

Goal 1:   End poverty in all its forms everywhere

Goal 2:   End hunger, achieve food security and improved nutrition and promote sustainable agriculture

Goal 3:   Ensure healthy lives and promote well-being for all at all ages

Goal 4:   Ensure inclusive and equitable quality education and promote lifelong learning opportunities for all

Goal 5:   Achieve gender equality and empower all women and girls

Goal 6:   Ensure availability and sustainable management of water and sanitation for all

Goal 7:   Ensure access to affordable, reliable, sustainable and modern energy for all

Goal 8:   Promote sustained, inclusive and sustainable economic growth, full and productive employment and decent work for all

Goal 9:   Build resilient infrastructure, promote inclusive and sustainable industrialization and foster innovation

Goal 10: Reduce inequality within and among countries

Goal 11: Make cities and human settlements inclusive, safe, resilient and sustainable

Goal 12: Ensure sustainable consumption and production patterns

Goal 13: Take urgent action to combat climate change and its impacts

Goal 14: Conserve and sustainably use the oceans, seas and marine resources for sustainable development

Goal 15: Protect, restore and promote sustainable use of terrestrial ecosystems, sustainably manage forests, combat desertification, and halt and reverse land degradation and halt biodiversity loss

Goal 16: Promote peaceful and inclusive societies for sustainable development, provide access to justice for all and build effective, accountable and inclusive institutions at all levels

Goal 17: Strengthen the means of implementation and revitalize the global partnership for sustainable development

---

This predominantly intergovernmental process led to the 2030 development agenda; despite the proliferation of goals and targets, it nonetheless still excludes many contemporary issues of critical importance to development prospects that were politically sensitive. Thus, the North insisted upon Goal 16, which calls for inclusive societies and institutions as well as justice. Yet, the remaining goals make no explicit mention of forced migration, chronic humanitarian crises, terrorism, religious intolerance, cyber warfare, capital flight, financial mismanagement, and other forms of disruption and fragility connected to weak governance. The expression "human rights" appears several times in the Preamble of the *Outcome Document*, but they are afforded only a passing mention as a task for education (SDG 4).[48]

Despite these omissions, the 2030 Agenda constitutes the UN's most comprehensive set of goals and now represents the principal focus of work by UNDS organizations. As a normative framework, its utility will depend on the degree of rigor attached to monitoring progress. The General Assembly resolution calls for monitoring to be "voluntary and country-led" (para. 74 (a)) with selective annual reviews at sessions of the High-Level Political Forum for Sustainable Development (under ECOSOC auspices). Every four years (starting in 2019), the forum is supplemented by a two-day "summit" for heads of state and government in the General Assembly. The Voluntary National Reviews (VNRs) presented to these meetings have grown in number from 22 in 2016 to 51 in 2019. Given the complexity of the SDGs, the VNRs will provide only partial coverage but will illustrate how countries include SDGs in their planning frameworks. The VNRs reflect to varying degrees the involvement of civil society in the national consultations.

SDG 13 concerns climate change, which was the focus of another UN meeting in Paris in December of the same year that resulted in a separate framework agreement.[49] Earlier in July 2015, the Third Financing for Development Conference was supposed to examine the resources required for the achievement of the SDGs. The discussions, which led to agreement on the Addis Ababa Action Agenda (AAAA), referred to several established UN norms; a refreshing absence of typical vitriolic North–South rhetoric helped to focus attention on the many potential sources of development support in addition to external aid.[50] The three key conferences of 2015—resulting in the 2030 Agenda, the Paris Agreement, and the AAAA—have helped restore the UN's leadership role in setting the global development agenda.

UN operations

Given the substantial size of the aid business in terms of resources, personnel, and organizations, it is often forgotten how controversial ODA was in the immediate post-war years. Short-term humanitarian assistance helped to resettle migrants and restore livelihoods, but long-term international charity for development purposes initially was anathema to the dominant powers. Under the auspices of the League of Nations, there were transfers of technical assistance (TA), but in line with historical precedent, the requesting countries covered the full costs, both local and international.[51]

Kick-starting TA in the UN's early years required resources that were limited in regular (or core) budgets of the specialized agencies. US President Harry S. Truman gave UN TA a boost after Washington had launched the 1948 Marshall Plan to support European recovery. Truman signaled a change of heart on external aid with Point Four of his inauguration speech in January 1949:

> We must embark on a bold new program for making the benefits of our scientific advances and industrial progress available for the improvement and growth of underdeveloped areas … we should make available to peace-loving peoples the benefits of our store of technical knowledge in order to help them realize their aspirations for a better life … This should be a cooperative enterprise in which all nations work together through the United Nations and its specialized agencies wherever practical.[52]

Point Four gave a green light for the first substantial US contributions to the new Expanded Programme of Technical Assistance (EPTA), beginning with a grant of $20 million in 1950. Discussions also began on a more substantial fund to prepare the ways for capital lending through pre-investment studies, which later became the UN Special Fund.[53]

Pre-funded grant assistance, and all subsequent ODA, faced the challenge of matching identified needs. To demonstrate the commitments of requesting countries, the UN devised various mechanisms for cost-sharing, including OPEX (operational and executive personnel). For OPEX operations, the UN identified international experts and supplemented their basic salaries met by requesting countries. These supplements were phased out when local experts replaced external expertise. Cooperative arrangements were underpinned by the UN's Standard Basic Assistance Agreements (SBAAs), which required the requesting governments to provide for all the local costs of international experts.

However, the principles of cooperation soon began to yield as the discipline of cost-sharing unraveled and the terms of the SBAAs were relaxed. UN agencies, for reasons of continuity, requested guaranteed shares from EPTA and began to promote their expertise with recipient countries, generating their own "demand." These distortions were described at the time in the following terms:

> it sometimes seemed that the chief reason for undertaking a particular project was not the fact that the applicant government had placed it high on its list of priorities, but merely that a particular agency had money available and was willing to finance it.[54]

In 1965, the EPTA and the Special Fund became the components of the UN Development Programme (UNDP), which was supposed to be both a central funding mechanism for the UNDS and a coordinator for a system that had become a "jungle of proliferating agencies," according to Robert Jackson.[55] He was asked to forge a new blueprint for the UNDS, which took the form of the 1969 *Capacity Study*.[56] His report was the most comprehensive attempt to that date to bring more order and coherence to the UNDS by strengthening UNDP. In addition to enhancing coordination, the purpose was to achieve a better match between the supply and demand for the UN's TA services. The approved solution was to designate the UNDP's "resident representatives" (RRs) as the local eyes and ears in developing countries who were to assist in formulating needs through country programs. Each country was also to have an "Indicative Planning Figure" (IPF), a pre-allocated envelope of resources determined by country size and level of development. RRs were part of geographical regional bureaus, which were to work closely with the UN's regional commissions, with a view to a possible future merger.

The First UN of member states rejected some of Jackson's central proposals, including in particular the designation of a director-general as the supreme overseer for the UNDS and the creation of a "development resources panel" comprising the heads of UNDP, the World Bank, the IMF, UNCTAD, UNICEF, WFP, and DESA. Had they materialized, these proposals could have ensured a greater degree of policy and operational coherence. Instead, efforts at better coordination could only be pursued at the country level. In 1977, UNDP's RRs were renamed "UN resident coordinators" for operational activities. Their role of matching needs to resources and helping in-country coordination could not fully overcome agency salesmanship, especially as UNDP was no longer the predominant funding source.

UN organizations began to solicit funds directly from willing bilateral donors, who manifested limited interest in centralized funding; soon such bilateral project funding—alternatively called "soft" or "non-core"—became the predominant sources of operational financing for the specialized agencies. For its part, UNDP itself became disillusioned with the cumbersome nature of the tripartite project management process (involving governments and agencies besides itself) and in the 1970s moved beyond its funding role and became its own executing agency. For this purpose, it created the Office for Project Execution (later to become the independent UN Office of Project Services, OPS); as such, it became a direct competitor for operational resources rather than the objective coordinator at the UNDS's center. The contradictory roles created tensions until 2018, when UNDP lost the management of country coordination, which was relocated in the UN Secretariat under the direction of the UN deputy secretary-general.

In the meantime, more UNDS organizations created their own regional and country representation offices, adding to the complexities of local and international coordination. Donor resources, mainly from the OECD/DAC countries, also grew appreciably, enabling an expansion of operations both for development and for humanitarian activities. Funding was available for both core and non-core (or project- and program-specific) purposes. Since the turn of the century, non-core funding has grown while core resources have stagnated, which affords donors more direct control over the use of their funds. For the UNDS as a whole, the proportion of non-core funding has grown to some four-fifths; for individual organizations, it was even higher. The preponderance of earmarking within non-core funding has reduced the autonomy of individual UNDS organizations; donor agendas predominate, which reinforces and even exacerbates the supply-driven nature of UN assistance.

`To help rebalance demand and supply, UN organizations have developed integrated programming frameworks. These strategic plans are based on an assessment of development needs; they are intended to match available core and non-core resources. In practice, individual organizations draw up frameworks with an eye to donor preferences, which do not necessarily correspond to country priorities. Another way to dilute the impact of donor preferences is for organizations to establish trust funds to support broad thematic programs and within which donors are encouraged to pool funding.

The UN's development impact

The original purpose of UN technical assistance was to facilitate the transfer of expertise, filling temporarily the skills gap in developing countries to complement needed external capital. The breadth of expertise on offer through the UN grew with the expansion of the UNDS through its steady accretion. Growth was not merely horizontal. As more and more country offices opened, UN TA reached into almost every part of the developing world.

External expertise was intended to improve local skills and thereby work itself out of a job or be taken over financially by the requesting government. Funding from EPTA, and later UNDP, supported many technical experts to countries, often under OPEX arrangements, especially in the earliest years of independence—for example, the Congo, Ghana, Libya, Ethiopia, and Pakistan were among the first beneficiaries that came to rely on UN expertise. In many countries, the UN helped create central planning bodies that guided the early stages of development. For example, a UN expert fielded to Singapore in the 1960s devised the industrial strategy of the city-state on which much of its subsequent prosperity has been based. After the initial assignment, the costs of the expert were taken over by the government. When China began to re-open to the world in the late 1970s and seek development partners, its first invitations were to the UN, which has remained a trusted partner. In South Africa, the UN provided support to the national liberation movement before the democratic era.

While other alternative multilateral and bilateral sources of technical expertise exist, most developing countries have placed their trust in the UNDS to help develop local capacity, including from the 1970s funding for growing numbers of national experts. The UNDS has been instrumental in the creation of many national institutions, while also providing expertise in many specialist areas. For instance, UNESCO has helped in the preservation of cultural heritage, FAO in the establishment of food and agricultural research capabilities, ICAO and IMO in the enhancement of transport safety, and ITU and UPU in building communication capacities. Similarly, the ILO has given valued advice on the development of social protection systems. UNIDO has supported the emergence of small and medium enterprises across a range of sectors.

The UN has also been active during periods of reconstruction after conflict, for example in Timor Leste and Liberia. With more countries graduating to middle- and upper-income status, it is particularly in poorer, fragile, and conflict-prone states where the traditional development services of the UN remain relevant, often in conjunction with humanitarian assistance and the full range of UN functions.[57] The UNDS is being drawn increasingly into peacebuilding (now often called "sustaining the peace") functions, which include prevention and early warning, as well as development management in war's aftermath.

There are other areas in which the UNDS can continue to have an operational impact, including health and the environment. Global health campaigns require the trust and cooperation of all member states and the mobilization of numerous local actors. The eradication of smallpox in 1977 under WHO's auspices is frequently cited as a quintessential UN success story. Ridding the world of polio and guinea worm may be the next health milestones to figure as assets on the UN's balance sheet. Today, the UN (principally WHO, UNICEF, and local partners) vaccinates more than half the world's children and has saved millions of lives. When the HIV/AIDS pandemic began to spread in the 1980s, the UN helped to find solutions to combatting the disease and coordinating the response, albeit more tardily than could have been expected. The handling of the Ebola outbreak in 2015 in West Africa and again in 2019 in the Congo met mixed evaluations, as did WHO's oversight of the coronavirus pandemic in 2019–2020.

Climate change is another global crisis that requires a UN-orchestrated response. Progress in helping to roll back ozone depletion from the 1980s has been described as the single most successful international agreement. Now a second healing process will be required to diminish the huge potential losses to livelihoods through global warming.

Conclusion

This chapter's illustrations highlight the breadth of UN ideational and operational activities. The latter suggest two types of functions for which the UNDS will continue to be relevant. First, in circumstances of fragility and conflict, only the UN has the mixture of legitimacy, experience, and wide range of expertise to help. The most recent reform proposals include the strengthening of UN capacity in all phases of peacebuilding and should bind the UNDS's organizations into closer collaboration on the ground with the UN's security and humanitarian operations. By having the central pillars—international peace and security; human rights; humanitarian action; and sustainable development—working more harmoniously and on a more limited range of activities, the UN could and should help overcome the system's fragmentation for concrete delivery in the neediest of countries.

Second, the principal strength of the UNDS undoubtedly will continue to be in areas where it successfully combines vision, ideas, goals, norms, and policy, accompanied by operational testing and verification. The UN can legitimately claim credit for "ideas that changed the world";[58] they have led to global principles, norms, conventions, and standards. These and future global agreements and treaties will continue to benefit from research and informed advocacy emanating from the UNDS. It follows that the most legitimate focus for the system's operations is on the same conventions and norms that its organizations have helped develop, promulgate, and foster.

Indeed, UN history documents how understandings of "development" have grown and evolved from what was narrowly defined in the Charter—exemplified, for instance, by the additions of such considerations as gender and the environment. Even harsh critics would have to admit that such adaptation is laudable, if surprising when emanating from a place that can frequently be characterized as having limited imagination or being held in check by political shenanigans.

The paucity of funding for its ideational role—along with the gap between UN normative frameworks and operational realities—has aptly been viewed as "a threat to its credibility."[59] Stand-alone activities with little or no pertinence for UN norms and standards should be phased out whether donors favor them or not. Examples of the effective marriage of norms and operations include: the ILO's work in enhancing labor standards and working conditions; UNICEF's activities in helping countries meet their obligations under the Convention on the Rights of the Child; the work of UNODC in encouraging adherence to the UN Convention Against Corruption; FAO projects to raise food standards; and UNIDO's work on metrology. They all involve convening relevant stakeholders, undertaking learning activities, proposing institutional and technical solutions, monitoring progress, and providing feedback.

The UNDS confronts the challenge of assisting countries to meet the UN's most comprehensive development agenda to date in the 2030 Agenda and its 17 SDGs. History will judge the world organization's effectiveness by its success in encouraging member states to engage with the agenda and pursue its goals as well as forthrightly monitor performance. Over the first 75 years of the UN development system, there have been numerous indications of dynamism among the various members of the Second UN and the Third UN; they provide a rare sign of hope amidst the resurgence of new nationalisms and inward-looking perspectives among the member states of the First UN.

NOTES

1 Dan Plesch and Thomas G. Weiss, eds., *Wartime Origins and the Future United Nations* (London: Routledge, 2015).
2 M. Patrick Cottrell, "Lost in Transition? The League of Nations and the United Nations," in *Charter of the United Nations*, ed. Ian Shapiro and Joseph Lampert (New Haven, CT: Yale University Press, 2014), 91–106.
3 Leland M. Goodrich, "From League of Nations to United Nations," *International Organization* 1, no. 1 (1947): 3.
4 Patricia Clavin, *Securing the World Economy: The Reinvention of the League of Nations* (Oxford: Oxford University Press, 2013).
5 League of Nations, *The Development of International Cooperation in Economic and Social Affairs, Report of the Special Committee* (Geneva: League of Nations, 1939).
6 David Mitrany, *A Working Peace System* (Chicago, IL: Quadrangle Books, 1966).
7 Lord Boyd Orr, Director-General of FAO, in a letter to Robert Jackson, quoted in UNDP, *A Study of the Capacity of the United Nations Development System* (Geneva: United Nations, 1969), DP/5, 33n.
8 Craig N. Murphy, *The United Nations Development Programme: A Better Way?* (Cambridge: Cambridge University Press, 2006).
9 Richard Jolly, *UNICEF (United Nations Children's Fund)* (London: Routledge, 2014).
10 Stephen Browne, *United Nations Industrial Development Organization* (London: Routledge, 2012).
11 Yves Berthelot and Paul Rayment, "The ECE: A Bridge Between East and West," in *Unity and Diversity in Development Ideas*, ed. Yves Berthelot (Bloomington, IN: Indiana University Press, 2004), 51–131.
12 Stephen Browne and Thomas G. Weiss, "How Relevant Are the UN's Regional Commissions?" *FUNDS Project Briefing no. 1* (New York: FUNDS, 2013).
13 Kenneth Dadzie, "The UN and the Problem of Economic Development," in *United Nations, Divided World: The UN's Roles in International Relations*, ed. Adam Roberts and Benedict Kingsbury, 2nd edn. (Oxford: Clarendon, 1995), 297–326.

14 For a discussion, see Thomas G. Weiss, David P. Forsythe, Roger A. Coate, and Kelly-Kate Pease, *The United Nations and Changing World Politics*, 8th updated and enlarged edn. (London: Routledge, 2019), 259–283.

15 Joseph A. Schumpeter, *The Theory of Economic Development: An Inquiry into Profits, Capital, Credit, Interest, and the Business Cycle* (New Brunswick, NJ: Transaction Books, 1934), translated from the 1911 original German, *Theorie der Wirtschaftlichen Entwicklung*.

16 Gilbert Rist, *The History of Development* (London: Zed Books, 1997).

17 Janez Stanovnik, an early Yugoslav delegate to the UN (and later the Executive Secretary of the ECE), was scarcely exaggerating: "There was no one single great name in economic writings in the period of 1945 to 1955 who was not in one way or the other associated with the United Nations." Oral History transcript, United Nations Intellectual History Project, 2007. CD-ROM available upon request from the Ralph Bunche Institute for International Studies. Indiana University Press published 15 volumes. See www.unhistory.org.

18 P. N. Rosenstein-Rodan, "Problems of Industrialization of Eastern and South-Eastern Europe," *The Economic Journal* 53 (London: Royal Economic Society, 1943), 202–211; Arthur W. Lewis, "Economic Development with Unlimited Supplies of Labour," *The Manchester School* 22 (1954): 139–191.

19 John Toye and Richard Toye, *The UN and Global Political Economy: Trade, Finance and Development* (Bloomington, IN: Indiana University Press, 2004).

20 Stephen Browne and Sam Laird, *The International Trade Centre* (London: Routledge, 2011).

21 The NIEO debate led to the establishment in 1974 of the Centre on Transnational Corporations (CTC) in New York. The CTC toiled for two decades on an international code of conduct on trans-national corporations. The CTC closed in 1993 under pressure from some industrialized countries, and its information activities merged with UNCTAD, which resulted in the annual *World Investment Reports*. See Tagi Sagafi-Nejad in collaboration with John Dunning, *The UN and Transnational Corporations* (Bloomington, IN: Indiana University Press, 2008).

22 A summary of the research showing the anti-growth effects of structural adjustment policies and the Washington consensus is in James Raymond Vreeland, *The International Monetary Fund: Politics of Conditional Lending* (London: Routledge, 2007), 73–94. A quasi-official IMF review of this evidence appears in *World Economics* 8, no. 2 (2007): 97–118.

23 International Labour Organization, *Employment, Growth and Basic Needs: A One-World Problem, Report of the Director-General of ILO* (Geneva: ILO, 1976).

24 Dag Hammarskjöld Foundation, *What Now? Another Development* (Uppsala, Sweden: DHF, 1975).

25 In 2010, INSTRAW was merged into UN Women.

26 Devaki Jain, *Women, Development, and the UN: A Sixty-Year Quest for Equality and Justice* (Bloomington, IN. Indiana University Press, 2005). See also Ellen Chesler and Terry McGovern, eds., *Women and Girls Rising: Progress and Resistance around the* World (London: Routledge, 2016).

27 Louis Emmerij, Richard Jolly, and Thomas G. Weiss, *Ahead of the Curve? UN Ideas and Global Challenges* (Bloomington, IN: Indiana University Press, 2001).

28 J. P. Singh, *United Nations Educational, Scientific and Cultural Organization (UNESCO)* (London: Routledge, 2011).

29 See, for example, Future UN, *Surveys*, www.futureun.org/Surveys.

30 UN Population Division, *Publications*, www.un.org/en/development/desa/population/publications/index.asp.

31 *Development and Environment, Report of a Panel of Experts Convened by the Secretary-General of the United Nations Conference on the Human Environment, Founex, Switzerland, 4–12 June 1971*, paragraphs 2 and 4, reproduced as Annex I of UN document A/CONF.48/10, 22 December 1971.

32 World Commission on Environment and Development, *Our Common Future* (Oxford: Oxford University Press, 1987). See Nico Schrijver, *The UN and the Resource Management: Development without Destruction* (Bloomington, IN: Indiana University Press, 2009).

33 https://ipbes.net/ipbes-global-assessment-first-comprehensive-global-biodiversity-assessment-2005.

34 Thomas G. Weiss and Ramesh Thakur, *Global Governance and the UN: An Unfinished Journey* (Bloomington, IN: Indiana University Press, 2010).

35 Thomas G. Weiss, Tatiana Carayannis, and Richard Jolly, "The 'Third' United Nations," *Global Governance* 15, no. 1 (2009): 123–142. See also Thomas G. Weiss and Tatiana Carayannis, *The "Third" United Nations: How Knowledge Brokers Help the UN Think* (Oxford: Oxford University Press, forthcoming).

36 Giovanni A. Cornia, Richard Jolly, and Frances Stewart, eds., *Adjustment with a Human Face* (Oxford: Clarendon Press, 1987).

37 Amartya Sen, *Development as Freedom* (New York: Alfred A. Knopf, 2000).

38 Richard Jolly et al., *UN Contributions to Development Thinking and Practice* (Bloomington, IN: Indiana University Press, 2004).

39 Mahbub ul Haq, *Reflections on Human Development* (Oxford: Oxford University Press, 1995), 14.

40 Michael G. Schechter, *United Nations Global Conferences* (London: Routledge, 2005).

41 United Nations, *Report of the World Summit on Social Development*, UN document A/CONF.166/9, 19 April 1995, para. 26.

42 Jolly et al., *UN Contributions*.

43 Jolly, *UNICEF*.

44 UNICEF, *Declaration on the Survival, Protection and Development of Children and a Plan of Action for Implementing the Declaration in the 1990s* (New York, September 1990), www.unicef.org/wsc.

45 Thomas J. Bollyky, *Plagues and the Paradox of Progress* (Cambridge, MA: MIT Press, 2018).

46 UN, *World Summit Outcome*, General Assembly resolution 60/1, 24 October 2005.

47 UN, *The Future We Want*, Outcome Document of the UN Conference on Sustainable Development, UN document A/RES/66/288, 20–22 December 2012, para. 246, emphasis added.

48 UN, *Transforming Our World: The 2030 Agenda for Sustainable Development* (UN document A/RES/70), 25 September 2015.

49 UN, *Paris Agreement, Twenty-First Session of the Conference of the Parties to the United Nations Framework Convention on Climate Change* (Paris: UN, 2015).

50 UN, *Report of the Third International Conference on Financing for Development, Addis Ababa 13–16 July 2015*, UN document A/CONF.227/20.

51 Gilbert Rist, *The History of Development* (London: Zed Books, 1997).

52 US Government, *Department of State Bulletin* (Washington, DC, 30 January 1949), 123.

53 Olav Stokke, *The UN and Development: From Aid to Cooperation* (Bloomington, IN: Indiana University Press, 2009).

54 Hugh Keenleyside, *International Aid: A Summary with Special Reference to the Programmes of the United Nations* (New York: Heinemann, 1966), 164.

55 Murphy, *The United Nations Development Programme*, 142.

56 UN, *A Study of the Capacity of the United Nations Development System* (Geneva: United Nations, 1969).

57 Stephen Browne and Thomas G. Weiss, eds., *Peacebuilding Challenges for the UN Development System* (New York: Future UN Development System Project, 2015).

58 Richard Jolly, Louis Emmerij, and Thomas G. Weiss, *UN Ideas That Changed the World* (Bloomington and Indianapolis, IN: Indiana University Press, 2009).

59 Bruce Jenks, *Global Norms: Building an Inclusive Multilateralism* (Uppsala, Sweden: Dag Hammarskjöld Foundation, 2017), Development Dialogue Paper no. 21, 4.

ADDITIONAL READING

Stephen Browne, *Sustainable Development Goals and UN Goal-Setting* (London: Routledge, 2017).

Stephen Browne, *The UN Development Programme and System* (London: Routledge, 2012).

Patricia Clavin, *Securing the World Economy: The Reinvention of the League of Nations* (Oxford: Oxford University Press, 2013).

Richard Jolly, Louis Emmerij, and Thomas G. Weiss, *UN Ideas That Changed the World* (Bloomington, IN: Indiana University Press, 2009).

Sara Lorenzini, *Global Development: A Cold War History* (Princeton, NJ: Princeton University Press, 2019).

Dan Plesch and Thomas G. Weiss, eds., *Wartime Origins and the Future United Nations* (London: Routledge, 2015).

Olav Stokke, *The UN and Development: From Aid to Cooperation* (Bloomington, IN: Indiana University Press, 2009).

John Toye and Richard Toye, *The UN and Global Political Economy: Trade, Finance and Development* (Bloomington, IN: Indiana University Press, 2004).

Thomas G. Weiss and Ramesh Thakur, *Global Governance and the UN: An Unfinished Journey* (Bloomington, IN: Indiana University Press, 2010).

Thomas G. Weiss and Sam Daws, eds., *The Oxford Handbook on the United Nations* (Oxford: Oxford University Press, 2018), 2nd edn.

Thomas G. Weiss and Rorden Wilkinson, eds., *International Organization and Global Governance* (London: Routledge, 2018), 2nd edn.

2

THE UN AND DEVELOPMENT

Objectives and governance

José Antonio Ocampo

One of the success stories of the United Nations has been its capacity to serve as the forum to agree on global development goals. This success includes those set not only in the UN Development Decades but also in the global UN conferences convened since the 1970s and the series of summits that started with the 1990 World Summit for Children. It includes the three major agendas approved in 2015: Agenda 2030 and the Sustainable Development Goals (SDGs), which succeeded the Millennium Development Goals (MDGs); the Addis Ababa Action Agenda, adopted at the third Financing for Development (FFD) Conference, following a process that had been launched in Monterrey in 2002; and the Paris Agreement within the United Nations Framework Convention on Climate Change, adopted at the 1992 Rio de Janeiro Earth Summit.

This success reflects not only the UN's convening power and its character as the most representative global institution but also its strong historical partnership with civil society. However, although goal-setting has helped place many new issues on the global agenda, it has generally been characterized by a complex governance structure and weak monitoring and accountability for international commitments.

This chapter analyzes the major elements of this topic. Development is understood here in its broad sense, encompassing its economic, social, and environmental dimensions, well captured in the SDGs. It begins with the objectives of international cooperation in relation to development and is followed by the transition from the MDGs to the SDGs. It then analyzes the governance of the system, including the proposal to create a robust UN Council on economic, social, and environmental issues, and ends with brief forward-looking conclusions.

The objectives of international development cooperation

There are three basic objectives[1] of international cooperation in the economic, social, and environmental fields: managing interdependence and providing the associated global public goods; promoting common international social norms and standards, which can be referred to as "universal social goods"; and reducing inequalities in development among countries. These objectives reflect not only the three dimensions of the UN's conception of sustainable development but also the concept of "development" which is used in the UN in a dual sense: to refer to developing countries and, in the terminology of the Preamble to the UN Charter, to the promotion of "social progress and better standards of life in larger freedom"—a concept that applies, of course, to all societies.

This typology coincides with the historical origin of different forms of cooperation. Prior to World War I, international cooperation was essentially related to managing such technical interdependence as navigation treaties, contagious diseases, telegraph and postal services, and intellectual property rights (IPRs). The creation of the International Labour Organization (ILO) in the Treaty of Versailles in 1919 gave birth to the second form of cooperation; to a lesser extent, the League of Nations also provided limited economic and social cooperation, and there was an attempt to coordinate the economic responses to the Great Depression of the 1930s, which largely failed. The third form of cooperation was born after World War II (WWII) and was linked to dismantling the colonial order.

All forms of international cooperation blossomed after WWII. The first two objectives gave birth to the elaborate system of funds, programs, and specialized agencies of the UN development system, including the Bretton Woods institutions (BWIs), but also some international institutions that were not formally part of it—notably those in the trade area, the General Agreement on Tariffs and Trade (GATT) and later the World Trade Organization (WTO).[2] Cooperation in the environmental field was a late arrival, which started with the United Nations Conference on the Human Environment held in Stockholm in 1972.

The second form of cooperation includes the economic and social rights that became part of the 1948 Universal Declaration of Human Rights and of the 1966 International Covenant of Economic, Social and Cultural Rights. It also covers the multitude of UN conventions in the social field approved by the UN General Assembly and by the intergovernmental organs of the specialized agencies; and the principles and plans of action agreed since the 1970s in UN conferences and summits.

The third form of cooperation became largely the subject of the official development assistance (ODA) administered by developed countries, and coordinated by the Organisation for Economic Co-operation and Development (OECD). South–South cooperation has become an additional and dynamic part of this form of cooperation in recent decades. Also relevant were the different forms of UN technical cooperation launched since the late 1940s, the creation of the World Bank's International Development Association (IDA) in 1960, and the adoption of the principle of "special and differential treatment" in trade agreements. The UN Conference on Trade and Development (UNCTAD), created in 1964, led the way on the latter, which was adopted first by GATT and in a moderate form by the WTO after its creation in 1994.

The three forms of cooperation are conceptually distinct in terms of both national sovereignty and the demands for international cooperation. The first responds to the need for collective action to avoid the under or over-provision of the goods or services that are non-rival and non-excludable in consumption (which is what welfare economics defines as "public goods"), or that generate strong externalities (positive or negative). At the national level, the demand for collective action is reflected in the provision and regulation of those goods and services by the state, but also by different forms of communal or private (generally not-for-profit) cooperation. At the international level, the demand for collective action to manage interdependence requires sharing national autonomy, as well as "responsible sovereignty," defined by Inge Kaul and Donald Blundin as sovereignty exercised in a way that is fully respectful of the sovereignty of others.[3]

Managing interdependence involves issues of (economic) efficiency, whereas those that relate to the second and third objectives of cooperation relate to equity—equality of citizens and of nations, respectively. In the second case, the origin of "publicness" is the decision by society that certain goods and services should be provided to all as citizens because of their social rather than technical attributes, or rules that they should respect in their interaction with each other (e.g., non-discrimination, protection of weaker members of society). In their provision or the enforcement of the associated rules, the state continues to exercise full autonomy, though following internationally agreed principles/norms—"sovereignty embedded in broader values and principles," the concept that, as Bruce Jenks argues,[4] was at the center of early post-WWII conceptions of international cooperation.

In turn, the third form of cooperation is related to the demand for equality, but in this case equality among nations. It includes ODA, special credit channels for developing countries, and rules that create preferences for them in the trade or technology transfer, among other fields. It aims at compensating the large inequalities that characterize the world economy. National sovereignty to adopt development strategies should be the rule. However, to the extent that economic interdependence generated by globalization reduces room for the effective exercise of such sovereignty, international cooperation should aim at enhancing it—at increasing the "policy space" that countries should enjoy, to use the concept that was coined in UN (particularly UNCTAD) debates.

From the MDGs to the SDGs

In terms of setting global development goals, the MDGs and, particularly, the SDGs represent some of the most ambitious UN decisions. The MDG experience can be praised on several grounds. It set a concise set of clear and measurable social and environmental goals, with a high level of visibility. They served not only for advocacy but also as a framework for numerous global, regional, and national debates and, most importantly, for the design of the development strategies of several countries. The BWIs strongly backed them, as did the ODA community and numerous civil society organizations (CSOs), thus realizing the aim of using the representative character of the UN to lead global action. Although accountability continued to be weak, the monitoring process and common database put in place by the UN, with the support of many other organizations, represented a significant advance. It furthermore included high-quality regular reports on the MDGs as well as those of the MDG Gap Task Force (MDG-8) on the global partnership for development.

However, the MDGs were deficient in many ways. Although they were drafted on the basis of the Millennium Declaration, the selection of the goals and targets was a highly centralized process that lacked participation by the UN of member states. It was perceived to be donor-centric, a view that was enhanced by its similarity with the OECD Development Assistance Committee's (OECD/DAC's) 1996 agenda.[5] Several targets were relevant only for the poorest countries and left little room for the adoption of targets appropriate for other countries (e.g., for middle-income countries). Moreover, MDG-8 on the "global partnership for development" was added after the summit as a rather diluted catch-all goal.

Beyond that, many critics pointed out that the MDGs mostly left out environmental sustainability, but particularly the *economic* development issues, including one crucial socio-economic variable: employment. In that regard, the 2005 Summit that reviewed the Millennium Declaration added the objective of "achieving full and productive employment and decent work for all." However, it was included as a target for MDG-1 rather than a new goal, thus significantly reducing its scope. More generally, the MDGs captured only a small segment of the "internationally agreed development goals"—that is, the goals agreed in the UN summits and conferences, which constitute the broader UN development agenda, and there was only weak commitment from many specialized agencies. The targets were also clearly incomplete—as it was argued, among others, on MDG-3 on gender equality and empowerment of women.

For the launch of the discussion of what came to be called "Agenda 2030," the UN considered three major reports: that prepared in 2012 by a task force of UN agencies; the report of the High-Level Panel convened by the Secretary-General for this purpose; and the Secretary-General's own report to the 68th session of the UNGA debate on "Post 2015 Development Agenda: Setting the Stage."[6] These reports are referred to hereafter as "UN Task Force," "High-Level Panel (HLP)," and "SG Report," respectively. An additional useful document is the summary of the elaborate "global conversation" on the post-2015 agenda set up by the UN Development Group (UNDG).[7]

Important agreements arose from these reports. The first was that the new agenda should integrate the three dimensions of *sustainable development*: economic, social, and environmental. The second was that the agenda should be *universal*—that is, it should apply to *all*, and not only to developing countries. The third area of consensus was that, although goals should be guided by universal vision and principles, they should take into account regional, national, and local circumstances and priorities. In particular, they should leave ample space for national policy design and adaptation to local settings. This was critical to guarantee the "ownership" of this agenda by national governments and societies—without which it would not be realized. The fourth was that goals should be "bold but practical"—that is, they should be achievable within the chosen time framework—and include clear measurable indicators that should be subject to monitoring and accountability.

Finally, and perhaps most significantly from the point of view of the process, there was the implicit agreement that the post-2015 agenda should be adopted by the UNGA and not the way that the MDGs had been formulated with a hurried sign-off at a global summit. The process was to be open and consultative. In particular, it should converge with the discussion that had already started of the open working group on the SDGs to implement the agenda agreed in the 2012 Conference on Sustainable Development.

Both the UN Task Force and the HLP also proposed that the new agenda should incorporate not only areas that were covered by the MDGs, but also some that were left out of that agenda as well as "emerging issues." Two common themes on which the two reports agreed were peace and security, and good national governance. This understanding reflected the conviction that the most limited progress and even the retrogression in development had affected most severely countries afflicted by armed conflict, and that "peace and good governance were core elements of wellbeing, not an optional extra," in the HLP's words.[8] In turn, the list of emerging issues that the UN Task Force proposed was a long one: the persistence of or increase in inequalities, including gender inequalities; large and growing knowledge gaps between and within countries, and loss of traditional knowledge; shifting demographics (rapid population growth in Africa, population aging, internal and international migration, urbanization and the growing population living in slums); and a growing environmental footprint (shrinking forests, growing scarcity of water, land degradation, climate change, biodiversity loss) and incidence of natural disasters.

More broadly, the UN Task Force proposed a vision based on the fundamental principles of respect for human rights, equality, and sustainability. They proposed an agenda with four interdependent dimensions: inclusive social development, through universal access to basic social services and the eradication of hunger; inclusive economic development, including productive employment and decent work, and reduction of income poverty and inequalities; environmental sustainability, which requires, among other things, new consumption and production patterns; and peace and security, which includes national governance based on the rule of law and the principles of political inclusion and participation.

In turn, the HLP report began by stating: "Our vision and our responsibility are to end extreme poverty in all its forms in the context of sustainable development and to have in place the building blocks of sustainable development for all."[9] It then proposed five "big, trans-formative shifts": leaving no one behind, taking into account income, gender, ethnicity, dis-abilities, and geography; placing sustainable development at the core, integrating its three dimensions; transforming economies for jobs and inclusive growth; building peace and effective, open and accountable institutions for all; and forging a new global partnership.

The major difference between the two reports was in the proposed vision: while sharing the theme of sustainability, the HLP proposed that fighting multidimensional poverty should be at the center of the agenda, whereas the UN Task Team gave primacy to respect for human rights and overcoming inequality. In UN terminology, the latter was a "rights-based approach" to development. It was also closer to the basic values agreed in the UN Millennium Declaration: freedom, equality, solidarity, tolerance, respect for nature, and shared responsibilities.

The emphasis on overcoming inequality, and not only poverty in its multiple dimensions, was also at the center of the UN Task Force, the SG Report, and the UNGA discussion that followed. It involved not only international inequalities but also the rising domestic inequalities that have affected a large number of countries—developed and developing alike—in recent decades. This meant that rising domestic income inequality was one of the most important "emerging trends" that had to be addressed by Agenda 2030. In its 2013 report, the UN Com-mittee for Development Policy (CDP) also argued that the reduction of inequality should be included as a specific goal in the post-2015 agenda, with measurable targets, adding a specific reference to overcoming the high levels of abject poverty.[10]

The UNGA discussion generated a heated debate on the institutional issues, in particular about how to include peace and security as well as national governance on the agenda. Develop-ing countries raised, in particular, the need to respect national sovereignty in the choice of institutions, and to avoid adopting *measurable* targets in this area, given the imperfections and controversial character of all existing indicators of national governance—including those used by the World Bank.

Developing countries also raised the need to include good *global* governance in the agenda and to improve significantly MDG-8 on the global partnership for development. The agree-ment also went well beyond the multi-stakeholder partnerships proposed by the HLP to include *intergovernmental* cooperation, including in finance, trade, technology, and systemic issues. It also included the commitment to "Broaden and strengthen the participation of developing countries in the institutions of global governance" (target 16.8 of the SDGs), to reaffirm a principle that had been agreed in the first UN Conference on Financing for Development.[11] The UN Task Force also called for the UNGA to reaffirm the principle of "common but differentiated respons-ibilities" agreed in the 1992 Rio Earth Summit, but the HLP shied away from even mentioning it and implicitly reformulated it as "shared responsibilities in accordance with respective cap-abilities."[12] This reflects the wide disagreement that still exists among UN member states about the application of this principle beyond the environmental area.

The results of the open and extensive debates, which involved multiple consultations with academia and civil society, were the 17 SDGs approved in 2015. The SDGs meet the criteria that were agreed at the outset: they include all the dimensions of sustainable development; they are universal in scope; and they leave ample space for national policy design. The SDGs also reflect in a better way the broader agenda agreed in the UN summits and conference, and bring back economic development to the UN agenda—a major issue for developing countries. Inter-national organizations, including the BWIs, the official development assistance community, and global civil society, have all recognized the new agenda. Several national governments have incorporated them into their national agendas, and several major municipal governments have done the same. However, while this complex agenda was translated into 169 targets, several of which cannot be measured in precise terms, it still leaves aside some issues that, as we see below, are part of the global development agenda.

Two additional important innovations were related to the mechanisms put in place for the follow-up of Agenda 2030. The first was the creation of the High-Level Political Forum (HLPF), which combines very well the political profile of the UNGA with the responsibility of the Economic and Social Council (ECOSOC) to follow up on the implementation of the outcomes of all major UN conferences and summits in the economic, social, and environmental fields. According to the relevant 2013 General Assembly resolution, that body would convene the HLPF every four years at the heads-of-state level to provide political leadership; meanwhile, ECOSOC would undertake the regular follow-up of the SDGs during its annual ministerial meetings. The second was the mechanism that was put in place to follow up on the implementation of Agenda 2030 at the national level, the Voluntary National Review (VNRs), which built upon the "annual ministerial reviews" adopted by the 2005 World Summit for countries to voluntarily report to other UN members how they are fulfilling the different goals and targets. This mechanism resembles OECD's "peer reviews" and was preferred to evaluations by the UN Secretariat.

The VNRs have been successful, as suggested by the rising number of countries willing to do their reviews in ECOSOC's annual sessions: 22 countries in 2016, 43 in 2017, and 46 in 2018. However, the process of review could and should be improved. According to the CDP's evaluation:

> VNRs could become more effective instruments to share lessons learned and promote mutual learning by including more explicit and detailed discussions on national strategies for implementing the 2030 Agenda. Substantive coverage of the VNRs should be more comprehensive; reporting should not be selective and leave out major areas, particularly considering that the 2030 Agenda is intended to be indivisible and integrated.[13]

Such coverage is combined with the reports of DESA on the SDGs at the global level, which improved on the previous ones on MDGs. Both have been supported by an elaborate system of indicators of the MDGs and now the SDGs, which is coordinated by the UN Statistical Division but with collaboration from a large number of international organizations. Evaluations and pressure from international civil society are also very important complements in the follow-up of these goals.

The governance of global development cooperation

In terms of governance, global development cooperation faces three crucial issues: the incomplete character of the international agenda; the imperfections in the existing governance structures; and some problems of coherence of the system.[14] For the first issue, there are areas of interdependence where cooperation is well developed and accepted (such as contagious diseases and transportation rules), others in which there are significant gaps (climate change, global macroeconomic and financial stability, and international tax cooperation), and some in which there is no or very limited cooperation (economic migration).[15] Furthermore, powerful countries or powerful private actors tend to fill vacuums in the regulatory space.

In the intergovernmental process, power is reflected in the role assumed by groups of major countries—for instance, the Group of 7 (G-7) or Group of 20 (G-20), and their control of decision-making in different organizations (notably of the BWIs by developed countries), the inadequate financing given to international organizations to achieve their assigned tasks, and the different degrees of power and autonomy of the secretariats[16] of different international organiza-tions. The major issue is the limited capacity of many developing countries—and some smaller developed countries—to be part of the decision-making process.

In most of these cases, the problem is how to guarantee the inclusiveness of international cooperation, and the legitimacy associated with it, while ensuring effective decision-making and efficient performance. To try to match power relations with some level of inclusiveness, the BWIs adopted a system in which they combine weighted votes, essentially based on the quotas/capital that take into account the economic relevance of different countries, with a small number of basic votes given equally to all members, and a constituency system that guarantees that all countries have a representative at the table. However, the process of redefining the weighted vote to take into account the growing share of developing countries in the world economy has been extremely slow.

In turn, the WTO model is based on consensus-building through a system of "concentric circles," as characterized by WTO's former director-general Pascal Lamy:[17] negotiations are made within and then between coalitions to facilitate building consensus—a process which, in a sense, matches the way parliamentary decisions are taken within countries, as negotiations within and then between political parties. The consensus principle also gives all countries the possibility of blocking an agreement, though the effective capacity to do so depends on the power of individual countries. However, this system has proven to be relatively ineffective in terms of decision-making and has thus been strongly criticized.

The transition from the G-7 to the G-20 as the major decision-making body of major coun-tries was, of course, a step forward in terms of representation of developing countries; it was effective in helping mitigate the 2007–2009 North Atlantic financial crisis, strengthening finan-cial regulation, and promoting new areas of international cooperation, notably in taxation. However, it excludes most countries and has not been particularly effective after its initial decisions.

The UN decision-making rule based on "one country, one vote" is, of course, the most inclusive and has facilitated consensus-building at different times, but frequently it leads powerful countries to disregard the associated decisions; it has also been characterized in recent times by lack of agreement on major issues among the increasingly diverse community of developing countries. In several cases, it led to the use of the UN for consensus-building, but then to actions by organization beyond the core UN. This is what John Toye and Richard Toye called the "twin-track system":

> The UN General Assembly provides a world forum where economic ideas, interests and policy proposals are presented, discussed, and negotiated. Its authority is, and can continue to be, a moral authority […] Once the process of UN discussion and nego-tiation produces agreements, however, their implementation is delegated to executive agencies in which the countries that will foot most of the subsequent bills place their confidence.[18]

The creation of IDA in the World Bank group and the adoption of the principle of special and differential treatment by GATT are interesting historical cases already mentioned, to which can be added the 2014–2015 decisions on sovereign debt resolution. Their inclusive character implies, however, that, under any arrangement, the General Assembly and ECOSOC should be recognized as the most open and democratic and, therefore, as the most appropriate forums for debate and consensus-building. Gert Rosenthal characterizes ECOSOC—and by extension, other UN processes—as "quite successful in promoting the development debate, identifying emerging issues, and offering guidelines for policy makers," and

> the non-binding nature of decisions and resolutions has been an asset in furthering the policy debate, which has contributed to the organization's considerable achievements in the development of ideas, in its advocacy role, and in its ability to shape public awareness.[19]

Beyond the UN system, global civil society also plays an essential role in placing new issues in the agenda and in overseeing the implementation of international agreements. The UN Intellectual History Project captured this role well with the concept of the "three UNs": member states, international secretariats, and civil society.[20] In any case, it is interesting to note that that role predates the UN, as reflected in the anti-slavery movement of the late eighteenth and early nineteenth centuries, the struggle of the sequence of socialist internationals for better labor standards, and the fight of the international feminist movement for the right to vote for women. Today, it is, of course, much more active and heterogeneous. It takes place in a parallel manner to intergovernmental processes, as reflected, among many other areas, in the persistent struggles of the feminist movements and the international movement of indigenous peoples. ECOSOC is the most open forum to civil society, and therefore plays a useful role in giving it voice in intergovernmental processes.

In terms of coherence, any instrument to enhance intergovernmental cooperation must take into account that the current system's design was radically decentralized. Proposals to create an apex organization to direct and coordinate the UN system have been on the agenda for the past quarter-century. In 1992, UNDP's *Human Development Report* proposed replacing ECOSOC with a 22-member Development Security Council, with the capacity to take decisions and not just to formulate recommendations, following the powers that the UN Security Council has—hence its proposed name. According to the proposal, the new Council would serve as the framework to design global policy frameworks in all key economic and social areas, preparing a global budget of development resource flows, and provide a policy coordination framework for the smooth functioning of international development and financial institutions.[21] The Commission on Global Governance made a similar proposal for an "Economic Security Council" three years later.[22] Similarly, the 2006 Panel on System-Wide Coherence proposed the creation of a Global Leaders' Forum of ECOSOC (also called L27, made up of half of ECOSOC's members).[23]

Along these lines, the General Assembly president in 2009 convened the Stiglitz Commission, which proposed the creation of a Global Economic Coordination Council (GECC).[24] Its major role would have been the direction and coordination of the UN system, including the BWIs as well as WTO—to be brought into the UN system. It would also have had as special responsibilities the identification of gaps in the current system of cooperation, and of the spillovers among the areas of responsibilities of individual agencies that would need attention (e.g., environmental effects of trade policies and social effects of budgetary policies). It would have been a small decision-making body at the heads-of-state level, supported by subsidiary ministerial bodies, combining the participation of systemically important countries with universal representation through a mechanism similar to that of the BWIs—a constituency system with weighted votes based on economic weight of countries mixed with some basic votes that were equal for all. The latter element is essential to guarantee that the most important countries must be at the decision-making table, or otherwise they will tend to ignore its decisions. In any case, the GECC would have left to the more specialized bodies the specific decisions in their areas of work.

One alternative would be for the G-20 to be transformed into a more representative and thereby legitimate mechanism of international economic cooperation—in a sense, into a GECC. This is similar to the Palais Royal Initiative's proposal to reform the international monetary system: a three-level governance structure for the global economy that would have a reformed G-20 at the top, based on a constituency system.[25]

If the current G-20 continues and exercises its role as "the premier forum for our international economic cooperation,"[26] it would have to change its operating style, and avoid stepping onto the mandates and governance structures of representative international institutions. It would also have to avoid adding issues onto its agenda, which lead to no or very limited action. Essentially, it would have to operate as a "steering committee,"[27] to help generate consensus among the most powerful countries. According to Kemal Dervis,[28] it would operate as an informal mechanism that interacts with the formal international organizations, playing a complementary role, with the informal setting being particularly important, according to his view, to permit bolder proposals. Furthermore, the interaction between formal and informal processes works best when it facilitates a variable geometry of informal dialogues, as not all countries are equally relevant for specific international decisions.

Under any arrangement, ECOSOC should continue to be the intergovernmental organ in charge of the economic, social, and environmental responsibilities given to the UN Secretariat, funds, and programs—the core UN organization, to distinguish it from the UN system as a whole, which also includes the specialized agencies. It should play at least in part the role given by UN Charter Article 62, according to which it "may co-ordinate the activities of the specialized agencies through consultation with and recommendations to such agencies and through recommendations to the General Assembly and to the Members of the United Nations." The additional function of following up on the SDGs and the plans of action of major UN summits and conferences may be particularly important in this regard. An interesting case is the follow-up of the Financing for Development Summits from Monterrey to Addis Ababa, which has generated a new way of interacting with the BWIs. The Charter does not mention humanitarian affairs, an area in which ECOSOC came to be the main mechanism of coordination at the global level. The Council should also continue to play the task of convening global debates on development crises and emergencies, with the objective of contributing in this way to a timely and effective global response.

As already pointed out, a definite asset of ECOSOC is the confidence in it of developing countries. Given that it provides possibly the most open intergovernmental forum on economic and social issues, civil society also has a preference for ECOSOC as a forum. With the increasing openness of the UN to the private sector, ECOSOC's convening power has also been evident in this area. Further, its network of subsidiary and expert bodies is also a source of strength, as shown in the success of many of them.

The UNGA will also continue to play an important role in global development cooperation, reflecting its capacity to serve as an effective mechanism for consensus-building and generating new ideas for international cooperation. In this regard, the convening of UN summits and conferences, as well as high-level technical groups (also convened at times by the Secretary-General), has played an important role. However, there is, in this regard, a potential conflict with the responsibilities of ECOSOC, which has surfaced on many occasions. So, it should be understood that the UNGA is the main *political* organ and has universal membership (a characteristic that ECOSOC lacks), but ECOSOC has the major responsibility for following up on world economic, social, and environmental issues.

Conclusion: looking to the future

The world still needs stronger mechanisms to fulfill the three objectives of international cooperation: managing interdependence, providing universal goods, and reducing international inequalities in levels of development of different countries. The UN is uniquely positioned to provide a forum and facilitate consensus-building in all of these areas, with the active participation of civil society and the private sector. However, the coherence of the system as a whole through the creation of a special Council, as well as of mechanisms that guarantee the implementation of global development cooperation, should continue to be on the agenda. This requires, of course, a persistent commitment to multilateral cooperation, with major powers recognizing its virtues over unilateral action and a return to the unsuccessful eras of confrontation.

As pointed out, in terms of the UN governing bodies, the High-Level Political Forum is a novel model, which can enhance the complementarities and comparative advantages of the UNGA and ECOSOC while avoiding duplication. The objective is to provide political leadership by the heads of state with the regular follow-up of the SDGs by ECOSOC during its annual ministerial meetings. It should be complemented by ECOSOC's broader responsibility to follow up on all UN conferences and summits. A final but crucial issue is the maturing and improvement of the mechanism adopted for countries' own evaluations, the Voluntary National Reviews.

NOTES

1 This section and that on governance draw partially from José Antonio Ocampo, ed., "Global Economic and Social Governance and the United Nations System," in *Global Governance and Development* (Oxford: Oxford University Press, 2016), Chapter 1. See also United Nations, *World Economic and Social Survey: Retooling Global Development* (New York: United Nations Department of Economic and Social Affairs, 2010), Chapter VI; and on global public goods, see Inge Kaul, Pedro Conceicao, Katell Le Goulven, and R. Mendoza, eds., *Providing Global Public Goods: Managing Globalization* (New York: Oxford University Press, 2003); and Inge Kaul and Donald Blundin, "Global Public Goods and the United Nations," in *Global Governance and Development*, ed. Ocampo, Chapter 2.

2 The International Trade Organization (ITO) was agreed in Havana in 1948 but not approved by the US Congress. Thus, the GATT agreement, signed in 1947, became the major instrument of trade cooperation until the creation of WTO in 1995.

3 Kaul and Blundin, "Global Public Goods."

4 Bruce Jenks, "UN Development Cooperation: The Roots of a Reform Agenda," in *Global Governance and Development*, ed. Ocampo, Chapter 5.

5 OECD/DAC, *Shaping the 21st Century: The Contribution of Development Co-operation* (Paris: OECD/DAC, 1996).

6 UN, *Realizing the Future We Want, Report of the UN System Task Team on the Post-2015 UN Development Agenda*, June 2012; UN, *A New Global Partnership: Eradicate Poverty and Transform Economies through Sustainable Development, Report of the High-Level Panel of Eminent Persons on the Post-2015 Development Agenda*, May 2013; UN, *A Life of Dignity for All: Accelerating Progress Towards the Millennium Development Goals and Advancing the United Nations Development Agenda beyond 2015, Report of the Secretary-General*, 26 July 2013.

7 UN, *The Global Conversation Begins: Emerging Views for a New Development Agenda*, 2013.

8 UN, *A New Global Partnership*, 9.

9 Ibid., opening statement of the executive summary.

10 UN Committee for Development Policy, *Report on the Fifteenth Session*, 18–22 March 2015.

11 As stated in UN, *Monterrey Consensus on Financing for Development*, 2002, para. 62, to "broaden and strengthen the participation of developing countries and countries with economies in transition in international economic decision-making and norm-setting."

12 UN, *A New Global Partnership*, 3 and 9.

13 UN CDP, *Report on the Twenty-First Session*, UN document E/2019/33, 11–15 March 2019. See a more detailed evaluation of the 2018 VNRs in UN CDP, "Voluntary National Reviews Report—What Do They (Not) Tell Us," *CDP Background Paper*, no. 49 (July 2019).

14 There are other issues, particularly strengthening the mechanisms for monitoring, accountability and, ultimately, enforceability of international commitments, to which I refer in this chapter only in relation to the MDGs and SDGs.

15 The area of international trade has come under threat from a resurgence of nationalism on the part of some of the major economies (including the United States and United Kingdom).

16 Following UN practice, I use this term here to refer to the elected officials and the international civil service that administer the different international organizations.

17 Pascal Lamy, "Statement to Delegations" (Geneva: World Trade Organization, 2005), www.wto.org/english/news_e/news05_e/stat_lamy_nov05_e.htm.

18 John Toye and Richard Toye, *The UN and Global Political Economy: Trade, Finance, and Development* (Bloomington, IN: Indiana University Press, 2004), 280.

19 Gert Rosenthal, "The Economic and Social Council of the United Nations," in *The Oxford Handbook on the United Nations*, ed. Thomas G. Weiss and Sam Daws, 2nd edn. (Oxford: Oxford University Press, 2007), 143.

20 Thomas G. Weiss, Tatiana Carayannis, and Richard Jolly, "The 'Third' United Nations," *Global Governance* 15, no. 2 (2009): 123–142; and Tatiana Carayannis and Thomas G. Weiss, *The "Third" United Nations: How Knowledge Brokers Help the UN Think* (Oxford: Oxford University Press, forthcoming). See also UN, *Delivering as One, Report of the Panel on United Nations System-Wide Coherence*, UN document A/61/583, 20 November 2006, para. 59.

21 UNDP, *Human Development Report 1992: Global Dimensions of Human Development* (New York: Oxford University Press, 1992), 82–83.

22 Commission on Global Governance, *Our Global Neighbourhood* (Oxford: Oxford University Press, 1995).

23 UN, *Delivering as One*, para. 59.

24 UN, *Report of the Commission of Experts Convened of the President of the UN General Assembly on Reforms of the International Monetary and Financial System* (New York: UN Stiglitz Commission, 2009); José Antonio Ocampo and Joseph E. Stiglitz, "From the G-20 to a Global Economic Coordination Council," *Journal of Globalization and Development* 2, no. 2 (2011): article 9.

25 Palais Royal Initiative, "Reform of the International Monetary System: A Cooperative Approach for the 21st Century," in *Reform of the International Monetary System: The Palais Royal Initiative*, ed. Jack T. Boorman and André Icard (New Delhi: Sage Publications, 2011), 24.

26 G20, "Leaders' Statement, The Pittsburgh Summit, 24–25 September 2009," para. 19.

27 Paul Martin, "The G20: From Global Crisis Responder to Global Steering Committee," in *Global Leadership in Transition: Making the G20 More Effective and Responsive*, ed. Colin I. Bradford and Wonhyuk Lim (Seoul and Washington, DC: Korea Development Institute and Brookings Institution Press, 2011), 13–15.

28 Kemal Dervis, "Towards Strengthened Global Economic Governance," in *New Ideas on Development after the Financial Crisis*, ed. Nancy Birdsall and Francis Fukuyama (Baltimore, MD: The Johns Hopkins University Press, 2011), 191–212.

ADDITIONAL READING

Richard Jolly, Louis Emmerij, and Thomas G. Weiss, *UN Ideas That Changed the World* (Bloomington, IN: Indiana University Press, 2009).

Inge Kaul, Pedro Conceicao, Katell Le Goulven, and R. Mendoza, eds., *Providing Global Public Goods: Managing Globalization* (New York: Oxford University Press, 2003).

José Antonio Ocampo, ed., *Global Governance and Development* (Oxford: Oxford University Press, 2016).

Gert Rosenthal, "The Economic and Social Council of the United Nations," in *The Oxford Handbook on the United Nations*, ed. Thomas G. Weiss and Sam Daws (Oxford: Oxford University Press, 2018), 2nd edn., 165–167.

John Toye and Richard Toye, *The UN and Global Political Economy: Trade, Finance and Development* (Bloomington, IN: Indiana University Press, 2004).

UN, *Report of the Commission of Experts Convened of the President of the UN General Assembly on Reforms of the International Monetary and Financial System* ("Stiglitz Commission") (New York: UN, 2009).

3

EMERGING POWERS, A DECLINING WEST, AND MULTILATERALISM

Kishore Mahbubani

The world stands at a curious moment of history on multilateralism. For three powerful reasons the case for strengthening multilateralism has never been stronger. First, the 7.5 billion plus people on planet earth now live in a small interdependent global village, with global challenges leaping effortlessly across sovereign borders, including financial crises, pandemics, terrorism, and especially global warming. All villages need strong village councils. Now, more than ever, our village needs stronger village councils, including the United Nations (UN), International Monetary Fund (IMF), World Bank, and World Trade Organization (WTO).

Second, the West, including Europe and the United States, which originally championed the 1945 rules-based order, need stronger multilateral institutions more than ever. With only 12 percent of the population of the global village and a declining share of economic and military power, the West's long-term geopolitical interests will shift from trying to preserve Western dominance to generating safeguards to protect the West's minority position in a new global configuration of power. The best way to protect minority rights is strengthening the rule of law and the institutions that promote it. As most organizations of global governance are designed for this purpose, the West should work to strengthen, not weaken, them.

Third, emerging powers—including China, India, Indonesia, and Brazil—have grown and prospered by participating actively in the forces of globalization that were unleashed by the 1945 rules-based order. China, for example, has become the biggest beneficiary of the open global trading system and emerged as the world's biggest trading nation. Hence, the emerging powers should be providing leadership to strengthen multilateralism. In theory, therefore, multilateralism should be strengthening.[1]

In practice, multilateralism is weakening, also for three reasons. First, the Trump administration is clearly hostile to multilateralism. Trump's former national security advisor, John Bolton, explicitly called for weakening the UN: "If the UN secretary building in New York lost 10 stories, it wouldn't make a bit of difference." He has also said: "If I were redoing the Security Council, I'd have one permanent member: The United States." Trump has leveled similar invective at the UN, once asking reporters, "when do you see the United Nations solving problems? They don't. They cause problems."[2] However, even the previous US administrations that paid lip service to the UN often tried to weaken it.

Second, while theoretically Europeans support stronger multilateralism (as expressed eloquently in the speeches of French President Emmanuel Macron), in practice they have shown no courage in defending the UN from a three-decade-long assault on the UN system by successive US administrations. As a result, Europe has effectively been complicit in a long-standing US strategy to keep the UN weak. Even during the Cold War, when Moscow and Washington disagreed on everything, both actively conspired to keep the UN feeble by, for example, selecting pliable secretaries-general, such as Kurt Waldheim, and bullying them into dismissing or sidelining competent or conscientious UN civil servants who showed any backbone, squeezing UN budgets, and planting CIA and KGB agents across the UN system. This chapter documents how Europe undermined its own long-term geopolitical interests by weakening the global multilateral system.

Third, while the emerging powers, especially China and India, support stronger multilateralism in theory, they too have been reluctant to challenge the Western domination of global multilateral institutions. In early 2009, after the global financial crisis shook the West, its governments agreed in theory that their insistence on controlling the leadership of the IMF and World Bank was unjustified. Hence, at the Group of 20 (G-20) meeting in London in April 2009, Western nations explicitly issued the following statement: "We agree that the heads and senior leadership of the international financial institutions should be appointed through an open, transparent, and merit-based selection process."[3] Despite this commitment, the United States and Europe retained control of both the IMF and World Bank in the following decade. Neither China nor India challenged this explicit hypocrisy. In part, this happened because short-term geopolitical rivalries between these two powers trumped their common long-term interest in having a greater say in the IMF and the World Bank.

This chapter explores this curious gap between theory and practice in multilateralism in the early twenty-first century. Firstly, it demonstrates, through two case studies of the WHO and IAEA, how the West has been unwisely weakening key multilateral institutions. Secondly, it spells out how the policy of weakening multilateral institutions is fundamentally against the long-term interests of Western societies. Thirdly, it suggests how emerging powers, especially China and India, can provide better leadership for the multilateral system.

How the West weakens multilateralism

One undeniable fact underpins the case for multilateralism: we live in a small interdependent global village. Curiously, the most eloquent expressions of this reality often have emanated from such previous Western leaders as Bill Clinton, Al Gore, and Tony Blair.[4]

Future historians will be puzzled that even though such Western political leaders as well as thought leaders among journalists and in Western universities have taken the lead in developing a strong global intellectual consensus that we now live in one world, Western governments have taken the lead in weakening the multilateral institutions that our interdependent world needs. To add some nuance to this claim, it is important to emphasize that the United States and European countries are motivated by different considerations. The United States, as the world's dominant great power, finds that multilateral institutions constrain its unilateral tendencies. Hence, Washington has consistently pushed for the selection of weak UN secretaries-general and reductions in budgets to keep the entire UN system weak. The Europeans do not share the same desire to weaken that system but nonetheless resent their large share in the budget. Hence, they have joined the United States in working hard to keep UN budgets down. In so doing, the Europeans have failed to ask the obvious strategic question: would Europe's own long-term strategic interests be better served by a stronger or weaker global multilateral system? This chapter therefore documents how Europe has undermined its own long-term interests by conspiring with Washington to restrain the growth of the budgets of key UN institutions.

This section illustrates this point by looking carefully at two case studies, the World Health Organization (WHO) and International Atomic Energy Agency (IAEA). They demonstrate more clearly than other cases how the West, especially Europe, is undermining its own long-term interests by squeezing their budgets. Both Europe and North America are vulnerable to global pandemics. Similarly, the West has feared the illegal proliferation of nuclear weapons. To control these two threats, the West should have strengthened both the WHO and the IAEA in recent decades, but instead, in an act of strategic folly, the West has steadily weakened them.

In the first decades of the twenty-first century, the danger of global pandemics was obvious from the SARS virus in 2002–2003, the H1N1 bird flu virus in 2009, and the Ebola outbreaks in 2014 and 2019. As we move inexorably toward living in a more and more compact global village, one common threat is the rapid spread of pandemics. Distances have disappeared. Viruses move rapidly across continents. Hence, it is in the planet's interest to strengthen the global health institutions, especially the WHO. Yet, as Kelley Lee points out, we have done the opposite.[5] Lee dissects many flawed policies affecting the WHO, in particular three strategic errors.

The first allows short-term and often sectional special interests to override enlightened long-term interests in stronger institutions. As the fastest-shrinking and most affluent members of the global village, Western countries have a clear interest in strengthening the WHO to improve global health conditions and to develop its capability and legitimacy to fight major global epidemics. SARS began in a small village in China. From there it went to Hong Kong, and from there it leapt to two cities on opposite sides of the global village, Singapore and Toronto. The WHO helped ameliorate this crisis and gets high marks from respondents worldwide in a poll. Rather than strengthen the WHO and provide more resources, however, the major contributors have starved it.

In 1970–1971, the WHO received 62 percent of its budget from core (or regular) budgetary funds (RBFs) and 18 percent from non-core (or extra-budgetary) funds. By 2006–2007, the ratio had reversed to only 28 percent from core and 72 percent from non-core resources. The WHO can make long-term plans only from its core budget because non-core resources can disappear overnight. Why have Western countries reduced their contributions to core budgets? The simple answer is that all member states make decisions about the allocation of such funds. So even though the Western countries, especially European ones, contribute the largest amount to the WHO's "income," they are outvoted when it comes to the "expenditures." Europeans thus prefer non-core contributions, because they control expenditures. However, in seeking short-term control, the Europeans did not ask the larger and long-term strategic question about whether they were thereby undermining their own long-term interests by keeping a key global institution, the WHO, weak.

One key point should be emphasized. The total US and European finance for the UN system is paltry. In pursuing this penny-wise and pound-foolish strategy, the West has weakened a key global institution like the WHO that could play a key role in protecting both the United States and Europe global pandemics. To date, no major Western leader has urged the reconsideration of this short-sighted policy.

To make matters worse, the "Geneva Group" of 14 major Western donors introduced zero real growth to the RBFs of all UN organizations, including the WHO. This policy continued under both the more internationally minded Clinton-Gore administration and the less enlightened Bush-Cheney administration. In short, in Washington and elsewhere, the Western decision to starve UN organizations seemed driven by a myopic desire to control the global agenda and against its own interests.

The second strategic error was to allow the traditional Western interest in biomedicine, with its focus on individual behavior and biology, to trump growing global interest in social medicine, with its emphasis on understanding and transforming social conditions underlying health and disease. Policies toward the WHO are heavily influenced by the big pharmaceutical corporations, whose bottom lines reflect individual health spending, not collective well-being. Lee adds that "the rise of neoliberal-based fiscal policies brought even greater restrictions on public spending on health."[6] The *New York Times* reported that at the 2018 World Health Assembly in Geneva, the US delegation

> sought, unsuccessfully, to thwart a WHO effort aimed at helping poor countries obtain access to lifesaving medicines. Washington, supporting the pharmaceutical industry, has long resisted calls to modify patent laws as a way of increasing drug availability in the developing world, but health advocates say the Trump administration has ratcheted up its opposition to such efforts.

The same article quoted Ilona Kickbusch, director of the Global Health Centre in Geneva at the Graduate Institute of International and Development Studies, on the "growing fear" among public health experts that the Trump administration was damaging institutions like the WHO: "It's making everyone very nervous, because if you can't agree on health multilateralism, what kind of multilateralism can you agree on?"[7]

The third strategic error has been to dilute the role of the WHO as the leading global health agency and to augment the resources of the World Bank for health. The latter's lending on health went from roughly half of the WHO budget in 1984 to more than two and a half times larger in 1996. The West prefers to lend money through the World Bank which is controlled by it, rather than the WHO. Moreover, the creation of large private foundations, especially the Bill and Melinda Gates Foundation, also undermined the central role of the WHO. As Anne-Emanuelle Birn says, "In part-funding selected initiatives, the [Gates] Foundation has influenced the decisions of other donor agencies, and thus global health priorities in general."[8] As a result, Lee concludes, "for the WHO, it has meant a substantial bypassing of its role as the lead UN health agency."[9]

As the most prosperous occupants of an ever-shrinking global village, Western populations have a clear interest in preventing the emergence of epidemics. No Western state has the moral or political authority to investigate the internal health conditions of other states. The WHO does. Similarly, neither the World Bank nor the Gates Foundation has the authority or legitimacy to galvanize instant global cooperation to deal with an epidemic. The vast majority of developing countries often hesitate to welcome the World Bank or the Gates Foundation, which are perceived as keen to investigate the responsibility for generating any new global epidemic. But they normally open their doors to WHO representatives whom they perceive to be defending global, not narrower, interests.

The mistakes in dealing with global health are replicated in the security arena for nuclear proliferation. The logical consequence of a fear about such proliferation should be to strengthen the global institution that deals with this problem. The Commission of Eminent Persons who reviewed the future of the IAEA in 2008 found that despite the Western rhetoric after 9/11, the IAEA had also been subjected to the same zero-budget-growth policies applied to all UN organizations.[10]

One of the IAEA's key roles is the inspection of nuclear power plants to ensure compliance with international standards and verify the absence of diversion of fuel for weapons. The IAEA needs to keep on its regular payroll a strong and large team of dedicated nuclear inspectors, who will stay with the IAEA only if they have guaranteed competitive salaries and career prospects. The IAEA can provide these good terms and conditions only from reliable and predictable assessed, not voluntary, contributions. However, exactly the opposite has occurred. Europe's myopia in weakening the inspection capacity of the IAEA is difficult to understand in the light of both the dangers of faulty nuclear power plants (in Chernobyl) and illegal nuclear proliferation on its doorstep (in Libya). Hence, Europe is once again undermining its own long-term interests in weakening the IAEA.

These brief case studies are not aberrations but rather common bill-of-fare for all UN organizations, whether they are technical or more political. The UNDS has suffered generally from the increase in tied funds and circumscribed autonomy.

Migration: why weaken multilateralism now?

The West is weakening the very institutions that it needs to strengthen its long-term security. It should undertake cold and dispassionate analyses of its future threats.[11] No major inter-state wars are poised to break out in Europe because of the stable military balance of power. Instead, the main threats range from illegal immigrants to dangerous viruses (like SARS and Ebola), and from lone terrorists carrying Weapons of Mass Destruction (WMD) to cyber-attacks.

For most of the second half of the twentieth century, Europe worried mostly about a military invasion from the Soviet Union. This threat has effectively gone, although Russia will remain a strategic competitor in other dimensions. A central threat to Europe will come from illegal migration from Africa. In many areas, predictions are perilous but not in demographics. In 1950, the EU's combined population (379 million)[12] was nearly double that of Africa's (229 million). Today, Africa's population (1.2 billion in 2015)[13] is double that of the EU (513 million in 2018).[14] By 2050, Africa's population is projected to be nearly five times larger: 2.49 billion[15] versus 524 million at present.[16] The Mediterranean is all that separates Europe from the populous continent of Africa. Hence, without more economic development and jobs to Africa, it will inevitably export more African migrants to Europe. Indeed, there has already been a significant increase of Africans having to enter Europe, legally and illegally. The Pew Research Center reported in 2018 that "the population of sub-Saharan migrants [in Europe] has been boosted by the influx of nearly 1 million asylum applicants (970,000) between 2010 and 2017."[17] Pew also reported that "in 2017, about 5.2 million North African immigrants lived in EU countries, Norway and Switzerland, compared with about 3 million in 1990."[18]

To protect its long-term security, Europe should be working energetically to strengthen the institutions that could accelerate the social and economic development of Africa, including those of the UN development system, to help prevent boatloads of Africans from trying to cross the tiny Mediterranean. Europe has already paid a terrible political price when it experienced a small surge of illegal migrants, from Africa and the Middle East. In 2015–2016, this surge of illegal migrants fostered the rising success of populist parties, including in the governments of Hungary, Poland, and Italy in 2019 and as increasing minorities even in Germany and France.

Many European commentators have condemned these populist parties with great moral conviction. They blame the populist leaders, not the traditional centrist parties, for the emergence of populism. Yet, centrist parties from the right and the left have dominated the European political scene for decades. In their period of political domination, they have created or supported policies that have led to the surge of migrants, which has consequently led to the rise of populism. Those who vote for populist parties are not morally deficient. They communicate loud political signals about their insecure future that have been ignored by the traditional elites from centrist parties.

"We must confront a flood of people pouring out of the countries of the Middle East, and meanwhile the depth of Africa has been set in motion. Millions of people are preparing to set out" is the description by Hungary's populist leader Viktor Orban. While often derided by the Western media, he captures the fears of ordinary Europeans in the face of a potential mass migration to Europe:

> It is a modern-day global mass migration, which we cannot see the end of: economic migrants hoping for a better life, refugees and drifting masses mixed up together. This is an uncontrolled and unregulated process, and ... the most precise definition of this is "invasion."[19]

Most centrist European leaders will be reluctant to admit that they have been responsible for the rise of populist leaders by refusing to pay heed to the fears of their own people. If European leaders want to address such fears of mass migration and also address the long-term threat to their security, they should first ask themselves whether it has been wise for Europe to weaken global multilateral institutions as well as the UNDS for short-term financial gains. Some simple strategic common sense might be the following calculation. For every dollar spent by the UNDS in Africa, Europe would probably pay the largest share of, say, 30 cents. Yet 70 cents would also be contributed by the rest of the world to develop Africa. The main beneficiaries of the development of Africa, after the residents of the continent, would be Europe. Therefore, to protect their own long-term interests, they should do the opposite of what they currently are doing— namely, increase rather than decrease their funding of the UNDS.

This is not the only area where the Europeans will need to make a strategic U-turn in their African policies. To promote economic development, Europe should welcome the efforts of other major economic powers to invest in Africa. For example, China has emerged as the largest new investor in Africa; Figure 3.1 shows how over the last two decades China has become the continent's largest trading partner.

Instead, Europe is opposing or criticizing Chinese investment in Africa. In April 2018, 27 of the 28 EU member nations (except Hungary) signed a report stating that the Belt and Road Initiative (BRI) "runs counter to the EU agenda for liberalizing trade and pushes the balance of power in favor of subsidized Chinese companies."[20] The reasons for European opposition are complex, but one key reason is loyalty to the trans-Atlantic alliance. Yet Europe, not the United States, will suffer if Africa fails to develop. Europeans have been critical of Chinese investment practices, which should be improved. However, the best way to improve them is to work with China. When China convenes a high-level China–Africa conference, virtually all African leaders attend. A better way forward would consist of a joint African–Chinese–European partnership to develop Africa. In failing to understand and grasp these new geopolitical opportunities, Europe is undermining its own long-term geopolitical interests.

Similarly, Europe is also undermining its own interests by conspiring with the United States to retain control of the most important global economic institutions, the IMF and the World Bank. As indicated, Europe and the United States had promised at the G-20 leaders' meeting in London in April 2009 that future leaders of these international financial institutions would be selected in a "meritocratic process." Instead, all subsequent heads of the IMF and the World Bank again came from Europe and the US, respectively.

Future historians undoubtedly will cite Western myopia in insisting on maintaining control of these two organizations rather than fostering a global sense of ownership. In insisting on maintaining control, the West does not seem to understand how fundamentally the world has changed. A simple boat metaphor captures the profound change. In the past, when the world's

Since 2000, **China** has catapulted from being a small investor in Africa to becoming its biggest economic partner.

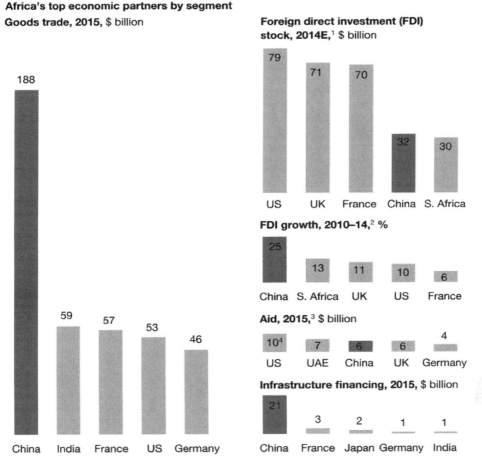

Africa's top economic partners by segment

Goods trade, 2015, $ billion

Foreign direct investment (FDI) stock, 2014E,[1] $ billion

FDI growth, 2010–14,[2] %

Aid, 2015,[3] $ billion

Infrastructure financing, 2015, $ billion

[1]Estimated according to compound annual growth rate from 2009 to 2012.
[2]For countries other than China, we made projections using historical data.
[3]Office of Development Assistance and other official flows, 2015 for Organisation for Economic Co-operation and Development (OECD) countries, 2012 for China.
[4]According to United States Agency for International Development data, US foreign aid to Africa was $11.9 billion in FY 2015 and $7.4 billion in FY 2016. The discrepancy with OECD data shown is likely due to the fact that US fiscal years start in October, whereas OECD data is for calendar years.

Source: Bilateral trade database, International Trade Centre trade map, 2015; Bilateral FDI database, UN Conference on Trade and Development, 2012; Foreign Aid Explorer, USAID; Ministry of Commerce, People's Republic of China, 2015; "Infrastructure Financing Trends in Africa–2015," The Infrastructure Consortium for Africa, 2015

Figure 3.1 China has become Africa's biggest economic partner.[1]

Note
1 www.weforum.org/agenda/2018/09/three-myths-about-chinas-investment-in-africa-and-why-they-need-to-be-dispelled.

population lived in 193 separate countries, it was as though they were living in 193 separate boats. Now, as a result of our world shrinking, the 7.5 billion members of the global population no longer live in 193 separate boats. They live in 193 separate cabins on the same boat. To stay with the metaphor, we also have captains and crews taking care of each cabin but none of the boat.

If the world population is aboard the same ship, it is surely in the interest of the West to give the remaining 88 percent of humanity an equal sense of ownership of the fate of the boat. Western control of these two institutions is driven by the short-term considerations of national prestige in retaining Western control, not by a rational and strategic evaluation of whether long-term Western interests are best served by ceding control of two key global institutions. Indeed, both the IMF and World Bank could be more effective globally if they were perceived as genuinely owned by the 193 countries of the world.

Equally important, the insistence of the West in retaining the control of these two key institutions is forcing other states to create parallel institutions that have the potential of deploying more capital and resources than the IMF or World Bank. For example, over 125 countries have signed up to join China's BRI, which may mobilize up to a trillion dollars to support the BRI. Similarly, China has also set up the Asian Infrastructure Investment Bank (AIIB) with the support of many other countries. The five BRICS (Brazil, Russia, India, China, and South Africa) have also set up a development bank, which could prove be a game changer in the global financial order. In November 2019, it was reported that the BRICS had proposed "creating a cryptocurrency for settling payment transactions between the countries."[21]

These major changes and developments suggest why the West should reconsider its decades-long policies of trying to weaken UN institutions and retain control of the IMF and the World Bank. These policies reflect a different global environment when the threats to the West, especially to Europe, were different. Thus, it would be wiser for the West to re-examine the premises on which its policies to global multilateral institutions were based.

Can the Global South, especially Asia, save multilateralism?

Since enlightened policies on multilateralism are unlikely to come from the West in the short term, can emerging economic and political powers, especially from China and India, provide the leadership not only to preserve but also to strengthen the current, however weak, institutions of global governance as well as promote the culture and practices of multilateralism more generally? Despite Asia's diversity and a recent tradition of mutual suspicion between Beijing and New Delhi, there is hope that its return will result in strengthening multilateralism. As Asian norms and practices infect the global political chemistry, this could result in a strengthening of the global multilateral architecture.

This bold statement will come as a surprise since Asia is sometimes viewed as a troubled continent with such geopolitical flash points as India-Pakistan, the South China Sea, and the Korean peninsula. Yet, there has been no major inter-state war since the Sino-Vietnamese War of 1979; by and large, the guns have been silent in East Asia, Southeast Asia, and South Asia, while conflict is concentrated primarily in West Asia, mainly because of Western interventions in Afghanistan, Iraq, and Syria.

Indeed, Asia should not have experienced peace because the biggest power shifts have taken place in Asia and will continue there. Until 1820, the two largest economies were always those of China and India, as illustrated in Figure 3.2. It is especially noteworthy how fast China and India are returning to their natural number one and two positions, as depicted in Figure 3.3.

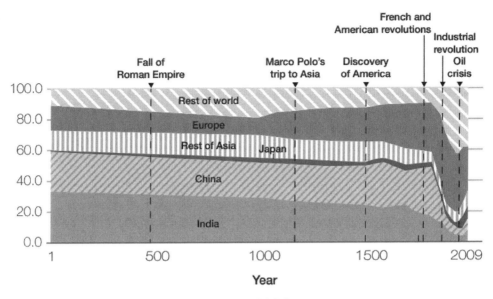

Figure 3.2 Evolution of regional and country shares of global GDP.

History teaches us that such shifts of power are accompanied by armed conflicts. Scholars have long worried that Asia would emerge as a region of conflict. Richard Betts, for example, remarked that "one of the reasons for optimism about peace in Europe is the apparent satisfaction of the great powers with the status quo," while in East Asia there is "an ample pool of festering grievances, with more potential for generating conflict than during the Cold War, when bipolarity helped stifle the escalation of parochial disputes."[22] Aaron L. Friedberg has remarked similarly:

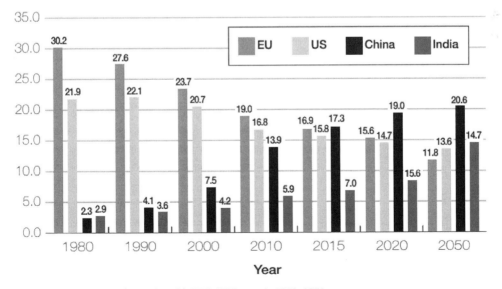

Figure 3.3 Percentage share of world GDP (PPP terms), 1980–2050.

Data sources: 1980–2020—IMF Database (2016 Economic Outlook). Accessed 3/3/2017—PwC GDP.

while civil war and ethnic strife will continue for some time to smoulder along Europe's peripheries, in the long run it is Asia that seems far more likely to be the cockpit of great-power conflict. The half millennium during which Europe was the world's primary generator of war (as well as wealth and knowledge) is coming to a close. But, for better or for worse, Europe's past could be Asia's future.[23]

Barry Buzan and Gerald Segal, in the immediate aftermath of the Cold War, said of East Asia that

there is little that binds its states and societies together but much that divides them. Any chance of finding unifying common ground against the West has long since disappeared ... history, therefore, strongly reinforces the view that Asia is in danger of heading back to the future.[24]

The Western consensus that armed conflict was inevitable in Asia has proved wrong after 30 years. These dramatic failures to understand the dominant peaceful dynamic of Asia demonstrate that there is a real need for Western scholars to re-examine their understanding of Asia.

Is the United States a peaceful country and China an emerging militaristic one? Former US president Jimmy Carter, for one, has noted that the United States is "the most warlike nation in the history of the world" and been at peace for only 16 years of its over 240 years since its founding in 1776.[25] As China's economy grows, it will certainly emerge as a major military power but perhaps will follow Sun Tzu, who advocated that "to fight and conquer in all your battles is not supreme excellence; supreme excellence consists in breaking the enemy's resistance without fighting."[26] Of the five permanent members of the UN Security Council, China is the only one that has not fought in any foreign wars outside of its borders since World War II.

The culture of peace in Asia is also reflected in ASEAN, the world's second most successful regional organization after the European Union, despite the fact that ASEAN seemed destined to fail.[27] At its founding in 1967, Southeast Asia was the most conflict-ridden region in the world, with the Vietnam war raging. With its ethnic and religious diversity, Southeast Asia was labeled as the "Balkans of Asia" because in a relatively small and densely populated space, some 240 million Muslims, 120 million Christians, 140 million Buddhists, and 7 million Hindus reside in addition to millions of Confucianists and Taoists. No region is better suited to undergo a clash of civilizations.

Does that mean that ASEAN is a perfect organization? Far from it. Yet, its strength lies in its weakness. It does not represent a threat to any great power but rather an opportunity. Hence, as the brilliant former Singaporean foreign minister, George Yeo, said, "ASEAN's leadership is the most preferred because all others would be threatened by others' leadership."[28]

Despite Brexit, the European Union remains a far more successful organization than ASEAN. It has deeper cooperation among its members. It also has no prospect of war, which ASEAN has not achieved; but within ASEAN there have been no wars since its founding. However, it is ahead of the EU in some respects. If any objective observer of multilateral organization had been asked even five years ago which organization is likely to break up first, ASEAN or the EU, the answer would have been ASEAN. Nonetheless, with Brexit looming and growing discomfort among some Central Europeans over a borderless EU, ASEAN's looser articles of association seemingly have made it resilient and durable.

More importantly, while the EU member states have kept peace within the EU, they have initiated it or participated in conflicts on the periphery of the EU, including in the former Yugoslavia, the Middle East (Iraq and Syria), and North Africa (Libya). By contrast, the ASEAN countries have not participated in external armed conflicts. Hence, there is hope that the eco-system of peace ASEAN has developed could infect and spread elsewhere in Asia. In this way, Asia could develop its own multilateral security culture and norms that could later serve as a model. In short, the world needs to develop a deeper understanding of the new political and strategic culture developing in Asia.

Similarly, other Asian-generated multilateral institutions could provide exemplary models of governance for development. As mentioned, a good example is the Asian Infrastructure Investment Bank (AIIB) set up by China in January 2016. Washington opposed AIIB's establishment and urged its allies not to join. In the end, most countries ignored the pressure, including the United Kingdom, Germany, Australia, and India.

Paradoxically, the AIIB has ended up having higher governance standards than the IMF and the World Bank, where the United States has insisted on retaining its veto power by consistently raising the "super majority" needed for decisions on major issues. It formerly was 75 percent when Washington's voting share was around 25 percent. As the US voting share shrank to 16 percent, it insisted that the "super majority" should be raised to 85 percent. By contrast, China has pledged not to raise the AIIB "super majority," even though China will lose its veto. As a democratic country, the United States has been less democratic in its management of global multilateral institutions than China, a non-democratic country. Similarly, the size of the AIIB management and staff has been kept leaner than that in the IMF and World Bank, where resident boards in Washington, DC participate in key decision-making on a daily basis. By contrast, the AIIB board is non-resident, demonstrating that its standards of corporate governance are higher than those of the IMF and the World Bank.

As indicated, the United States and Europe should no longer insist on control over the IMF and World Bank. Instead, they should allow a fully meritocratic selection process and allow Asian and other Global South countries to exercise leadership. Fortunately, Asia has produced a strong number of development economists, like Manmohan Singh, the former PM of India, Goh Chok Tong, the former PM of Singapore, Montek Singh Ahulwalia, the former Chief Planner of India, and Sri Mulyani, the current finance minister of Indonesia, who could serve as president of the World Bank. Similarly, Asia has equally strong candidates to lead the IMF, including Raghuran Rajan, the former governor of the Central Bank of India, Tharman Shanmugaratnam, the former Finance Minister of Singapore and Chairman of the International Monetary and Financial Committee (IMFC), and Zhou Xiaochuan, the former governor of the People's Bank of China. Such a change in leadership would be an important symbolic gesture to demonstrate that the West is willing to allow the remaining 88 percent of the world's population, outside the Western world, to feel a sense of ownership of these major multilateral development institutions.

Similarly, the West could generate a greater sense of global ownership of the UN Security Council, the most powerful international security organization, by changing the composition of its members. The council's 15 members are composed of the five permanent ones (China, France, Russia, the United Kingdom, and the United States) and 10 elected ones. Yet the P-5 dominate because of their veto power and continuity in office.[29]

The UN set up the Open-Ended Working Group on Security Council reform in 1993 with a view toward altering the composition and rules to reflect contemporary geopolitical realities. No progress has been made. The Security Council cannot remain a fossil representing yesterday's great powers. It must integrate tomorrow's great powers. The challenge here is to create a political consensus on who should be the new great powers to be included.[30] The council will soon face a critical challenge. If it does not change its composition to include rising powers like Brazil and India, it will lose its credibility.[31]

Conclusion

Multilateral cooperation for development and for security would benefit from rethinking the nationalities of senior personnel, the operating procedures of institutions, and the composition of essential UN and other organizations. Since the UN system was created in 1945, the global population has soared and the size of the global GNP has exploded. Common sense dictates that the budget of the UN system should also be increased significantly to meet growing multilateral demands. Yet, no UN Secretary-General has felt able to propose a simple suggestion to increase the UN budget because of the negativity of the P-5 that dominates UN decision-making. Similarly, in making key UN appointments—including leadership of the UNDP, WFP, and UNICEF—the Secretary-General abides by the wishes of the P-5, not the larger geopolitical community. In short, the domination of the UN system by the P-5 is pernicious and distorting. A more representative Security Council would break this distorting stranglehold and help the entire UN system.

To bring about significant change in the current multilateral system, we need to create a global consensus that our small, interdependent global village requires strengthened, not weakened, organizations of global governance, including the UN system. Fortunately, even though many Western governments are resisting reform and rejuvenation of the UN, some of their populations are calling for the strengthening of global multilateral institutions in the face of such existential threats as climate change. Gradually, emerging powers as well as other members of the Global South will have to assume greater responsibility and enhanced leadership if we are to begin strengthening, rather than weakening, the global multilateral order.

NOTES

1 Kishore Mahbubani, *The Great Convergence* (New York: Public Affairs, 2013), 44–47.
2 John Wagner, "Trump Re-Ups Criticism of United Nations, Saying It's Causing Problems, Not Solving Them," *The Washington Post*, 26 December 2016, www.washingtonpost.com/news/post-politics/wp/2016/12/28/trump-re-ups-criticism-of-united-nations-saying-its-causing-problems-not-solving-them.
3 International Monetary Fund, 2009, *London Summit—Leaders Statement*, www.imf.org/external/np/sec/pr/2009/pdf/g20_040209.pdf.
4 See, for example, Bill Clinton, *Speech in Mukono, Uganda*, 23 March 1998, http://clinton3.nara.gov/Africa/19980324-3374.html; Al Gore, "A New Security Agenda for the Global Age," *U.S. Foreign Policy Agenda* 5, no. 2 (2000): 35–38; and Tony Blair, *Speech at Labour Conference*, 28 September 1999, www.theguardian.com/politics/1999/sep/28/labourconference.labour14.
5 Kelley Lee, *The World Health Organization (WHO)* (New York: Routledge, 2009).
6 Ibid., 79.
7 Andrew Jacobs, "Opposition to Breast-Feeding Resolution by U.S. Stuns World Health Officials," *New York Times*, 8 July 2018, www.nytimes.com/2018/07/08/health/world-health-breastfeeding-ecuador-trump.html.
8 Ibid., 116.
9 Ibid., 117.
10 IAEA, *Report of the Commission of Eminent Persons on the Future of the Agency*, 23 May 2008, www.belfercenter.org/sites/default/files/files/publication/gov2008-22gc52inf-4.pdf.
11 For a discussion by the author, see Mahbubani, *Has the West Lost It? A Provocation* (London: Allen Lane, 2018), 44–53.
12 EEA, 2016, *Population Trends 1950–2100: Globally and within Europe*, www.eea.europa.eu/data-and-maps/indicators/total-population-outlook-from-unstat-3/assessment-1.
13 UN Population Division, 2019, *UN World Population Prospects 2019*, https://population.un.org/wpp/Download/Standard/Population.
14 Eurostat, 2019, *Population and Population Change Statistics*, https://ec.europa.eu/eurostat/statistics-explained/index.php/Population_and_population_change_statistics.

15 https://population.un.org/wpp/Graphs/Probabilistic/POP/TOT/903.

16 Eurostat, 2019, *The EU's Population Projected up to 2100*, https://ec.europa.eu/eurostat/web/products-eurostat-news/-/DDN-20190710-1.

17 "At Least a Million Sub-Saharan Africans Moved to Europe Since 2010," *Pew Research Center*, 22 March 2018, www.pewresearch.org/global/2018/03/22/at-least-a-million-sub-saharan-africans-moved-to-europe-since-2010.

18 Phillip Connor, "International Migration from Sub-Saharan Africa Has Grown Dramatically since 2010," *Pew Research Center*, 28 February 2018, www.pewresearch.org/fact-tank/2018/02/28/international-migration-from-sub-saharan-africa-has-grown-dramatically-since-2010.

19 Viktor Orban, "Speech at the Opening of the World Scientific Forum, November 7, 2015," quoted in Ivan Krastev and Stephen Holmes, *The Light That Failed: A Reckoning* (London: Allen Lane, 2019), 35.

20 Dana Heide, Till Hoppe, Stephan Scheuer, and Klaus Stratmann, "EU Ambassadors Band Together Against Silk Road," *Handelsblatt Today*, 17 April 2018, www.handelsblatt.com/today/politics/china-first-eu-ambassadors-band-together-against-silk-road/23581860.html.

21 Yogita Khatri, "BRICS Member Nations Propose Creating a Cryptocurrency for Payment Settlements," *The Block*, 15 November 2019, www.theblockcrypto.com/post/47230/brics-member-nations-propose-creating-a-cryptocurrency-for-payment-settlements.

22 Richard K. Betts, "Wealth, Power and Instability," *International Security* 18, no. 3 (Winter 1993–1994): 64.

23 Aaron L. Friedberg, "Ripe for Rivalry," *International Security* 18, no. 3 (Winter 1993–1994): 7.

24 Barry Buzan and Gerald Segal, "Rethinking East Asian Security," *Survival* 36, no. 2 (1994): 7.

25 David Brennan, "Jimmy Carter Took Call about China from Concerned Donald Trump: 'China has not wasted a single penny on war,'" *Newsweek*, 15 April 2019, www.newsweek.com/donald-trump-jimmy-carter-china-war-infrastructure-economy-trade-war-church-1396086.

26 Sun Tzu, *The Art of War*, trans. Lionel Giles (M.A. Pax Librorum Publishing House, 2009), www.paxlibrorum.com/books/taowde.

27 Kishore Mahbubani and Jeffery Sng, *The ASEAN Miracle* (Singapore: NUS Press, 2017), 3.

28 Ibid.

29 See Sebastian von Einsedel, David Malone, and Bruno Stagno, eds., *The United Nations Security Council: From Cold War to the 21st Century* (Boulder, CO: Lynne Rienner, 2016).

30 For a proposal by the author on getting from here to there, see Mahbubani, *The Great Convergence*, 244.

31 See Mahbubani, *The Great Convergence*, 111–116.

ADDITIONAL READING

Parag Khanna, *The Future Is Asian* (New York: Simon and Schuster, 2019).

Kishore Mahbubani, *The Great Convergence* (New York: Public Affairs, 2013).

Kishore Mahbubani, *Has the West Lost It? A Provocation* (London: Allen Lane, 2018).

Marty Natalegawa, *Does ASEAN Matter? A View from Within* (Singapore: ISEAS, 2018).

4

ENVIRONMENT AND DEVELOPMENT IN THE UN

Maria Ivanova

In September 2019, the United Nations Environment Programme (UNEP) presented an activist youth organization, Fridays For Future, which had been organizing climate strikes in over 2,000 locations around the world, with its highest honor—the Champions of the Earth award. Speaking on behalf of the organization at the award ceremony in New York, 15-year-old Kallan Benson declined the prize, stating that young people could not accept it. "Instead," she stressed, "we offer to hold it for you to earn. You at the United Nations hold the power to save humanity from itself. You must act in time to become the real champions of the Earth."[1]

This powerful act of protest emphasized the importance of the environmental crisis and the significance of the UN as the primary organization at the international level with the responsibility and authority for solving inherently global problems. Mounting global challenges such as climate breakdown and mass extinction of species outstrip the capabilities of any one state, organization, and the UN to address alone. They demand intentional engagement of the three UNs—the UN of the member states, the UN of the secretariat and various UN agencies and programs, and the UN of independent experts, civil society, the private sector, and nongovernmental organizations (NGOs).[2] Yet, the gap between the intergovernmental negotiations and engagement of nongovernmental actors has widened and deepened. At the 25th Conference of the Parties to the climate change convention, COP25, in December 2019 in Madrid, Spain, tensions between environment and development flared up, protesting activists were removed from the plenary room, and collective action suffered.

Engagement of all three UNs had begun in 1972 at the first UN Conference on the Human Environment, the Stockholm Conference. The Stockholm Conference was the first global UN meeting with NGO participation. Although NGOs were not allowed to speak at the plenary sessions or participate in working groups, they delivered information to the public, shaped perceptions, and raised awareness, initiating a trend of engagement of nongovernmental actors at the UN. Subsequently, environmental agreements would rely on all three UNs to ensure ambition and implementation and to bring environmental concerns into global consciousness and mobilize global citizenship. Yet, the United Nations has remained state-based, prone to lowest-common-denominator dynamics, and averse to ensuring compliance and implementation through robust enforcement mechanisms. This chapter explains the trajectory of global environmental governance, including the milestone global conferences where core

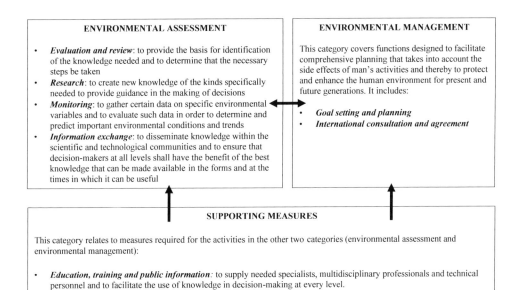

Figure 4.1 Framework for environmental action of the Stockholm Action Plan.[1]

Note

1 The figure is adapted from the Action Plan for Human Environment, 1972. Available online: https://bit.ly/2K3c4zT.

norms and institutions were created, two of the key global environmental conventions for major environmental problems, and the challenges to compliance and implementation. The tension between environment and development that shaped the initial intergovernmental discussions in the 1970s persists and, unless resolved, will continue to obstruct action for addressing global environmental concerns.

Global environmental conferences

Global environmental conferences have become an indelible feature of international politics that offer opportunities for leadership and social change. In 1972, governments convened at the UN Conference on the Human Environment in Stockholm and identified key global environmental problems, set global goals, and created global institutions (see Figure 4.1). A series of global conferences on environment and sustainable development followed. The UN Conference on Environment and Development (the Rio Earth Summit) took place in 1992, the World Summit on Sustainable Development (the Johannesburg Summit) in 2002, and the Rio+20 Conference on Sustainable Development in 2012. States have also been convening at global gatherings on particular issues and developing multilateral environmental agreements on ozone, climate, chemicals and hazardous waste, and biodiversity, among others, and their COPs (conferences of the parties) are often gathering places for the three United Nations. In 2022, governments plan to convene Stockholm+50 to commemorate the half-century mark of the creation of UNEP and the Stockholm Conference. Critics of global summits argue that these large gatherings are irrelevant, wasteful, and even counterproductive because they convene and empower nation states—an outdated governance unit. Yet the rapid growth of issues, actors, and agendas actually makes global conferences more relevant than ever. They galvanize international attention, offer opportunities to set goals and commit resources to ensure compliance and implementation, and provide critical junctures where states, secretariats, civil society, and the private sector converge and can shape ideas and institutions for decades.

Environment-development tensions and the role of the Third UN

The global political agenda for the 1972 Stockholm Conference was captured in the powerful motto, "Only One Earth." However, the interconnectedness of ecological realities was challenged by a highly fragmented and divided political reality. Many developing countries had only gained formal independence within the previous decade, and their main concern in the 1960s and 1970s was using economic growth to ensure their autonomy. In the context of post-colonialism, environment and development were pitted against each other.

Confronted with the environmental aspects of modern poverty, such as urban blight, epidemic disease, and sickness from unsanitary conditions, dirty water and food, and lack of energy, clothing, and shelter, many leaders in the Global South viewed the nascent environmental initiatives in the North as an implicit denial of their right to industrialize and develop. As an observer of the negotiations noted, developing countries saw environmental concerns as "a neat excuse for the industrialized nations to pull the ladder up behind them."[3] Henrique Cavalcanti, a member of the Brazilian delegation at the Stockholm Conference, recalled his vivid impression that "we [the North and South] lived in very different worlds."[4]

Suspicious of the industrialized world's political agenda, governments of many developing countries argued that environmental measures would negatively influence patterns of world trade, the international distribution of industry, and the comparative costs of production, as well as imposing limits on population growth, and would undercut whatever competitive advantages developing countries enjoyed.

The problems were clearly global and required global collective action. A common understanding and sense of urgency was critical and integrating scientific input into the political discussions was imperative. To this end, Maurice Strong, the secretary-general of the Stockholm Conference, convened a panel of 27 independent economists and scientists from the developing world in Founex, Switzerland, in June 1971. The initial nine-day meeting was followed by smaller conferences organized by the UN regional commissions in Asia, Africa, Latin America, and the Middle East and is an important example of the Third UN's impact. The *Founex Report* elaborated and endorsed the concerns of developing countries, while at the same time countering claims that development and environment were diametrically opposed. It established that environmental concerns were both more widespread and more relevant to developing countries' situation than they had appreciated.[5] The report affirmed that the environment should not be viewed as a barrier to development but as part of it. It also cemented developing countries' role in the conference process, as it assigned specific tasks for delegations to complete before Stockholm such as producing national reports on environmental concerns that they were encountering.

Ultimately, the Stockholm Conference set up the landscape for international environmental governance, creating an anchor institution for the global environment, the United Nations Environment Programme (UNEP), with the mandate to coordinate the environmental activities in the UN system, undertake assessment of the world environment, and provide policy guidance and support for implementation.[6] Subsequently, UNEP initiated and facilitated the creation of a series of multilateral environmental agreements, also known as global environmental conventions, on ozone, climate change, biodiversity, and chemicals and hazardous waste, among others, and domestic environmental institutions in countries across the globe. The conventions became important instruments of global environmental governance.

The role of civil society grew over the years as NGOs used global conferences to advance networking and advocacy.[7] The World Commission on Environment and Development chaired by then-Norwegian prime minister Gro Harlem Brundtland engaged a number of experts and produced the seminal report *Our Common Future* in the run-up to the 1992 Rio Earth Summit.[8] Once again, a product of the Third UN had a significant impact on global environmental politics as the report defined sustainable development, put it firmly on the map of international affairs, and influenced the agenda of the summit, which transformed the international environmental stage by catalyzing a wave of new norms, policies, and institutions for the global environment. It established sustainable development as a new global paradigm and created consensus around the need to resolve a range of environmental issues through conventions on climate change, biodiversity, and desertification.

In 2002, the World Summit on Sustainable Development in Johannesburg affirmed the centrality of sustainable development as the core principle in international affairs and stimulated a political debate on reform of the international environmental institutions. In 2012, governments reconvened in Rio de Janeiro for the Rio+20 Conference on Sustainable Development. They committed to launching new global goals—what became the Sustainable Development Goals (SDGs) in 2015—and to reforming the environmental and sustainable development institutions. Many of the environmental conventions that UNEP had initiated articulated global goals that formed the basis for several of the SDGs, including goals 12 (responsible production and consumption), 13 (climate action), 14 (life below water), and 15 (life on land). The idea of sustainable development was institutionalized as a fundamental global goal and the UN system committed to assisting member states in attaining it. The 2030 Development Agenda thus reflects the march of integrating environment and development, a trajectory that began in Stockholm in 1972.

Global environmental conventions: ozone and climate

Global environmental conventions are an integral part of the international environmental governance system and an important element of the problem resolution value chain, which includes scientific assessment, policy development through a global convention, and assistance with compliance and implementation of the international commitments. They are essential legal instruments to raise awareness, gather information, and promote coordinated action toward resolving environmental problems. Since the early 1970s, the number of environmental treaties and the number of states party to them have increased, and the spectrum of issues covered has expanded, moving from conservation to protection of natural resources to combating climate change.

The creation of a robust body of international environmental law is one of the landmark successes in global environmental governance. Governments created international agreements on conservation and on pollution, broadly defined. The conservation treaties include the conventions on wetlands, trade in endangered species, migratory species, world heritage, biodiversity, and desertification, among others. The pollution treaties include the conventions on ozone layer protection, on chemicals and hazardous waste, on mercury, and on climate change. The creation of these agreements was to a great extent because of the efforts by UNEP to engage scientists, raise awareness, and work with governments in committing to collective action. The agreements on ozone and climate stand out as a success story and a persistent challenge.

The depletion of the ozone layer is perhaps the most significant and urgent global environmental problem that is close to being resolved and an example of the influence of UNEP as an international organization. UNEP identified, analyzed, developed an action agenda, and enabled governments to act toward the resolution of the problem. Scientific knowledge was an important foundation for the political process that led to this success. The 1985 Vienna Convention for the Protection of the Ozone Layer promoted international cooperation through systematic scientific observations and research, information exchange, and public awareness. It mandated parties to create legislation and regulate activities with potentially harmful effect on the ozone layer but provided no specific goals and mechanisms for their implementation. With significant leadership from UNEP, in 1987, 24 countries convened in Montreal and "promised to halve the production and use of ozone-destroying chemicals by 1999."[9] The Montreal Protocol committed countries to specific actions to control ozone-depleting substances, including banning the use of and trade in these chemicals. It contained economic incentives for participation and compliance, provisions for technology transfer, and stipulations for assessment of efficacy and for readjustment.[10] The creation of a financing mechanism to support the implementation of the convention—the Multilateral Fund—was a significant institutional innovation. The fund has been critical to ensuring collaboration from developing countries and supporting the successful implementation of the treaty. Since its inception, the Multilateral Fund has received more significant and more stable funding than UNEP's core financial mechanism, the Environment Fund.

The leadership role of the Second UN, of UNEP and its executive director at the time, Dr. Mostafa Tolba, was critical to the successful resolution of ozone depletion.[11] Scholars of the ozone regime and practitioners explain that Tolba "pushed UNEP to assume responsibility for getting a treaty because he felt so strongly that a formal agreement was essential for planetary survival"[12] and demonstrated "the very model of how a UN agency should operate in a complex international negotiation."[13] UNEP took the lead in managing the agreement and created the necessary institutional structures to support it. The Multilateral Fund financed member-state actions with the support of other UN development system (UNDS) organizations such as the UN Development Programme (UNDP) and UN Industrial Development Organization (UNIDO). National ozone units were set up within governments to support the implementation of the treaty, and the ozone secretariat within UNEP supported international collaboration. These robust institutional structures facilitated a close to 100 percent level of compliance with the reporting obligations over the years the Protocol has been in force and an equally high implementation rate.

While Montreal Protocol implementation has been a success, to a large extent this is because of the engagement of scientific communities, the existence of commercially viable substitutes for ozone-depleting substances, and the NGOs that helped mobilize public opinion. Because of the implementation support mechanisms, attaining climate change obligations remains a serious challenge. The 2015 Paris Agreement on Climate Change was the pinnacle of a progression of negotiations that had begun within the United Nations in the 1970s with a series of conferences bringing together scientists, governments, and UN organizations—that is, all three United Nations.

Two UN institutions, UNEP and WMO (the World Meteorological Organization), were instrumental and highly influential in the creation of the international climate regime. In 1988 they established the Intergovernmental Panel on Climate Change (IPCC) to provide policymakers with regular assessments of the scientific basis of climate change, its impacts and future risks, and response strategies for mitigation and adaptation. In 1992, at the Rio Earth Summit, governments signed the UN Framework Convention on Climate Change (UNFCCC), modeled after the successful 1985 Vienna Convention. Since 1995, when the first Conference of the Parties of the UNFCCC met in Berlin, governments have been assembling annually in an effort to coordinate action to abate climate change.

Three milestones stand out in the subsequent 20-year history of the international climate regime. In 1997, at COP3, governments agreed to the Kyoto Protocol, which set emission reduction targets only for developed countries since they were the largest emitters historically.[14] In 2009, COP15 in Copenhagen became known as "the low-point" in the history of the climate regime[15] when no legally binding agreement could be reached.[16] Six years later, in 2015, at COP21 in Paris, 197 Parties to the Convention (195 countries and the European Union) unanimously adopted the Paris Agreement, which articulated ambitious long-term goals and a renewed global response to the threat of climate change—applicable to all parties and comprehensive in scope.

The Paris Agreement was hailed as a monumental achievement and a game changer[17] because it was successful on all core criteria for effectiveness of an international treaty as outlined by scholars, researchers, and the UN Secretary-General: universal participation, significant emission reduction commitments, transparency and accountability, finance, and high compliance rates.[18] The agreement is ambitious and universal; it possesses a binding, yet flexible legal nature, clear procedures for accountability, and a credible financial structure. By early 2020, 189 parties of the 197 signatories to the convention had ratified it.[19] The compliance rates can only be assessed after countries have had a chance to implement their commitments. The COP gatherings after Paris have sought to create the mechanisms and a "rulebook" to ensure that countries limit greenhouse gas emissions and keep the temperature rise within 1.5 degrees.[20] According to the special 2018 report of the IPCC, time to mobilize action is running out.[21] However, mounting disagreements threaten implementation as the ongoing tension between environment and development, and between developing and developed states, persists. Suspicion and reticence to act first are the most significant roadblocks to implementation. The largely unsuccessful COP25 held in 2019 in Madrid, Spain showcased this reality starkly.

Compliance and implementation: the role of the three UNs

Global environmental conventions combine the UN's normative and operational roles by articulating the global goals to which member states aspire and by highlighting the need for operational assistance to ensure compliance with the norms and implementation of the international commitments. Multiple studies have attempted to evaluate the implementation of global environmental conventions but none offers a systematic empirical assessment of the commitments member states have made, and the extent to which they have been able to fulfill them. Without empirical measurement of the level of implementation, the extent of fulfillment of international obligations remains largely unknown. As a result, there is no baseline against which to assess performance, actions, or even expectations. What is clear, however, is that the system of international agreements is largely failing and is doomed to continue to fail unless urgent action is taken.[22] The ozone case illustrates the ability to resolve global problems with global collective action but the climate change agreements remain unheeded, while greenhouse gas emissions continue to rise.

Implementation of the Paris Agreement is critical, yet contentious. The tensions between the need for development and the requirements of environmental protection have strained the negotiations, much like in the run-up to the 1972 Stockholm Conference. Negotiators started COP25 with an astonishing level of disagreement—the text for Article 6 on voluntary cooperation or what has been termed "rocket boosters" toward a safe climate future had 672 square brackets (denoting contested parts of the text).[23] As the meeting moved forward and the number of brackets decreased, countries still failed to reach agreement on the final text. Importantly, negotiators eliminated language on human rights, sparking protests. Market-based mechanisms and financial aid for cooperation were the most contested issues. Countries could not decide how and whether to carry over Kyoto carbon units, how to ensure that there is no double-counting of carbon credits, and how to ensure accountability and transparency of financial aid.[24] Different groups had different expectations and red lines. Just as at the 1972 Stockholm Conference, the main divide lay clearly between developed and developing states and resulted in limited progress. "I am disappointed with the results of COP25," UN Secretary-General António Guterres remarked on its outcome. "The international community lost an important opportunity to show increased ambition on mitigation, adaptation and finance to tackle the climate crisis. But we must not give up, and I will not give up."[25] Continuing to push for greater action by member states will be critical and an important role for the Third UN.

Member states have been caught in a repeating cycle of seemingly irreconcilable demands. Major donors like the United States insist on higher aid transparency. Developing countries argue that industrialized states are hypocritical since they themselves are not phasing out CO_2 and decreasing fossil fuel production and greenhouse gas emissions as fast as pledged. Additionally, without any aid to build capacity pre-2020, expectations for immediate action after 2020 were deemed unrealistic. In climate negotiations, leadership has come from small states and from the European Union. In 2015, the Marshall Islands led a high-ambition coalition that many member states joined over time. In 2019, Costa Rica advanced the San Jose Principles,[26] and the European Union committed to be carbon neutral by 2050 and announced the "European Green Deal," which would earmark at least 25 percent of the EU long-term budget for climate action.

The ability to measure, explain, and improve implementation is critical and the role of civil society in demanding action and requiring accountability is indispensable. The efforts of the youth movement Fridays For Future, Fire Drill Fridays led by Jane Fonda in Washington, DC, and the international movement Extinction Rebellion starkly illustrated the power of the Third UN in 2019. Young people all over the world are joining climate protests, demanding immediate action from their governments. During COP25, half a million people participated in a climate strike led by Swedish student Greta Thunberg. Climate activists protested and urged ambitious action from industrialized states and over 300 were banned from the venue.[27] By not allowing activists in the plenary, member states rolled back the slim progress the UN had made over the last years in engaging civil society. In the context of weak decisions taken at COP25, these actions raise significant concerns regarding the future of climate change action as governments are not responding and the Second UN remains insufficiently empowered to resolve global environmental problems.

On other issues than climate, however, members of the Third UN enjoy more fruitful interaction with governments and UN agencies. Earth Day Network is cooperating with UNEP's Science Division to use 2020 Earth Challenge Data for reporting on the implementation of the SDGs.[28] 2020 Earth Challenge is part of the 50th Earth Day campaign that focuses on climate change—and aims to be "the largest-ever global citizen science initiative, which will arm everyday individuals with the tools they need to report on the health and wellbeing of the environment, from water quality, to air quality, to the species around them."[29] Earthrise, a movement aimed at mobilizing millions around the world in April 2020, was designed to raise global awareness about the environment.

While civil movements have grown stronger and become more vocal on climate issues, civil society activism cannot be a substitute for public oversight of international action by national governments.[30] State action is critical, especially because climate change bears all the features that challenge strengthening processes and mechanisms of accountability, as Peter Newell has outlined: often the worst effects are not felt by those perpetuating the problem in the near or long term; those with most to lose often have the least voice; the patterns of causation and irresponsibility are often complex and contested; and the governance mechanisms to deal with the problem are often weak, under-resourced, and operate across poorly coordinated scales.[31]

Importantly, while civil society has reacted to the influence that the private sector exercises in climate politics, only states can develop and impose meaningful regulations on major carbon emitters.[32]

The coherence challenge

Environmental concerns were not among the issues the United Nations was envisioned to tackle at its creation. Peace and security, human rights, and development were among the pressing issues of the time. In the 1960s, global resource management emerged as an important concern and a number of UN agencies became active in the environmental field. Over time, governments created new institutions, while the existing ones took on greater responsibilities in the environmental field. The 1992 Rio Earth Summit catalyzed the development of new environmental conventions (on climate, biodiversity, and desertification) and new institutions (the Global Environment Facility and the Commission on Sustainable Development), and prompted the UN agencies to undertake more environmental activities. However, "the flourishing of new international institutions," UN Secretary-General Kofi Annan remarked, "poses problems of coordination, eroding responsibilities and resulting in duplication of work as well as increased demand upon ministries and government."[33] Over time, the multiplicity of environmental institutions resulted in unproductive competition, fragmentation of effort, and loss of focus. Efforts at increasing coherence and coordination continue and remain a challenge.

Once launched, the conventions became autonomous entities with separate legally independent structures, decision-making bodies, and procedures, each with its own Conference of the Parties, secretariat, and subsidiary bodies. Fifteen agreements rely on UNEP for their secretariat; others are hosted by UNESCO (the World Heritage Convention) and IUCN (the Ramsar Convention on Wetlands). And some, like the climate and desertification conventions (UNFCCC and UNCCD), are independent. Moreover, the convention secretariats are geographically dispersed across Nairobi, Montreal, Geneva, Bonn, and Paris. As one government official put it in 2018, "we have kept creating small new kingdoms." They became a strong political force in many governments as they mobilized public attention and resources, while UNEP did not manage to support countries in the implementation of the conventions it had helped create.

Little progress has been made on resolving global environmental concerns in the 50 years since the world recognized their urgency, besides the problems of ozone depletion. Tensions between the priorities and expectations of industrialized and developing countries have thwarted progress. Developed countries have kept promising financing but have not delivered and developing countries have had difficulty utilizing resources effectively. States first committed to contribute 0.7 percent of national income to official development assistance in 1970. This target has been restated repeatedly at the highest level at international conferences, but in 2018 only five countries contributed at that level—Sweden, Luxembourg, Norway, Denmark, and the United Kingdom—and the world's largest donor, the United States, has never even committed to this target. Its $34 billion total in 2018 represented only 0.17 percent of its national income. Ultimately, the rhetoric of industrialized countries making promises and not delivering has damaged global trust and shaped the political context for negotiations.

The Global South, on the other hand, has pressed for more support and held negotiations hostage to the delivery of financing. Importantly, when finance has been forthcoming in the context of well-crafted and managed institutions, as in the case of the ozone regime, problems have been resolved. In the absence of functioning institutions, qualified personnel, and many of the legal checks and balances, however, many developing countries have been unable to utilize resources effectively. "When there is no integrity on the part of the leadership, no systematic approach to governance, civil liberties, rule of law, donor aid is simply wasted," notes Daniel Kaufmann, former director of global programs at the World Bank.[34] Historically, developing countries have often approached international negotiations with a victimization mentality—they have suffered from the consequences of the development patterns of the countries that are now economically advanced, and have had no means to act. The victimization narrative has affected many international negotiations and was particularly obvious in the climate change debates where the issues of who was responsible, who should act, and how action would be financed were particularly divisive and often resulted in stalemate.

Ultimately, both the North and the Global South have failed to implement their environmental agreements to safeguard biodiversity, reverse desertification, reduce pollution, deal with persistent organic chemicals and hazardous waste, or address climate change. Suspicion on the part of the Global South of any new promises and caution on the part of the North to commit any resources have resulted in a lack of intergovernmental progress and propagation of a new governance approach—partnerships between international organizations, governments, industry, and NGOs to translate principles into projects. Without genuine government engagement, however, partnerships cannot succeed. Public pressure, accountability, and the possibility of innovation for a new economic model could mobilize governmental action. The role of the knowledge sector will be particularly critical as it advances understanding, accountability, and learning, and empowers the next generation to act.

Conclusion

"Each generation is given two things: one is the gift of the world, and the other is the duty of keeping it safe for those to come. The generations of yesterday trust those of today not to take more than their share, and those of tomorrow trust their elders to care for it," write the activists of Extinction Rebellion. "The contract is broken, and it is happening on our watch."[35] Living a meaningful life requires that we restore our integrity and deliver on this sustainability contract.

In the three-quarters of a century since its creation, the United Nations and its specialized agencies, funds, programs, and secretariats have been awarded the Nobel Peace Prize 11 times for their work on the resolution of global problems across several areas—peace, refugees, social justice, chemical weapons prohibition, and measures to deal with climate change.[36] The Paris Agreement is perhaps the most ambitious international agreement on stemming a climate crisis and highlighted three imperatives that face the UN and need to be addressed: dealing with the interconnectedness of global problems in an effective and equitable manner; engaging more actors more effectively; and ensuring effective implementation.

The 17 SDGs set the 2030 Agenda; they took on a range of interconnected challenges across the environmental, economic, and social dimensions of development—the culmination of the UN's work on the environment that began in the 1960s. The linkages present opportunities as well as trade-offs and even conflicts. The United Nations, however, does not possess the necessary mechanisms to mitigate such conflicts and ensure productive integration. Numerous UN organizations are now active in the sustainability and climate areas, yet the incentives for engagement remain sector-based and project-driven. Importantly, a much larger number of non-state actors is involved in action across sectors and levels of governance.

Yet the United Nations remains state-centric and is often beleaguered by lowest-common-denominator dynamics. "The UN system has not yet moved beyond episodic participation towards meaningful, durable incorporation of non-state actors into global political processes," writes Nora McKeon.[37] At the same time, the rise of civil society movements clearly shows that non-state actors cannot be ignored, and UN leaders actively seek ways to engage youth and industry in the process of environmental governance. Addressing climate change will be the biggest test for the UN as the universal global organization because it "is not the quest of one nation," Christiana Figueres, the executive secretary of the climate convention who led the successful COP21 resulting in the Paris Agreement, writes.

> This time it's up to all of us, to all the nations and peoples of the world. No matter how complex or deep our differences, we fundamentally share everything that is important: the desire to forge a better world for everyone alive today and all the generations to come.[38]

Moreover, the United Nations could earn the honor of the award that the young people of Fridays For Future are holding for it.

NOTES

1 Quoted in *Concord Friends Journal (Quakers)*, www.concordfriendsmeeting.org/aggregator/sources/7.
2 Thomas G. Weiss, Tatiana Carayannis, and Richard Jolly, "The 'Third' United Nations," *Global Governance* 15, no. 2 (2009): 123–142; and Tatiana Carayannis and Thomas G. Weiss, *The "Third" United Nations: How Knowledge Brokers Help the UN Think* (Oxford: Oxford University Press, forthcoming).
3 Wade Rowland, *The Plot to Save the World: The Life and Times of the Stockholm Conference on the Human Environment* (Toronto: Clarke, Irwin & Co, 1973), 47.
4 Interview of Henrique Cavalvanti by the author, 2007.
5 UN, *Report of the Secretary-General on United Nations Committee of the Human Environment* (UN document A/CONF.48/PC/11), 1971.
6 These are the key functions, or mandate, of UNEP as adapted from the text of the UN General Assembly resolution 2997 (XXVII). On the anchor institution concept, see Maria Ivanova, *Can the Anchor Hold? Rethinking the United Nations Environment Programme for the 21st Century* (New Haven, CT: Yale School of Forestry & Environmental Studies, 2005).
7 Dianne Otto, "Nongovernmental Organizations in the United Nations System: The Emerging Role of International Civil Society," *Human Rights Quarterly* 18 (1996): 107; Nora McKeon, *The United Nations and Civil Society: Legitimating Global Governance—Whose Voice?* (London: Zed Books Ltd., 2013).
8 World Commission on Environment and Development, *Our Common Future* (Oxford: Oxford University Press, 1987).
9 Glen Garelick, "Environment a Breath of Fresh Air: Delegates of 24 Nations Sign a Historic Pact on Ozone," *Time Magazine*, 28 September 1987.
10 Carol Annette Petsonk. "The Role of the United Nations Environment Programme in the Development of International Environmental Law," *American University Journal of International Law & Policy* 5, no. 2 (1990): 369–370.
11 Peter S. Thacher, "Multilateral Cooperation and Global Change," *Journal of International Affairs* 44, no. 2 (1991): 433–455; Carol A. Petsonk, "Recent Developments in International Organizations: The Role of the United Nations Environment Programme (UNEP) in International Environmental Law," *American University Journal of International Law and Policy* 5, no. 2 (1990): 367; and Richard E. Benedick, *Ozone Diplomacy: New Directions in Safeguarding the Planet* (Cambridge, MA: Harvard University Press, 1991).
12 Penelope Canan and Nancy Reichman, *Ozone Connections: Expert Networks in Global Environmental Governance* (Sheffield, UK: Greenleaf Publishing, 2002), 48.
13 Richard E. Benedick, "US Environmental Policy: Relevance to Europe," *International Environmental Affairs* 1, no. 2 (1989): 47.

14 Kyoto Protocol, Article 3.
15 Annalisa Savaresi, "The Paris Agreement: A New Beginning?" *Energy and Natural Resources Law* 34, no. 16 (2016).
16 The Copenhagen Accord, however, articulated a global goal of limiting warming to 2 °C, a global goal of assisting climate action in developing countries with $100 billion per year, and a global strategy harnessing voluntary mitigation actions and contributions. See Harro van Asselt, "Copenhagen Chaos? Post-2012 Climate Change Policy and International Law," *Amsterdam Law Forum* 2, no. 2 (2010): 9–16; and Daniel Bodansky, "The Copenhagen Climate Change Conference: A Post-Mortem," *American Journal of International Law* 104, no. 1 (2010): 230.
17 Coral Davenport, "Nations Approve Landmark Climate Accord in Paris," *New York Times*, 12 December 2015; and Fiona Harvey, "World Bank President Celebrates 'Game Changer' Paris Talks," *The Guardian*, 13 December 2015.
18 Ban Ki-moon, "The Paris Climate Challenge," *Boston Globe*, 25 November 2016; Scott Barrett, *Environment and Statecraft* (New York: Oxford University Press, 2003); Institute for Sustainable Development and International Relations, 2016, *Judging the Paris Agreement: A Comparison with IDDRI's 10 Criteria for Success*; and Robert Stavins, "Paris Agreement—A Good Foundation for Meaningful Progress," 12 December 2015, www.robertstavinsblog.org/2015/12/12/paris-agreement-a-good-foundation-for-meaningful-progress.
19 United Nations Framework Convention on Climate Change, 2017, *Paris Agreement-Status of Ratification*, http://unfccc.int/paris_agreement/items/9444.php.
20 For a detailed explanation of the Paris Agreement "rulebook," see Jennifer Huang, "A Brief Guide to the Paris Agreement and 'Rulebook'," Center for Climate and Energy Solutions, June 2019, www.c2es.org/site/assets/uploads/2019/06/paris-agreement-and-rulebook-guide.pdf.
21 Intergovernmental Panel on Climate Change, 2018, *Special Report Warming of 1.5oC*, www.ipcc.ch/sr15.
22 See James Gustave Speth, *Red Sky at Morning: America and the Crisis of the Global Environment* (New Haven, CT: Yale University Press, 2004), 84.
23 "COP25: Key Outcomes Agreed at the UN Climate Talks in Madrid," *Carbon Brief*, 15 December 2019, www.carbonbrief.org/cop25-key-outcomes-agreed-at-the-un-climate-talks-in-madrid.
24 Under the Kyoto Protocol carbon market, developing countries could get carbon credits or emissions offset units as part of the Clean Development Mechanism if they supported sustainable development initiatives. Countries that received and still hold the most credits include India, Brazil, China, South Korea, and Mexico. Carry-over of these credits to the post-2020 process was supported by some countries, while others saw it as "diluting" climate action and lowering the ambition on overall emission reduction. As the carbon market under the Paris Agreement allows for trade among countries, the issue of accounting and avoidance of double-counting through adjustments was crucial for effectiveness of the mechanism and for cutting emissions. Some countries, Brazil for example, were against introducing adjustments and wanted to account for carbon credits generated within the country and sold overseas.
25 *Statement by UN Secretary-General António Guterres on the Outcome of COP25*, https://unfccc.int/news/statement-by-the-un-secretary-general-antonio-guterres-on-the-outcome-of-cop25.
26 The San Jose Principles set out rules for carbon markets that, among others, include adjustments to avoid double-counting and prohibit carry-over of Kyoto credits.
27 Fridays For Future, www.fridaysforfuture.org.
28 Earth Day Network, "Global Citizen Science Effort Marks the 50th Anniversary of Earth Day," www.earthday.org/2019/10/22/global-citizen-science-50th-anniversary-of-earth-day.
29 Earth Day Network, "Earth Day 50th Anniversary," www.earthday.org/earthday/countdown-to-2020.
30 Peter Newell, "Civil Society, Corporate Accountability and the Politics of Climate Change," *Global Environmental Politics* 8, no. 3 (2008): 149.
31 Ibid., 123.
32 Ibid., 149.
33 UN General Assembly, *Agenda Item 30: Environment and Human Settlements–Report of the Secretary-General*," UN document A/53/4631998.
34 Quoted in Michela Wrong, *It's Our Turn to Eat* (London: Fourth Estate, 2009), 208. Wrong explains that a World Bank review by its internal anti-corruption unit into four Kenya projects approved between 2000 and 2005 and worth $375 million found that three of them suffered from serious irregularities. Those included "bribing of public officials to abuse of office, inflated expenses, fraudulent claims, conflict of interest, the concerted rigging of bids, failure to carry out allotted tasks, and blatant nepotism."

35 Extinction Rebellion, "About Us," https://rebellion.earth/the-truth/about-us.
36 One agency, the United Nations High Commissioner for Refugees (UNHCR), received the prize twice, in 1954 and 1981.
37 Nora McKeon, *The United Nations and Civil Society*, foreword.
38 Christiana Figueres and Tom Rivett-Carnac, *The Future We Choose* (London: Manilla Press, 2020), 161.

ADDITIONAL READING

Ken Conca, *An Unfinished Foundation: The United Nations and Global Environmental Governance* (Oxford: Oxford University Press, 2015).

Christiana Figueres and Tom Rivett-Carnac, *The Future We Choose* (London: Knopf, 2020).

Maria Ivanova, *A Revisionist History of the World's Premier Environmental Institution: UNEP at Fifty* (Cambridge, MA: MIT Press, forthcoming in 2021).

Nico Schrijver, *Development without Destruction: The UN and Global Resource Management* (Bloomington, IN: Indiana University Press, 2010).

5

GENDER EQUALITY AND THE UNITED NATIONS

Saraswathi Menon

This chapter begins by tracing the early bold beginnings when member states and organizations of the UN system established conventions and policy frameworks about women, most notably with the adoption of the Convention of All Forms of Discrimination Against Women and its related accountability for reporting. It continues with the catalyzing effect of the four global UN conferences on women to reflect breakthroughs in standards and approaches as well as forums for women's movements to exchange ideas and organize around specific issues. The chapter then describes the institutional contributions of various parts of the UN and the UN development system. It examines the 2010 creation of UN Women, in response to continuing pressure from women's movements, which improved the UN's work across the pillars of its work and contributed to framing the Sustainable Development Goals. It then analyzes UN responses in the face of the rise of political and religious fundamentalism and the consequent backlash against gender equality. The chapter concludes with the need for the UN to be bolder, to work organically across human rights, development, and sustaining peace, and above all to address such structural issues of gender inequality as the care contribution to social reproduction, sexual and reproductive health and rights, and multidimensional discrimination.

The United Nations has long both led and responded to advances in women's struggle for equality and rights.[1] With the UN's establishment and the creation of a platform on which governments reached negotiated agreements on political, economic, and social priorities, and directed the UN system of organizations to act in support of these priorities, the women's movement has looked for support for its agenda in seeking equality worldwide. The UN through standard- and norm-setting, through support at the national level, and through advocacy in partnership with women's organizations has contributed to change, and yet challenges remain. At times, this support has been critical and opened new avenues of knowledge and action; yet too often the UN has fallen short of a transformative agenda.

Many gains are visible in terms of women's empowerment and rights, but discrimination and gender inequality persist worldwide. Despite increasing visibility and political mobilization, violence against women continues unabated. An average of 35 percent of women worldwide experience physical and/or sexual violence in their lifetimes, and this percentage reaches 70 percent in some countries.[2] There are 122 women for every 100 men of the age group 25–34 living in poverty. In India, the average age of death for Dalit women is nearly 15 years lower than that of upper-caste women. Many countries do not guarantee reproductive health rights. Some 750 million girls and women in the world were married before the age of 18.

Globally, women earn on average 23 percent less than men, but with variations from 33 percent less in South Asia to 14 percent less in the Middle East and North Africa.[3] Women in all countries bear a disproportionate burden for unpaid care. Women are responsible for collecting water in 80 percent of households without their own water source. Insufficient investments in basic infrastructure such as water and sanitation and basic social services accentuate this burden. Women's political participation has expanded, largely through affirmative action, but on average they hold just 23.7 percent of parliament seats and few countries have crossed the 30 percent target of women in parliament. In armed conflicts, sexual and gender-based violence are used as weapons of war. Women are absent and thus their needs inconsistently considered in peace negotiations and post-conflict recovery. The last 70 years have seen advances in terms of women organizing for change, their conditions of well-being, and their political leadership. Yet, the battle is far from won.[4]

This chapter evaluates the record of the UN in fostering change as well as the challenges it faces in addressing these persistent deprivations of gender equality. It begins with an overview of the UN's political engagement with women's rights. It continues with a survey of the evolution in women's rights, the world conferences on women and the accompanying backlash, the contributions of the UN system, and the creation of UN Women. In looking toward the future, the chapter concludes with an assessment of the UN's overall contribution.

UN history: the early years

The UN's first breakthroughs were to establish processes that provided a framework to discuss issues faced by women across countries. One of the earliest UN bodies, the Commission on the Status of Women (CSW), was established by ECOSOC in 1946 with the purpose of meeting annually to "promote women's rights, documenting the reality of women's lives throughout the world, and shaping global standards on gender equality and the empowerment of women."[5] In the 1950s and 1960s, issues such as married women's rights, legitimacy of children, and maternity protection were on the agenda. Although the topics stayed close to a traditional view of women as homemakers and mothers, the CSW presciently did not restrict itself to the status of women in newly independent nations but dealt with the advancement of women as a universal issue. Today the Sustainable Development Goals (SDGs) again attempt to restore that balance, an issue to which the chapter returns.

The CSW directly contributed to the establishment of a framework of rights for women, drafting such early international conventions on women's rights as the 1953 Convention on the Political Rights of Women, the first international instrument to recognize and protect the political rights of women. It also adopted one of the first international agreements on women's rights in marriage, namely the 1957 Convention on the Nationality of Married Women, and the 1962 Convention on Consent to Marriage, Minimum Age for Marriage and Registration of Marriages. The CSW also contributed to the work of UN organizations such as the International Labour Organization's (ILO's) 1951 Convention concerning Equal Remuneration for Men and Women Workers for Work of Equal Value, which first enshrined the principle of equal pay for equal work.[6]

In 1963, the General Assembly requested the CSW to draft a Declaration on the Elimination of Discrimination against Women, which the Assembly adopted in 1967. By 1979, CSW experts had drafted the legally binding Convention on the Elimination of All Forms of Discrimination Against Women (CEDAW),[7] a path-breaking women's bill of rights that for the first time made the state accountable for discrimination and violence against women in the home. It thus broke down the artificial barrier between public and private that bedevils the achievement of gender equality. It came into force in 1981.[8]

CEDAW provides the most comprehensive statement of women's rights. It is predicated on the notion of substantive equality going beyond equivalence or equity, which reduced fairness to existing social norms. Instead, equality requires the transformation of political, economic, cultural, and social attitudes and norms on which discrimination is based; this yardstick is the basis to assess the UN's contribution to gender equality. CEDAW was further strengthened by the Optional Protocol to the Convention adopted in 1999, which introduced the right of petition for survivors of discrimination and the series of general recommendations that expand the convention's scope to new areas such as access to justice, and conflict and post-conflict settings, among others.[9]

One hundred and eighty-five countries have ratified CEDAW with the United States, Sudan, and Iran among the most prominent exceptions. The establishment of the 23-member CEDAW Committee that conducts a periodic review process every four years for all member states has created an unsurpassed system of accountability. Women's organizations in all countries have engaged actively in the review process, preparing shadow reports to the official government reports that have alerted the CEDAW Committee to evidence of persistent discrimination. The UN System too engages by supporting government and shadow reporting and with UN country teams providing confidential information directly to the CEDAW Committee.

World conferences on women: advances and backlash

A burgeoning women's movement across countries demanded greater attention to women's issues. The United Nations established 1975 as International Women's Year to remind the international community of states that "discrimination against women continued to be a persistent problem in much of the world,"[10] and it later declared 1976 to 1985 as the Decade for Women. Four international conferences over the decades provided a strong impetus to pulling together different strands of the push for equality; they also addressed the variations in the status of women across countries. The convening power of the UN was visible in the extent of official and civil society participation and in the range of concerns that the conferences took up.

The first UN global gathering was the World Conference on Women in 1975 in Mexico City. The conference was a highlight of International Women's Year with over 2,000 participants. It was the largest meeting to that date to deal specifically with women's issues. Of the 133 member states at the time, 125 sent official delegations. The conference issued a World Plan of Action for the Implementation of the Objectives of the International Women's Year, offering a comprehensive set of guidelines for action through 1985. The text urged governments to establish and implement national strategies and priorities for the advancement of women.[11]

The second such meeting was the World Conference of the United Nations Decade for Women: Equality, Development and Peace, which met in Copenhagen from 14 to 30 July 1980, with official delegations from 145 countries. The title of the decade and conference explicitly recognized all pillars of the UN system, although the focus was largely on development and legal rights. The Programme of Action called for stronger national measures to ensure women's ownership and control of property, as well as improvements in protecting women's rights to inheritance, child custody, and nationality. The conference benefited from the drafting of CEDAW and thus highlighted that equality was more than legal recognition: discrimination should be eliminated for true equality. Three main measures of equality were equal access to education, employment opportunities, and adequate health care.[12]

The third gathering was the 1985 World Conference to Review and Appraise the Achievements of the UN Decade for Women, at which over 140 countries reviewed the achievements in terms of equality, development, and peace. The conference adopted the Nairobi Forward-Looking Strategies for the Advancement of Women, which sought to integrate women in development processes. The focus on poverty, health, and education continued. In addition, three key new categories were included to measure progress: constitutional and legal measures, equality in social participation, and equality in political participation and decision-making. The Nairobi conference called for the establishment of appropriate governmental machinery for monitoring and improving the status of women.

> Such machinery can play a vital role in enhancing the status of women, inter alia, through the dissemination of information to women on their rights and entitlements, through collaborative action with various ministries and other government agencies and with non-governmental organizations and indigenous women's societies and groups.[13]

Recommendations called for adequate funding, national and sectoral plans and specific targets for women's development, and institutional mechanisms to address especially vulnerable groups of women. Since then more than 100 countries have been tracking the gender allocation of budgets.

Many observers have referred to Nairobi as the birth of global feminism and the beginnings of a shift from women in development (WID) to gender and development (GAD). The UN effort began to move away from just incorporating women into development processes as objects to looking at women as agents of change and examining the impact of development and other policies on their well-being and opportunities. Against a backdrop of growing economic pressures in Copenhagen and Nairobi, the women's movement protested the crises spawned by structural adjustment policies and the neoliberal agenda.[14]

By the time of the Fourth World Conference on Women in Beijing in September 1995, the women's movement had come of age; the official conference with 189 official delegations and the parallel NGO conference with thousands of participants together addressed the most comprehensive set of issues to that date. The Beijing Declaration and Platform for Action aimed at accelerating the Nairobi Forward-Looking Strategies and at removing all the obstacles to women's active participation in all spheres of public and private life through a full and equal share in economic, social, cultural, and political decision-making. The 12 critical areas of concerns displayed the full range of gender equality issues: women and the environment; women in power and decision-making; the girl child; women and the economy; women and poverty; violence against women; human rights of women; education and training of women; institutional mechanisms for the advancement of women; women and health; women and the media; and women and armed conflict.

The Beijing conference marked a high point in the UN's political engagement with gender equality. Other global ad hoc conferences of the 1990s also raised significant issues related to gender equality and equity: environment and development (UNCED, Rio de Janeiro, 1991); human rights (Vienna, 1993); population and development (ICPD, Cairo, 1994); and the World Social Summit (Copenhagen, 1995).[15] After Beijing, however, despite an articulate women's movement, the political UN failed to respond with consistent advances in setting standards, which reflected a brutal and deep backlash to women's rights. All religions stereotype women and the rise of fundamentalisms of all stripes—in Islam, Christianity, Judaism, and Hinduism—attacked women's rights consistently on sexual and reproductive health and rights (SRHR) and on access to public spaces, including education. Some of the resistance is reflected in laws not passed or reversed.

The spillover to the political UN is visible. The international community of states could not agree on a new and forward-looking agenda on gender equality after the Beijing Conference. Instead, centers of neoliberal and religious fundamentalist thinking spanning the North and Global South resisted negotiations at the CSW and resolutions and other UN forums. In 2013, governments even failed to reach agreement on as innocuous a theme as rural women at the CSW.

UNCED, ICPD, and Beijing were 20-year review conferences (as opposed to 10-year reviews in other domains). Interestingly, language at UNCED+20 included reference to "the rights of women, men and youth to have control over and decide freely and responsibly on matters related to their sexuality, including access to sexual and reproductive health, free from coercion discrimination and violence." This language extended the Beijing Platform commitments to men and youth. At ICPD+20 the resistance to reproductive rights was stronger. At Beijing+20 the areas of contention included sexuality and reproduction, equal inheritance, unpaid care work, and early marriage.[16]

Significantly, the critical Vienna Human Rights Conference recognized women's rights as human rights, and the Copenhagen Social Summit had unmarked anniversaries. Holding onto the gains of CEDAW and Beijing became the hallmark of progressive efforts at the UN.

In the early 2000s, as a natural sequel to Beijing and the activism of women's peace movements in conflict-affected countries, the agenda of women, peace, and security was introduced in the Security Council. Its 2000 path-breaking resolution 1325 recognized women not just as victims of violent conflict but also as key participants and leaders of conflict prevention, peace negotiations, peace building, and economic and social recovery. The Security Council has, through a series of subsequent resolutions, emphasized women's contribution in the broadest meaning of sustaining peace.[17] A host of women-led peace movements from Central Asia to Africa to Latin America provided evidence of the agency of women before, during, and after conflict. The CEDAW General Recommendation complemented Security Council resolutions. Even here, however, the gains were under duress, reflecting the whim of governments. In early 2019, the United States ensured through threat of veto that Security Council members excluded from a resolution wording on the assurance to provide reproductive health services to women survivors. Significantly, none of the 169 targets in the SDGs specifically addresses the needs of women and girls in conflict.[18]

Contributions by the UN system

While the intergovernmental UN often took two steps forward and one step backward on gender equality, the UN system integrated women into their mandates, which in turn influenced the international community of states. For instance, the UN statistical system made significant contributions to monitoring the situation of women. Statistics on women were an early substantive addition to the agenda of the UN Statistical Commission. From the 1950s, the UN Population Division supported newly established statistical offices to collect sex-disaggregated data in their censuses and household surveys. The UN Statistical Division has regularly provided relevant gender data in their publication *The World's Women*, which first appeared in 1991. They have conducted extensive training of national statistical offices.

The UN's gender statistics include a minimum set of 52 indicators related to gender. They include: average number of hours spent on domestic chores and care work, by sex, age, and location; average number of hours spent on unpaid domestic chores, by sex, age, and location;

average number of hours spent on unpaid care work, by sex, age, and location; and gender gap by occupation, age, and among persons with disabilities.[19] More recently, methodologies for collecting data about such emerging areas as violence against women and care work have been used; they have been tested by national statistical systems and endorsed by the UN Statistical Commission.

There have been other imaginative attempts to measure gender inequality, notably as captured in composite gender indices presented in UNDP's annual *Human Development Report*. They have used available data and been modified to highlight different dimensions of gender inequality over successive issues of the report. As with all composite indices, choices are made regarding indicators and their weights in the index and so the final assessment serves to highlight critical issues while encouraging readers to dig deeper into data and national contexts to fully understand the extent of discrimination. In short, these indices have often served advocacy more than a measurement of the situation of women and girls.[20]

Work on human rights was primarily associated with the work of the CEDAW Committee, and work on peace and security was linked to the series of resolutions in the Security Council; but the work by organizations in the UN development system (UNDS) most readily absorbed the advancement of women into their regular work, initially by adding women in development programs. For instance, the UN Educational, Scientific and Cultural Organization (UNESCO) sought to increase the enrollment of girls in education and science; the World Health Organization (WHO) to deal with the specific issues of women's health through specific programs; and the ILO to increase women's access to paid employment. Through its electoral reform programs, the UN Secretariat sought to expand the public and political presence of women.

These programs reflect the premise that once women were included in ongoing development and political processes, their advancement would follow. As with so much of the UN's development work, the division into sectoral mandates often diminished results. Working across the development spectrum to tackle the political, social, and economic empowerment of women occurred only rarely. More problematic still was the failure to work across the UN system. Over time this was further complicated by the UN system responding to the persistence of conflict and natural disasters by the creation of a fourth humanitarian pillar to address the failed aspirations of human rights, development, and peace in the midst of or following armed conflict. The gender dimensions of humanitarian crises were reflected in the mandates of organizations such as the World Food Programme (WFP), the Office for the Coordination of Humanitarian Affairs (OCHA), and the Office of the UN High Commissioner for Refugees (UNHCR), exacerbating fragmentation and undermining integrated efforts to address substantive equality.

Today: UN Women

A long-standing demand of the women's movement had been the creation of a single UN institution that could overcome such atomization and spearhead change in the UN. From 2008 to 2010, over 300 civil society organizations from across the world came together in the Gender Equality Architecture Reform (GEAR) Campaign to ask the UN to form a new agency dedicated to gender equality.[21] The General Assembly's 2010 resolution 64/289 created UN Women; it was a symbolically important bridge between rhetoric and action. It probably was the first time that the UN altered its architecture in response to activism and a rare example of the consolidation of UN bodies. The resolution merged four existing offices: the United Nations Fund for Women (UNIFEM) that provided grant funding for women's projects in developing countries and was under the aegis of UNDP; the Institute for Training and Research on Women (INSTRAW) that was headquartered in Santo Domingo and pursued "action research"; the

Division for the Advancement of Women (DAW) that was located within the Department of Economic and Social Affairs (DESA) and prepared documents for intergovernmental deliberations; and the Office of the Special Adviser on Gender Issues (OSAGI) that was responsible for tackling gender equality within the UN.

UN Women was established amid a backlash on women's rights in many parts of the world, where numerous hard-fought gains were questioned by conservative forces; fundamentalist religious groups attacked reproductive and property rights. Elsewhere, rather than expanding the legal framework for equality, similar forces introduced revisions to restrict rights for people classifying themselves as lesbian, gay, bi-sexual, and transgender (LGBT). Economic crises have accentuated inequality with spillover on gender inequality. Violent extremism has shared a common feature—attacks on women's rights such as in the actions of Boko Haram. Women's organizations have been weakened and marginalized as a result.

Three crucial elements of the new organization drew from previous mandates and earlier work. First, UN Women continued to work on the UN's pillars of activities—human rights, humanitarian action, sustainable development, and peace and security. However, negotiations leading to its creation included opposition to using "women's rights" in the name, which reflected the atmosphere of resistance to gender equality. Second, UN Women's universal mandate supported gender equality everywhere and not only in developing countries, but without a clear allocation of funds and responsibility beyond advocacy. Third, the organization was tasked with normative, development, and coordination mandates. In keeping with the umbrella resolution on coherence within the UN system, a key new element was to support and make the entire system accountable for gender equality.

As a patchwork of existing offices, the governance of UN Women reflected two inherited planning and funding streams. As a recipient of very limited funds from the UN's assessed budget, UN Women prepared a biennial Strategic Framework and Budget for General Assembly approval. Governments shaped UN Women through the founding resolution primarily as a development organization dependent on voluntary contributions and governed by an Executive Board akin to UNDP, the UN Population Fund (UNFPA), the UN Children's Fund (UNICEF), and WFP. The required Five-Year Strategic Plan is in line with the UN's other development funds and programs and with the development-oriented Quadrennial Comprehensive Policy Review (QCPR).

The establishment of UN Women did not reflect the full range of CEDAW rights pursuing substantive equality. In effect, given the governance model and funding arrangements in place, UN Women prioritized development, while continuing to work on the peace and security pillar and introducing a humanitarian effort. An early result was the rapid establishment of regional offices and an expanded country presence that replicated similar independent arrangements of many other UNDS organizations. The new Executive Board endorsed UNIFEM's thematic priorities; those from the largest of the predecessor organizations. These themes were political participation; economic empowerment; ending violence against women; and women, peace, and security. Programmatic work at the country level, policy and analytical work, and engagement with intergovernmental processes continued.

UN Women's seat at the table with the UN country team (UNCT) increased engagement with the rest of the UNDS. Country-based organizations had included programs promoting girls and women within their mandates, and UN Women was expected to foster greater collaboration across individual organizations to address multidimensional gender inequalities. It became the 11th co-sponsor of UNAIDS, thus ensuring the inclusion of the specific needs of women in the battle against HIV. With the new resident coordinator (RC) system, UN Women has the potential to play a stronger advisory role across the system.

The inter-agency group of gender offices in UN organizations was reactivated, and a framework for accountability (the System–Wide Action Plan on Gender Equality) was adopted along with a gender marker, which required each UN organization to report performance. Each organization set its own targets across an agreed set of indicators on program, management human resources, finance, and other dimensions; each organization is thereby accountable to its own stakeholders, the UN system, and the public. As revealed by successive global perception surveys, UN Women was recognized early by members of the global public as one of the more relevant UN organizations.[22]

UN Women continued to champion women, peace, and security. The executive director supplemented the annual open discussions at the Security Council on the topic with briefings on specific country situations. UN Women has collaborated in joint training on sexual violence with the Department of Peace Operations (DPO)—formerly the Department of Peacekeeping Operations (DPKO)—and for elections with the Department of Political and Peacebuilding Affairs (DPPA)—formerly the Department of Political Affairs (DPA). UN Women works closely with the Peace Building Support Office (PBSO) on sustaining peace in line with the Secretary-General's seven-point Action Plan on Gender Responsive Peacebuilding. At the country level, UN Women has provided advisers for UN peace operations and special political missions; it has supported investigations by a variety of tribunals and other processes with experts who establish the basis for combating impunity after an armed conflict ends.

While UN Women has expanded its development, coordination, and advocacy work, its current funding is insufficient for its universal mandate. The normative work on gender equality continues to be spearheaded by the CEDAW Committee for the accountability on reporting and follow-up that every country is to meet. A closer synergy across the normative, development, and peace and security work would require a deeper engagement by UN Women with CEDAW processes.

One of the benchmarks of progress within the UN is gender balance in staffing. Despite years of setting targets, the UN has not practiced what it preaches. In 2017, the UN established a task force to reach gender parity by 2030. In 2014, the UN's male international staff were 61 percent male and 71 percent of those working in the field. A further criticism has been the poor representation of women from developing countries among senior staff. Out of the six committees in the General Assembly, only one has a female chair. The president of the 74th General Assembly, María Fernanda Espinosa, was only the fourth woman to hold the presidency.

Perhaps as revealing as staffing patterns is an organization's capacity on gender equality. One of the UN's most rapidly growing areas of expertise is conflict-related sexual violence, in response to the 2008 Security Council resolution 1820 that labeled such violence as a tactic of war. Other areas of expertise do not seem to be progressing apace. For UN organizations to be effective, relevant and broad-based expertise is critical. A 2015 survey of gender experts in the UN system revealed that the proportion of women was above 10 percent in only three organizations (UN Women, ILO, and FAO).[23]

Some of the most important breakthroughs for the UN have come in the realm of ideas, analysis, and influence. The series on *The World's Women*[24] has exposed the facts of the status of women across the world. The *Human Development Report 1995* took gender inequality beyond the measurement of gaps by showing that the human development achievement of an entire country was diminished by the existence of gender inequality and by unpaid work.[25] UN Women's *World Survey on the Role of Women in Development* has made inroads into analyzing sustainable development from a feminist perspective. Its flagship publication, *Progress of the World's Women*, has provided insights into analytical frameworks as captured in the sub-titles of the last three: *In Pursuit of Justice* (2011),[26] *Transforming Economies, Realizing Rights* (2015),[27] and *Families in a Changing World* (2019–2020).[28]

Change but not transformation

Fragmentation is not the only problem that besets the UN's work. Throughout the decades of the UN's political and organizational work, the structural underpinnings of gender inequality were intermittently addressed. Women and girls were viewed as weak, a group who merely required opportunities to join the existing development process. Even the term "gender mainstreaming" connotes joining an existing flow rather than changing it. As a result, it is essential to underline three critical issues mentioned earlier that have been sidestepped or marginalized, the result of which has been a less than transformative impact of the UNDS in fostering gender equality.

First, the role of women in production extended to a critical role in social reproduction through unpaid care work, which has made it possible for the household and society to engage in economic production.[29] Second, women's sexual and reproductive health and rights have been bound up with cultural and religious practices that have promoted abuse and violence and prevented control over their own bodies. Third, gender inequality has been closely intertwined with such other forms of discrimination as class, caste, race, ethnicity, and sexuality—thus compounding discrimination.

None of these issues was ignored. The ILO spearheaded work on unpaid care work and the informal sector in the 1980s.[30] In Beijing, the attempt to include a reference to unpaid work was debated but made progress. Governments recognized sexual and reproductive health and the rights of women at ICPD, but the issue has remained contentious. Concerns have been raised about comprehensive sexuality education and the access of refugees or survivors of conflict to reproductive health services. Among the organizations that have pioneered work in this area have been UNFPA, WHO, and UNAIDS. CEDAW and other UN human rights forums in Geneva have paid growing attention to the multi-dimensionality of gender discrimination and inequality.

Without a comprehensive understanding of these and other structural issues, development programs often have not resulted in the expected benefits. Increasing paid work without providing social services and better sharing of care work within the household merely increases the burden on women. As neoliberal policies held sway, austerity programs in many industrialized countries reduced social services, again increasing the burden on women who picked up the slack of caring for the elderly and sick. Environmental disasters and conflict have made tasks such as collecting firewood and water more onerous and dangerous for women and girls.

The UN has attempted, with mixed results, campaigns against harmful cultural practices such as female genital mutilation (FGM), often because of a reluctance to take on religious and other traditional, patriarchal leaders. The bodies of women are too often the battleground of religious fundamentalists of all persuasions. The UN's prevailing approach remains building consensus in order to move the global agenda forward. This has sometimes led to a reluctance to be bold or even consistent, with organizations deciding to reverse positions—including UN Women in the case of sex workers—despite the negative implications for access to medical, legal, and social services. Perhaps the single most difficult issue is the multi-dimensionality of discrimination. From Dalit to indigenous women, violence has been a means to exercise terror and dominance over communities.

The formulation of the SDGs offered the women's movement and UN Women an opportunity to highlight the structural issues of gender equality as universal priorities. Previously, setting goals for gender equality tended to oversimplify persistent challenges. The MDGs, for instance, had settled for parity as a proxy for equality and in effect condoned low rates of achievement for girls and boys, and women and men. Setting targets around disparities was inadequate because the assumption is that everything else was equal. However, achievement varies because of what is not measured—patriarchy and multidimensional discrimination.

A deeper engagement with the formulation of the SDGs by the women's movement and UN Women focused on a gender equality goal and the integration of gender-specific targets in other goals. Advocates argued for an examination of structural issues such as sexual and reproductive health and rights, unpaid care work, absence of violence, control of and not just access to resources, and participation in decision-making at all levels: in the community, in the private sector, in political bodies, and also, importantly, within the home. This case for substantive gender equality was buttressed by the emphasis in the SDGs on universality and addressing inequality within and across countries, moving away from the misleading averages of the MDGs.

After considerable debate, the adoption in 2015 of SDG 5 on Gender Equality, with nine targets and 14 indicators, represented progress. In brief, the targets are the following: end all forms of discrimination against all women and girls everywhere; eliminate all forms of violence against women and girls in the public and private spheres; eliminate all harmful practices such as child, early, and forced marriage and FGM; recognize and value unpaid care and domestic work through the provision of public services, infrastructure, and social protection policies and the promotion of shared responsibility within the household and the family; ensure women's full and effective participation and equal opportunities for leadership at all levels of decision-making in political, economic, and social life; ensure universal access to sexual and reproductive health rights (SRHR); undertake reforms to give women equal rights to economic resources, as well as access to ownership and control over land and other forms of property, financial services, inheritance, and natural resources; enhance the use of enabling technology, especially ICT; and adopt and strengthen sound policies and enforceable legislation. However, the continuing opposition to fully empowering women can be gauged from the restrictive phrases attached to some of the targets, such as "as nationally appropriate" to target 4 on unpaid care work; and "in accordance with national laws" to target 7 on economic rights.

The incorporation of gender into the other SDGs was uneven, although gender dimensions were included in the goals on poverty, hunger, health, education, water and sanitation, employment, safe cities, and peaceful and inclusive societies. The real test of the SDGs will be in the measurement of progress. Six of the 17 SDGs lack gender-specific indicators, including water and sanitation, industry and innovation, and sustainable consumption. The absence of targets or indicators capturing the specific situation of women living in conflict situations was noted. In many cases, the failure to translate macro or environmental changes to deprivation is a reflection not just of ignoring gender discrimination but also of failing to translate targets into people's lives more broadly. The SDGs remain a statement of commitment and a promise to act. Until national legal frameworks, budgets, and policies are aligned with these commitments, and until investment is made in tracking meaningful indicators, public accountability for the SDGs will remain a chimera.

Conclusion

The UN's political and system-wide engagement with gender equality has expanded over the last seven and a half decades. The UN has benefited from the vision of such staff leaders in the Second UN as Helvi Sipila, who led the planning for the first World Conference on Women in Mexico, and Michelle Bachelet, the first executive director of UN Women and now the UN High Commissioner for Human Rights.[31] Nonetheless, the main impetus for change has come mainly from outside—from the Third UN, including the women's movements at the local, national, and global levels and the men and women who have stood in solidarity with them.

Persistent pressure from the women's movement has made a difference. At times, the engagement has reflected resistance to change by the first UN of member states; both the political UN and the systems of organizations have been weak in dealing with the structural barriers to substantive equality.

Yet at other times, the engagements of and interactions among the three UNs have opened new avenues. The UN has been successful in setting new norms and standards for women's rights and expanding knowledge on gender equality. The UN's resolutions, programs, analyses, and advocacy often provide a measure of validation and support for women struggling to claim their rights. As with so much else, the interplay between pushing norms and ideas at the UN and progress in the material lives of women and girls cannot be a simple trajectory. It requires public action by all.

NOTES

1 The author is grateful to Candice Jaimungal for her research help.
2 WHO, *Global and Regional Estimates of Violence against Women: Prevalence and Health Effects of Intimate Partner Violence and Non-Partner Sexual Violence* (Geneva: WHO, 2013); and UNFPA Pacific Sub-Regional Office, "Violence Against Women (VAW) in the Pacific," 1 August 2013, http://countryoffice.unfpa.org/pacific/2013/07/31/7502/violence_against_women_vaw_in_the_pacific.
3 UN Women, *Progress of the World's Women 2015–2016: Transforming Economies, Realizing Rights* (New York: UN Women, 2015), 96.
4 UN Women, *Turning Promises into Action: Gender Equality in the 2030 Agenda for Sustainable Development* (New York: UN Women, 2018).
5 UN Women, *A Brief History of the Commission on the Status of Women*, www.unwomen.org/en/csw/brief-history.
6 Ibid.
7 Ibid.
8 Ibid.
9 Ibid.
10 United Nations System, *Chief Executives Board for Coordination, First World Conference on Women*, www.unsystem.org/content/first-world-conference-women-1975-0.
11 Ibid.
12 Anniamma Emmanuel, "Feminist Movements in Global Perspective: United Nations and the Rights of the Women," *The Indian Journal of Political Science* 71, no. 3 (2010): 837–852.
13 Earth Summit 2002, *Toolkit for Women, 3rd World Conference on Women, Nairobi 1985*, www.earthsummit2002.org/toolkits/women/un-doku/un-conf/narirobi-2.html.
14 Emmanuel, "Feminist Movements."
15 United Nations System, *Chief Executives Board for Coordination, Fourth World Conference on Women*, www.unsystem.org/content/fourth-world-conference-women-1995-0.
16 Gita Sen, *UN Women, The SDGs and Feminist Movement Building* (New York: UN Women, 2018).
17 UN Women, *The Beijing Platform for Action: Inspiring Then and Now*, https://beijing20.unwomen.org/en/about.
18 Radhika Coomaraswamy, *Preventing Conflict, Transforming Justice, Securing the Peace: A Global Study on the Implementation of the United Nations Security Council Resolution 1325* (New York: UN Women, 2015).
19 United Nations Statistics Division, 2019, *The United Nations Minimum Set of Gender Indicators*, https://genderstats.un.org/files/Minimum%20Set%20indicators%202018.11.1%20web.pdf.
20 UNDP, *Human Development Reports*, www.hdr.undp.org.
21 Gita Sen, *The SDGs and Feminist Movement Building* (New York: UN Women, 2018).
22 FUNDS Project, *Future UN Surveys*, www.futureun.org/Surveys.
23 Elisabeth Prugl, *Gender Experts and Gender Expertise: Results of a Survey* (New York: UN, 2015).
24 United Nations Statistical Division, *The World's Women 2015* (New York: UN Statistical Division, 2015).
25 UNDP, *Human Development Report 1995* (Oxford: Oxford University Press, 1995).
26 UN Women, 2011, *Progress of the World's Women: In Pursuit of Justice*, www.unrol.org/files/Progress%20of%20the%20Worlds%20Women%202011-2012.pdf.

27 UN Women, 2015, *Progress of the World's Women 2015–2016*, http://progress.unwomen.org/en/2015.

28 UN Women, 2019, *Progress of the World's Women, Families in a Changing World, 2019–2020*, www.unwomen.org/en/digital-library/progress-of-the-worlds-women.

29 Antonella Picchio, *Social Reproduction: The Political Economy of the Labour Market* (Cambridge: Cambridge University Press, 1992).

30 Luisella Godschmidt-Clermont, *Unpaid Work in the Household: A Review of Economic Methods* (Geneva: ILO, 1989).

31 These categories come from Thomas G. Weiss, Tatiana Carayannis, and Richard Jolly, "The 'Third' United Nations," *Global Governance* 15, no. 2 (2009): 123–142. See also Tatiana Carayannis and Thomas G. Weiss, *The "Third" United Nations: How Knowledge Brokers Help the UN Think* (Oxford: Oxford University Press, forthcoming).

ADDITIONAL READING

Ellen Chesler and Terry McGovern, eds., *Women and Girls Rising: Progress and Resistance around the World* (London: Routledge, 2015).

Devaki Jain, *Women, Development, and the UN: A Sixty-Year Quest for Equality and Justice* (Bloomington, IN: Indiana University Press, 2005).

Gita Sen, *UN Women: The SDGs and Feminist Movement Building* (New York: UN Women, 2018).

Bonnie G. Smith, *The Oxford Encyclopedia of Women in World History* (Oxford: Oxford University Press, 2008).

United Nations, several annual reviews contain essential data and analyses about women and gender, including UNDP, *Human Development Report*; UN Statistical Division, *The World's Women*; and UN Women, *Progress of the World's Women*; also the Proceedings of the Committee on CEDAW.

6

HUMAN RIGHTS AND SUSTAINABLE DEVELOPMENT

Together at last?

Natalie Samarasinghe

The formulation "peace, development, and human rights" has long been used as shorthand for the founding aims or pillars of the United Nations, with "sustainable" now prefacing "development" to reflect the importance of climate and environmental issues; in addition, the magnitude of humanitarian operations means that often they constitute a fourth pillar. The interdependent nature of the pillars is strongly implied in the Preamble to the UN Charter, which establishes the world organization's purpose as collective action to maintain international peace and create the conditions for it through cooperation on social progress and equal rights for all.

The Preamble presents human rights and development as mutually reinforcing, referring to "faith in human rights, in the dignity and worth of the human person" and to "social progress and better standards of life in larger freedom." These phrases capture the essence of a rights-based approach to development, articulated decades later by Nobel laureate Amartya Sen, who wrote:

> Human rights express the bold idea that all people have claims to social arrangements that protect them from the worst abuses and deprivations—and that secure the freedom for a life of dignity. Human development, in turn, is a process of enhancing human capabilities—to expand choices and opportunities so that each person can lead a life of respect and value. When human development and human rights advance together, they reinforce one another—expanding people's capabilities and protecting their rights and fundamental freedoms.
>
> *(Human Development Report, United Nations Development Programme, 2000, 2)*

This approach positions development and human rights not only as objectives with intrinsic value but as practically necessary to each other's achievement. For instance, the extent to which a person's basic needs are met will have an impact on their ability to claim their human rights. At the same time, a rights-based approach to fulfilling these needs, which seeks to empower people and address the inequalities that lie at the heart of poverty, is likely to lead to better and more sustainable development outcomes.[1]

An appraisal of the UN's machinery and resources, however, casts the development pillar as the star of the show, with human rights a mere supporting actor. The UN development system (UNDS) encompasses around two dozen specialized agencies, funds, and programs; five regional commissions; five training and research institutes; and several offices or departments, including the Office for the Coordination of Humanitarian Affairs (OCHA), Office for the High Commissioner for Human Rights (OHCHR), Department of Economic and Social Affairs (DESA), Department of Political and Peacebuilding Affairs (DPPA), Office on Drugs and Crime (UNODC), and Office for Project Services (UNOPS). Together, they address virtually every aspect of human endeavor and planetary resource. The system is coordinated, at least on paper, by the intergovernmental Economic and Social Council (ECOSOC), one of the UN's six principal organs. It accounts for over 70 percent of the UN system's funding ($33.6 billion in development and humanitarian assistance in 2017),[2] and roughly two-thirds of its 109,000 staff.[3]

Far from being an equal pillar, the UN's human rights work has 1,300 staff and receives only 3.7 percent of the UN's regular budget ($201.6 million), in addition to voluntary contributions ($143 million in 2017, the highest amount ever received). The body responsible for coordinating UN activity on human rights, meanwhile, is part of the UN Secretariat: the Office of the High Commissioner for Human Rights (OHCHR). It was created in 1993—nearly half a century after the UN's founding—with a mandate to prevent human rights violations, secure respect for all human rights, promote international cooperation on human rights, and strengthen and streamline the UN system in the field of human rights. It services the intergovernmental Human Rights Council (HRC) in Geneva, as well as the human rights components of UN peace missions or political offices and UN country teams.

In terms of political currency, supporters of human rights are once again the defensive. Rising geopolitical tensions and resurgent authoritarianism have contributed to a backlash against rights and freedoms. Across the world, demagogues and extremists have sought to curtail or undermine human rights. Many have succeeded. These trends have exacerbated long-standing rifts at the UN, where human rights have always been a source of contention—resulting, for example, in cyber-bullying at the 2019 Commission on the Status of Women (CSW)[4] and difficult discussions on issues such as migration in the General Assembly.

Development, on the other hand, is in the ascendancy. Along with the Paris Agreement on Climate Change, the adoption of the 2030 Agenda for Sustainable Development was one of the few bright spots during a period in global affairs characterized by a drift away from international agreements. With 17 Sustainable Development Goals (SDGs) and 169 targets, the agenda is significantly broader and more ambitious than its predecessor framework, the Millennium Development Goals. It is universal in nature and encompasses issues such as climate change, human rights, corruption, and violence. Nonetheless, it enjoys a high degree of support from governments who have agreed to align the agendas of the General Assembly and ECOSOC with the goals.

Some argue that the SDGs are a practical manifestation of the interdependence of human rights and development implied in the UN Charter. The 2030 Agenda[5] was developed through the most inclusive process in UN history. It incorporates human rights language, most notably in its rallying cry to "leave no one behind," and includes 12 specific references to "human rights," including two to the Universal Declaration of Human Rights and international human rights treaties. It covers issues related to all human rights, including the right to development, through dedicated goals on inequalities and on peace, justice, and strong institutions, as well as its broader framework.[6] And it has the potential to bring significant financial resources, organizational capacity, partnerships, and political support to the UN's human rights work.

Others argue that despite significant efforts by some world leaders, UN officials, and grassroots groups, the 2030 Agenda represents a missed opportunity to take forward a rights-based approach to development. Most of the human rights language is in the declaratory elements of the agenda and reflects watered-down text from previous drafts, for instance in relation to sexual and reproductive rights. Just one of the goals, SDG 4 on education, makes reference to human rights. While all goals correspond to existing human rights instruments, only one—the

Convention on the Rights of the Child—is listed in the section on "means of implementation." And every goal has been critiqued from a human rights perspective.

There are also broader criticisms about the 2030 Agenda's overall emphasis on economic growth and the weakness of its monitoring and accountability arrangements, which include the rest of governments' self-assessment and peer review as well as reliable, disaggregated data that is not yet available for all targets, and which include only vague provisions in relation to corporate responsibilities.[7]

This chapter explores whether the SDGs do indeed represent a coming together of the human rights and development agendas. It traces the evolution of both agendas, focusing on their relationship as well as the consequences of their not being aligned which has, on occasion, contributed to a failure to prevent mass atrocities. The chapter ends with some thoughts on the future as the UN marks its 75th anniversary in 2020.

Rights and development: stronger together

Articulated in the 1948 Universal Declaration of Human Rights and codified in dozens of legally binding international, regional, and national treaties, human rights are held to be universal, indivisible, interdependent, and interrelated.[8] The categorization of rights—and what constitutes a right—remains a matter of considerable debate, drawing in arguments framed in terms of state sovereignty and of cultural relativism.[9] However, the following descriptions are commonly used:[10]

- Civil and political rights, such as the rights to: life, political participation, and asylum; freedom of speech, religion, and assembly; and freedom from torture, slavery, and arbitrary detention. Associated with liberalism, they are sometimes called "first-generation rights" because they reflect early writings on human rights, and "negative rights" because their implementation is said to require states to refrain from doing something.
- Economic, social, and cultural rights, such as the rights to education, food, shelter, health, work, social security, and an adequate standard of living. Associated with socialism, they are sometimes called "second-generation rights" because of their association with nineteenth- and twentieth-century economic and social movements, and "positive rights" because they require states to take measures to implement them.
- Collective rights, such as the rights of minorities and indigenous peoples, and the rights to peace, development, and a healthy environment. Associated with de-colonization, they are sometimes called "solidarity rights" because they pertain to groups of persons, and "third-generation rights" because the process of defining and codifying them is still ongoing at the UN (the right to self-determination is a notable exception).

Yet despite this rich body of laws, norms, and common understandings expressed in countless documents, statements, and meetings, the area of human rights remains one of the most contested areas of the UN's work.

The concept of development, meanwhile, has undergone a number of transformations since 1945.[11] Anchored in economic growth during the early years, it is now considered a multidimensional undertaking, which encompasses social development and environmental protection and is predicated on sustainable peace and security. While there is often significant disagreement on priorities and approaches, states have agreed to more ambitious plans and more detailed programs of action on this than on any other areas of the UN's work—which provides one reason for the reluctance to pursue synergies between the two agendas.

However, this reticence is based on a fallacy. Both conceptually and in practice, human rights and development are stronger together.[12] Human rights can encourage a shift from traditional notions of development assistance as charity, with donors and recipients, toward issues of social justice, with rights holders and duty bearers. They bring with them legal and normative tools and mechanisms. They demand priority be given to the most deprived and excluded, to inclusion and participation, and to transparency and accountability. This lends itself to moral legitimacy and practical actions that are especially useful in the context of globalization.

Sustainable development, in turn, can bring a long-term perspective to the fulfillment of rights and encourage better and more strategic planning. It highlights the socio-economic context in which rights can be realized—or threatened. Its concepts and tools "provide a systematic assessment of economic and institutional constraints to the realization of rights"[13]—as well as of the resources and policies available to overcome them.

However, for much of the UN's history, development and human rights unfolded along largely distinct tracks.[14] Dominated by policymakers and economists, the former focused on economic growth and social progress. Dominated by political activists and lawyers, the latter concentrated on political pressure and legal advances.

Human rights

The protection and promotion of human rights has had a difficult trajectory within the UN. This area of work, perhaps more than any other, sees the UN grapple with fundamental questions of legitimacy, universality, and sovereignty. At the same time, it has produced some of the UN's most transformative successes, at the normative level and on the ground. Five distinct analytical categories are helpful to understand the range of UN activities.

Instruments

Early drafts of the UN Charter made scant mention of human rights. The Soviet Union objected to language on civil and political rights, the United Kingdom and France to language that they considered problematic as colonial powers, and the segregated United States to language asserting racial equality. Eventually, efforts by other states and civil society groups led to the inclusion of human rights.[15] These references paved the way for the creation of a Commission on Human Rights (CHR), which was tasked with drafting a Universal Declaration of Human Rights (UDHR).

Adopted in 1948, the Declaration brought together civil, political, economic, social, and cultural rights as a "common standard of achievement for all peoples and nations." The General Assembly asked for it to be translated into a legally binding covenant; but after much debate on the first iteration of this treaty, the assembly decided to produce two documents: an International Covenant on Civil and Political Rights (ICCPR) and an International Covenant on Economic, Social and Cultural Rights (ICESCR).[16]

This reflected the broad perception among member states that implementation of first-generation rights was different from that of second-generation rights. The former were supposedly enforceable by judicial proceedings; they also could be put in place immediately (although the upholding of the right to a fair trial, for instance, depends on prior investment in judicial, security, and education systems). The latter, meanwhile, were perceived as too context-specific to be justiciable, and needed to be realized progressively, as they required resources. This sequencing has subsequently been rebutted by UN bodies, but it remains prevalent.[17]

The covenants are two of the UN's nine core human rights treaties (see Table 6.1). The others focus on particular issues or social groups. In addition to protecting specific rights, they

Table 6.1 The core international human rights instruments

According to the Office of the UN High Commissioner for Human Rights, there are nine core international human rights instruments. Each of these instruments has established a committee of experts to monitor implementation of the treaty provisions by its states parties.

Acronym	Human rights treaty	Date adopted
ICERD	International Convention on the Elimination of All Forms of Racial Discrimination	21 Dec 1965
ICCPR	International Covenant on Civil and Political Rights	16 Dec 1966
ICESCR	International Covenant on Economic, Social and Cultural Rights	16 Dec 1966
CEDAW	Convention on the Elimination of All Forms of Discrimination Against Women	18 Dec 1979
CAT	Convention Against Torture and Other Cruel, Inhuman or Degrading Treatment or Punishment	10 Dec 1984
CRC	Convention on the Rights of the Child	20 Nov 1989
ICMW	International Convention on the Protection of the Rights of All Migrant Workers and Members of Their Families	18 Dec 1990
CRPD	Convention on the Rights of Persons with Disabilities	13 Dec 2006
ICPED	International Convention for the Protection of All Persons from Enforced Disappearance	20 Dec 2006

have made broader normative contributions, including in the development sphere. For example, the Convention on the Rights of the Child brought civil, political, economic, social, and cultural rights into a single, binding treaty. Meanwhile, Article 32 of the Convention on the Rights of Persons with Disabilities states that development assistance should be provided to enable developing countries to implement the convention.

Monitoring mechanisms

All core human rights treaties require states to submit regular reports to a committee of independent experts. While there is no sanction for not submitting a report, these "treaty bodies" can make recommendations to states and, if states have agreed, consider specific cases. For example, a state that has ratified the Optional Protocol to the ICESCR has recognized the competence of its treaty body to receive communications from individuals who have exhausted all available domestic remedies. Pronouncements on individual cases can have practical and normative outcomes. The communication *Mohamed Ben Djazia and Naouel Bellili vs. Spain*, for example, confirmed that the right to adequate housing is vested in all persons, including those living in public and private rental accommodation. It also highlighted the importance of special protection measures for vulnerable groups.[18]

Meanwhile, "General Comments" issued by treaty bodies serve as guidance on the interpretation and implementation of rights. For example, in General Comment 3, the Committee on Economic, Social and Cultural Rights addressed concerns that the principle of progressive realization effectively gives states a free pass to do nothing on economic, social, and cultural rights. It maintained that states must take deliberate, concrete, and targeted steps within a reasonably short timeframe after ratification.[19]

In General Comment 15, the Committee inferred the right to water from Articles 11 and 12 in the ICESCR on the rights to an adequate standard of living and to the highest attainable standard of physical and mental health. It noted that states have international obligations in relation to this right, including a positive duty to facilitate the realization of the right to water in other countries "[d]epending on the availability of resources […] for example through provision of water resources, financial and technical assistance, and provide the necessary aid when required."[20]

Protecting rights

The UN Charter does not explicitly authorize the monitoring of human rights, and scholars have argued that the term "protection" was deliberately left out of the document, reflecting many states' deep reluctance to be held accountable for human rights violations. This reluctance was spelled out in 1947 at the first meeting of the CHR, when member states declared that it had no power "to take any action in regard to any complaints." In combination with reservations on the justiciability of economic, social, and cultural rights, exceptions to this rule tended to focus on systematic abuses of civil and political rights—such as enforced disappearances—or on prominent country situations such as Israel–Palestine or South Africa.

There was, however, some overlap with the development agenda in the robust critique of colonialism put forward by non-self-governing territories and newly independent states. Their commentary encompassed issues of economic growth, trade, and development; it eventually fed into the articulation of the "new international economic order" and other demands for accelerated development in the 1970s.

In 2006, the CHR was replaced by the Human Rights Council, which included a new feature: the Universal Periodic Review (UPR). This is widely considered to be the HRC's most significant innovation, with every UN member state being subject to review by peers once every four years. The process is far from perfect. States can reject all recommendations generated, and the sheer number of recommendations produced (over 8,000 during the UPR's second cycle) is impractical. Nonetheless, UPR has contributed to changes on the ground, such as the decriminalization of marital rape in the Republic of Korea,[21] and there are now calls for it to be reflected in reporting on the SDGs.[22]

The Special Procedures, meanwhile, have made a significant contribution to the protection of development-related human rights. Appointed by the HRC, these independent experts can conduct studies, provide advice, visit countries (with their consent), consider appeals, and engage with specific cases. For instance, the special rapporteur on the implications for human rights of the environmentally sound management and disposal of hazardous substances and wastes has issued opinions on cases such as the Bhopal toxic gas leak, the Flint water crisis, and the Fukushima Daiichi nuclear disaster.[23] Meanwhile, the special rapporteur on the right to a safe, clean, healthy, and sustainable environment submitted a statement to the case *Friends of the Irish Environment CLG v. The Government of Ireland, Ireland and the Attorney General* in 2018 which concluded, "climate change clearly and adversely impacts the right to life." Therefore, governments have an "obligation to mitigate climate change by rapidly reducing its greenhouse gas emissions."[24]

But while the UN's human rights infrastructure has developed considerably, state cooperation remains a crucial and often missing ingredient. UN officials and organs, with the support of civil society, can encourage, prod, push, and sometimes embarrass states. There are few options when a state is unable or unwilling to comply with its obligations, but naming and shaming is a prominent item in the UN's toolbox.

Mainstreaming

Since its creation in 1993, OHCHR has been part of various efforts to integrate human rights into all areas of the UN's work. Its head office in Geneva supports the HRC, treaty bodies, and special procedures; it also engages with the development and humanitarian agencies based there. Its office in New York interacts with the Security Council, General Assembly, and ECOSOC as well as the departments for peace operations and for political and peacebuilding affairs. Its network of regional and country offices works with UN regional commissions and country teams. OHCHR also provides human rights advisers when requested by resident coordinators (RCs).

The integration of human rights into the work of UN country teams (UNCTs) has been one of the world organization's biggest challenges and a major contributing factor in some of its most egregious failures. UNCTs are primarily focused on development or humanitarian assistance, which requires the consent of the host state and some degree of cooperation with national governments and other pertinent actors. These constraints can put the UN in an uncomfortable position when it comes to advocating for human rights, particularly when this position is at odds with the government and a principled stand may cost access to vulnerable populations.

Traditionally, RCs have tended to come from a development rather than a political or human rights background. Many have not felt empowered to advocate on behalf of the UN system as a whole[25]—or civilians in need of protection—with their ability to do so linked to a wide range of variables. They include human resource and capacity constraints in RCs' offices, institutional support, and backup within the UN system, and the level of internal cohesion and mutual accountability within UNCTs.

Preventing atrocities

At times, UNCTs' reluctance to speak out on human rights abuses has had tragic consequences. In 2012, an internal review panel on UN action in Sri Lanka concluded that there had been a systemic failure to protect civilians.[26] A report raising similar concerns in relation to Myanmar was released in 2019 and concluded: "Without question serious errors were committed and opportunities were lost in the UN system following a fragmented strategy rather than a common plan of action."[27]

It endorsed recommendations contained in the 2012 report, including that every UNCT should have staff with expertise in political analysis and human rights; that UNCT planning tools should incorporate a frank analysis of the human rights situation; that all UN bodies should embed human rights into their vision and strategy; and that RCs should be evaluated in part on their human rights performance. In response to that report, Secretary-General Ban Ki-moon launched the "Human Rights Up Front" initiative in 2013, which largely embraced these recommendations. His successor, António Guterres, has further implemented them through specific measures, including: placing the RC system under the UN Deputy Secretary-General, as opposed to UNDP; improving coordination, monitoring, analysis, and responses to unfolding crisis situations; creating better lines of communication between UN headquarters and field offices; and decentralizing decision-making to give officials on the ground greater room for manoeuvre.[28]

Development

Failures like those in Myanmar and Sri Lanka represent the sharp end of the development–rights nexus. They have proved deadly for civilians and damaging for the UN. They cannot be excused, but overcoming them requires an understanding of the long journey to integrate development and rights in a manner that reflects the notional interdependence set out in the Charter. Given the limitations of space, this section provides only a brief summary of developments with particular focus on human rights-related milestones.

Over the decades, the UNDS has made substantive contributions to advancing the human rights agenda. Entities such as the UN Development Programme (UNDP) have provided thought leadership, including in formulating a rights-based approach to development. Others, such as the UN Population Fund (UNFPA), have been vigorous advocates for translating norms into binding laws and standards. Others still, like the UN Educational, Social and Cultural Organization (UNESCO), have provided technical assistance to support implementation by member states.[29]

However, for a variety of reasons, many parts of the development system have been reluctant, even hostile at times, to human rights approaches. One reason is the decentralized nature of the development system.

Decentralization = depoliticization?

In its early years, the UNDS comprised bodies like the UN Children's Fund (UNICEF), which grew out of the humanitarian relief programs created in the aftermath of World War II; technical agencies established by the UN's predecessor, the League of Nations, such as the International Labour Organization (ILO); and even older entities, notably the nineteenth-century technical unions, the International Telecommunications (formerly Telegraph) Union (ITU) and Universal Postal Union (UPU). The Charter gave ECOSOC a role in overseeing and coordinating their work, but it was never allowed to fulfill these functions, as each entity established its own independent, governing structure. The UN's potential for broader contributions to macroeconomic policy and development planning was also undermined, as major economic powers—which are not afforded special status or powers within ECOSOC—tended to gravitate to the World Bank and International Monetary Fund (IMF), where voting was weighted in their favor.

Some scholars have argued that this decentralized structure was a conscious choice, a way of avoiding the fate of the League of Nations by ensuring that international cooperation on technical matters could continue in spite of political impasses.[30] In practice, politics infused the UNDS from its earliest days, not least during the heated debates on resettling refugees in the aftermath of World War II. Nonetheless, officials sought to maintain an apolitical veneer—and that façade has now become ingrained in many of the system's constituent parts. The UNDS's diffuse nature, meanwhile, has kept states, UN officials, and policy wonks busy for years with endless debates about improving coordination and coherence.[31]

These challenges increased as development moved to center stage at the UN. By the mid-1960s, decolonization had nearly tripled the UN's original 1945 membership and former colonies emphasized programs to alleviate poverty and accelerate economic growth. With this new membership configuration, and with the Cold War impeding actions on international peace and security as well as human rights, development became a legitimate pursuit in and of itself, not solely as a precondition for peace.

Existing UN organizations increasingly took on development activities alongside humanitarian work, driven in part by the need to find longer-term solutions to crises such as famines, and in part by the increasing focus on accelerating economic growth in developing countries.[32] By the end of the 1960s, there was growing acceptance that developed countries should allocate a percentage of their Gross National Income (GNI) to official development assistance (ODA). The General Assembly endorsed a target of 0.7 percent of GNI in 1970.

In the 1970s, member states set targets in relation to education, employment, and health,[33] as work by the ILO and others found that growth had intensified inequalities between and within countries; and its spoils had failed to trickle down to the poorest—and most vulnerable—countries and individuals. For the UNDS, this marked the beginning of a period of rapid investment that would lead to intense competition between development entities over resources and, at times, a lowered priority for human rights in light of donor and recipient demands.[34]

There were two notable exceptions. The first was the UN system's entry into the environmental sphere. In 1972, it convened the Stockholm World Conference on the Human Environment, which considered the environmental consequences of economic growth, and the seeming trade-offs between environmental protection and development.

The second was gender and development. Previously, UN gender-related development activities had focused on narrow areas, such as women's literacy. The 1976 World Conference on Women and Development looked at issues relating to civil and political rights, as well as economic, social, and cultural rights. It produced recommendations on areas such as health, education, employment, social services, nutrition, and family planning that continue to form the basis of programming today.[35]

The influence of the "Washington Consensus" in the 1980s saw development programs return to a focus on neoliberal growth and free-market policies but with more emphasis on deregulation and privatization, and a more constrained role for the state—particularly in developing countries.[36] This approach was enthusiastically adopted by the Bretton Woods institutions through their structural adjustment programs—widely seen today as fueling a "lost decade" of development opportunity in Africa and Latin America.[37] At the time, most of the UNDS "ended up either endorsing the policies of the financial agencies, or at best offering low-key critiques."[38] Many implemented these policies on the ground. The Economic Commission for Africa, which analyzed the impact of debt servicing and stabilization, was one of a few notable exceptions.

Human development

The 1990s saw another major shift in development thinking and practice, this time with the UNDP leading the charge. The end of the Cold War ushered in prospects for a shift in the global development paradigm, with greater opportunities for coordination across macro-economic policies, as well as action on non-economic (or social) elements of development. In 1986, UN member states endorsed the Declaration on the Right to Development, which proclaimed that everyone is "entitled to participate in, contribute to, and enjoy economic, social, cultural and political development, in which all human rights and fundamental freedoms can be fully realized."[39] The declaration also marked a step-change in human rights at the UN, with activity moving toward collective rights, such as the rights of indigenous peoples and the rights to peace and a healthy environment, and to collective duties, by the international community of states in relation to development, for instance, but also by entities such as transnational corporations. This work increased in prominence, if not tangible outcomes, with the growth of public resistance to unchecked globalization aided by burgeoning civil society movements and developments in media and technology.

Within the UNDP, Mahbub ul Haq and Amartya Sen elaborated the notion of human development[40] as a means to address the serious questions that had been raised in the 1980s about the effectiveness and sustainability of development aid, paving the way for a rights-based approach to development. Neither the exponential increase in economic output nor ODA had managed to narrow global gaps in wealth and opportunity—indeed, many had increased. Meanwhile, targeted initiatives—notably the eradication of smallpox—had succeeded.

Building on work by Giovanni Andrea Cornia, Frances Stewart, and Richard Jolly, which had formed a core element of UNICEF's riposte to structural adjustment, Ul Haq and Sen argued that public policies needed to be more focused and public institutions strengthened. In 1990, UNDP published its first *Human Development Report*. This path-breaking report was anchored in Sen's work on human capabilities, often framed in terms of whether people are able to "be" and "do" certain things in life,[41] such as be well fed and healthy, and participate in education and voting. As such, freedom of choice is central to this approach.[42]

The report also introduced the Human Development Index (HDI) as a measure of development progress. Gross Domestic Product (GDP) and economic growth had become the leading indicators of development progress in many parts of the world, although GDP was never intended to serve as a measure of well-being. The HDI put greater emphasis on development outcomes, specifically life expectancy at birth and mean and expected years of schooling, alongside GNI per capita. Since 2000, the index has gone through several adjustments, and companion indices have been created. However, as Ul Haq predicted, it is still the main index each year that inspires and cajoles states into action: "We need a measure of the same level of vulgarity as GNP—just one number—but a measure that is not as blind to social aspects of human lives as GNP is."[43]

The 1990s also saw a number of global, ad hoc UN conferences that generated declarations, conventions, and plans of action that reflected development and human rights concerns. The principal ones are listed below:

- The 1990 World Summit for Children in New York and World Conference on Education for All in Jomtien adopted global targets for primary school education.
- The 1992 UN Conference on Environment and Development in Rio de Janeiro created the conventions on biodiversity, climate change, and desertification. It also launched the *Agenda 21* framework on strengthening the role of children and youth, women, non-governmental organizations, local authorities, business and industry, workers, indigenous peoples, farmers, and others in development.
- The 1993 World Conference on Human Rights in Vienna emphasized the relationship between democracy, development, and human rights. It also created the post of High Commissioner for Human Rights.
- The 1994 International Conference on Population and Development in Cairo focused on such issues as women's rights, education, health, and access to family planning.
- The 1995 Fourth World Conference on Women in Beijing set out recommendations for action in relation to women in the environmental, social, political, and economic spheres.
- The 1995 World Summit for Social Development in Copenhagen highlighted the linkages between poverty, employment, and social integration.

Together, these gatherings generated a significant number of targets around three core themes: inclusive globalization, equality, and poverty eradication. Of the three, poverty eradication emerged as the "super norm" and primary focus for states, in particular donors.[44] For example, while the Organisation for Economic Co-operation and Development's Development Assistance Committee (OECD/DAC) grouping of major bilateral donors adopted six international development goals—income poverty, education, gender disparity, maternal and child deaths, reproductive health, and environmental sustainability—poverty reduction was their overarching purpose.[45]

Scholars have argued that the 1995 Copenhagen agenda prevailed because it was more palatable to governments. Presented by economists, it put forward a familiar perspective, with solutions that straddled growth, access to resources, and basic needs. The frameworks developed in Beijing, Cairo, and Rio, on the other hand, were more challenging because they focused on structural inequalities and societal relations, and raised questions about the negative consequences of economic growth.[46]

The era of goals

Ahead of the Millennium Summit in 2000, Secretary-General Kofi Annan released the report *We the Peoples*.[47] It reflected the broad sweep of the previous decade's conferences, complemented by some forward-looking language on technology and global governance, as well as a special focus on Africa, much of which had experienced substantial negative growth in the 1980s and 1990s. The report's core development recommendations, though, were very much in line with the OECD/DAC agenda. This orientation can be ascribed in part to Annan's pragmatism, and his desire for the UN to assert leadership over what had become a sprawling development agenda[48] and movement, encompassing hundreds of goals and thousands of actors with insufficient coordination and prioritization. The summit provided an opportunity to do so, as would another summit 15 years later.

Millennium Development Goals

At the Millennium Summit in 2000, world leaders endorsed the Millennium Declaration, which closely reflected Annan's report. The development section of General Assembly resolution 55/2 emphasized poverty reduction and contained a number of objectives on the areas identified in Annan's report: poverty, primary education, under-five mortality, HIV/AIDS, slums, gender equality, youth employment, new technologies, and multi-stakeholder partnerships. These were eventually translated into eight Millennium Development Goals (MDGs) with 21 targets and 60 indicators.[49]

The UN has described the MDGs as the largest and most successful anti-poverty movement in history.[50] Between 1990 and 2015, the proportion of people living in extreme poverty was more than halved, as was the under-five mortality rate. Primary school enrollment rose by 8 percent in developing countries, two-thirds of which achieved gender parity. Significant progress took place in fighting malaria, tuberculosis, and HIV/AIDS. While critics maintain that these trends were already in train, researchers have calculated that some 20–30 million lives were saved because of accelerated rates of progress arising from the MDGs.[51]

However, many targets were missed by the 2015 deadline. The MDGs were also criticized for the closed-door approach to their formulation, their focus on quantitative over qualitative outcomes, and their emphasis on low-hanging fruit. While the MDGs embraced the notions of human development,[52] they were a simplification of the many goals identified in the 1990s.

The UN conferences held during that decade had emphasized human rights and equality, and the need for partnerships between governments, businesses, and civil society. The MDGs reflected neither. They were also silent on inequalities, globalization, and economic systems and structures. At the same time, they "neglected the centrality of growth and the private sector for poverty reduction and dangerously exaggerated the role and capacity of the state."[53] In short, they mainly served donors' needs, giving them a quantitative, results-driven framework that allowed measurement and a global legitimacy their own goals had lacked.

Sustainable Development Goals

Five years after the MDGs were adopted, Annan's second major report, *In Larger Freedom*,[54] and the 2005 World Summit *Outcome Document* in General Assembly resolution 60/1 emphasized the links between the UN's pillars. Specifically, member states recognized that human rights were essential to achieving the MDGs and committed to integrating them into development and cooperation policies. Subsequent conferences strengthened this message, most notably Rio+20 in 2012. That gathering also marked the beginning of the search for the MDGs' successors: the 2030 Agenda for Sustainable Development, with 17 Sustainable Development Goals (SDGs), 169 targets, and 232 indicators.

In crafting these new goals, member states and UN officials sought to address many of the shortcomings of the MDGs. Instead of endorsing only the objectives, states decided to negotiate the text for every goal and target. A high-level panel was set up, co-chaired by three heads of government, thereby significantly raising the profile of the process. The UN conducted its largest survey to date,[55] complemented by consultations worldwide. The process was lengthy, but it helped to foster a sense of genuine ownership of the new goals among member states and, to some extent, civil society actors.

MDG targets were refined and expanded to capture a more holistic vision. For example, the MDG on gender had just three targets: school enrollment, seats in parliament, and share of women in wage employment in the non-agricultural sector. The SDG on gender includes targets on different forms of violence, on land ownership and legal rights, on sexual and reproductive health care, and on gender-responsive budgeting. Many areas that were absent from the MDGs—such as inequalities and good governance—were included. Some structural inequalities (e.g., in trade and financial institutions) and global governance gaps (e.g., in migration, regulation of business, and financial speculation) also feature in the 2030 Agenda, although they are not attached to specific targets.

Conceptually, the new framework moved from a narrow focus on economic and social issues to a rounded, people-centered approach. The interdependence of human rights and sustainable development is evident in many goals. In total, some 90 percent of the 169 targets reflect core international human rights and labor standards.[56]

They embrace social and economic rights, by calling for universal health coverage, full employment, and universal access to education, housing, water, and sanitation. Learning from the MDG experience, the 2030 Agenda requires disaggregated data so that progress can be measured not in crude averages but monitored for all social groups. Crucially, the 2030 Agenda seeks to move away from the binary donor–recipient paradigm. It is universal, for all states to achieve. It is nationally and locally owned, with countries and communities determining targets and monitoring progress through "voluntary national reviews" (VNRs). The agenda is predicated on stakeholders playing a meaningful role in monitoring and delivery.

Many scholars and practitioners see the SDGs as a positive evolution of the MDGs, and one that has helped to bring the human rights and development agendas closer together.[57] Between September 2015 and April 2018, over 40 percent of the Human Rights Council's resolutions, decisions, and statements (excluding UPR outcomes) mentioned the 2030 Agenda. Meanwhile, a number of countries have integrated reports to UN human rights bodies into their VNRs. For instance, Belgium reported in its VNR that it had developed indicators on violence against children following recommendations by the UN Committee on the Rights of the Child. Costa Rica integrated information from its review under the Committee on the Elimination on All Forms of Discrimination Against Women (CEDAW).

A number of the treaty bodies, including the two mentioned above, have explored synergies between human rights and SDGs. As of mid-2019, the Human Rights Council had 12 thematic mandates with particular relevance to development, including the rights to education, food, health, housing, poverty, water, and sanitation. The OHCHR has published guidance on well-functioning and inclusive National Mechanisms for Reporting and Follow-Up.

In practice, however, serious challenges remain. A tenth of humanity still lives in extreme poverty. A third does not have safe drinking water. One in two people lacks access to proper sanitation, social protection, and essential health services. It is still the case that women, older people, LGBT+ people, those with disabilities, and those from a rural, minority, or indigenous community are more likely to be disadvantaged or subjected to human rights abuses.

In relation to the SDGs, gaps in data are undermining the commitment to leave no one behind, as is the lack of funding for human rights bodies—UN and otherwise. The political backlash against human rights ensured that references to issues such as reproductive rights were watered down in the 2030 Agenda, while areas such as climate justice, global governance, and stakeholder inclusion were left out almost entirely. Meanwhile, human rights defenders, including those working in areas such as government and corporate accountability, are increasingly under attack.

Conclusion: looking ahead

As states gear up for "a decade of action and delivery" on the SDGs, the context for realizing the goals is challenging. The situation is even trickier for human rights protection. A confluence of crises—climate, environmental, political, economic, social, and health—is threatening the human rights and development gains from previous decades. Rapid changes in technology and demography also require urgent attention. The social contract is fraying as governments are increasingly unable to provide a credible guarantee to their citizens while inequalities deepen. Nationalist sentiment, xenophobia, and extremism are on the rise, as the world grows more polarized.

There are opportunities too. Modest changes, such as increasing core or non-earmarked funding for OHCHR and for development entities, would significantly improve their ability to plan and deliver. So would extending to all senior appointments the spirit behind the changes initiated in 2015–2016 to make the selection of the Secretary-General more inclusive and transparent.[58] As Brian Urquhart and Erskine Childers wrote long ago, "no amount of reform will compensate for the lack of leadership."[59]

Fully integrating human rights into the 2030 Agenda could provide the foundation for a "global green new deal"[60] and a new social contract—drawing on the agendas developed in the 1990s, the promise of new technologies, and contemporary debates on the rights of future generations. Moreover, expanding SDG 17 could be a route to addressing global governance gaps, notably in economic governance,[61] and finding meaningful ways to include stakeholders in UN decision-making and delivery. This could usefully see them absorb tasks that they can deliver as well as or better than the world organization, freeing up resources for it to focus on areas such as human rights standard-setting that others cannot easily take on.[62]

The 75th anniversary of the United Nations in 2020 provides an opportunity to take forward the above and make progress toward people-centered multilateralism and a truly global partnership for sustainable human development.

NOTES

1 Office of the High Commissioner for Human Rights, *Frequently Asked Questions on a Human Rights-Based Approach to Development Cooperation* (Geneva: UN, 2006).

2 Chief Executives Board for Coordination and Report of the Secretary-General, (UN document A/74/73-E/2019/4), 18 April 2019.

3 Chief Executives Board for Coordination, *Personnel Statistics: Data as at 31 December 2018*, UN document CEB/2019/HLCM/HR/17, 19 August 2019.

4 See, for example, Sonah Lee, "The Case of Harassing a UN Diplomat via 1,000s of Text Messages," *PassBlue*, 14 May 2019, www.passblue.com/2019/05/14/the-case-of-harassing-a-un-diplomat-via-1000s-of-text-messages; and "Feminist Leadership Delivers on Women's Human Rights as CSW," *Development Alternatives with Women for a New Era*, 26 March 2019, dawnnet.org/2019/03/feminist-leadership-delivers-on-womens-human-rights-at-csw.

5 *Transforming Our World: The 2030 Agenda for Sustainable Development*, UN General Assembly resolution A/RES/70/1, 21 October 2015.

6 See, for example, The Danish Institute for Human Rights, 2018, *The Human Rights Guide to the Sustainable Development Goals*; and Center for Economic and Social Rights, 2015, *Strong Commitments in Final SDG Text despite Sordid Final Compromises*.

7 See, for example, Thomas Pogge and Mitu Sengupta, "The Sustainable Development Goals (SDGs) as Drafted: Nice Idea, Poor Execution," *Washington International Law Journal* 24, no. 3 (2015): 571–587; Kate Donald and Sally-Anne Way, "Accountability for the Sustainable Development Goals: A Lost Opportunity?" *Ethics & International Affairs* 30, no. 2 (2016): 201–213; and Bertrand G. Ramcharan, *"Human Rights and the SDGs: A Side-Lined Priority?" FUNDS Briefing No. 31*, July 2015.

8 Vienna Declaration and Programme of Action, adopted by the World Conference on Human Rights in Vienna on 25 June 1993.

9 Graeme Reid, "The Trouble with Tradition: When 'Values' Trample Over Rights," *World Report 2013* (New York: Human Rights Watch, 2013).

10 Karel Vasak, "Human Rights: A Thirty-Year Struggle: The Sustained Efforts to Give Force of Law to the Universal Declaration of Human Rights," *UNESCO Courier* 30, no. 11 (1977): 29. A critique of his categorization can be found in Patrick Macklem, "Human Rights in International Law: Three Generations or One?" *London Review of International Law* 3, no. 1 (2015): 61–92.

11 See, for example, Margaret J. Anstee, "Millennium Development Goals: Milestones on a Long Road" in *The Millennium Development Goals and Beyond: Global Development After 2015*, ed. Rorden Wilkinson and David Hulme (London: Routledge, 2012), 19–34.

12 See, for example, Mac Darrow, "New Aid Modalities: An Opportunity or Threat to Principled Engagement on Human Rights?" in *Applied Legal Philosophy: Principled Engagement: Negotiating Human Rights in Repressive States*, ed. Mac Darrow1Morten B. Pedersen and David Kinley (Farnham, UK: Ashgate Publishing Ltd., 2013), 227–248.

13 Rajiv Balakrishnan, "Human Development: Meanings, Mechanisms and Measurement," in Social *Redevelopment in Independent India: Paths Tread and the Road Ahead*, ed. Rajiv Balakrishnan and Muchkund Dubey (New Delhi: Pearson Education, 2008), 34.

14 Siobhán McInerney-Lankford, "Human Rights and Development: A Comment on Challenges and Opportunities from a Legal Perspective," *Journal of Human Rights Practice* 1, no. 1 (2009): 51–82.

15 Jan Herman Burgers, "The Road to San Francisco: The Revival of the Human Rights Idea in the Twentieth Century," *Human Rights Quarterly* 14, no. 4 (1992): 447–477.

16 Office of the UN High Commissioner for Human Rights, *Status of Ratification—Interactive Dashboard*, https://indicators.ohchr.org.

17 Office of the UN High Commissioner for Human Rights, *Key Concepts on ESCR*, www.ohchr.org/EN/Issues/ESCR.

18 Committee on Economic, Social and Cultural Rights, *Mohamed Ben Djazia and Naouel Bellili v. Spain*, Communication No. 5/2015 (E/C.12/61/D/5/2015), 20 June 2017.

19 Committee on Economic, Social and Cultural Rights, *General Comment No. 3: The Nature of States Parties' Obligations* (Art. 2, par. 1), 14 December 1990.

20 Committee on Economic, Social and Cultural Rights, *General Comment No. 15: The Right to Water* (E/C.12/2002/11), 20 January 2003.

21 *Statement by Natalie Samarasinghe to the All-Party Parliamentary Group on the UN*, Houses of Parliament, London, 27 March 2017; and Hans Fridlund, "A Butterfly Effect—Steps to Improve UPR Implementation," *Open Democracy*, 24 January 2017.

22 See, for example, Danish Institute for Human Rights, *Linking the Universal Periodic Review to the SDGs* (Copenhagen: Danish Institute for Human Rights, 2018), which found that over 50 percent of UPR recommendations were linked to specific SDGs.

23 Cases listed on the independent website of the special rapporteur, www.srtoxics.org.

24 Grantham Research Institute on Climate Change and the Environment, *Friends of the Irish Environment CLG v. The Government of Ireland, Ireland and the Attorney General*, www.lse.ac.uk/GranthamInstitute/litigation/friends-of-the-irish-environment-v-ireland.

25 Ana Maria Lebada, "New Year, New United Nations: Structural Reforms Begin," Policy brief, International Institute for Sustainable Development—SDG knowledge hub, 22 January 2019.

26 Charles Petrie, *Report of the Secretary-General's Internal Review Panel on United Nations Action in Sri Lanka*, UN document ST(02)/R425/Sri Lanka, November 2012.

27 Gert Rosenthal, *A Brief and Independent Inquiry into the Involvement of the United Nations in Myanmar from 2010 to 2018*, 29 May 2019.

28 See, for example, United Nations Association—UK, *UN briefing: Human Rights Up Front*, 23 October 2019, www.una.org.uk/news/un-briefings-human-rights-front.

29 Dharam Ghai, "UN Contributions to Development Thinking and Practice," *Development in Practice* 18, no. 6 (2008): 767–772.

30 See, for example, J. Müller, *Reforming the United Nations: The Quiet Revolution* (The Hague, Netherlands: Kluwer Law International, 2001). For different perspectives, see R. I. Meltzer, "Restructuring the United Nations System: Institutional Reform Efforts in the Context of North–South Relations," *International Organization* 32, no. 4 (1978): 993–1018; and Ken Conca, "Greening the United Nations: Environmental Organisations and the UN System," *Third World Quarterly* 16, no. 3 (1995): 441–457.

31 Silke Weinlich, *Reforming Development Cooperation at the United Nations: An Analysis of Policy Position and Actions of Key States on Reform Options* (Bonn: German Development Institute, 2011).

32 Anstee, "Millennium Development Goals."

33 Ibid.

34 Darrow, "New Aid Modalities."

35 Margaret Snyder, *Transforming Development: Women, Poverty and Politics* (Bradford, UK: ITDG Publishing, 1995).

36 Matthew M. Taylor, "Development Economics in the Wake of the Washington Consensus: From Smith to Smithereens?" *International Political Science Review* 29, no. 5 (2008): 543–556.

37 Taylor, "Development Economics."

38 Ghai, "UN Contributions to Development Thinking."

39 "Declaration on the Right to Development," General Assembly resolution 41/128, 4 December 1986.

40 Khadija Haq, "The Inaugural Mahbub ul Haq Memorial Lecture: Amartya Sen and Mahbub ul Haq: A Friendship That Continues Beyond Life," *Journal of Human Development* 9, no. 3 (2008): 329–330.

41 United Nations Development Programme, *About Human Development*, http://hdr.undp.org/en/humandev.

42 See, for example, Desmond McNeill, "'Human Development': The Power of the Idea," *Journal of Human Development* 8, no. 1 (2007): 5–22.

43 Mahbub ul Haq quoted in Pedro Conceicao, "Human Development and the SDGs," in *Sustainable Development Goals: Transforming our World*, ed. United Nations Association—UK (London: Witan Media, 2019).

44 Sakiko Fukuda-Parr and David Hulme, "International Norm Dynamics and the 'End of Poverty': Understanding the Millennium Development Goals," *Global Governance* 17, no. 1 (2011): 17–36.

45 Development Assistance Committee, *Shaping the 21st Century: The Contribution of Development Cooperation* (Paris: OECD, 1996).

46 Rosalind Eyben, "The Road Not Taken: International Aid's Choice of Copenhagen Over Beijing," *Third World Quarterly* 27, no. 4 (2006): 595–608.

47 Kofi A. Annan, *We the Peoples: The Role of the United Nations in the 21st Century* (New York: United Nations, 2000).

48 Fukuda-Parr and Hulme, "International Norm Dynamics," 20.

49 UN, *Millennium Development Report 2015* (New York: United Nations, 2015).

50 Ibid.

51 Krista Rasmussen and John W. McArthur, "Change of Pace: Accelerations and Advances during the Millennium Development Goal Era," *World Development* 105 (May 2018): 132–143.

52 David Hulme, "The Making of the Millennium Development Goals: Human Development Meets Results-Based Management in an Imperfect World," *Working Paper 16*, Brooks World Poverty Institute, December 2007.

53 Fukuda-Parr and Hulme, "International Norm Dynamics," 29.

54 Annan, *In Larger Freedom: Towards Development, Security and Human Rights for All.*

55 MYWorld, *The United Nations Global Survey for a Better World*, https://myworld2030.org.

56 Danish Institute for Human Rights, *Human Rights and the 2030 Agenda for Sustainable Development: Lessons Learned and Next Steps* (Copenhagen: Danish Institute for Human Rights, 2018), 9.

57 See, for example, Inga Ingulfsen and Anna Koob "Human Rights and the Sustainable Development Goals: Are the SDGs Living up to Their Promise to Leave No One Behind?" Foundation Center, 15 February 2018; and Lily Caprani, "Five Ways the Sustainable Development Goals Are Better than the Millennium Development Goals and Why Every Educationalist Should Care," *Management in Education* 30, no. 3 (2016): 102–104.

58 See, for example, Yvonne Terlingen, "A Better Process, a Stronger UN Secretary-General: How Historic Change Was Forged and What Comes Next," *Ethics & International Affairs* 31, no. 2 (2017); and Natalie Samarasinghe, "Selecting the Ninth Secretary-General, a Practical Step Towards Development Reform?" *FUNDS Briefing 34*, October 2015.

59 Erskine Childers and Brian Urquhart, *Renewing the United Nations System* (Stockholm: The Dag Hammarskjöld Foundation, 1994), 36.

60 Kevin P. Gallagher and Richard Kozul-Wright, "A New Multilateralism for Shared Prosperity: Geneva Principles for a Global Green New Deal," Boston University and UN Conference on Trade and Development, April 2019.

61 Dimitry Uzunidis and Lamia Yacoub, "Global Governance and Sustainable Development: Rethinking the Economy," *Journal of Innovation Economics and Management* 1, no. 3 (2009): 73–89.

62 Natalie Samarasinghe, *A Truly Global Partnership—Helping the UN to Do Itself Out of a Job*, submission to Global Challenges Foundation New Shape Prize 2017, https://globalchallenges.org/new-shape-library/59cfe0e09bb755680d442bbf/details.

ADDITIONAL READING

Philip Alston and Mary Robinson, *Human Rights and Development: Towards Mutual Reinforcement* (Oxford: Oxford University Press, 2005).

Danish Institute for Human Rights, *The Human Rights Guide to the Sustainable Development Goals*, https://sdg.humanrights.dk/en/node/10.

Jack Donnelly, *Universal Human Rights in Theory and Practice* (Ithaca, NY: Cornell University Press, 2013).

Sakiko Fukuda-Parr, *Millennium Development Goals: Ideas, Interests and Influence* (London: Routledge, 2017).

Macharia Kamau, Pamela Chasek, and David O'Connor, eds., *Transforming Multilateral Diplomacy: The Inside Story of the Sustainable Development Goals* (London: Routledge, 2018).

Amartya Sen, *Development as Freedom* (Oxford: Oxford University Press, 1999).

UNDP, *Human Development Report 2000* (New York: Oxford University Press, 2000).

7

SUSTAINING PEACE AND THE 2030 DEVELOPMENT AGENDA

Sigrid Gruener and Henrik Hammargren

How do the UN's sustaining peace resolutions relate to the 2030 Agenda for Sustainable Development, and to what extent do they interact? An analysis of relevant data makes the potential connection between the Sustainable Development Goals (SDGs) and sustaining peace clearer: approximately 1.8 billion people, including half of the world's extremely poor, live in fragile and conflict-affected settings.[1] Without significant new action, the forecasts for 2030, the deadline that the international community of states has set for achieving the SDGs, indicate an increase to 2.3 billion and over 80 percent of the world's poorest people. Migration is an additional factor that has a significant impact on sustainable development, with an estimated 272 million people on the move,[2] of which 70.8 million are forcibly displaced because of conflict or other crises.[3] These facts point to an urgent need for an approach that links sustaining peace with the 2030 Agenda and the UN's work on supporting development. Hence, the crucial question is: to what extent are efforts to advance these agendas pursued in tandem?

Through the twin resolutions on the review of the United Nations peacebuilding architecture (commonly referred to as "the sustaining peace resolutions"), adopted through General Assembly resolution 70/262 and Security Council resolution 2282 in April 2016, member states made a commitment to approach more comprehensively both peacebuilding and sustaining peace, with conflict prevention at the core.

The resolutions recognize sustaining peace as a goal and a process that encompasses activities aimed at preventing the outbreak, escalation, continuation, and recurrence of armed conflict, addressing root causes, assisting parties to conflict to end hostilities, ensuring national reconciliation, and moving toward recovery, reconstruction, and development. The resolutions were reaffirmed in April 2018 with two additional parallel resolutions—General Assembly resolution 72/267 and Security Council Resolution 2413—which invite relevant UN bodies and organs to advance, explore, and improve their implementation.

By endorsing the 2030 Agenda for Sustainable Development, world leaders signed on to an ambitious framework in 2015 that, with its 17 goals and 169 targets, aims to set the world on a course of sustainable development and "to leave no one behind." Although the many conflict-prone and fragile states are not explicitly mentioned among the SDGs, Goal 16 calls for peaceful, just, and inclusive societies, equal access to justice, and strong institutions for effective governance. It provides a framework to promote resilience and strengthens the convergence of initiatives that support social and economic change with cooperation around environmental issues such as addressing natural resource scarcity, development of alternative energy sources, and adaptation to climate change. It provides a platform for integrating peacebuilding into national development plans, ensuring that resources are allocated to efforts required to address risks and to sustain peace. The explicit connection in the 2030 Agenda between sustainable development and peace, and the emphasis in the sustaining peace resolutions on the need to address root causes, encourage an examination of critical development issues such as inequality, exclusion, human rights violations, pockets of poverty, high unemployment, and unequal access to social services through the lens of conflict prevention.

From the UN Charter to the sustaining peace resolutions

In order to understand the current interpretation of peacebuilding, it is essential to explore its development over time within the UN system. The evolution involves conceptual and institutional elements; this section also parses the original resolutions and looks toward a review in 2020.

"Peacebuilding" in the UN system: the concept

With or without explicit policies or operational arrangements, efforts to build peace have always featured as a core element of actions across the UN system, although the term "peacebuilding" does not feature in the UN Charter. The concept can be said to have sprung from the content of Article 1:

> To maintain international peace and security, and to that end: to take effective collective measures for the prevention and removal of threats to the peace, and for the suppression of acts of aggression or other breaches of the peace, and to bring about by peaceful means, and in conformity with the principles of justice and international law, adjustment or settlement of international disputes or situations which might lead to a breach of the peace.

From the outset, member states of the First UN and international civil servants of the Second UN have explored a broad range of innovative ways to support and maintain peace, notably through preventive diplomacy, the invention of peacekeeping missions, and targeted development actions in defense of human rights. But the fragmentation of the UN system—in part a reflection of the Charter's division of responsibilities between the organization's development, human rights, and peace and security pillars—has hampered the process of placing what became known as "peacebuilding" at the center of the UN's operations.

The starting point for understanding the concept is Secretary-General Boutros-Ghali's groundbreaking 1992 report *An Agenda for Peace*, following a Security Council session as he assumed his mandate and the implosion of the Soviet Union and the end of the Cold War.[4] The report advanced the UN's traditional approaches of peacemaking, peacekeeping, and preventive diplomacy by introducing a new concept of peacebuilding, which he defined as "action(s) to identify and support structures which tend to strengthen and solidify peace in order to avoid a relapse into conflict."[5] The report was later updated with a 1995 "Supplement" to address specific challenges related to the volume and nature of intra-state conflict, along with the security and institutional dimensions of peacebuilding, including the UN's own limitations.[6] The two documents were essential to reframing the UN's responses in civil wars that erupted following the Cold War. A challenge that emerged early in its implementation involved how to define and situate peacebuilding in relation to other development and security efforts of the UN system. While strides have been made in this regard, in particular with the sustaining peace resolutions, the challenge remains two and a half decades later.

Increasing demands for peacekeeping and a new Secretary-General led to the creation of the Department of Peacekeeping Operations (DPKO) in 1992, with the purpose of strengthening planning and coordinating UN peacekeeping missions as well as providing administrative and technical support. From the perspective of addressing overall development and inputs by the various organizations of the UN development system (UNDS), the specific challenges in the context of armed conflicts became obvious. The UN Development Programme (UNDP) introduced the crucial notion of "human security" in its *Human Development Report 1994*.[7] The UN's engagement in fragile and conflict-affected regions of the world faced continued demands during the 1990s, with a rapid escalation of intra-state conflicts, in particular the failure to prevent genocide in Rwanda, the fall-out from the implosion of the former Yugoslavia, the "failure" of the state of Somalia, and the recognition of the limitations of humanitarian interventions. In the wake of these developments Secretary-General Kofi Annan embarked on an ambitious agenda for reform.

Part of this initiative involved a review of UN peace operations and an assessment of the UN's capacity to effectively respond to global threats. The outcomes from this process included *The Report of the Panel on United Nations Peace Operations* (2000) and the creation of a High-Level Panel on Threats Challenges and Change (2003).[8] The panel issued a four-part report, *A More Secure World: Our Shared Responsibility*, in December 2004. The report reaffirmed the UN's recognition of states' right to self-defense, but it also argued that post-conflict peacebuilding should be a core UN function. The report prescribed revitalization of the Security Council and the General Assembly, and the creation of a new Peacebuilding Commission (PBC).

In 2005, Secretary-General Kofi Annan presented a five-year progress report on the implementation of the Millennium Declaration of 2000, which the General Assembly had requested. The report, *In Larger Freedom: Towards Development, Security and Human Rights for All*, presented six months before the 2005 World Summit, set out priorities for action in the fields of development, security, and human rights; it suggested changes within global institutions, especially of the UN itself.[9] The second of the four parts of the report, "Freedom from Fear," asked member states to agree on a new security consensus. More importantly, it proposed the creation of an intergovernmental body, the Peacebuilding Commission, to fill what Annan had referred to as the "gaping hole" of the UN institutional and structural capacity to address the transition from war to peace.

The evolution of Peacebuilding Architecture, 2005–2015

The so-called Peacebuilding Architecture (PBA) was created as an outcome of the 2005 World Summit and is composed of the Peacebuilding Commission (PBC), the Peacebuilding Support Office (PBSO), and the Peacebuilding Fund (PBF). The PBC is a subsidiary organ to both the Security Council and the General Assembly. It has three main purposes: to bring together all relevant actors in order to marshal resources and to advise on and propose integrated strategies for post-conflict peacebuilding and recovery; to focus attention on the reconstruction and institution-building efforts necessary for recovery from conflict and to support the development of integrated strategies to lay the foundation for sustainable development; and to provide recommendations and information to improve coordination of all pertinent partners within and outside the UN, to develop best practices, to help to ensure predictable financing for early recovery activities, and to extend the period of attention given by the international community to post-conflict recovery.[10]

The PBC's first five years of functioning were primarily devoted to discussing administrative and procedural issues, especially its working formats, which includes the Organizational Committee and Country Specific Configurations.[11] Although its creation was hailed as an important innovation, the PBA encountered difficulties, notably its relationship to other UN bodies, especially the Security Council and General Assembly. It also had problems in demonstrating the PBC's and PBF's positive impacts in the field.

The first review of the PBA in 2010 was mandated by the founding resolutions and was facilitated by three member states: Ireland, Mexico, and South Africa. The final report highlighted six critical issues: the complexity of peacebuilding; the imperative of national ownership; the illusion of sequencing; the urgency of resource mobilization; the importance of contributions by women; and the need for connection with the field. It concluded that the PBA had fallen short of the initial expectations and argued that a concerted effort was needed to place peacebuilding at the heart of the UN's overall work. Lacking an implementation mechanism and political will from member states, little follow-up or change resulted.

Five years later, the 2015 review took a different tack. It built on the language in the General Assembly resolution that accepted the report from the 2010 review that called for "a further comprehensive review" after five years. Three main differences distinguished this review from the previous one. The first was that the Terms of Reference (ToR) for the review were designed with a two-stage process, the first to be conducted by an independent, seven-person Advisory Group of Experts (AGE) and a chair to be designated by the Secretary-General. The second part of the review involved an intergovernmental process led by two co-facilitators, Australia and Angola. The third and most important distinction was the scope of the review; it took seriously the call to be comprehensive, which the AGE interpreted broadly as the overall "architecture" of the PBC, PBSO, and PBF.

One of its objectives was to examine the continued relevance and functioning of the three entities, including their mandate, structure, resources, and working methods. In addition, its scope encompassed an analysis of relevant policy developments since the establishment of the PBA; the complementarity of the PBC to UN operational entities; and continuing or emerging gaps or constraints that limited the UN's ability to prevent the recurrence of armed conflict.

The first phase of the 2015 review concluded in June of that year with the AGE's comprehensive report, *The Challenge of Sustaining Peace*.[12] The main findings included the emphasis on peacebuilding not only as a set of activities for post-conflict situations but also for prevention; the primacy of politics; and a recognition that peacebuilding is the responsibility of all pillars of the UN system that must work together. This framework directly addressed the silos and fragmentation that undermine the organization's efforts. The AGE report, intended to be the main input to the intergovernmental process, was not addressed to the Secretary-General but directly to the presidents of the General Assembly and the Security Council.

The 2016 resolutions that introduced "sustaining peace"

The intergovernmental process resulted in the twin Sustaining Peace resolutions, adopted by both the General Assembly and Security Council in April 2016. The resolutions echoed much of the AGE's analysis and recommendations but in addition incorporated findings from two other parallel reviews, namely the High-Level Independent Panel on Peace Operations (HIPPO)[13] and the Global Study on the Implementation of Security Council Resolution 1325 on Women Peace and Security.[14]

The sustaining peace resolutions were recognized as a remarkable achievement, which established and framed the concept of sustaining peace as a core UN principle. Member states thus sent a clear and powerful message to the UN system and to themselves that many of the structures, practices, and policies for addressing or preventing violent armed conflicts were insufficient or inadequate. As a result, the UN system, including the members of the UNDS, could not continue business as usual. The resolutions emphasized the need for greater coherence at all levels and introduced a new conceptual framework, which significantly stressed building peace as an ongoing process that spans prevention of conflict to the consolidation of peace after violence has subsided.

The resolutions lacked explicit reference to the 2030 Agenda. Partly this omission could be explained because the agenda had only been adopted in September 2015. However, it is also likely that the political sensitivity of issues of peace and conflict prevented their inclusion among the SDGs. The only specific mention is in the Preamble: "Recalling General Assembly resolution A/70/1, entitled *Transforming our world: the 2030 Agenda for Sustainable Development*, which adopted a comprehensive, far-reaching and people-centered set of universal and transformative Sustainable Development Goals and targets." In addition, the sensitivity among some member states about the possible over-politicization and securitization of development played a role as well.

Since the 2016 resolutions, member states have on numerous occasions affirmed the indivisibility of sustaining peace and achieving the SDGs. One of the first of such occasions was in a joint meeting held by the PBC and the Economic and Social Council (ECOSOC) during June 2016 on "the 2030 Agenda for Sustainable Development and Sustaining Peace." The nexus between peace and development was discussed in view of the adoption of the 2030 Agenda. Member states agreed that comprehensive approaches were needed for effective implementation of the SDGs, particularly in fragile states and those emerging from war. The role of the UNDS for sustaining peace was specifically recognized, in particular in order to address the root causes of armed conflict.

In January 2018, the Secretary-General issued his report on *Peacebuilding and Sustaining Peace*, in line with paragraph 30 of the resolutions, which had called for a progress report on implementation. He provided a set of recommendations for addressing the remaining gaps, grouped into four categories: coherence, financing, leadership, and partnerships.[15] The report highlighted that

> the 2030 Agenda for Sustainable Development with its commitment to leave no one behind contains the blueprint of the common vision of society towards which the world is trying to move. Inclusive and sustainable development not only is an end in itself but also happens to be the best defense against the risks of violent conflict.

The report pointed out that the twin resolutions acknowledged development as a central goal in itself, but went on to recognize the valuable contributions by the UNDS to peacebuilding, in particular through growth and poverty eradication.

In 2018, member states reaffirmed the value of the sustaining peace resolutions in two additional parallel resolutions—General Assembly resolution 72/276 and Security Council resolution 2413. Significantly, the texts invited relevant UN organizations, including those of the UNDS, to advance implementation. They mandated a report by the Secretary-General, which in May 2019 covered the four fundamental elements of sustaining peace enumerated in the 2018 report.[16] Its main aim was to show evidence of efforts by different parts of the UN system to operationalize the sustaining peace resolutions and to provide information on how the ongoing reforms initiated by the Secretary-General—most critically, those related to the UNDS and the peace and security pillar—support their implementation.

This interim report was a forerunner to a detailed report that the Secretary-General will present during the 74th session of the General Assembly and the third comprehensive review of the PBA in 2020.

The 2020 review

In 2020, for the third time since its creation and following the reviews in 2010 and 2015, member states will take stock of the functioning of the PBA. As this book goes to press, a few concerns are obvious, which will undoubtedly be explored in identifying ways to strengthen efforts to sustain peace.

The first and informal phase of the review will assess progress made in the implementation of the various resolutions on the PBA. The central considerations will include: consultations on various aspects of peacebuilding and sustaining peace in the PBC (open, exceptionally, to all member states); an independent assessment from eminent persons selected by the Secretary-General; and regional and thematic consultations convened by regional organizations and independent think tanks. The findings will provide input to the Secretary-General's 2020 report on peacebuilding and sustaining peace and will be transmitted to the presidents of the General Assembly and the Security Council. The second and formal intergovernmental phase will draw upon the Secretary-General's report and the findings of the informal phase; it is expected to conclude with the adoption of two new procedural resolutions by the assembly and the council.

Overall the review is regarded as an opportunity not only to examine progress since 2015 toward implementation in a variety of contexts, but also to provide insights into whether and how the new generation of resident coordinators (RCs) and UN country teams (UNCTs) are positioned to improve joined-up analyses, including the dynamics of armed conflict and efforts to bring all of the UN's assets to bear in support of national priorities.

Key considerations for implementation

Implementation is always more problematic than agreement on measures. Among the central considerations in the near term are the challenge of coordination, the relationship of other UN reforms, the links to the SDGs, and the nexus of human rights and peacebuilding.

Prevention: a system-wide challenge

The sustaining peace resolutions have brought about a fundamental shift in the UN system at both policy and operational levels. Initial concerns about insufficient clarity in the concept of sustaining peace and its loosely defined relationship to peacebuilding have given way to a recognition by practitioners that the lack of prescriptiveness can be a strength that allows for tailored responses to specific needs and challenges in diverse contexts.

The twin resolutions recognize the importance of the international community of states focusing on preventing "the outbreak, escalation, recurrence, or continuation of conflict," not merely as a post-conflict priority. It also is a prerequisite for identifying and addressing risks before they translate into a return to violent conflict, especially in fragile contexts; an essential need is thus for assisting belligerents to end hostilities, ensure national reconciliation, and move toward recovery, reconstruction, and development. The resolutions emphasize that efforts to sustain peace are a system-wide responsibility; they thus emphasize greater efforts to address the fragmentation among the pillars of UN activities, which exist at all levels with an overriding negative impact. They call for renewed efforts to ensure comprehensive and coherent political, development, and human rights initiatives to address the root causes of conflict, including corruption, organized criminal activity, and inadequate public security.

Operationalizing sustaining peace calls for the PBC to focus on its three main functions: advising, bridging, and convening. The PBC can provide advice that is complementary and useful to the UN's three principal organs—the General Assembly, ECOSOC, and Security Council—thereby also bridging the work of these three bodies. The process of electing member states to the Organizational Committee of the PBC creates the conditions for a broad sense of ownership and reinforces the fact that peacebuilding belongs to the UN as a whole.[17] If PBC members assume responsibility for representing and reporting back to the body that elected them and take a proactive approach to encourage the organs to draw on the advice and convening power of the PBC, its bridging role can thereby be strengthened.

The PBC has an important and recognized role in providing a forum at which conflict-affected countries can be assisted with their prevention and peacebuilding priorities. One of its main strengths is its convening power; as such, it has the possibility to use a flexible format to discuss the wide range of issues on sustaining peace, contributing with different perspectives and analysis provided by various actors, including regional organizations, international financial institutions (IFIs), civil society, and the private sector. In particular, the PBC has the mandate to provide a holistic, long-term perspective that can provide policy recommendations for UN decisions in countries in transition as well as in situations where the Security Council may be focused on an immediate crisis.

Inextricable linkages to ongoing UN reforms

After assuming office in 2018, Secretary-General António Guterres initiated a series of efforts to address challenges within the UN system and to make the organization better positioned to deliver on the 2030 Agenda. Of particular note are three reform streams: for the international peace and security pillar; the UNDS; and management. These reforms thus far have moved toward more effectiveness in prevention and in sustaining peace. New regional divisions were created within the peace and security pillar to allow for better shared analysis, planning, and programming across the Department of Political and Peacebuilding Affairs (DPPA) and the Department of Peace Operations (DPO) and to promote regional approaches to cross-border issues. Efforts to work across the peace, development, and humanitarian nexus include integrated inter-agency committees at headquarters and the engagement of Peace and Development Advisors (PDAs) at country, as well as more recently at regional, levels.

The reforms within the UNDS and the repositioning of the RC system were intended to strengthen in-country capacities to conduct conflict and context analysis and to translate such analysis into more conflict-sensitive programming. The empowered and impartial RCs are expected to "bring to the role an appreciation of the breadth of assets of the United Nations in the service of sustaining peace."[18] To facilitate their work across the usually separate efforts for peace, humanitarian action, human rights, and development and to advance engagement in prevention and political mandates, these reforms have elevated the RC position within the UNCT and created a direct reporting line to the Secretary-General through his deputy. Greater capacity within RC offices should enhance their ability to engage in a diverse range of processes, including the coordination not only of UN funds and programs but also of specialized agencies. The process aims to apply the UN Sustainable Development Cooperation Framework (UNSDCF) based on a Common Country Analysis (CCA); it also should be grounded in national ownership and anchored in national development priorities which is a central tenet of sustaining peace.

RCs are now the official representative of the UN in-country, not connected to any specific agency, which is intended to allow them to act in a more independent and impartial manner and to provide stronger leadership and coherence within UNCTs. The Secretary-General's 2018 report underscores that setting the direction for implementing the sustaining peace resolutions is largely the onus of senior leadership at country level, specifically the RC and the deputy special representatives of the Secretary-General (DSRSG) in mission settings. RCs are "responsible for coordinating development strategies that are risk informed and help to build peaceful and inclusive societies." Concerns have been raised about the lack of financial resources' at their disposal acting as a hindrance to their empowerment. Another serious challenge facing RCs is maintaining the support of the host government while having the mandate to speak out on human rights violations and to engage in political debates, including in the service of sustaining peace.

Sustaining peace and the 2030 Agenda: a complex relationship

The sustaining peace resolutions and Agenda 2030 are broadly understood as being mutually reinforcing. Implementation of the SDGs can be viewed as key to advancing the sustaining peace agenda. Similarly, peacebuilding and sustaining peace have been recognized as a prerequisite for achieving the SDGs, even if they are not explicitly included among the list of 17 goals. Both convictions, however, acknowledge that not all development leads to peace, and not all peace leads to development. While the SDGs constitute a critical mechanism for sustaining peace, efforts are needed to ensure quality development that avoids patterns of marginalization and social exclusion, and that peace provides safety and stimulates creativity across all sectors of society, including rule of law and legitimate politics.

The Preamble of the 2030 Agenda makes clear the link between sustainable development and peace, which is echoed in the sustaining peace resolutions that point to the need to address root causes of conflict. SDG 16—admittedly the most sweeping and least specific of the 17 goals—is most clearly connected to the process and objectives of sustaining peace. Indeed, it often is referred to as the "peace goal." It calls on member states to address issues of corruption by enhancing accountability and transparency. However, other objectives are also referenced for their potential preventive impact. The specifics, including nuances in the interconnectivity between the SDGs and the sustaining peace resolutions, should be clarified in every context in order to maximize the effectiveness of the 2030 Agenda.

There are diverging perspectives regarding exact linkages and preferences among some member states (particularly from the Global South) to maintain a clear separation between the UN's work on peace and security and that focused on development. One issue relates to national ownership and the extent to which peacebuilding and sustaining peace threaten or strengthen national sovereignty. Another concern is that an increased focus on peacebuilding and sustaining peace could distort the focus on poverty elimination by linking development aid to security—thereby narrowly focusing on the security-related issues and priorities that interest aid providers. Tensions about those issues grouped under the banner of *securitization of development* have increased because of counter-terrorism strategies and the transformation of national security interests into development objectives. However, some voices have flipped this argument into a call for the 2030 Agenda as a means to renew thinking and approaches with a developmental focus placed on security. This debate on the *developmentalization of security* is far from over and is likely to continue to polarize positions.

The nexus of human rights and peacebuilding

The resolutions on sustaining peace reaffirm that "development, peace and security, and human rights are interlinked and mutually reinforcing"; they emphasize the importance of a comprehensive approach to sustaining peace, wherein "respect for, and protection of, human rights and fundamental freedoms" are essential.[19] The 2018 Secretary-General's report goes further to specify that "the international human rights framework provides a critical foundation for sustaining peace."[20] It elaborates that

> the collective work of the UN system to advance human rights should help to identify the root causes of and responses to conflict. In that respect, it will remain imperative for the peace and security and development pillars to make better use of the existing human rights mechanisms, such as special procedures, the treaty bodies and the universal periodic review, and their recommendations in support of Member States.[21]

Despite the evidence and growing recognition of the synergies between human rights and peacebuilding, and calls over decades to "mainstream human rights," there are still tensions between what still are often viewed as competing agendas that need to be overcome. These include the criticism of human rights principles and mechanisms, and of many peacebuilding strategies, as being culturally insensitive or irrelevant.[22] In practice, the work of UN organizations and other international actors working on peacebuilding and human rights at the country level also often lacks coordination and takes place within distinct local frameworks. That said, the disconnect is often more pronounced at the global policy level.

The more integrated and holistic approach proposed by the sustaining peace resolutions requires examining the ways that synergies between peacebuilding and human rights can be strengthened, and the silos broken down. This is particularly crucial in the current political climate of resistance to and retreat from human rights, and against the notion of sustaining peace. The challenge is to find the right balance and use the 2020 PBA review to identify positive examples and to further advance the human rights and peacebuilding nexus, without losing the previous gains.

Renewed partnerships for peace

The sustaining peace resolutions as well as the 2030 Agenda clearly recognize the importance of partnerships in achieving sustainable peace and development. The 2018 Secretary-General's report refers to an "ecosystem of partners working in support of Governments," underscoring the role of regional and sub-regional organizations in building and sustaining peace.

In supporting national leadership, the resolutions call for the UN's relationships with government, civil society, regional organizations, and the private sector to change. The focus should stress the organization's normative role and efforts to strengthen local capacities as well as to help enable the creation and maintenance of inclusive dialogue spaces that can encourage local ownership. Partnerships with private-sector actors are seen to hold promise for providing access to greater resources, innovation, and employment. Yet, these shifts must be pursued with caution as they can be detrimental to inclusive sustainable development if the right regulatory frameworks are absent. Private-sector partnerships should complement efforts to strengthen inclusive institutions as well as long-term policies that address economic, social, and political aspirations of all segments of society.

An operational paragraph in the parallel resolutions requests the Secretary-General explicitly to explore options for strengthening the UN–World Bank collaboration in conflict-affected countries, among other things in order to enable and encourage regular exchanges on priority peacebuilding. In response, both organizations initiated a joint study on prevention in 2016, the first such report in the history of the two institutions. The study, *Pathways for Peace: Inclusive Approaches to Preventing Violent Conflict*, was hailed as a success for being a step toward fostering greater collaboration to deliver at country level.[23] It recognized the separate comparative advantages of the World Bank and the UN in the prevention of violent conflict and called for closer collaboration in the field, including in the form of joint risk assessments and agreed indicators.

The study drilled into some specific aspects of the sustaining peace resolutions, including root causes and the role of grievances. It advocated recognizing exclusion and inequality as powerful potential drivers of armed conflict; it highlighted the need for greater intersectionality between security and diplomatic instruments; and it called for using all tools available for prevention, including humanitarian and development programs. In its recommendations, *Pathways* urges international actors to invest more in upstream prevention by presenting the economic arguments for this approach, including the cost savings involved in the long term.

The sustaining peace resolutions, along with several other normative frameworks and policies, call for the inclusion of a broad spectrum of society in preventing and resolving armed conflicts. The *Pathways* study concluded: "For all countries, addressing inequalities and exclusion, making institutions more inclusive, and ensuring that development strategies are risk-informed are central to preventing the fraying of the social fabric that could erupt into crisis." This path reinforces the point prominently raised in the joint resolutions that the UN's efforts to sustain peace must support legitimate and inclusive national peacebuilding processes. Multi-layered, broad-based participation in design, implementation, and monitoring is essential and should build on vertical relationships that penetrate beyond elite circles, hopefully even to the most local level.

This general awareness and acceptance that peacebuilding and development processes must be inclusive and actively reduce marginalization customarily lacks practical application. Deepening inclusion and addressing marginalization requires a focus on spaces for realizing the right of every individual to participate in public affairs. The UN's role is critical in opening those spaces and in engaging national governments in ongoing and frank discussions about the imperative of inclusion, which is especially pertinent in the face of measures to actively restrict the ability of civil society to be effective in peace-related projects.

The resolutions also stress the importance of women's leadership and participation as well as efforts to increase meaningful and inclusive participation of youth in conflict prevention and peacebuilding. They both create clear links to the implementation of Security Council resolution 1325 on Women, Peace and Security and resolution 2250 on Youth, Peace and Security. Both are essential components to fully operationalize sustaining peace.

In 2016, shortly after the adoption of the sustaining peace resolutions, the PBC adopted a gender strategy to "ensure a more structural integration of gender perspectives in all its work."[24] It places gender equality at the center of the sustaining peace resolutions, as well as the 2030 Agenda. It sets out, among other things, the desirability of integrating gender perspectives in all its efforts; engaging such gender-specific priority areas as women's economic empowerment, women's inclusion in early warning, conflict prevention, and conflict resolution; and advocating dedicated technical expertise and funding for gender-responsive peacebuilding.

At a fundamental level, partnerships are meaningless without adequate, predictable, and sustained financing for sustaining peace. The resolutions emphasize "the need for predictable and sustained financing to UN peacebuilding activities, including through increased contributions, and strengthened partnerships with key stakeholders, while also noting the significance that non-monetary contributions can play in peacebuilding efforts." The Secretary-General's 2018 report on implementation of the resolutions pointed to discouraging trends in donor funding that resulted in insufficient resources to address conflict risks and to support countries going through fragile transitions. The report made several recommendations for advancing the application of the sustaining peace framework and to address existing gaps, including in financing.

Although some steps have been taken for the reforms to begin in response to the Secretary-General's recommendations, those related to financing have been especially limited, even with regard to replenishment of the PBF, the funding mechanism within the UN system specifically set up to finance peacebuilding activities. Observers consider the PBF to have an unusual niche in the Secretary-General's toolkit as a catalytic, flexible, and risk-tolerant fund. It is necessary to help bring together the wider UN system and other partners to jump-start processes, address critical financing gaps, and respond to urgent peacebuilding opportunities. The PBF is regarded as particularly critical in transition settings—among UN insiders, it is often referred to as falling off the so-called financing cliff. This flexibility is especially acute in contexts that require cross-border or multi-country approaches to tackle the underlying drivers of armed conflict. At country level, the PBF is an essential funding mechanism for RCs that connects to and complements the SDG Fund and the Central Emergency Response Fund (CERF).

Yet, the challenge remains to meet the PBF's target of $500 million in annual replenishments through voluntary contributions while diversifying the donor base. Member states are looking for greater evidence of the catalytic effect of the PBF and calling for greater synergies between the PBF and the work of the PBC. There have been limited cases in which unspent peacekeeping budgets have been transferred to the PBF as per one of the Secretary-General's recommendations in his 2018 report. Member states have repeatedly expressed reluctance to consider using assessed contributions to reach the PBF's target replenishments.

The 2018 report also calls for an exploration of innovative finance options to support peacebuilding, an under-developed area generally understood as any instrument beyond traditional grants that mobilizes new capital or improves the efficiency or effectiveness of existing capital. The humanitarian sector has experimented with initiatives that hold promise for peacebuilding. A white paper by the Humanitarian Investing Initiative (a partnership between the World Economic Forum, the World Bank, and the International Committee of the Red Cross) notes that challenges to mobilize more resources to address humanitarian needs in contexts of fragility, conflict, and violence (FCV) include: an "insufficient number of truly investible opportunities, the need for more awareness of new financing approaches, issues of collaboration among stakeholders, and the lack of organizational capacity among many actors in the space."[25] These challenges are especially pronounced with regard to peacebuilding, where the application of financing tools is less developed.

As innovative finance is unlikely to be a panacea to achieve the level of resources required to meet global peacebuilding needs, donor contributions are likely to remain at the heart of financing such efforts in the near term. There is, however, more room for exploring opportunities for leveraging resources from official development assistance (ODA) and non-ODA sources, especially those invested by the World Bank—its financing has doubled from $7 billion to $14 billion for low-income countries affected by FCV as part of the 18th replenishment of the International Development Association (IDA18).[26] Beyond the need for additional resources for peacebuilding, a radical rethink is also needed about how financing is structured, and how to leverage strong partnerships for more effective resourcing.

Conclusion

With 2020 marking the UN's 75th anniversary, the atmosphere in the world organization and within the international community of states is fraught—there are basic conversations and debates about its purpose, role, and performance over previous decades, including in peacebuilding and sustaining peace. It is useful in this context to recall the opening words of the Charter, and specifically the commitment to "save succeeding generations from the scourge of war" and "to promote social progress and better standards of life in larger freedom," and for these ends "to unite our strength to maintain international peace and security." It calls for recognition that successfully mobilizing for a decade of action to deliver on the 2030 Agenda,[27] as called for by the Secretary-General, requires that the sustaining peace resolutions also be operationalized and become doctrine across the pillars and at all levels of the UN's work.

It is impossible to challenge the proposition that peaceful and inclusive societies are essential to achieving sustainable development; and the reverse is also true. The 2020 review of the PBA should provide new insights into whether and to what degree these objectives are being pursued in a coherent and synchronized manner. It will also augment the urgency of strong, principled, and courageous leadership at all levels of the UN system.

NOTES

1 OECD, *States of Fragility 2018* (Paris: OECD Publishing, 2018), https://doi.org/10.1787/9789264302075-en.

2 "The number of international migrants reaches 272 million, continuing an upward trend in all world regions, says UN," *UN DESA News*, 17 September 2019, www.un.org/development/desa/en/news/population/international-migrant-stock-2019.html.

3 UNHCR, 2019, *Refugee Statistics*, www.unrefugees.org/refugee-facts/statistics.

4 Boutros Boutros-Ghali, *An Agenda for Peace: Preventive Diplomacy, Peacemaking and Peace-Keeping* (New York: UN, 1992), UN documents A/47/277–S/24111, 17 June 1992, Report of the Secretary-General pursuant to the statement adopted by the Summit Meeting of the Security Council on 31 January 1992, 1–23.

5 Ibid., 5.

6 Boutros Boutros-Ghali, *"Supplement" to An Agenda for Peace* (New York: UN, 1995), UN documents A/RES/50/60 and S/RES/1995/1.

7 UNDP, *Human Development Report 1994* (New York: Oxford University Press, 1994), http://hdr.undp.org/sites/default/files/reports/255/hdr_1994_en_complete_nostats.pdf.

8 *Report of the High-Level Panel on Threats, Challenges and Change*, UN document A/59/565, 2 December 2004.

9 Kofi Annan, *In Larger Freedom: Towards Development, Security and Human Rights for All* (New York: UN, 2005), www.un.org/ruleoflaw/files/A.59.2005.Add.3[1].pdf.

10 *World Summit Outcome*, General Assembly resolution A/RES/60/1, 24 October 2005, 24–25.

11 For more information on the early years of the PBC see Sarah Hearn, Alejandra Kubitschek Bujones, and Alischa Kugel, *The UN Peacebuilding Architecture: Institutional Evolution in Context* (New York and Geneva: CIC NYU and Geneva Peacebuilding Platform, 2015); and Rob Jenkins, *Peacebuilding: From Concept to Commission* (London: Routledge, 2013).

12 UN, *The Challenge of Sustaining Peace: Report of the Advisory Group of Experts for the 2015 Review of the UN Peacebuilding Architecture Review* (New York: UN, 2015).

13 UN, *Uniting Our Strengths for Peace—Politics, Partnerships and People: Report of the High-Level Independent Panel on Peace Operations* (New York: UN, 2015).

14 UN, *Preventing Conflict, Transforming Justice, Securing Peace: A Global Study on the Implementation of UN Security Council Resolution 1325* (New York: UN, 2015).

15 *Report of the Secretary-General on Peacebuilding and Sustaining Peace*, UN documents A/72/707–S/2018/43, 18 January 2018.

16 *Report of the Secretary-General on Peacebuilding and Sustaining Peace*, UN documents A/73/890 and S/2019/448, 30 May 2019.

17 Seven members are elected by the General Assembly, seven by the Security Council, and seven by ECOSOC; they are joined by the top five providers of military personnel and civilian police to UN missions and the top five providers of assessed contributions to UN budgets and of voluntary contributions to the PBF. UN 2020, *Peacebuilding Commission Membership*, www.un.org/peacebuilding/commission/membership.

18 Language included in the resident coordinator's job description. UNSDG, 2020, https://unsdg. un.org.

19 For additional reading on peacebuilding and human rights see Michelle Parlevliet, guest editor, "Breaking the Silos: Linking Human Rights and Peacebuilding," *Journal of Human Rights Practice* 9, no. 3 (2017): Special Issue.

20 *Report of the Secretary-General on Peacebuilding and Sustaining Peace*, 6.

21 Ibid.

22 See, for example, Michael Ignatieff, "The Attack on Human Rights," *Foreign Affairs* 80, no. 6 (2001): 102–116, www.michaelignatieff.ca/assets/pdfs/TheAttack.pdf.

23 United Nations and World Bank, *Pathways for Peace: Inclusive Approaches to Preventing Violent Conflict* (Washington, DC: World Bank, 2018).

24 *UN Peacebuilding Commission's Gender Strategy* (New York: UN, 2016), www.un.org/peacebuilding/ sites/www.un.org.peacebuilding/files/documents/07092016-_pbc_gender_strategy_final_1.pdf.

25 *Humanitarian Investing—Mobilizing Capital to Overcome Fragility* (Geneva: World Economic Forum, 2019).

26 World Bank, 2017, *IDA18 Replenishment*, http://ida.worldbank.org/replenishments/ida18-replenishment.

27 UN, 2020, *SDGs: Decade of Action*, www.un.org/sustainabledevelopment/decade-of-action.

ADDITIONAL READING

The Carnegie Commission on Preventing Deadly Conflict, *Preventing Deadly Conflict: Final Report* (New York: Carnegie Corporation of New York, 1997).

Sarah Cliffe and David Steven, *An Integrated Approach to Prevention—The Links between Prevention, the 2030 Agenda, and Sustaining Peace* (New York: Center on International Cooperation, 2017), https://cic.nyu. edu/sites/default/files/cic_prevention_sdgs_sp_2017.pdf.

Rob Jenkins, *Peacebuilding: From Concept to Commission* (London: Routledge, 2013).

United Nations and World Bank, *Pathways for Peace: Inclusive Approaches to Preventing Violent Conflict* (Washington, DC: World Bank, 2018), www.pathwaysforpeace.org.

United Nations, lead author Graeme Simpson, *The Missing Peace: Independent Progress Study on Youth, Peace and Security* (New York: UN, April 2018), www.un.org/peacebuilding/news/missing-peace-independent-progress-study-youth-peace-and-security.

8

SUSTAINING PEACE

Changing architecture and priorities for UN peacebuilding

Gert Rosenthal

The present chapter builds on the report on the implementation of the recommendations contained in the report of the Advisory Group of Experts (AGE) for the 2015 Review of the United Nations Peacebuilding Architecture (PBA), which the author prepared in his capacity as chair and later updated for the Future UN Development System Project (FUNDS).[1] Almost half a decade after the presentation of the AGE report, there have been other more significant developments. They include the adoption of the 2030 Sustainable Development Agenda,[2] and Secretary-General António Guterres's reform proposals, notably those touching on the peace and security pillar,[3] all in the context of a deteriorating international environment toward multilateral diplomacy in general, and the United Nations in particular.

This chapter's particular relevance for this book is that "peacebuilding" or "sustainable peace" brings together the UN's work in what are conventionally known as its "four pillars," drawing on its comparative advantage in matters of international peace and security as well as human rights, to also become a major player in the areas of humanitarian action and sustainable development.

Peacebuilding architecture

The intergovernmental decision to create the Peacebuilding Commission (PBC), the Peacebuilding Support Office (PBSO), and the Peacebuilding Fund (PBF)—collectively known as the "peacebuilding architecture" (PBA)—was broadly hailed as one of the most significant achievements of the 2005 World Summit on the occasion of the 60th anniversary of the United Nations. This chapter does not detail the conceptual framework of peacebuilding and the way the concept has evolved over time, which are the subject of numerous other accounts. However, five years after its creation,[4] the first formal review of the peacebuilding architecture was viewed as one of unrealized hopes. At the time, the recommendations contained in the review were formulated by three ambassadors to the UN in New York (the permanent representatives of Ireland, Mexico, and South Africa) with the aim of narrowing the gap between aspirations and performance.[5] The General Assembly, in taking note of the review, recommended in resolution 65/7 of 29 October 2010 a more in-depth exercise in 2015, on the 10th anniversary of the PBA. It appears that by 2015 the "unrealized hopes" had, if anything, increased and intensified according to some surveys.[6]

The 2015 review

Accordingly, in 2015 both the General Assembly and the Security Council approved a new review.[7] It was not limited to the entities mentioned, but covered the UN system as a whole, including the development organizations that customarily had been ignored for the maintenance of international peace and security. It had two phases. First, an independent advisory group prepared its own assessment and recommendations for the presidents of the General Assembly and the Security Council.[8] Second, an intergovernmental phase was intended to translate the recommendations of the AGE into consensual policy decisions codified in a resolution with the objective to improve the UN's performance.

The first phase of the review concluded at the end of June 2015 with the presentation of the report of the seven-member AGE.[9] The report began with a brief description of the changing contexts confronted by the UN in attempting to deal operationally with the challenges of peace, security, development, and the defense of human rights. It then assessed the world organization's performance after 2005 with specific reference to peacebuilding. It concluded with general and specific recommendations aimed at dealing with the challenges identified, as well as enhancing the UN's performance in what the review called "sustainable peace."

The main conclusion was that the unrealized hopes from the peacebuilding architecture were misplaced: rather than inherent shortcomings of the PBC, the PBSO, and the PBF, the problems were deeper: more systemic and structural. Peacebuilding entailed numerous and complex activities that fell under the purview of several principal organs—the Security Council on matters of international peace and security, the Economic and Social Council (ECOSOC) and the General Assembly on development and governance, and human rights through its subsidiary body, the Human Rights Council. However, they functioned in separate "silos" and carried out their narrow mandated activities with little or no interactions among them.

Moreover, these shortcomings were not limited to the UN's intergovernmental bodies; they also took place within the structure of the Secretariat, in headquarters and in the field. Indeed, the Security Council tended to perceive peacebuilding as activities that occurred only after the end of a violent conflict, which thus relegated it to a relatively peripheral role because ending the war always took priority. The AGE review argued that peacebuilding actually can and should occur during all phases of violent conflicts—before, during, and after—and that peacebuilding should be framed as part of the toolbox of preventive measures at the UN's disposal.[10]

Another overarching conclusion was the institutional and organizational implications for the conceptualization of peacebuilding. While the Security Council's mandate is to maintain international peace and security, it also is the principal organ most involved in peacebuilding. However, most members of the council do not perceive themselves as peace builders, even though virtually all resolutions about peace operations contain numerous references to the panoply of classic peacebuilding functions such as state-building, capacity development, and promoting the rule of law. The review pointed to the obvious fact that part of those activities, and especially the development aspects, also falls within the purview of the General Assembly and ECOSOC, and thus requires a much clearer definition of who does what to counter the long-standing and well-known fragmentation of the system. Even more importantly, the principal organs had to coordinate the activities that fell within their respective jurisdictions in order to come up with a coherent policy.

As stated, the same type of fragmentation observed at the intergovernmental level also took place in the internal distribution of responsibilities among the different departments in the Secretariat as well as between them and the rest of the UN system. There was even less coordination among the various actors in the UN's field presence, where operational peacebuilding takes place. Each program, fund, or agency represented in a UN country team

(UNCT) had differing mandates, differing bureaucratic cultures, and differing interactions with host governments, often making the work of UN resident coordinators tortuous. In some extreme cases, rather than promoting coherence and cooperation, differences among members of a UNCT led to even more fragmentation, as organizations competed for space and resources.

The AGE made an additional point when it referred to the crucial role of domestic stakeholders, who need to reach a common understanding about how to accommodate different views and interests without resorting to violence. The report invokes "inclusive national ownership" as a process that must be forged between the state and civil society in order to ensure that peace becomes sustainable. It further suggests that the UN can play an essential enabling role in that endeavor; indeed, it may have a comparative advantage as the only institution that can bring to bear a full range of services.[11] Nonetheless, the United Nations will never be the only external actor, and often not even the main one. Hence and in addition to national ownership, the AGE report emphasized the importance of partnerships with regional organizations, multilateral lending agencies, and non-state actors.

To address fragmentation, the AGE insisted on the decisive role that the PBC, an advisory body to the three pertinent principal organs, could and should play. In other words, the PBC could only be effective if the three intergovernmental organs accepted working with it in a partnership mode, something that happened rarely. The AGE raised a final central point: a commitment to peacebuilding involved predictable long-term financing. In that regard, the PBF had played a critical catalytic role in helping to mobilize additional resources, and the AGE recommended strengthening this role, including the possibility of providing predictable funding through assessed contributions within the UN's regular budget. Other more specific recommendations were in the appendices.[12]

The second phase of the review was based on the recommendations of the AGE report. After lengthy negotiations, in April 2016 member states adopted twin resolutions: 70/262 in the General Assembly and 2282 (2016) in the Security Council. With virtually identical texts, the titles of both resolutions differed somewhat. The assembly's was "Review of the United Nations Peacebuilding Architecture," whereas the council labeled its "Post-Conflict Peacebuilding." The generic term on the council's agenda was, in fact, at odds with one of the main conclusions, namely that peacebuilding occurs in all phases of armed conflict. While the AGE report informed member states for the second phase of the review, the resolutions clearly reflected the main thrust of the conceptual framework and virtually all of its central recommendations. The exception was the reluctance of member states to commit to assessed contributions for the PBF.

The General Assembly and the Security Council simultaneously found common ground, which could be viewed as a major achievement. In adopting both resolutions, member states agreed that peacebuilding is a system-wide responsibility that should go beyond post-conflict situations. The resolution clearly states the intent of moving toward coherence and cooperation by the principal organs, and confers on the PBC the "bridging" role advocated by the AGE. The PBF's vital potential role was recognized, although, as noted, the AGE's recommendation of mobilizing assessed contributions to ensure the long-term sustainability of the fund was not endorsed.[13] Instead, while welcoming the contributions to the PBF, the resolution simply noted the proposals and invited the Secretary-General to explore options.[14]

Regarding the specific recommendations found in the AGE report, many found an echo in the 2016 joint resolutions A/70/262–S/2282 (2016) that emerged from the review's second stage. In addition, the AGE's crucial reframing in the report's title, "sustaining peace," has entered the Secretariat's discourse as well as that of its key intergovernmental bodies, despite continuing discussions regarding the rather ambiguous definition of the term as set forth in paragraph 8 of the resolutions.[15]

Parallel developments

At least seven parallel developments to the review process deserve mention. The first is the adoption in September 2015 of the landmark 2030 Agenda for Sustainable Development through resolution 70/1. It not only offers a strategic framework for the UN's work for the next decade and a half, but also incorporates into the Sustainable Development Goals (SDGs) a specific commitment in Goal 16 to "promote peaceful and inclusive societies for sustainable development, provide access to justice for all and build effective, accountable and inclusive institutions at all levels." Proposals related to the work of the world organization in peacebuilding fit neatly into this broader framework, both a strength and a potential weakness, if expectations are unmet.

A second characteristic refers to the exceptional leadership of the PBC during the past years. Permanent representatives in New York animated an unusually productive and extended period in the PBC's work—before, during, and after the review process. This period also coincided with a change in PBSO leadership in 2014, which led to its strengthening. It also resulted in a concerted effort in promoting stronger interactions by the PBC with its organizational committee and its country configurations, on the one hand, and with the principal intergovernmental organs of the UN, on the other.

The third characteristic is related to the beginning of the mandate on 1 January 2017 of the ninth Secretary-General, António Guterres, as well as to the procedure that led to his selection.[16] The somewhat more open selection process meant that candidates published vision statements and held informal dialogues with all delegations not only of the Security Council but also of the General Assembly and civil society. As part of his campaign, Guterres emphasized conflict prevention, including the need to address root causes. He also used the term "sustainable peace" repeatedly,[17] and offered to confront fragmentation of the UN system.

The fourth characteristic is the Secretary-General's wide-ranging reform proposals dealing with the peace and security pillar, the development pillar, and management, which have clear connections to the joint resolutions A/70/262–S/2282 (2016). Most significant is the area of pursuing greater coherence in the organization's overall work and breaking down the "silos" around which different aspects of its work are organized.

A fifth characteristic with potentially far-reaching consequences was the formation of an informal "Group of Friends of Sustainable Peace" to maintain the momentum for the fuller implementation of the April 2016 resolutions. Under the initial coordination of Mexico, and with a cross-regional membership of over 35 delegations, the "friends" became an advocate for systematically addressing peacebuilding. The formation could also presage a new trend in the way intergovernmental organs manage their interactions by clustering around topics rather than regional groupings or the North–South cleavage.[18] A similar advocacy group also surfaced around the implementation of SDG 16, with the establishment of an increasingly active "Pathfinders for Peaceful, Just and Inclusive Societies," made up of some 30 member states, international organizations, global partnerships, civil society, and the private sector.[19]

The sixth characteristic is the latest Quadrennial Comprehensive Policy Review (QPCR) of Operational Activities for Development of the United Nations System, which was adopted at the end of 2016 and is supportive of sustainable peace in the broader context of the 2030 Development Agenda. General Assembly resolution 71/243 of December 2016 recognizes explicitly that "a comprehensive whole-of-system response … is fundamental to most efficiently and effectively addressing needs and attaining the Sustainable Development Goals." It also calls upon the entities of the UN development system to "enhance coordination with humanitarian assistance and peacebuilding efforts at the national level."[20]

Seventh, the mostly encouraging aspects took place despite the international environment of increasing skepticism regarding the post–World War II international order, its institutional manifestations, and multilateralism in general. This skepticism is not limited to the traditional nationalistic and authoritarian states that resist any type of perceived encroachment on their sovereignty; it has found renewed resonance in some Western democracies as well.[21]

Implementation: an assessment

An assessment after only five years is challenging but necessary. Four approaches provide a partial basis for evaluation.

Follow-up activities on Resolutions A/70/262–S/2282 (2016)

Several years after the twin resolutions on sustainable peace, enough available data and analysis provide the basis to assert important tangible and intangible results. They include a moderate change in mindset regarding how member states view peacebuilding, with increasing frequency called "sustaining peace." At the same time, there is still much work pending.

In general, member states have advanced in assimilating the conceptual framework of sustaining peace, including through high-level meetings, retreats, and seminars to identify how to improve implementation. Further analytical work has also helped clarify and expand the policy framework.[22] The initial opportunity to analyze the first phase of the review (and in preparation for the second phase) was the open debate organized during the Venezuelan presidency of the Security Council on "Post-Conflict Peacekeeping: Review of the Peacebuilding Architecture." This debate took place in February 2016 and had no formal outcome,[23] but it was followed shortly thereafter in May by the "High-Level Thematic Debate on the United Nations, Peace and Security" organized by the president of the General Assembly. The latter attracted broad participation from member states, reaffirmed support for peacebuilding and sustaining peace, and confirmed the importance of synergies among the principal organs and the PBC.[24]

Subsequently, both the Security Council and the General Assembly have continued building on the two landmark resolutions. For example, in January 2017, the Security Council under the presidency of Sweden organized a ministerial-level open debate on the "Maintenance of International Peace and Security," which focused on "Conflict Prevention and Sustaining Peace." In addition to the Secretary-General's remarks,[25] all 15 council members and some 75 non-members participated—an unusually large number taking advantage of Rule 37 of the Rules of Procedure.[26] Not to be outdone, the president of the General Assembly also organized a high-level dialogue on "Building Sustainable Peace for All: Synergies between the 2030 Agenda for Sustainable Development and Sustaining Peace." This January 2017 event took place in plenary and interactive sessions. The Secretary-General's opening remarks[27] were followed by 81 presentations by member states. Subsequently, under the agenda item "Peacebuilding and Sustaining Peace," the United Kingdom organized during its Security Council presidency a debate on "The role of reconciliation in maintaining international peace and security on 19 November 2019."[28] The Secretary-General made an introductory statement, stressing that reconciliation is part of a comprehensive approach to sustaining peace.[29]

The Security Council's members now adopt formal reactions to the mandated reports that the PBC presents annually.[30] In addition, the assembly's president convened an April 2018 high-level meeting on peacebuilding and sustaining peace to focus on the Secretary-General's January 2018 report.[31] The assembly and council also adopted another set of twin resolutions—A/72/276–S/2413 (2018)—in April 2018; the most significant operative paragraph reaffirms the 2016 joint resolutions and encourages further action by member states and the UN system to implement the decisions. These resolutions have not only kept alive the earlier policy recommendations but have provided renewed impetus, including comprehensive reviews of the UN peacebuilding architecture by the Secretariat.

The Secretary-General's reports

The Secretary-General's extensive 2018 report was followed by an interim report in May 2019,[32] which maintained momentum by offering an overall assessment of developments on sustainable peace since the 2016 resolutions. Both reports updated previous analysis on the matter and covered operational and policy coherence; questions of leadership, accountability, and capacity in supporting peacebuilding and sustaining peace; financing for peacebuilding in general and more specifically for the peacebuilding fund; and partnering for peacebuilding, especially with the World Bank and the African Union (AU).[33] The Secretary-General concluded both reports by pointing out "the considerable progress already achieved" and committed himself to working with member states to "set out additional, targeted changes to ensure that the United Nations does not lose sight of the linkages between its work in peace, development, human rights and humanitarian action."[34]

One of the most significant recommendations pertained to the PBF, especially the call for a "quantum leap" in contributions "which should be un-earmarked and provided for a longer term to ensure that support is both responsive and predictable." The report notes that there seems to be wide support for strengthening the role of the PBF, with its positive accomplishments. It has demonstrated a capability to invest "in a timely, catalytic and risk-tolerant way."[35] On the other hand, there is disagreement about how the Secretary-General's recommendation of a "quantum leap" in contributions to the PBF should be financed.[36]

The PBF's Strategic Plan for 2017–2019 contemplates investing some $500 million in 40 countries.[37] During the first two years, this goal seems on track, with $157 million approved for 31 countries in 2017 and an estimated $183 million approved for 40 countries in 2018. The management of the PBF also reports a qualitative improvement in the allocation of resources, aimed at four priority areas, with increasing importance assigned to supporting transitions, cross-border activities, and innovative approaches for women's and youth empowerment. Increased contributions have augmented operations, with member-state funding growing from $53.5 million in 2015 and $57.7 million in 2016 to $92.4 million in 2017 and $128.9 million in 2018. In short, progress was noticeable over the last few years in "strengthening" the PBF's financial capacity.

Nonetheless, the number of major voluntary contributors remains limited. Moreover, as stated, there is a marked resistance on the part of some of the major contributors to the UN regular budget to consider assessed contributions as a source of predictable funding, which presumably would help attract additional voluntary contributions. This resistance is due, in part, to the donors' reluctance to go through the complex process of decision-making that takes place in the General Assembly's Fifth Committee.

The PBC's evolution

The original 2005 joint resolutions A/60/180–S/1645 (2005) conceived the PBC as a forum "to marshal resources and to advise on and propose integrated strategies for post-conflict peace-building and recovery." It also sought to focus attention on the reconstruction and institution-building necessary for recovery from conflict and especially to provide recommendations and information to improve the coordination of all relevant actors within and outside the UN. Its advocacy was concentrated in what were denominated "country configurations," which played a useful role in some specific country settings and led to disappointment in others. The Secretary-General noted in his 2019 report:

> As a flexible and dedicated intergovernmental platform, the Peacebuilding Commission has continued to promote policy coherence in support of conflict-affected countries by convening partners from within and outside the United Nations, through country-specific, regional and thematic discussions … [which] provided regular venues for discussion of political, socioeconomic, development and security challenges and risks at the national and regional levels. The advisory role of the Commission to the Security Council has also continued to advance, especially as the Council is considering the review and drawdown of peacekeeping operations and special political missions.[38]

Indeed, the PBC's expanding convening power has resulted in useful and timely debates during successive annual meetings.[39] It has also expanded its thematic agenda.[40] Further, it has consolidated its primary role vis-à-vis the country configurations, which continue to be accountable to the PBC.

More important, there has been progress in the PBC's "bridging" role envisioned in the AGE report and the subsequent resolutions, at least as judged from the increasing engagement by the PBC with the Security Council, General Assembly, and ECOSOC.[41] Not only has the Security Council invited the PBC chairs with greater frequency to discuss both thematic and country-specific topics, but it also has reached out to the PBC for briefings and advice for several countries, including the Central African Republic, Guinea-Bissau, Burkina Faso, and Mali. There also was more engagement between ECOSOC and the PBC, as illustrated by the meeting held between both bodies in November 2018, on the linkages between climate change and challenges to peacebuilding and sustaining peace in the Sahel. In March 2019, the General Assembly and the PBC held their first ever joint meeting, in the format of an informal interactive dialogue to discuss priorities on sustaining peace and peacebuilding.[42] Further, in implementing its gender and youth strategies, the PBC convened a meeting on the margins of the 63rd session of the Commission on the Status of Women to discuss the linkages between gender, social protection, peace, and development.

Finally, the 2010 and 2015 reviews proposed that the seven members elected to the PBC by each of the principal organs should be somehow accountable not only to their own governments but also to the principal organ that elected them. The logic behind this recommendation was to instill a sense of PBC ownership by each of the principal organs. However, this proposal to date remains unimplemented, since member states that aspire to join the PBC utilize vacancies in their regions irrespective of the voting blocs more as launching pads for their own diplomacy than as a commitment to "represent" the principal organ that facilitated their election.

Interactions between the reform process and sustaining peace

To reiterate, the AGE report had two main recommendations: to break down the UN system's fragmentation—especially from the three principal organs across the main pillars of activity (peace and security, development, promotion of human rights, and humanitarian assistance)—and to emphasize prevention. They form the essence of the 2016 resolutions and are integral to the Secretary-General's reform proposals. Particularly pertinent for the development system was the decision to separate the functions of the resident coordinator from those of the UNDP resident representative for the "new generation of United Nations country teams."[43] In this regard, the tangible results of peacebuilding efforts take place on the ground, where the UN's country teams interact with domestic and other governmental and non-governmental actors.

The most immediate and direct impact of the reform proposals was to insert the PBSO in the new Department of Political and Peacebuilding Affairs (DPPA). Arguably, a better location for the PBSO in the revised organizational structure of the Secretariat would have been at the level of the Executive Office of the Secretary-General (EOSG), to be consistent with the bridging concept that respected the PBC's advisory role to the three principal organs across the main pillars of activities. However, this deliberate decision was taken to decentralize the organizational structure and keep the EOSG limited to its coordination, monitoring, and accountability functions. At the time of writing, the location of the PBSO in what had formerly been the Department of Political Affairs has reportedly not limited its ability to engage with the other departments responsible for the development, human rights, and humanitarian assistance pillars.

Another notable post-2015 measure with relevance for the peacebuilding architecture and development, including the SDGs, was the closer relationship between the UN and the World Bank. One illustration, among others, was the joint publication in 2018 of *Pathways for Peace*.[44] That the Bank and the UN joined forces in producing a common document was in itself remarkable, given their different mandates, systems of governance, and bureaucratic cultures. It suggested that both institutions could also improve their work together on sustaining peace. The document makes a "business case" for the cost-effectiveness of prevention.

Half full or half empty?

As with most UN endeavors, the formulation and application of policies normally goes through a complex process of consultations and negotiations among the organization's 193 member states, complemented by the dynamics of constant interactions between the intergovernmental organs and the Secretariat. The review process for the peace architecture and its subsequent implementation correspond to the "half-full/half-empty syndrome" applied to the UNDS by Stephen Browne and Thomas G. Weiss.[45] However, the achievements over the last three years suggest that the glass is somewhat more than half full, notwithstanding that the implementation of the twin resolutions of 2016 has also faced obstacles and setbacks, certainly in relation to the expectations of most member states when they adopted those resolutions.

Overall, the two-stage review process proved to be successful. The report produced by the independent panel of outside experts took an objective look at what was wrong with the PBA, without the constraints that affect in-house reviews, where diverse criteria and interests, as well as well-established routines and working methods, often shape the outcome of this type of exercise. Therefore, the collective opinion of seven diverse specialists provided a blueprint on which the intergovernmental second phase could build, giving rise to an interesting combination of an outcome that reflected an independent assessment which translated into a sense of ownership on the part of both the General Assembly and the Security Council. Instead of experts providing material for the Secretariat to formulate its own proposals, the AGE reported back directly to both principal organs.

There now is certainly a better understanding of the role of peacebuilding or sustaining peace in the broader agenda of the United Nations; stated differently, there has been progress in articulating a conceptual framework. In addition, numerous recommendations became policy within the system's architecture. Among the intangible benefits is a perceptible improvement in the PBC's interactions with the principal organs as well as its advocacy. It also appears that the subsidiary bodies, known as the country configurations, have acted more coherently than earlier, respecting their role as part of a larger structure. Certainly, the PBF has registered significant tangible achievements in terms of total funding, number of eligible countries (and cross-border situations), and levels of financing of projects and programs.[46] Further, tangible benefits on the ground have been documented, for example in Cote d'Ivoire and Sierra Leone.[47]

On the half-empty side, there have also been challenges, three of which stand out: specific areas of contention; continued resistance to ending or at least mitigating fragmentation; and, perhaps most importantly, insufficient long-term, predictable funding for the PBF. First, the term "sustainable peace" is still contested by some countries, which either fear the "securitization" of development or, for some permanent members of the Security Council, the encroachment of non-members into its jurisdiction. The roots of these concerns are in the traditional tensions between the restricted council and the universal assembly, which finally led to the compromise wording found in SDG 16. Some delegations believe that additional work is needed to reach a common understanding of the precise meaning of "sustaining peace" or "sustainable peace." However, the ambiguities contained in resolutions A/70/262–S/2282 (2016) are, for this author, as close to consensus as feasible; differences have not impeded the widespread usage of "sustainable peace."

Second, the continued resistance to ending or at least mitigating fragmentation remains a deeply ingrained characteristic of the UN's work; change comes slowly. In other words, there is still a long way to go to break down institutional silos and foster greater coherence in the work of the three principal organs as well as to reinforce processes across the different pillars of the organization's activities, despite the Secretary-General's latest reform proposals urging more convergence.

Third, the AGE report stressed the importance of the PBF as a singularly meaningful instrument at the UN's disposal to be able to offer rapid financial assistance and play a catalytic role in mobilizing funds from bilateral and multilateral financial institutions. Neither assessed contributions nor a small percentage of the peacekeeping budget earmarked for the PBF has resulted; hence, there is still no solid basis for predictable, long-term planning. The opening of the report by the Secretary-General expressed clear concerns about the PBF's future: "The Fund's financial health remains in question at a time when the demand for its assistance has reached historic highs."[48]

Conclusion

In short, the implementation of General Assembly resolution 70/262 and Security Council resolution 2282 (2016) marks an important step forward. Achievements have gone beyond the author's personal expectations when the AGE report appeared in June 2015, as substantiated by the Secretary-General's two progress reports of January 2018 and May 2019. This encouraging assessment provides a foundation as the General Assembly prepares its third five-year review of the peacebuilding architecture in 2020. Indeed, as an epilogue to this chapter, on 31 October 2019 the presidents of the General Assembly and the Security Council approved the terms of reference for this new review, which will build on the progress achieved so far, and tackle the challenges still to be overcome.[49]

NOTES

1 Gert Rosenthal, "Assessing the Reform of the UN's Peacebuilding Architecture: Progress and Problems Two Years On," *FUNDS Briefing 47*, June 2017, www.futureun.org/en/Publications-Surveys/Article?newsid=105.

2 General Assembly resolution 70/1, 25 September 2015.
3 See: https://reform.un.org.
4 General Assembly and Security Council resolutions 60/180 and 1645, 20 December 2005.
5 UN, *2010 Review of the United Nations Peacebuilding Architecture*, UN documents A/64/868–S/2020/393, 21 July 2010.
6 Only 20 percent of respondents believed that the PBC was performing effectively. See FUNDS, "Survey on the UN's Peacebuilding Record—The Results Are Out!" www.futureun.org/en/Publications-Surveys/Article?newsid=63.
7 UN, *Letter Dated 15 December 2014 from the President of the General Assembly and the President of the Security Council to the Secretary-General* (UN documents A/69/674–S/2014/911), 17 December 2014.
8 This highly unusual procedure was crucial since most resolutions task the Secretary-General with designating panels that report back to him, prior to his basing his own report to the intergovernmental bodies on the findings of the designated panel.
9 *The Challenge of Sustaining Peace: Report of the Advisory Group of Experts for the 2015 Review of the United Nations Peacebuilding Architecture*, UN documents A/69/968–S/2015/490, 29 June 2015.
10 The Security Council recognized this matter as early as 2001 but without assimilating it for decision-making. See: *Statement by the President of the Security Council* (UN document S/PRST/2001/5), 20 February 2001.
11 Stephen Browne and Thomas G. Weiss, eds., *Peacebuilding Challenges for the UN Development System* (New York: Future UN Development System Project, 2015).
12 *The Challenge of Sustaining Peace*, "Part IV, The Way Forward: Conclusions and Recommendations," paras. 120–191.
13 Some of the main contributors objected for a number of reasons including the risk of submitting such funding to the Byzantine process of negotiations within the General Assembly's Fifth Committee.
14 The Secretary-General complied with this mandate. See: *Report of the Secretary-General on Peacebuilding and Sustaining Peace*, UN documents A/72/707–S/2018/43, 18 January 2018, especially paragraph 49, pp. 14–15.
15 "Recognizing that 'sustaining peace,' as drawn from the Advisory Group of Experts report, should be broadly understood as a goal and a process to build a common vision of a society, ensuring that the needs of all segments of the population are taken into account, which encompasses activities aimed at preventing the outbreak, escalation, continuation and recurrence of conflict, addressing root causes, assisting parties to conflict to end hostilities, ensuring national reconciliation, and moving towards recovery, reconstruction and development, and emphasizing that sustaining peace is a shared task and responsibility that needs to be fulfilled by the Government and all other national stakeholders, and should flow through all four pillars of the United Nations engagement at all stages of conflict, and in all its dimensions, and needs sustained international attention and assistance."
16 Thomas G. Weiss and Tatiana Carayannis, "Windows of Opportunity for UN Reform: Historical Lessons for the Next Secretary-General," *International Affairs* 92, no. 2 (2017): 309–326; and Stephen Browne and Thomas G. Weiss, "Ninth Secretary-General Takes Office Amidst Clarion Calls for Change," *FUNDS Briefing no. 44* (2017).
17 *Statement by the Secretary-General to the Security Council on International Peace and Security*, 10 January 2017, www.un.org/sg/en/content/sg/speeches/2017-01-10/secretary-generals-remarks-maintenance-international-peace-and-security.
18 See, for instance, the *Statement by Juan Jose Gómez Camacho at the Seminar on Sustaining Peace*, 7 June 2016, www.ipinst.org/2016/06/2016-new-york-seminar-sustaining-peace#2.
19 See: SDG 2020, SDG 16, www.sdg16.plus.
20 Operative paragraphs 14 and 24, respectively.
21 See, for example, *Statement by the Secretary-General to the Fifth Committee on Improving the Financial Situation of the Organization*, 4 June 2019, www.un.org/sg/en/content/sg/speeches/2019-06-04/remarks-the-fifth-committee.
22 See, for example, Youssef Mahmoud and Anupah Makoond, *Can Peacebuilding Work for Sustaining Peace?* (New York: International Peace Institute, 2018).
23 UN, *Security Council, 7629th Meeting* (UN document S/PV.7629), 23 February 2016, www.securitycouncilreport.org/atf/cf/%7B65BFCF9B-6D27-4E9C-8CD3-CF6E4FF96FF9%7D/spv_7629.pdf.
24 UN, *Report of the Peacebuilding Commission on Its Tenth Session* (UN documents A/71/768–S/2017/76), 27 January 2017, 7. A summary of the meeting is contained in an annex to the letter addressed by the president of the General Assembly to all member states on 20 May 2016.

25 See: *Statement by the Secretary-General's to the Security Council.*

26 For a full report on the meeting, see UN, *Security Council, 7629th Meeting.*

27 António Guterres, "Remarks to the General Assembly High-Level Dialogue on 'Building Sustainable Peace for All: Synergies between the 2030 Agenda for Sustainable Development and Sustaining Peace,'" *UNSG*, 24 January 2017, www.un.org/sg/en/content/sg/speeches/2017-01-24/secretary-generals-building-sustainable-peace-all-remarks.

28 For a report on the meeting see: UN, *Security Council, 8668th Meeting*, 19 November 2019, https://undocs.org/en/S/PV.8668%20(Resumption1).

29 See: *Statement by the Secretary-General to the Security Council on the Role of Reconciliation Processes*, 19 November 2019, www.un.org/sg/en/content/sg/speeches/2019-11-19/role-of-reconciliation-processes-remarks-security-council.

30 See: *Statement by the President of the Security Council*, 28 July 2016, www.securitycouncilreport.org/atf/cf/%7B65BFCF9B-6D27-4E9C-8CD3-CF6E4FF96FF9%7D/s_prst_2016_12.pdf; *Statement by the President of the Security Council*, 21 December 2017, https://undocs.org/en/S/PRST/2017/27; and *Statement by the President of the Security Council*, 18 December 2018, https://undocs.org/S/PRST/2018/20.

31 *Report of the Secretary-General on Peacebuilding and Sustaining Peace, 2018.*

32 *Report of the Secretary-General on Peacebuilding and Sustaining Peace, 2019.*

33 Gustavo de Carvalho, *Building a Better UN–AU Peacekeeping Partnership*, Institute for Security Studies, 9 June 2019, https://issafrica.org/iss-today/building-a-better-un-au-peacekeeping-partnership; "Joint Communique on United Nations-African Union Memorandum of Understanding on Peacebuilding," *AU Press Releases*, 20 September 2017, https://au.int/en/pressreleases/20170920/joint-communique-united-nations-african-union-memorandum-understanding; and Alexandra Novosseloff and Lisa Sharland, *Partners and Competitors: Forces Operating in Parallel to UN Peace Operations* (New York: International Peace Institute, 2019), www.ipinst.org/2019/11/partners-and-competitors-forces-operating-in-parallel-to-un-peace-operations.

34 Similarly, the 2019 *Report of the Secretary-General on Peacebuilding and Sustaining Peace* indicates: "The present interim report offers an early indication of progress: headway is being made on the vast majority of my recommendations, except for the important ones on securing adequate financing for peacebuilding. I urge the membership to ensure that progress is also made in those areas, in order to support collective efforts to advance the sustaining peace paradigm overall," para. 53.

35 Ibid., para. 47.

36 Yearly reports on the performance of the PBF are available for the period covered in this chapter: *The Peacebuilding Fund*, UN documents A/71/792, 14 February 2017, A/72/740, 9 February 2018, and A/73/829, 29 April 2019.

37 UN, *United Nations Peacebuilding, Strategic Plan 2017–2019*, www.un.org/peacebuilding/sites/www.un.org.peacebuilding/files/documents/pbf_sp_2017-19_final_180327.pdf.

38 *Report of the Secretary-General on Peacebuilding and Sustaining Peace*, 2019, para. 3.

39 See the reports of PBC at their 9th, 10th, 11th, 12th, and 13th sessions: UN, *Peacebuilding Commission Annual Session*, www.un.org/peacebuilding/commission/annual-session.

40 For example, *Statement by the Secretary-General to the PBC*, 7 September 2018, www.un.org/peacebuilding/news/secretary-generals-remarks-peacebuilding-commission: "Allow me to also highly commend the PBC for promoting the crucial role of women in peacebuilding and adopting a gender strategy, the first of its kind for a UN intergovernmental body."

41 For example, the President of ECOSOC and the Chair of the PBC co-chaired a joint meeting of ECOSOC and PBC on "Linkages between climate change and challenges to peacebuilding and sustaining peace in the Sahel" on 13 November 2018.

42 The president of the General Assembly circulated a written summary to all delegations on 25 June 2019. Since it was an informal meeting, neither the letter nor the summary have official symbols.

43 *Repositioning of the United Nations Development System in the Context of the Quadrennial Comprehensive Policy Review of Operational Activities for Development of the United Nations System* (UN document 72/279), 31 May 2018.

44 World Bank and United Nations, *Pathways for Peace: Inclusive Approaches to Preventing Violent Conflict* (Washington, DC: World Bank, 2018).

45 Browne and Weiss, "Ninth Secretary-General Takes Office Amidst Clarion Calls for Change."

46 UN, *United Nations Peacebuilding Fund*, www.un.org/peacebuilding/fund.

47 A sample of the scope, depth, and impact of the PBA's activities can be found in the ample documentation produced by the PBSO. See: www.un.org/peacebuilding/documents.

48 UN, *The Peacebuilding Fund: Report of the Secretary-General* (UN document A/71/792), 14 February 2017, last line of summary on front page.

49 UN, *Letter Dated 31 October 2019 from the President of the General Assembly and the President of the Security Council to the Secretary-General*, 31 October 2019, www.un.org/pga/74/wp-content/uploads/sites/99/2019/11/Letter-Review-of-the-UN-Peacebuilding-Architecture-31-October.pdf.

ADDITIONAL READING

Cedric De Coning and Eli Stamnes, eds., *UN Peacebuilding Architecture: The First Ten Years* (London: Routledge, 2016).

Cedric De Coning, Chiyuki Aoi, and John Karlsrud, eds., *UN Peacebuilding Doctrine in a New Era* (London: Routledge, 2017).

Graciana del Castillo, *Obstacles to Peacebuilding* (London: Routledge, 2017).

Rob Jenkins, *Peacebuilding: From Concept to Commission* (London: Routledge, 2013).

Youssef Mahmoud and Anupah Makoond, *Can Peacebuilding Work for Sustaining Peace?* (New York: International Peace Institute, 2018).

Roland Paris, "Peacebuilding," in *The Oxford Handbook on the United Nations*, ed. Thomas G. Weiss and Sam Daws (Oxford: Oxford University Press, 2018), 479–504.

9

WHAT DOES "LEAVE NO ONE BEHIND" MEAN FOR HUMANITARIANS?

Peter J. Hoffman

The records of humanitarianism and development over the past 30 years suggest stunning progress at the global level and in historical perspective; but upon closer examination, they tell a more subtle story of stark and enduring inequalities in outcomes coupled with troubling process issues of inefficiency, incoherence, and non-accountability. Disaggregated data between and within countries reveals that despite sizeable resources directed into humanitarianism and development, some populations remain poor, vulnerable, and unacknowledged. Moreover, discrete efforts by these respective sectors bespeak the creation of silos rather than a harmonized "humanitarian–development nexus."

In terms of development, the Sustainable Development Goals (SDGs) of September 2015 sought to rectify shortfalls by rethinking problems and solutions that would transform the pursuit of development from merely attending to symptoms, such as poverty and disease, to also tackling structural drivers and quality-of-life aspects, including the promotion of sustainability, inequality, peace, and justice. However, the SDGs did not address deficiencies in humanitarianism; in fact, with the exception of some perfunctory references, the SDGs failed to mention many of the acute horrors that lie behind most contemporary humanitarian crises—for example, human rights abuse, terrorism, protections of civilians in armed conflict, and aid manipulation. Three main problems linger for humanitarians: the operational challenge of too many victims of emergencies receiving no or inadequate assistance; the organizational challenge of an all-too-frequent disconnect with development; and the identity-based challenge of giving voice and choice to affected populations. To galvanize the international humanitarian system to confront unequal treatment of those in need (the displaced, the sick or injured, the starving, etc.), better cohere humanitarianism with development work, and cultivate inclusivity and agency of the afflicted, in 2016 the concept of "Leave No One Behind" was formally introduced to the humanitarian sector. This chapter outlines the birth, effect, and overtones of "Leave No One Behind" in humanitarianism.

Inspiration and idea

The concept of "Leave No One Behind" (LNOB) is an expression of solidarity; it connotes mutual support and a shared goal. The idea can be traced to the Latin phrase *nemo reside*, which animated Roman Legions in antiquity and in the modern era pervades the tenets of fighting forces.[1] In the same way that soldiers feel a sense of duty to comrades, humanitarians are compelled to help those suffering. However, embedding the specific norm and language of LNOB into the sensibilities of the humanitarian sector emerged only in recent years, out of context of durable and growing disparities between those who suffer from armed conflicts and disasters, and those who receive assistance. It was also motivated by accountability concerns. At the heart of this idea is a humanitarian sensitivity that feedback from affected populations is vital to building trust, which is central to addressing power imbalances in provider–recipient relations in addition to the efficiency and effectiveness of programming.[2]

From the founding of the International Committee of the Red Cross (ICRC) in the late nineteenth century, one of the primary humanitarian principles has been impartiality—the belief that aid should be provided without "discrimination as to nationality, race, religious beliefs, class or political opinion."[3] However, implementing impartiality has proven difficult, and some crises as well as certain populations within crises have experienced neglect or marginalization, and this has been compounded by affected populations having no avenue for providing feedback on or input into humanitarian action.

The perception that humanitarianism could do better has ballooned since the 1990s—better in reaching all those in need, better in not merely servicing needs but ending needs, and better in being more accountable to donors and affected populations. The experiences of the "well-fed dead" in the Balkans and aid manipulation following the Rwandan genocide were benchmarks of failures and sparked calls for reform. Numerous standards and governance schemes by aid agencies and donors are illustrative of efforts to improve delivery, tackle root causes, and increase participation of intended beneficiaries (see Box 9.1). What is lacking is not ideas about the importance of addressing all in need and being accountable to them; the complications have been in implementation.

Box 9.1 Standards and governance for and by the humanitarian sector and donors

The Code of Conduct for The International Red Cross and Red Crescent Movement (1994)

People in Aid (1995)

Active Learning Network for Accountability and Performance in Humanitarian Action (ALNAP) (1997)

The Sphere Project (1997)

The Humanitarian Accountability Partnership International (2003)

People in Aid Code of Good Practice (2003)

Good Humanitarian Donorship (2003)

HAP Standard in Accountability and Quality Management (2007)

International Aid Transparency Initiative (2008)

HAP Standard in Accountability and Quality Management—update (2010)

Inter-Agency Standing Committee Transformative Agenda (2011)

Joint Standards Initiative (2011)

Core Humanitarian Standards on Quality and Accountability (2014)

The most recent movement toward a more ambitious and accountable humanitarianism began in January 2012 when UN Secretary-General Ban Ki-moon announced his priorities for sustainable development, peace and security, human rights, democracy, women and youth, and also a strengthening of the international humanitarian system through better coordination, more robust capabilities, and greater accountability.[4] As part of this statement he proposed a "first-of-its-kind World Humanitarian Summit to help share knowledge and establish common best practices," which would be pivotal in launching many new initiatives in the humanitarian sector. While humanitarians were preparing for the World Summit, in the development space the notion of LNOB was first articulated in a September 2015 General Assembly resolution proclaiming the *2030 Agenda for Sustainable Development*, which contained the SDGs.[5] Although the SDGs offered an elaborate vision for development—17 goals with 169 targets—they were conspicuously silent on humanitarian issues.

The humanitarian sector, however, was not far behind in presenting its own grand strategy. In October 2015, a global consultation with around 1,200 participants from 153 countries was convened to synthesize inputs from eight regional and thematic consultations with humanitarian actors (over 23,000 people from 150 countries participated) held in 2014 and 2015; these were to form the basis for proposals to be unveiled at the upcoming World Humanitarian Summit (WHS). In January 2016, the High-Level Panel on Humanitarian Financing presented its findings.[6] This report noted, first, the importance of shrinking needs through breaking the silos of humanitarianism and development, commenting that while humanitarian action addresses emergencies, development builds resilience to emergencies. Second, the report suggested exploring new funding mechanisms to mobilize greater resources. Third, it underscored that greater efficiency could be achieved, on the one hand, through distributing cash and, on the other, listening to affected populations.

The Secretary-General continued the momentum in February 2016 and attended partially to an injudicious and debilitating lacuna in the SDGs when he declared the *Agenda for Humanity*. This vision vows five "responsibilities" to be measured and achieved through 24 "transformations"—a word that indicates the ambitions of the undertaking, certainly unrealistic in the context of the usual pace and quality of change in intergovernmental organizations. "Core responsibility three: leave no one behind"[7] stipulated:

> Leaving no one behind is a central aspiration of most political, ethical or religious codes and has always been at the heart of the humanitarian imperative. The pledge to leave no one behind is the central theme of the 2030 Agenda and places a new obligation on us all to reach those in situations of conflict, disaster, vulnerability and risk first so that they benefit from and contribute to sustainable long-term development. The World Humanitarian Summit provides a first test of the international community's commitment to transforming the lives of those most at risk of being left behind.[8]

There are two key elements to the *Agenda for Humanity*: First, it unequivocally states that LNOB humanitarianism is about more than addressing needs; it also concerns working to reduce needs, risks, and vulnerabilities. Second, it asserts that realizing LNOB requires a fusing of humanitarianism and development—"To achieve [reduction of need, risk, and vulnerability], institutional providers will need to set aside such artificial institutional labels as 'development' or 'humanitarian', working together."[9] The logic of bringing together two usually separate pursuits is encapsulated in the discourse of a "humanitarian–development nexus" that offers a root-cause analysis and envisions a smooth and reinforcing continuum between short-term emergency assistance and long-term aid for building socio-economic capabilities. This rationale is also underscored by the fact that many requests for funding humanitarian assistance recur year after year. From 2000 to 2017, 27 countries had more than five consecutive years of UN-coordinated appeals, and in the contemporary period, the average duration of a humanitarian appeal for funding has grown, averaging seven years; over 90 percent are for at least three years in a row.[10]

The proposed linking of humanitarian action to development objectives would also be manifested in the creation of shared measurements as the *Agenda for Humanity* calls for "every country to commit to collecting comprehensive data and analysis to better identify, prioritize and track the progress of the most vulnerable and disadvantaged groups towards the Sustainable Development Goals."[11] To fulfill LNOB, the agenda specifies seven "transformations":[12]

- *Address displacement*: Lessen flows across borders and internal displacement by 50 percent by 2030.
- *Address migration*: Establish lawful means for mobility for family, work, or education purposes to be accepted, and protect those who are preyed upon by criminals (e.g., human traffickers) during migration.
- *End statelessness*: References the *Convention Relating to the Status of Stateless Persons* and the *Convention on the Reduction to Statelessness*, to end the problem by 2024.
- *Empower and protect women and girls*: Greater participation by women in decision-making, access to livelihoods, and protection of sexual and reproductive rights.
- *Ensure education for all in crisis*: Create safe environments and provide resources for education, including secondary schools and vocational training.
- *Empower youth*: Foster greater participation by young people in resolving conflicts and helping societies recover.
- *Include the most vulnerable*: Reach a larger array of frequently forsaken populations, not just women and girls but also those with disabilities and the elderly.

The parameters of LNOB as presented in the *Agenda for Humanity* are essentially an admission that regardless of humanitarianism's traditional principle of impartiality, it has not been inclusive; it has failed to serve certain sectors, in particular the displaced, women, and youth. In short, the agenda seeks to broaden the ends and means of humanitarianism. A report by the UN's Office for the Coordination of Humanitarian Affairs (OCHA) summarized:

> The 2030 Agenda calls on humanitarians locally, nationally, and internationally to work differently with one another and with counterparts in development, peace operations, climate change, and gender equality to move people out of crisis: reducing vulnerability, doubling down on risk management, and tackling root causes of crises and conflict.[13]

The LNOB vision of cohering humanitarianism and development was also backed at the April 2016 meeting of the International Dialogue on Statebuilding and Peacebuilding. This forum released a statement committing members "to advancing the *Agenda for Humanity* as a way to transcend the divide between humanitarian and development action to achieve collective outcomes supporting the implementation of the 2030 Agenda to fragile and conflict affected areas."[14] The communiqué specified the urgent need for pooled data, enhanced collaboration, and collective outcomes.

Normative developments for applying LNOB to humanitarianism crystalized at the May 2016 World Humanitarian Summit in Istanbul. The meeting produced many initiatives that take up the theme of LNOB. First, the *Grand Bargain* made 51 commitments by 18 donors and 16 aid agencies (mainly those of the UN and Red Cross/Red Crescent societies) to set in motion a "participation revolution," creating channels for feedback of people receiving aid and enhancing the role of local and national organizations in decision-making. It specified that 25 percent of global humanitarian funding would be directed through local and national bodies by 2020, thus not "leaving behind" local capacities. Second, the *Charter for Change* spelled out eight commitments to promote the localization of humanitarian aid, which advocate developing local capacities and avoiding disruptive recruitment practices so that communities are not "left behind." Third, the *Global Partnership for Preparedness* is a coordinating mechanism led by vulnerable countries to foster readiness in response to climate change-fueled disasters, which means national governments are not "left behind." Fourth, *Education Cannot Wait* aims to fund quality education for school-aged children displaced by disasters and safe places to deliver it, with the objective of providing it to all by 2030, and therefore education and children are not "left behind." Fifth, *Connecting Business Initiatives* incorporates business actors into humanitarian systems for reducing risk and providing aid, harnessing the private sector to "leave no one behind." Sixth, the *Charter on the Inclusion of Persons with Disabilities in Humanitarian Action* recognizes a sector that is frequently the most vulnerable and marginalized; it pledges inclusion in determining programming and facilitating greater access to humanitarian aid to ensure those with disabilities are not "left behind." Seventh, the *New Way of Working* (NWOW) affirms the collaboration of humanitarian and development architectures and working with local and national partners in the achievement of "collective outcomes"; the purpose is to build capacities for reducing risk and vulnerability that can shrink the number of those in need, which heralds "leaving no one behind." *NWOW* is the most representative of the "humanitarian–development nexus" as a singular practice in pursuit of the SDGs.

Although LNOB is formally measured through what would amount to seven transformations, its importance lies in the effort to have humanitarianism respond to a wider range of demands—those in immediate need but also those who are vulnerable and at risk. Moreover, placing this within the larger context of WHS's redesign of humanitarianism, the principle of LNOB is apparent in other localization and accountability schemes, such as the *Grand Bargain* and *Charter for Change*, which vow that the capacities in at-risk countries and the views of affected populations will not be "left behind."

Impacts and influence

LNOB is a relatively recent innovation, but progress can be gleaned by reviewing performance since 2016. The significance of the idea can be measured in the effect of its three-fold agenda: broadening the scope of humanitarianism from needs to encompass vulnerabilities and risks; re-conceptualizing humanitarianism as a system that coheres with development actors and goals; and expanding humanitarianism's scale to include not only international but also national and local ownership, including participation by affected populations. Resource flows, service delivery, and agency behavior are indicators of whether a qualitative shift in mindset working toward "leaving no one behind" has taken hold. Three facets connecting material impacts and normative influences are revealing: affected populations, funding, and data and programming.

Affected populations

The size of populations in humanitarian crises has soared, and gaps in coverage among those in need persist. The introduction of LNOB in 2016 has fueled a better mapping out of how affected populations are "left behind" by humanitarian assistance. For example, the International Federation of Red Cross and Red Crescent Societies (IFRC) has scrutinized those left "out": "out of sight" (those who are not known or recognized, such as the undocumented or victims of sexual violence); "out of reach" (those who are inaccessible because of physical or political obstacles); "out of the loop" (those who are unintentionally excluded, e.g., the disabled, the elderly); "out of money" (those who suffer because there are insufficient resources); and "out of scope" (those who are beyond the usual jurisdiction of humanitarians, such as migrants or victims of urban violence).[15]

The magnitude of global humanitarian needs is a useful barometer for measuring the LNOB principle; they give a sense of how vast and complicated the challenge is as well as whether progress has been made. In addition to the structural strains of the international humanitarian system emanating from the burgeoning number of affected populations—from both armed conflicts and natural disasters—there are also differences over the numbers of those in need, and limits on who can realistically be reached by humanitarians, let alone who is actually reached.

Some surveys contend there are presently about 200 million people in need, but other estimates are closer to 130–140 million.[16] Whatever the number, the disparity between needs and delivery remains. OCHA's data for the past five years exhibits that the numbers of those in need are rising, as are the numbers of those who they aspire to aid, but the gap between these populations is also growing.[17] In 2015, 77.9 million were in need, with 57.5 million to receive aid, but estimates and aspirations skyrocketed in 2016, with 125.3 million in need and 87.6 million to receive aid. In the last few years, the numbers continue the upward trend but more slowly; in 2017, 128.6 million in need, 92.8 million to receive aid; in 2018 the respective figures were 135.7 million and 90.9 million, and in 2019, 131.7 million and 93.6 million. Other data makes similar estimates; for 2017, 130.5 million in need and 95.4 million targeted for aid; for 2018, 141.2 million in need and 101.2 million targeted.[18] Furthermore, many of those in need are experiencing it for longer periods. The average length of a crisis has grown—in 2008 it was 6.2 years, by 2014 it had dropped to 5.2 years, but in 2017 it shot up to 7.5 years and in 2018 it hit 9.3 years.[19]

Beyond the overall numbers, a crucial characteristic of those in need is whether they are displaced—this affects where and how to deliver assistance and also may be suggestive of the nature and duration of their needs. Displacement has snowballed over the past decade.[20] In 2008, it was already 42.7 million; it reached over 65 million by the time LNOB entered into humanitarian discourse, and in 2018 it exceeded 70 million. Moreover, many of the uprooted are internally displaced, making it difficult for international agencies to reach them. They include "refugees" who cross borders, have designated rights under international humanitarian law, and far more often are in spaces that are more hospitable to aid delivery as compared to IDPs, who may be purposely neglected or even attacked by actors that may be responsible for their displacement.

The long-standing upward trends of humanitarian needs and displacement suggest not only that LNOB is necessary but also what a struggle it is to achieve. If the humanitarian system is already scrambling to address those "left behind," its capacity to come to grips with a more extensive casting of "left behind" is doubtful. The scales are daunting: those in need at the high end of estimates number 200 million, but they are dwarfed by the figures of those who are vulnerable or at risk because of poverty or armed conflict: between 1.8 and 2 billion.[21] If vulnerabilities and risks can be limited, this would surely lower needs; but currently all categories of affected populations are rising. Indeed, despite LNOB, the numbers of those "left behind" are growing, which is a telling comment on its significance in the context of drivers and consequent conditions.

Funding

Financial resources are essential to realizing any type of aid work; its amount, where it is directed, and how it is used determine not only the number of lives saved but also the quality of those lives and the capacities of those populations. With the institution of LNOB, there should be sufficient funding for all crises, it should build the capacities of actors that have traditionally been "left behind" in terms of resourcing, and the funds should give recipients more say in how aid is used.

Figure 9.1 shows that the funding for the humanitarian sector has surged over the past 30 years, going from less than $1 billion to almost $29 billion. At the same time, however, notable gaps have opened between what is requested and what is received. Data from OCHA's UN-coordinated appeals from 2009–2018 tells a similarly dire story of a growing gap in the UN system: according to their calculations the 2009 gap was 28 percent, in 2014, 39 percent, and in 2018, 44 percent.[22] This gap in UN funding is woeful but it may also be a sign of a shift in funding through other humanitarian actors. For example, funding through the ICRC and IFRC has grown markedly in the past decade, up around 30 percent in the last few years alone, and their gap is strikingly smaller, respectively only about 7 percent and 17 percent.[23]

The ongoing changes in channels of funding in the humanitarian sector, however, remain fundamentally between intergovernmental organizations and international NGOs, and to a lesser extent also for national governments that host crises. Although the *Grand Bargain* promised to dramatically increase the role of local and national aid providers—to channel 25 percent of all funding through them by 2020—the data suggests that there has been miniscule progress.[24] In 2018, 96 percent of funding was through the major international actors (based in the West), only 3.1 percent through local and national responders, and 0.3 percent for Southern international NGOs. The headway that has been made toward the *Grand Bargain*'s aim has been paltry—in 2016, 2 percent was channeled through local and national responders, in 2017, 2.8 percent, and in 2018, 3.1 percent. A closer look at these advances also shows that they have been almost entirely by aid going to national governments, which accounts for over 80 percent of this growth, while the proportion of funding through local and national NGOs has declined: in 2017 it accounted for 17 percent, but in 2018 it fell to 15 percent.

Additionally, the funding that does come into the system, regardless of the channel, is concentrated in relatively few crises (i.e., populations).[25] About 44 percent of appeals receive half or less of requested funds. Over roughly the last decade, 10 countries have received 59–66 percent of all humanitarian aid, with a noticeable growing proportion at least since 2014. In the last few years, appeals for crises in Syria, Yemen, Somalia, Ethiopia, Nigeria, and the Democratic

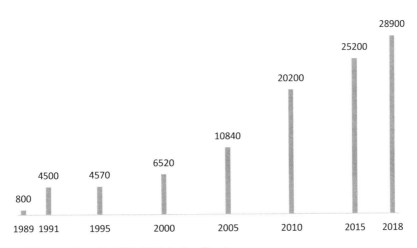

Figure 9.1 Humanitarian aid, 1989–2018 (in $ millions).

Republic of the Congo have loomed large and account for around three-quarters of all aid requested; for example, in 2018, appeals associated with these emergencies constituted 77 percent of all humanitarian aid requested.

One aspect that gets little attention but is important in terms of the quality of funding is the composition of the resulting aid. Food, medicine, and shelter, usually through a voucher system, are traditionally the staples of humanitarian assistance; but some observers have viewed this as reductionist. A 2016 OCHA report invoked the lamentation, "we are still giving people what we have, not what they need," and compared the humanitarian system to a "cargo cult" more concerned with the delivery of available resources than considering requirements or impacts.[26] In recent years, though, there has been a change in thinking to providing cash—in both the humanitarian and development arenas—which gives greater decision-making power to the recipient.[27] This practice has been increasing; in 2015, 55 percent of aid was distributed as cash rather than vouchers, and in 2018 the number had climbed to 78 percent.[28]

Funding patterns suggest that there are more resources in the humanitarian system but only a trickle potentially have an impact on "leaving no one behind." There remain sizeable gaps in funding, and especially in how and where funds are directed. But when it does arrive, the resources show potential to give more authority, and therefore more dignity, to recipients.

Data and programming

A paramount element in achieving LNOB is data inasmuch as it underscores what is being measured and how, and ultimately how it shapes reporting and programming—in particular, accountability. The importance of data as a reflection of embedding LNOB can be seen in the behavior of humanitarian actors. One of the central premises of fulfilling LNOB is to integrate humanitarian and development actors in devising a common set of objectives: "collective outcomes." A far more extensive representation of data as signifying the gravity of LNOB is in the reporting on LNOB and also the substance of what that data says.[29] While the number of stakeholders reporting their adherence to overall commitments to the *Agenda for Humanity* has dropped—in 2017, 142 reported, and in 2018, only 104—reporting on the beneficiaries of LNOB grew, except for a slight dip in education.

The highlights of the data on the seven so-called LNOB transformations illustrate considerable progress:

- Address displacement: The signing of the *Global Compact on Refugees* (2018) along with reports documenting protections for refugees and an increase in advocacy and resources for IDPs.
- Address migration: The *Global Compact for Safe, Orderly and Regular Migration* (2018) has stimulated greater advocacy for migrants, especially children, along with initiatives for income generation and social services.
- End statelessness: This transformation is by far the least reported on, and aside from UNHCR's regular documentation and advocacy, only four states note activities in this area.
- Empower and protect women and girls: More reporting on gender equality programming and funding for sexual and reproductive rights as exemplified by the Inter-Agency Standing Committee's support for the *Policy and Accountability Framework on Gender Equality and the Empowerment of Women and Girls in Humanitarian Action* (2017).
- Ensure education for all in crisis: Most reports comment on increasing financial support and providing education to displaced populations and host communities.

- Enable youth: *The Compact for Young People in Humanitarian Action* (2016) has been a touchstone for establishing programming to build capacity among youth and increase their participation in responding to crises.
- Include the most vulnerable: Following the *Charter on the Inclusion of Persons with Disabilities in Humanitarian Action* (2016), many humanitarian agencies have developed disability-sensitive programming.

The data on affected populations and on the humanitarian sector, culled from the reporting by stakeholders, reflects the difficulty generalizing about the significance of LNOB. While the information on "transformations" points to headway, it is not apparent there is widespread momentum—the data is fundamentally anecdotal and does not indicate a sea change. Furthermore, to apprehend agency and accountability for those "left behind," the data must be more granular, specifically disaggregated by gender, age, and disability.[30]

At the level of programming, there has been remarkable progress in linking humanitarian and development work. Although NGOs have often had mandates in both areas, historically the UN has had more silos. However, in November 2017, the Joint Steering Committee (JSC) to Advance Humanitarian and Development Collaboration was formed as a platform co-chaired by the under-secretary-general for humanitarian affairs/emergency relief coordinator and the UN Development Programme (UNDP) administrator to integrate their programming as per the *New Way of Working*.[31] The creation of this entity fortifies the idea of cohering agendas, analytics, and actions. Since its inception up through the end of 2019, there have been five JSC meetings. The operational impact is seen in the senior on-the-ground authorities from both sets of agencies (Resident Coordinators of Humanitarian Country Teams and UN Country Teams from the development system) fashioning joint metrics and missions that traverse the entirety of the humanitarian–development nexus.[32]

The material impact and normative influence of LNOB is most evident in data. More empirical information is available about who is being left behind and how—greater coherence and collaboration between analytics of humanitarian and development actors have contributed to this. At the same time, there continues to be a requirement for more and better data to understand which populations are still being left behind, and with respect not just to development but also humanitarian needs.[33] The increases in funding have not necessarily been commensurate with ensuring that no one is "left behind" because of the concentration on certain crises and persistent gaps between requests and funds received. Additionally, advances made in channeling funds through actors at the local and national level broadly evidence recognition that capacities in the Global South must be developed, and those that do exist are underutilized and require encouragement and supplementing by the North. Yet, actual allocations have been primarily via national governments, while locals and NGOs from the Global South are in effect "left behind" as humanitarian agents that contribute to decision-making and impel accountability.

Technical and political

LNOB is presented as a breakthrough in humanitarian principles and practice, but it raises the issue of its "meaning"—not just about how it is understood but also how it is valued and resonates with the identity of an actor. A deeper analysis of LNOB implies two distinctive meanings; first, as a technical or operational version that reconceptualizes the problem of and solution to the nature and plight of affected populations; or second, as a political phenomenon that rearticulates the relationship between humanitarians and affected populations. The result of these varied meanings produces contestation and incoherence in the humanitarian sector because different constituencies act on different understandings and ascribe different value to LNOB. Ultimately, the question humanitarians confront is: does the meaning of LNOB give new meaning to humanitarianism?

The technical perspective on LNOB considers the characteristics of affected populations—what accounts for being "left behind"—and positions humanitarianism as part of a larger set of global response tools to crises; what it requires to "leave no one behind." The usual view of humanitarians is that emergency needs are the problem—that is, hunger, disease, and the like. In LNOB the structural conditions that produce these problems are conceived far more broadly. Armed conflict, poverty, displacement, the durability of crises (such as in protracted refugee situations), migration and urbanization, and climate change are factored in. Thus, rather than needs alone, vulnerabilities and risk also feature prominently in understanding what LNOB means, and it values humanitarians doing more, i.e., taking actions that address root causes. This also positions humanitarianism to augment and compensate for the omission in the SDGs. Moreover, achieving this wider formulation necessitates humanitarian agencies working with development actors. From this point of view, LNOB creates an opportunity for humanitarians to access new and bigger funding streams. Therefore, in this framing LNOB is also understood as an interweaving of mandates, resources, and operations, and valuing substantive cooperation, if not wholesale integration, between the humanitarian and development sectors.

The critical interpretation of LNOB is that it is a political project, a disputed discourse and practice that grounds yet veils power relationships. LNOB is predicated on a far-reaching reorientation of the humanitarian system to help those who have the least capacity to survive in emergencies combined with the poorest chance of receiving assistance, but the actual practices that come with this reorientation alter the relationship between humanitarians and affected populations. Consequently, LNOB must be understood as more than new organizational and operational arrangements; its reality also engenders a dynamic that communicates a new set of humanitarian values to victims that are draped in utopian promises but bespeak instrumentalization and efficiency over responsibility and solidarity.

The type and level of resources, their channels, and the contextual conditions of assistance connote power. The hard truth is that there are profound limits on humanitarianism regardless of the morality, logic, and LNOB's operational protocols. A recent review of the sector summarizes the chronic acute impediments on humanitarianism: "In reality, humanitarian action is fundamentally about triage—and with increases in global risks and constraints on resources and access, humanitarians will never have the capacity to address all needs arising from conflicts and disasters."[34] Put simply, the drivers of need are simply greater than the volume of response; despite tinkering with the conception of humanitarian aid and increases in resources for it, the former has outpaced the latter and always will. Thus, "leaving no one behind" is an impossibility; an idealistic aspiration more than a realistic goal.

Aside from the systemic challenges inherent in growing the size of affected populations and placing limits on resources and capacities that undermine LNOB, critical perspectives bring to the fore five ways that humanitarian actors may resist LNOB. First, before no one can be left behind, there must be information indicating there are those being left behind. However, to collect this type of data can be problematic; for humanitarians, it is a form of surveillance. Knowledge of the need and size of affected populations can be used not only for the purposes of aid programming but also by political actors to provoke fears or fatigue among donors or host populations.

Second, LNOB presumes its version of impartiality can guide operations, but there are other concerns regarding distributive principles. Most humanitarian agencies concentrate on those immediately in need, especially as this is their mandate under international humanitarian law.

They do not want to go too far "upstream" in directing resources to more indistinct aspects that may potentially produce need but are not definitively at the level of need just yet—humanitarians see that as the domain of development. To many humanitarians, shifting resources away from glaring needs to the longer-term issues of the vulnerable and at risk is not morally justifiable. For instance, to hypothetically save 100 people in the future at the cost of concretely dooming 10 who are currently suffering is not a bargain that humanitarians would make. Equally problematic is the fact that some aid operations can be more efficient and seemingly leave fewer behind by delivering aid in easy-to-access places. Hence, the cost of delivery is less than for hard-to-reach places, which leave more funds to buy more aid that is then available for more people in need; but populations that are difficult to physically connect with are those who get "left behind." Médecins Sans Frontières (MSF), for example, prioritizes those whose needs are greater. Relief displays solidarity with affected populations; it is not a straightforward exercise to "leave no one behind," but rather to target particular populations who suffer the most from extreme neglect. Similarly, an agency with a specific mandate that focuses on a subset of victims may try to respond to a "left-behind" segment in a grander scheme, such as UNICEF, but at the operational level it entails "leaving behind" others in their planning and allocation of resources. Smaller agencies, particularly local and national ones, may not be able to operate at the LNOB scale, and thus this principle is an entry barrier for this work, meaning that these potential capacities and actors are "left behind."

Third, an issue for some humanitarians is the integration of humanitarianism with development. Doing so is controversial not only because it involves undertaking work that is beyond the conventional work of humanitarians, but also because it compromises the principle of independence. In addition to historically having different perspectives on metrics of distress and types of aid to provide, humanitarianism and development have differed over the client; for development, it has been governments, but for humanitarianism, it has been the people. Resistance by humanitarians to cooperation with development actors started in the 1990s with fears that attempts at coherence watered down or coopted humanitarianism; enmity swelled in the early 2000s after collaborations were carried out in theaters of the Global War on Terrorism (GWOT), which led to charges of humanitarianism being distorted or maligned. As such, some in the humanitarian sector have opposed a "do-it-all" humanitarianism and demanded a "back-to-basics" strategy.[35] This attitude argues that the implementation of LNOB results in the principles of humanitarianism being "left behind."

Fourth, another source of discontent with LNOB stems from international humanitarian agencies placing a premium on their own role and presence relative to local and national actors. While it might be claimed that this preference is based on the parochial interests of organizational prestige and economic survival given it attracts donor money, there are other views. Some humanitarians, for example, claim that international agencies being gatekeepers allows them to circumvent or mitigate biases that may exist within local and national actors that would manipulate resources. At the same time, other humanitarians worry that the role of international aid agencies, which are fundamentally coping tools, will be decreased by abiding LNOB. This circumstance would be worrisome as it justifies avoiding deeper involvement and is a step toward international disengagement and disavowal of duty to affected populations. That is, providing resources to local and national parties represents a minimal expense and is a tacit stepping stone toward a neoliberal conferral of authority that ends the responsibility of great powers and international organizations. In any case, empirically the increase in resources to frontline actors beyond international agencies has been modest in amounts and qualitative effect. A 2018 analysis of the humanitarian system points out, "Relations between international actors and the governments of affected states continue the trend of improvement … [w]hile little has been achieved in handing over power and resources to local civil society organisations."[36] Beyond some symbolic gains, the "participation revolution" called for by the *Grand Bargain* and that also epitomizes a LNOB ethos with regard to local capacity-building has thus far been inconsequential, and this signals discomfort with the politics of LNOB.

Fifth, another opprobrium derives from what it takes for humanitarian actors to reach those who have been "left behind" because of problems of violence that influence access. In places where international aid workers have been attacked or threatened—a growing threat—international staff are evacuated, and the burden of aid delivery shifts entirely to local staff, although decision-making and management authority usually remain with internationals.[37] In an attempt to "leave no one behind," it is Global South aid workers who are "left behind."

Beyond the humanitarian sector, contemporary global debates among states and in intergovernmental organizations on what humanitarianism is also shape prospects for LNOB. While these debates have existed since the formation of the international humanitarian system in the late nineteenth century and heightened during the 1990s, the introduction of new donors and the establishment of new agencies from the Global South have amplified discord within the humanitarian sector.[38] To some, LNOB has an elitist quality: yet another case of the North presuming that it is the savior of the suffering, and whose humanitarians must instruct counterparts in the South. Yet, LNOB may be challenged as global shifts in power will surface in resource flows and reverberate on humanitarian action. In a related fashion, affected populations may also be averse to LNOB. The prospect of emergency relief is appealing but fears of political strings may be a deterrent. Those who have been victimized by armed conflict may be especially sensitive about aid that emanates from a belligerent with an agenda—obscuring accountability for violence, creating dependency, normalizing the emergency, and influencing population management. Certain populations may be intrinsically opposed to Western aid agencies and, rather than endure what they see as colonialism, prefer to be "left behind."

Conclusion

Humanitarianism is rooted in providing concrete emergency relief, but it routinely comes to an existential crossroads over what more it could be. Starting in the 1990s, from inside and outside the international humanitarian system, there have been calls for reinvention to make programming more efficient, equitable, effective, and accountable. "Leave No One Behind" is part of the latest wave of attempts to remake humanitarianism by acting in conjunction with development and building local capacities. Regardless of the morality or logic of those aims, they are invariably fraught with political consequences for the humanitarian phenomenon, which bristles at any such insinuation. Much of the analysis of LNOB and work to achieve it has concentrated on the nuts and bolts of measuring needs and foregrounding the conditions of affected populations, who suffer from the dual challenges of emergencies and being "left behind" in responses. Frequently lost in the exuberance of LNOB's popular rhetoric is that this technocratic reform does not weigh the repercussions for the identity of humanitarianism. In this light, LNOB is a more facile and dogmatic slogan than sensible and feasible practice. Indeed, operationalizing it has raised hackles among some humanitarians who fret over the political implications of integration with development, a new one-size-fits-all regimen that constrains decision-making by agencies and does not address the dearth of substantive levels of accountability. Therefore, LNOB presents a quandary for humanitarians in a three-fold configuration of core problems— the operational, organizational, and identity-related. To address the operational problem of scale and scope of affected populations, an organizational solution of conjoining efforts with development is posed, but it provokes an identity challenge for humanitarians.

LNOB may prove to make an invaluable contribution in bringing resources to bear on the acute problems besetting affected populations. However, it is also possible that the political project of "Leave No One Behind" will itself be left behind by humanitarians.

NOTES

1 For example, the US Army Ranger Creed states, "I will never leave a fallen comrade to fall into the hands of the enemy."
2 Mary B. Anderson, Dayna Brown, and Isabella Jean, *Time to Listen: Hearing People on the Receiving End of International Aid* (Cambridge, MA: CDA Collaborative Learning Projects, December 2012).
3 The International Committee of the Red Cross, www.redcross.int/en.
4 Ban Ki-moon, *Remarks to the General Assembly on His Five-Year Action Agenda: "The Future We Want,"* 25 January 2012, www.un.org/sg/en/content/sg/speeches/2012-01-25/remarks-general-assembly-his-five-year-action-agenda-future-we-want.
5 General Assembly resolution A/RES/70/1, *Transforming Our World: The 2030 Agenda for Sustainable Development*, 25 September 2015, https://sustainabledevelopment.un.org/post2015/transformingour world. Multiple passages reference "no one would be left behind" in the pursuit of sustainable development: preamble, paras. 4, 26, 48, 72, 74(e).
6 High-Level Panel on Humanitarian Financing, *Too Important to Fail—Addressing the Humanitarian Financing Gap*, January 2016, http://earlyrecovery.global/sites/default/files/hlp_report_too_important_ to_fail-addressing_the_humanitarian_financing_gap.pdf.
7 *One Humanity: Shared Responsibility: Report of the Secretary-General for the World Humanitarian Summit*, 2 February 2016, https://reliefweb.int/sites/reliefweb.int/files/resources/Secretary-General%27s%20 Report%20for%20WHS%202016%20%28Advance%20Unedited%20Draft%29.pdf.
8 Ibid., para. 72.
9 Ibid., para. 108.
10 Development Initiatives, *Global Humanitarian Assistance (GHA) 2019*, 12; OCHA, *An End in Sight: Multi-Year Planning to Meet and Reduce Humanitarian Needs in Protracted Crises* (New York: OCHA Policy and Study Series, July 2015), 4.
11 *One Humanity: Shared Responsibility*, para. 80.
12 Agenda for Humanity, *Platform for Action, Commitments, and Transformations*, www.agendaforhumanity. org. In the initial presentation of the Agenda in the Secretary-General's February 2016 speech, there was a transformation that was specific to gender-based violence and sexual violence, but it has since been seemingly folded into the one on empowering and protecting women and girls, while a new one that more broadly refers to disadvantaged populations was established.
13 OCHA, *Leaving No One Behind: Humanitarian Effectiveness in the Age of the Sustainable Development Goals* (New York: OCHA Policy Analysis and Innovation Section, Policy Development and Studies Branch, 2016), 5.
14 *Stockholm Declaration on Addressing Fragility and Building Peace in a Changing World*, 5 April 2016, www. pbsbdialogue.org/media/filer_public/1e/23/1e237c73-5518-4a03-9a87-b1aa6d914d20/stockholm_ declaration.pdf.
15 International Federation of Red Cross and Red Crescent Societies, *World Disasters Report 2018: Leaving No One Behind* (Geneva: IFRC, 2018).
16 *GHA 2019*, 22; Paul Knox Clarke, *The State of the Humanitarian System* (London: ALNAP, 2018), 17; OCHA, *Global Humanitarian Overview (GHO) 2019*, 4; OCHA, *World Humanitarian 2018*, 6.
17 *GHO 2015*, 4; *GHO 2016*, 4; *GHO 2017*, 2; *GHO 2018*, 3; *GHO 2019*, 4.
18 *World Humanitarian 2017*, 6; *World Humanitarian 2018*, 6.
19 OCHA, *GHO 2019*, 18.
20 OCHA, *GHO 2019*, 14; *GHA 2019*, 23.
21 *GHA 2019*, 16; World Bank data cited in OCHA, *GHO 2019*, 13.
22 OCHA, *Global Humanitarian Review 2019*, 19.
23 *GHA 2019*, 35.
24 Ibid., 64.
25 *GHA 2019*, 27, 34–35; and Knox Clarke, *The State of the Humanitarian System*, 17.
26 OCHA, *Leaving No One Behind: Humanitarian Effectiveness in the Age of the Sustainable Development Goals* (New York: OCHA Policy Analysis and Innovation Section, Policy Development and Studies Branch, 2016), 34.

27 ODI and Center for Global Development, *Doing Cash Differently: How Cash Transfers Can Transform Humanitarian Aid (Report of the High-Level Panel on Humanitarian Cash Transfers)* (ODI, September 2015); Joseph Hanlon, Armando Barrientos, and David Hulme, *Just Give Money to the Poor: The Development Revolution from the Global South* (Sterling, VA: Kumarian Press, 2010).

28 *GHA 2019*, 13.

29 OCHA, *No Time to Retreat: First Annual Synthesis Report on Progress since the World Humanitarian Summit* (OCHA Policy Branch, November 2017), 39; OCHA, *Staying the Course: Delivering on the Ambition of the World Humanitarian Summit—Agenda for Humanity Annual Synthesis Report 2018* (New York: OCHA Policy Branch, December 2018), 39–57.

30 OCHA, *Staying the Course*, 41.

31 The establishment of the Joint Steering Committee was a recommendation of the Report of the Secretary-General, *Repositioning the United Nations Development System to Deliver on the 2030 Agenda: Ensuring a Better Future for All*, 11 July 2017, para. 81.

32 Victoria Metcalfe-Hough, Wendy Fenton, and Lydia Poole, *Grand Bargain Annual Independent Report 2019* (London: HPG/ODI, June 2019), 3.

33 Since 2018 the Overseas Development Institute has produced an annual "Leave No One Behind" Index, but it makes no reference to humanitarian issues.

34 IFRC, *World Disasters Report 2018*, 214.

35 Humanitarian Policy Group, *Time to Let Go: Remaking Humanitarian Action for the Modern Era* (London: ODI, April 2016); Marc Dubois, *The New Humanitarian Basics* (London: HPG Working Paper, May 2018).

36 Knox Clarke, *The State of the Humanitarian System*, 21.

37 Data on attacks on aid workers shows increases, particularly among local staff as a proportion of all attacks, and this intensifies in the wake of the withdrawal of international staff. See the Aid Worker Security Database, https://aidworkersecurity.org. This security situation results in a pull-out of inter-nationals, though they retain leadership; see Antonio Donini and Daniel Maxwell, "From Face-to-Face to Face-to-Screen: Remote Management, Effectiveness and Accountability of Humanitarian Action, in Insecure Environments," *International Review of the Red Cross* 95, no. 890 (2014): 383–412.

38 Atta Al-Mannan Bakhit, *Humanitarian Challenges: Perspective from the South and Islamic Countries*, Annual WFP Partnership Consultation, October 29–30, 2014.

ADDITIONAL READING

Atsushi Hanatani, Oscar A. Gómez, and Chigumi Kawaguchi, eds., *Crisis Management Beyond the Humanitarian–Development Nexus* (London: Routledge, 2018).

Peter J. Hoffman and Thomas G. Weiss, *Humanitarianism, War, and Politics: Solferino to Syria and Beyond* (Lanham, MD: Rowman & Littlefield, 2018).

International Federation of Red Cross and Red Crescent Societies, *World Disasters Report 2018: Leaving No One Behind* (Geneva: IFRC, 2018).

Homi Kharas, John W. McArthur, and Izumi Ohno, eds., *Leave No One Behind: Time for Specifics on the Sustainable Development Goals* (Washington, DC: Brookings, 2019).

OCHA, *Leaving No One Behind: Humanitarian Effectiveness in the Age of the Sustainable Development Goals* (New York: OCHA Policy Analysis and Innovation Section, Policy Development and Studies Branch, 2016).

10

MIGRATION AND DEVELOPMENT IN THE UN GLOBAL COMPACTS

Nicholas R. Micinski

In 2015, more than 1.2 million people crossed the Mediterranean, many hoping to migrate to or apply for asylum in Europe, making migrants and refugees a priority on the global agenda.[1] While this number was large for Europe, the majority of refugees and asylum seekers reside in host countries in the Global South. At the center of debates about migration and development is global inequality—inequality in the burden-sharing of refugees and inequality in the global economy that makes migrating to the Global North so rewarding. The Sustainable Development Goals (SDGs) and the global compacts for refugees and migrants incorporate more complex understandings of migration and development; they also represent new opportunities to address global inequalities head on.

In 2018, the UN member states adopted the two compacts to renew efforts to help displaced people around the world. Both documents emphasize the role that less developed economies play as a push factor for migration, while also acknowledging the benefits of migration and diaspora to development. Long before the compacts, the UN system was engaged in research, policy promotion, and project implementation connecting migration and development. Historically, UN agencies and special representatives have been key actors in linking "migration and development" and have exercised principal roles in its global governance.

This chapter examines the role of the UN in the emergence and evolution of migration and development policies. First, it describes the concept of the migration–development (M–D) nexus, the types of M–D projects, and the contradictory assumptions of the M–D nexus. Migration includes both emigration and immigration, in addition to forced displacement and labor migration. Development is conceived broadly to mean human, social, and economic development for states in the Global South as well as the Global North. Second, the chapter traces over two decades how the M–D nexus became embedded throughout the UN system. The chapter turns to the key innovations in the global compacts for migration and development and the role that UN development actors will play in implementation—including the UN Development Programme (UNDP), the International Organization for Migration (IOM), the International Labour Organization (ILO), and the Office of the UN High Commissioner for Refugees (UNHCR).

The migration–development nexus

The M–D nexus emphasizes the interdependence between migration and development policies. A policy discourse has emerged around the nexus (largely from the Global North), which proposes to maximize the positive gains that migration can bring to both countries of origin and reception in both the North and Global South.[2] M–D policies aim to address the root causes of migration—like poverty and poor governance—by shifting the focus from migrant-receiving states to migrant-sending states. M–D policies target migrants before they depart in order to remove push factors for emigration and engage diaspora to invest in their communities back home. The M–D nexus is a Janus-faced coin: it identifies both development components of migration and migration components of development. For example, the lack of development, poverty, and political instability are seen as key drivers for migration and displacement. Development programs target different stages of migration—like pre-departure, resettlement, repatriation, or local integration—to remove economic push factors before they leave or to improve the quality of life of migrants and refugees during or after they have moved. While displacement creates certain vulnerabilities and exacerbates inequality, development initiatives have the potential to provide livelihoods and other forms of support. However, Daniel Naujoks points out that vulnerable migrants and refugees are often left out of many of the benefits of development.[3]

The other side of the coin is that emigration from developing countries impacts their development by bringing new resources and opportunities from abroad. Ninna Sørensen et al. used the term "migration–development nexus" in an influential journal article that shifted policy debates from the negative aspects of immigrant integration to the positive contributions of emigrants to economic development in migrant-sending countries.[4] The authors described different ways that migrants are a resource for development: for example, the diaspora send remittances, migrant entrepreneurs organize transnational investments, and migrant women provide economic stability for their families by working abroad. However, immigrants and refugees can have a negative impact on development because they are an additional burden on government services and labor markets in receiving countries.[5]

M–D projects broadly fit within four types of goals: to build state capacity to manage migration; to improve security related to migration or displacement; to achieve more traditional development outcomes, like improving education, health, or employment; and to facilitate research and knowledge-sharing. For example, the European Union (EU) funds M–D projects to build state capacity throughout Africa to train border guards, install biometric technologies at checkpoints, and establish birth registration systems; while funding for security goes to projects that engage migrants in peacebuilding and conflict prevention.[6] Some funding goes to campaigns to raise awareness about the risks of emigration and about migrants' rights. One typical M–D project aimed to create "jobs and economic opportunities through sustainable management of the environment in transit zones and departure in Niger."[7] Other M–D projects target economic opportunities, job training, food security, resilience, health and social services, education, and other youth activities. Sometimes states use M–D projects to engage their diaspora abroad to foster deeper relationships and to increase remittances and investments. Other projects focus on moving remittances from informal to formal channels and reducing transaction costs. The UN itself has promoted three types of transfers (3Ts) involved in migration and development: the transfer of people between different places, the transfer of knowledge, and the transfer of financial capital.[8]

The M–D policies that emerged in the Global North can be classified into three types of regimes: policies that focus on *containing and controlling* immigrants into countries with development as a second thought; policies that *selectively* choose immigrants with higher skills or social status and selectively disburse development aid; and policies that *liberalize* labor markets, asylum processes, or dual citizenship in migrant-receiving countries to encourage development.[9] The tension within M–D policy regimes is reflective of Hollifield's "liberal paradox": liberal states need open markets to facilitate free trade and economic growth, but must restrict the movement of people to guard against political risks for their citizens.[10] Similarly, M–D projects push for more open markets and capital flows, but reinforce borders and control the movement of migrants or potential migrants. This stands in contrast to neoliberal theories that posit that economic growth is based on free trade and the free movement of people.

Despite its popularity among policy analysts in the Global North, the M–D nexus is based on questionable and contradictory assumptions. First, most M–D programs between developed (donor) and developing countries assume that development aid targeted at reducing poverty will also reduce emigration, but a plethora of economic studies show a different relationship.[11] In the poorest countries, increases in GDP per capita are associated with increased emigration.[12] Economic development only decreases emigration in countries with per capita incomes (PPP) above $10,715; for example, economic development in Namibia ($11,229), Libya ($11,956), or Albania ($13,345) could decrease emigration.[13] This "migration hump" is so labeled because the relationship can be charted as an inverse U–curve. Second, M–D programs assume that remittances are a potential source for economic development; but this relationship is also unclear. Remittances reduce household-level poverty when families hit challenging times, but the evidence is mixed and inconclusive that remittances significantly contribute to economic growth.[14] Remittances can have a negative impact as well by increasing price inflation or reducing labor market participation.[15] Third, M–D programs assume that irregular immigration in developed countries is connected to a lack of state capacity to manage migration in developing countries. This leads to M–D funding for state-building activities in migration-sending countries like new security technologies and databases, training for border guards, and birth registration drives. The impact of this assumption is more documentation and control of potential migrants, rather than reducing poverty as a push factor. Unsettlingly, state-building activities could undermine democratic institutions by increasing a state's capacity to control and repress its citizens, creating even more push factors for emigration. Finally, longer walls and more border guards do not prevent irregular migration; instead, migrants and refugees are pushed to take more precarious routes or pay higher fees to smugglers.[16]

The UN's history of migration and development

Most scholars point to the 1994 International Conference on Population and Development as the first moment within the UN when migration was linked with development.[17] At the conference, 179 countries adopted the Programme of Action (often called the Cairo Programme of Action) that articulated an agenda for improving the well-being of all individuals, and placed inequality and human rights—and the rights of migrants—at the center of development. While earlier UN conferences on population in 1974 and 1984 included references to migration, the 1994 Programme of Action systematically addressed how states would tackle the root causes of migration through development. The document described the approach to development for documented and undocumented migrants, in addition to refugees and asylum seekers, and the role of international organizations.[18] In addition, the Programme of Action calls on states to increase the integration of immigrants through long-term residency, facilitate family reunification, prevent discrimination and xenophobia, and prevent trafficking and exploitation. The agreement also predicted future bilateral and multilateral agreements on return and readmission of irregular migrants.[19] Following the conference, the General Assembly added to the title of the Population Commission; it became the Commission on Population and Development (CPD). The assembly also appointed the CPD to assess the implementation of the Programme of Action.

The CPD agenda regularly featured migration and development throughout the 1990s and 2000s. In 1997, the 30th session of the CPD focused on international migration and development, with the report somewhat controversially rejecting population growth, environmental change, poverty, and poor governance as the root causes of international migration.[20] Rather, the report emphasized that individuals migrate for a mix of reasons including inequality and wage differentials. In addition, the report found that the "use of official development assistance to reduce migration pressures may not be effective because the level of aid required is usually very high and because piecemeal aid initiatives are unlikely to be successful."[21] Instead, the CPD called for better data on migration and a coherent theory of migration and development.[22] Following on, the United Nations Institute for Training and Research created the International Migration Policy Programme in 1998 to facilitate research, data gathering, and training on migration management.

Another way that migration and development were linked was in the 1990 International Convention on the Protection of the Rights of All Migrant Workers and Members of Their Families. The convention defined the human rights of migrant workers and promoted humane and equitable working conditions. While the treaty entered into force in 2003, by 2019 only 39 states were signatories (for example, Mexico, Morocco, and Turkey), signaling more disagreement than consensus on migrant workers' rights. Many officials within the UN system interpreted the failure to gain broad support for the treaty as an eroding of support for future international cooperation on migration.

A third way that migration and development were connected was through Regional Consultative Processes (RCP). The Inter-Governmental Consultations on Asylum, Refugees and Migration, founded in 1985, helped to facilitate informal discussions, sharing best practices, and attempting to find common approaches to migration among 16 countries.[23] Throughout the 1990s and 2000s, RCPs were established in other regions (although they are not necessarily about geographic proximity) like Eastern Europe, Central America, West Africa, and Southern Africa. More recently, IOM has been a key initiator, funder, and coordinator of RCPs worldwide. Another important regional initiative was the 1989 International Conference on Central American Refugees (CIREFCA), which UNHCR and UNDP implemented jointly, channeling more than $400 million to development projects in the region to help the displaced people.[24]

Despite the overarching pessimism about a global migration regime, ideas about a "missing regime" circulated amongst academics and policy makers, including the New Regime for Orderly Movements of People (NIROMP) coordinated by Bimal Ghosh. Former UN Assistant Secretary-General Michael Doyle led the Migration Working Group, which published a report in 2003 on migration and the UN system that resulted in the creation of the Global Commission on International Migration (GCIM).[25] The GCIM held further consultations and discussion from 2003–2005, which led to the report: "Migration in an Interconnected World: New Directions for Action."[26] The GCIM report featured an entire chapter on migration and development, emphasizing the lack of integration of migration into development policies and the lack of capacity in most countries to plan for M–D policies. The report also raised concerns that the brain drain of health professionals could undermine efforts to achieve the Millennium Development Goals (MDGs).[27] Interestingly, the report argues that governments should not confiscate remittances because they are a private resource.[28] Finally, the GCIM points to hometown associations and other diaspora initiatives that funnel investments from abroad back to their country of origin.

Secretary-General Kofi Annan responded to the GCIM report by creating the Global Migration Group and appointing in 2006 Peter Sutherland, an Irish politician who was the founding director-general of the World Trade Organization (WTO) and former chairman of Goldman Sachs, as the special representative of the Secretary-General (SRSG) on international migration. The Global Migration Group (GMG) began as a coordination meeting among UN agencies working on issues related to migration in Geneva.[29] Twenty-two UN organizations or entities met to share information on migration and coordinate their related programs. For example, UNHCR leads on refugee issues, IOM on migrants or mix migration flows, ILO on migrant workers, UNDP on M–D policies, United Nations Office on Drugs and Crime (UNODC) on human trafficking, and Office of the High Commissioner for Human Rights (OHCHR) on the rights of migrants and refugees—to name just a few. The GMG met regularly with agencies and conducted work through working groups and task forces related to data and research; migration, human rights, and gender; capacity development; and migration and decent work. For example, the working group on data created migration profiles that facilitated uniform measurement of migrant stocks, population size, and development indicators (like life expectancy, literacy rates, education, and GDP) for the 2030 agenda. Another GMG working group focused on mainstreaming migration into national development strategies and published a handbook on the topic in 2010.[30] It articulates a similar vision of the M–D nexus described above, especially as represented by the 3Ts (transfer of people, transfer of knowledge, and transfer of financial capital), and provides checklists and sample terms of references for national M–D committees to incorporate all stakeholders. The overall reputation of the GMG was somewhat weak because it lacked commitment by UN agencies as the exclusive coordination tool; rather, the GMG was a space for consultation and information-sharing among the agencies.[31]

For years, the General Assembly called for a high-level event at the UN related to migration and development. Finally, in 2006 Sutherland's appointment led to preparations for the UN High-Level Dialogue on International Migration and Development. The agenda focused on the impact of migration and development, human rights of migrants, capacity-building, and best practices.[32] The summary document reported:

> Participants felt that it was essential to address the root causes of international migration to ensure that people migrated out of choice rather than necessity. They observed that people often had to migrate because of poverty, conflict, human rights violations, poor governance or lack of employment.[33]

This language represented a significant shift in the approach to M–D since the 1997 CPD report that focused on wage inequality rather than more general root causes of migration. This shift is representative of a wider acceptance within the UN and other international policy circles that M–D policies should focus on "root causes" like poverty, conflict, and governance—while academics still question the measurable impact of each as a push factor and the efficiency of M–D aid.

States agreed at the High-Level Dialogue to create a new space for states to engage outside the UN system: the Global Forum on Migration and Development (GFMD). The forum is a state-led, informal, and non-binding process where states from both the North and Global South share best practices and engage in debates about migration and development. By 2014, SRSG Sutherland concluded: "The Forum created a safe space in which stakeholders from around the world can gather, learn, deliberate, and foster cooperation—far from the destructive distractions of domestic politics."[34] The GFMD holds roundtable discussions on data and research on migration and development; diagnostic tools for what countries need; and evaluations of current policies. Despite being outside the UN system, the secretary-general attends the meeting every year and the GFMD's small support unit is supplemented by staff from the SRSG and the GMG. GFMD has grown in the last decade: the forum did not initially include civil society and did not have discussions on the human rights of migrants on the agenda until 2010.[35] More recently, Civil Society Days have become a staple of the GFMD that include trade unions, migrant and diaspora organizations, the private sector, and recruitment agencies, in addition to side events organized by the ILO, IOM, World Bank, and other UN agencies.

The GFMD's main focus has been on migration and development, in addition to discussions of social cohesion, irregular migration, and data. Looking at recent outcome documents, M–D tops the number of recommendations behind only governance and cooperation; among M–D recommendations, the forum focused most on remittances and diaspora policies.[36]

At the 2008 GFMD, UN Secretary-General Ban Ki-moon emphasized that

> only by safeguarding the rights of migrants and ensuring that they are treated with the dignity and respect due to any human being, can governments create the conditions for migrants to contribute to development. Exploitation is the antithesis of development.[37]

Despite the Secretary-General's comments, the intersection of human rights, exploitation, and development has never become a priority. The GFMD remains relentlessly positive; for example, the 2018 tagline was "Honoring international commitments to unlock the potential of all migrants for development"[38]—reflecting states' understandings of migrants as a resource for development. Note that the tagline is "migrants for development," not development for migrants. Much of the policy focus in the first decade of the GFMD was on integrating migration policies into national development strategies. One long-standing critique is that the GFMD, and global migration governance in general, is a "talking shop" and obsessed with research and data, rather than commitments.[39] Supporters counter that informal, non-binding meetings are a space for socialization and norm diffusion.[40]

The evolving discourse on migration and development—primarily during the GFMD annual meetings—expanded the M–D agenda beyond simply migrants driving development. For example, the statements from country representatives at the GFMD mentioned more often a topic previously largely avoided: the human rights of migrants.[41] By 2013, the UN had hosted the second High-Level Dialogue on International Migration and Development and discussed issues as diverse as the "human rights of all migrants," labor migration, exploitation, public opinion, and M–D in the post-2015 development agenda. The next year the Swedish chairperson made inclusive development a key part of the discussions at the 2014 GFMD in preparation for the SDGs.

Unlike the MDGs, migration was included in the 2030 Agenda for Sustainable Development. Despite not being listed as a separate goal,[42] the intersectional nature of migration makes it relevant to all 17 Sustainable Development Goals (SDGs), and migration is explicitly included in seven of the 169 targets (see Box 10.1) and at least seven of the 232 official indicators. Throughout the consultations for the SDGs, UN agencies and the GMG contributed position papers on how migration should be included in the 2030 agenda. These position papers echo previous understandings of the M–D nexus by noting the value of remittance and diaspora investments, but are outspoken on labor and human rights of migrants.[43] This framing of migration and development was largely included in the finalized SDGs, particularly with a focus on measuring and reducing the cost of remittances and ending human trafficking. The SDGs prioritize data collection by requiring all indicators to disaggregate migration status as one of the demographic variables. Migration intersects with other targets like brain drain related to healthcare workers and securing the mobility of students. Others have pointed to the inclusion of migration in SDG 8.3 on decent work for all and Goal 5.4 to "recognize and value unpaid care and domestic work" because they acknowledge the gendered impact on migration and work.[44] A shortcoming of the SDGs is the absence of refugees and internally displaced persons in development.

Box 10.1 Migration in the SDGs

The SDGs cover a range of policy areas that intersect with migration issues. Below are the goals, targets, and indicators that explicitly mention migration or migration-related areas. [Emphasis added.]

Goal 5. Achieve gender equality and empower all women and girls

- 5.2 Eliminate all forms of violence against all women and girls in the public and private spheres, including *trafficking* and sexual and other types of exploitation

Goal 8. Promote sustained, inclusive and sustainable economic growth, full and productive employment and decent work for all

- 8.7 Take immediate and effective measures to eradicate forced labour, end modern slavery and *human trafficking* and secure the prohibition and elimination of the worst forms of child labour, including recruitment and use of child soldiers, and by 2025 end child labour in all its forms
- 8.8 Protect labour rights and promote safe and secure working environments for all workers, including *migrant workers*, in particular women migrants, and those in precarious employment
  - 8.8.1 Frequency rates of fatal and non-fatal occupational injuries, by sex and *migrant status*
  - 8.8.2 Level of national compliance with labour rights (freedom of association and collective bargaining) based on International Labour Organization (ILO) textual sources and national legislation, by sex and *migrant status*

Goal 10. Reduce inequality within and among countries

- 10.7 Facilitate orderly, safe, regular and responsible *migration and mobility* of people, including through the implementation of planned and well-managed *migration policies*
  - 10.7.1 *Recruitment cost* borne by employee as a proportion of monthly income earned in country of destination
  - 10.7.2 Number of countries with *migration policies* that facilitate orderly, safe, regular and responsible *migration and mobility* of people
- 10.c By 2030, reduce to less than 3 per cent the transaction costs of *migrant remittances* and eliminate *remittance corridors* with costs higher than 5 per cent
  - 10.c.1 *Remittance* costs as a proportion of the amount remitted

Goal 16. Promote peaceful and inclusive societies for sustainable development, provide access to justice for all and build effective, accountable and inclusive institutions at all levels

- 16.2 End abuse, exploitation, *trafficking* and all forms of violence against and torture of children
  - 16.2.2 Number of victims of *human trafficking* per 100,000 population, by sex, age and form of exploitation

Goal 17. Strengthen the means of implementation and revitalize the Global Partnership for Sustainable Development

  - 17.3.2 Volume of *remittances* (in United States dollars) as a proportion of total GDP
- 17.18 By 2020, enhance capacity-building support to developing countries, including for least developed countries and small island developing States, to increase significantly the availability of high-quality, timely and reliable data disaggregated by income, gender, age, race, ethnicity, *migratory status*, disability, geographic location and other characteristics relevant in national contexts

Source: UNSTATS, "SDG Indicators," Sustainable Development Goals. Accessed 6 September 2019. https://unstats.un.org/sdgs/indicators/indicators-list.

One major critique of the UN's adoption of the M–D nexus, and the development industry writ large, is that the M–D nexus has depoliticized the policy choices and economic systems that sustain inequality.[45] For example, M–D policies are often state-centric and assume that state-led development projects benefit individuals and local communities. The M–D policies and the SDGs naturalize or normalize the conditions that make emigration, and thus M–D aid, necessary because they assume that more integration into the global economy is always a good thing but further economic integration could, for example, kill off local economies, especially small-scale farmers who are forced to migrate to cities or to richer countries.[46] The UN's solutions are technical fixes—e.g., reducing the transaction costs for remittances—rather than political—e.g., the legal and economic inclusion of migrants and refugees. Technical solutions aim to improve livelihoods for migrants without giving them rights to local integration or citizenship. Instead of probing the underlying causes of lower development and global inequality, the M–D nexus focuses on smoothing the edges of development by creating spaces for migrants to participate in the economic system without changing it.

New York Declaration for Refugees and Migrants

The UN hosted the Summit for Refugees and Migrants on 19 September 2016. Member states agreed the New York Declaration for Refugees and Migrants, which consolidated their previous commitments on migrants and refugees and laid out a negotiation process for the two global compacts. The NY Declaration was a significant accomplishment because it affirmed the principles of human rights for all migrants and agreed to greater international cooperation on migration.

The NY Declaration detailed a more complex understanding of the impact of migration and displacement on the development prospects of origin, transit, and receiving countries. This more nuanced conceptualization of the M–D nexus goes beyond simply remittances and diaspora. The declaration calls for mainstreaming migration in national plans for development, peacebuilding, humanitarian assistance, and human rights;[47] it also advocates for community-based development programs aimed at helping refugees and local communities.[48] One of the document's most progressive elements advocates for the integration of refugees into labor markets in order to drive development.[49] Finally, the declaration calls for more coordinated and joint responses to migration and development.

Overall, migrants' rights advocates hailed the NY Declaration as an ambitious response to the global crisis, while states were willing to sign the declaration because it was a non-binding agreement. The most tangible institutional outcome of the summit was that the International Organization for Migration officially joined the UN system as a "related organization," notwithstanding criticism that the IOM had not altered sufficiently its mandate to reflect the UN's normative principles.[50]

Global Compact for Safe, Orderly and Regular Migration

The momentum from the success of including M–D in the SDGs and the NY Declaration continued in the Global Compact for Safe, Orderly and Regular Migration (also referred to as the Global Compact for Migration, or GCM). During the negotiation phase of the GCM, two thematic consultations looked at development and poverty as drivers of migration and the contributions of migrants and diaspora to development. The co-facilitators recognized a significant shift in the discourse around migration to a more complex understanding of "migration decision-making processes": that people move for mixed reasons including economic, social, and political factors. In addition, country delegations and specialists discussed the "migration hump" and acknowledged that global inequality and wage differentials were important factors for migration, not only poverty.[51] The co-facilitators wrote that "migration is not a problem to be solved, but a reality to be well-managed."[52]

After nearly two years of negotiations, the finalized text was to be adopted in December 2018 by an intergovernmental meeting in Morocco. However, in mid-September 2019, extremists in Europe used social media to push misinformation that the GCM created a "right to migrate," which would violate state sovereignty.[53] The online campaign—which included a petition to "Stop Migration Pact"—reached a fever pitch when the Belgian government collapsed over the GCM.[54] Ultimately, 152 countries adopted the compact with five countries voting against and 12 countries abstaining.[55]

The final text outlined 23 objectives ranging from better data collection and information provision to saving lives of migrants and preventing trafficking. The GCM is anchored in the UN's previous work on human rights, development, and migration. The most extensive discussion of M–D in the GCM is around diaspora engagement and remittances (Objectives 19 and 20), but other objectives and actions articulate a more nuanced understanding of M–D (see Box 10.2). For example, Objective 18 encourages skills partnerships between countries of destination and origin and Objective 21 acknowledges the impact on development from migrants who have returned. Objective 20 recognizes the importance of access for migrant women to banking and remittances. The compact calls for implementation through research centers, data collection, a new capacity-building mechanism, and a startup fund to finance projects.[56] The compact also established a new architecture of global migration governance in which states and UN agencies coordinate through a new UN Network for Migration led by IOM and meet to reflect

---

Box 10.2 Development in the Global Compact for Migration (GCM)

References to development are scattered throughout the 23 objectives and 187 actions in the GCM. Below are summaries of the most relevant objectives and actions.

1 **Collect and utilize accurate and disaggregated data as a basis for evidence-based policies**

   d   Collect and analyze disaggregated data on the contribution of migrants and diasporas to sustainable development

2 **Minimize the adverse drivers and structural factors that compel people to leave their country of origin**

   d   Invest in SDGs and Addis Action Agenda at the local, national and regional level
   e   Invest in human capital development to reduce youth unemployment and brain drain
   f   Strengthen cooperation between humanitarian and development actors

18 **Invest in skills development and facilitate mutual recognition of skills, qualifications and competences**

   a–d Develop standards for mutual recognition of foreign qualifications
   e–h Build bilateral and global skills partnerships between countries of destination and origin and the private sector

---

19 Create conditions for migrants and diasporas to fully contribute to sustainable development in all countries

  b   Integrate migration into development planning at local, national, regional, and global levels

  c   Research non-financial contribution of diaspora to development

  d   Establish national ministries, offices, or advisory boards for diaspora

  e–f Target diaspora investment and entrepreneurship

  g   Enable diaspora voting and political involvement in country of origin

  i–j Help private sector and diaspora transfer knowledge and skills

20 Promote faster, safer and cheaper transfer of remittances and foster financial inclusion of migrants

  a   Reduce transaction cost for remittances to below 3 percent and eliminate remittance corridors over 5 percent

  b   Promote UN International Day of Family Remittances

  c   Prevent money laundering through remittances corridors

  g   Develop programs to promote investments by remittance senders in local development

  h–i Enable migrant women to open bank accounts and financial literacy training

21 Cooperate in facilitating safe and dignified return and readmission, as well as sustainable reintegration

  h–i Support returned migrants to reintegrate and contribute to development

on their progress every four years in an International Migration Review Forum. These new institutions are in their early days and their impact is not yet apparent.

Global Compact on Refugees

The Global Compact on Refugees (GCR) was negotiated in parallel to the GCM from 2016–2018. To many analysts, the GCR was more advanced than the GCM because it built on the well-developed international refugee regime, anchored in the 1951 refugee convention, 1967 protocol, and the norm of non-refoulement. In addition, UNHCR has a solid mandate and clear role as the lead UN agency for refugees—unlike IOM, which was previously not in the UN system and had no normative mandate or specific role within the UN system. At the core of the GCR is the Comprehensive Refugee Response Framework (CRRF) that introduces a step-by-step approach to long-term planning that engages all stakeholders from the outset. In the case of an emergency, states can activate a Support Platform and host solidarity conferences to engage donors and development actors in early planning. Finally, states committed to reflect on their progress at the Global Refugee Forum every four years.

The M–D nexus does not generally refer to refugees because theoretically increased development should reduce economic migration, not forced migration. However, based on the assumption that inadequate state capacity leads to irregular migration, some M–D policies target capacity-building for states to create more predictable responses to large movements of refugees. The GCR established an Asylum Capacity Support Group within UNHCR to facilitate capacity-building for early warning and contingency planning, refugee registration, and security. The CRRF introduces a new framing of M–D by advocating for reduced pressure on host communities by encouraging refugee self-reliance—meaning jobs, business development, and alternative livelihoods. In this framing, development can empower refugees by starting new businesses that contribute to local economies. The compact is unclear about how refugees and other vulnerable populations will be transformed into "self-reliant" entrepreneurs.

The GCR also has references to how development can help refugees. For example, the compact highlights that additional resources are needed to achieve the SDGs in communities with large refugee communities. The document suggests that development cooperation should be for both host and refugee communities, and that resources should also be allocated to countries of origin to encourage repatriation. Finally, new M–D aid should be additional to resources already allocated to host countries. The GCR affirms that planning should be guided by the UN Resident Coordinator, who should cooperate with humanitarian and development actors as well as empower country leadership and local ownership throughout implementation. The document emphasizes local integration of refugees who can contribute to development through new jobs and livelihoods. The compact envisions planning for environmental impact and sustainable development when working for refugees (para. 79) and supporting states to build civil registries (para. 82) to prevent statelessness. In addition, the private sector and cities or local municipalities should be included as stakeholders in planning.

Conclusion

This chapter began by describing the concept of the M–D nexus and the UN's role in promoting and institutionalizing M–D within the UN development system (UNDS). The M–D nexus emphasizes the positive contributions of migrants to development, but often it neglects how development can improve the lives of migrants. Migration and development grew in popularity and importance in both UN and non-UN forums—CPD, SRSG for Migration, GFMD, GMG, High-Level Dialogue, SDGs, NY Declaration—culminating most recently in the global compacts for migration and on refugees.

During the early years, the CPD was critical of the "root causes" of migration—instead focusing on inequality and wage differentials—and was skeptical that the development aid could have a substantial impact on migration. The more that M–D became institutionalized, the more all-purpose M–D has become—funding such projects as skills trainings, youth workshops, and birth registration drives. Within the UN system, M–D programs focused on incorporating diaspora engagement and remittances into national development planning. This simplistic understanding of M–D has become more sophisticated in the global compacts and promises to open new avenues for increasing the impact of M–D policies. While M–D is not a solution for every problem in migration or development, the UNDS is recognizing the importance of supporting migrants to use their skills, capital, and communities to improve lives in both their countries of origin and destination.

NOTES

1 UNHCR, "Operational Portal: Mediterranean Situation," 3 December 2019, https://data2.unhcr.org/en/situations/mediterranean.
2 Sandra Lavenex and Rahel Kunz, "The Migration–Development Nexus in EU External Relations," *Journal of European Integration* 30, no. 3 (2009): 439–457.

3 Daniel Naujoks, "The Mobility Mandala: Conceptualizing Human Mobility in the Sustainable Development Framework," *International Studies Association, 27 March 2019* (Toronto).

4 Ninna Sørensen, Nicholas Van Hear, and Poul Engberg-Pedersen, "The Migration–Development Nexus: Evidence and Policy Options," *International Migration* 40, no. 5 (2002): 49–73.

5 Naujoks, "The Mobility Mandala," 20.

6 European Commission, "Themes," EU Emergency Trust Fund for Africa, https://ec.europa.eu/trustfundforafrica/thematic.

7 In 2017, the EU allocated €30 million for the "Création d'emplois et d'opportunités économiques à travers une gestion durable de l'environnement dans les zones de transit et départ au Niger" to be implemented by the Belgian, Italian, and Dutch development agencies.

8 Sohpie Nonnenmacher, Ashmita Naik, and Laura Chappel, *Mainstreaming Migration into Development Planning: A Handbook for Policy-Makers and Practitioners* (Geneva: Global Migration Group, 2010), 16.

9 Sørensen, Van Hear, and Engberg-Pedersen, "The Migration–Development Nexus."

10 James F. Hollifield, *Immigrants, Markets, and States: The Political Economy of Postwar Europe* (Cambridge, MA: Harvard University Press, 1992).

11 Nicholas R Micinski and Thomas G Weiss, "The European Migration Crisis: Can Development Agencies Do Better?" *FUNDS Brief 37*, 2016, www.futureun.org/media/archive1/briefings/FUNDS_Brief37_European_Migrant_Crisis_Jan2016.pdf.

12 Philip Martin and J. Edward Taylor, "The Anatomy of a Migration Hump," *Development Strategy, Employment, and Migration: Insights from Models* (Paris: Organisation for Economic Co-operation and Development, 1996), 43–62; Henry Telli, "Less Poverty, More Emigration: Understanding Migrant Flows from Developing Countries," *Migration and Development* 3, no. 1 (2014): 54–72; Hein de Haas, "Turning the Tide? Why Development Will Not Stop Migration," *Development and Change* 38, no. 5 (2007): 819–841.

13 This number has been adjusted for inflation to 2018 US dollars. The original study determined the threshold to be $7,348 in PPP 2000 prices. See: Jean-Claude Berthelemy, Monica Beuran, and Mathilde Maurel, "Aid and Migration: Substitutes or Complements?" *World Development* 37, no. 10 (2009): 1589–1599. Examples of GDP per capita PPP in 2018 are from *World Economic Outlook Database*, April 2019, International Monetary Fund, www.imf.org/external/pubs/ft/weo/2019/01/weodata/index.aspx.

14 Adolfo Barajas et al., "Do Workers' Remittances Promote Economic Growth?" *International Monetary Fund Working Paper*, 2009; Ronald Ravinesh Kumar, "Exploring the Interactive Effects of Remittances, Financial Development and ICT in Sub-Saharan Africa: An ARDL Bounds Approach," *African Journal of Economic and Sustainable Development* 1, no. 3 (2012): 214–242; Gyan Pradhan, Mukti Upadhyay, and Kamal Upadhyaya, "Remittances and Economic Growth in Developing Countries," *European Journal of Development Research* 20, no. 3 (2008): 497–506; Simon Feeny, Sasi Iamsiraroj, and Mark McGillivray, "Remittances and Economic Growth: Larger Impacts in Smaller Countries?" *Journal of Development Studies* 50, no. 8 (2014): 1055–1066; D. O. Olayungbo and Ahmod Quadri, "Remittances, Financial Development and Economic Growth in Sub-Saharan African Countries: Evidence from a PMG-ARDL Approach," *Financial Innovation* 5, no. 9 (2019): 1–25.

15 Barajas et al., "Do Workers' Remittances Promote Economic Growth?" 5–6.

16 Derek Lutterbeck, "Policing Migration in the Mediterranean," *Mediterranean Politics* 11, no. 1 (March 2006): 59–82; Peter Andreas, *Border Games: Policing the US–Mexico Divide* (Ithaca, NY: Cornell University Press, 2000).

17 United Nation Population Fund, "International Cairo Programme of Action 1994," 5–13 September 1994, www.unfpa.org/sites/default/files/event-pdf/PoA_en.pdf.

18 Ibid., 83–92.

19 Ibid., 89.

20 ECOSOC, "Concise Report on World Population Monitoring, 1997: International Migration and Development," Commission on Population and Development, 30th session, 24–28 February 1997, Document no. E/CN.9/1997/2, 21–22.

21 Ibid., 23.

22 Ibid., 24–25.

23 Alexander Betts and Lena Kainz, "The History of Global Migration Governance," University of Oxford, Refugee Studies Centre Working Paper No. 122, July 2017, 4.

24 Alexander Betts, "Nowhere to Go: How Governments in the Americas Are Bungling the Migration Crisis," *Foreign Affairs* 98, no. 6 (2019): 122–133.

25 United Nations Migration Working Group, "Background Report on Migration Prepared for the Senior Management Group," United Nations, 18 March 2003.

26 Global Commission on International Migration, "Migration in an Interconnected World: New Directions for Action," United Nations, October 2005.

27 Ibid., 24.

28 Ibid., 27.

29 Nicholas R. Micinski and Thomas G. Weiss, "Global Migration Governance: Beyond Coordination and Crises," in *The Global Community: Yearbook of International Law and Jurisprudence 2017*, vol. 1 (Oxford: Oxford University Press, 2018), 175–194.

30 Global Migration Group, *Mainstreaming Migration into Development Planning: A Handbook for Policy-Makers and Practitioners* (Geneva: IOM, 2010).

31 Susan F. Martin, "International Migration and Global Governance," *Global Summitry* 1, no. 1 (2015): 64–83.

32 Betts and Kainz, "The History of Global Migration Governance," 5.

33 United Nations, "Summary of the High-Level Dialogue on International Migration and Development," UN document no. A/61/515, 13 October 2006, 2.

34 GFMD, "Report of the Swedish Chairmanship of the Global Forum on Migration and Development 2013–2014: Unlocking the Potential of Migration for Inclusive Development," Government Offices of Sweden, October 2014, 5.

35 François Crepeau and Idil Atak, "Global Migration Governance: Avoiding Commitments on Human Rights, Yet Tracing a Course for Cooperation," *Netherlands Quarterly of Human Rights* 34, no. 2 (2016): 133.

36 Wies Maas and Khalid Koser, *Towards Global Governance of International Migration: 15 Years of Intergovernmental Recommendations and Conclusions* (The Hague, The Netherlands: The Hague Process on Refugees and Migration, 2010), 22, 30.

37 GFMD, "Protecting and Empowering Migrants for Development: Second Meeting of the GFMD, Report of the Proceedings," Manila, Philippines, 27–30 October 2008, 5.

38 GFMD website, www.gfmd.org, Marrakesh, Morocco, 2018.

39 Crepeau and Atak, "Global Migration Governance"; Corey Robinson, "Making Migration Knowable and Governable: Benchmarking Practices as Technologies of Global Migration Governance," *International Political Sociology* 12, no. 4 (2018): 1–20.

40 Stefan Rother, "The Global Forum on Migration and Development as a Venue of State Socialisation: A Stepping Stone for Multi-Level Migration Governance?" *Journal of Ethnic and Migration Studies* 45, no. 8 (2019): 1258–1274.

41 Tendayi Bloom, "Coordinating the Future of International Migration Policy," United Nations University, 12 March 2014, https://gcm.unu.edu/publications/articles/coordinating-the-future-of-international-migration-policy.html.

42 Parvati Nair, "Should Migration Have Been a Separate Goal?" United Nations University, 25 September 2015, https://unu.edu/publications/articles/migration-a-separate-goal.html.

43 GMG, "Realizing the Inclusion of Migrants and Migration in the Post-2015 United Nations Development Agenda," Joint Discussion Paper, April 2015; GMG, "Realizing the Inclusion of Migrants and Migration in the Post-2015 United Nations Development Agenda," Joint Communiqué, 2014; GMG, "Integrating Migration in the Post-2015 UN Development Agenda," Joint Position Paper, 2013.

44 Nicola Piper, "Migration and the SDGs," *Global Social Policy* 17, no. 2 (2017): 231–238.

45 Samid Suliman, "Migration and Development after 2015," *Globalizations* 14, no. 3 (2017): 415–431; Raul Delgado-Wise, "The Global Compact in Relation to the Migration–Development Nexus Debate," *Global Social Policy* 18, no. 3 (2018): 328–331.

46 Kathleen Sexsmith and Philip McMichael, "Formulating the SDGs: Reproducing or Reimagining State-Centered Development?" *Globalizations* 12, no. 4 (2015): 582; and Suliman, "Migration and Development after 2015," 419.

47 UN, "New York Declaration for Refugees and Migrants," document no. A/RES/71/1, para. 47, 9.

48 Ibid., para. 90, 14.

49 Ibid., para. 84, 15.

50 Nicholas R. Micinski and Thomas G. Weiss, "International Organization for Migration and the UN System: A Missed Opportunity," *FUNDS Briefing No. 42*, January 2016, www.futureun.org/media/archive1/briefings/FUNDS_Brief42_IOM_UN_Migraton_Sept2016.pdf.

51 UN, "Addressing Drivers of Migration, Including Adverse Effects of Climate Change, Natural Disasters and Human-Made Crises, through Protection and Assistance, Sustainable Development, Poverty

Eradication, Conflict Prevention and Resolution—Issue Brief #2," Second informal thematic session on drivers of migration, 22–23 May 2017, New York, https://refugeesmigrants.un.org/sites/default/files/issue_brief_ts2_final.pdf.

52 UN, "Addressing Drivers of Migration … Co-Facilitators' Summary," Second informal thematic session on drivers of migration, 22–23 May 2017, New York, https://refugeesmigrants.un.org/sites/default/files/ts2_cofacilitators_summary.pdf.

53 Laurens Cerulus and Eline Schaart, "How the UN Migration Pact Got Trolled," *Politico*, 3 January 2019, www.politico.eu/article/united-nations-migration-pact-how-got-trolled.

54 Laurens Cerulus and Sarah Wheaton, "Belgium Sets Up Minority Government after Migration Dispute Breaks Coalition," *Politico*, 9 December 2018, www.politico.eu/article/belgium-sets-up-minority-government-after-migration-dispute-breaks-coalition.

55 The United States, Israel, Poland, Hungary, and the Czech Republic voted against the compact, while Algeria, Australia, Austria, Bulgaria, Chile, Italy, Latvia, Libya, Liechtenstein, Romania, Singapore, and Switzerland abstained.

56 Nicholas R. Micinski, "Implementing the Global Compact for Migration: The Role of States, UN Agencies, and Civil Society," Friedrich Ebert Stiftung, Global Policy and Development, June 2018, http://library.fes.de/pdf-files/iez/14547.pdf.

ADDITIONAL READING

Hein de Haas, "Turning the Tide? Why Development Will Not Stop Migration," *Development and Change* 38, no. 5 (2007): 819–841.

Thomas Faist, Margit Fauser, and Peter Kivisto, eds., *The Migration–Development Nexus: A Transnational Perspective* (New York: Palgrave Macmillan, 2011).

Ronald Skeldon, *Migration and Development: A Global Perspective* (London: Routledge, 1997).

Ninna Sørensen, Nicholas Van Hear, and Poul Engberg-Pedersen, "The Migration–Development Nexus: Evidence and Policy Options," *International Migration* 40, no. 5 (2002): 49–73.

Samid Suliman, "Migration and Development after 2015," *Globalizations* 14, no. 3 (2017): 415–431.

PART II

Resources, partnerships, and management

11

FUNDING THE UN*

Support or constraint?

Max-Otto Baumann and Silke Weinlich

Adequate and predictable funding to multilateral development organizations is key to promoting global sustainable development. Funding volumes and practices matter. They affect the scale and scope of solutions that can be offered. They reveal the extent to which multilateral organizations are owned by member states when looking at who shares the risks and costs of multilateral activities, and they demonstrate the level of trust placed in an organization. Through resource politics, states exercise influence and control over an organization. This influence can serve to support and strengthen multilateral organizations by helping them to be efficient, effective, and innovative. Or, it can also undermine international organizations by making their work harder, hampering development effectiveness, and eroding multilateral assets.

The UN development system (UNDS) illustrates both kinds of financial engagement, often in parallel. Over the last three decades, member states collectively multiplied their contributions; new, private actors emerged as significant donors. This growth in funding allowed the UNDS to expand significantly in scale and scope. At the same time, the practice of earmarking funding and the dependence on a small number of Western member states have been placing constraints on the UNDS. Despite a broad acknowledgment of the negative repercussions, efforts to curb earmarking practices and broaden the donor base have so far been mostly in vain. Adopting the UN Funding Compact in 2019, member states and the UNDS for the first time formulated a potential systemic approach to bring about a more predictable, flexible, and multilateralism-friendly funding so that the UNDS becomes fit for supporting member states in their transformations toward sustainable development.[1]

This chapter begins by describing the current funding patterns of the UNDS, analyzes the main drivers, and assesses repercussions. It then takes stock of responses by individual organizations as well as by the system as a whole. The chapter concludes with some reflections about the inherent challenges in finding remedies to the unsustainable funding structures that endanger the system's multilateral assets.

Main funding patterns

The UN development pillar, or "system," comprises more than 30 funds, programs, specialized agencies, and other entities that play a role in sustainable development.[2] While UNDS entities have specific thematic mandates and also substantially differ in their sizes and profiles—some focusing more on direct support and service delivery, others more on capacity-building and policy advice—they are all supposed to represent and further the UN's international standards and normative commitments, including human rights. The majority of entities have mandates to further sustainable development, yet there are also some parts of the UNDS that have partly or fully humanitarian mandates. Institutionally, the UNDS is marked by weak central authority and high fragmentation. In a typical developing country, there are on average a dozen UN entities that coordinate their activities, more or less successfully.[3] The majority of the UNDS's activities are funded by voluntary contributions. There is not a centralized funding mechanism; instead, individual entities mobilize most of their resources themselves. When analyzing the funding of the UNDS over the last two decades, three patterns emerge, namely a strong increase in resources, a dependency on Western contributors, and a shift toward earmarked funding.[4]

First, the UNDS has over the years greatly benefited from an increase in resources. As Figure 11.1 shows, resources have more than doubled over the last 15 years and were at $33.6 billion in 2017, the last year for which data are available. Humanitarian resources grew at a faster pace than development-related resources and now make up 46 percent of contributions.[5] This growth is also mirrored in the distribution of resources among UNDS entities. Overall, funds are concentrated in a relatively small number of organizations. The World Food Programme (WFP), the United Nations Children's Fund (UNICEF), the Office of the United Nations High Commissioner for Refugees (UNHCR), and the United Nations Relief and Works Agency for Palestine Refugees in the Near East (UNRWA), with large humanitarian portfolios, account for more than half of overall funding in 2017. The United Nations Development Programme (UNDP), the World Health Organization (WHO), the Food and Agriculture Organization of the United Nations (FAO), and the United Nations Population Fund (UNFPA), all with a development focus, together received around 30 percent. The other 35 entities accounted for the remaining 17 percent.[6]

The mostly steady increase in resources has allowed the UNDS to be the largest collective development actor with funding in 2017 equal to about 23 percent of total official development assistance (ODA). The UNDS has been receiving roughly one-third of all ODA contributions to multilateral development organizations as registered by the OECD (see Figure 11.2 for a comparison with other funding channels). This testifies to the trust that contributors place in the

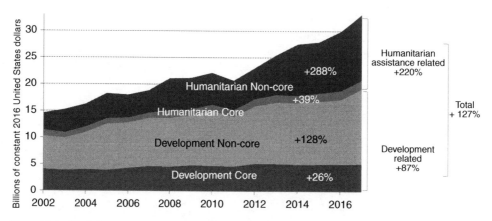

Figure 11.1 Real change over time of funding for UN-OAD, 2002–2017.

Source: Secretary-General (2019), Funding Analysis of Operational Activities for Development—Addendum 2, p. 4 (graph and data were shared by Andrew Macpherson who gave permission to reprint).

UNDS and the value that they see in funding it. Yet considerable as it may be, the funding cannot match the UNDS's potential tasks. UN Charter Article 1 states the overall mission: "to achieve international co-operation in solving international problems of an economic, social, cultural, or humanitarian character, and in promoting and encouraging respect for human rights and for fundamental freedoms for all." Various UN organizations have broad mandates in many policy areas, and the idea that all developing countries are eligible for UN assistance has led to a worldwide field presence. The 2030 Agenda requires vast resources for implementation, although it is clear that development aid can only play a catalytic role; private investments and other funding are essential. With climate change-related disasters on the rise and humanitarian needs chronically underfunded, resource requirements for both are substantial.

The Funding Compact, focusing on the development side only, indeed aims to raise additional funds for the UNDS, albeit in a very specific form. To do justice to the integrated challenges inherent in the Agenda 2030 and the Sustainable Development Goals (SDGs), funding targets exist for three funds that finance collective work of UNDS entities: the UN Peacebuilding Fund (PBF), the Joint SDG Fund, and the Special Purpose Trust Fund that facilitates UN coordination structures. In particular, the Joint SDG Fund aims to foster a new approach by UN country teams whereby they help unlock innovative finance for governments and national partners.

Second, a handful of donors from the Organisation for Economic Co-operation and Development's Development Assistance Committee (OECD/DAC) dominate the funding of the UNDS. They do so not only directly but also through funding other multilateral institutions that have grown into important UN funding sources. While there has been a diversification of sources over the last decades, it is taking place at a slow pace and has not fundamentally changed the reliance on a small number of Western donors. In 1982, states contributed more than 90 percent of all UNDS funding; today, their share is down to 74 percent. The remaining share is contributed by private actors and nongovernmental organizations (at 13 percent), the European Union (EU, at 7 percent), and global funds (6 percent). Only a few UN organizations benefit from this influx of non-governmental funding. UNICEF and WHO received around 20 percent of their total revenue from non-state contributors; and together with UNHCR, they accounted for over 80 percent of the UN's non-state funding.[7] While this funding lessens the dependence on governments, some of it may come with its own challenges—e.g., in terms of influence of actors such as the Bill and Melinda Gates Foundation, or further fragmentation of the multilateral development system through the creation of global funds.[8] Within the group of government funders, a relatively small group of countries pays the largest shares. As highlighted by the UN Secretary-General in his 2019 funding report, seven countries accounted for over two-thirds of all government contributions to the UNDS. When looking only at development activities, half of all funding was contributed by the United States, the United Kingdom, and Germany.[9] Other long-standing supporters of the UNDS include Sweden, Japan, Norway, Canada, the Netherlands, Switzerland, and Denmark.[10]

Funding from developing countries has been increasing, yet remains marginal when taking a system-wide perspective. In 2017, funding from non-OECD members amounted to 11 percent of overall UNDS contributions. China comes first, followed by the Russian Federation, Colombia, Saudi Arabia, and Qatar. These top five countries contributed 51 percent of the total funding for UN operational activities originating from non-OECD/DAC countries.[11] In particular, the drastic increase in Chinese resources from roughly $50 million in 2008 to $320 million in 2017 points to the potential for more resources from the wealthiest members of the Global South. Indeed, China has begun to invest resources especially in smaller UN organizations with Chinese leadership. Yet, when compared with Chinese contributions to the World

Bank or the Asian Infrastructure Investment Bank (AIIB) and its bilateral spending on South–South cooperation, resources invested in the UNDS seem modest.[12]

The rise of emerging powers in the Global South so far has bypassed the UN, at least in terms of financial contributions. Given that the UNDS is widely considered a trusted partner of developing countries, the growth in South–South cooperation could have also led to an influx of resources, the more so as the UNDS for decades has actively championed South–South cooperation both at the intergovernmental and field levels.[13] Moreover, the modest sums indicate that many developing countries still interact with the UNDS more as a resources-transfer mechanism for their benefit rather than seizing responsibilities and greater ownership of a set of organizations with key responsibilities for the implementation of universal norms, standard-setting, and global public goods. Overall, the concentrated funding patterns increase the dependency and potential vulnerability of UN organizations. On the one hand, funding grants power and influence, which can become problematic in multilateral organizations that need to be impartial and should be able to balance particular interests. On the other hand, changes of government and policies in important donor countries can lead to sudden and significant funding shortfalls, as witnessed by organizations such as UNFPA, UNESCO, or UNIDO in recent years.

Third, the increase in resources reflects mainly the growth in earmarked contributions. At an all-time high in 2017, 79 percent of all resources for operational activities (humanitarian and development-related) and 73 percent of all development-related resources were tied to specific purposes. Earmarked or non-core funding has three characteristics: it is voluntary, it preserves the national identity of a grant, and it by-passes statutory governance bodies of multilateral organizations.[14] As Figure 11.1 shows, core funding has been rising at a much slower pace than earmarked funding. Core contributions mean funding provided without restrictions to the budgets of an organization, controlled by the respective intergovernmental governing body of that organization. Core contributions come in two forms: mandatory contributions, which are a legal obligation of membership according to an agreed scale of assessment, and voluntary contributions, the size of which is determined by the donor individually.[15]

Earmarking in the UNDS has a long tradition. Already in the 1950s and 1960s, funding rules at many UN organizations changed in order to allow earmarked contributions. These changes were initiated by actors willing to provide more financing to the UN in order to expand its activities into new areas.[16] Until the 1990s, however, the majority of resources were in the form of core funding. From 1992 on, a stagnation and sometimes decline in core resources set in, which accompanied a sharp increase in earmarked resources. By 1997, the majority of all contributions to the UNDS were earmarked. Such contributions have outgrown core resources for the majority of organizations. For the five largest operational organizations, earmarked resources have been exceeding core contributions by a large margin. In 2017, UNICEF, WFP, UNDP, UNHCR, and WHO each received between 74 and 87 percent of their total revenue through earmarked contributions.[17] Smaller, more thematically or geographically focused agencies like UNFPA (62 percent), UNRWA (45 percent), and UN Women (57 percent) have maintained higher levels of core funding but have also recently witnessed an increase in earmarked funding.

As Figure 11.2 shows, the inverse proportions and the dominant share of earmarked resources distinguish the UNDS from other multilateral development actors such as the World Bank, regional development banks, and the EU. While also registering an increase in earmarked funding, these organizations so far are more solidly grounded in core funding.[18] By earmarking, contributors narrow the room for maneuver by a multilateral organization

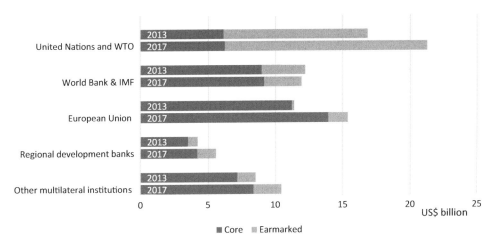

Figure 11.2 Multilateral assistance channels of OECD-DAC countries, core and earmarked, 2013 and 2017 (in 2017 constant US$).

Source: Own compilation based on OECD creditor database (as of December 2019). Values are in constant 2016 prices. The figures for the World Trade Organization (WTO) have been integrated into the channel "United Nations." Figures are accessible here: https://stats.oecd.org/Index.aspx?DataSetCode=MULTISYSTEM.

and increase their own ability to control the delegated activities. They can use the assets of UN organizations (e.g., impartiality, broad country presence, expertise, and convening power) for their own bilateral priorities. They also receive more detailed information on how funds are spent and results. Several factors may explain why the UNDS receives such high levels of earmarked funding. Contributors have been pointing to UN organizations' broad thematic portfolios and (perceived) deficits in organizational transparency and performance. Furthermore, unlike in multilateral development banks, high shares of core funding do not translate into larger voting rights; instead, earmarking seems to be the preferred (and sometimes the only) way to ensure (perceived) control in a multilateral setting.

Varieties of earmarked funding

In much of the academic literature, earmarked funding has traditionally been treated as one category and juxtaposed to multilateral core funding. However, earmarked funding comes in many forms and differs along a variety of dimensions. It has evolved over the years, often as a flexible means to work around existing structures. In order to identify specific instruments of earmarked funding that at least share some important characteristics and collect comparable data about the system's earmarked portfolio, the UNDS now distinguishes between four instruments (which in themselves carry significant variation, as argued elsewhere[19]): UN inter-agency pooled funds, single-agency thematic funds, local resources, and project-/program-specific contributions.[20] They are worth parsing.

Inter-agency pooled funds (also known as "multi-partner trust funds") bring together several donors and several UN organizations. They are typically, but not necessarily, administered by the Multi-Partner Trust Fund Office (MPTFO), which is hosted by UNDP. Some of these instruments are defined by sectors (country-based humanitarian pooled funds), others by their purpose of improving coordination (One UN Funds, Joint Programs), and yet others by their function of promoting global thematic priorities (Global Funds).

Agency-specific thematic funds can be multi- or single donor, but they benefit a single UN entity. They represent an attempt to reconcile the request by donors for the thematic specifications of allocations with the need for greater flexibility in how and where UN organizations spend funds. Examples include UNDP's Funding Windows on climate, governance, crisis recovery, and poverty eradication[21] as well as UNFPA's Maternal and Newborn Health Thematic Fund.[22]

Figure 11.3 shows that these two types of pooled funding so far account for a small portion of total UNDS resources. Both inter-agency and thematic funds are explicitly mentioned in the UN Funding Compact with the aim of doubling their shares in the overall UNDS development-related funding mix to 10 and 6 percent respectively by 2023. Pooled funding has gained more traction in humanitarian affairs, where it amounts to some 11 percent. The Grand Bargain, the humanitarian predecessor of the Funding Compact that was agreed in 2016 at the World Humanitarian Summit, had defined a global target of 30 percent of humanitarian contributions non-earmarked or softly earmarked by 2020.[23]

Local resources are source-based. While all UN member states and private actors may contribute to other forms of funding, in this case the government of a developing country itself contributes funding for UN activities within its own borders and also specifies their use. This practice is particularly common in Latin America. Local resources in fact accounted for more than half of developing countries' contributions to the UNDS in 2017,[24] although the share of China's local resources has been going down over the last five years.

Project- and program-specific funding is often described as contributions by one donor and for activities by one organization, usually but not exclusively at country level. There is little transparency for this type of funding, and various stakeholder compositions are possible and in fact common. For many years, this type of funding has been making up the largest portion of non-core contributions to the UNDS. The UN considers it the most restrictive and therefore harmful form of funding—for both development and humanitarian affairs. As a small disincentive, the Funding Compact, therefore, imposes a 1 percent levy on project- and program-specific funding, which will help fund the UNDS's coordination structures.

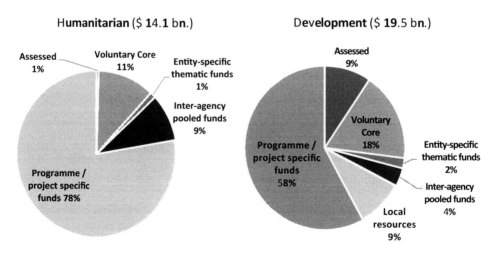

Figure 11.3 Contributions to UNDS.

Source: Own compilation, based on Secretary-General (2019) Report on the implementation of the QCPR, Statistical Annex on funding data, www.un.org/ecosoc/en/2019-operational-activities-development-segment.

Why the substantial increase in earmarking?

Most frequently, the rise of earmarked funding is explained by looking at the supply side—e.g., the policies of donor countries, mostly from OECD/DAC countries. Observers stress that several issues came together to facilitate the increase in earmarked resources from the 1990s onwards.[25] Despite hopes for a peace dividend, and in the absence of the obvious foreign political rationales, ODA declined, at the United Nations and elsewhere. The downward trend was reversed by a reorientation of development policy toward thematic priorities. In particular, the Millennium Development Goals (MDGs) helped mobilize resources; the focus on thematic priorities led to a significant increase in resources for the UNDS.

At the same time, increasingly critical national constituencies demanded more efficiency and visibility for their contributions to multilateral organizations. With greater aid volumes, scrutiny of these funds and the need for accountability also increased. OECD/DAC countries were dissatisfied with the perceived inefficiencies and shortcomings of multilateral organizations or with their restricted mandates. This concern translated into funding for highly specialized, newly founded vertical funds such as the Global Fund to Fight AIDS, Tuberculosis and Malaria (Global Fund), and the vaccine alliance GAVI. It also led to more earmarked funding that encouraged more transparency, accountability, and communication about efficiency and results. New multi-donor trust funds also enabled a more coordinated approach among groups of donors to support a common cause.

The factors that brought about the increase in earmarking also helped to perpetuate its rise. Such international factors as donors' wishes to exert more influence and ensure their thematic priorities in organizations with multilateral governance were important. Domestic and bureaucratic factors have also been crucial: many governments have divided the financial responsibilities for the diverse UN organizations across line ministries. Often, there is little knowledge about the other ministries' activities and insufficient coordination. Vested interests exist in the respective organizations or programs/projects, hampering whole-of-government approaches. Some donor countries take a large part of their funding decisions at the country level; others have big ODA shares tied to programmatic priorities determined at the center. There is often a strong path-dependency to allocation decisions, including the division between bi- and multilateral channels or among multilateral channels. Finally, in many donor countries, domestic actors ask for greater accountability and demonstration of concrete results.[26] This requirement often goes hand in hand with a demand for quantifiable outputs, rather than wider societal or political outcomes that are much harder to pin down, as Paul Yanguas has argued.[27] For humanitarian affairs, it is widely accepted that earmarked funding allows the mobilization of funding for new crises and rapid reactions in emergencies. Yet, earmarking allows donors to pick and choose and exert influence on the work of multilateral organizations and their implementation partners.

Yet, we should not assume that UN entities have been innocent by-standers in the rise in earmarked contributions, although their role is harder to pin down. Multilateral organizations have generally embraced the additional voluntary contributions that allowed them to evolve, stay relevant, and expand the scope and scale of activities. In fact, UN organizations have played an active part in mobilizing earmarked resources, a process facilitated by a decentralization of decision-making authority to the country level where strong incentives for field offices exist to sustain themselves financially. Coordination mechanisms inside and across entities—notwithstanding some positive examples—have so far not enforced a firmer corporate stand against earmarked funding proposals that fall outside an organization's thematic priorities or are too restrictive. Given the lopsided ratio of core to non-core resources, core resources are used increasingly to actively leverage non-core contributions.[28]

Consequences of earmarking

Earmarking is not per se detrimental to UN development cooperation. As described, UN organizations have long actively pursued this form of funding as a welcome source for increasing revenue and scope. Even today, their stance on earmarking remains ambivalent, as they balance the (perceived) need for additional resources with the problematic aspects of earmarking. Earmarked funding can be credited with energizing the UN, making it more results-oriented and conscious of efficiencies. It has been key to quickly mobilizing resources particularly in the humanitarian but also in the development realm.

While often described as turning the UN into an "implementer" or "service contractor," UN field staff often see the relatively close involvement of donors that accompanies earmarking in terms of dialogue and partnerships. When donors pool their resources, either in a trust fund or some joint program, this creates a form of UN "mini-lateralism" with benefits such as risk-sharing, greater efficiency, and enhanced respect for UN global norms. Such arrangements promote one of the UN's original aspirations; namely, in the words of Charter Article 1, "to be a centre for harmonizing the actions of nations in the attainment of [...] common ends." In fact, pooled funding presents the only opportunity to finance joint or collective activities by UN organizations, which has become even more necessary for the Agenda 2030's pursuit of SDGs, which calls for integration and scale.[29]

However, these generally positive attributes should be viewed in the larger institutional and political context.[30] In general, UN organizations plan, both at headquarters and in the field, on the basis of both core and earmarked resources. As long as the latter align with an organization's values and program, they can be considered generally supportive. However, earmarking can and often does have very disruptive effects, particularly for those organizations or field offices that almost exclusively rely on earmarked resources. Each earmarked contribution requires the negotiation of a contract and reporting results, which can re-direct attention away from core tasks and consume limited personnel capacities.[31] The fragmented nature of earmarked revenue requires field offices to piece together the implementation of medium-term programs from a multitude of short-term earmarked contributions that arrive in unpredicted and unpredictable ways during the entire program period. The unpredictability and potential inflexibility of incoming resources also affects staffing and staff structures;[32] it creates strong incentives for staff to become entrepreneurial in the competition for resources, both within and across UN organizations. Individual entrepreneurship—and the desire of every staff member to be their own project manager—in turn undermines the UN's attempts to deliver as one and presents a serious obstacle to any reforms.[33]

These issues could be dismissed as simply administrative annoyances. However, as such terms as "bilateralization," "commercialization," and "privatization" of UN development politics suggest, the implications of earmarking go beyond purely administrative issues.[34] Given nearly three decades of a high ratio of earmarked funding, earmarking by now profoundly shapes almost all aspects of how UN organizations think and operate. The rationale behind multilateral organizations lies in the delegation of responsibilities as a way to increase member states' capacity for collective action. As Devi Sridhar and Ngaire Woods state,

> The general proposition is that multilateralism offers governments a chance to delegate authority to an international institution to take the political heat off themselves or to tie their hands in a way that is conducive to long-term goals but not to short-term political interests.[35]

Many forms of earmarking in fact undermine this proposition, by reducing the decision-making autonomy of international organizations.

This starts with resource allocation: earmarked funding patterns, over which UN entities have limited influence, tend to reflect donor interests and arguably prevent the UN's providing some sort of multilateral corrective to bilateral priorities. This reinforces donor darling/aid orphan dichotomies, but it also leaves the UN with ineffective ways to address cross-country challenges and emergencies. One major factor explaining why the WHO, despite increases in overall revenue in the preceding years, was slow to respond to the Ebola crisis in 2014 was that its core budget stagnated for years. For example, in 2011, the WHO let go of some 300 staff because of budgetary constraints; meanwhile, earmarked resources could not be used for the Ebola response. Similar problems related to the lack of flexibility in resource allocation exist at each budget level—whether global programs, country programs, or individual projects. These problems manifest themselves in the form of under- and over-funded areas for UN agencies receiving resources that are not well aligned with their strategic plans, restricting their ability to shift resources to respond to needs and improve results, as a recent analysis for the WHO showed.[36]

The influx of earmarked funding has also directed UNDS activities toward operations and service delivery and constrained organizations in their ability to bolster the normative, convening, and knowledge functions that could be described as the UN's unique core functions. UNICEF, for example, officially embraced children's rights as its mandate in the 1990s following the 1990 Children's Summit, which implies working for legal and institutional changes; however, on the ground, service-delivery functions continue to play an important role. Results can be measured more easily and thereby help with further resource mobilization. However, such an approach may be adequate in emergency situations, but it fails to push for more structural and transformative changes.[37] A recent study finds that around 20 percent of all development resources are spent on normative functions across the UNDS.[38] Earmarking thus seems hard to reconcile with an approach by which the UN would work more normatively at the country level, focusing on policies and advocacy and doing so informed by its global norms and agreements, as the editors suggest in a more globally oriented, collective action-based UN development cooperation.

The strong dependence on earmarked funding creates a donor orientation in all phases of the programming, implementation, and evaluation cycle that is difficult to square with the UN's multilateral assets. Projects funded by earmarked resources tend to have specific targets that might be rather piecemeal. From the perspective of the UN, such targets create a "tyranny of the urgent." In the aid effectiveness literature, results orientation and performance measurement have been connected to unintended consequences such as "tunnel vision," "myopia," and "measure fixation."[39] Dealing with contingencies, learning, and adjustments along the way becomes more difficult in a setting where donors expect prompt and visible results. Anticipating donors and their political needs, UN organizations design programs and projects for measurable outputs, which are not necessarily aligned with longer-term, sustainable outcomes. An evaluation by the UN's independent Joint Inspection Unit (JIU) concluded that earmarking, in combination with results-based management practices, has produced UN "leadership that is responsive but not responsible."[40]

Relatively small, donor-driven projects can also undermine ownership by host governments that might have neither the patience nor capacity to deal with a large number of insufficiently integrated projects that each have their own logic. Such projects will probably not catch the attention of political leaders unless they are linked to political priorities. They are then also significantly less likely to be scaled up or taken over by the government. The UN's own surveys have registered dissatisfaction by developing countries with earmarking, though their attitudes are not totally negative (which might be explained by improvements in UN programming that resulted in better alignment of projects to country programs).[41]

At the global level, earmarking engenders its own kinds of disruptions to the UN's multi-lateral governance.[42] With the ever-growing proportion of earmarked resources, the UN's center of gravity has shifted to the country level, where the majority of these resources are raised, negotiated, and spent. Decreasing core budgets means that governing bodies become less influential, to the frustration of many developing countries. While donors—including non-state donors such as private actors and philanthropic foundations—can wield the informal power of their purses, developing country officials feel sidelined despite their formal voting rights. The practice of earmarking has also given rise to persistent discussions about perceived injustices about the cross-subsidization of non-core resources through core resources, potentially dis-incentivizing traditional and new donors from assuming collective responsibility through core contributions. Such issues absorb diplomatic and administrative capacities, driving micro-management through UN governing bodies. More importantly, perhaps, they stifle the multi-lateral ambition of member states. They erode the multilateral fabric that consists in the belief that collective action can occur, that putting the national interest behind the common good is appropriate, and that strong institutions are a value in themselves.[43]

Fight-back or surrender? Responses to earmarking

In spite of a now widely shared understanding of the undermining effects of current funding practices, persistent appeals for more reliable and sustainable funding have been mostly in vain. Several attempts by individual member states and groups of them as well as by UN organizations have failed to bring about positive change on a larger scale. Over the last two decades, UN organizations have sought to reduce and mitigate restrictively earmarked funding in favor of more softly earmarked contributions. Among the first to adjust their resource mobilization strategies was the WHO, which already in 1999 sought closer collaboration and long-term strategic agreements with donors to reduce uncertainties in revenue streams.[44] Similar strategies of foster-ing partnerships—both informal and contract-based—with donors have been and continue to be pursued across the UNDS. Bilateral strategic dialogues and meetings between small donor clubs such as the Utstein group and organizations form part of this.

Other responses across the UNDS range from attempts for greater standardization in the management of non-core contributions through standard contracts and reporting to efforts that unlock new funding sources, which include both funding from governmental donors from the North and Global South and private sources. Partnerships with emerging economies of the Global South are being actively pursued, as well as with the already risen China. In addition, many UN organizations have also reinforced their efforts to engage private companies and philanthropies.

Many organizations have also tried to accommodate the needs of donors, thus attempting to reduce the need for earmarking—or to demonstrate that core funds are well spent. Improvements of organizational efficiency, a greater results orientation, and increased trans-parency have been very high on their agendas; constant improvements have been signaled to donors. More recently, efforts to increase donor visibility on core contributions were included in the Funding Compact—a strategy not without risk. Core contributions are technically a form of pooled funding through which contributions lose their national identity; attempts nevertheless to highlight donor contributions can pose a threat to the legitimacy and neutrality of organizations that belong to all member states. Thematic funding—first introduced by UNICEF in 2003 and later adopted by other UN special funds and programs—aims to recon-cile the needs of donors for thematic specifications with the needs of organizations for more flexible allocation of funds.

The WHO has initiated funding dialogues that allow it to wield public pressure on donors to match their funding to the mandates agreed for the organization. It has also published donor-funding profiles as an incentive for donors to maintain or improve their funding. Other organizations have replicated this approach; yet, they often remain trapped in their financial dependency on donors that impedes straightforward criticism about harmful donor practices and their own challenges in digesting earmarked funding. Overall, these separate strategies have been ineffective, as earmarking has continued to increase over the last decade. In the context of the most recent UNDS reform process, the Secretary-General made a rare intervention in UNDS matters and proposed a Funding Compact in which both sides—UN bodies and member states—were to commit to tangible changes that would allow the other side to adjust behavior. The Funding Compact mirrors the Grand Humanitarian Bargain that was concluded in 2016 between the UN, major donors, and NGOs; it sought to improve the quality and quantity of humanitarian funding by reducing the share of tightly earmarked funding and increasing multi-year commitments. The UNDS pledged greater coordination, transparency, and efficiency; member states committed to higher shares of core funding, more pooled funding, and more multi-year contributions. In addition, all states were asked to contribute to pooled funds and to increase core with the intention of increasing the overall number of governments providing UNDS funding.

While not necessarily new in content, the Funding Compact represents the first systemic answer to the UNDS's unhealthy funding situation: it brings together both member states and the system and takes a universal approach that includes all states. After almost a year of negotiations, in which specific indicators were established, the Funding Compact was formally adopted in spring 2019. The high-level attention now accorded to resource mobilization and the explicit link to the most ambitious UNDS reforms in recent times provide some hope that this initiative will be more successful than previous ones.

Conclusion

The imperfect way that the UNDS has been funded for many years entails adverse consequences, ranging from negative impacts on individual organizations and their work, thereby impeding cooperation, to undermining multilateral assets and the credibility of the UNDS as a universally owned system. Earmarked funding is not necessarily detrimental, yet without a secure funding base for core functions, a more regulated and less fragmented approach and full cost-recovery has come with a high price tag. The Funding Compact states that:

> [Current funding patterns] … constitute lost opportunities, by hindering the system's ability to respond in integrated, flexible and dynamic ways to Member States' demands and national priorities. Ultimately, they compromise the multilateral nature of United Nations support to the 2030 Agenda.[45]

Elsewhere we have argued that a worrisome set of collective action problems are at play, which further erode the UNDS's multilateral assets. The more that contributors, under current conditions, engage in earmarking, the more it becomes a rational strategy for others to mimic, even if such practices diminish the unusual multilateral assets that make delegation to the United Nations so attractive in the first place. Relatedly, the provision of core funding becomes less and less attractive, potentially also for those countries from the Global South that are now in a position to contribute. Moreover, the more that UN organizations accept overly restrictive earmarking arrangements, the more that it becomes rational for other organizations to do the same, even if in the long run it is in no one's interest.

It is too early to tell whether the Funding Compact can slow down such a vicious circle. Its systemic and detailed commitments and follow-up mechanisms provide a source of cautious optimism. At the same time, the problems that it tackles are complex, especially in the context of the ongoing crisis of multilateralism.

NOTES

* With financial support from the German Federal Ministry for Economic Cooperation and Development (BMZ).

1 *Implementation of General Assembly Resolution 71/243 on the Quadrennial Comprehensive Policy Review of Operational Activities for Development of the United Nations System, 2019: Funding Compact. Report of the Secretary-General,* UN documents A/74/73/Add.1–E/2019/14/Add.1, 2 April 2019.

2 These are nine special funds and programs: (UNDP [including UNCDF and UNV], UNEP, UNFPA, UN Habitat, UNHCR, UNICEF, UNRWA, UN Women, WFP); 14 specialized agencies (FAO, IAEA, ICAO, IFAD, ILO, IMO, ITU, UNESCO, UNIDO, UNWTO, UPU, WHO, WIPO, WMO); 12 UN Secretariat departments (DESA, ECA, ECE, ECLAC, ESCAP, ESCWA, OCHA, OHCHR, UNCTAD, UNDPA, UNISDR, UNPBSO); and numerous other research and training institutions and other entities. See UN, *Annex to the Secretary-General's 2017 Report on Funding: Technical Note on Definitions, Sources and Coverage,* www.un.org/ecosoc/sites/www.un.org.ecosoc/files/files/en/qcpr/sgr2017-annex-technical-note.pdf.

3 Max-Otto Baumann, *Mission Impossible? Country-Level Coordination in the UN Development System* (Bonn, Germany: Deutsches Institut für Entwicklungspolitik, 2018).

4 For a more long-term perspective, see Bruce Jenks, "Financing the UN Development System and the Future of Multilateralism," *Third World Quarterly* 35, no. 10 (2014): 1809–1828; Silke Weinlich, "Funding the UN System," in *Post-2015 UN Development,* ed. Stephen Browne and Thomas G. Weiss (London: Routledge, 2014), 75–94.

5 Until autumn 2018, the UN registered all activities of UNHCR, UNRWA, and OCHA as well as emergency operations by UNICEF, humanitarian emergencies of UNFPA, and WFP's humanitarian operations as humanitarian, in the absence of common definitions on development or humanitarian activities. From then on data has been collected using OECD/DAC purpose codes. See UNDG, 2019, *Data Standards for United Nations System-Wide Reporting of Financial Data,* https://undg.org/wp-content/uploads/2019/03/UN_DataStandards_Digital_Final.pdf.

6 UN, *Funding Analysis of Operational Activities for Development: Addendum 2* (UN documents A/74/73–E/2019/4 Add. 2), 18 April 2019.

7 UN Multipartner Trust Fund Office and Dag Hammarskjöld Foundation, *Financing the UN Development System: Time for Hard Choices* (Uppsala: Dag Hammarskjöld Foundation, 2019), 41–42.

8 Stephen Browne, "Vertical Funds: New Forms of Multilateralism," *Global Policy* 8, no. S5 (2017): 36–45; Karolin Seitz and Jens Martens, "Philanthrolateralism: Private Funding and Corporate Influence in the United Nations," *Global Policy* 8, no. S5 (2017): 46–50.

9 *Funding Analysis of Operational Activities for Development: Addendum 2,* 8–9.

10 Silke Weinlich, *Reforming Development Cooperation at the United Nations: An Analysis of Policy Position and Actions of Key States on Reform Options* (Bonn, Germany: Deutsches Institut für Entwicklungspolitik, 2011).

11 UN MPTFO and Dag Hammarskjöld Foundation, *Financing the UN Development System,* 45–46.

12 Mao Ruipeng, *China's Growing Engagement with the UNDS: Changing Rationale, Funding Preferences and Future Trends.* (Bonn, Germany: Deutsches Institut für Entwicklungspolitik, 2020).

13 Silke Weinlich, "Emerging Powers at the UN: Ducking for Cover?" *Third World Quarterly* 35, no. 10 (2014): 1829–1844; Carolina Milhorance and Folashade Soule-Kohndou, "South–South Cooperation and Change in International Organizations," *Global Governance* 23, no. 3 (2017): 461–481.

14 Silke Weinlich, Max-Otto Baumann, Erik Lundsgaarde, and Peter Wolff, *Earmarking in the Multilateral Development System: Many Shades of Grey* (Bonn, Germany: Deutsches Institut für Entwicklungspolitik, 2020).

15 The UN Secretariat and UN specialized agencies such as WHO and FAO receive mandatory core contributions from the UN's membership, yet increasingly they also seek to attract voluntary core funds. UN funds and programs rely exclusively on voluntary resources. The World Bank and other multilateral development banks technically rely on voluntary core contributions that, however, are raised in collective capital increases and replenishment processes.

16 The Netherlands provided the first earmarked contribution to UNDP for industrial development at a time when this topic was advocated by the Soviet bloc and many developing countries and resisted by the United States. See Erin R. Graham, "The Institutional Design of Funding Rules at International Organizations: Explaining the Transformation in Financing the United Nations," *European Journal of International Relations* 23, no. 2 (2016): 365–390.

17 UN MPTFO and Dag Hammarskjöld Foundation, *Financing the UN Development System*, 34.

18 See also OECD, *2019 Multilateral Development Finance Report: Recharging Multilateral Development Co-operation to Achieve the 2030 Agenda Together* (Paris: OECD, 2018).

19 Weinlich, Baumann, Lundsgaarde, and Wolff, *Earmarking in the Multilateral Development System*.

20 UNDS entities are requested to report separately on revenues received from vertical funds. A new category was added in 2018 that also asks for numbers on in-kind contributions of goods and services earmarked for specific programs or projects. See UN CEB-HLCM/UNDG 2019, *Data Standards for United Nations System-Wide Reporting of Financial Data*.

21 See UNDP Funding Windows, www.undp.org/content/undp/en/home/funding/funding-windows.

22 See UNFPA Maternal and Newborn Health Thematic Fund, www.unfpa.org/maternal-and-newborn-health-thematic-fund.

23 For an update on the implementation of the Grand Bargain, see Victoria Metcalfe-Hough, Wendy Fenton, and Lydia Poole, *Grand Bargain Annual Independent Report 2019* (London: Humanitarian Policy Group, ODI, 2019).

24 UN, *Funding Analysis of Operational Activities for Development: Addendum 2*.

25 See Vera Z. Eichenauer, Bernhard Reinsberg, and Katharina Michaelowa, "The Rise of Multi-Bi Aid and the Proliferation of Trust Funds," in *Handbook on the Economics of Foreign Aid*, ed. B. Mak Arvin and Byron Lew (Cheltenham, UK: Edward Elgar Publishing Limited, 2015), 527–554; Graham, "Follow the Money: How Trends in Financing Are Changing Governance at International Organizations."

26 See Piera Tortora and Suzanne Steensen, *Making Earmarked Funding More Effective: Current Practices and a Way Forward* (Paris: OECD, 2014); Nilima Gulrajani, *Bilateral versus Multilateral Aid Channels: Strategic Choices for Donors* (London: ODI, 2016).

27 Paulo Yanguas, *Why We Lie about Aid: Development and the Messy Politics of Change* (London: Zed Books, 2018).

28 For an analysis of the role of UN staff in earmarking practices, see Baumann, Lundsgaarde, Weinlich, and Wolff, *Earmarking in the Multilateral Development System*.

29 Silke Weinlich and Bruce Jenks, "Current and Future Pathways for UN System-Wide Finance," and UN Multi-Partner Trust Fund Office, "UN Pooled Funding: 'Healthy' Financing for Better Multilateral Results," in *Financing the UN Development System*, 119–123, 101–105.

30 Klaus H. Goetz and Ronny Patz, "Resourcing International Organizations: Resource Diversification, Organizational Differentiation, and Administrative Governance," *Global Policy* 8, no. S5 (2017): 5–14; Katharina Michaelowa, "Resourcing International Organisations: So What?" *Global Policy* 8, no. 5 (2017): 113–123.

31 UN, *Review of Donor Reporting Requirements Across the United Nations System* (Joint Inspection Unit report, JIUREP/2017/7).

32 Jörn Ege and Michael W. Bauer, "How Financial Resources Affect the Autonomy of International Public Administrations," *Global Policy* 8, no. S5 (2017): 75–84.

33 Timo Mahn, "The United Nations in Development: Confronting Fragmentation?" in *The Fragmentation of Aid: Concepts, Measurements and Implications for Development Cooperation*, ed. S. Klingebiel et al. (London: Palgrave Macmillan, 2016), 247–260; and Baumann, *Mission Impossible?*

34 Timo Mahn, *The Financing of Development Cooperation at the United Nations: Why More Means Less* (Bonn, Germany: Deutsches Institut für Entwicklungspolitik, 2012).

35 Devi Sridhar and Ngaire Woods, "Trojan Multilateralism: Global Cooperation in Health," *Global Policy* 4, no. 4 (2013): 325–335.

36 OECD, *Multilateral Development Finance Report: Recharging Multilateral Development Co-operation to Achieve the 2030 Agenda Together* (Paris: OECD, 2019).

37 Julia K. Hagn, *UNICEF: Caught in a Hypocrisy Loop* (Nomos, Germany: Baden-Baden, 2018).

38 *System-Wide Outline of Functions and Capacities of the UN Development System, Consultant's Report*, June 2017, sg-report-dalberg_unds-outline-of-functions-and-capacities-june-2017.pdf.

39 Sarah Holzapfel, *Boosting or Hindering Aid Effectiveness? An Assessment of Systems for Measuring Donor Agency Results* (Bonn, Germany: Deutsches Institut für Entwicklungspolitk, 2014); Peter Smith, "On

the Unintended Consequences of Publishing Performance Data in the Public Sector," *International Journal of Public Administration* 18, no. 2–3 (1995): 277–310.

40 UN, *Results-Based Management in the United Nations Development System: Analysis of Progress and Policy Effectiveness* (Joint Inspection Unit report JIU/REP/2017/6), ii–iv.

41 UN, *Report on QCPR Monitoring Survey of Programme Country Governments in 2017*, 23 February 2018, www.un.org/ecosoc/sites/www.un.org.ecosoc/files/files/en/2018doc/sgr2018-survey-report-pgc.pdf.

42 Graham, "Follow the Money."

43 Dag Hammarskjöld Foundation, "Why the United Nations Should Embrace the Concept of Global Public Goods," in *Financing the UN Development System*, 138–140; and Michaelowa, "Resourcing International Organisations."

44 WHO, *Proposed Programme Budget for 2000–2001: Implementation of Resolution EB103.R6. Report by the Secretariat* (Geneva: WHO, 1999).

45 *Funding Compact*, 3.

ADDITIONAL READING

Klaus H. Goetz and Ronny Patz, "Resourcing International Organizations: Resource Diversification, Organizational Differentiation, and Administrative Governance," *Global Policy* 8, no. 5 (2017): 5–14.

OECD, *2019 Multilateral Development Finance Report: Recharging Multilateral Development Co-operation to Achieve the 2030 Agenda Together* (Paris: OECD, 2018).

UN Multipartner Trust Fund Office and Dag Hammarskjöld Foundation, *Financing the UN Development System: Time for Hard Choices* (Uppsala, Sweden: Dag Hammarskjöld Foundation, 2019).

Silke Weinlich, Max-Otto Baumann, Erik Lundsgaarde and Peter Wolff, *Earmarking in the Multilateral Development System: Many Shades of Grey* (Bonn: German Development Institute, 2020).

12

PRIVATE FINANCE AND PARTNERSHIPS AT THE UN

Barbara Adams

Over the last three-quarters of a century, member states have provided neither adequate nor reliable funding to the UN system at the level needed to enable it to fulfill the mandates that they have authorized. This reality has been compounded by the insistence for many years of Western governments on a doctrine of zero-growth of the regular (assessed) UN budget. Governments have responded to global challenges by establishing a growing number of formal and informal institutions and arrangements that are partly within, but to a large extent outside of, the UN system. These arrangements have embraced the concept of "partnership," notably promoted as a primary way to meet the commitments in the 2030 Agenda for Sustainable Development and to achieve the Sustainable Development Goals (SDGs).

In 2017, total UN funding of the UN system—including the UN Secretariat as well as its programs, funds, and specialized agencies—was $48.3 billion. Operational activities for development and humanitarian assistance accounted for about 71 percent, peacekeeping operations for 19 percent, and norm-setting, policy, and advocacy activities for 10 percent.[1] UN funding for operational activities for development in 2017 reached $33.6 billion, an increase of 12.6 percent over 2016. However, as the Secretary-General's report states, this growth was attributable primarily to an increase in non-core funding.[2] Within this overall context, member states have acknowledged repeatedly "the need to address the imbalance between core and non-core resources." In 2018, they agreed to a Funding Compact, in which they "commit to bringing core resources to a level of at least 30 percent in the next five years."[3]

The structural underfunding of the UN system and its dependence on a limited number of largely Western donors have led to a search for new funding sources, particularly in the for-profit, private sector. The enthusiasm with which some member states and UN entities have pursued engagement with the private sector encompasses the search not only for funding but also for its expertise and influence. This engagement has encouraged the adoption of a business and investor mindset and it has outpaced the rules and procedures for non-state and for-profit actors' accountability to the UN Charter, including its instruments, norms, and values.

Exploring these developments, this chapter begins with a brief history of support from the private sector over the world organization's 75-year history. It continues with a discussion of the main UN interfaces with the private sector, the shifting funding patterns, the approaches to risk assessment, and the implications for the future of the United Nations.

Private funding: a brief history

In the UN's early years, private actors—whether private-sector companies or philanthropic foundations—for the most part kept their distance from the world body. One notable exception was John D. Rockefeller, Jr., who donated the money to purchase the land on which the UN's headquarters now stand. This distance gave way to open animosity in 1973 when the UN established the Centre on Transnational Corporations (UNCTC) and the Commission on Transnational Corporations,[4] which critically monitored business activities. In the 1980s, US companies and lobbying groups, along with the Heritage Foundation, constituted the driving force behind the political hostility of the Reagan administration toward, and financial pressure on, the UN.

Another notable exception is the experience of UNICEF. Its first national committees were established in 1946 and 1947; in 2017, they had grown to number 34. They are vital to the work of the organization, "raising about one-third of UNICEF's annual income/expenditures through contributions from corporations, CSOs, and more than 6 million individual donors worldwide."[5]

The inadequate financing of the UN system spurred the exploration of other initiatives and responses. In 1993, the Ford Foundation sponsored a High-Level Panel, chaired by former Chairman of the US Federal Reserve, Paul Volcker, and former Deputy Governor for International Relations of the Bank of Japan, Shijuro Ogata. *Financing an Effective United Nations*, the panel's report, concluded:

> Current proposals for additional, nongovernmental sources of financing are neither practical nor desirable. For now, the system of assessed and voluntary contributions provides the most logical and appropriate means of financing the U.N., as it permits and encourages member governments to maintain proper control over the U.N.'s budget and its agenda.[6]

After Kofi Annan became Secretary-General in January 1997, his reform program included initiatives that would see the UN systematically open up to the business sector, actively seeking out private actors for financial and political assistance. That year, the US refusal to pay its regular UN budget contributions in full and on time prompted the announcement of US billionaire Ted Turner to fill the gap by donating $1 billion to the UN over a period of 10 years through a US public charity, the United Nations Foundation (UNF). His decision marked a fundamental shift in the relationship between the United Nations and private funders. In 1999, the Secretary-General urged world business leaders to join with the UN in a "global compact of shared values and principles, which will give a human face to the global market."[7] This marked the origin of the UN Global Compact, now one of the most important vehicles for cooperation between the UN and the business sector. The two initiatives of Kofi Annan, one focused on funding and the other on relationship-building, were accompanied over time by the establishment of a UN Trust Fund to receive the related state and non-state contributions, respectively the United Nations Fund for International Partnerships (UNFIP) and the Global Compact Trust Fund.

Along with the changing relationship of the UN with the business sector, private funding for UN-related activities has grown steadily since the mid-1990s. In 2012, specified voluntary contributions from foundations, corporations, and civil society to the UN system amounted to some $2.5 billion, increasing to about $3.3 billion in 2013, or 14 percent of all specified voluntary contributions to the UN system.[8] In 2017, these contributions represented the largest growth area to UN entities, accounting for 13 percent of total voluntary contributions.[9]

This trend was not only driven by UN secretaries-general Annan and Ban Ki-moon, but has also come to be strongly supported by some member states. By 2017, the UN trust fund set up to receive contributions from Turner was also receiving contributions from member states, resources that might otherwise have been disbursed directly to the UN. For example, in 2017 Denmark, the Netherlands, Norway, Sweden, the United Kingdom, Germany, Italy, France, and China contributed to the Global Compact Trust Fund, with Denmark making the largest contribution of $1,805,326.[10]

Member states have also discussed partnerships between the UN and private actors in the context of the "partnership resolutions" of the General Assembly, the first one adopted in 2000 in resolution 55/215. The German government began the initiative with the goal of promoting the Global Compact at the intergovernmental level, only a few weeks after its official launch on 26 July 2000.

Since that time, the topic of partnerships has been an established item on the General Assembly agenda. Its resolutions "Towards Global Partnerships" between 2000 and 2003 reflected the skepticism of many governments toward the concept of public–private partnerships and the shift in power from purely intergovernmental bodies to partnerships with private actors. However, from 2005 onwards, the General Assembly "encouraged" the development of public–private partnerships in many areas of the UN; it routinely "welcomed" innovative approaches to the use of partnerships to realize UN goals and programs.[11]

This trend continued in the assembly's resolution in December 2012 on the Quadrennial Comprehensive Policy Review (QCPR). Here again governments emphasized

> the importance of broadening the donor base and increasing the number of countries and other partners making financial contributions to the United Nations development system in order to reduce the reliance of the system on a limited number of donors.[12]

In 2018, after many months of deliberation and negotiations, member states adopted General Assembly resolution 72/279 on "Repositioning of the United Nations Development System." This resolution has ushered in a series of reforms to the UN development system (UNDS) aimed at improving its ability to deliver on the 2030 Agenda for Sustainable Development. Implementation of the resolution has been framed by a new UN Sustainable Development Cooperation Framework (UNSDCF), the guiding document to shape UNDS engagement at country level. This document emphasizes the importance of partnerships, including with the private sector.[13]

The resolution also established a Funding Compact between the UN and member states with guidelines for financing the UNDS in order to achieve results on the SDGs of the 2030 Agenda. It heavily emphasizes greater coherence of UN entity programming, and inter-agency pooled and entity-specific thematic funds.[14] A new trend of appealing to private-sector partners to participate in these funds is evident from the UN Development Programme's (UNDP's) "The Lion's Share Fund," and from UNICEF's Thematic SDG Funds. The Secretary-General's 2019 Report on Implementation of QCPR notes:

> of the $557 million contributed to entity-specific thematic funds in 2017, 70 per cent went to funds with a development focus and the other 30 per cent to funds with a humanitarian focus. The private sector was the largest source of those contributions, accounting for nearly a third of the system-wide total in 2017.[15]

Funding UN regular budget and core activities

In response to the growing gap between financial needs and available resources of the "regular" or "assessed" budget, voluntary contributions from individual governments and other donors have been increasingly used as an additional income source for the UN. While the activities of most UN funds and programs have been financed completely through voluntary contributions, a growing share of the core activities of the UN Secretariat itself are now also dependent on non-assessed, or voluntary, contributions; they are not subject to the same member-state reporting and oversight procedures for multilateral accountability and adherence to UN core business and values.

The (internal) Schedule of Individual Trust Funds for the biennium 2012–2013 showed that 35 UN general trust funds received contributions from about 40 non-state donors, including foundations, research institutes, private companies, and Ban Ki-moon himself. Most of these contributions, totaling $101 million, were relatively small, with only a few exceeding $1 million.[16]

By far the largest contribution in 2012–2013 came from the UNF, which gave $92.5 million to the UNFIP. The UNF and UNFIP as its interface within the UN system, as well as the Global Compact, have been instrumental in opening up the UN to private and particularly corporate money and influence. It is to that story that this chapter now turns.

The UNFIP, UNOP, and UNF

The UNFIP has played a central role in the evolving relationship between the UN system and the private sector. The details of this relationship are in a 1998 agreement that stated that the foundation has responsibility for formulating its program priorities; on that basis, UN departments, funds, programs, and specialized agencies can submit project proposals. An advisory board established by the Secretary-General reviews them, but the actual decisions regarding proposed projects are made by the UNF's Board. Over the years, the imbalance between the advisory function of the UNFIP board and the decision-making power of the UNF board has raised concerns that UNF decisions on policy or programmatic issues do not sufficiently involve Advisory Board members and should be made more transparent and accountable.[17]

At the end of 2016, cumulative allocations to UNFIP projects reached approximately $1.4 billion, of which $450 million came from billionaire Ted Turner and $990 million was mobilized as co-financing from other private donors.[18] A large share of the revenue from other donors came from the Bill and Melinda Gates Foundation, which between 1999 and 2017 gave $286 million in grants, mainly for projects in the areas of health and agriculture.[19]

Not all of the UNF's revenues and expenditures have been allocated to UNFIP. A significant share of UNF expenditures were devoted to activities outside the UN system, including in the areas of public health and reproductive rights.

The UNF has also played a leadership role in the Global Fund to Fight AIDS, tuberculosis, and malaria as an alternate member of the Global Fund's board. In 2009, the UNF supported the Friends of the Global Fund through a $2.7 million grant from the Gates Foundation.[20] In an effort to strengthen the relationship between the UN and the business community, in 2010 the UNF integrated the Business Council for the United Nations (BCUN) into its programmatic activities. That same year it created its Global Entrepreneurs Council, which encouraged young entrepreneurs to support UNF campaigns and help to create new ones.

Over the last 15 years, the UN Foundation changed from being primarily a grant-making institution to one increasingly launching its own initiatives outside the UN. These included contributing to the Energy Future Coalition, brokering between donors and implementing agencies (inside and outside the UN system), and campaigning on behalf of the Secretary-General and his key priorities—including scaling up engagement in "transformative multi-stakeholder partnerships" with the private sector, civil society, philanthropists, and academia.[21]

The UN Foundation has been a driving force behind the "global partnerships" initiated by the Secretary-General since 2010, notably in two initiatives: "Sustainable Energy for All" and "Every Woman, Every Child." Its representatives have become close advisors to the Secretary-General; its resources have hired additional UN staff and become a key outreach and campaigning arm for UN senior staff.[22]

UNOP: the gateway for private companies

In 2006, then-UN Secretary-General Annan created the UN Office for Partnerships (UNOP), which since then has been responsible not only for the management of UNFIP, but also for the management of the UN Democracy Fund (UNDF) and particularly for partnership advisory services and outreach. In order to provide UNOP with an additional financial mechanism for mobilizing resources of non-state actors through public–private partnerships, the Secretary-General established in 2009 an additional vehicle, the Trust Fund for Partnerships.[23] While its resources are limited, its primary role is as a "gateway for public–private partnerships with the United Nations system."[24]

In the last few years, UNOP has become actively involved in organizing high-level events with top business representatives and corporate philanthropists to promote market-based solutions to development and to mobilize private funds to solve global problems. An example is the 2013 Forbes 400 Philanthropy Summit, held in the UN Trusteeship Council and sponsored by Credit Suisse and attendees, including UN Secretary-General Ban and over 150 entrepreneurs and philanthropists. The latter represented, according to *Forbes Magazine*, "close to half a trillion of the world's wealth, [who] discussed how they can use their wealth, fame and entrepreneurial talent to eradicate poverty."[25] UNOP co-hosted events (e.g., Social Innovation Summit and the Investor Summit on Climate Risk) have conveyed similar messages.

Thus, while the direct financial flows from private donors to the UN through UNFIP/ UNOP have been declining and volatile, UN interactions with corporations and corporate philanthropists have intensified steadily. As a result, the number of corporations with partnerships or alliances with or through UNOP has grown to include almost 100 transnational corporations (TNCs), among them Bank of America, BP, Coca-Cola, Goldman Sachs, Nestlé, Shell, and Wal-Mart.[26]

The change from funder to facilitator outgrew the initial relationship agreement between the UN and the UNF and generated complications, as the UN Office of Internal Oversight Services pointed out in 2013:

> Third party donors and other co-financing partners had made significant contributions to projects financed by the Foundation (approximately 63%). The source of such funding, however, was not known to the United Nations until after the project documents were received by UNFIP for disbursement of funds. In one instance, a project had to be reconsidered as the United Nations had concerns about the donor. Inadequate review of donors by UNFIP may result in a reputational risk to the United Nations and conflict with its ethical values.[27]

After two decades, the UN updated in December 2014 its Relationship Agreement, issuing regulations and guidelines for more transparent governance. However, unlike the previous agreements, this version was not made public. Furthermore, it included an annex that "grandfathers in" existing programs and projects under the previous rules covering third-party and member-state contributors.[28]

The UN Global Compact

Initiated by Annan in 1999, the UN Global Compact (UNGC) was originally designed as a corporate social responsibility (CSR) initiative to "mainstream" a set of principles related to human rights, labor, the environment, and corporate corruption. Global Compact principles serve as the framework for cooperation with the business sector.[29]

In 2006, the US non-profit Foundation for the Global Compact was established. The Global Compact is coordinated by the UN Global Compact Office, which originally was based inside UN headquarters premises in New York. The UNGC is open to all businesses that commit to 10 principles. The main sources of finance for the UNGC are contributions from member states and fees from the private sector. Donations from the latter and membership fees are collected by the Foundation for the Global Compact, and tax deductible in many countries. In 2015, these amounted to $15.7 million (over 80 percent of overall contributions).[30]

Contributions by member states are for the Global Compact Trust Fund, established by the Secretary-General in 2001. In 2015, such contributions totaled $18.3 million: $2.7 million (down from 3.5 million in 2013) from member states and $15.6 million from the foundation (up from 2 million in 2013).[31] Additional support has come by way of staff seconded to the Global Compact Office, both from member states and from private corporations; in 2013, these included ENEL, China Petroleum, Chemical Corporation, Sinopec, and Fuji Xerox Company Ltd.[32]

The Global Compact has a combined annual budget of roughly $18 million, the bulk of which is spent on staff, consultants, and conferences.[33] Since 2010, when the Foundation and the Global Compact Trust Fund began to keep a joint account, money from public sources has been more or less static, while the income from private sources has more than tripled. A 2010 report by the UN Joint Inspection Unit (JIU) drew attention to the lack of government representatives on the Global Compact Board, calling it highly unusual for an intergovernmental organization such as the UN. It added that this weak government oversight is duplicated in the Global Compact Government Group, which is formally entrusted with overseeing the use of government resources.[34] The JIU also concluded that the General Assembly Partnership resolutions do not close the governance gap, failing to address and guide either the objectives of the Global Compact to promote responsible corporate citizenship or its business-led advocacy in policy processes, the latest example being toward the Post-2015 Agenda. The 2017 JIU report, *The United Nations System: Private Sector Partnerships Arrangements in the Context of the 2030 Agenda for Sustainable Development*, reiterated these governance and accountability concerns and recommended a revised mandate for the Global Compact:

> The General Assembly, based on a report by the Secretary-General, should initiate a revision of the current mandate of the Global Compact, which should include, inter alia:[35]
> - A clearer role of the Global Compact, at the global and national levels, in effectively engaging the business sector to support the implementation of the 2030 Agenda
> - An enhanced role for Member States in its governance structure
> - An updated definition of the relationship between the Global Compact Office and the Foundation for the Global Compact, with an emphasis on the transparency of the Foundation's fundraising activities
> - A clear definition of the relationship between the Global Compact headquarters and the Global Compact Local Networks.

As contributions to the Global Compact come from both private sources and member states, the usual oversight mechanisms of the UN system do not apply. Its outsourced status contrasts with the role attributed to the Global Compact and its 10 principles as provider of the framework for UN cooperation with the business sector. Also, while the Global Compact and its principles are used by the UN Office for Project Services (UNOPS) as a measure for sustainable procurement, its accountability and oversight mechanisms do not report on its central role within the United Nations for business–UN relations.

The UNGC's work in connection with the 2030 Agenda illustrates an approach weighted toward bringing corporate political influence into government and governmental agencies processes rather than the reverse. At its Leaders Summit 2013, the UN Secretary-General unveiled the Post-2015 Business Engagement Architecture, designed to "ensure that the views and contributions of businesses and the private sector feed into the Post-2015 process."[36]

Financing operational activities of the UN system for development

The UNDS's organizations are facing similar funding challenges to the UN itself: stagnating or even shrinking core funding and growing dependence on non-core, mostly earmarked contributions. From a democratic governance perspective, a crucial difference is whether an organization is funded mainly through core (unrestricted) or non-core resources. According to several reports from the Secretary-General, core resources provide the highest quality, flexibility, and efficiency of pooled funding; they are central to ensuring the independence and neutrality of the UN. By contrast, as member states noted in 2014, non-core resources can have adverse effects, via increased transaction costs, fragmentation, competition, and overlap among entities; they also risk distorting program priorities regulated by intergovernmental bodies and processes.

The independent evaluation of the UNDP *Strategic Plan 2008–2013* found that a major reason for non-delivery of outputs was the under-resourcing of projects due to earmarking of funds, causing an "imbalance in resource mobilization across outcomes or outputs." A related problem is that the recovery of institutional costs associated with non-core activities is not guaranteed. The reports of the Secretary-General have repeatedly expressed concerns that support to non-core-funded activities may be subsidized by core resources, thereby reducing core resources for program activities, especially at the country level.[37]

Restructuring and encouraging private funders

UN funds, programs, and specialized agencies have responded to the shift to earmarked resources with various measures, all of which have served to further erode core funding and increase dependence on earmarked contributions. In an effort to broaden their donor base, members of the UNDS have intensified engagement with the corporate sector and philanthropic foundations. Private funding for the UNDS has for years benefited UNICEF, whose resources emanate from its national committees and philanthropic foundations; these have increased greatly over the past decade. Based on this model, UNHCR has begun to appeal to individuals and corporations, and UN Women has made this a priority for its resource mobilization strategies.

Today, corporate philanthropy, above all the Bill and Melinda Gates Foundation, not only commits higher levels of resources, but it also plays a more active role in international development cooperation. The Gates Foundation is among the top five contributors to WHO and the UN Capital Development Fund (CDF). It also plays a key role in the global health funds, as a major funder of the global vaccine alliance (GAVI) and the largest private donor to the Global Fund. In addition, foundations and other private actors contribute indirectly through global funds, such as the Global Fund and GAVI, both of which have given significant amounts to UNICEF. With over US$400 million in 2013, the Global Fund has become the largest single contributor to UNDP, which acts as an implementing agency.[38] Representatives of the Gates Foundation are on the Boards of both GAVI and the Global Fund and thus exert significant influence on their strategies and funding decisions.

The results have been mixed. An official evaluation of UNDP partnerships with global funds and philanthropic foundations lists some benefits but just as many risks and challenges.[39] The former include increased resources and enhanced impact, particularly in projects that address the environment and health. The latter include the fact that the partnerships do not always meet the priority needs of partner countries, and they tend to foster competition among UNDS entities. The evaluation concluded that given the ad hoc nature of most of these UNDP partnerships, there is little evidence that the results are sustainable even for the success stories.

Despite uneven results, UNDS organizations continue to seek increased funding from private companies and philanthropies (see Box 12.1). This effort has resulted in hundreds of different funding arrangements between UN entities and corporate actors; they range from small, ad hoc donations for specific projects to global multi-stakeholder partnerships with long-term perspectives. Most UN funds, programs, and agencies have established their own special offices for cooperation with the private sector, such as UNDP's Innovations and Development Alliances Group, UNICEF's Division of Private Fundraising and Partnerships, and UNESCO's Division of Cooperation with Extra-Budgetary Funding Sources.

UNDP, for example, received $13 million from the Coca-Cola Company between 2006 and 2013 in support of their joint initiative "Every Drop Matters," which supports local groups, mainly in Eastern Europe and Central Asia, to undertake projects that improve access to water, water quality, and water management.[40] UNICEF's "Schools for Africa" initiative, which seeks to increase access to quality basic schooling for all, particularly the most disadvantaged, has received over $20 million from the Gucci fashion company since its launch in 2004.[41]

UNICEF's Private Fundraising and Partnerships financial report for the year ending on 31 December 2018 is illustrative of a widespread trend, reporting that "total private sector revenue was $1.43 billion." Of this total, contributions to regular resources (RR) represented $690.6 million—the highest amount ever generated from the private sector in any given year—and contributions to other resources (OR) were $740.9 million, of which $578.9 million was other resources regular (ORR) and $162.0 million other resources emergency (ORE).[42]

Box 12.1 Appeal to individual giving

Another crucial and growing source of funds comes from individuals who are committed to the objectives of individual UN organizations. Such funds are also categorized as emanating from non-state or private sources, but they have no strings attached and are thus different from corporations and philanthropies. The World Food Programme's (WFP's) *Strategy for Partnership and Engagement with Non-Governmental Entities (2020–2025)* details its plans for individual giving and brand strengthening as well as market analysis: "Individual giving is the largest source of donations among non-governmental entities in the global fundraising market, and it continues to grow … The goal is to create a model that becomes self-financing within five years and delivers a significant level of flexible income to WFP." The WFP strategy acknowledges that "there is a concern that increasing WFP's fundraising from individuals might reduce income for other United Nations agencies and non-governmental partners," but it states further that: "This is based on a belief that the overall individual giving market is limited. However, analysis conducted by a number of peer organizations with large individual fundraising operations shows that the market is both large and growing significantly—increasing the opportunities for all organizations." While WFP addresses the possible tension with important partners, it ignores the distortion of accountability away from member states to individuals and downplays the important and unique role a UN agency could and should play with governments.

In 2019, UNICEF redoubled efforts to grow private-sector fundraising, particularly from individuals. Through the Supporter Engagement Strategy, UNICEF enhances supporter relationships with a view to reducing donor attrition and increasing donor acquisition. Continuing the current level of investment funds will be critical to support ongoing growth, particularly in individual giving. UNICEF regular resources grew in 2018—"comprising $66.1 million by National Committees and $0.8 million by country offices. Individual giving remained the primary source of contributions to regular resources."[1] The appeal of individual giving is evident when one recognizes that such resources are virtually always core resources; in addition to this flexibility, they require very little reporting. In 2014, 92 percent of the total amount of individual contributions was remitted as core funding.

Similar to UNICEF, UNHCR has in the last few years successfully developed and invested in its private-sector fundraising. Refugees and internally displaced persons (IDPs), like children, are appealing images for individuals. Such contributions have increased and become a key financial source for UNHCR, and they are likely to continue growing. In 2017, UNHCR mobilized $276 million from individual contributors, nearly doubling in four years ($137 million in 2014). The number of individuals giving to UNHCR in 2014 was close to 1 million, and in 2017 over 1.92 million.[2] UNHCR anticipated that by the end of 2018, there would be a total of 2.5 million individuals contributing a total of $500 million.[3]

Notes

1 *Private Fundraising and Partnerships: Financial Report for the Year Ended 31 December 2018, Report by the United Nations Children's Fund* (Economic and Social Council document E/ICEF/2019/AB/L.6), 12 July 2019, para. 9.

2 *Global Report 2017, United Nations High Commissioner for Refugees*, 2018, 42.

3 *UNHCR's 2018–2019 Financial Requirements, United Nations High Commissioner for Refugees Global Appeal 2018–2019*, 2018, Figure 5.

Uncharted territory: corporate contributions

For UN Women, in 2018, the private sector, including corporations, foundations, and individuals donating through UN Women's National Committees, provided 5 percent of contributions, with a 29 percent increase from $17.9 million in 2017 to $23 million in 2018.[43] This upward trend drew on funding from Foundation Chanel, the Alwaleed Bin Talal Foundation, the Bill and Melinda Gates Foundation, BNP Paribas, and BHP Billiton Foundation, to name a few, and the latter is now counted among the top 20 contributors to UN Women.[44] The partnership with BHP was signed despite numerous reports of BHP's involvement as co-owner with Vale of Samarco in the Brazil mine disaster in 2015 as well as continuing litigation. For example, in May 2018, shareholders filed a lawsuit against BHP Billiton in Australia, alleging that the company misled them as it was aware of the safety risks prior to the disaster, but failed to take any action to prevent it.[45] In August 2018, the company settled a similar lawsuit filed by US shareholders, agreeing to a $67 million compensation without admitting liability.[46]

In a private-sector promotional brochure, UNESCO lists various incentives for companies to partner with the agency, including "image transfer" through association with a prestigious UN entity, access to the agency's wide and diverse private networks, and nameless benefits from the agency's role as a neutral and multi-stakeholder broker.[47] These potential benefits for companies apply generally to all UN funds, programs, and agencies; so it is worth asking: What does "image transfer" mean for the reputation of the UN? Is there not the risk that the cooperation with controversial corporations (like Shell, Coca-Cola, Microsoft, and BHP Billiton) adversely affects the image of the UN as a neutral broker and undermines its reputation?

The UN Food and Agricultural Organization (FAO) referred to this risk in a 2005 assessment of its partnership projects, stating that non-state entities with interests that differ from the FAO mission may bring "undue influence" or "reduce the Organization's credibility by damaging its image of impartiality."[48] This adds to the issues raised with regard to earmarked funding, including fragmentation, competition and overlap among entities, disregard of UN program priorities, and high transaction costs, all of which create obstacles to progress.

Despite these risks, nearly all UN funds, programs, and agencies intend to increase private funding for their operational activities. In general they follow a multi-layered fundraising strategy, which includes sustaining core contributions from governments and increasing those from emerging economies; exploring "core-like" funding modalities, including pooling resources in Multi-Donor Trust Funds; expanding contributions from the private sector, civil society, and philanthropic foundations; and participating in new global multi-stakeholder partnerships. UN organizations are devoting staff and resources to analyzing potential private-sector donors and positioning themselves as an attractive brand. In 2017, the JIU listed among the "most cited motivational factors" with the UN system the desire to "Build brand image and higher visibility among civil society, including consumers, other business groups and the media."[49]

Mixed blessings and messy definitions

Inadequate financing for the UN system and its mandates has prompted UN organizations and their member states to embrace a range of non-state funders. The resulting contributions primarily from philanthropy and the business community now represent the largest growth area, rising from 8 percent in 2016 to 13 percent one year later, representing some $4.4 billion (see Figure 12.1).[50] This aggregate figure is misleading because for some UN entities, such contributions are truly substantial, whereas for others, they are little or nothing. Moreover, lumping together NGOs with philanthropic and private donors disguises whether these contributions are commitments to the purpose and values of the UN—usually the case for NGOs—or rather reflect more self-interested concerns such as market access and building a brand image. Figure 12.2 shows six entities which have received the bulk of such private funding: UNDP, UNFPA, UNHCR, UNICEF, WFP, and WHO. Indeed, UNICEF and WHO "both received around 20 percent of their total revenue from non-state contributors, and together with WFP and UNHCR accounted for over 80 percent of the UN's non-state funding."[51]

Definitions and categorizations used by the UN entities are not standard across the UN system. UNHCR categorizes private individuals as distinct from foundations, companies, and philanthropists; UNICEF classifies resources raised by their National NGO Committees as from the private sector. UNDP, UNFPA, WHO, and WFP classify foundations, private sector, and NGOs as separate categories. This discrepancy is illustrative of the lack of common terminology within the UN system to define business actors or private-sector entities. The UN Secretary-General's Guidelines on a principle-based approach to the cooperation between the United

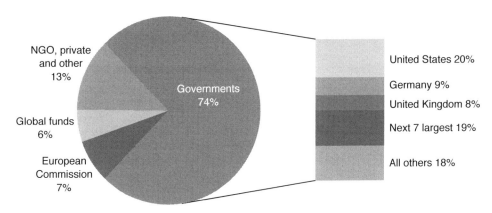

Figure 12.1 Main groups of funding sources, 2017.

Nations and the business sector define the business sector as: "either for-profit, and commercial enterprises or businesses; or business associations and coalitions (cross-industry, multi-issue groups; cross-industry, issue-specific initiatives; industry-focused initiative); including but not limited to corporate philanthropic foundations."[52]

> The WHO Framework for Engagement with Non-State Actors (FENSA), negotiated Private sector entities are commercial enterprises, that is to say businesses that are intended to make a profit for their owners. The term also refers to entities that represent, or are governed or controlled by, private sector entities. This group includes (but is not limited to) business associations representing commercial enterprises, entities not "at arm's length" from their commercial sponsors, and partially or fully State-owned commercial enterprises acting like private sector entities.[53]

Some UN entities, including the WHO, consider private philanthropic foundations as non-profit entities and therefore as separate types of actors. Other UN organizations consider business actors as non-governmental organizations, non-state actors, (non-party) stakeholders, or in certain cases even as part of civil society.

Recognizing risk and conflicts of interest

In recent years, there has been growing acknowledgment that the enhanced interaction with the private sector brings a variety of risks and side effects for the UN. A *Lancet* article by Chelsea Clinton and Devi Sridhar asked, "Who pays for cooperation in global health?" Their comparative analysis details a number of consequences:

> The move towards the partnership model in global health and voluntary contributions … allows donors to finance and deliver assistance in ways that they can more closely control and monitor at every stage … away from traditional government-centred representation and decision-making; and towards narrower mandates or problem-focused vertical initiatives and away from broader systemic goals sought through multilateral cooperation.
>
> By using financing and governance mechanisms within the old institutions, as well as by creating new agencies, donors can more likely achieve their goals for a few

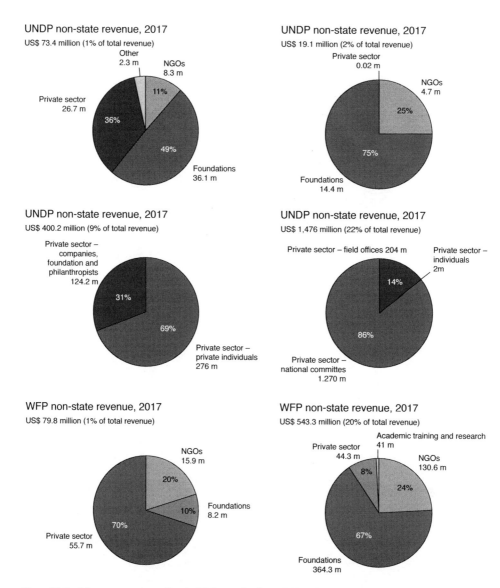

Figure 12.2 Non-state revenue for six UN organizations, 2017.

Source: Financing the UN Development System: Time for Hard Choices, September 2019, www.daghammarskjold.se/wp-content/uploads/2019/09/financial-instr-report-2019-interactive.pdf.

reasons. First, they have structurally aligned the objectives of global agencies with their own objectives. Individual governments (or small groups of governments and like-minded others) can use the new funding mechanisms, agencies, or initiatives as a way to define and pursue a separate mandate, for example with HIV/AIDS.

Over time, the rearrangement of WHO's priorities to align with funds was inevit-able, with donors earmarking 93% of voluntary funds in the 2014–15 budget. Influ-ence is heavily concentrated among the top donors. Undeniably then, a direct link exists between financial contributions and WHO focus.[54]

WHO Director-General Margaret Chan reaffirmed the importance of public interest safeguards in a speech at the 8th Global Conference on Health Promotion in June 2013: "In the view of WHO, the formulation of health policies must be protected from distortion by commercial or vested interests." The WHO has identified the following risks in its FENSA:

a   conflicts of interest;
b   undue or improper influence exercised by a non-State actor on WHO's work, especially in, but not limited to, policies, norms and standard-setting;
c   a negative impact on WHO's integrity, independence, credibility and reputation; and public health mandate;
d   the engagement being primarily used to serve the interests of the non-State actor concerned with limited or no benefits for WHO and public health;
e   the engagement conferring an endorsement of the non-State actor's name, brand, product, views or activity;
f   the whitewashing of a non-State actor's image through an engagement with WHO;
g   a competitive advantage for a non-State actor.[55]

Moreover, the 2017 UN report on enhanced cooperation between the United Nations and relevant partners, in particular the private sector, warns:

> The lack of a system-wide approach to due diligence results in the inefficient use of financial and human resources, as multiple United Nations agencies often screen the same partners, and poses significant reputational risk to the Organization. It sometimes leads to contradictory decision-making across entities, undermining the integrity and increasing the vulnerability of the Organization.
>
> Due diligence exclusionary criteria also vary. For example, 61 per cent of United Nations entities exclude companies in the tobacco industry from partnership consideration as a policy measure; 19 per cent of United Nations entities view companies from that sector as high-risk prospective partners but do not exclude them from partnership consideration; and 20 per cent do not have specific policies in place that apply to the tobacco industry.[56]

In addition, two reports from the UN's Joint Inspection Unit (JIU) in 2017 also analyzed the UN systems' mechanisms and policies on ethics and integrity, as well as on partnerships with the private sector. The JIU Report *Review of Mechanisms and Policies Addressing Conflict of Interest in the United Nations System* observed that while the topic of personal conflict of interest is well covered, hardly any organizational conflict of interest policy exists among UN systems organizations.[57] WHO's FENSA does contain specific provisions on the management of conflict of interests, institutional as well as individual:

> In actively managing institutional conflict of interest [...], WHO aims to avoid allowing the conflicting interests of a non-State actor to exert, or be reasonably perceived to exert, undue influence over the Organization's decision-making process or to prevail over its interests.

The JIU Report *The United Nations System: Private Sector Partnerships Arrangements in the Context of the 2030 Agenda for Sustainable Development* addressed the inadequate UN system attention to due diligence procedures and recommended, *inter alia*, that:

The Secretary-General of the United Nations and all the executive heads of participating organizations should identify and agree on a minimum set of common standard procedures and safeguards for an efficient and flexible due diligence process, to be applied system-wide in a transparent way by the United Nations operational staff engaged in the initiation and implementation of partnerships with the private sector.[58]

Moving forward on due diligence

As part of the reorientation of the UN development system (UNDS) to a system-wide approach, the newly structured United Nations Sustainable Development Group (UNSDG) issued in 2019 the *Common Approach to Prospect Research and Due Diligence for Business Sector Partnerships*. It notes:

> The private sector plays a pivotal role in advancing the 2030 Agenda for sustainable development and within it, the importance of business sector partnerships has been reaffirmed by Member States as a vital and critical component to accomplish the Sustainable Development Goals (SDGs). As the United Nations (UN) aims to scale up its engagement with business, it needs to do so in a way that optimizes the benefits of collaboration, manages potential risks, and ensures integrity and independence of the organization. The December 2017 Report of the Secretary-General calls for a coherent and streamlined approach on due diligence standards and procedures across the United Nations system as part of stepping up the scale and scope of partnerships with the business community to accompany the requirements of the 2030 Agenda.[59]

The new common approach establishes a set of exclusionary criteria when conducting due diligence for prospective partners, which are spelled out in Table 12.1. The report also addresses "sectors with high-risk in operational context" and references the fact that "the extractive industry is another example of sector operating often in fragile environmental or political contexts, making considerations around their long-term impact an important element to inform collaboration." It does not address, however, whether these criteria will be applied retroactively to re-examine a number of engagements with the private sector that underwent perfunctory or contested due diligence processes and at the entity level only; UN Women's partnership with BHP is a prime example.

Conclusion

Few observers dispute the pressing need for more adequate and reliable resources for both standard-setting and operational activities by organizations of the UN system. Nonetheless, the significant shift to tied funding by governments and to new resources from the for-profit private sector are not without shortcomings and critics. As the UN embraces private-sector funding and partnerships with for-profit corporations as a central means to implement its development agenda, it needs not only to match this enthusiasm with a much-needed and overdue upgrade of the rules and tools covering relationships and responsibilities, but also to strengthen its institutional capacity for monitoring and independent oversight.

Concerns about engagement with the for-profit sector extend beyond those related to funding and partnering with the UNDS. They also extend to the potential distortion of the purpose of the United Nations itself. The reorientation toward the private sector omits attention

Table 12.1 Common set of exclusionary criteria

1 Appearance on the United Nations Security Council Sanctions List[1] or the United Nations Ineligibility List, or in violation of UN sanctions, relevant conventions, treaties, and resolutions	Entities directly engaged in activities inconsistent with the UN Security Council Sanctions, Resolutions, and other similar measures
2 Direct and core involvement in the manufacturing or trading of controversial weapons subject to bans under International Treaties	Entities directly and primarily[2] involved in the sale, manufacture, or distribution of weapons banned by UN treaties, including anti-personnel mines, cluster bombs and ammunitions, and biological, chemical, or nuclear weapons, for instance
3 Direct involvement or complicity[3] in systematic or egregious human rights abuses through operations, products, or services	Entities engaging in any of the following: • causing or directly contributing to gross human rights abuses through their own business activities (such as forced or compulsory labor or child labor and human rights violations, including rights of indigenous peoples and/or other vulnerable groups); or • tolerating or knowingly ignoring such practices by an entity associated with it; or • knowingly providing practical assistance or encouragement that has a substantial effect on the perpetration of the gross human rights abuse
4 Weapons manufacturing or sales as a core business	Entities directly and primarily involved in the sale, manufacture, or distribution of weapons
5 Tobacco manufacturers	Entities for whom the core business[4] is the production and wholesale distribution of tobacco products
6 Systematic failure to demonstrate a commitment or to meet in practice the principles of the United Nations, including statements or principles that are consistent with and reflect the Universal Declaration of Human Rights, the Rio Declaration and the ILO Declaration on Fundamental Principles and Rights at Work, the UN Global Compact, or the United Nations Guiding Principles on Business and Human Rights	Entities that systematically[5] fail to demonstrate a commitment to meet the stipulated principles (human rights, labor, environment, and anti-corruption)

Notes
1 www.un.org/sc/suborg/en/sanctions/un-sc-consolidated-list.
2 "Primarily" here is intended to mean businesses that generate above 10 percent of their total revenues from the activity, which hold market share leadership on excluded activity (i.e., ranking among the top 10 players in a market or globally), or which is publicly presented and promoted focusing on excluded activity.
3 For a more extensive definition of "complicity," see the following publications: "Guiding Principles for Business and Human Rights" and "Embedding Human Rights into Business Practice" at www.unglobalcompact.org/library/1441; and *Report of the Special Representative of the SG on the Issue of Human Rights and Transnational Corporations—Clarifying the Concepts of Sphere of Influence and Complicity*, UN document A/HRC/8/16.
4 "Core business" refers to the primary area or activity that a company was founded on or focuses on in its business operations.
5 Systematic nature of such violations is measured through an assessment of issues using indicators such as: materiality, incidence and frequency, corporate response and remedial action, company specificity and peer assessment, etc. Specific tools and guidelines for this assessment will be developed and will follow this framework.

to the broader analysis taking place in the UN discussions on Financing for Development (FfD) and on economic policies. The report of UN Inter-Agency Task Force on FfD, entitled *Financing for Development: Progress and Prospects 2018*, discusses the framework that is needed for private-sector investment to be effective in advancing sustainable development (see Box 12.2).

Box 12.2 Excerpts from UN, *Financing for Development: Progress and Prospects 2018* (New York, 2018)

The IATF report highlights the importance of long-term investment horizons in risk assessment, to ensure that major risks, such as those from climate change, are incorporated into investment decision-making. The report notes that "pension funds, insurance companies and other institutional investors hold around US$80 trillion in assets" but the majority of these resources are invested in liquid assets, such as listed equities and bonds in developed countries. Investment in infrastructure represents less than 3 percent of pension fund assets, with investment in sustainable infrastructure in developing countries even lower.

The report emphasizes the need for analysis that takes into account the different stages of development of a country. Not all countries are (equally) attractive to investors/partners.

This approach lacks measures of accountability in line with member-state decisions in the UN Human Rights Council such those laid out in the Human Rights Council resolution 17/4: *Guiding Principles on Business and Human Rights: Implementing the United Nations "Protect, Respect and Remedy" Framework* (UNGP).[60] The UNGPs, adopted by consensus in 2011, provide a roadmap to both states and businesses and are structured on three pillars: state duty to protect human rights, the corporate responsibility to respect human rights, and access to remedy.

Additionally, the Human Rights Council resolution 26/9, *Elaboration of an International Legally Binding Instrument on Transnational Corporations and Other Business Enterprises with Respect to Human Rights*, has "establish[ed] an open-ended intergovernmental working group [IGWG] on transnational corporations and other business enterprises with respect to human rights … to elaborate an international legally binding instrument to regulate, in international human rights law, the activities of transnational corporations and other business enterprises."[61] During its deliberations in October 2017, the IGWG received a joint submission from Business at OECD, the Foreign Trade Association, the International Chamber of Commerce, and the Global Voice of Business "which collectively represent millions of companies around the world [and] have been constructively engaged in the business and human rights agenda for many years." That submission stated: "We underscore our opposition to impose direct international human rights obligations on transnational corporations (TNCs) and other business enterprises (OBEs), which takes the debate back to the politically-charged era of the UN norms."[62]

In a recent UN initiative with the private sector, in June 2019 Secretary-General Guterres signed a *Strategic Partnership Framework* with the World Economic Forum (WEF) to accelerate the implementation of the 2030 Agenda for Sustainable Development.[63] This UN–WEF Memorandum of Understanding enumerates the focus areas of financing the 2030 Agenda, climate change, health, digital cooperation, gender equality and the empowerment of women, education, and skills and commits to multi-stakeholder partnerships and the promotion of public–private partnerships as the main means of implementation.

The WEF describes itself as an "international organization for public-private cooperation" with a mission that "engages the foremost political, business, cultural and other leaders of society to shape global, regional and industry agendas." The institution advocates voluntary and stake-holder approaches to governance as it "carefully blends and balances the best of many kinds of organizations, from both the public and private sectors, international organizations and academic institutions."

The lack of commitment to rigorous assessment and oversight in line with UN norms and human rights standards and the embrace of the "win-win" mindset have exacerbated a host of concerns among some seasoned observers and former UN staff, as well as many CSOs, that the UN itself is being converted into a public–private partnership.[64]

NOTES

1 *Implementation of General Assembly Resolution 71/243 on the Quadrennial Comprehensive Policy Review of Operational Activities for Development of the United Nations System, 2019: Funding Analysis, Report of the Secretary-General* (UN document A/74/73/Add.2), 22 April 2019, para. 1.
2 Ibid.
3 *Implementation of General Assembly Resolution 71/243 on the Quadrennial Comprehensive Policy Review of Operational Activities for Development of the United Nations System, 2019: Funding Compact, Report of the Secretary-General* (UN document A/74/73/Add.1), 2 April 2019.
4 United Nations Centre on Transnational Corporations (UNCTC), https://uia.org/s/or/en/1100024712.
5 *National Committees for UNICEF, Report of the UNICEF National Committees*, PowerPoint presentation, 15 January 2019.
6 Independent Advisory Group on United Nations Financing, *Financing and Effective United Nations* (New York: Ford Foundation, 1993); also published as UN document A/48/460, para. 99, 23.
7 *Statement by UN Secretary-General Kofi Annan to the World Economic Forum* (UN document SG/SM/6881), 31 January 1999.
8 *Budgetary and Financial Situation of the Organizations of the United Nations System, Note by the Secretary-General*, UN document A/69/305, 12 August 2014, Tables 2 and 2B.
9 UN document A/74/73/Add.2, para. 13.
10 *Schedule 3.14.1G, Global Compact Trust Funds AGK, Voluntary Contributions Receivable* (DM/OPPBA document Financial Statements for the year ended 31 December 2017), Schedule of Individual Trust Funds, 2018, 190.
11 General Assembly resolution 60/215, 22 December 2005.
12 Quadrennial Comprehensive Policy Review of Operational Activities for Development of the United Nations System (General Assembly resolution 67/266), 21 December 2012, para. 35.
13 "United Nations Sustainable Development Cooperation Framework—Internal Guidance, United Nations Sustainable Development Group," June 2019, para. 76–77.
14 UN document A/74/73/Add.1, para. 26.
15 UN document A/74/73/Add.2, para. 41.
16 *Financial Statements for the Biennium 2012–2013 Ended 31 December 2013. Schedule of Individual Trust Funds, United Nations Department of Management/Office of Programme Planning, Budget and Accounts*, New York, 2014.
17 Barbara Adams and Jens Martens, *The United Nations Foundation—A Foundation for the UN?* (Berlin/Bonn/New York: Global Policy Forum, March 2018), 6.
18 *United Nations Office for Partnerships Report of the Secretary-General* (UN document A/71/159), 15 July 2016.
19 Adams and Martens, *The United Nations Foundation*, Tables 1 and 3.
20 *United Nations Office of Partnerships, Report of the Secretary-General* (UN document A/65/347), 3 September 2010.
21 *Statement by the United Nations Secretary-General Ban Ki-moon*, "The Secretary-General's Five-Year Action Agenda," 25 January 2012.
22 Adams and Martens, *The United Nations Foundation*, Annex.
23 *Organization of the United Nations Office for Partnerships, Secretary-General's Bulletin*, UN document ST/SGB/2009/14, 19 December 2009.
24 *United Nations Office for Partnerships, Report of the Secretary-General*, UN document A/64/91*, 12 December 2009.

25 Forbes, *Special Issue on Philanthropy*, 2 December 2013; and "Forbes 400 Philanthropy Summit," United Nations Office of Partnerships, 2013 Events Summary, www.un.org/partnerships/content/past-events.

26 UN document A/65/347, Annex I.

27 *Audit of the Management of the United Nations Fund for International Partnerships, UN Office of Internal Oversight Services Report 2015/001* (Internal Audit Division Assignment #2013/522/01), 15 January 2019, para. 18.

28 Adams, *The United Nations Foundation—A Foundation for the UN?*, 8, Box 1.

29 UN Global Compact, *The Ten Principles of the UN Global Compact*, United Nations Global Compact, www.unglobalcompact.org/AboutTheGC/TheTenPrinciples/index.html.

30 *United Nations Global Compact Activity Report 2015*, United Nations Global Compact Headquarters, 2017, 20.

31 *United Nations Global Compact Activity Report 2013*, United Nations Global Compact Headquarters, May 2014, 31.

32 Ibid., 36.

33 Ibid., 31; and *United Nations Global Compact Activity Report 2015*, 20.

34 *United Nations Corporate Partnerships: The Role and Functioning of the Global Compact, Report of the Joint Inspection Unit* (document JIU/REP/2010/9), v.

35 *United Nations Office for Partnerships Report of the Secretary-General* (General Assembly document A/68/186), 1 and 10.

36 *United Nations Global Compact Activity Report 2013*, 12.

37 UN document A/74/73/Add.2, 7.

38 Barbara Adams and Jens Martens, *Fit for Whose Purpose? Private Funding and Corporate Influence in the United Nations* (Bonn/New York: Global Policy Forum, September 2015), 48.

39 *Evaluation of UNDP Partnership with Global Funds and Philanthropic Foundations, Report of the Independent Evaluation Office* (New York: UNDP, 2012), para. 25.

40 UNDP, "Press Release 2 March 2013, The Coca-Cola Company and UNDP Cooperate on 'Every Drop Matters,'" www.undp.org/content/undp/en/home/presscenter/pressreleases/2013/03/22/the-coca-cola-company-and-undp-cooperate-on-every-drop-matters-.html.

41 UNICEF, "Press Release, 2 June 2015, Gucci–UNICEF Partnership Turns 10: Over 7.5 Million Children Reap Reward," www.unicef.org/media/media_82165.html.

42 *Private Fundraising and Partnerships: Financial Report for the Year Ended 31 December 2018: Report by the United Nations Children's Fund* (UN document E/ICEF/2019/AB/L.6), 12 July 2019, para. 5.

43 *UN Women Compendium of Financial Partners Contributions 2018, United Nations Entity for Gender Equality and Women's Empowerment*, 2019, 4.

44 Ibid., 9.

45 "BHP Billiton & Vale Lawsuit (re dam collapse in Brazil)," *Business & Human Rights Resource Centre*, www.business-humanrights.org/en/bhp-billiton-vale-lawsuit-re-dam-collapse-in-brazil.

46 Darren Gray, "BHP Settles US Class Action over Samarco Dam Failure for $67 Million," *The Sydney Morning Herald*, 9 August 2018.

47 *Engage with UNESCO—Leave Your Mark, UNESCO and the Private Sector, United Nations Educational Scientific and Cultural Organization*, 2014, https://unesdoc.unesco.org/ark:/48223/pf0000228855, 9.

48 Rachel Sauvinet-Bedouin et al., *Evaluation of FAO's Cross-Organizational Strategy Broadening Partnerships and Alliance* (Rome: FAO, 2005), para. 189.

49 UN document JIU/REP/2017/8.

50 *Implementation of General Assembly resolution 71/243 on the Quadrennial Comprehensive Policy Review of Operational Activities for Development of the United Nations System, 2018, Report of the Secretary-General*, UN document A/73/63, 20.

51 Dag Hammarskjöld Foundation and UN Multi-Partner Trust Fund Office, *Financing the UN Development System: Time for Hard Choices* (Uppsala, Sweden: DHF, 2019), 41.

52 *Guidelines on a Principle-Based Approach to the Cooperation between the United Nations and the Business Sector*, issued in 2000, revised and reissued in 2009, and revised in 2015 (General Assembly resolution 68/234), 2015, 3; and *Secretary-General Proposes Global Compact on Human Rights, Labour, Environment, in Address to World Economic Forum in Davos*, UN Press Release SG/SM/6881, 1 February 1999.

53 "Framework of Engagement with Non-State Actors" (World Health Assembly resolution WHA69.10), 28 May 2016, 7.

54 Chelsea Clinton and Devi Sridhar, "Who Pays for Cooperation in Global Health?" *The Lancet* 390, no. 10091 (15 July 2017): 324–332.

55 Ibid., 6.
56 United Nations, *Global Compact Activity Report 2015* (New York: United Nations Global Compact Headquarters, 2017), 20.
57 JIU, *Review of Mechanisms and Policies Addressing Conflict of Interest in the United Nations System*, JIU/REP/2017/9 (Geneva: UN, 2017).
58 JIU, *The United Nations System: Private Sector Partnerships Arrangements in the Context of the 2030 Agenda for Sustainable Development*, JIU/REP/2017/8 (Geneva: UN, 2017).
59 UNSDG, *UNSDG Common Approach to Prospect Research and Due Diligence for Business Sector Partnerships*, www.ilo.org/wcmsp5/groups/public/-dgreports/-integration/documents/genericdocument/wcms_726770.pdf.
60 OHCHR, *Guiding Principles on Business and Human Rights* (New York and Geneva: UN, 2011), www.ohchr.org/documents/publications/guidingprinciplesbusinesshr_en.pdf.
61 UN Office of the High Commissioner for Human Rights, 2014, *Elaboration of an International Legally Binding Instrument on Transnational Corporations and Other Business Enterprises with Respect to Human Rights*, Geneva (UN document A/HCR/RES/26/9).
62 *Letter to the UN Treaty Process on Business and Human Rights*, "Response of the International Business Community to the 'Elements' for a Draft Legally Binding Instrument on Transnational Corporations and Other Business Enterprises with Respect to Human Rights," 20 October 2017, www.business-humanrights.org/sites/default/files/documents/Joint%20business%20response%20to%20IGWG%20elements%20paper%20-%2020.10.2017%20-%20FINAL.pdf.
63 "World Economic Forum and UN Sign Strategic Partnership Framework," *World Economic Forum*, 13 June 2019, www.weforum.org/press/2019/06/world-economic-forum-and-un-sign-strategic-partnership-framework.
64 Harris Gleckman, "How the United Nations Is Quietly Being Turned into a Public–Private Partnership," *Open Democracy*, 2 July 2019.

ADDITIONAL READING

Barbara Adams, "Money Talks at the World Health Organizations: An Alternative World Health Report," *Global Health Watch* 5 (ZED Scholar, 15 December 2017).
Barbara Adams, "United Nations and Business Community: Outsourcing or Crowding in?" *Development* 59, nos. 1–2 (21–28 and 2 May 2017): 21–28.
Barbara Adams and Jens Martens, *Fit for Whose Purpose? Private Funding and Corporate Influence in the United Nations* (Bonn/New York: Global Policy Forum, September 2015).
Barbara Adams and Jens Martens, *The United Nations Foundation—A Foundation for the UN?* (Berlin/Bonn/New York: Global Policy Forum, March 2018).
Jens Martens and Karoline Seitz, *Rules of Engagement between the UN and Private Actors: Towards Regulatory and Institutional Framework* (Aachen/Berlin/Bonn: Global Policy Forum Europe, September 2019).

13

THE "THIRD UN"

Civil society and the world organization

Roberto Bissio

Speaking at the opening of the UN General Assembly in September 2018, UN Secretary-General António Guterres warned that "multilateralism is under fire precisely when we need it most."[1] A few weeks later, addressing the World Economic Forum in Davos, he continued:

> In several parts of the world, we see the civil society space shrinking. We see media freedom being negatively impacted. And we see the expression of forms of authoritarianism or this new fantastic expression that was invented, "illiberal democracy"—This is clear. The human rights agenda is in trouble and we need to make sure that we mobilise the international community—and again the civil society has a key role to play in this—for human rights to be protected.[2]

It is not difficult to conclude that the attacks on multilateralism and on civil society have a similar origin. The human rights agenda, which is currently "under fire," is the *raison d'être* for civil society. It cannot exist without the freedom to associate and to speak, but human rights are also at the very core of the UN, and are mentioned seven times in the UN Charter, "making the promotion and protection of human rights a key purpose and guiding principle of the Organization."[3]

Civil society has a history of supporting specific UN agendas or processes, as was the case during the cycle of UN conferences in the 1990s, or introducing new initiatives, as with the ban on landmines or the creation of the International Criminal Court. However, now multilateralism itself needs to be defended. Significantly enough, even when addressing the assembly of the global corporations, Guterres did not appeal to the billionaires to come to the rescue, but he asked for help from the very civil society whose space is shrinking.

This chapter discusses the role of non-governmental organizations (NGOs) in the work of the UN and particularly its development system. It includes a historical review of NGO engagement and the shift in perception of the role of civil society from an agent in implementing development to an ally in defending multilateralism.

A short history

The "Third UN" is a term coined by Thomas G. Weiss, Tatiana Carayannis, and Richard Jolly to encompass non-governmental organizations (NGOs), academics, consultants, experts, independent commissions, and other individuals and their informal networks working side by side with the other two (the first composed of the member states, the second of secretariats).[4] The relation between the three has never been a static one. It began evolving since the words "We the peoples" were inscribed in the first words of the Preamble to the UN Charter in 1945. Article 71 coined the term "non-governmental organizations" to designate private international non-profit associations with which the Economic and Social Council (ECOSOC) would engage in "consultations." Eventually their voices registered in UN deliberations and influenced some agendas; but they never had a vote, a prerogative of member states.[5]

"Trade union confederations, faith groups, disarmament movements, and business associations were among the first forty-one organizations to be admitted in 1948."[6] The enormous variety of purpose, methods, and constituencies of these entities led to their being designated by what they were not, "*non*governmental organizations," rather than by what they were. The number of NGOs accredited by ECOSOC grew to 400 by 1970, 600 by 1980, and nearly a thousand by 1990. While their presence was obvious in earlier global conferences,[7] it was the post-Cold War cycle of agenda-setting, global, ad hoc UN conferences that attracted the attention of the public worldwide. For instance, the 1992 "Earth Summit" in Rio de Janeiro (known as UNCED) allowed over 3,000 organizations to enter the official spaces while some 20,000 more were part of a parallel "Global Forum," raising the public profile and political weight of the conference and the Agenda 21 that resulted. The Earth Summit was also the first time that computer-mediated communications (e-mail and discussion groups) were used widely in an international conference, through a service provided by NGOs. The ability of civil society to spread news and documents, organize, and react fast surprised diplomats, international civil servants, and even the press at a moment when most of the media relied on fax and teletype, and the commercial use of the Internet was forbidden because it was a service subsidized by the US government.

The emerging Internet helped Southern-based NGOs to engage in international debates that formerly had been impossible because of the costs of physical participation. Through its Non-Governmental Liaison Service (NGLS), the UN actively assisted NGOs, particularly from the Global South, to participate meaningfully in the conferences of the 1990s by organizing the funding for travel, advising NGOs, and helping UN bodies interface with them. Significantly, in 1995 when the Internet only accounted for 1 percent of telecommunicated information, the NGLS published a handbook on using electronic mail for NGOs in developing countries, which was entitled *@t ease with e-mail*.[8]

NGONET, an initiative created to promote Southern NGO engagement in global decision-making through the use of new technologies, gathered an impressive collection of 48,000 pages of documents contributed by civil society organizations (CSOs) throughout the preparatory process of UNCED.[9]

This technical possibility of Southern-based organizations to participate in UN processes directly, instead of through hierarchical structures centered in New York, London, and Paris, coincided with a change in the rules for NGO accreditation by ECOSOC. They became less restrictive and regional and national organizations, particularly from the South, were able to interact with one another as well as the First UN of member states and the Second UN of secretariats.

The number of accredited NGOs tripled between 1990 and 2000. As of 1 September 2018, officially 5,161 NGOs enjoyed active consultative status with ECOSOC;[10] in addition, over 1,450 NGOs are in formal association with the Department of Public Information (DPI) in 2019.[11]

This growing interest to participate in the UN agenda-setting conferences was parallel to the growing anti-globalization movement. Those mobilizations peaked in the final years of the twentieth century, when the negotiations led by the Organisation for Economic Co-operation and Development (OECD) for a Multilateral Agreement on Investment were indefinitely postponed in 1998 because of massive civil society opposition. The following year, the World Trade Organization's (WTO's) ministerial meeting in Seattle collapsed in the midst of substantial street demonstrations and the refusal of countries from the Global South to accommodate the demands of the industrialized North.

That momentum also created a backlash. In the words of James Paul, the US government, alarmed at the gathering worldwide criticism of globalization and neoliberalism, led a sharp attack on the (UN) conferences as unproductive, expensive, and pie-in-the-sky, with (Washington charged) little policy relevance in the real world. The US Congress even passed legislation in 1996 threatening to restrict US dues payments if global conferences continued. Some other governments agreed, nervous that their own unpopular policy options might be challenged if future conferences were convened. Annan and his team felt constrained to abandon the conference idea, even if this meant distancing the UN from the progressive NGO movements and the great energy and support they brought to the world body. Annan announced in 1996 that he would oppose any further conferences, though in fact several remained in the pipeline. The last major conferences of the 1990s tradition took place in 2002: the first "Financing for Development" Summit in Monterrey, the Summit on Aging in Madrid, and the Johannesburg Summit on the Environment. From that time forward, UN conferences would be much less frequent and far less ambitious, and the PrepComs would be short, infrequent, and carefully crafted to keep NGO participation to a minimum.[12]

The millennium paradigm shift

In 2000 then-UN secretary-general Kofi Annan tried to compromise with the backlash by announcing in February in Davos the creation of the "Global Compact." The objective was to attract business leaders to the UN, including joining forces with the OECD, the International Monetary Fund (IMF), and the World Bank in a common manifesto in July, entitled "Better World for All," which became the basis for the Millennium Development Goals (MDGs), added by the secretariat as an Annex to the Millennium Declaration in September.

Then-UN deputy secretary-general and UNDP administrator Mark Malloch-Brown later explained how those goals were advocated by "Western donors in the OECD/DAC [Development Assistance Committee] [that] didn't have the global authority and legitimacy" to get universally agreed. He confesses that he and a small group "liberally stole from them this package that became the Millennium Development Goals," written up in the basement of the UN headquarters in "relative casualness," so much so that they almost forgot to include a section on the environment. "The document had gone to the printing presses as I passed the head of the UN's environmental programme," says Malloch-Brown:

> I was walking along the corridor, relieved at job done, when I ran into the beaming head of the UN environment programme and a terrible swearword crossed my mind when I realised we'd forgotten an environmental goal … we raced back to put in the sustainable development goal.[13]

Apart from MDG 7 on the environment and MDG 8 on implementation, the other six MDGs were already included in the "Better World for All" document, which in turn extracted them from the OECD document "Shaping the XXI Century." The objectives that were to guide development policies for 15 years were not only lacking any NGO input into their formulation but also conveniently forgot to consult developing countries, while donor countries had their say through their "club," the OECD, and the Bretton Woods institutions, then tightly controlled by the Group of 7 (G-7).

All of the MDG targets were agreed at UN conferences of the 1990s, but critics argued that they were picked and chosen out of context, ignoring many other agreed goals and reducing the development agenda to an anti-poverty program. On the one hand, the limited set of goals excluded "social problems in the North forgetting that each government committed itself [in the Social Summit of 1995] to addressing social issues in each country of the world."[14] The Tobin Tax, on which the General Assembly had recommended an analysis in June 2000,[15] was left out of MDG 8. Developing countries disapproved of the paradigm change because they understood development as "focused on economic transformation, growth and industrialisation."[16] The negotiated outcome of the Monterrey Summit on Financing for Development in 2002 referred to internationally agreed development goals, but not to the MDGs as such. Later in that year, the Johannesburg Summit on Sustainable Development included in its Plan of Implementation a similar commitment "to achieving the internationally agreed development goals, including those contained in the United Nations Millennium Declaration and in the outcomes of the major United Nations conferences and international agreements since 1992."[17]

The MDGs were not an explicit part of the Millennium Declaration and were not negotiated by governments. Nevertheless, from then on, the phrase "the Internationally Agreed Development Goals including the MDGs" became the standard formulation in all UN negotiated documents. While the "First UN" (member states) tried to remind the "Second UN" (secretariats) of the wider scope of agreements of the 1990s, the UNDS embraced the MDGs as a chance to rescue their budgets from "aid fatigue." Similarly, development NGOs in the North, as part of the greater development "industry," promoted the MDGs to revitalize ODA and gain a seat at the table. This movement peaked with the "Make Poverty History" campaign and the "Live 8" concerts, which ran in parallel to the G-8 summit chaired by Tony Blair in Gleneagles, Scotland.

NGOs or CSOs?

The twenty-first century started with a changing landscape for the Third UN. On the one hand, the Rio Conference had introduced the notion of "major groups" to channel non-state actors' participation in its follow-up: farmers, indigenous peoples, local authorities, scientists, trade unions, women, youth, business, and NGOs. Technically, any organization allowed to address the UN has to be recognized as an NGO by ECOSOC's Committee on NGOs, be it a small association of farmers or the International Chamber of Commerce. However, in the context of the Rio follow-up, through the Commission on Sustainable Development (CSD) or its successor, the High-Level Political Forum (HLPF), they are clustered in these nine major groups, to which a new one of "other stakeholders" was added in 2015. In 1995, the Beijing Conference on Women and the Copenhagen Social Summit both introduced the term "civil society" or "civil society and other stakeholders," which can be understood as a recognition of the variety of constituencies beyond the formalized and frequently donor-led NGOs; however, in practice its use legitimized the unrestricted and un-vetted access of transnational corporations (TNCs).

The UN currently defines civil society as "the 'third sector' of society, along with government and business. It comprises civil society organizations and non-governmental organizations." The UN Department of Economic and Social Affairs (DESA) developed an integrated Civil Society Organizations (iCSO) system, which "facilitates interactions." The iCSO "provides online registration of general profiles for civil society organizations" and "facilitates the application procedure for consultative status" of those wishing to do so. In practice, that approach defines NGOs as a subset of CSOs that has been vetted and approved by the inter-governmental NGO Committee. The database of CSOs currently registers over 24,000 organizations.

With the new millennium and heightened security considerations, physical access to UN premises became limited, while the open practice of preparatory committees to negotiate resolutions through transparent processes that NGOs could influence was shifted to closed rooms or to other forums entirely. The World Bank and the WTO became more involved in policy-making areas previously reserved for UN agencies.

Simultaneously, structural adjustment programs of the World Bank were increasingly leading to the privatizing of public services around the world. Corporations assumed service delivery for those able to afford it; NGOs attracted funding to deliver them to the very poor, or to become watchdogs of their "focused" delivery, substituting for a role spontaneously taken by the middle classes when those services are universal.

The expansion of the NGO role in service delivery was not uncontroversial. Already in 1999, sociologist James Petras estimated that "there are at least 50,000 NGOs in the Third World receiving over $10 billion in funding from international financial institutions, Euro-US-Japanese governmental agencies and local governments." He considered them a micro-level complement to the macroeconomic "assault on the industrial base, independence and living standards of the Third World" introduced by structural adjustment policies.[18]

From within the NGO community, addressing the annual World Bank conference on development economics on behalf of Médecins sans Frontières (MSF), Morten Rostrup argued in 2001 that

> the fact that MSF delivers health care in the world today is a sign of a serious failure, nothing else. For MSF the crucial question will be: Should NGOs really compensate for the state's retreat? Isn't the state's legitimacy being eroded by privatization of fundamental public services? Is it really the role of an NGO to provide health care as part of a permanent or sustainable solution?[19]

In a similar vein, the 2008 Accra conference on aid effectiveness between the OECD donors and "partner countries" elevated NGO status in the ODA-led development circles by calling CSOs "independent development actors in their own right whose efforts complement those of governments and the private sector."[20] Government funding of NGOs, once anathema, became the norm, particularly for big international NGOs; even Amnesty International, built under strict independence, started to accept public funds.

Nonetheless, for the UN, the role of independent citizen organizations was never limited to that of implementing development policies. In 2005, Annan established the UN Democracy Fund (UNDEF), "with the primary mandate to support democracy through civil society."[21] UNDEF presents itself as "a unique model in the UN family, working to do transformative things with grants in relatively small amounts, using direct support to create enabling environments for civil society around the world."[22] UNDEF is the first UN body to have the word "democracy" in its name, and the first to focus exclusively on promoting CSOs as agents of change. However, the UNDEF is hardly a counterweight to the increased role of corporations in UN affairs. UNDEF grants to national and regional non-profit organizations are small and their number limited. Of some 2,307 project proposals in 2018, only 54 could be funded for a total of less than $11 million.

Post-2015

The Third UN's role in the system changed again with the debate around the post-2015 Agenda. The OECD donors and the Second UN (international civil servants across the system) were preparing to continue the same strategies that they had been implementing since 2000. British filmmaker Richard Curtis even produced a campaign video to that effect, featuring Usain Bolt and titled "No Point Going Half Way." This short film would—in the words of a UNDP press release—"help explain why we should finish what we started with the Millennium Development Goals, as we can end poverty by 2030."[23] That slogan implied a 15-year extension of the same policies, proclaimed as successful even though the global halving of extreme income poverty (measured by the World Bank standard of $1.90 a day) was mainly concentrated in a single country: China.

Meanwhile, the First UN of member states pursued a different tack. Led by middle-income countries, which felt excluded from the MDG strategies, the Rio+20 conference (back in Rio de Janeiro two decades after the previous meeting) approved the notion of "Sustainable Development Goals" (SDGs) and kicked off a government-led negotiation process toward them.

The Third UN saw an opportunity and participated actively in this process, attending numerous consultative meetings at all levels, writing reports, signing petitions, and mobilizing public opinion. Among other steps forward was the inclusion in the 2030 Agenda of a chapter on inequalities (SDG 10), the incorporation of "sustainable agriculture" as a way to overcome hunger (SDG 2), a chapter on sustainable consumption and production (SDG 12) demanding developed countries take the lead, and many references to justice and gender equality throughout the text.

Contrary to the MDGs, the SDGs did not emerge from a closed basement meeting but from a long, transparent, and participatory discussion. Ambition and a wide sense of "ownership" were the benefits, and the costs were losses in conciseness and precision.

Nevertheless, government accountability is strictly confined to national parliaments and citizens in the 2030 Agenda. The term "civil society" is mentioned in the resolution but only for implementation; in all references, civil society appears together with the private or business sector as part of a list of actors without a differentiated role.

Further, Target 17.17 encourages and promotes "effective public, public–private and civil society partnerships" but the indicator that will account for that commitment only measures "the amount of US dollars committed to (a) public–private partnerships and (b) civil society partnerships." As this is the sole indicator related to civil society in the whole framework, it might lead to the belief that the main value of civil society is in its potential to contribute money, which is the least adequate role for most CSOs—foundations and philanthropies excepted.

Civil society voices celebrated the 2030 Agenda as "highly ambitious" and underlined its "transformational" aspirations; but at the same, many found it

> irritating that the International Chamber of Commerce (ICC) as coordinator of the Global Business Alliance for 2030 (an umbrella group of major global industry associations and business organizations) can claim to play a key role in implementing the 2030 Agenda, offering "comprehensive engagement with the full diversity of business expertise."[24]

Shrinking space after 2015 and UN "repositioning"

The year 2015 ended with the approval of three major strategic documents for the UN system: the Addis Ababa Action Agenda (AAAA) on Financing for Development, the 2030

Agenda on Sustainable Development, and the Paris Agreement on Climate Change. However, 2016 saw a new administration in the White House, which early on dissociated itself from the Paris Agreement and suspended the US membership at UNESCO; it not only blocked further multilateral trade negotiations at the WTO but de facto paralyzed the trade body by not allowing for vacant seats in its Appellate Body to be filled, thus rendering dispute resolutions impossible.

In his "Repositioning the United Nations Development System to Deliver on the 2030 Agenda,"[25] Guterres elaborates on the strategy to defend multilateralism by making it relevant for society:

> Beyond accountability to Member States, the United Nations must continue to open up, reach out and be more responsive to the larger public that it serves. Reinvesting in public advocacy and communications for sustainable development results would make it easier for the world to understand and take part in global United Nations commitments. Development experts and practitioners should also turn to the Economic and Social Council as a vibrant space for development exchanges and analysis. In addition, as the system expands its outreach to external partners, Member States might wish to strengthen stakeholder engagement in the deliberations of the Council, especially by civil society, including women's and youth groups.[26]

This policy is not only valid for the UN headquarters: "United Nations country teams must increasingly champion collaborative and open dialogue with all stakeholders, including the furthest behind, as it supports national institutions."[27]

The UNDS strategic document makes the same point in its Annex:

> the United Nations system should use its convening role to help expand meaningful participation by civil society, especially marginalized groups, to ensure that the United Nations development system supports Governments in reaching the furthest behind first and leaves no one behind.[28]

Such a recommendation goes beyond a public-relations exercise aimed at improving the UN's image. UNDP's Independent Evaluation Office, for example, after assessing evaluations covering 93 countries and all five regions over 15 years of country programs, concluded in 2018 that "the sustainability of UNDP programme results is most often directly related to the extent of national ownership, sustained attention to national capacity-building, and engagement with civil society."[29]

Among the top 10 recommendations most commonly formulated by the evaluations of UNDP country programs, two directly refer to civil society: increase civil society and community-level engagement in interventions; and create additional spaces for civil society influence in policy and decision-making.

VNRs: an opportunity?

The Voluntary National Reviews (VNRs) on SDG implementation submitted to ECOSOC's High-Level Political Forum (HLPF) have become in many countries an opportunity for national interactions between governments and civil society, frequently facilitated by the UN resident coordinator. All OECD members (except the United States) participate in the reporting process, which has involved in a UN process CSOs from developed countries outside the traditional circle of "development NGOs," as the national reporting discusses domestic policies beyond official development assistance.

The DESA "Handbook for the Preparation of VNRs" notes in its 2019 edition[30] that

> stakeholders from different countries and sectors have been coordinating efforts to produce "spotlight reports", reflecting their perspectives on implementation of the 2030 Agenda. National civil society coalitions on the SDGs have been established in several countries and usually take the lead on drafting those reports.[31]

DESA reminds governments that

> efforts could include reaching out to legislative bodies, the public, civil society and the private sector, and communicating entry points for stakeholder participation in VNR preparation and implementation of the 2030 Agenda. Additionally, efforts could be taken to identify representative voices from marginalized groups and to enable their meaningful engagement in the process.

By the end of 2020, over 200 VNRs will have been officially submitted (with many countries reporting two or even three times), which shows a high degree of political commitment by the First UN to the 2030 Agenda. By then, the only UN members with over 1 million inhabitants having failed to submit a single report will be Angola, Cuba, Eritrea, Haiti, Iran, Myanmar, Nicaragua, South Sudan, the United States, and Yemen.[32]

Yet, Sakiko Fukuda-Parr, vice-chair of the Committee for Development Policy, reports that less than half of the VNRs submitted in 2018 address any commitment to giving priority to helping those furthest behind: "Without clearer strategies, plans and analysis, VNRs don't serve their follow-up and review purpose, and do little to encourage Member States who are off-track to switch trains and head in the right direction."[33]

Encouraged by the UN to claim a seat on the table in the elaboration of their national VNRs, CSOs have developed an appetite to be present when the VNR is submitted to ECOSOC; a new generation of NGOs is thus being attracted to UN headquarters. However, their alternative "spotlight reports" (a name that plays on the traditional designation of "shadow reports" in human rights proceedings) are not recognized, listed, linked, or mentioned in any official UN database. This absence is notable because the system registers all kinds of voluntary "partnerships." CSOs not based in New York and interested in attending their countries' presentations in New York face major difficulties—particularly those from the Global South with visa restrictions, too little travel support, and limited participation opportunities. Physical space is constrained, and time is too short to make presentations or formulate questions. When governments do not welcome dissent, a situation that is inherent with the "shrinking space" that the Secretary-General denounced, the Second UN is not prepared to defend its defenders.

The NGLS and the Department for Public Information were merged into the Civil Society Unit of the UN Department of Global Communications (DGC). NGOs associated with DGC are supposed to "help build knowledge and support for the world organization at the grassroots level"[34] but this support does not work the other way around, from the UN to NGOs. A "best case" example of an attempt to create space is in Box 13.1. It illustrates how the UN can help redress shrinking civic space through active diplomacy, civil society campaigning, and convening like-minded governments that are committed to sustainable development.

Box 13.1 Escazú agreement: a regional attempt to expand civic space

"Shrinking civic space" can be a life-or-death matter. In 2016, at least 120 environmental defenders were killed in Latin America, mainly in Brazil and Colombia, and that toll grew to around 200 in 2017.[1] On 3 March 32018, two years after the murder of Berta Cáceres in Honduras, the UN Economic Commission Latin America and the Caribbean (ECLAC) hosted the states from the region in Escazú, Costa Rica, to adopt a mandatory legal convention to redress that situation and promote three key "access rights."

The Escazú agreement is inspired by Principle 10 of the 1992 Rio Declaration on Environment and Development: environmental issues are best handled with participation of all concerned citizens, at the relevant level. At the national level, each individual shall have appropriate access to information concerning the environment that is held by public authorities, including information on hazardous materials and activities in their communities, and the opportunity to participate in decision-making processes. States shall facilitate and encourage public awareness and participation by making information widely available. Effective access to judicial and administrative proceedings, including redress and remedy, shall be provided.

Principle 10 was reaffirmed by the 2012 "Future We Want" declaration. It sets out three fundamental "access rights" as key pillars of sound environmental governance: to information, to public participation, and to justice.

Access to information empowers citizens and incentivizes them to participate in decision- and policy-making processes in an informed manner. Public participation is increasingly being seen as a vital part of addressing environmental problems and achieving sustainable development by encouraging governments to adopt policies and enact laws that take community needs into account. Access to justice provides the foundation of "access rights," as it facilitates the public's ability to enforce their right to participate, to be informed, and to hold regulators and polluters accountable for environmental harm.

The Escazú Convention, known officially as the "Regional Agreement on Access to Information, Public Participation and Justice in Environmental Matters," was signed by 24 countries and will enter into force when ratified by 11.[2] Some hail it as "the first ever legally binding treaty on environmental rights,"[3] but it addresses the very preconditions for civil society to organize and get actively involved.

The convention requires governments to take measures to prevent, investigate, and punish threats and attacks against "human rights defenders in environmental matters."[4] For the first time in international law, the convention requires governments to ensure that vulnerable populations, like indigenous peoples or vulnerable communities, can exercise their full rights to information, participation, and justice. Actions governments must take range from providing free legal assistance to creating more accessible communication channels between affected communities and political officials.

Finally, under the agreement, governments must guarantee opportunities for public participation in projects that will significantly impact the environment. They must involve the public early on in the decision-making process, and after a decision has been made, they must inform citizens of how their input shaped the final outcome.

Implementation is the responsibility of national governments. The agreement admits no reservations and ECLAC will function as its secretariat and host of a "clearing house on access rights," including legislative, administrative and policy measures, codes of conduct, and good practices. A Consultative Committee was created to support compliance "and formulate recommendations" with "significant participation of the public."

Notes
1 See www.globalwitness.org/en/campaigns/environmental-activists/at-what-cost.
2 As of September 2019, Guyana and Bolivia have ratified.
3 See www.unece.org/fileadmin/DAM/env/pp/wgp/WGP-22/Other_material/Updated_LAC_P10_
   Two-Pager_Final_6.12.2018.pdf.
4 See https://repositorio.cepal.org/bitstream/handle/11362/43583/1/S1800428_en.pdf.

Space is not optional

"According space to civil society is not optional," states the UN High Commissioner for Human Rights in a 2018 report, "Procedures and Practices in Respect of Civil Society Engagement with International and Regional Organizations."[35] The language is clear: everyone has the right, individually and in association with others, to promote and to strive for the protection and realization of human rights and fundamental freedoms at the community, national, regional, and international levels, to exercise the freedoms of opinion and expression, of peaceful assembly, and of association, and to have access to information and participate in public affairs. International law also protects the lives, liberty, physical integrity, and privacy of civil society actors.

With inputs from numerous UN organizations, the report provides an overview of how the Second UN values civil society contributions, in three ways in particular. The first is advocacy and awareness raising. The report quotes examples provided by FAO, UNAIDS, DESA ("strengthening the participation of the most underrepresented"), the UN Office for Disarmament Affairs ("mobilize victims" and "forming civil society networks"), and Peacebuilding Support Office ("critical advocacy role").

The second type of contribution is expertise and knowledge. The report credits CSOs with the establishment of "a system of international pressure on the development of human rights, as shown by the 2017 Nobel Prize for Peace awarded to the International Campaign to Abolish Nuclear Weapons," while the International Civil Aviation Organization credits NGOs with technical contributions to the development of standards.

The third contribution involves implementation, monitoring, and evaluation. Many agencies including IFAD, FAO, UNAIDS, UNESCO, UNHCHR, and the Peacebuilding Support Office quote civil society participation in the design and implementation of projects, as "civil society has the added advantage of having close links with grass-roots organizations and individuals and could therefore help to increase the effectiveness of UN interventions."

The report goes on to list a variety of advisory bodies to channel civil society inputs and different modalities of accreditation and access to meetings. It highlights access to information as "a precondition for any meaningful engagement" and underlines that "the absence of justice and appeal mechanisms in regional and international institutions […] was incompatible with the spirit of the Charter of the United Nations."[36]

The High Commissioner concludes, "the effective functioning of international and regional organizations is inexorably linked to civil society participation" and formulates 14 concrete recommendations to improve that participation and protect the participants from threats and reprisals. Box 13.2 lists those recommendations.

Box 13.2 Recommendations of the UN High Commissioner on Human Rights for the effective engagement of civil society

In order for States and organizations to provide and foster effective engagement, OHCHR and the contributors to the present report recommend that they:

a   Adopt policies and frameworks for civil society engagement that recognize the contribution of civil society, and establish clear, effective, human rights-based and gender-sensitive channels of participation and engagement; and establish institutional mechanisms to promote a systematic and meaningful civil society engagement, such as advisory boards;

b   Expand the transparency of decision-making processes and access to public meetings, including by making information available in a timely manner, in relevant languages, with minimum restrictions and by employing new communications tools to maximize outreach, based on explicit policies that comply with human rights;

c   Put in place transparent, fair and gender-sensitive accreditation processes that deliver prompt decisions in compliance with human rights standards, including by establishing grievance mechanisms for redress, and address any erroneous accreditation decisions;

d   Review the practice and procedures of the Economic and Social Council Committee on Non-Governmental Organizations for granting consultative status so that it complies fully with international standards, such as non-discrimination, accountability and transparency, and ensure that they are fit for the purpose of securing full, diverse and timely civil society participation;

e   Adopt and implement robust policies on access to information, including by appointing focal points and ensuring secure information channels;

f   Ensure the safety and security of persons seeking to engage with regional and international organizations, including online, prevent any acts of reprisals by State or non-State actors against them and, when such reprisals do occur, condemn them and ensure accountability and access to an effective remedy;

g   Enable the prompt and objective review by independent accountability mechanisms of restrictions imposed on civil society engagement at the international and regional levels, for example through a review panel or an Ombudsperson;

h   Report regularly on civil society engagement, including on measures taken to bolster engagement and diversify civic society partners;

i   Reach out proactively to underrepresented parts of civil society with a view to ensuring the diversity of civil society participation, by including women, children, young people, older persons, persons with disabilities, ethnic, national, linguistic and racial minorities, migrants and indigenous people;

j   Explore avenues to enable the participation of those segments of civil society and individuals that are not associated with or organized in NGOs, including social movements;

k   Consider different institutional arrangements, such as the creation of civil society advisory boards, liaison units in secretariats of international organizations and the development of tools to increase capacity for effective civil society participation;

l   Ensure that those bodies responsible for civil society engagement have the resources necessary and provide other forms of support to the least represented civil society actors, including training and funding for travel. Special considerations should be given to organizations that face challenges in gaining access to the resources necessary to function effectively, including as a result of restrictions placed on access to foreign funding. In parallel, expand remote participation through videoconferencing and conference hubs and, where possible, organize meetings and conferences in accessible and less costly places or venues;

m   Guard against abuses of process, exploitation of procedural flaws and modalities of participation, including undue use of points of order during meetings and restrictive language in relation to modalities of stakeholder engagement;

n   Promote civil society participation in the implementation of the Sustainable Development Goals and the High-Level Political Forum reviews, also with a view to ensuring that no one is left behind.

While the report leaves no doubt on how important civil society is for the UN, it does not address the reverse question: is the UN relevant for civil society? In fact, during the meetings of the World Social Forum in the first decade of this century, participants were frequently divided between those who saw the UN as part of the establishment to be changed versus those who viewed it as an ally. Development NGOs were clearly among the latter, but many locally based CSOs in different countries recognized the value of the UN for its normative role, from human rights to standard-setting, as well as for providing opportunities for engaging in global and regional issues and for contesting their own governments' policies on substantive issues.

After hearing from many of the world's top women politicians in March 2019 in a debate on "Women in Power" during the session of the Commission on the Status of Women (CSW), Guterres convened a town hall meeting for civil society activists. "The central question of gender equality is a question of power," he stressed, noting that

> we continue to live in a male-dominated world with a male-dominated culture … We will only be successful if we are able to combine the institutional approaches, like the ones the UN develops, with the approaches at the civil society [level], the grassroots movements and the public opinion in general.

He concluded that "power is not given, power is taken" and added that "we have to push back" against the resistance to change.[37]

In an opinion piece published by *The Guardian*,[38] Guterres uses similar language of mobilization on the climate crisis:

> Young people, the UN—and a growing number of leaders from business, finance, government, and civil society—in short, many of us—are mobilizing and acting.
>
> But we need many others to take climate action if we are to succeed. We have a long way to go. But the movement has begun.

Conclusion: multilateralism needs civil society … and vice-versa

Can such a movement include tax justice, on top of gender equality and climate? Or social justice? Or plain justice, in a world where access to courts and remedies is out of reach for most of the under-privileged? That is ultimately the Third UN's aspiration; if successful, it will have ultimately rescued the First UN and the Second UN from many present threats.

Civil society has historically engaged with the UN in a variety of roles: an advocate for a multiplicity of causes; a watchdog over its activities; a provider of expertise; and an implementing agent. Today, civil society is asked to defend multilateralism itself. However, the species of multilateralism that civil society will defend is not about the survival of the extant international bureaucratic machinery. It is about a United Nations system that understands power and its asymmetry and the need to use it to transform the world politics as it was supposed to do when it was founded three-quarters of a century ago.

NOTES

1 António Guterres, "Address to the 73rd General Assembly," 25 September 2018, www.un.org/sg/en/content/sg/speeches/2018-09-25/address-73rd-general-assembly.
2 António Guterres, "Address to the World Economic Forum Annual Meeting," 24 January 2019, www.weforum.org/agenda/2019/01/these-are-the-global-priorities-and-risks-for-the-future-according-to-antonio-guterres.
3 UN, "What We Do," www.un.org/en/sections/what-we-do/protect-human-rights.
4 Thomas G. Weiss, Tatiana Carayannis, and Richard Jolly, "The 'Third' United Nations," *Global Governance* 15, no. 2 (2009): 123–142. See also Tatiana Carayannis and Thomas G. Weiss, *The "Third" United Nations: How Knowledge Brokers Help the UN Think* (Oxford: Oxford University Press, forthcoming).
5 Peter Willets, *Non-Governmental Organizations in World Politics: The Construction of Global Governance* (London: Routledge, 2011).
6 James A. Paul, "Civil Society and the United Nations," in *Global Civil Society: Shifting Powers in a Shifting World* (Uppsala, Sweden: Uppsala University Press, 2011), www.globalpolicy.org/images/pdfs/NGOs_and_the_United_Nations_Paul_James.pdf.
7 Michael E. Schechter, *United Nations Global Conferences* (London: Routledge, 2005).
8 NGLS/UNCTAD and FES, "@t Ease with E-mail: A Handbook on Using Electronic Mail for NGOs in Developing Countries," New York, 1995, www.jca.apc.org/~mtachiba/at-ease/index.html.
9 International Development Research Center (IDRC), "The Earth Summit CDROM," in *Information, Communication and IDRC*, Ottawa, no. 1, December 1993, https://idl-bnc-idrc.dspacedirect.org/bitstream/handle/10625/40576/98353-n1-1993.pdf?sequence=1&isAllowed=y.
10 UN, "List of Non-Governmental Organizations in Consultative Status with the Economic and Social Council as of 1 September 2018" (UN document E/2018/INF/5), https://undocs.org/E/2018/INF/5.
11 Civil Society Union, "About Us," https://outreach.un.org/ngorelations/content/about-us-0.
12 Paul, "Civil Society," 5.
13 Quoted from the video interview by Mark Tran, "Mark Malloch-Brown: Developing the MDGs Was a Bit Like Nuclear Fusion," *The Guardian*, 16 November 2012, www.theguardian.com/global-development/2012/nov/16/mark-malloch-brown-mdgs-nuclear.
14 *Statement by Roberto Bissio at the Opening of the Geneva 2000 Forum*, "I Was in Geneva," 25 June 2000, UN document UNRISD/NEWS/22/00/1, www.unrisd.org/80256B3C005BCCF9/(httpAuxPages)/D04C6DE046955DA8C1256BE4002E48B9/$file/22e.pdf.
15 Statement by John Langmore, "Results of the Special Session on Social Development," also in document UNRISD/NEWS/22/00/1.
16 Sakiko Fukuda-Parr and David Hulme, "International Norm Dynamics and 'The End of Poverty': Understanding the Millennium Development Goals (MDGs)," *BWPI Working Paper 96* (Brooks World Poverty Institute, June 2009), http://hummedia.manchester.ac.uk/institutes/gdi/publications/workingpapers/bwpi/bwpi-wp-9609.pdf.
17 UN, *Report of the World Summit on Sustainable Development, Johannesburg, South Africa, 26 August–4 September 2002* (UN document A/CONF.199/20), https://undocs.org/A/CONF.199/20.
18 James Petras, "NGOs: In the Service of Imperialism," *Journal of Contemporary Asia* 29, no. 4 (1999): 429–440.
19 Rostrup, Morten, "The Role of Nongovernmental Organizations in Providing Health Care," *Proceedings of the Annual World Bank Conference on Development Economics*, 1–2 May 2001, Washington, DC, www.msf.fr/sites/default/files/2001-05-01-Rostrup.pdf.

20 OECD, *Accra Agenda for Action* (Paris: OECD, 2008), www.oecd-ilibrary.org/development/accra-agenda-for-action_9789264098107-en.

21 UNDEF, "UNDEF Update—No. 42. 2019," www.un.org/democracyfund/sites/www.un.org.democracyfund/files/Newsletter/uu42_july_2019.pdf.

22 Ibid.

23 UNDP, "Global Goals Campaign Launched with UNDP as Key Partner," 3 September 2015, www.undp.org/content/undp/en/home/presscenter/pressreleases/2015/09/03/global-goals-campaign-2015.html.

24 Jens Martens, "The 2030 Agenda—A New Start Towards Global Sustainability?" *Spotlight 2016*, www.2030spotlight.org/en/book/605/chapter/i1-2030-agenda-new-start-towards-global-sustainability.

25 UN, *Repositioning the United Nations Development System to Deliver on the 2030 Agenda: Our Promise for Dignity, Prosperity and Peace on a Healthy Planet, Report of the Secretary-General* (UN documents A/72/684–E/2018/7), https://undocs.org/A/72/684.

26 Ibid., para. 112.

27 Ibid., para. 134.

28 Ibid., para. 13.

29 Independent Evaluation Office of UNDP, *Annual Report on Evaluation 2018* (New York: UNDP, June 2019), 19, http://web.undp.org/evaluation/documents/annual-report/2019/ARE2018.pdf.

30 DESA, *Handbook for the Preparation of Voluntary National Reviews*, October 2018, https://sustainabledevelopment.un.org/content/documents/20872VNR_hanbook_2019_Edition_v2.pdf.

31 See the website for the *Global Spotlight* report at www.2030spotlight.org/en.

32 Sustainable Development Knowledge Platform, Voluntary National Reviews Database. See UN, "Sustainable Development, VNRs," https://sustainabledevelopment.un.org/vnrs.

33 Elena Marmo, "VNRS, National 'Spotlight' Reports and the Future of the HLPF," www.socialwatch.org/node/18319.

34 See UN, "Civil Society," www.un.org/en/sections/resources-different-audiences/civil-society/index.html.

35 See *Report of the United Nations High Commissioner for Human Rights*, UN document A/HRC/38/18, 18 April 2018, http://ecnl.org/wp-content/uploads/2018/05/2018-HC-report-on-civic-space-in-UN-A-HRC-38-18.pdf.

36 Ibid., para. 41.

37 See UN Women, " 'Power Is Not Given, Power Is Taken,' UN Chief Tells Women Activists, Urging Push-Back against Status Quo," 13 March 2019, www.unwomen.org/en/news/stories/2019/3/news-secretary-general-holds-civil-society-town-hall.

38 António Guterres, "The Movement to Take Climate Action Has Begun—But We Have a Long Way to Go," *The Guardian*, 3 October 2019.

ADDITIONAL READING

Barbara Adams, Cecilia Alemany Billorou, Roberto Bissio, Chee Yoke Ling, Kate Donald, Jens Martens, and Stefano Prato, eds., *Reshaping Governance for Sustainability: Transforming Institutions, Shifting Power, Strengthening Rights, a Global Civil Society Report on the 2030 Agenda and the SDGs*, July 2019, www.2030spotlight.org/sites/default/files/spot2019/Spotlight_Innenteil_2019_web_gesamt.pdf.

Roberto Bissio, "The 'A' Word: Monitoring the SDGs," *FUNDS Briefing no. 26*, February 2015, www.futureun.org/en/Publications-Surveys/Article?newsid=61&teaserId=1.

Tatiana Carayannis and Thomas G. Weiss, *The "Third" United Nations: How Knowledge Brokers Help the UN Think* (Oxford: Oxford University Press, forthcoming).

Dag Hammarskjöld Foundation, Third World Network, Global Policy Forum, Friedrich Ebert Stiftung, DAWN, Terre des hommes, and Social Watch, eds., *No Future without Justice: Report of the Civil Society Reflection Group on Global Development Perspectives*, Development Dialogue no. 59, June 2012, www.daghammarskjold.se/wp-content/uploads/2012/06/dd59_web_optimised_single.pdf.

Peter Willets, *Non-Governmental Organizations in World Politics: The Construction of Global Governance* (London: Routledge, 2011).

14

THE UN AND THE WORLD BANK

Collaboration toward stronger global governance?

Richard Jolly[1]

Many observers may have forgotten that at the 1944 Bretton Woods Conference, the clear intention was for the World Bank and the International Monetary Fund (IMF) to be integral parts of the United Nations, under the authority of the UN secretary-general. Nonetheless, powerful voices like Harry Dexter White, the chief US negotiator, and Henry Morgenthau, secretary of the US treasury, were determined that the UN should never tell the World Bank or the IMF what to do. Notwithstanding, the Bank and the IMF became part of the UN organigram, though by the time of the Bank's first meeting in 1946, the de jure organizational chart had given way to de facto separation. Reflecting on this relationship, John Toye and Richard Toye commented: "this tension between the formal UN status and the de facto operational independence of the IMF and the World Bank has been a constant feature of the international scene ever since."[2]

Much has been lost over the years because of this separation and the resulting tensions, although perspectives on how much depend on whether one believes that closer relations would have brought broader UN ideas and economic thinking on development into the Bretton Woods institutions (BWIs) or, in contrast, limited their creation and adoption within the UN itself. This also depends, of course, on an overall assessment of the quality of the UN's development work in comparison with that of the World Bank and the IMF, as well as what the impact would have been on the volume of (concessional) resources for development which both institutions were able to raise. This chapter reflects on these issues as well as on the future: whether in the next decades of the twenty-first century, closer relations can help both institutions reform and better meet the new and fundamental challenges facing the world.

1945–1980: early years of post-war development

In retrospect, the de facto separation between the UN and the BWIs over their first half-century was costly for both organizations—in analysis, policy recommendations, and action. For the first quarter-century after their founding, the UN including parts of the UN Development System (UNDS) was the center of international analytical work on developing countries while the Bank and the IMF focused mainly, if decreasingly, on developed countries. The BWIs undertook analysis and issued reports on individual countries, but their global reports focused on the developed world. In contrast, the UN was the creative generator of reports and new thinking and policy on developing countries. The UN's Department of Economic and Social Affairs (DESA, formerly the Department of Economic Affairs) issued annual reports on the world economy, comprising analyses of the developed economies, the planned economies, and the so-called under-developed countries (later called "developing countries"). The UN was the only international body issuing such a comprehensive report on the world economy, with the Bank, the IMF, and later the Organisation for Economic Co-operation and Development (OECD) confining themselves to the developed countries.

The UN also focused on research and global policy recommendations. In the 1950s, the UN sponsored three major and pioneering reports on development: *Measures for Full Employment*; *Measures for Economic Development*; and *Measures for International Economic Stability*.[3] Each was the product of an international panel of distinguished economists set up by the UN—the last one including two economists later to win Nobel Prizes, Arthur Lewis and Theodore Schultz. This report recommended low-interest loans to poorer countries. Because of World Bank opposition, via its president Eugene Black, a former Wall Street banker, concessional loans were absent until 1959 when the World Bank set up the International Development Authority (IDA).

Beginning about 1960, the UN and the UNDS adopted the first of what eventually became some 50 quantitative goals for development, usually after detailed and careful analysis and consultation with governments.[4] The first goals related to education, and the next to accelerating the growth of GNP in developing countries, adopted in response to the call by US president John F. Kennedy for the 1960s to be the "Development Decade." These and later goals met with almost universal support from national governments and other international agencies, but never from the Bank and the IMF. Even the 0.7 percent target for development assistance as a proportion of developed country GNP was never adopted by the BWIs. Only in 2000, nearly 40 years later, did the BWIs for the first time adopt international quantitative goals in the form of the Millennium Development Goals (MDGs) and after 2015, their successor, the Sustainable Development Goals (SDGs).

The nearest that the Bank came to promoting broader UN perspectives on development was under its president Robert McNamara (from 1968 to June 1981) who gave priority to poverty reduction, which had long been part of development thinking and policies in many parts of the UN. McNamara's support and often his annual speeches helped shift donors and much of the international development community to follow this focus. McNamara and Hollis Chenery, the World Bank's first chief economist, also endorsed "basic needs," a concept and priority emerging from the International Labour Organization's (ILO's) World Employment Programme over the 1970s. And in 1978, the Bank launched its annual *World Development Report*, which in their first few issues focused on the need for poverty reduction, set in the context of the global economy and emerging issues such as adjustment, debt, growth, and what the Bank termed human development—investment in human resources in then-UN parlance.

For a few years, the World Bank seemed to be giving a strong international lead, with rapidly increasing funding as well as analysis, on many issues that the UN had originally championed, thus providing the basis for closer partnership. Unfortunately, this emphasis did not last. With the departure of McNamara as president in 1981[5] and with the rise of debt and balance-of-payments problems in most countries of Africa and Latin America, the Bank returned to a more conventional economic and financial agenda, giving highest priority to restoring macroeconomic balances and structural adjustment. The focus on poverty reduction was downgraded in terms of policy and analysis, although lending for poverty, education, and health grew. Even in the 1970s, many Bank staff had not taken McNamara's poverty message seriously, some referring to poverty reduction as "the favorite toy of McNamara and of Mahbub ul Haq."[6] Ernie Stern, the Bank's senior vice-president, always argued that economic growth was the best way to achieve poverty reduction, and regional staff argued that drafting poverty briefs on countries would involve additional work with no obvious justification.[7]

Even with McNamara's strong public statements on poverty, the Bank over the 1970s and 1980s was a latecomer in recognizing the importance of supporting primary education, managing the environment, protecting vulnerable groups during structural adjustment, and, more generally, the importance of non-economic aspects of development, including participation and even democracy.[8] All of these are areas where closer links between the World Bank and the UN could potentially have increased and broadened international support for developing countries.

1980–2000: debt, structural adjustment, and transition

Beginning in the 1980s, mounting debt and balance-of-payments problems afflicted many countries in Africa and Latin America, often the consequence of the sharp rises in oil prices in the mid- and late 1970s. The Bank aligned itself formally and more closely with the IMF, pressuring borrowing countries to adopt a narrow economic agenda and the constraints of structural adjustment. The specifics of formulating these conditions were usually the work and focus of short-term missions of the Bank or IMF visiting from Washington. This was in sharp contrast to most UN funds, programs, and specialized agencies that were led by in-country representatives who had a close day-to-day opportunity to observe the impacts of adjustment policies in the countries where they were living.

Over the 1980s and 1990s, there were fierce public debates about the content and impact of the policies of structural adjustment, which became known as the "Washington Consensus." The UN's Economic Commission for Africa (ECA) argued that the policies were ideologically driven, embodying the neoliberal, free-market, and smaller-state philosophy set out in the 1981 Berg Report.[9] ECA viewed structural adjustment in Africa as a deliberate attempt to displace the Lagos Plan of Action,[10] a broader economic-political regional strategy that had been agreed by all African countries. Adebayo Adedeji, the ECA's executive secretary, led the fight but mostly from a position of institutional weakness, even though he chaired an inter-agency committee bringing together most UN organizations involved with Africa. In the mid-1980s, the ILO tried to organize a major international conference on alternatives, but this had to be limited to a much smaller consultation after pressure from the industrial countries.

The UN Children's Fund (UNICEF) was also outspoken and produced several reports on the way that children were hurt by cutbacks in education, health, and other social services. Based on information from its country offices, UNICEF also issued strong statements within the UN and held a face-to-face meeting with Jacques de Larosière, the IMF's managing director. More importantly, from 1984, UNICEF promoted proposals for alternative approaches. They were later spelled out in *Adjustment with a Human Face*,[11] a two-volume study that drew heavily on case studies of Brazil, Chile, Peru, Jamaica, Botswana, Ghana, Zimbabwe, Philippines, Sri Lanka, and South Korea, providing an overview of the impacts of structural adjustment on a diverse range of developing countries.

Toward the end of the 1980s, both the World Bank and the IMF publicly recognized the need to give more attention to the negative impacts of structural adjustment on people, especially on the poor and other vulnerable groups. A special fund was created for providing flexible and additional, though limited, support for such groups. Yet in practice, the macroeconomic policies of the BWIs were little changed, mostly on the argument that structural adjustment was the *sine qua non* for the restoration of economic growth in the medium to longer run.

In retrospect, the Bank's view of structural adjustment placed too much faith in market forces, and the IMF's in how austerity would rapidly help achieve balance in the economies of developing countries. Both also paid too little attention to institutions as well as to the often devastating and long-run impacts on poverty, equity, education, and health. Both also ignored the analytical work of other parts of the UN, including the Economic Commission for Latin America and the Caribbean (ECLAC) and the UN Conference on Trade and Development (UNCTAD) on trade and investment.

Much research within the BWIs and in the academic research community has since been devoted to investigating whether structural adjustment policies stimulated or retarded economic growth. After much debate and analysis, in 2005 Robert J. Barro and Jong-Wha Lee concluded, "IMF programs have a negative effect in the short-run that is not statistically significant, and a strong statistically significant negative effect on economic growth in the long-run."[12] So, as James Vreeland concluded, the newly emerging consensus was that IMF programs hurt economic growth.

The impact of structural adjustment policies in the 1980s and 1990s was a harsh demonstration of this finding. Over the whole of this 20-year period, GNP growth per capita in Latin America amounted to 9 percent compared to 80 percent from 1960–1980. In Sub-Saharan Africa the figures were even worse: from 1980–2000, per capita income declined by 15 percent, compared to its growth by 36 percent from 1960–1980.[13] Not all the declines in growth over the 1980–2000 period could be attributed to the policies of structural adjustment—domestic weaknesses of policy and action and difficulties of trade and armed conflict also affected specific countries. Nevertheless, misguided structural adjustment policies were an important factor, and it can only be surmised how the lives of people in Latin America and Sub-Saharan Africa and their economies might have improved had UN doubts about structural adjustment been taken more seriously over this period.

With the collapse of the Berlin Wall in 1989 and later of the Soviet Union, another sharp difference opened up between UN and BWI thinking and policy approaches. The Economic Commission for Europe (ECE) had been, from the 1950s to the 1980s, the only international economic forum where representatives of East and West Europe met regularly. After the collapse, the ECE argued in a succession of its annual *Economic Surveys* that transition to a more capitalist system needed to be gradual and evolutionary, allowing time to build new institutions, regulations, and structures before simply moving to a market economy. Stabilization and structural and institutional reform were vital and could not be separated from one another. ECE also argued for a new Marshall Plan to provide support while this process proceeded.

The BWIs—and some economists especially in the United States—argued for "shock therapy" and a "big bang," to let markets take over without hesitation.[14] This approach won the day, and over the 1990s led to soaring unfettered capitalism, the rise of the oligarchs, the collapse of social services, and increases in mortality. One argument of proponents of dramatic change was that any delay might bring back the forces behind the previous regime; but this line of argument ignored the fact that public opposition and disillusion had led to the downfall in the first place as well as the importance of replacing the former institutions, which were ill suited to the efficient functioning of markets.

There is a widespread belief that the quality of BWI economic analytical work and forecasting is and has been professionally better and more accurate than that of the UN. The record challenges that belief. The recent history of DESA shows that it has been consistently more accurate in economic forecasting than either the World Bank or the IMF. Inevitably, none of the institutions has a perfect record, but a statistical review in 2018 showed that when short-term forecasts were compared with outcomes two or three years later, DESA forecasts over a 30-year period since the 1980s generally performed better.[15] During the early years of structural adjustment in the 1980s, it was notable that the World Bank's forecasts for recovery by African countries were over-optimistic; in particular that structural adjustment would be short-lived. After a few years, the World Bank quietly dropped such forecasts from its annual reports.

The quality of the UN's work is also illustrated by the standing of some of their staff members and economic advisers. Few observers realize that nine UN officials have won Nobel Prizes in economics, a number far in excess of those who have worked for the BWIs.

Costs to the UN of separation from the World Bank and the IMF

Over the years, there have been costs to the UN as well as the Bank from the lack of closer working relationships. UN organizations have often suffered from weak economic analysis, especially at field level. Attention to cost-effectiveness has often been lacking and sometimes non-existent, certainly more deficient than if collaboration between the BWIs and the UN had been as close as originally envisaged. Individual countries have frequently received contradictory advice and there has been a tendency for economic strategy, policy, and sectoral projects supported by the Bank to be unnecessarily distant from sectoral plans and priorities supported by different parts of the UNDS. Multilateral funding has increasingly been channeled to the Bank or to Bank-led projects, in spite of their projects often having much higher unit costs, partly as a consequence of the Bank's annual lending targets. In parallel, most UN organizations have been increasingly starved of core funding and dependent on uncertain and limited amounts of supplementary resources.[16] Closer collaboration might have achieved a better balance in donor funding.

Differences and donor preferences between the UNDS and the Bank also reflect differences in the government ministries that send representatives to them. For the world organization, representatives usually come from departments of foreign affairs or specialized ministries like health, agriculture, education, or social services. For the Bank and the IMF, representatives usually come from ministries of finance and the center of decision-making is not in the field but in Washington.

Differences of approach and hierarchy are reinforced by differences in voting systems. In the UN, each country has one vote and developing countries have had an overall majority since the 1960s. In the BWIs, votes are in proportion to shares, with the shares allocated by a formula that has always ensured a majority of votes to the industrialized countries. There is also an additional proviso that on fundamental matters, votes must exceed a high threshold, with the threshold set so that support from the United States is required if such a resolution is to pass. World Bank and IMF voting systems are designed to ensure donor influence, and the BWIs remain the preferred institutions of the donor countries and the West. In contrast, the UN is usually more popular and more consistently supported by developing countries.

Whatever the founding and financial logic, the result is that all parts of the UNDS and of the World Bank have suffered from separation and differences in perceptions, approach, priorities, and focus. These differences have had consequences for borrowing and investment as well as planning and delivery in developing countries. Donor countries themselves have also been affected. Moreover, collaboration between the BWIs and different parts of the UN has been made difficult, from which both sets of institutions have suffered.

Twenty-first-century possibilities for closer collaboration

Major new opportunities for cooperation opened with the Millennium Summit of 2000. For the first time, the Bank and the IMF accepted international goals and joined with the UN and governments in supporting the MDGs. This support was reinforced in 2015 with the adoption of the SDGs, a broader range of goals covering production and prosperity as well as people, peace, and partnerships. Reductions of inequality, nationally and internationally, were also included. An era of closer collaboration began, with BWI representatives in countries often joining with UN colleagues in meetings for sharing and coordination within the country. After his election in 2012, World Bank president Jim Yong Kim made unprecedented efforts to reach out to the UN Secretary-General Ban Ki-moon and to encourage partnerships with different parts of the UNDS.

Nevertheless, collaboration is still far from sufficient or complete. Too often, it is one-sided and bureaucratic, with the Bank having more influence on economic matters in the UN than the UN funds and programs or specialized agencies have on the Bank. There is also the criticism that common positions from the international institutions lead to the agencies ganging up on governments, limiting the freedom of choice and maneuver of the governments concerned.

Global changes and weaknesses

Over the last two decades, the UN and the Bank have both lost influence, with the shifts in global politics and the world economy, especially the rise of China and India, economic advances in other emerging economies, and the shift of development approaches from concessional aid to "business investment" and "blended finance." New measures are needed to strengthen global economic governance and to reform the institutions that can support it, including the UNDS.

UN organizations are increasingly marginal and lack resources, especially core support, though they still command more confidence and support in most parts of the developing world, especially in comparison with the IMF and Bank.[17] In terms of global economic and social management, ECOSOC has never achieved the role envisaged for it, or even lesser roles that have been proposed and tried at different times.[18]

In the years before the 2008 global financial crisis, there was widespread questioning of the Bank's role in a world in which private flows of capital and access to a variety of private capital market funds had grown rapidly. However, post-crisis meetings of the Group of 7 (G-7) and Group of 20 (G-20) to mobilize action identified new roles for the Bank and the IMF and agreed proposals for modest changes in their governance. These were far less than those proposed in 2009 by the Stiglitz Commission of Experts set up by the UN on the Reform of the International Monetary and Financial System,[19] which were bold, fundamental, and far-reaching but sidelined by the developed countries.

Policy and access to capital by would-be borrowing countries is only one test. Arguably, another with more and ever-growing importance is whether the Bank provides the proactive leadership and resources for the supply of global public goods in such key areas as mitigation of and adaptation to climate change, measures to ensure global stability and reduce inequalities, and worldwide actions to control migration. These are vital, as is increasing support for the least developed and other categories of poor and vulnerable countries to achieve fairer, fuller, and wider engagement in the global economy.

The real test is not the strengths and weaknesses of existing international institutions in some abstract sense but their political, economic, and social adequacy to command the support, exercise the leadership, and take the initiatives required for a more humane, more peaceful, and better-functioning world economy. Oxford University's Ian Goldin comments, "if there is one thing that keeps us awake at night it is the absence of global leadership and even awareness of the scale of global challenges ... Global politics is gridlocked."[20] His book identifies five areas of global public goods where international action is urgently needed but woefully missing or inadequate: climate change, cyber-security, pandemics, migration, and finance. There are, of course, other risks that should be addressed, including controlling nuclear weapons and protecting nuclear installations as well as the traditional concerns for peace, security, and diminishing the risks of conflict. In the world of the twenty-first century, better global governance is not an option. It is a question of what form or forms it will take, what support it will have, and who will take the lead.

To identify such needs is to focus not only on priority areas for action but, less emphasized, complementarities between the UN, the World Bank, and the regional development banks and other regional institutions in initiating and effectively supporting such action. The UNDS may be weak in economic management but has long been stronger in non-economic areas of social analysis and action—for instance, the ILO, UNICEF, and World Health Organization (WHO)—that have expertise and field experience.[21] UN organizations also have global legitimacy—and the Regional Commissions and Development Banks have regional legitimacy—in a way that many other institutions operating globally lack.

Challenges, priorities, initiatives, and reform

Two decades after the Millennium Summit, much has changed. The balance of power and influence within the global economy has fundamentally shifted. Chinese and Indian economies have greatly expanded, representing much larger shares in the global economy, and they are now independent actors in many areas. Brazil and several other large countries at the same time are abandoning earlier alliances. In the United States, President Donald Trump has gleefully acted outside the rules-based order, and the United Kingdom decided to leave the European Union (EU) by a small majority in a referendum. Thus, two of the major founding supporters of the United Nations and essential players in global governance have been turning their backs on multilateral structures; moreover, they have often sought to undercut global approaches in parallel with other influential countries displaying major doubts. What is not clear are the consequences of these developments, including the timing and nature of possible new forms of global influence and governance, and their effect on the roles and positions of the UNDS and the BWIs.

Regional cooperation can help and in Asia, Africa, and Latin America it is alive and well despite setbacks. Effective regional initiatives and progress may be easier to achieve than stronger global action. After the Asian financial crisis of 1997–2000, initiatives within East Asia created agreements, institutions, and practices that have largely prevented recurrence, achieving the "never again" ambitions of countries within the region. In Africa and Latin America, regional efforts have also grown, along with efforts to expand the roles and capacities of their regional development banks. China's Asian Infrastructure Investment Bank (AIIB) has more than 70 members and capital equivalent to half that of the World Bank. The 2018 General Assembly resolution 73/216 recognized the AIIB's potential for financing sustainable development and formally expressed the UN's desire to cooperate with it. Regional action may be the immediate way forward, opening positive collaborative possibilities now that may be more amenable to political support than global efforts.

However important are such regional initiatives and actions, the UN, the World Bank, and the IMF remain the only universal institutions in the economic, financial, and political arenas. This position gives them opportunities and responsibilities for giving a lead to new forms of global governance, stronger and better adapted to the future world economy. This will require closer collaboration, in particular between the UNDS and the World Bank, building on the SDGs but going far beyond them. Collaboration will need to focus on priorities, new initiatives, and reform.

Priorities for collaboration

Three priorities should be at the top of the list for World Bank and UNDS collaboration: climate change, reducing inequalities, and providing resources for poorer countries. The last would help ensure a more balanced global economy as part of channeling the funding for these countries to implement the SDGs. All three priorities would accelerate broader action toward the SDGs, climate change directly focusing on SDG 13 (take urgent action to combat climate change and its impacts), moderating inequalities on SDG 10 (reduce inequalities within and among countries) and SDG 1 (end poverty everywhere and leave no one behind).

Climate change and environmental action is an urgent priority and one where collaboration has much to build on. Since the first global environmental conference in Stockholm in 1972, the UN has taken a lead on environmental matters, reinforced after the Earth Summit in Rio and a succession of follow-up global conferences including a UN Summit on Climate Change in 2019. The International Panel on Climate Change (IPCC) has established an internationally acknowledged reputation for its periodic scientific reports, based on the consensus findings of leading scientists from all parts of the world.[22]

Pursuing equity and diminishing inequalities in and between countries worldwide is also a global priority, with a diversity of required actions and perhaps new potential for effective collaboration. The UN has long emphasized the need for greater equity in development, in income, gender, and other key areas, and especially in terms of access to education, health, and other social services, fundamental for ensuring an equitable start for future generations. In its earlier years, the UN also emphasized the need for greater equity in access to assets, especially to land. Recently, the Bank and the IMF have recognized the need for much stronger action to diminish inequalities in these areas. The scope for collaboration at country, regional, and global level is enormous, especially when awareness about unsustainable inequalities is growing. That said and unlike climate change, awareness about inequalities has still not generated serious calls for urgent action to reduce inequalities, nationally and globally.

More resources for the least developed countries and small island states are a third priority, important for reducing inequalities between countries and serious imbalances in the global economy. Additional resources for these poorer countries would also help them take actions to adapt to and offset the consequences of climate change.

Each of these three priorities focuses on areas in which the UNDS has long been involved and has given an important lead in the past, analytically in reports, usually also in UN resolutions, and frequently in calls for action. Building on support for the SDGs from countries can open new opportunities for the UN and the BWIs to collaborate in new international initiatives. Strong leadership within the institutions can also help build on the goals of the SDGs, without the need to wait for new endorsements or resolutions.

Diminishing inequalities inevitably arouses opposition and sharp debates on appropriate action. Recent research by the IMF and the World Bank has shown the ways that extremes of inequality have lowered economic growth and diminished development. Awareness of the injustices of using tax havens to avoid national regulations has grown, as has awareness of corruption, leading to vast outflows of resources often from poorer countries. Strong leadership will be needed to build a new professional and political consensus for action in all regions of the world. Support for poorer countries is less controversial, and the time is ripe for contributing and allocating larger amounts of resources to reduce this dimension of global inequality.

Pursuit of these priorities needs to go far beyond closer collaboration between the UN and the BWIs. Both institutions should use their convening powers to bring together regional banks and new institutions like the AIIB, global corporations, governments, and analysts to spread awareness and mobilize international action on a global scale. Such meetings could start by building a consensus for concerted action toward the three priorities within the frame of the SDGs.

Three further measures should help strengthen the implementation of these priorities. One is for the international and funding agencies to be more counter-cyclical in their support of countries. For a long time, an important weakness of World Bank lending and IMF support has been their tendency to reinforce rather than counteract the upswings and downswings of individual countries and the developed world in general.[23] Counter-cyclical international action will help countries in all parts of the world to gain in stability and steadier economic growth.

A second measure is to build support for human rights. The Bank has often been constrained by its lawyers who have specifically argued that its Charter prevents formal support of human rights, interpreting any attention to rights as a political approach to development. This has not prevented World Bank presidents, especially James Wolfensohn and Jim Yong Kim, from advocating boldly the importance of human rights. Yet direct support for a rights-based approach to development has been left to the UN, notably the UN High Commissioner for Human Rights (UNHCHR).

Over the last two decades, UN funds and programs have pioneered international action for a rights-based approach to development, an approach that embraces not merely human rights as part of the goals and objectives of development but also, equally important, a commitment to bringing rights into the processes used to pursue them. Closer collaboration between the UNDS and the Bank on a rights-based approach to development could thus lead to a real advance, but it would require recognition within the Bank that they have much to learn from UN organizations as well as recognition within the UN that the Bank's emphasis on prioritization, for example, has something to contribute to rights-based approaches.

A stronger embrace of human development is a third area. For almost three decades, the UN Development Programme (UNDP) has produced a series of path-breaking reports elaborating a human development paradigm, in sharp contrast to neoliberal economics. Some 700 National Human Development Reports have now been produced in about 140 developing countries, each applying in country context the human development paradigm and methodology. These reports have identified many areas for fruitful collaboration at the country level between the Bank and many members of the UNDS. Collaboration with the Bank would depend on the World Bank broadening its use of the term "human development" from support for education and health to take on the fuller and deeper concept of human development. In the definition of Nobel laureate Amartya Sen, this means putting people at the center of policy-making, not as a bi-product of increasing the rate of economic growth but directly in strengthening human capacities and broadening human choices.[24]

Political reform and global governance

In the long term, there is an obvious need to address political concerns of representation and reform both of the UN and the BWIs. The measures of voting reform concluded in 2015 in the BWIs were too little and too late, held up by delays in the US Congress. The issues are highly and obviously political, to which an outside commentator can add little.

It may, however, be useful to take inspiration from earlier contributions by more detached commentators. Hans Singer, the distinguished international economist, argued many years ago that a change of voting formulas in both the UN and the BWIs was necessary and would help closer collaboration between them.[25] In his view, voting within the UN on economic matters should be adjusted to give greater weight to the size of a country's economy, not simply weighting by GDP but linked to a group system under which categories of countries—industrialized countries, emerging countries, developing counties, the least developed countries, for instance—should have some form of block vote. If possible, he argued, this change should parallel similar ones within the World Bank, not only to bring shares of votes into line with the present size of today's economies but also to pay attention to the overall distribution of votes so as to lay the basis for a genuine focus on global management of the world economy.

Mahbub ul Haq argued for the creation in the UN of an Economic Security Council, with a small representation elected from the North and the Global South but with a two-tier voting system.[26] Only with a majority from both the North and Global South could such a measure be passed.

Kishore Mahbubani takes on the difficult issue of changing the UN voting structure in a recent book,[27] noting that the developing countries, and those of Asia in particular, are still strong supporters of the UN, more so than most of the West.[28] Asian optimism is heavily influenced by the region's economic successes, but other achievements, moving from destructive war and outdated ideological structures to a pragmatic capitalism, have also been important.

As regards voting structures, Mahbubani puts forward a proposal for fundamentally changing the membership of the Security Council, emphasizing that his proposal is linked to changes in the economic balance of the global economy. His formula creates a new Security Council of 21 seats, with a permanent seat for each of the seven dominant political economic powers in the world today, the allocation of seven semi-permanent seats to the next 28 countries ranked by population or income, and a final seven seats from the remaining countries. He argues that these changes would open the door for deliberations by the Security Council on a wider range of economic as well as political issues.

An altered Security Council would enable it to play a more active role in global economic governance, on its own and in closer collaboration with the BWIs. This outcome could, of course, accelerate if revisions to the voting structures in the World Bank would give weight to population as well as to GDP. If these changes were brought together, the stage would be set for closer collaboration among the international institutions.

Conclusion: leadership for change

Whatever the changes, stronger leadership is needed from the Second UN—the organizations of the UNDS—and from the First UN of member states. The executive heads and senior staff within the secretariats of the UNDS must lead, mobilizing support from governments toward new initiatives, not only for incremental change but also for bolder steps. Once again, much more is required than formal steps of collaboration between the UN and the World Bank, let alone simple expressions of goodwill. In both institutions and governments, there must be a serious rethinking of current approaches and a willingness to listen and learn from countries and experience on a global scale. The UN and the World Bank must recognize the value of multi-disciplinary approaches and experience beyond neoliberal orthodoxy. Above all, the Bank must moderate the arrogant professional certainty that too often has framed BWI attitudes and actions. For example, when the ILO pressed for greater policy coherence with the Bank, the IMF, and the World Trade Organization (WTO), the IMF representative asked whether coherence meant that "you are coherent with us or that we are coherent with you?"[29] If such one-sided polarization of attitudes remains, a new relationship will not go far.

The different parts of the UNDS will also require a new openness and willingness to incorporate new economic thinking and stronger economic professionalism within their own programs, analyses, and actions. Bold leadership will be required for support in key departments like

DESA, in the funds and programs as well as in specialized agencies. Working more closely with the World Bank will require sharing of new perspectives and goals, based on recognizing the different professionalisms and experience of each.

While adapting to the new challenges and changing structures and balance in the global economy, all development organizations are required to transform their standard operating procedures. They have already moved some way from the Western-led approaches that characterized the first half-century of the UNDS and the BWIs, but there is much further to go. No longer do the political and ideological assumptions of the liberal democratic order, which underpinned both sets of institutions, persist in the world today. Exactly what should follow is far from clear.

The positions taken by China, India, and other emerging powers will be critical. If these countries follow the precedents of industrialized countries, little of consequence will happen. However, if the emerging powers are willing to use their growing economic weight and leverage for long-run advance and reform of international institutions, serious action could result toward meeting the global challenges of the twenty-first century. Without it, little can be expected beyond cosmetic tinkering.

The UN system and the BWIs grew out of the crisis of World War II and the economic depression of the 1930s. Today, there is no world war, but climate chaos and global warming present as great a planetary challenge for the future. The devastating consequences of Covid-19 in 2020 showed the worldwide costs when nations do not take action when faced with clear global warnings.

NOTES

1 This chapter was much improved by comments from Gerry Helleiner, Paul Isenman, José Antonio Ocampo, and Rob Vos. The author is solely responsible for the final text.
2 Cited by John Toye and Richard Toye, *The UN and Global Political Economy* (Bloomington, IN: Indiana University Press, 2004), 23.
3 Louis Emmerij, Richard Jolly, and Thomas G. Weiss, *Ahead of the Curve: UN Ideas and Global Challenges* (Bloomington, IN: Indiana University Press, 2001), Chapter 1.
4 The goals and their outcomes are summarized and reviewed in Richard Jolly, Louis Emmerij, Dharam Ghai, and Frederic Lapeyre, *UN Contributions to Development Thinking and Practice* (Bloomington, IN: Indiana University Press, 2004), 257–276.
5 Mahbub ul Haq, an adviser to McNamara and a strong supporter of poverty reduction strategy, departed soon after. He returned to ministerial positions in his country Pakistan over much of the 1980s. After this, he returned to the UN where, in 1990 as a member of UNDP, he set up the annual *Human Development Report*.
6 Devesh Kapur, John P. Lewis, and Richard Webb, *The World Bank: Its First Half Century* (Washington, DC: Brookings, 1997), 240.
7 Alex Shakow led a Bank effort to rescue the sinking poverty mission in September 1981. His report *Focus on Poverty* led to his later proposal that all CPPs should include a special poverty brief, which was opposed by regional staff on the grounds that it would involve "additional work with no obvious justification." Ibid., 337–338.
8 Richard Jolly, Louis Emmerij, and Thomas G. Weiss, *UN Ideas That Changed the World* (Bloomington, IN: Indiana University Press, 2009).
9 World Bank, *Accelerated Development in Sub-Saharan Africa: An Agenda for Action* (Washington, DC: World Bank, 1981).
10 Organization of African Unity, *Lagos Plan of Action for the Economic Development of Africa, 1980–2000* (Addis Ababa: Economic Commission of Africa, 1980).
11 Giovanni Andrea Cornia, Richard Jolly, and Frances Stewart, *Adjustment with a Human Face: Protecting the Vulnerable and Promoting Growth—A Study by UNICEF* (Oxford: Clarendon Press, 1988).
12 Cited in James Raymond Vreeland, *The International Monetary Fund: Politics of Conditional Lending* (London: Routledge, 2007), 90.

13 Mark Weisbrot, Robert Naiman, and Joyce Kim, *The Emperor Has No Growth: Declining Economic Growth Rates in the Era of Globalization* (Washington, DC: Center for Economic and Policy Research, 2001).

14 An overview of the ECE's proposals and of debates of the time is in Yves Berthelot and Paul Rayment, "The ECE: A Bridge between East and West," in *Unity and Diversity in Development Ideas*, ed. Yves Berthelot (Bloomington, IN: Indiana University Press, 2004), 111–120.

15 Jose Antonio Ocampo, Anis Chowdhury, and Diana Alarcón, eds., *The World Economy Through the Lens of the United Nations* (New York: Oxford University Press, 2018).

16 See Asmita Naik, "Can the UN Adjust to the Changing Funding Landscape?" *FUNDS Briefing*, no. 2 (March 2013), www.futureun.org/en/Publications-Surveys/Article?newsid=8.

17 Kishore Mahbubani comments on the deep fissure that exists between the dominant Western narrative (about the UN) and the narrative of the rest of the world, with the former presenting the UN as a vast, bloated, inefficient bureaucracy and "the majority of those who live outside the West retain[ing] massive trust in the UN system." Kishore Mahbubani, *The Great Convergence: Asia, the West and the Logic of One World* (New York: Public Affairs, 2013), 91. But even this may overstate the doubts of ordinary Americans in contrast to the politicians and commentariat. To cite just one recent survey of US opinion, The Better World Campaign reported in May 2011 that 56–59 percent of US public held a favorable opinion of the UN, UNICEF, and WHO and only 24 percent of the World Bank. See www.betterworldcampaign.org/news-room/articles-editorials/full-findings.html.

18 Thomas G. Weiss, *ECOSOC Is Dead, Long Live ECOSOC* (New York: Friedrich Ebert Stiftung, 2010).

19 Convened by the General Assembly president.

20 Ian Goldin, *Divided Nations: Why Global Governance Is Failing and What We Can Do About It* (Oxford: Oxford University Press, 2013), xii, 3, and 178.

21 WHO and UNICEF are consistently ranked by FUNDS global perception surveys as the most relevant and effective UN organizations. See FUNDS, *Surveys*, www.futureun.org/Surveys.

22 See the Independent Group of Scientists appointed by the Secretary-General, *Global Sustainable Development Report 2019: The Future Is Now—Science for Achieving Sustainable Development* (New York: UN, 2019), https://sustainabledevelopment.un.org/content/documents/24797GSDR_report_2019.pdf.

23 Ngaire Woods expands on this in "Bretton Woods Institutions," in *The Oxford Handbook on the United Nations*, ed. Thomas G Weiss and Sam Daws, 2nd edn. (Oxford: Oxford University Press, 2018), 283–298.

24 See Amartya Sen, "Foreword" and "Development as Capability Expansion," Ch. 1 *Readings in Human Development*, ed. Sakiko Fukuda-Parr and A. K. Shiva Kumar (New Delhi: Oxford University Press, 2003).

25 H. W. Singer, "Revitalizing the United Nations: Five Proposals," in H. W. Singer, *International Development Cooperation: Selected Essays by H. W. Singer on Aid and the UN System* (Basingstoke, UK: Palgrave Macmillan, 2001), 107–117.

26 Mahbub ul Haq's views on UN reform in general and for an Economic Security Council are set out in Khadija Haq and Richard Jolly, "Global Development, Poverty Alleviation and North–South Relations," in *Pioneering the Human Development Revolution: An Intellectual Biography of Mahbub ul Haq*, ed. Khadija Haq and Richard Ponzio (New Delhi: Oxford University Press, 2008), 63–87.

27 Mahbubani, *The Great Convergence*.

28 Kishore Mahbubani, "Why We—Especially the West—Need the UN Development System," *FUNDS Briefing* no. 4 (2013), www.futureun.org/media/archive1/briefings/Briefing-4-Mahbubani.pdf.

29 Gerry Rodgers et al., *The ILO and the Quest for Social Justice 1919–2009* (Geneva: ILO, 2009), 231.

ADDITIONAL READING

Ian Goldin, *Divided Nations: Why Global Governance Is Failing and What We Can Do About It* (Oxford: Oxford University Press, 2013).

Richard Jolly, Louis Emmerij, and Thomas G. Weiss, *UN Ideas That Changed the World* (Bloomington, IN: Indiana University Press, 2009).

Mark Mazower, *Governing the World: The History of an Idea* (London: Penguin, 2012).

Joseph E. Stiglitz, *Making Globalization Work* (New York: Norton, 2006).

15

THE WTO, THE UN, AND THE FUTURE OF GLOBAL DEVELOPMENT

Rorden Wilkinson

The various organizations of the United Nations development system (UNDS) face a number of challenges if they are to remain fit for purpose, able to tackle the most enduring and tenacious forms of human destitution, and able to help those fortunate enough to already be advancing up the development ladder. Most of these challenges are well known, even if they are not always addressed with appropriate verve and determination. However, reform, change, and evolution in the world organization have historically been slow, incremental, and accretive. The system suffers from the kind of diffusion and atomization that has put in place more than 30 separate bureaucracies and, occasionally, incommensurate evolutionary pathologies.[1] The scale of the task required to make more than a modest contribution to bettering the lived experiences of the majority of the world's population is daunting. And the speed with which the landscapes of global poverty and inequality[2]—not to mention the plight of the planet[3]—are changing poses problems for even the lithest of institutions.

There is, however, another challenge that is seldom recognized when thinking about the future of the UN in development. This challenge is the capture of a significant proportion of the global development agenda by agencies that lie outside—ideologically and otherwise—of the UNDS. In part, this challenge is non-governmental. Major philanthropic institutions like the Bill and Melinda Gates and the Stichting INGKA Foundations have resources and influence that are the envy of many an intergovernmental organization; and a plethora of nongovernmental organizations (NGOs), religious bodies, and civil society institutions act as service deliverers of development assistance on the ground. They often have no connection to formal UN machineries. Both, nonetheless, combine to put in place developmental agendas and strategies that challenge the UNDS—if not ideologically then certainly operationally—but which often lack the UN's legitimacy and accountability credentials.

In part, this challenge is also intergovernmental. A number of institutions that lie formally outside the UN system have operational mandates that confront and, on occasion, encroach upon the development activities of the UNDS. In these instances, the evolution of institutional remits and substantive operations has given rise to alternative and often contradictory approaches to development. In some cases, these approaches matter little. In others, formal bodies exist, the actions and activities of which represent serious challenges to established UNDS ways of thinking and acting.

While private non-state involvement in development is much debated and dealt with extensively elsewhere,[4] the intergovernmental challenge to the UNDS is less frequently the focus of attention. When it is, commentary has tended to center on instances when a clash of institutional cultures or ideologies occurs and wherein the UN plays a role in mediating the more evangelical aspects of, for example, World Bank and International Monetary Fund policies.[5] One intergovernmental challenge that is different—but which is infrequently commented upon in the development literature—comes from the increasing encroachment of the World Trade Organization (WTO) on global development.

This chapter has two purposes: to explore the role that the WTO plays in global development, and to set out the challenges that this role presents for the UNDS, particularly those organizations most involved in international trade—the UN Conference on Trade and Development (UNCTAD), International Trade Centre (ITC), and UN Industrial Development Organization (UNIDO)—though these latter bodies are not the specific subject of the chapter. It begins by probing why and how the WTO is a key development actor and the challenges that this poses. It then explores why reform of the WTO—like many of its UNDS counterparts—is important, not only to address problems with its own functioning but also to enable more effective development gains to be realized. The final section offers some concluding thoughts on the future of the WTO in global development.

The WTO: rhetoric and reality

At first glance, the claim that the WTO is a key player in global development appears to have little substance. The WTO is not ostensibly a development institution. It makes little more than a passing reference to playing a role in shaping global development.[6] The organization's supporters and detractors point out in equal measure that it is not—nor should it become—a development institution. Any developmental features of the organization's activities are understood as second-order consequences of its functioning. Moreover, there are other institutions designed specifically to explore the trade and development nexus: of which UNCTAD, ITC, and UNIDO, noted above, are but three.

The WTO is, however, ideologically and operationally central to both the means by which development is pursued and the mal-distribution of economic opportunities that make development so difficult to achieve.[7] It is also ideologically distinct from its counterparts in the UN system in the same way that the Bretton Woods institutions (BWIs) are different from their UN brethren. The WTO's centrality reflects the dominant approach to early twenty-first-century development, which is predicated on the assumption that it is by increasing the volume and value of trade that growth is generated and substantive economic gain realized—hence, the equation-cum-mantra: trade = growth = development. It is also central because of the way the multilateral trading system has functioned, the impact that its functioning has had, the outcomes that have resulted, and the representative shortfalls in the organization's system of operation. In addition, as a mechanism for generating trade openings, the WTO and its predecessor institution, the General Agreement on Tariffs and Trade (GATT), has persistently presided over trade negotiations that have produced asymmetrical bargains favoring the advanced industrial states over their developing and least developed counterparts.[8]

This matters on a number of levels. It matters because the WTO's centrality to the way that development is pursued, and the problems in actually achieving it, are at variance with many of the existing ideas about economic and social advancement championed by the UN system. It matters because although WTO negotiations have generated some small gains for developing countries—particularly the least developed—in the form of the measures agreed at the organization's last three ministerial conferences (Bali, 2013, Nairobi, 2015, and Buenos Aires, 2017),[9] the lion's share of benefits continues to accrue to their industrial counterparts. It matters because the most recent round of trade negotiation, which was intended to advance a comprehensive development agenda (the Doha Round), has all but been abandoned. Moreover, questions have been raised about the future of the organization by (i) the Trump administration;[10] and (ii) the failure of members to reach agreement on a ministerial declaration affirming the continued importance of the WTO to the global trading system at the 2017 Buenos Aires ministerial conference. It matters because the unwillingness of many—including in the organization as well as in the UNDS—to accept that the WTO is central to global development obfuscates the capacity to facilitate both substantive development gains globally and UN activities in the area.

In short, it is because trade is seen as a key vehicle for generating development that the WTO—as the core institution concerned with how trade is governed—has become a major player in global development. It is also because there are recognized problems with the WTO system that attention needs to be diverted toward the organization, particularly its reform. As it currently stands, relations between the constituent members of the UNDS and the WTO are amicable but thin.[11] UNCTAD and the WTO nominally "cooperate" in sponsoring the ITC, but this arrangement is more a means of holding one another at bay than an instance of meaningful collaboration. The WTO houses and manages the Standards and Trade Development Faculty (STDF)—a small-scale partnership co-established with the Food and Agriculture Organization, the World Organisation for Animal Health, the World Bank, and the World Health Organization. It also involves ITC and UNIDO, supporting the implementation of sanitary and phytosanitary standards and comprising a secretariat of just six with an average annual budget of approximately $4.3 million. These instances aside, in large measure, the WTO and the UNDS operate with competing and conflicting ideas about trade. The best that can be said is that both hold store in the importance of trade; thereafter ideas about how trade is best organized and encouraged, and the role of trade in promoting development, diverge.

In terms of a power relationship—and much like the way the IMF and World Bank hold sway in the UN system—the WTO has the upper hand. The UNDS has championed the interests of developing countries in compensating for unfavorable terms of trade and has influenced aspects of the trade agenda (particularly in agriculture);[12] but the WTO remains the main forum of global trade negotiations and the institution through which member states seek to pursue their trade objectives. Those UNDS organizations that engage in trade do so mainly as purveyors of research and technical assistance services, and occasionally of advocacy.[13]

Realizing that the WTO is a central player in global development is, however, only the start of a journey. Understanding how development has fared in the governance of global trade takes us further. From the very outset, the multilateral trading system was set up to enable the leading industrial states to pursue their trade objectives vis-à-vis one another. It was not designed to be a vehicle for realizing the trade objectives of their developing counterparts and—despite repeated attempts[14]—no significant adjustments in the trading system's governance have occurred to alter its focus.

In part, the inattention to issues of development is the consequence of the failure of a larger, more ambitious institutional project—the International Trade Organization (ITO)—in the immediate post-war period and the installation of a limited and what was originally intended to be a provisional form of trade governance in the shape of the GATT. In part, it is the consequence of an evolutionary history that has seen developing countries continually prove unable to alter aspects of the trade regime to suit their interests better. In part, it is the result of a negotiating machinery that pitches unequally matched states against one another in chaotic bouts of negotiating that has seen developed countries secure the lion's share of economic opportunities while offering developing countries very little of what they actually need.

These three elements—a trade institution that was designed primarily to serve the interests of industrialized countries, that has evolved in a fashion that largely mimics the purposes for which it was originally established, and a negotiating machinery that favors the economically more powerful over their weaker counterparts—have combined to produce a turbulent and contested trade politics, to which the recent record of trade negotiations bears witness.[15] Turbulence and contestation are manifest most dramatically during trade rounds, although they also play out in other WTO functions—as the current dispute over appointments to the organization's appellate body amply demonstrates.[16] This turbulence and contestation lends trade negotiations a great deal of sloth, which, in turn, gives rise to complex strategies of maneuver: states seek to gain advantages in negotiations through the formation of multifaceted and often cross-cutting coalitions while simultaneously seeking to secure advantages by linking movements forward in trade with deals brokered outside of WTO negotiations. Deals are finally brokered when these complex games have arranged the various pieces of a puzzle in such a way that they represent the best that can be achieved, or when delegations are worn down to the point at which *any* movement forward is perceived to be acceptable; otherwise, they stall seemingly irrecoverably, as is the case with the most recent Doha Round. For all of the energy that developing countries exert (and always have exerted) in pursuing their interests in trade rounds, it has consistently been the case that the disproportionate share of opportunities negotiated has fallen to the industrial states.

Why does all of this matter?

It matters at the most basic level because the perceived centrality of trade to global economic fortunes means that attention is directed disproportionately toward what goes on in the WTO rather than in the UNDS. It matters because getting trade right, rather than mopping up market failure, is a more effective way of developing. It matters because when a round of trade negotiations was set up ostensibly to be a "development round"—as Doha was—it actually evolved in a way that reduced the meaning of development to a focus on agricultural market access.[17] It matters because the outcomes that did result from the Doha negotiations repeat—rather than disrupt—a cycle of asymmetrical outcomes and continue to widen further the gap between the global haves and have-nots.

Negotiating trade deals that are asymmetrical is an unsustainable state of affairs; and reform of the multilateral trading system is essential if trade is going to be a driver of substantive and more equitable economic improvement. Yet, while there currently exists something of a consensus on the need to reform the WTO, many of the reform proposals that have been put forward would—if implemented—merely patch up an already problematic system. Few press for a more thorough overhaul of the system, one that does away with competitive negotiating as a machinery for generating economic opportunity. Such a system would install a governance structure that is more democratic, representative, accountable, and appropriate; and it would connect the way that we govern trade with the realization of broader social goods as well as the management of other aspects of global life.[18]

Reforming the WTO

Many of the reasons why the WTO needs reforming, why its relationship with the UNDS is so problematic, and why meaningful change has been so hard to bring about can be found in the way the system has evolved over time. Particularly important here are the roles of compromise, happenstance, opportunism, and unintended consequence.

To understand how the WTO might be reformed, it is worth recalling that the multilateral trading system was the product of a response to blockages in the post-World War II negotiations for the ITO. By the time the 1947 Havana Conference on Trade and Employment was convened, it was clear that divergent positions had emerged and the chances of salvaging the ITO project were slight. The response of the United States and the United Kingdom—the lead architects—was to begin a round of negotiations that eventually produced the GATT. Meanwhile, continuing disagreements about the content of the ITO Charter eventually led to the organization being abandoned. By default, the GATT assumed the role of steward of the nascent multilateral trading system.

It matters here that what currently passes for global trade governance emerged from happenstance and opportunism. The GATT was originally intended to be a provisional agreement drawn from Chapter IV of the ITO Charter and designed to begin the process of liberalizing trade among a limited group of 23 contracting parties. It was not designed to be an all-encompassing set of rules governing global trade in the way that the ITO had been; nor was it one intended to account for and deal with variations in economic development. These features set the tone for the evolution of the institution over time.

Yet, the parties that acceded to the GATT after it was created often did so with dramatically different interests to the founding 23 contracting parties. Once the first rounds of accession had taken in the remaining industrial states—whose interests were reasonably aligned with the original contracting parties—those that acceded were largely newly created, post-colonial developing states. Despite the growing number of signatories, subsequent GATT negotiations seldom involved new developing country signatories and were not binding on all of the contracting parties. Areas of significant economic concern to large groups of developing contracting parties (such as agriculture) were excluded or else subject to quota systems and other controls (for example, textiles and clothing) for long periods of time.[19] Custom and practice emerged as the modus operandi and substituted for substantive procedure. Processes of reform and institutional development tended to take the form of augmenting and extending early practice rather than substantively changing and evolving procedures and modes of operation to suit the changing complexion of the GATT contracting parties. When reform proposals were developed that attempted to tackle issues of development head on—as they did with the negotiation of Part IV of the GATT in 1964 (formally in force in 1966)—they had little impact on the trading fortunes of developing countries.[20] What the inattention to issues of development did achieve, however, was to increase developing country frustrations which, in turn, fueled the convening of the first UNCTAD in 1964.[21]

While UNCTAD emerged, in part, out of growing developing country dissatisfaction with the GATT and, in part, from a desire to see tangible efforts to boost their trade performance in the UN's first development decade, it failed to produce an institutional challenge to the GATT.[22] What resulted instead was the creation of a permanent UNCTAD secretariat; the launch of fact-finding exercises on issues of economic development; and an agreement that member states convene at four-yearly intervals to assess trade and development issues. It did not result in powers to go beyond the issuing of recommendations.

The outcome, then, was a process of institutional evolution for the governance of global trade that drew from and built upon happenstance and which proved resilient in the face of institutional challenges. This institutional evolution did not occur in accordance with a clear plan or vision. It did, however, preserve in large measure the character of the original GATT and the advantages that the first contracting parties accrued. And it pieced together a system of rules, norms, customs, and procedures as if it were a bricolage—many of the features of which have been preserved in the current WTO system, which are discussed below.

The nature of negotiating

The problems embedded in this bricolage are compounded by the way that bargains are struck among the participating parties. The system itself, the trade opportunities it affords, the rules governing the conduct of negotiations, and the procedures for the administration of the system—among other things—are all outcomes of competitive negotiations. Because the negotiations are competitive and member interests are determined by the advantages they seek to accrue and the concessions they aim not to give away, the resulting outcomes inevitably reflect the capability of members to realize strategic gains while protecting areas of special interest.[23] In other words, the interests of more powerful, economically more significant, and more capable members have usually prevailed. This, in turn, has contributed to—rather than attenuated—the growing disparities between developed and developing countries.

Understanding that this system is the product of—and generates outcomes that result from—negotiations between members varying dramatically in size, economic significance, and negotiating capacity is crucial. It helps explain why reform tends not to change fundamentally existing ways of operating; it ensures that the interests of the industrial states more often than not lie in supporting proposals for reform that make adjustments to suit their purposes but which leave the system largely intact; and it underscores why development in the WTO is understood differentially than in the UNDS. Of course, this does not preclude outcomes emerging from reform processes that bring genuine system-wide benefits; but it does mean that they are likely to be agreed only as part of an overall outcome that reflects prevailing relations of power and preserves the status quo.

Differences of perception

That said, WTO reform is not just a problem of institutional design and evolution. It is inevitably also an outcome of the differences in perception about the purpose of the WTO that exists across the membership. These differences derive from the interests of members. The way they clash is instructive when considering why seemingly unbridgeable divides exist—on development as well as on other issues. And they are important in explaining how the system has evolved as well as what influences proposals and responses in reform debates.

The divide in member perceptions over the purpose of the WTO lies along a spectrum from those that see the organization as a narrow mechanism for administering a set of agreed rules, to those that see its contribution as more than just international commercial regulation. Some members—largely developing countries—approach the WTO seeking to correct anomalous trade rules and obstacles to development, and to reinforce the value of multilateralism as a means of negating the power disadvantages they encounter in bilateral and North–South regional trade deals. Other members—such as the EU—see reform of the multilateral trading system as an opportunity to extend WTO governance and its role as a source of law and precedent. This is quite different from those who perceive the WTO to be a narrow technical machinery for overseeing the application of rules and obligations—and not a source of jurisprudence—and approach reform in this manner. This view most closely approximates that currently expressed by the Trump administration.

Differences in perception matter because they frame the way members engage in debates about reform and affect the capacity of the institution to deliver development outcomes; they inform the proposals members generate and the potential deals to which they agree; and the distances between these positions explain why striking a bargain on a substantive and meaningful program of reform is so difficult to achieve. Thus, the focus of reform for many developing countries is on achieving better and more effective participation, improved trade outcomes, and the resources to build capacity. For the EU and like-minded others, reform tends to focus on deepening existing commitments and harmonizing trade practices globally. For the United States—particularly under the Trump administration—reform of the WTO is about rolling back provisions seen as restricting or disadvantaging US economic activity and the capacity to act as a sovereign entity.

It would, however, be a mistake to assume that these positions are new. Developing countries have always sought to unpick enduring iniquities. The EU has consistently favored increased legalization and the extension of trade governance into related areas. And the United States has always worried about a system of trade governance encroaching on its sovereignty by bleeding beyond narrow commercial arrangements. In large measure, these positions were on display during the post-war ITO negotiations. They have been present throughout the history of the GATT and WTO. And they are very much in evidence today.

The trouble with rounds

The problem of reform is compounded by the continued use of big-ticket negotiating rounds as the means of pursuing market openings and further regulation. At least two issues are worth highlighting. First, rounds of negotiations come with an expectation that big market access or other gains must be negotiated. The smaller everyday gains that can be made from ongoing, technical, and piecemeal negotiations do not suffice. This is a problem at the aggregate level where the expectation is that a concluded round will produce significant global benefits. It is also a problem at the member level where all negotiating teams seek to bring home gains that outweigh those of their competitors. To many in the industrial world, striking deals that disproportionately help their developing counterparts will simply not suffice.

Second, rounds do not take place in isolation from the history of trade negotiations. Rather, they unfold in relation to the outcome of previous rounds. This means that delegations approach any new negotiation mindful of what has gone before, cognizant of any prior iniquities, and determined to improve upon any previous deal *relative* to the gains—perceived or otherwise—of their competitors. The consequence is that the results of one round inevitably shape the way future negotiations unfold; and they frequently combine to make development outcomes less rather than more likely.

Moreover, this "iterated" form of bargaining predictably accentuates the degree to which members are at loggerheads with one another. For developing countries, the asymmetries of previous rounds ensure they approach any new negotiation seeking to rectify past anomalies (and as time goes by, more determinedly so). While this position has also been the case for a number of industrial countries, their primary position is one of seeking to protect sectors of decreasing competitiveness and political sensitivity as well as opening up new areas of commercial opportunity. Thus, the problem is that in approaching any negotiation, those seeking some kind of rectification are encouraged to agree to new concessions in return for remedial action. Yet, it is because of the requirement—for all but the least developed—to offer something in return for that which is received, coupled with existing power inequalities between participating states, that asymmetries in outcome have been compounded by successive GATT/WTO rounds. The point here is that the use of exchange as the mechanism of both governing and distributing trade openings among members of vastly different capabilities in institutional confines that have traditionally favored the already powerful has produced bargains that are of dramatically different value to the participating states.

The art of reform

The preceding discussion provided a lens through which the problematic and the necessity of WTO reform can be understood. What, then, might a way forward look like?

One way may lie in looking back at how previous blockages in trade negotiations were overcome. In preparing for the Uruguay round (1986–1994), the GATT contracting parties established a negotiating group on the Functioning of the GATT System (FOGS). The purpose of the FOGS was to enhance how the GATT operated as a negotiating body; refine its role as an arbiter of trade disputes; improve its notification, surveillance, and dispute settlement functions; examine the *General Agreement*'s institutional structure; and increase the GATT's contribution to achieving greater coherence in global economic policy-making. However, it was not until the market access and other commercial aspects of the Uruguay round negotiations were faltering that contracting parties realized that common agreement could be reached in making improvements in almost all of these areas.

It is here that a potential solution may lie. If we treat the creation of the WTO as one moment in an ongoing process of institutional development, then the creation of a group that explores the Functioning of the WTO System (FOWTO) would be entirely appropriate. The group could pick up on the unfinished business of the Uruguay round, focus attention on areas of pressing need, and divert attention toward system reform and continual improvement, crucially taking a panoptic view of the balance of endeavors across member states with an eye on the WTO's contribution to global development.

What might this process entail? While this is ultimately for members to consider and design, it could nonetheless comprise:

- Reviewing in-depth the manner in which trade deals are negotiated;
- Developing a set of rules governing the conduct of negotiations that enable all interests to be represented;
- Lending clarity to the substantive agenda of negotiations and specifying how they will unfold;
- Enabling parties to the negotiations to establish a clear sequence of realizable aims;
- Requiring all members to make the process, progress, and substance of the negotiations transparent;
- Developing measures that allow for a process of arbitration to intervene in instances where differences of interpretation and/or blockages exist and which allow for redress;
- Offering technical assistance on the practice, substance, and organization of negotiations to smaller, less able, developing delegations; and
- Outlawing practices that give members undue advantages over their competitor states.

To really capitalize on the gains these endeavors could bring, a move away from highly pressured, big-expectation rounds toward less ambitious, piecemeal negotiations that operate on a continuing and continual basis could also occur. Seeing negotiations as an ongoing and continuous program of work on manageable issues would have utility in removing blockages and in reducing political tensions. They could also be run as individual projects in "task and finish" groups with the secretariat playing the role of overseer. Ministerial conferences could then move away from pressured negotiating points in the WTO calendar toward events focused on reviewing a program of work and its delivery. Moreover, getting rid of this lumpiness would help remove the WTO's version of "boom and bust" by making ministerial conferences more mundane, ordinary, and expected.

There are, however, other areas that require focus and which would bring gains. The key to any reform, nonetheless, would be to find a way to negate the divisions that arise from the divergent interests of members and to create incentives for cooperation. Equally as important would be a process that clarifies the purpose of the multilateral trading system so that members have a clear and shared understanding of the value and role of the WTO. This could be achieved through the negotiation of a ministerial declaration on the role of the WTO and the part members play in making the system function, akin to the declarations of understanding that were negotiated during the Uruguay round. This kind of clarification could go some way toward reconciling the tensions between narrow functionalist and technically oriented understandings of the organization and those that see it much more broadly. It would also be useful in sorting out the relationship with—and delineating the relations between—the WTO and members of the UNDS. An allied endeavor would be to clarify once and for all the status of the Doha Round.

The very real need to deal with social and environmental sensitivities notwithstanding, attention in the immediate term should focus less on expanding the trade agenda, and more on getting right what the WTO does. This should include—but not be limited to—clarifying dispute settlement functions, procedures, and outcomes; and expanding the trade policy surveillance, review, and research and analysis functions of the secretariat. Delivery should be a system mantra. Too many negotiations and agreements are either not or are only partially implemented, or else they do not fulfill their promise. Had this been the case after the Uruguay round then many developing country concerns could have been addressed. It would also mean that more could have already been made of the Trade Facilitation Agreement.

Other areas too require attention. A conscious effort needs to be made to get ahead, in a substantive and meaningful way, of new trade agendas—of which ecommerce is among the most pressing. Thought should also be given to the representation of public debate in the WTO. Recent research on ministerial conferences and the Public Forum, for instance, shows that business and the diplomatic community are very well represented, but that public (that is, non-state, not-for-profit) participation has fallen off considerably.[24] A properly constructed FOWTO could provide meaningful answers to these and other questions, and a way through the reform conundrum.

Conclusion

The current conjuncture provides a potentially fruitful opportunity to attend to aspects of the WTO's functioning and organization as well as its relationship with the UNDS; but there is a risk that a shift in gear toward a reform mode might prove satisfactory only in that it translates pent-up frustration into action. It does not guarantee that such a shift would bring about the kind of analysis, reflection, and action required to address the deeply rooted problems that generate the system's afflictions.

It is, nonetheless, worrisome that debate about WTO reform lacks innovation and risks resulting in meaningful change. This is because it does not allow more fundamental questions to be asked and concerns to be raised. In turn, this lends thinking about reform a path-dependent quality and ensures that all too often proposals are discussed that either attempt to recover lost functionality or else implement modest adjustments to the existing system. While incremental evolution is in principle a reasonable way to bring about measured reform, the bricolage-like qualities of the system require more than minor adjustments, particularly if it is to be enhanced. Rather than persisting with piecemeal approaches to reform, more thought should be given to dismantling the system, preserving what is good, discarding the ill, and then putting it back together in a way that enables trade-led development and growth to occur in a manner that offers greater equity of opportunity across the board and substantial corrective action for those that have been negatively affected by the system's past functioning.

While the ongoing standoff in the WTO—over Doha, dispute settlement appointments, and system purpose, among other things—reigns, a proverbial Rome threatens to burn. In his assessment of the record of the multilateral trading system at its 50th anniversary, Nelson Mandela put it thus:

> … when the founders of the GATT evoked the link between trade, growth and a better life, few could have foreseen such poverty, homelessness and unemployment as the world now knows. Few would have imagined that the exploitation of the world's abundant resources and a prodigious growth in world trade would have seen the gap between rich and poor widening. And few could have anticipated the burden of debt on many poor nations.
>
> As we celebrate what has been achieved in shaping the world trading system, let us resolve to leave no stone unturned in working together to ensure that our shared principles are everywhere translated into reality … let us forge a new partnership for development through trade and investment.[25]

Some three-quarters of a century into the system's journey, we continue to ignore the necessity for WTO reform, and its importance to and relationship with the UN development system. It is to upturning every stone and forging a new partnership for development that collective effort should now turn.

NOTES

1 Michael N. Barnett and Martha Finnemore, "The Politics, Power, and Pathologies of International Organizations," *International Organization* 53, no. 4 (1999): 699–732.

2 David Hulme, *Global Poverty: Global Governance and Poor People in the Post-2015 Era* (London: Routledge, 2015).

3 See, for instance, World Meteorological Organization, *WMO Provisional Statement on the State of the Global Climate in 2019* (Geneva: WMO, 2019), https://library.wmo.int/doc_num.php?explnum_id=10108.

4 See, for instance, Michael Moran, *Private Foundations and Development Partnerships* (London: Routledge, 2014); Jonathan J. Makuwira, *Non-Governmental Development Organizations and the Poverty Reduction Agenda* (London: Routledge, 2014); and David Hulme and Michael Edwards, *NGOs, States and Donors: Too Close for Comfort?* (Basingstoke, UK: Macmillan, 1997). For a recent review see: Robert Giloth, "Philanthropy and Economic Development: New Roles and Strategies," *Economic Development Quarterly* 33, no. 3 (2019): 159–169.

5 See, for example, Thomas G. Weiss, "Governance, Good Governance and Global Governance: Conceptual and Actual Challenges," and Jean-Philippe Thérien, "Beyond the North–South Divide: The Two Tales of World Poverty," in *The Global Governance Reader*, ed. Rorden Wilkinson (London: Routledge, 2005), 68–88 and 218–238.

6 The WTO's official role in development is set out here: www.wto.org/english/tratop_e/devel_e/devel_e.htm. For a good discussion of the WTO and issue linkage see José Alvarez, "The WTO as Linkage Machine," *American Journal of International Law* 96, no. 1 (2002): 146–158.

7 Robert Hunter Wade, "What Strategies Are Viable for Developing Countries Today? The World Trade Organization and the Shrinking of 'Development Space,'" *Review of International Political Economy* 10, no. 4 (2003): 621–644.

8 See Sylvia Ostry, *The Post-Cold War Trading System* (London: University of Chicago Press, 1997); Arvind Subramanian and Shang-Jin Wei, "The WTO Promotes Trade, Strongly but Not Evenly," *Journal of International Economics* 72, no. 1 (2007): 151–175; Rorden Wilkinson, "Back to the Future: 'Retro' Trade Governance and the Future of the Multilateral Order," *International Affairs* 93, no. 5 (2017): 1131–1147.

9 Erin Hannah, James Scott, and Rorden Wilkinson, "The WTO in Buenos Aires: The Outcome and Its Significance for the Future of the Multilateral Trading System," *The World Economy* 41, no. 10 (2018): 2578–2598; Rorden Wilkinson, Erin Hannah, and James Scott, "The WTO in Nairobi: The Demise of the Doha Development Agenda and the Future of the Multilateral Trading System," *Global Policy* 7, no. 2 (2016): 247–255; Rorden Wilkinson, Erin Hannah, and James Scott, "The WTO in Bali: What MC9 Means for the Doha Development Agenda and Why It Matters," *Third World Quarterly* 35, no. 6 (2014): 1032–1050. For a comprehensive view of international trade under the Trump administration see: Craig VanGrasstek, "The Trade Policy of the United States Under the Trump Administration," Robert Schuman Centre for Advanced Studies Research Paper No. RSCAS 2019/11 (2019), http://dx.doi.org/10.2139/ssrn.3330577.

10 For a recent view of WTO developments see David Tinline, "The World Trade Organisation Has Been Making More Progress Than You Think," *Prospect*, 3 October 2019, www.prospectmagazine.co.uk/economics-and-finance/the-world-trade-organisation-has-been-making-more-progress-than-you-think-wto-trump.

11 A list of these can be found here: www.wto.org/english/thewto_e/coher_e/igo_divisions_e.htm.

12 See John Toye and Richard Toye, *The UN and Global Political Economy: Trade, Finance, and Development* (Bloomington, IN: Indiana University Press, 2004); and Matias Margulis, "Negotiating from the Margins: How the UN Shapes the Rules of the WTO," *Review of International Political Economy* 25, no. 3 (2018): 364–391.

13 Erin Hannah, Holly Ryan, and James Scott, "Power, Knowledge and Resistance: Between Co-optation and Revolution in Global Trade," *Review of International Political Economy* 24, no. 5 (2017): 741–775.

14 Rorden Wilkinson and James Scott, "Developing Country Participation in the GATT: A Reassessment," *World Trade Review* 7, no. 3 (2008): 473–510.

15 See Rorden Wilkinson, *The WTO: Crisis and the Governance of Global Trade* (London: Routledge, 2006).

16 "WTO Chief Sees No End in Sight to U.S. Blockage," *Reuters*, 21 February 2019, www.reuters.com/article/us-usa-trade-wto/wto-chief-sees-no-end-in-sight-to-us-blockage-idUSKCN1QA2IW.

17 James Scott, "The Future of Agricultural Trade Governance in the World Trade Organization," *International Affairs* 93, no. 5 (2017): 1167–1184.

18 For further discussion of recent debate about WTO reform including proposals on ways forward see Brendan Vickers, Teddy Soobramanien, and Hilary Enos-Edu, eds., *WTO Reform: Reshaping Global Trade Governance for 21st Century Challenges* (London: Commonwealth Secretariat, 2019).

19 See Scott, "The Future"; and Tony Heron and Ben Richardson, "Path Dependency and the Politics of Liberalisation in the Textiles and Clothing Industry," *New Political Economy* 13, no. 1 (2008): 1–18.

20 John W. Evans, *The Kennedy Round in American Trade Policy: The Twilight of the GATT?* (Cambridge, MA: Harvard University Press, 1971).

21 Richard N. Gardner, "GATT and the United Nations Conference on Trade and Development," *International Organization* 18, no. 4 (1964): 685–704.

22 John Whalley, "Non-Discriminatory Discrimination: Special and Differential Treatment Under the GATT for Developing Countries," *The Economic Journal* 100, no. 403 (1990): 1318–1328.

23 Richard H. Steinberg, "The Hidden World of WTO Governance: A Reply to Andrew Lang and Joanne Scott," *European Journal of International Law* 20, no. 4 (2009): 1063–1071. Also, Andrew Lang and Joanne Scott, "The Hidden World of WTO Governance," *European Journal of International Law* 20, no. 3 (2009): 575–614.

24 Erin Hannah, Amy Janzwood, James Scott, and Rorden Wilkinson, "What Kind of Civil Society? Debating Trade at the WTO Public Forum," *Journal of World Trade* 52, no. 1 (2018): 113–142.

25 *Statement by H.E. Mr. Nelson Mandela at the 50th Anniversary Celebrations of the GATT*, 19 May 1998, www.wto.org/english/thewto_e/minist_e/min98_e/anniv_e/mandela_e.htm.

ADDITIONAL READING

Chad P. Bown and Douglas A. Irwin, "Trump's Assault on the Global Trading System: And Why Decoupling from China Will Change Everything," *Foreign Affairs* 98, no. 5 (2019): 125–137.

Bernard Hoekman, "Urgent and Important: Improving WTO Performance by Revisiting Working Practices," *Journal of World Trade* 53, no. 3 (2019): 373–394.

Kristen Hopewell, *Clash of Powers: US–China Rivalry in Global Trade Governance* (Cambridge: Cambridge University Press, 2020).

Rorden Wilkinson, *What's Wrong with the WTO and How to Fix It* (Cambridge: Polity, 2014).

16

UN ACCOUNTABILITY

From frameworks to evidence and results

Richard Golding

The online *Business Dictionary* defines accountability in the following way: "The obligation of an individual or organization to account for its activities, accept responsibility for them, and to disclose the results in a transparent manner."[1] Agreeing to be held accountable builds trust and success. When people are held accountable, they effectively understand that their work is valued. For international development activities, which are predominantly funded by governments, whether directly or through intergovernmental organizations or nongovernmental organizations (NGOs), the taxpayer largely represents the original source of such funds. However, the eventual recipients and beneficiaries invariably are remote, the funds having passed through multiple organizations in order to reach their eventual destinations. In some cases, they may never arrive. It is relatively straightforward to analyze and address issues of accountability within any given entity that has its own governance structure; but the task becomes quite complex and even daunting when analyzing accountabilities across many distinctive organizations, each with its own governing body and many common but also many diverse stakeholders.

Yet, they all have an obligation to collaborate and coordinate with one other across a global spectrum and especially in the context of the 17 Sustainable Development Goals (SDGs) and the United Nations Agenda 2030. The UN Development System (UNDS) characterizes this complex challenge in many ways. It now comprises over 30 distinct organizations and many other smaller entities; it also constitutes a major part of the UN system as a whole.

This chapter starts with an outline of what a typical framework of accountability comprises in the context of the UNDS and then examines in more detail the three components of such a framework within and across various UNDS organizations. The chapter concludes by stepping back and examining "the big picture" of holding the entire UNDS accountable for its contribution to progress with achievement of the SDGs, which provide a globally accepted set of objectives and against which to measure progress and impact. Ensuring system–wide accountability, of course, requires considerable coordination, cooperation, and cohesion across all organizations; there are some important new developments that have taken place to enable and facilitate this demand.

Accountability frameworks within the UN system

In 2011, the UN Joint Inspection Unit (JIU) issued a report[2] that summarized concisely the key components of any accountability framework within the context of the UN system. It is illustrated in Figure 16.1. This framework pre-dated the SDGs but illustrates the three core elements that together provide the basis for holding individual organizations, and indeed the entire system, to account. In one respect, it also anticipated what would become fundamentally important in meeting the global challenge of the SDGs.

The JIU report found that seven UN entities at the time already had or were well on the way to having a robust accountability framework in line with this model, and three others had the same at program level. The rest had not yet defined one. All UN organizations certainly had the key components of internal controls and some of the complaints and response mechanisms; but there was little evidence of any formal and meaningful political covenants with member states at that time.

Subsequently, the UN Secretary-General's 2019–2020 reform program for the UNDS and the publication of the management and accountability framework of the UN Development and Resident Coordinator System[3] showed evidence that the UNDS had implemented or were in the process of implementing all or most of these accountability framework components. The key "building blocks" for more comprehensive accountability are certainly present, enabling results and outcomes to be measured and reported transparently, whether those results and outcomes are expected or not. The question of how effective they are proving to be in terms of achieving the desired results is more complicated to assess.

Internal controls

The internal control environment comprises the core elements or foundations of accountability with which UN management and staff, and member states, will be most familiar, some of which have existed since the UN's creation. These seven elements are: internal audit; external audit and the UN Board of Auditors; audit and oversight committees; evaluation; the Joint Inspection Unit; risk management; and ethics and financial disclosure.

Internal audit

Almost all UN entities operate an internal audit function, which is a basic activity that holds management accountable for actions, processes, and, to a certain extent, outcomes. It is often,

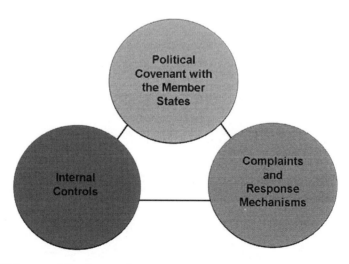

Figure 16.1 UN accountability framework.

though not always, part of a wider division or department of internal oversight alongside other functions such as evaluation and investigations (see below). The core UN, including the Secretariat and major departments (e.g., the Department of Economic and Social Affairs, DESA), is subject to internal audit reviews from the UN Office for Internal Oversight Services (OIOS). Other UN funds and programs—e.g., UNICEF, UN Development Programme (UNDP), and UN Population Fund (UNFPA)—as well as the specialized agencies have their own internal oversight functions. They all have well-established internal audit departments.

The OIOS was set up in 1994 with internal audit, inspection and evaluation, and investigations departments. Initially, most heads of internal oversight reported to the Secretary-General or executive head of the UN entity concerned. In some cases, this reporting line is still the case, but most now either report uniquely or jointly to their respective governing bodies and their audit and oversight committees. This reporting line is important in order to provide and enforce appropriate independence and objectivity and maintain the credibility of the internal audit function. It is also important that the budget and audit plans for the internal oversight and audit functions are not solely determined by the Secretary-General or executive heads but are ultimately approved by member states through governing bodies (often via an audit committee).

Internal audit reports are usually addressed to the head of the department or function being audited together with the Secretary-General or executive head of the entity concerned. The process for issue, distribution, and clearance of internal audit reports has been the subject of considerable discussion over the years. The advent of independent audit and oversight committees of governing bodies is an important advance, especially with regard to internal audits. Once agreed and finalized with appropriate management responses to any internal audit recommendations, the reports are available for public access on the OIOS or equivalent organizational website.

However, there have been instances in the past when reports have been either posted on websites or widely circulated *before* management comments and responses are agreed. This lack of formal clearance has sometimes caused serious friction between management, internal auditors, and governing body representatives. In general, most internal auditors will only circulate the first draft of a report with findings and recommendations to the auditee or appropriate management representative. The final version will only be shared more widely once the contents and any management responses have been agreed. This issue remains an important quality standard for internal auditors and facilitates the objective of auditors and management finding consensus. Since 2013, it has been policy to post all reports on the OIOS website 30 days after they have been agreed with management and reported to the audit and oversight committees and governing bodies. The fact that such reports are, once finalized, made available to the public demonstrates a high level of transparency and accountability by the UN system because they are rarely available for other organizations.

The heads of internal audit across the UN system have also formed a group known as the UN Representatives of Internal Audit Services (UN-RIAS) which meets at least once a year to share experiences and best practices. There is also a wider group simply known as RIAS, which includes heads of internal audit from other multilateral organizations outside the UN system. The UN's internal audit functions are usually members of the worldwide Institute of Internal Auditors (IIA) and, as a result, usually submit themselves to an independent external quality review every five years, in line with a recommendation from a 2016 JIU report.[4] The same report also recommended that all heads of internal audit within the UN system have a term limit to their appointment of no more than five or seven years. These conditions represent good examples of the UN following best practices and high professional standards. While the JIU report also included other more detailed recommended improvements, internal audit represents an important area of activity that directly contributes to holding UN organizations accountable for their internal controls (or, in some cases, lack thereof).

External audit

Each member of the UN system has a distinct governing body—variously called an assembly, executive board, or a council—of member-state representatives and, as such, it will produce its own annual accounts and financial statements. Within the UN system, these are all now produced to conform to the global International Public Sector Accounting Standards (IPSAS) and are audited annually by external auditors from certain governments that have such a professional capability. The core UN entities and its special funds and programs are currently each audited by teams from the governments of Chile, Germany, or India. The three heads of these government audit functions together form the UN Board of Auditors. They are responsible for timely execution and completion of the external audits for each entity and providing executive management with internal control reports and recommendations. The final audited accounts and reports are presented by the Board of Auditors to the Advisory Committee on Administrative and Budgetary Questions (ACABQ), a committee of the General Assembly.

The 13 UN specialized agencies also produce their own annual accounts according to IPSAS, and their audits are conducted by audit teams from one of the following governments: Canada, France, Ghana, Indonesia, Italy, Philippines, Switzerland, and the United Kingdom. Reports are submitted to the governing body. Representatives of the three governments on the UN Board of Auditors and representatives from the governments of each of the specialized agency's auditors also come together to form the UN Panel of External Auditors, at which they share their findings and experiences in order to improve system-wide financial reporting and internal controls.

Audit and oversight committees

Audit and oversight committees are relatively recent elements for the UN's governance and accountability. The first recorded instance was the World Food Programme's (WFP's) Audit Committee set up in 1984. At the outset, it had only advisory functions to the WFP executive director. It was not until 2004 that the terms of reference of this committee were changed and, in 2005, it submitted its first report directly to the WFP Executive Board. In 2004, UNESCO and UNFPA also set up such committees and reporting structures. In 2006, the JIU produced a report on *Oversight Lacunae*[5] and the Secretary-General published his *Comprehensive Review of Governance and Oversight*,[6] both of which recommended that independent audit and oversight committees be set up for all UN bodies. According to a 2019 JIU report in 2019,[7] such committees now operate in 18 UN entities with only five still pending: at International Atomic Energy Agency (IAEA), International Maritime Organization (IMO), joint UN Programme of HIV and AIDS (UNAIDS), Universal Postal Union (UPU), and the UN World Tourism Organization (UNWTO).

These committees are usually made up of independent professionals from outside the UN system; however, some may have had prior experience within the UN system or are retirees. Representatives from the private sector are also included. They usually serve three-year terms that are renewable once; they are voluntary. The experts usually have expertise in accounting, auditing, risk management, and financial disclosure. Such committees serve only in an advisory capacity to the governing body. They have no executive authority. They receive regular reports from executive management and from the appropriate internal oversight function as well as the external auditors.

An important aspect of the set-up of such committees has been that they now provide an independent expert body with inputs for internal audit and other internal oversight functions as well as to executive management. The independence and objectivity of the internal auditors is thereby strengthened; it also provides a necessary reporting channel should there be cases for which the executive head may be the subject of adverse or sensitive findings. Operating such committees is instrumental in helping the world organization demonstrate its seriousness about following best practices.

Evaluation

In 2014, a JIU analysis of the UN's evaluation system stated that:

> Evaluation is one of the main instruments that support the United Nations system in addressing accountability for results and added value, for learning and knowledge development, strengthening its leadership role in global governance, and instituting reforms that influence the lives of people worldwide. Thus, the continuous development of the evaluation function is critical to the United Nations system's ability to achieve its objectives, to account for success, and bring about necessary changes to improve international development and governance.[8]

Most UN organizations have their own evaluation departments, which reflects the awareness of the fundamental importance of measuring results. In some cases, it is part of a wider internal oversight function alongside internal audit and investigations. This is the case with the OIOS. However, some UN entities, such as the International Labour Organization (ILO), have their own evaluation division independent of the audit and investigation functions; its head reports directly to the director-general. The referenced JIU report included a recommendation that the appointment of heads of evaluation be for a fixed term of five to seven years in order to sustain independence and objectivity, the same as was recommended for heads of internal audit functions. Whatever internal reporting structure is adopted, evaluation is the core internal function for assessing the organization's achievements in terms of the results being achieved and whether or not they meet management, governing body, and beneficiary expectations.

Just as the internal auditors across the UN system meet in the RIAS organization, the heads of evaluation have formed the UN Evaluation Group (UNEG) in order to share experiences and best practices, and to sustain quality and professionalism. This sharing helps to strengthen accountability. UNEG actually has over 50 members and observers covering all UN organizations (including several departments of the UN Secretariat, the regional commissions, and others outside the UN system such as the World Bank and WTO).

One of UNEG's core functions is to maintain a system of evaluation norms and standards that UNEG members are expected to uphold in their work. These norms and standards have evolved over many years and are a critical element in providing assurance that when results are being assessed and evaluated, the process and methodology being applied are rigorous and consistent. In total, 14 areas are covered by these norms and standards. These are: internationally agreed principles, goals, and targets; utility; credibility; independence; impartiality; ethics; transparency; human rights and gender equality; national evaluation capacities; professionalism; enabling environment; evaluation policy; responsibility for the evaluation function; and use and follow-up. There is considerable detail specified for each of the above, and the UNEG also commissions independent external assessments to provide feedback on the application of the standards system-wide.

The processes of evaluation within the UN system are therefore well embedded and mature, which is encouraging for accountability and results. Of itself, evaluation practice does not provide assurance that results are as expected or optimized but it does provide significant comfort that whatever results are being achieved, they are professionally monitored, evaluated, and reported.

Joint Inspection Unit

The UN Joint Inspection Unit was founded in 1966 and, apart from external auditors of individual agencies and entities, was the first oversight body to be part of the UN system. It has 11 independent inspectors who are mandated by member states. The JIU asserts its mandate on its website[9] as being "the only independent external oversight body of the United Nations system mandated to conduct evaluations, inspections and investigations system-wide."

The JIU is funded by budgetary contributions from all UN organizations (including the specialized agencies) based on the size of their budgets; but the JIU determines its own program of reviews and evaluations. Inspectors usually produce some 6–10 reports per year. These reports are usually lengthy and often informative and useful in terms of providing comparative data across UN organizations on a variety of topics. They make recommendations for action, always targeted at either governing bodies or executive management in terms of the responsibility to implement the recommendations.

JIU reports have a mixed reception and reactions depending on the topic and the nature of the recommendations. However, there is no doubt that, on many issues, their insights and system-wide information are a valuable source of reference.

Risk management

While the topic of risk management may not instinctively be considered pertinent to accountability, effective and ongoing assessment and management of risks is, in fact, a key element of any accountability framework. Failure to adequately anticipate or manage critical operational, security, and reputational risks can have a significant negative impact on the performance of an organization and its ability to achieve its desired results and goals.

The identification, assessment, management, and reporting of risks across any organization has gradually become a robust practice—often referred to as Enterprise-Wide Risk Management (ERM). As with independent oversight committees, the origins of ERM within the UN system can be traced to 2006 and the JIU Oversight *Lacunae Report* and the Secretary-General's *Comprehensive Review of Governance and Oversight*. Both contained high-priority recommendations about the development and adoption of ERM practices. Progress was sluggish at first, but most UN organizations now have an institutionalized ERM process that enables senior management as well as member states to have a sense of the risks the organization faces, and how to mitigate and manage them. This sense contributes significantly to the ability to hold management and staff accountable for their actions, especially in inherently high-risk operational regions such as conflict zones, epidemics, and natural disasters.

Ethics and financial disclosure

It was again in 2006 that the UN Secretariat set up the UN Ethics Office which was responsible for ensuring implementation of the UN's ethics policies, code of conduct, and financial disclosure processes. The office helps to ensure that UN staff always behave ethically as well as lawfully, as well as avoiding any actual or perceived conflicts of interest. This office serves all the entities of the UN Secretariat as well as its funds and programs. Since then, ethics officers and departments have gradually been set up in the various specialized agencies, although some have combined responsibility for ethics and financial disclosure with other existing roles—such as internal oversight (in WMO and UNIDO) or the financial controller (ILO). Some, like UPU, have outsourced the function to an accounting and advisory firm.

Ethics policies and adherence to them have become a critical component of accountability for all staff. Conflicts of interest, whether real or perceived, can prove to be highly problematic or even disruptive to certain operations of any UN organization. In recent years, the development professionals have experienced a number of difficult cases of unethical and fraudulent behavior. As such, members of the UNDS and other non-UN bodies have had to respond quickly and robustly with much stronger ethical policies and staff training programs, especially for safeguarding of children, in order to satisfy increased donor demands. The latter have been held accountable by their taxpayers, especially when such malfeasance appears in the mainstream and social media channels.

The establishment of the UN Ethics Office in 2006 was partly, but not wholly, in response to the issues surrounding the Iraq Oil-for-Food Programme during 2003–2005. There were particular concerns about the impact on the UN's procurement functions and the staff working there. As a result, what appeared to be very stringent personal annual financial disclosure statements for UN staff (including their spouses and immediate family members) were made mandatory for all senior management plus all staff at all levels in key functions such as procurement and finance. It has taken some of the specialized agencies several years to implement similar policies and processes. Nonetheless, there now is a clear understanding and expectation by staff generally that they will be held accountable for any unethical behavior, financial irregularity, or conflict of interest.

Once again, like the issue of risk management, this topic has become a key platform of internal control for UN organizations. Risk management is required to demonstrate to member states and the public at large that UN staff are managing effectively.

Complaints and response mechanisms

The components of internal control provide the core foundations of any accountability framework; they have evolved and developed over a few decades across the UN system. Mechanisms for managing and responding to complaints and reporting incidents are more recent; but they are equally important in demonstrating clear accountability and transparency to stakeholders. There have long been various investigation functions within the UN system that respond to reports of malpractice, abuse, fraud, or other irregularities; but this core function has also been enhanced by other essential mechanisms—notably much stronger whistleblowing and protection processes. These various components are discussed below.

Investigations

The UN Secretariat has its own investigations department, which is part of the OIOS. It has grown and now handles more than 500 complaints or reported incidents per year.[10] It cannot and does not have to investigate and report on every case; but, following initial assessment, many are referred to other bodies for further review and investigation, others are pending further information, and a small minority are closed without further investigation. This high figure excludes UN peace operations whose reported incidents or complaints are handled in a parallel but distinct process due mainly to the need to refer such cases back to the troop-contributing governments.

The investigations department of the OIOS is one of the three primary contact points for all UN staff to report any misconduct or wrongdoing. The other primary contact points are the UN Ethics Office (for instances of retaliation or protection from retaliation) and Human Resources Management (for other issues).

Whistleblowing

While whistleblowing is not new, the processes for receiving and managing reports have become more robust and professional, especially in terms of protecting anonymity and minimizing the risks of retaliation. Another JIU report of 2018[11] on whistleblowing stated that, in the five-year period 2012–2016, there were 10,413 cases reported by whistle-blowers across 23 different UN entities—on average, approximately 90 cases per UN entity per year. This number is a very generalized indicator. Despite all the robust ethics policies, training programs, financial disclosure returns, and risk management strategies, problems still arise on a continuous basis across the system.

The UN's policy on whistleblowing is set out in *Protection against Retaliation for Reporting Misconduct*.[12] This policy, in addition to the need for staff to report to the OIOS, the Ethics Office, or Human Resources, also provides very specific conditions for staff members who may wish to report something to an external source. These cases should be very exceptional but are nonetheless possible and so are elaborated.

Overall, the UN has a robust set of policies and processes for dealing with complaints and managing whistleblower anonymity that would probably match or exceed those of most other organizations. More detailed analysis of the 90 or so annual cases would no doubt reveal reasons why not all of them may be relevant to the strength of the policies and procedures; but it still provides a framework within which to hold people accountable.

In dealing with complaints, the UN's special funds and programs also have an ombudsman function. The ombudsman service was founded in 2002 and is available to staff around the world with offices in key UN hubs—ranging from New York, Geneva, Vienna, Nairobi, Santiago, and Bangkok to Entebbe and Goma. The service helps staff to resolve workplace conflicts in an informal, confidential manner with the aim of maintaining a harmonious workplace. An ombudsman does not advocate for any party in a dispute. It can be a useful but more informal method of resolving a problem or dispute without or before resorting to reporting it to OIOS or the Ethics Office.

Furthermore, it should not be forgotten that most UN entities have some form of Staff Council which is designed to represent the interests of all staff in any organization and through which certain grievances can be made and resolved. As a further measure, staff disputes can also be heard at the Administrative Tribunal of the International Labour Organization (ILOAT) which aims to resolve employee–employer conflicts.

Political covenant with member states

As referenced at the outset, the 2011 JIU report highlighted a third, and arguably most important, element of a truly transparent and complete accountability framework. The requirement is for a clear political covenant between executive management and member states—in short, accountability by the Second UN of international civil servants to the First UN of member states whose citizens' taxes pay the bills.

The details of this covenant are the most recent yet undoubtedly the most needed aspect of a strong accountability framework. It is the one that truly brings all the elements together and binds them into an organizational culture of accountability and transparency. In business terms, it sets the tone at the top.

In many ways, the starting point of accountability in UN organizations should be mutual agreement on the strategic plans of any organization and its member states' political will to provide the resources and the empowerment to management necessary for the delivery of expected results. Member states are responsible for providing a clear mandate and setting priorities. Member states also play a role in oversight matters through entities such as the Board of Auditors, the JIU, OIOS, audit and oversight committees, and evaluations. Furthermore, as noted in the JIU report, member states are also usually responsible for selection and performance assessment of executive heads.

Back in 2011, few organizations formally included this approach specifically in their accountability frameworks or internal documents. The practice, however, has become more widespread. The UN Secretariat, UNDP, UNICEF, and WFP all initiated a political agreement or "covenant" with member states as the centerpiece of their accountability architecture. In addition, some such as the International Organization for Migrations (IOM), UNAIDS, UNDP, and UNHCR have included their accountability toward beneficiaries as an explicit stakeholder in the accountability framework of the organization.

The most important development for the UNDS in recent years has been the global adoption of the 2030 Agenda and the SDGs. They provide the current context for accountability frameworks for all members of the UNDS and the basis for political covenants with member states. All the elements of accountability described so far under the headings of internal control and complaints and reporting mechanisms are present; they are effective on an organization-by-organization basis. Systematically, all entities are working toward helping to achieve the SDGs or some subset of them. To be effective and be held accountable, there should be broad, overarching political covenants and other governance and accountability structures across the system to enable measurement of progress and success (or failures) in realizing the goals. Given this reality and the global consensus reached about the SDGs, some important reforms and new structures have been agreed and established.

Latest reforms of the UNDS since 2017 for the Second UN

In July 2017, Secretary-General António Guterres spelled out his vision of accountability in the concluding paragraphs of his report to the General Assembly and ECOSOC. It is captured in *Repositioning the United Nations Development System to Deliver on the 2030 Agenda*:

> The analysis conducted for the present report indicates that the UN development system is both willing and ready but is not fully equipped nor designed at the present time to live up to the ambition of the 2030 Agenda.
>
> There is an urgent need for the United Nations development system to move beyond coherence and coordination towards greater leadership, integration and accountability for results on the ground.[13]

The report's title indicates the transformative potential of the 17 SDGs. These two concise paragraphs draw attention to fundamental issues and challenges. As the UNDS was already two years into the 2015–2030 Agenda, and with the clock ticking, his statement could be interpreted as a somewhat damning assessment.

This assessment has resulted in reforms that led to a General Assembly resolution to reposition the UNDS in line with the recommendations. Guterres introduced them with the following words: "The resolution you adopt today ushers in the most ambitious and comprehensive reform of the UN Development System in decades."

If true, such a statement should have attracted significant attention not only from member states (whether contributing or receiving ODA) but also from the world's press and public. In reality, it received little public attention, but the General Assembly accepted the proposals, which are moving ahead. The reforms set out during 2017–2018 and under partial implementation aim to "move beyond coherence and coordination" with five priorities. The first is greater empowerment of Development Group (DG) management and staff through increased delegation of authority, essential because empowerment and accountability go hand in hand. The second consists of mainstreaming the SDGs into the strategic planning cycles of the DG entities. The third priority emphasizes better use of the newly empowered country-level structure with a "new generation" of UN country teams (UNCT) with a common back-office, a strengthened UN Resident Coordinator (RC) system, and a re-vamped regional structure. The fourth focus reflects the hopes for a new Funding Compact with member states for core resources across the DG entities with clear, quantifiable targets along with increased use of targets for inter-agency funding pool. The fifth priority consists of strengthening results-based management processes and reporting on inter-agency operations and outcomes aligned to the SDGs.

The above reforms have received further credibility through the set-up of a new Department of Operational Support (DOS) in January 2019. This department plays a key role and provides visible evidence of active support to these reforms which, in turn, should tangibly improve transparency and accountability as well as provide a UNDS structure that is more agile, effective, efficient, pragmatic, and decentralized.

Implementation of the first priority, concerning empowerment of management, has already resulted in multiple, highly detailed operational changes to delegate more responsibilities within the management hierarchies of the UN Secretariat. These changes clearly recognize the underlying principle that individuals cannot be held accountable for activities that they do not have sufficient authority to implement. These increased delegated authorities are positive and directly mitigate against the hitherto negative image that complexity and micro-management from member states and agency heads provided ready-made excuses for lack of progress on key objectives by members of the Second UN.

However, the point about mainstreaming the SDGs into the strategic planning cycles of DG organizations—essentially the entire UN system—may seem rather bland or even esoteric. However, it is fundamental as these planning cycles drive so much decision-making and activity in individual organizations; previously, these cycles were not well aligned. Some organizations have a strategic planning cycle of just two years while others have up to six years; others fall in between. Even where the lengths of the planning periods are aligned, they may have different start and end dates. For the first time, there are considerable efforts to get all UN organization onto the same time horizon for planning, budgeting, and resource mobilization. The likely norm of four years is fundamental to achieving sensible progress on coherence, accountability, and reporting.

The revised RC structure is worth examining more closely as it is crucial to the SDGs and to accountability. A better country presence has long been recognized as a fundamental necessity if the UNDS is to be credible in arguing that the operations of separately governed UN organizations can be cohesive and deliver as one. One of the criticisms had long been that each RC was on the payroll of UNDP. The clash between its operational and coordination roles impeded generating the right relationship, authority (where required), and respect from the other participants in the development activity in a country. Accountability was invariably a victim. When expectations were not fulfilled or things went wrong, it was rather easy to avoid accountability under the former RC structure.

With the support of the UNDP administrator, the RC now reports directly to the UN Sustainable Development Group (comprising all operational entities in the UNDS), rather than through UNDP, and ultimately to the UN deputy secretary-general, who herself played a significant role in the development of the SDGs. The Management and Accountability Framework of the UN RC system as part of the reforms now clearly sets out the relationships and accountability agreements at country level for the new RCs, including clarity of UN leadership for activities in the country plus clear working relationships with accountability indicators for results in strategic planning and programming; communications and advocacy; common services; and funding/resource mobilization. Further accountability agreements are expected for the regional and global levels.

Overall, these proposed changes and targets represent a more practical and tangible set of reform goals than many reform efforts from previous secretaries-general. However, the inherent constraints of a 75-year-old, fragmented UN system, with a long history of building silos and branding, mean that the single biggest challenge remains the alignment of goals, resources, activities, evaluations, and reporting back to member states, to donors, and ultimately to taxpayers.

On the funding side, an analysis of non-core (earmarked) funding, which has increased and dominated the scene for decades, shows that over 90 percent is allocated to single UN entities whereas only 6 percent is channeled through inter-agency pooled funds to a combination of organizations. Given the lack of inherent alignment of the large number of organizations in the UNDS and the 17 cross-cutting SDGs, this pattern is not only unacceptable but also illogical.

Hence, underpinning all proposed changes is the call for a Funding Compact between member states and the UN system. For many, this is a welcome surprise involving a distinctive commitment by member states. Its specific, quantifiable targets are illustrated in Figure 16.2. Achieving a core funding level of at least 30 percent for the UNDS within five years would be

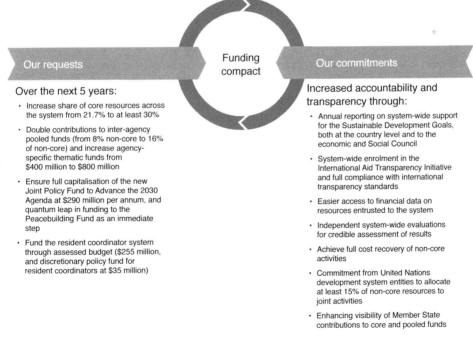

Figure 16.2 Proposed parameters for a Funding Compact.

a big and crucial change. If donors live up to this commitment, it may even herald a step function in the level of trust afforded to the UNDS and the UN system in general.

It is too early to say if the apparent reversal of the slow, downward trend for core funding, together with commitments to the revised RC system and the much-needed boost to inter-agency funding, are realistic. However, it would certainly provide fuel for improved entity-level and system-wide-level accountability that is essential to show progress by the UNDS toward helping to realize the SDGs.

On the wider, cross-cutting evaluation and reporting front, these latest reforms also contain some significant commitments, including independent system-wide evaluations for credible assessment of results, easier and more open access to all financial data resources, plus a further distinctive and welcome commitment for system-wide enrollment in the International Aid Transparency Initiative (IATI). Significantly, it includes full compliance with international transparency standards. This significant undertaking does not guarantee results but represents a clear and unambiguous commitment.

In this context, many large foundations, which do not always have open books, are also responding to increasing global expectations about transparency. The Bill and Melinda Gates Foundation, for example, now provides accessibility to their full grants database. It reports to the OECD, the Foundation Center, the US Internal Revenue Service, the IATI, and others. It also has a policy to enable the unrestricted access and reuse of all peer-reviewed, published research funded by the Foundation, including any underlying data sets.[14]

Over 1,000 other organizations, including increasing numbers of UN organizations, publish spending information through the IATI.[15] As of May 2017, the UNDS had published information on UN pooled funds to IATI for the first time. In one very basic sense, publishing such financial data and results through IATI publicly demonstrated a willingness to be held accountable by the public at large to a common international standard, a willingness that previously was absent. The long-term effect of sustaining this commitment has yet to be seen, but it is the right direction to pursue.

Reforms underway for the First UN of member states

In looking a little further back, one important occurrence took place in 2012 which, after a rather low-key start in many people's eyes, has now become a key focus of attention as member states consider their responsibilities with regard to the SDGs. It was the creation of a UN High-Level Political Forum (HLPF) for Sustainable Development. It meets annually for eight days with ministerial-level participation for three of those days; it reports to ECOSOC. In addition, every four years, it meets for two days at head-of-state level under the General Assembly's auspices. For ultimate accountability and monitoring of feedback on progress toward the SDGs, this appears to be a significant commitment by the First UN.

A further recent decision implemented the HLPF is the production of Voluntary National Reviews (VNRs) by governments that assess their own country's progress and contributions toward the SDGs. These VNRs are self-assessments and not independent evaluations, but they are nonetheless a welcome development in demonstrating commitment to the SDGs through reporting evidence that can then be publicly scrutinized. The VNRs were produced in 2018 and 2019; in 2019, 47 countries reported (seven for the second time).[16] The United Kingdom so far is the only permanent member of the Security Council to produce a VNR.

The very existence of this forum illustrates the growing importance of Political Economic Analysis (PEA) in determining both funding priorities and political risks in achieving desired goals in many parts of the world, and holding the right parties accountable for whatever results are achieved. The challenge is that such debate and analysis in the context of the HLPF needs to actively take account of differing political considerations across the world and not just those political and economic priorities of the donor countries.

Conclusion

The UNDS has embarked on a fresh, challenging, and critical phase in the run-up to 2030 and the outcomes of the 17 SDGs. Trying to account for all the activities of the UNDS, especially within the wider context of a global official development assistance (ODA) system, is still a daunting prospect. However, the Secretary-General and other organizational heads and senior staff have reached a consensus about embracing significant changes in order to better align and work together on realizing the SDGs. The reforms of the RC system, the strategic planning alignments, and the proposed core and inter-agency Funding Compact, together with the greater system-wide evaluation and reporting commitments, definitely should be welcomed. Greater engagement through the HLPF is also an opportunity.

The UNDS is making these commitments and changes at a time when the wider international development system and underlying political climate hardly bode well. In particular, rising populism and emphases on national priorities suggest some significant and potentially disturbing shifts resulting in potentially disruptive threats to previously reliable funding streams.

Comprehensive solutions are never easy, and the magnitude of improving UN accountability should not be underestimated. However, transparency and accountability are not ends in themselves but means to ends. Accountability is a tool to make development aid more effective in reducing and ultimately eliminating poverty. Ways should be found of harnessing the proven benefits of well-developed and mature internal control functions and reporting mechanisms as a platform for greater coherence and results-oriented global activities across the UN and the wider multilateral system. That is a prerequisite for the UNDS to deliver at scale the support required to realize the SDGs and Agenda 2030.

Accountability is not a panacea, for the UNDS or any other institution. However, frameworks are in place for UN accountability and measurements have begun. Being able to hold organizations accountable is essential but does not guarantee that expected results are achieved; but at least it is clear what has and has not been accomplished.

NOTES

1 Business Dictionary, *Definition of Accountability*, www.businessdictionary.com/definition/account-ability.html.
2 Mounir Zahran, *Accountability Frameworks in the United Nations System* (Geneva: JIU, 2011).
3 UN Sustainable Development Group, *The Management and Accountability Framework of the UN Development and Resident Coordinator System* (New York: UN, 2019).
4 Rajab M. Sukayri and Cihan Terzi, *State of the Internal Audit Function in the United Nations System* (Geneva: JIU, 2016).
5 JIU, *Oversight Lacunae in the United Nations System* (Geneva: JIU, 2006).
6 UN, *Comprehensive Review of Governance and Oversight within the United Nations and Its Funds, Programmes and Specialized Agencies* (UN document A/61/605), 1 December 2006.
7 Aicha Afifi, *Review of Audit and Oversight Committees in the United Nations System* (Geneva: JIU, 2019).
8 Sukai Prom-Jackson and George A. Bartslotas, *Analysis of the Evaluation Function in the United Nations System* (Geneva: JIU, 2014).
9 Joint Inspection Unit of the United Nations System, www.unjiu.org.
10 Office of Internal Oversight Services, *Activities of the Office of Internal Oversight Services for the Period from 1 July 2018 to 30 June 2019: Report of the Office* (UN document A/74/305), https://digitallibrary.un.org/record/3826607?ln=ar.

11 Eileen A. Cronin and Aicha Afifi, *Review of Whistle-Blower Policies and Practices in United Nations System Organizations* (Geneva: JIU, 2018).

12 UN, *Activities of the Ethics Office: Report of the Secretary-General* (UN document A/73/89), 8 June 2018.

13 UN, *Repositioning the United Nations Development System to Deliver on the 2030 Agenda: Report of the Secretary-General* (UN documents A/72/124–E/2018/3), 4 July 2018.

14 Gates Foundation, *The Bill and Melinda Gates Foundation's Information Sharing Strategy*, www.gatesfoundation.org/How-We-Work/General-Information/Information-Sharing-Approach.

15 International Aid Transparency Initiative, https://iatistandard.org/en.

16 UN, *Voluntary National Reviews Database*, https://sustainabledevelopment.un.org/vnrs.

ADDITIONAL READING

Anna Botham-Edighoffer, *The New Human Resources Management of the United Nations: A Study of the Reform Process between 1985 and 2005* (Berlin: Freie Universität Berlin, 2006).

Stephen Browne and Thomas G. Weiss, eds., *Post-2015 UN Development: Making Change Happen* (London: Routledge, 2015).

Viktor Jakupec and Max Kelly, *Foreign Aid in the Age of Populism: Political Economy Analysis* (New York: Routledge, 2019).

James O. C. Jonah and Amy Scott Hill, "The Secretariat: Independence and Reform," in *The Oxford Handbook on the United Nations*, ed. Thomas G. Weiss and Sam Daws, 2nd edn. (Oxford: Oxford University Press, 2018), 212–230.

Joachim Mueller, *Reforming the United Nations: A Chronology* (Leiden: Brill-Nijhoff, 2016).

Transparency, Accountability and Participation (TAP) Network, *SDG Accountability Handbook: A Practical Guide for Civil Society—2018*, https://sdgaccountability.org.

UN Sustainable Development Group, *The Management and Accountability Framework of the UN Development and Resident Coordinator System* (New York: UN, 2019).

17

TOWARD BETTER KNOWLEDGE MANAGEMENT IN THE UN

Steve Glovinsky

Do all organizations learn, or are some doomed continually to repeat past mistakes? This chapter argues that the organizations of the UN development system (UNDS) generally fall into the latter category, because of an inbuilt structural amnesia inherent in its leadership.

This argument has four parts. The first clarifies the often misunderstood concept of knowledge management (KM), and explains how successful learning organizations learn by using KM systems to convert staff knowledge into improved organizational effectiveness. The second part presents a review of various attempts by UNDS organizations to introduce KM, reflecting on the lack of progress that prompted the General Assembly in December 2016 to call on the UNDS to introduce or strengthen KM strategies and policies, instigating an improved second generation of KM strategies. The third part presents the unfortunate fate of three promising pre-2016 KM strategies to support the conclusion that only half the battle has been won, with the UNDS's "structural amnesia" the remaining sticking point. The fourth part presents a vision for a more networked UNDS focused on the Sustainable Development Goals (SDGs) to break through this blockage; it suggests some practical steps toward making the vision a reality.

Knowledge management and the learning organization

Knowledge is, very simply, what someone knows;[1] three key characteristics of knowledge are relevant for KM. First, knowledge is "sticky." It is associated with the person whose knowledge it is, acquired through study, observation, sharing, and experience. Importantly, it involves trust: to trust the validity of the knowledge, the source must be trustworthy. Knowledge presented without reference to its owner loses its value.

Second, knowledge can be explicit or implicit. Explicit knowledge is documented material published by domain experts, based on evidence or experience. Implicit knowledge is tacit, part of individual cognition reflected in conversations, stories, or actions. Tacit knowledge incorporates undocumented insights from practitioners and can be as valuable as the distilled documented knowledge from experts.

Third, knowledge is measured in person-years. If someone has worked in a profession for 20 years, they have 20 years of knowledge about that profession. An organization of 5,000 people with an average of 20 years' experience would have 100,000 years of knowledge to draw on.

One hundred thousand years is a lot of knowledge, which is why every organization striving for continuing relevance and effectiveness should be tapping into what its staff members, consultants, and clients know. This is where KM enters.

How can knowledge be managed? The answer is that it cannot—simply because knowledge resides within a person's mind and lived experience. However, knowledge flows—the process that transfers what someone knows to other people who need to know it—can be managed. Essentially, then, KM is a process that manages knowledge flows from people to people.

Using this definition, KM can be articulated in two ways. The first is people-to-people, in which members of an affinity group, or "community," share knowledge to help a colleague or the collective group solve a challenge, build a better tool, or improve on a process. Communities in this sense are people engaged in a common pursuit such as a hobby, a project, or a profession. The latter is a "community of practice" because the interactions focus on building proficiency in or continually sharpening a practice within their professional domain. The second way is people-to-organization (and to its people), in which an organization puts processes in place to direct knowledge flows in, through, and out of an organization, tapping the knowledge of its staff, consultants, and clients to continually improve the relevance and effectiveness of its policies, products, and processes. In essence, an organization applies KM to turn individual knowledge into organizational learning.

Organizational learning is the process through which an organization adapts and improves its products and processes based on feedback and evidence from experience, evaluation, or research.[2] Drawing on people's knowledge provides an organization with an unparalleled store of first-person, on-the-ground understanding about what is working, what is not, and what could. In this way, KM's contribution to organizational learning can be applied to improve decision-making, sharpen methods, enhance knowledge products, promote consultation, disseminate good practices, and minimize "reinventing the wheel."

In addition to KM's benefits to organizational learning, KM can also contribute to an organization's human resources strategy. Drawing on the knowledge of staff sends an empowering message that the organization values an employee's knowledge. Contributions to corporate knowledge-sharing networks can identify the staff with the best, most thoughtful, or most creative ideas, making them visible to their peers and enhancing their reputations. It can also build community—sharing knowledge among professional peers builds familiarity and trust; they learn on whom they can rely for sound advice and who relies on them. Continual interaction promotes collegiality amongst the members that, like the networks of old, builds informal connections that promote career advancement, facilitate cross-boundary collaboration, and increase cohesiveness as a group.

If KM's benefits seem so straightforward, why have so many organizations, including UN organizations, struggled to get it right? KM is a relatively new concept, emerging as an area of study only in the early 1990s. From the beginning, KM has been a difficult concept to nail down due, among other reasons, to the difficulty in finding quantifiable evidence of its impact. In absence until very recently of a commonly accepted definition, KM has been subject to wide interpretation.

One common interpretation of KM is as an empty buzzword. Who would be against knowledge and management as a way to improve organizational effectiveness? As with other buzzwords, uptake is frequently claimed but superficially addressed by any activity loosely perceived to qualify for the honorific until its replacement by the next buzzword.

Another interpretation is as a technology solution. In this version, KM is implemented simply by buying or building a software promoted by information technology enthusiasts and salespeople to organizational managers unaware that KM is, at its core, people-centered.

A third variation is as a document collection. Typically, the software is used to compile, at great effort and cost, a large amount of documented knowledge, usually without considering whether anyone actually wants to use it; often they do not. Documented knowledge—evaluation material, project progress reports and findings, research papers—is an important component of a KM system, but effective KM requires both "collection" and "connection." So-called best practices, for example, are typically highly context specific and not easily transferable. Reading about a best practice is not as helpful to a practitioner facing a challenge as a visit from the person who thought up the best practice, and whose knowledge can then be tapped to help find a way forward within a different context.

A fourth interpretation confuses KM with information management. Unlike knowledge, "information" merely consists of data or features that describe the characteristics of an entity, independent of any reference to what an individual "knows."

A fifth interpretation is as a low-cost, low-impact pursuit. In this version, KM generally consists of interactive social networks or websites moderated by staff on volunteered time, with no linkage to or interaction with corporate business processes.

These versions of KM have generally resulted in low engagement rates and minimal impact, creating additional work without generating corresponding value. The result is that these initiatives usually fade away and produce skepticism and resistance to attempts to try again.

Even a well-designed KM strategy cannot be assured of lasting success. In addition to its other benefits, KM's knowledge-sharing dimension introduces a horizontal, inclusive, and collegial environment that breaks through hierarchies and silos. As such, KM can drive a cultural shift in formal top-down organizations, a common characteristic of UN organizations.[3] For these organizations, KM is by its nature a transformational initiative, and succeeding with transformational initiatives in UN organizations presents formidable challenges.

The next two sections present an overview of the UN development system's experiences with knowledge management. They track KM's general progress over time, and then focus in on three instances where the transformational version was attempted.

The trajectory of KM in the UNDS

In 2016 Petru Dumitriu of the Joint Inspection Unit (JIU), the UN system's independent oversight body, prepared a report on KM in the UN system, "based on the conviction that knowledge is a valuable core asset of [UN] organizations and its best comparative advantage," and that "the effective utilization of the knowledge capital, both in the organizations and system-wide, was critical for achieving the goals of the United Nations System organizations."[4] The report covered 28 organizations, including the UN Secretariat, the UN's special funds and programs, and the specialized agencies. It based its findings on an extensive literature and document review plus 55 meetings, 175 interviews, and almost 7,000 responses to a perception survey by managers and staff about KM.

Findings of the JIU report

The report revealed a wide variation of KM interpretations, strategies, and initiatives across the system, as well as widely varying experiences with successful implementation. It found 15 different definitions for knowledge management, varying from the simple to the sophisticated. Of the 27 organizations plus the individual departments of the UN Secretariat that were covered, only 16 (11 organizations and five Secretariat Departments) had developed KM strategies at some point between 2007 and 2016 (see Figure 17.1). And of these 16, only the International Atomic Energy Agency (IAEA) and UN Habitat were maintaining long-term strategies; several

	2007	2008	2009	2010	2011	2012	2013	2014	2015	2016	2017	2018	2019	2020
UNDP			2009 - 2011					2014 - 2017						
UNEP								2014 - 2017						
UNFPA			2009 - 2014											
UN-Habitat				2010 - 2013				2014 -2019						
WFP											*Work in progress →*			
FAO					2011 - 2014									
IAEA							2013 - 2021							
IFAD		2008 - 2010											2019 - 2025	
ILO	2007 - 2009			2010 - 2015							*Work in progress →*			
UNESCO						2012 - 2015								
WHO				2010 - 2015										
WIPO									2015 - 2018					
DPKO &DFS				2010 - 2013					2015 - 2018					
OCHA						2012 - 2013								
ECA								2014 - no expiry date						
ESCWA									2015 - Towards Vision 2030					

Figure 17.1 Knowledge management strategies in the UN system, 2007–2020.

others, including several identified as groundbreaking—the International Labour Organization (ILO), the UN Development Programme (UNDP), the Food and Agricultural Organization (FAO), and the World Health Organization (WHO)—had let their KM strategies lapse at some point, at least temporarily. Other organizations, including the Office for the Coordination of Humanitarian Affairs (OCHA) and the World Meteorological Organization (WMO), had incorporated KM activities into their broader corporate strategies.

The report did not address the relative strengths and weaknesses of the different strategies and activities. However, document reviews and consultations by the author with KM officers in several UN offices and organizations revealed KM efforts that had adopted some of the questionable approaches cited earlier: strategies focused on technology platforms; KM combined (or confused) with information management; absence of performance or impact indicators; discussion groups not linked to corporate business processes. These shortcomings helped explain why some of the KM strategies and initiatives failed to gain traction.

In spite of the mixed experience, the JIU found a very favorable environment for the UN system to press ahead with KM. The perception survey was most telling: there was broad consensus that staff of UN system organizations considered their organizations knowledge-based entities, and that knowledge-sharing be embedded among the core competencies of all staff.[5] The report made a strong case for UN organizations to continue to pursue KM, especially in light of the UN's ability to implement the holistic and collaborative approach on which the 2030 Agenda for Sustainable Development is based.

The report also emphasized the key characteristic of an effective KM effort highlighted in this chapter's first section; namely, as a means to incorporate the knowledge of staff into the policies and programs of the UN system organizations, as a key driver of organizational effectiveness. Particularly for these organizations, for which knowledge is the primary source of credibility and influence, and with an advantage of tapping into a globally distributed knowledge base, knowledge-sharing should be a key component of knowledge management. It is worth citing at length one of the main conclusions:

> Several knowledge management benefits were acknowledged and emphasized during the review:

(a) Improved organizational effectiveness by ensuring that programmes are designed based on the latest knowledge, capitalizing on past experience and expertise acquired by the staff;

(b) Improved organizational efficiency and reduced costs through strengthening the ability to respond quickly to emerging issues on the ground, rapid mobilization of organizational expertise and experience, avoidance of previous mistakes and duplication of efforts;

(c) Facilitation of the adoption of an integrated approach to programming, by establishing and empowering communities of practice and networks that cut across sectors and geographic locations.[6]

The report also concluded: "knowledge management remains a challenge for the United Nations system organizations in their attempt to systematically and efficiently develop, organize, share and integrate knowledge to achieve their cross-cutting goals."[7]

In light of these findings, the report's recommendations focused on three key actions. First, the UN system's organizations should approach KM as a system-wide effort and develop strategies, policies, or guidelines based on existing practices and experiences. Second, knowledge acquired by staff should be recognized in human resource policies and practices. Third, common system-wide KM initiatives should be stimulated both generally and in the specific context of the 2030 Agenda for Sustainable Development.

The JIU report had a major impact. Based on the report's recommendations, General Assembly resolution 71/243 of December 2016, presenting the results of a four-year review of the UNDS's operational activities (the Quadrennial Comprehensive Policy Review, QCPR), included a statement calling on the UNDS "to introduce or strengthen knowledge management strategies and policies, with a view to enhancing transparency and improving its capabilities to generate, retain, use and share knowledge."[8] The report also triggered a new generation of UN KM strategies that were deliberately designed to ensure that KM was, in fact, the critical element in organizational learning.

The first of these new efforts set the benchmark: the KM strategy for the International Fund for Agriculture and Development (IFAD) for 2019–2025, approved by its Executive Board in May 2019.[9] The strategy took advantage of a new organizational structure featuring a decentralized delivery model that was relocating Rome-based staff to the field to establish an increased country presence. IFAD applied KM "to connect and motivate people to generate, use and share good practice, learning and expertise to improve IFAD's efficiency, credibility and development effectiveness." It was "placing people at the core of the strategy, recognizing that it is the knowledge of its staff and consultants that ultimately drives the quality of its operations and of the institution overall."

The strategy's three action areas—knowledge generation, knowledge use, and an enabling environment—were supported from scaling up the virtual interaction among its globally distributed staff, and tapping into these conversations to improve organizational effectiveness. Knowledge-based publications, intervention models, project development, and operational programs and policies were to be informed by the on-the-ground realities of its field operations, as related by staff, consultants, and partners; and supplemented by monitoring, evaluation, and strategically focused research. The organization would rely on evidence-based and experiential knowledge to remain relevant and cost-effective, and achieve the strategic goal of producing better development results for poor rural people and greater impact toward the 2030 Agenda's goals 1 (reduction of poverty) and 2 (zero hunger).

IFAD's "next generation" KM strategy squarely placed its people at the center, focusing on how individual knowledge could benefit both the organization and its staff. In addition, several features of the formulation process may be worth noting by other UNDS organizations. First, it was opportunistic, presented as a response to a genuine concern about how the staff were going to adjust to the decentralized delivery model, and to address IFAD's high-level priorities for development effectiveness. Second, it was strongly championed by IFAD's president and other senior managers; it was motivated by the JIU report and QCPR mandate calling for all UN organizations to prepare a KM strategy; and it was presented as an Executive Board document, helping ensure compliance. Third, management and staff widely supported it after extensive consultations to derive a formulation which managers were prepared to support and staff were prepared to do. Fourth, it benefited from a detailed situation analysis, including a knowledge resource inventory, organizational network analysis, knowledge architecture review, assessment against a KM maturity model, and scan of comparative experiences. Fifth, it was presented in a user-friendly language and format, including a theory of change, action plan, and results framework, which improved staff comprehension. Sixth, it was relatively budget-neutral and not overly ambitious in terms of implementation.

Other UN organizations adopted a similar model, including UN Women and UNICEF.[10] While not all of the JIU recommendations have yet been taken up by all the organizations, the key messages in the report have captured the attention of at least some champions in UN leadership.

While there were shortcomings in early KM attempts, some of the strategies were, in fact, as soundly designed as IFAD's. These efforts did not survive, mainly because the right solutions were not sustained. Deeper factors of leadership were at work, and these should be addressed before the second generation of KM strategies has a chance of being sustainable.

UN "structural amnesia"

As explained, introducing a well-formulated KM strategy or system is essentially an exercise in organizational reform, with the potential to produce transformational change in such traditional hierarchical bureaucracies as those in the UN. The history of reform efforts by UNDS organizations, however, is fraught with failed or limited-success initiatives.[11] There is a common pattern: an incoming head of a UN organization or office brings to the job his or her personalized ambition and vision. Usually labeled a "reform" or a "reorganization" and launched with great fanfare, it triggers an inevitable upheaval and produces varying results. When the leader moves on—typically every four or five years—the replacement follows the same process of reinvention. The result is that, no matter how successful, major UN change initiatives have a limited shelf-life, precluding prospects for sustained organizational improvement. The process can be seen as a structurally inbuilt form of organizational amnesia—a deliberate effort to disregard past experience in order to create something "new."

The following cases concern three UN entities. They took place between 2004 and 2016, before the JIU study; they illustrate how structural amnesia led to the demise of promising KM initiatives.[12]

UNDP, 2004

UNDP gained a reputation as the UNDS's pioneer in KM when, in 1999, it introduced voluntary knowledge-sharing networks organized around UNDP's thematic priorities, demonstrating that staff in UNDP offices were eager to help their colleagues find solutions for their day-to-day challenges. The networks were popular, growing eventually to encompass two-thirds of all UNDP staff. They became the backbone of the concept of the "practice architecture," which proposed thematic-based career tracks for qualified staff as an alternative to the managerial or administrative tracks. In 2002, the key official driving UNDP's groundbreaking knowledge efforts presented a proposal to leverage the knowledge-sharing networks into a corporate KM strategy for improving organizational effectiveness. It entailed 33 initiatives, to be introduced in a carefully phased approach across five axes: networks and communities; content management; systems and tools; staff policy alignment; and technology infrastructure. In February 2003, funds were approved for an initial 18-month phase.

In April, however, the official left and was replaced. Rather than proceeding with the phased effort, the new official opted for an intensive "Big Bang" approach, starting all the initiatives simultaneously. The project was approved in January 2004, but the magnitude of the effort and the inadequate time and effort available to bring staff on board generated resistance across the organization. The initiative was discontinued by the end of 2004, with the successful knowledge-sharing networks and the proposed practice architecture among the casualties.

UN country team in India, 2010

In 2005, the UN country team (UNCT) in India, chaired by the resident coordinator (RC), adapted UNDP's knowledge-sharing networks to create a public-facing facilitation service that linked professionals with similar job objectives working in government, the private sector, academia, nongovernmental organizations (NGOs), and donors. Branded "Solution Exchange," professional colleagues joined e-mail networks each moderated by a full-time facilitator and a research associate. A member would post a query seeking help with a challenge; the community would respond with experiences and knowledge resources (e.g., books, experts, organizations); the facilitation team would synthesize the results into a "consolidated reply." Over the three years of the pilot (2005–2007), seven UNCT agency offices created 12 professional community networks, with between 2,000 and 4,000 members in their specialized areas; for example, the ILO for work and employment; the UN Educational, Scientific and Cultural Organization (UNESCO) for education; and the FAO for food and nutrition security.

Solution Exchange's success exceeded expectations. By the end of 2007, when it was incorporated into the UNCT's Development Assistance Framework for 2008–2012, over 15,000 professionals had subscribed and 8,000 of them had shared their knowledge in response to 536 queries. Evaluations carried out in 2007 and 2010 concluded that Solution Exchange had "impacted program implementation; influenced national policies; improved capacities of individuals and organizations; enhanced knowledge and changed attitudes,"[13] and that it had "occupied a unique niche in India's development scene, paving the way for new collaborative ventures, creating space for discussions that have fed into policy formulation, and impacting the policy process in several important development sectors."[14]

By the time of the second evaluation, however, the RC and most of the original UNCT had taken positions elsewhere, and their replacements focused on other priorities. The evaluation noted that

> Solution Exchange is in danger of grinding to a halt if further funding is not found immediately. We feel that it would be a huge loss to the Indian and global development community if SE is not continued. We therefore strongly recommend that the UN system funds this venture in the short term until such time that other sources of funding can be mobilized.[15]

The UNCT was unpersuaded, and the initiative disappeared soon after.

UN Economic Commission for Africa, 2016

In September 2012, the then newly appointed executive secretary of the UN Economic Commission for Africa (ECA) announced his intention to "make ECA the premier think tank on Africa's transformation." The idea that an economic commission could be a think tank was not new; the Economic Commission for Latin American (ECLA) under Raúl Prebisch (1950–1963) demonstrated that regional commissions could perform well as think tanks. However, marshaling in-house experts and consultants to generate a scholarly publication is no longer sufficient to reach key decision makers in a world of proliferating social media "influencers." Today's aspiring think tanks need to work differently: they must draw from a wide range of perspectives, experiences, and documented evidence to produce a compelling case, and present it in multiple formats through a targeted multifaceted communications campaign.

ECA's updated think-tank business model took the form of new corporate strategies for publications, information technology, communications, and KM, in order to enhance ECA's influence, effectiveness, visibility, and relevance. Under ECA's KM strategy, knowledge would flow from ECA's policy specialists through its program advisers to its national clients and professional networks (adapting the Solution Exchange model) and then back again, so that the policies and programs prepared by the specialists addressed the field realities. To ensure that this knowledge would benefit the organization, the knowledge flows were applied to three business processes: product development, ensuring that whatever was produced by ECA reflected the latest global knowledge; organizational learning, factoring knowledge into business processes so that, for example, project preparation guidelines included a due diligence step to account for network consultations; and capacity development, making continual improvements in staff training based on insights from experience.

Over the first quarter of 2014, ECA's senior management team approved the four corporate strategies, with very little discussion, which were translated into a project for strengthening ECA's think-tank capacity. The project's resource and staffing requirements became a subject of considerable negotiation, and limited resources followed only in September 2015. Under the KM component, the reduced funds were applied to start up two knowledge-sharing networks for African planners and statisticians, which were well received by the respective professional communities. However, after another year the executive secretary left, and his vision for ECA as a premier think tank departed with him. The networks and activities foreseen in the strategies were dropped, and the remaining resources allocated to an unrelated effort to refurbish ECA's library. Whereas in the other two examples the KM efforts collapsed after a change of leadership, ECA's experience represents a case where the senior management applied passive resistance until the leader moved on.

These three cases were promising attempts to introduce KM systems; but they were not sustained because leadership dynamics—transitions or resistance—cut short progress. Why, if the efforts had built up staff interest and support and demonstrated cost-effective usefulness, was there no outcry from users to continue it? Simply put, when an enlightened leader who welcomes staff engagement and interaction takes another post and is replaced by a more traditional one, the organizational culture reverts to the formal top-down hierarchical mindset. This culture discourages dissent; staff will grumble among themselves, but anyone who speaks out does so at the risk of their career prospects. Moreover, enlightened leaders are not common in the UN, where inspirational qualities are not factored into a largely political and politicized selection process.

KM's trajectory in the private sector paints a very different picture. Over the same timeframe as the UN's experience, KM has progressed from theory to mainstream practice. Knowledge organizations in the private sector have long committed to KM for enhancing their effectiveness, since the results show up in their bottom lines. KM has generated extensive attention through publications, media, professional journals, and enterprises like KM World, which hosts events and surveys progress in the field. It has become a degree-granting discipline at several universities. And it was recently assigned a classification—30401—by the International Organization for Standardization (ISO).[16] An ISO classification is a major milestone in a professional discipline, signifying that it is sufficiently mature to have performance and quality standards that can be codified, taught, and mastered.

There is a simple explanation for the dramatic difference between these two trajectories. In the private sector, if a KM effort championed by a previous CEO improved the bottom line, the successor CEO would not eliminate it. UNDS organizations, on the other hand, have no such "bottom-line" benchmark; leaders or managers achieve recognition by showcasing their own achievements.

Envisioning a knowledge-empowered UNDS

Given that UN leaders have no incentive to embrace a predecessor's achievements, how can UN development organizations break through the never-ending cycle of reorganization and reform, so that the system can finally move forward? Now that its KM initiatives are beginning to come together, how can they be sustained?

One solution is to take a page from the private sector and create a bottom line against which to judge the performance of UN leaders. Specifically, it should be possible to introduce an annual "effectiveness score" for the head and senior leadership of an organization derived from the extent to which the organization maintains or improves its performance over their tenure. This evaluation, for example, could adapt the methodology of the Multilateral Organization Performance Assessment Network (MOPAN).[17] It could become a yearly exercise so that trends could be tracked; it could assign the whole-organization value to the head, who would then assign values to the members of the senior management team on that basis. Incoming leaders motivated to achieve a high score would both refrain from dismantling successful initiatives and promote continuous organizational learning through knowledge-sharing-based KM strategies.

Another possible solution could prove to be even more far-reaching. One concept prevalent among theorists who study organizations is the "post-bureaucratic organization."[18] Bureaucracies modulate organization-individual relations through centralized "role-based controls," by which adherence to rules, norms, and culture ensures that individuals produce what is expected. A bureaucracy is a disciplinary regime that seeks "to normalize individuals by aligning their thinking, their sources of motivation, and ultimately their behavior with overarching moral standards." Post-bureaucracies—expressed as "network-shaped organizations"—rely on de-centered "trust-based controls," where individual freedom is encouraged, personal relationships are based on mutual trust, and shared values create bonds that produce results. A network is an "actuarial regime," which is less concerned with how things are being done; rather, "it sets people in motion" and "operates according to a principle of power which is more economical and less obtrusive."

These two organizational types are not mutually exclusive but can build on and enhance each other. Bureaucracies can provide a sense of identity and direction missing in the more amorphous network regime; networks can provide the passion, personal commitment, and self-actualization that are absent in a discipline-based regime.

What if the UNDS were to move in this direction? Could its bureaucratic organizations coexist with system-wide professional networks? Consider, as an illustration, gender equality.

Most UNDS organizations have offices for gender equality, staffed by professionals for whom gender equality is a career focus. The UNDS also has UN Women, an organization with a gender-equality mandate. In the blended bureaucracy/network model, UN Women could become the convening body for a system-wide gender-equality network developing common principles, standards, and guidelines that network members, backed by a cohesive and influential community, could introduce within their respective host organizations.

The model could be applied to most any UN organizations mandated to address a development issue—the UN Environment Programme (UNEP) for environment; the FAO for agriculture; the ILO for work and employment; even the UN Office for Project Services for operational services, given that every office of every UN organization has an operations unit.

These knowledge-sharing networks could be the source of effective organizational learning across the system. They would be profession-based, since a key motivation for participation is that it should benefit a participant's reputation and career progression—which in this case would facilitate staff movement across organizations.

These networks would not be specifically aligned to the 17 SDGs—the multi-disciplinary nature of the SDGs is ill suited to accommodate a professional network's all-important professional career progression dimension, which is needed to motivate participation and ensure effectiveness. However, the SDGs provide the essential framework for UN global networks to flourish: aligning their focus and direction around unity of purpose. The networks could contribute professionals to multi-disciplinary SDG teams working globally, regionally, nationally, or locally; team members could contribute their unique professional perspectives, backed by and in continuous consultation with their network peers. Working through multi-disciplinary teams, the networks could break down organizational silos and facilitate a focused, coordinated effort toward delivering the 2030 Agenda. It is worth citing the JIU report:

> As all Member States are committed to implementing the 2030 Agenda, the United Nations system is also expected to fuel more collaborative patterns and synergies at the national level. With the bar raised that high, it appears that knowledge can play the role as the ultimate federative factor of the 17 goals and 169 targets. Knowledge is the main connector among United Nations Charter organs, specialized agencies, funds and programmes and the multitude or non-State stakeholders. Knowledge is the common denominator of all United Nations mandates and actions and transcends thematic and geographic borders. More than goods, services and capital, knowledge is what fuels the dynamics of our globalized and interdependent world.[19]

Thus, introducing global knowledge-sharing networks driven by the unifying ambition of the SDGs would go far in adapting the UNDS to better address the multitude of complex challenges in today's world.

Next steps

The first step toward systematically institutionalizing KM into the organizations of the UNDS would be to pursue the JIU report's recommendation that UN leadership develop a common, system-wide KM culture and address KM as a whole-of-system issue. The UN Development Coordination Office (UNDCO) under the deputy secretary-general includes a KM portfolio that could take on this responsibility. It could start by reviving an earlier attempt coordinated by IFAD and UNDP to bring together the system's KM managers in a "collaboration forum." Centralized support would help create a favorable environment for the forum to build commonalities and consensus across UN organizations to align KM strategies and initiatives. Chances of success are promising: the UNDS's organizations are in the same business, with common challenges and opportunities. They are not, in principle (although perhaps not always in practice), competing with one another and should welcome opportunities for collaboration. Moreover, KM latecomers could be added and thereby leapfrog the mistakes, false starts, and wasted investments by early adopters. The JIU perception survey found that the most important factor conducive to promoting a KM strategy and introducing or institutionalizing KM-related arrangements, cited by 30.7 percent of the 6,634 respondents, was the existence of good practices in other organizations in the UN system, a sentiment that bodes well for a centrally coordinated effort.[20]

Second, one or several UN organizations, with support and encouragement from the UNDCO, could pursue the suggestion developed in this chapter to support the creation of system-wide professional networks, setting themselves up as conveners and inviting their professional peers across the UN system to join. As results become apparent, other UN organizations could follow the lead and set themselves up as network conveners. In addition to building cohesive professional communities that promote coherent positions across UN organizations, and realigning the UN's work for supporting the SDGs, the introduction of inter-organizational knowledge-sharing networks would break down the rigidities of top-down structures, instigate shifts in organizational culture, and increase prospects for transformational change. In fact, knowledge-sharing networks could become the essential glue that finally brings the UNDS closer—without the threatening prospect of organizational integration—thus fulfilling one of the key objectives of the current reforms.

Finally, one or more willing UN organizations could develop and introduce the bottom-line "effectiveness score" for UN heads and senior managers, becoming a pilot that could, if successful, be introduced more widely across the system. Structural amnesia would be mitigated or even eliminated, and UN organizations would become true learning organizations.

Conclusion

If the three earlier KM initiatives described in this chapter had been sustained, those organizations might have better realized their potential as true learning organizations in the manner described. Instead, in the absence of organizational learning, these organizations are, in all likelihood, still making the same mistakes they were making when they began. The recent developments laid out in this chapter finally make it possible for the development organizations of the UN to apply KM systems to enhance their effectiveness and remain relevant, valuable, and valued. If this window of opportunity is not grasped, they will remain ill equipped to help countries realize the SDGs and shape the world's future.

NOTES

1 This definition, the simplest of a wide range of versions, and the characteristics detailed here are derived from the work and presentations of Larry Prusak, a noted KM authority, as quoted by Steve Glovinsky, "The Story of Knowledge Networks at the UNDP," *Knowledge Management for Development Journal* 8, nos. 2–3 (2012): 186–189.

2 For more on this concept, see Linda Argote and Ella Miron-Spektor, "Organizational Learning: From Experience to Knowledge," *Organization Science* 22, no. 5 (2011): 1123–1137.

3 David De Long, "Building the Knowledge-Based Organization: How Culture Drives Knowledge Behaviors," *Working Paper*, Center for Business Innovation, Ernst & Young LLP, May 1997.

4 Petru Dumitriu, *Knowledge Management in the United Nations System* (UN document JIU/REP/2016/10) (Geneva: JIU, 2016), iii and 1.

5 Ibid., 13–14; and Annex 1.

6 Ibid., 50.

7 Ibid., iii.

8 General Assembly resolution A/RES/71/243, "Quadrennial Comprehensive Policy Review of Operational Activities for Development of the United Nations System," 21 December 2016, para. 70, 17.

9 IFAD *Knowledge Management Strategy*, submitted to the 126th Session of the Executive Board, 2–3 May 2019.

10 UN Women's recently issued KM Strategy includes a principle that KM is people-centered, with an objective to develop a knowledge-sharing culture and an emphasis on communities of practice. UNICEF's networks are growing and becoming more dynamic.

11 For a detailed account of the UN's reform experience, see Joachim Miller, *Reforming the United Nations: A Chronology* (Leiden, The Netherlands: Brill-Nijhoff, 2016).

12 These cases are elaborated in an earlier article by the author: Steve Glovinsky, "How Knowledge Management Could Transform the UN Development System," *FUNDS Briefing no. 45*, February 2017.

13 Smita Premchander and Richard McDermott, *Project Evaluation of Solution Exchange* (Bengaluru, Karnataka, India: Sampark; Denver, CO: McDermott Consulting, 2007).

14 Priya Deshingar, Simon Hearn, Laxman Rao, and Pramod Sharma, *Formative Evaluation of Solution Exchange* (London: Overseas Development Institute, 2010).

15 Ibid.

16 International Organization for Standardization, 2018, *Knowledge Management Systems—Requirements*, ISO document 30401:2018 www.iso.org/obp/ui/#iso:std:iso:30401:ed-1:v1:en.

17 MOPAN is a network of 18 donor countries with a common interest in assessing the organizational effectiveness of multilateral organizations that receive development and humanitarian funding. See *MOPAN Methodology Manual*, www.mopanonline.org/ourwork/ourapproachmopan30.

18 Christian Maravelias, "Post-Bureaucracy—Control through Professional Freedom," *Journal of Organizational Change Management* 16, no. 5 (2003): 547–566.

19 Dumitriu, *Knowledge Management in the United Nations System*, 51.

20 Ibid., Annex I, Question 10, 6. Other responses were: the interest of mid-level managers—29.4 percent; the personal vision of the executive head—23.8 percent; the initiative of knowledge champions—16.1 percent.

ADDITIONAL READING

Scott E. Bryant, "The Role of Transformational and Transactional Leadership in Creating, Sharing and Exploiting Organizational Knowledge," *Journal of Leadership and Organizational Studies* 9, no. 4 (2003): 32–44.

Heather Creech and Terri Willard, *Strategic Intentions: Managing Knowledge Networks for Sustainable Development* (Winnipeg: International Institute for Sustainable Development, 2001).

Petru Dumitriu, *Knowledge Management in the United Nations System* (Geneva: JIU, 2016), UN document JIU/REP/2016/10.

Steve Glovinsky, "How Knowledge Management Could Transform the UN Development System," *Future UN Development System Project Briefing no. 45* (New York: FUNDS, 2017).

Liana Razmerita, Kathrin Nielsen, and Pia Nielsen, "What Factors Influence Knowledge Sharing in Organizations? A Social Dilemma Perspective of Social Media Communication," *Journal of Knowledge Management* 20, no. 6 (2016): 1225–1246.

Laura Roper and Jethro Pettit, "Development and the Learning Organization: An Introduction," *Development in Practice* 12, nos. 3–4 (2002): 258–271.

PART III

Imagining the future of the UN in development

18

CHANGE IN THE UN DEVELOPMENT SYSTEM

Theory and practice

John Hendra and Ingrid FitzGerald

This chapter sets out the current efforts to reposition the UN Development System (UNDS) to deliver Agenda 2030; it analyzes these changes against previous reform efforts and the theory of change (ToC) adopted by the UN Development Group (UNDG) in early 2016,[1] and the need to enhance the UN's impact and contribution toward achieving the Sustainable Development Goals (SDGs). It begins with the current context and imperative for reform before revisiting earlier efforts. It continues with the current reform approach and practice, assessed against the ToC for the UNDS "as a system." It concludes by setting out a way forward and action required for accelerated change.

Substantive context and imperative for UNDS reform

There are at least five critical imperatives for the current UNDS reform. The first, and most immediate, is the adoption of the 2030 Agenda for Sustainable Development which requires a more integrated approach by the entire development community. A transformative, integrated, and universal sustainable development agenda requires a transformative UNDS that is able to work in a much more integrated and coherent way. In short, the "system" should be more than the sum of its parts in order to effectively address the cross-cutting, multi-sectoral nature of the SDGs.

The second imperative reflects the rapidly changing international development landscape. Indeed, these changes have accelerated even since the adoption of the SDGs; they have had an impact on political and financial support for the UN system. If the UNDS is to remain relevant and enhance its impact in the face of multiple, complex, and intersecting crises and challenges, change is not optional; it is essential.

The third is the declining support for multilateralism, including among traditional supporters of the UN system. The turn to nationalism, populism, and conservatism in many countries, coupled with a shift toward financial and political unilateralism and "de-globalization," is undermining support for, investment in, and the legitimacy of the multilateral system and its institutions.[2] While it may still be true that "if we didn't have the UN we would need to invent it,"[3] what is less clear is what kind of institution it would be, and whose interests it would serve, if we did so now. Against this backdrop, the UNDS is challenged to make the case for multilateralism, and to demonstrate it can deliver results.

The fourth imperative, which is beyond the scope of the present chapter, is the need to strengthen integration and cohesion across the four pillars of the UN system: international peace and security, humanitarian action, and human rights in addition to sustainable development. Operating in silos no longer reflects the realities of the countries and peoples served by the United Nations.

The fifth and critical concern is the rolling back of the normative standards and commitments that are the *raison d'être* for and that ground the UN system—including challenges to the primacy and universality of human rights, and threats to the funding of core treaty bodies.[4] To be truly "fit for purpose," the UNDS must reaffirm and recommit to promoting the realization of human rights as well as delivering development. This requires supporting governments to implement the SDGs and the 2030 Agenda, in which many, albeit not all, human rights commitments are embedded.[5] It also requires upholding in a balanced and integrated manner the wider framework of human rights norms and standards to which member states have committed.

History of UNDS reform efforts

The current UNDS repositioning is arguably the most far-reaching reform effort to date, perhaps even more than the package of reforms that UN Secretary-General Kofi Annan introduced in 1997. His initial reform package was designed to achieve better management and coordination across the UN system, and stronger human rights protection and peacekeeping operations.[6] It included strengthening the UN Resident Coordinator (RC) as the UN Secretary-General's representative in country and leader of the UN country team (UNCT). All UN funds and programs were requested to develop a joint country program document—the UN Development Assistance Framework (UNDAF)—and to increase use of common presences (UN Houses) and common services. At Headquarters, the Secretary-General established the UN Development Group (UNDG) with the UNDP administrator as chair; he also requested more cohesive meetings of executive boards. These reforms laid the groundwork for the operations of today's UNDS.

Building on these developments, in 2006, the High-Level Panel on System-Wide Coherence recommended a package of reforms. Member states took them up, in part, in the 2008 General Assembly resolution 62/277 which set out the following five key priorities: "Delivering as One" (DaO) at the country level; harmonization of business practices; funding; governance; and gender equality and the empowerment of women (which led to the establishment of UN Women).

As it was originally conceived, DaO was intended to achieve greater alignment with national planning, promote national ownership and leadership, and ensure greater effectiveness and efficiency through implementation of four "Ones": One Programme (the UNDAF), One Budget, One Leader (an empowered UN RC), and One Office. In practice, there was considerable experimentation in the eight countries that piloted DaO with some countries also introducing "One Voice" (one communications strategy and common advocacy), "One Fund" (a common country-pooled fund), and "One Set of Management Practices." In addition, some pilots developed monitoring frameworks for the DaO initiative itself, as well as for development results.[7]

The independent evaluation of DaO identified critical enabling factors for change that remain relevant for the current generation of UNDS reform initiatives: the importance of national ownership and engagement of government; the need for a strong tripartite alliance between the UNDS, donors, and governments; and the importance of funding mechanisms that drive coherence. Also critical was the role of mid-level staff, whose engagement and commitment increased over time and helped drive a UN-wide approach. Finally, the evaluation noted that while DaO was designed to promote efficiency and effectiveness, in practice it also improved the UN's strategic relevance and positioning, and strengthened delivery of results, in particular on cross-cutting issues such as gender equality.

Feedback from successive surveys of member states confirmed this finding, which high-lighted that the UNCTs implementing DaO are seen as more relevant and easy to work with than those that are not.[8] The DaO experience showed that country-led, bottom-up reform can work with the right partnerships, incentives, and horizontal working arrangements in place. Where the DaO initiative faltered was often when it came up against institutional, structural bottlenecks that could only be resolved at the HQ level.

A "second generation" of DaO built on the pilot experience. In 2014, an integrated package of support to countries wishing to adopt the DaO approach was codified with the UNDG's adoption of Standard Operating Procedures (SOPs).[9] The voluntary nature of DaO has meant uneven adoption of the pillars and core elements across UNCTs. Many member states indicated interest in adopting DaO, and only 8 percent expressed a lack of interest; but the rate of imple-mentation prior to the current repositioning remained low.[10]

At the global level, the 2012–2016 Quadrennial Comprehensive Policy Review (QCPR) resolution set out substantive mandates for the UNDS and outlined priorities for its improved functioning. They include many of the elements that are central to the current UNDS reform effort, including an emphasis on national ownership, joint programming at country level, strengthening the leadership of the UN RC, and sustainable financing of the UN RC system.

Current reform practice: repositioning the UNDS

As highlighted, the 2030 Agenda is perhaps the boldest development agenda ever agreed, and requires equally bold changes by all—governments; the private sector; civil society; parliaments; and international organizations, including the UNDS itself. Member states recognized the need for change over a year before the 2030 Agenda was approved, when they called for a transparent and inclusive ECOSOC-initiated dialogue on the longer-term positioning of the UNDS, taking into account the post-2015 development agenda.[11]

As a result, 18 months of intergovernmental discussions began—dubbed "the ECOSOC Dialogues"—around what the UNDS's future functions, funding, governance, organizational arrangements, capacity, impact, and partnerships should be in order to better align with the 2030 Agenda. The second phase of these dialogues was informed by an independent Team of Advisors (ITA) commissioned by the ECOSOC Bureau and co-chaired by former UNEP executive director Klaus Toepfer and former ILO director-general Juan Somavia. Meanwhile, several member states, think tanks, and the UNDG also tabled their own specific proposals for reform.[12]

Building on the 2015–2016 ECOSOC Dialogues, and after intensive negotiations, the General Assembly adopted the landmark QCPR resolution 71/243 in December 2016. It called for a "UNDS that is more strategic, accountable, transparent, collaborative, efficient, effective and results-oriented."

The then newly appointed Secretary-General António Guterres set out his vision for a repo-sitioned UNDS in two landmark reports in 2017: *Repositioning of the UN Development System to Deliver on the 2030 Agenda: Ensuring A Better Future for All*[13] and *Our Promise for Dignity, Prosperity and Peace on a Healthy Planet*.[14] These reports reflected his broader UN reform program and responded to the specific "asks" of him in the 2016 QCPR resolution.

Intensive intergovernmental negotiations on the Secretary-General's proposals for change followed, and on 31 May 2018, the General Assembly unanimously adopted resolution 72/279 on the repositioning of the UNDS, ushering in the most comprehensive reform in decades.[15]

In short, the current repositioning differs from previous reforms in at least three ways. First, unlike other UNDS reforms which focused on enhancing efficiencies or facilitating greater system-wide coherence, the current repositioning has its roots in the pressing need for the UNDS to change its approach and significantly raise its game against such a different, transformative 2030 Agenda. In the outcome document adopted in September 2015, member states highlighted the "integrated and indivisible" nature of the SDGs and the need for "coherent and integrated support to the implementation of the new Agenda by the United Nations development system."[16]

Second, the current reform is different from previous reforms that came predominantly from within the "Second UN" of the UNDS itself—whether driven by a new Secretary-General as in Kofi Annan's 1997 reform or by an independent "DaO" High-Level Panel, which was informed by innovative proposals from the field. Instead, the momentum for the current reform emanated from the "First UN" of member states which decided to start a process to reposition the UNDS four years before resolution 72/279; thus, one should not underestimate the extent to which the current reform is owned by member states, and their conviction that the repositioning process be implemented as envisioned.

What's more, unlike many other intergovernmental discussions on development, it was frequently developing countries, in particular several African countries, the small island developing states (SIDS), and middle-income countries (MICs), that were pushing for more fundamental change while many donor countries continued to focus on enhancing efficiencies.

Third, this momentum for repositioning was then clearly picked up by the new Secretary-General who was elected on a platform of reform and through a more open and transparent selection process than previous UN leaders. His own reform agenda was also informed by his experience as the UN High Commissioner for Refugees from 2005 to 2015. Hence, being more "fit" for the 2030 Agenda went beyond just a repositioned UNDS; it is reinforced through broader reforms initiated by Guterres for peace and security, management, and gender parity.

Four new major secretariat departments became operational in 2019: Peace Operations; Political and Peacebuilding Affairs; Operational Support; and Management Strategy, Policy and Compliance. They were accompanied by a comprehensive gender parity strategy and a major decentralization through a new simplified and streamlined delegation of authority. As Secretary-General Guterres highlighted,

> the goal of Reform is a 21st Century United Nations focused more on people and less on process, more on delivery and less on bureaucracy. The true test of reform will be measured in tangible results in the lives of the people we serve—and the trust of those who support our work.[17]

Repositioning the UNDS is built around eight major interrelated mandates as set out in General Assembly resolution 72/279, the status of which is briefly highlighted here, as of the September 2019 UN SDG Summit. First, the establishment of a new generation of UNCTs, through a revitalized, strategic, and results-oriented UNDAF; a new approach to physical presence with appropriate criteria to ensure tailored responses to country needs and priorities; and the advancement of common business operations, including common back-offices and common premises.

At the center of the reform is the need for the UNDS to work in a more integrated manner to support delivery of the 2030 Agenda. Instead of "one size fits all," UNCT presence is to be more needs-based and better tailored to ensure the best configuration on the ground, as well as enhanced coordination, transparency, efficiency, and greater impact of UN support to national

SDG needs. In this context, all UN organizations are called upon to strengthen their capacities and skills to better promote progress against those SDGs lagging behind; they are also supposed to reduce gaps, overlaps, and duplication across entities.

A key means to achieve this is a revitalized, new UN Sustainable Development Cooperation Framework (UNSDCF), which should respond coherently to key national needs and not simply be what the UN has to bring to the table. Instead, it should serve as the most important instrument for planning, coordination, and implementation of UN development work in a country. It is also intended to help determine appropriate criteria regarding the configuration of the UNCT on the ground. The guidance for this new framework was issued in June 2019;[18] substantive and operational guidance for implementation was finalized for roll-out before the end of 2019.

Second, through implementation of the Secretary-General's proposals for a reinvigorated, independent, and impartial RC system, the functions of UN RCs are now distinct from those of the Resident Representative of the United Nations Development Programme (UNDP). The accountability between Resident Coordinators and the Secretary-General is clearer; this includes a matrixed, dual-reporting model to structure the relationship between RCs and members of UNCTs.

A major milestone was the successful transition to a renewed RC system as of 1 January 2019 and the roll-out in May 2019 of a new country-level Mutual Accountability Framework to provide clarity on the relationship and reporting lines between RCs and UNCTs. In 2020–2021, a new RC assessment and selection process is to be developed, and RC system tools and skillsets strengthened.

Third, the introduction of a hybrid funding formula, which includes a doubling of cost-sharing amongst UN entities; voluntary funding; and a 1 percent levy on strictly earmarked donor funding to projects to help secure adequate and predictable funding for the RC system. This was a compromise alternative to the Secretary-General's proposal to fully fund the RC system through the regular (assessed) UN budget.

As of September 2019, a total of almost $200 million had been committed to the Special Purpose Trust Fund for the RC system, including voluntary contributions from 38 member states, complemented by a doubling of cost-sharing by organizations of the UNDS. However, a significant gap remains,[19] and more voluntary contributions will be required.

Fourth, the transformation of the United Nations Development Operations Coordination Office (DOCO) into a stand-alone office with managerial and oversight functions of the RC system (now the Development Coordination Office, DCO). The DCO reports directly to the deputy secretary-general in her capacity as chair of the United Nations Sustainable Development Group (UNSDG) and provides an annual report to ECOSOC.

Fifth, a two-phased approach to repositioning the UN's work at the regional level was adopted: an immediate optimization of working arrangements under existing mandates and resources followed by a review of options for the longer-term repositioning of the UN's significant regional assets. The regional review was accompanied by intergovernmental consultations on a region-by-region basis, which concluded at the end of 2019.[20]

Sixth, the resolution reiterated the QCPR's request for the development of a system–wide strategic document that will outline how, at the global level, the UNDS will better align its efforts to support the 2030 Agenda. In addition, it will build on individual UN organizations' comparative advantages, reduce overlaps and duplication, and ensure a more cohesive and integrated UN approach to support the achievement of the SDGs. An outline of the system–wide strategic document was presented during the 2019 ECOSOC session and received feedback from member states.

Seventh, the proposal of the Funding Compact was welcomed as a means to improve the quality and predictability of resources for the UNDS. Both member states and the UNDS together have recognized the need to address the sharp imbalance between core and non-core resources; they need to change their behavior if the UN is to deliver better results against the ambitious 2030 Agenda. In short, member states are being asked to commit to increase the level of core, pooled, and thematic funding as the UNDS commits to increased transparency, visibility, coherence, and efficiency as well as better reporting on collective work, spending, and results. The Funding Compact was developed through a series of Funding Dialogues, was endorsed by the 2019 ECOSOC Session, and is now under implementation.[21]

Eighth, the call was endorsed for a review of Multi-Country Offices (MCOs) to improve support against the 2030 Agenda and the Samoa Pathway. The MCO review was conducted in 2019 and is being finalized in consultation with concerned member states.[22]

Finally, in addition to the reform mandates encompassed by resolution 72/279, there are a number of other key changes proposed at the global level to better enable delivery of country-level results. They include steps taken to reconfigure the UNSDG, the successor to the UNDG comprising the majority of the organizations of the UNDS; the establishment of a Joint UN Steering Committee to support country teams in advancing humanitarian–development collaboration; ensuring a robust process for the repositioning of the UN's Department of Economic and Social Affairs (DESA); reinforcing independent system-wide evaluations; and strengthening the UN's partnership system.

A theory of change for the UNDS: functioning as a "system" for relevance, strategic positioning, and results

As identified during the ECOSOC dialogues, there was a clear need to develop a robust and shared understanding of how reform happens in the UNDS, and how the UNDS can better function as a system in support of the 2030 Agenda. To this end, a "theory of change" (ToC) for UNDS reform was developed in 2015. It was designed to be both exploratory and iterative—an initial working draft was subject to focus group discussions with over 150 colleagues in the field and at UN headquarters, a summary version of which was endorsed by the UNDG in early 2016.[23]

If the SDGs are the "what"—the development results to which the UNDS will be contributing—then the "theory of change" is very much about the "how." The ToC argued that a UNDS to effectively support the SDGs should better "function as a system" in an integrated and coherent manner with more relevance, strategic positioning, and impact. While some options, such as clarifying the division of labor among agencies, may offer "quick fixes," it is only by recognizing what it has to offer as a system that the UNDS can best support implementation of the 2030 Agenda.

A system—a regularly interacting, interdependent group (of organizations)—is a unified whole, and more than the sum of its parts. The UNDS is best understood as a "complex system"—a system of interacting components (entities) that react both to their environments and to one another, and that are characterized by co-evolution, inter-relationships, and dynamic, non-linear change.[24] This means that different approaches to change are needed that are dynamic, flexible, and diversified. Creating space for, and fostering experimentation and innovation is key in this regard, and as the ToC highlighted, much more of this is needed in the UNDS and in support of the SDGs at all levels.

Functioning as a system requires greater coherence and integration in delivering the key functions the UNDS will need to perform in order to support implementation of the 2030 Agenda and the SDGs. In this context, the ToC also highlighted the importance of looking at how change toward greater coherence and functioning as a system has occurred in sectors and organizations outside the UNDS.

For example, based on the premise that multi-stakeholder approaches are necessary to solve large-scale social problems that cannot be effectively addressed by organizations working alone—similar to the horizontal, interconnected challenge of meeting the SDGs—studies of "collective impact"[25] have identified six key conditions that enable true alignment and lead to greater impact. First, a common agenda, a shared vision for change that includes a common understanding of the problem, and a joint approach to solving it through agreed-upon actions. Second, a shared measurement system, an agreed way to measure and report on success/results, and consistent data collection and reporting on a core list of indicators, which is key to alignment and accountability. Third, mutually reinforcing activities, such as a coordinated and mutually reinforcing plan of action, are essential. Fourth, continuous communication, including regular in-person meetings of CEO-level leaders, supported by regular communication within the network of partner organizations. Fifth, a support organization, since creating and managing collective impact requires a distinct organization and staff with very specific skills to serve as the backbone for the entire initiative. Sixth and finally, an enabling environment, including having in place funding for the necessary facilitation, coordination, and measurement to enable participating organizations to work in concert is key.[26]

The ToC also identified areas where the UNDS has underinvested, including in system-wide change management and internal communications. The UNDS is often too ready to bureaucratize guidance and needs instead to open up much more space for experimentation, as was the case in the DaO pilots. This requires moving away from a "command-and-control" approach to change toward being more values- and purpose-driven. Further, the country level has largely focused and driven UNDS reform efforts, which while necessary is insufficient: systemic global change is also needed.

In addition to continuing to roll out DaO and boosting investment in the RC system, the ToC in 2016 identified six areas that need greater attention and investment. They are: using greater joint financing and pooled funding to help drive and support coherent responses; promoting transformative leadership at all levels as a key accelerator for driving change, as well as investing in the capacities and facilitating greater mobility of staff; investing in strategic capacity—"thinking" for and about the UNDS "as a system"—in addition to a system-wide change management function; establishing shared metrics for both development and coherence results; building the evidence for the contribution of collective efforts to development outcomes and impact; and mobilizing greater support for innovation and experimentation at all levels in support of the 2030 Agenda.

Does the current UNDS reform meet theory? What else is needed?

So how does the current repositioning of the UNDS, as outlined in resolution 72/279, stack up against previous reform efforts and the ToC developed in 2016? To what extent does the conceptualization of the current reform align with the ToC, and what are the implications for implementation?

In its broadest sense, the current reform scores relatively well. Its primary focus is on the "what"—the transformative nature of the 2030 Agenda—and the imperative for the UNDS to change to enable it to have greater impact on people's lives. The reform demonstrates a continuous high level of ambition and leadership by the secretary-general, deputy secretary-general, and, increasingly, the UNDS as a whole. Finally, while priority interests may differ, as indicated, there is unprecedented understanding and support from member states, in both the Global South and North, for the overall reform.

From the perspective of lessons learned from previous UNDS reform initiatives, it also scores well. While resolution 72/279 did not cover all the proposed changes set out by the secretary-general, its implementation is more "as a package" than any previous reform. It addresses not only the country level but also the global and regional levels of the UNDS, which is distinct and needed in the context of the ambitious 2030 Agenda. While meeting the test of leadership with an appetite for change at various levels, the reform is also strategic, focused, and sequenced; there is an accompanying recognition that no success is possible without significant attitudinal and behavioral change.

Measured against an external perspective such as the prerequisites for achieving "collective impact," the current UNDS repositioning also fares well given its common agenda (integrated support to Agenda 2030); a plan for mutually reinforcing activities (the new UN Sustainable Development Cooperation Framework); recognition of the importance of the enabling environment, especially with regard to funding (Funding Compact; new Joint SDG Fund); and the critical importance of a distinct backbone organization and staff as "often organizations involved in implementation are not able to take on this additional role" (separate, independent, full-time Resident Coordinator with a new Development Coordination Office). While more attention is required to develop shared measurement systems and ensure continuous communication, the emphasis in studies of "collective impact" on the need for a distinct backbone support organization is notable, and perhaps the key to the current UNDS repositioning.

In focus group discussions that informed the original ToC paper, UN field and headquarters staff consistently highlighted the urgency of change; that leadership, funding, and political will are the three key factors most needed to drive reform; and that incentives—along with attitude and behavioral change—are as important as structural change, if not more so. So, are these three key factors met by the current repositioning?

First, at the heart of the overall UN reform program is visible leadership as well as increased accountability and transparency. All four main UN reforms have strongly embraced the UN System Leadership Framework and its eight defining characteristics: leadership that is norm-based, principled, inclusive, accountable, multidimensional, transformational, collaborative, and self-applied.[27] The Secretary-General personally added a ninth attribute: action-oriented.

The attributes of the leadership framework are embedded in new UN RC job descriptions as well as in the new Management and Accountability Framework developed to realize the dual-reporting system mandated by resolution 72/279. In contrast to previous reforms, the current repositioning, and especially decisions made by the Secretary-General with his own prerogatives, has seen changes to both global and regional leadership roles in addition to alterations at the country level. The deputy secretary-general now chairs the UNSDG, while duplicative and overlapping structures at regional level are under scrutiny.

Second, unlike previous reforms, the current repositioning squarely addresses the imperative of changing the way that the UNDS is funded, if it is to respond in a more predictable manner to individual countries' SDG priorities without compromising the multilateral nature of UN support. While it is unclear how successful the Funding Compact will be in improving how the UNDS is funded, with the strong political engagement around it, and also its commitment to wide-ranging reform as an essential component, it is the first serious dialogue on how to change the funding of the UNDS in over two decades.

In line with the ToC and lessons learned from previous UNDS reforms, it is critical that emphasis be placed on at least doubling inter-agency pooled funding as the interconnected nature of the SDGs has highlighted the need for more flexible, dynamic, and integrated inter-agency cooperation—hence, with the incentive of common financing. Innovative UN pooled financing instruments are in place, including the Spotlight Initiative, the Peace-Building Fund, and the Joint SDG Fund. The latter is a new country-focused instrument designed to incentivize integrated and transformative policy shifts and thereby leverage additional resources; member states have been asked to contribute annually some $290 million.

A future challenge will be to ensure that the renewed RC system is adequately and predictably funded. As indicated, the secretary-general had proposed funding the entire RC system as part of the assessed UN regular budget, seeing it as a core function, just like peace operations. When some major contributing countries balked, the hybrid solution emerged. Whether funding will continue at the same level of voluntary resources to the special purpose trust fund is unknown. While many member states and UNDS organizations alike have been less than keen about the third element of the hybrid—the 1 percent coordination levy on tightly earmarked third-party, non-core contributions—it is important that it is fully operational, and generating income, as soon as possible.[28]

Third, with regard to political will, here too the repositioning seems positive. For many member states, much of the UNDS and especially the RC system has been a black box; so the enhanced transparency and increased accountability by the Secretary-General's reporting has been welcomed. As two observers note,

> the decisions entailed in the resolution break with the implicit philosophy of the UN as a decentralized system of semi-autonomous agencies, which is at odds with the requirements of the 2030 Agenda for collective efforts. The actions … point in the right direction, but much remains to be done.[29]

Likewise, in assessing the merits of the current reform as represented by resolution 72/279, there are limits. In particular, some key elements never made it into the resolution—for instance, enhancing the overall governance of the UNDS beyond more regular engagement by the secretary-general with ECOSOC, and measures to improve the functioning of the executive boards of UN funds and programs.

In addition, such long-standing issues as overlapping mandates or addressing accountability beyond an agency's explicit mandate were not addressed, or a set of new issues including the UN's role in developed countries in light of the universal nature of the 2030 Agenda. Further, while the establishment of the Funding Compact is important as a systemic response to the many challenges inherent in the way that the UNDS is funded, there is little focus on improving how the UNDS develops partnerships, including with private finance, or on the future implications of the relationship between the UNDS and the financially dominant World Bank.

That said, both the ToC and further analysis help identify a number of areas that either still should be addressed, or that are still in the very early stages of implementation and require reinforcement. While much emphasis has been placed on the reinvigorated RC system and structural elements, not enough has been on the substantive vision and especially what and how the UNDS will do and act differently against an ambitious agenda for change.[30] As Deputy Secretary-General Amina Mohammed said in a 2019 public forum:

> still today … we are still saying to countries "you need an SDG plan." We don't say in the budget these are all your SDG expenditures, not good enough, need to be better—so let's improve your budget. We are still talking and prescribing from an international perspective. That really doesn't have traction. … We have to find a different way of doing this.[31]

Many development actors are looking at more integrated and systemic approaches. That view reflects both the potential that implementation could be best organized through transformative changes that recognize and facilitate strong interdependencies across SDGs, and the risk that their transformative potential will not be realized unless the interactions among them—both synergies and trade-offs—are better grasped and acted upon.[32]

A second area requiring greater emphasis is the normative role of the UNDS. From the outset, civil society organizations were critical of the SDG framework's uneven attention to human rights; this lacuna remains a significant risk for implementation of the 2030 Agenda. While "cherry-picking" the SDG framework has been strongly discouraged, given the plethora of targets and indicators, some countries have chosen this approach, which has the potential to undermine Agenda 2030. This could result in an "MDGs plus" approach to SDG implementation whereby "sensitive" and hard-to-measure targets and indicators are dropped in favor of more "traditional" objectives.

This possibility is even more worrying at a time when resistance to the human rights agenda, and human rights violations, could undermine the reform and damage the UN's reputation and legitimacy. The SDGs were not intended to replace the UN's normative standards and commitments, nor should they. As UN Human Rights Commissioner Michelle Bachelet noted:

> The 2030 Agenda is a vital opportunity to realise the promise of the Universal Declaration of Human Rights and the Declaration on the Right to Development. It explicitly recognises that respect for *all* human rights—civil, political, economic, social and cultural—is central to the work of constructing more equal, resilient and sustainable societies.[33]

Efforts to spell out the human rights standards and commitments embodied in the SDGs in national SDG reporting, and to reflect these commitments, as well as the recommendations of human rights mechanisms, are underway.[34] This is all the more critical in the current global context, where support for countries to realize human rights commitments, both within the SDG framework and more broadly, is more vital than ever.

A third issue is the need for greater innovation and experimentation. On one level, change is happening. The ToC paper noted in 2016:

> looking forward, it will be important to facilitate strategic experimentation in support of the SDGs ... in such areas as greater integration of humanitarian action and development at country level, differentiated country support and presence, global partnerships in support of the SDGs, and how to stimulate increased global and regional functioning as a system.[35]

These areas are addressed, in theory, by the current UNDS repositioning.

In some cases, it is too early to determine the impact of potentially promising innovations such as UNDP's 60 Accelerator Labs serving 78 countries. The labs are designed to facilitate the introduction of new services, backed by evidence and practice, and by accelerating the testing and disseminating of sustainable development solutions within and across countries.[36] Other entities, such as UNICEF, have prioritized innovation for development with adolescent participation and will soon launch additional innovative priorities around learning, child health, and identity. Perhaps most encouraging has been the corporate commitment by both UNICEF and UNDP to collaborate in the 60 countries where the first wave of accelerator labs is underway.[37]

A fourth and critical issue in the ToC is the need for a concerted change management effort within and across UN organizations. This requires targeted incentives, effective internal communication, accountability mechanisms for management and staff that support UN coherence, and skill- and capacity-building for collaboration, partnership, and joint implementation. To date there has been insufficient investment in internal change management, incentives and performance mechanisms, and strengthened internal accountability to support reform efforts.

Senior management has engaged in the reform, but there has been a more limited effort to engage mid-level staff, including national staff, who will need to drive change if the reform is to succeed. The current reform is highly centralized and has to date been "top down" in its implementation. Without the buy-in and ownership of UN staff, which proved so critical in the DaO countries, it is less likely that the reform will gain traction on the ground. It is also crucial to nurture a new generation of younger staff, who will understand and be committed to change. This requires dedicated investment over time, and is all the more critical in light of the urgent need to implement policies on protection against sexual exploitation and abuse (PSEA) and sexual harassment in the wake of serious incidents in a number of UN organizations. Staff surveys show low levels of trust in UN senior management to implement these policies and impose consequences on perpetrators,[38] and trust is a prerequisite for successful implementation of UNDS reform.

Fifth, shared metrics for both results and coherence are weak; it is necessary to build the evidence base for the contribution of collective efforts to development outcomes and impact. This requires a fundamental shift in the way that the UNDS plans for and measures results, including how to ensure that the UNDS is actually measuring a key element of the 2030 Agenda, "Leaving No One Behind." The UN has a critical role to play in driving innovation in the use of data and evidence for decision-making, including increased use of disaggregated data for monitoring outcomes for the most marginalized and vulnerable, and of big data, for real-time tracking and trend analysis, building on existing initiatives such as Global Pulse.[39]

With such a complex reform agenda, and with so many moving parts, it will be critical that the focus remains on "what this is all for"—that is, greater impact and ensuring that no one is indeed left behind. One lesson from DaO that is worth repeating is the necessity to ensure that the emphasis is kept on relevance and the strategic intent of the reform, otherwise for many it too easily becomes "too much about process."

Sixth, the pressure of individual organizational accountability, flagged as a constraint in the independent evaluation of DaO. The risk is that the pressures on individual organizations to mobilize non-core resources and demonstrate comparative advantages remain dominant. Competing and overlapping mandates and "mandate creep," as well as the imperative need to raise resources, continue to undermine collaboration. While partners and governments have strengthened their call for coherent and integrated support for SDG implementation, all too often donor-funding modalities and priorities continue to promote competition rather than cooperation. Moreover, development partners largely continue to assess individual organizational performance rather than collective results. Against this backdrop, many members of the UNDS have yet to see the benefits of collective action versus the incentives for going it alone.

Further, and finally, the current generation of reforms may have unintended consequences. The separation of the RC function from UNDP and the lack of funding available to RCs have the potential to isolate and undermine the RC function—the very opposite of what was intended. In particular, one potential unintended consequence is that the largest UN funds and programs and humanitarian–development entities develop specific partnerships and joint initiatives—with no engagement by the RC or normative agencies—thereby resulting in a further marginalization of the UN's normative role at a time when most observers deem it critical to achieving the 2030 Agenda. It will also be important to ensure that the reconfiguration of UNCTs in line with a new generation of UNSDCFs doesn't result in the sidelining—or exclusion—of smaller agencies—often the very agencies with normative mandates and expertise that is vital to ensure a human rights-based approach to SDG implementation and leaving no one behind.

Conclusion: a way forward

A strong, cohesive, effective, and coherent UNDS is required to support delivery of Agenda 2030 and the SDGs. This is the central premise of the current UNDS reform effort, which is more far-reaching, comprehensive, and targeted to achieve real change than previous reform initiatives. The current UNDS reform builds on earlier generations of reform; it addresses the key dimensions of systemic change to achieve collective impact, including leadership, common objectives and targets, and a strong coordination backbone.

Such an ambitious UNDS reform agenda requires accelerated efforts for implementation. The repositioning has moved much more quickly than previous reform efforts with the new UN RC system and UNDCO, the recruitment of a new generation of UNDP staff, and new UN coordination personnel. That said, the pace of reform to date has been uneven, with some elements under development (such as the regional piece) or late starting (such as the roll-out of the new UNSDCF). Looking forward, it will be critical to better sequence and leverage linkages between different reform initiatives at headquarters, regional, and country levels.

To accelerate these efforts, it will also be essential to ensure a focus on the following priorities. The first is a common plan for SDG implementation, not only through the UNSDCF at country level but also at the regional level and in headquarters. The second is the establishment of a common set of metrics for measuring not only implementation of the reform itself but also the impact of working together on achieving development outcomes. The critical role the UN needs to play in ensuring data is available, and disaggregated, to measure progress and ensure no one is left behind is key in this regard. The third priority is much greater attention to change management, including for staff at mid-level in countries, to incentivize and reward collaborative action and actively discourage silos and competition; support for initiatives to build partnership skills at all levels is also essential. The fourth is a system-wide approach to innovation that enables testing and learning across, as well as within, organizations. The fifth priority is to ensure that individual organizations' accountability and "mandate" emphasis, resource mobilization, and positioning priorities do not undermine reform efforts in favor of the status quo. The sixth is a strengthened focus on the linkages between the humanitarian, peacebuilding, and development agendas, including common country programming. The seventh priority, perhaps most critically, is a renewed commitment by the UNDS to promoting the realization of human rights commitments, both within the framework of the SDGs and in their own right.

Realizing the aspirations of this far-reaching development agenda, and the reform effort that supports it, requires a shift from a top-down, centralized approach to country-led implementation and ownership of the reform; from a still fragmented and competitive UNDS to "delivering as a system"; and from a focus on process to substance: sustainable development with the realization of human rights at the core.

This chapter has examined the conceptual framing of the current reform against previous reform efforts, the 2016 UNDG ToC, and the need to deliver the SDGs and Agenda 2030. What is needed is to move from a theory of change to action for change. The extent to which key tensions and dilemmas of the reform effort—including ensuring sustainable funding, achieving better balance between functioning as individual entities and as a system, and delivering both the operational and normative agendas—are addressed in its implementation will be the litmus test for success—and for a UN development system that is "fit" to truly leave no one behind.

NOTES

1 The authors published a full version independently. See John Hendra and Ingrid FitzGerald, "Who Wants (to) Change? A 'Theory of Change' for the UN Development System to Function as a System for Relevance, Strategic Positioning and Results," *United Nations University Centre for Policy Research* (Tokyo: UN University, 2 August 2016).

2 María Fernanda Espinosa Garcés, "Multilateralism and the Challenges of the United Nations," 5 April 2019, www.un.org/pga/73/2019/04/05/multilateralism-and-the-challenges-of-the-united-nations; Louis Charbonneau, "Multilateralism under Threat," *Human Rights Watch*, 24 June 2019, www.hrw.org/news/2019/06/24/multilateralism-under-threat.

3 Paul Heinbecker, "The UN: If It Didn't Exist We Would Have to Invent It," *Policy Options*, 1 October 2006, https://policyoptions.irpp.org/magazines/climate-change/the-un-if-it-didnt-exist-we-would-have-to-invent-it.

4 Nick Cumming-Bruce, "Budget Cuts May Undercut the UN's Human Rights Committees, *The New York Times*, 24 May 2019, www.nytimes.com/2019/05/24/world/un-budget-cuts-human-rights.html.

5 According to the Danish Human Rights Institute, "more than 90% of the targets directly reflect elements of international human rights and labour standards." Danish Human Rights Institute 2019, *Integrated Review and Reporting on SDGS and Human Rights: A Key to Effective, Efficient and Accountable Implementation*, 3.

6 UN, *Renewing the United Nations: A Programme for Reform: Report of the Secretary-General* (UN document A/51/950), 14 July 1997; and Stephan Klingbiel, *Effectiveness and Reform of the UNDP* (London: GDI, 1999), 93.

7 UN, *Independent Evaluation of Delivering as One: Main Report* (New York: United Nations, 2012) www.un.org/en/ga/deliveringasone/pdf/mainreport.pdf; and UNDG, *Monitoring and Evaluation Framework for Delivering as One: Draft*, 7 July 2014, https://undg.org/wp-content/uploads/2014/12/Item-2-Draft-Delivering-as-One-ME-Framework_7_July-2014.docx.

8 UN, 2018, *Report of the Secretary-General Implementation of General Assembly Resolution 71/243 on the Quadrennial Comprehensive Policy Review of Operational Activities for Development of the United Nations System*, www.un.org/ecosoc/sites/www.un.org.ecosoc/files/files/en/qcpr/2018-sg-report-adv.pdf.

9 UNDOCO, 2016, *UNDG Standard Operating Procedures for 'Delivering as One' 2015 Progress Report*, https://undg.org/wp-content/uploads/2016/11/UN-DOCO_2015-SOPs-Report_final.pdf.

10 *Report of the Secretary-General Implementation of General Assembly Resolution 71/243*, 67.

11 UN, *Progress in the Implementation of General Assembly Resolution 67/226 on the Quadrennial Comprehensive Policy Review of Operational Activities for Development of the United Nations System*, ECOSOC resolution 2014/14, 14 July 2014, OP 44.

12 For background and position papers, including by the UNDG and the final report of the ITA, 16 June 2016, see the "ECOSOC Dialogue" section of www.un.org.

13 UN, *Repositioning the United Nations Development System to Deliver on the 2030 Agenda: Ensuring a Better Future for All, Report of the Secretary-General*, UN documents A/72/124—E/2018/3, 11 July 2017.

14 UN, *Repositioning the United Nations Development System to Deliver on the 2030 Agenda: Our Promise for Dignity, Prosperity and Peace on a Healthy Planet, Report of the Secretary-General*, UN documents A/72/684–E/2018/7, 21 December 2017.

15 General Assembly resolution 72/279, 31 May 2018.

16 General Assembly resolution 70/1, 25 September 2015.

17 Detailed background about current UN reforms is at www.reform.un.org.

18 UNSDG, "United Nations Sustainable Development Cooperation Framework Guidance," June 2019, https://undg.org/wp-content/uploads/2019/06/UN-Cooperation-Framework-Internal-Guidance-25_June-2019.pdf.

19 For the latest on total contributions to the RC System Special Purpose Trust Fund, see https://soc.un.org.

20 UN, *Progress in the Implementation of General Assembly Resolution 71/243 on the Quadrennial Comprehensive Policy Review of Operational Activities for Development of the United Nations System*, UN document E/RES/2019/15, 12 July 2019.

21 The full Funding Compact is available as Addendum 1 to *Implementation of General Assembly Resolution 71/243 on the Quadrennial Comprehensive Policy Review of Operational Activities for Development of the United Nations System, 2019—Report of the Secretary-General*, UN documents A/74/73–E/2019/4, 15 April 2019.

22 UN, *Progress in the Implementation of General Assembly Resolution 71/243*.

23 See Hendra and FitzGerald, "Who Wants (to) Change?"; and for the UNDG approved summary, see UN, "A 'Theory of Change' for the UN Development System to Function 'As a System' for Relevance, Strategic Positioning and Results," Summary Paper Version 1.0, 26 January 2016, www.un.org/ecosoc/sites/www.un.org.ecosoc/files/files/en/qcpr/theory-of-change-summary-paper.pdf.

24 See, for example, blog posts by Owen Barder and Ben Ramalingam, available at Owen Barder "Complexity, Adaptation, and Results," *Center for Global Development*, 2012, www.cgdev.org/blog/complexity-adaptation-and-results.

25 Kay Hanleybrown, John Kania, and Mark Kramer, "Channeling Change: Making Collective Impact Work," *Stanford Social Innovation Review* (2012), www.ssireview.org/articles/entry/collective_impact.

26 John Kania and Mark Kramer, "Collective Impact," *Stanford Social Innovation Review* (2011), www.ssir.org/articles/entry/collective_impact#.

27 *United Nations System Leadership Framework, Annex to Report of the CEB High-Level Committee on Programmes*, UN document CEB/2017/1, 6 November 2016.

28 Some observers see the levy as a potential innovative instrument to incentivize better funding behavior. See Silke Weinlich, "In My View: The New UN Co-ordination Levy—Can It Set the Right Incentives?" in *Multilateral Development Finance: Towards a New Pact on Multilateralism to Achieve the 2030 Agenda Together* (Paris: OECD, 2018), 217–218.

29 Max-Otto Baumann and Silke Weinlich, "Unfinished Business: An Appraisal of the Latest UNDS Reform Resolution," *German Development Institute Briefing Paper*, no. 13 (2018).

30 A review of current functions and capacities in June 2017, in response to the 2016 QCPR "ask," showed that the UNDS is yet to fully transition from the MDGs to the SDGs and Agenda 2030. See Dalberg Advisors, "System-Wide Outline of the Functions and Capacities of the UN Development System," *Consultant's Report*, June 2017.

31 See ODI's LinkedIn page, 10 July 2019, www.linkedin.com/posts/odi_data-leavenoonebehind-activity-6546327736414277633-NsOf.

32 See Jeffrey Sachs, J. Schmidt-Traub, G. Kroll, C. Lafortune, and G. Fuller, *Sustainable Development Report* (New York: Bertelsmann Stiftung and Sustainable Development Solutions Network, 2019), x; and David Donoghue and Amina Khan, "Achieving the SDGs and 'Leaving No One Behind': Maximizing Synergies and Mitigating Trade-Offs," *ODI Working Paper*, no. 560 (London: ODI, 2019).

33 *Statement by Michelle Bachelet to the Human Rights Council Intersessional Meeting on Human Rights and the 2030 Agenda: Empowering People and Ensuring Inclusiveness and Equality*, 16 January 2019, www.ohchr.org/EN/NewsEvents/Pages/DisplayNews.aspx?NewsID=24072&LangID=E.

34 For a summary of tools and resources developed by OHCHR for this purpose see *Voluntary National Reviews: Human Rights Mechanisms, Approaches and Tools*, https://sustainabledevelopment.un.org/content/documents/21101OHCHR_VNR_one_pager.pdf.

35 Hendra and FitzGerald, "Who Wants (to) Change?" 14.

36 See UNDP, *Accelerator Labs*, https://acceleratorlabs.undp.org.

37 Ibid.; and UN, *Innovation Network*, www.uninnovation.network.

38 Most staff do not report sexual harassment, and 40 percent lacked confidence that senior leaders would take action. Nineteen percent did not report because of fear of retaliation. See IISD, *Survey Finds One Third of UN Workers Experienced Sexual Harassment in Last Two Years*, https://sdg.iisd.org/news/survey-finds-one-third-of-un-workers-experienced-sexual-harassment-in-last-two-years.

39 UN, *Global Pulse*, www.unglobalpulse.org.

ADDITIONAL READING

Duncan Green, *Fit for the Future? Development Trends and the Role of International NGOs* (Oxford: Oxfam GB, 2015).

Fay Hanleybrown, John Kania, and Mark Kramer, "Channeling Change: Making Collective Impact Work," *Stanford Social Innovation Review* (Winter 2012), www.ssireview.org/articles/entry/collective_impact.

John Hendra, *Making the UN "Fit for Purpose": Lessons from the 'Delivering as One' Experience*, Development Dialogue Paper no. 11 (Uppsala, Sweden: Dag Hammarskjöld Foundation, 2014).

John Hendra and Ingrid FitzGerald, "Who Wants (to) Change? A 'Theory of Change' for the UN Development System to Function as a System for Relevance, Strategic Positioning and Results" (Tokyo: UN University, August 2016).

Bruce Jenks and Bruce Jones, *United Nations Development at a Crossroads* (New York: NYU Center on International Cooperation, 2013).

19

LOOKING TO THE UN'S FUTURE

Carsten Staur

The adoption of the 2030 Agenda for Sustainable Development and the 17 Sustainable Development Goals (SDGs) in September 2015 created a new political momentum for the United Nations, which was amplified by the adoption of the Addis Ababa Action Agenda on Financing for Development in July 2015 and the Paris Agreement on Climate Change in December 2015. This momentum has dwindled because of a number of political changes worldwide and a renewed pressure not only on the UN system but also on other multilateral organizations and on multilateralism in general. The growth of new nationalisms across the globe is noticeable, and the slowdown accelerated with the announcement by the Trump administration of the US withdrawal from the Paris Agreement. It is unlikely that we will soon see a return to the enthusiasm of 2015. Much can change in a few years.

The UN Secretary-General has responded to these developments by initiating a sweeping reform process, encompassing the management of the system, the effectiveness and coherence of peacekeeping operations and special political missions, and a thorough reform of the UN development system. He stressed that "sustainable and inclusive development is an end in itself. It is also our best tool for building resilience, preventing crises, ensuring human rights are a lived experience and sustaining peace."[1]

The mandate of the United Nations development system (UNDS) is to assist member states in their implementation of the 2030 Agenda with the noble aim of "leaving no one behind." The success of this endeavor will be the most important, and in political terms probably the only, yardstick for measuring the recent major reform initiatives undertaken within the UNDS. Reviewing the functions and capacities of that system, including overlaps and gaps, is not an end in itself or simply an exercise in bureaucratic efficiency. It should be closely linked to the system's successful advocacy for and assistance in the delivery of the 2030 Agenda and the SDGs.

The SDGs have become a global language: a conceptual framework that not only captures what needs to be done but also gives clear direction in terms of indicators and goals and may lead to better priority-setting and sequencing. This will make it much easier to tie financing, investment projects, and reporting together across public, private, and civil society actors. It will also make it possible to accelerate the scaling of ideas and approaches. The fact that the vast majority of countries have reported at least once on their efforts to attain the SDGs is an indicator of how widespread the use of the SDG framework is.

It is important to get the UNDS—the UN Secretariat itself, the funds and programs, and the specialized agencies—to provide more targeted and integrated policy advice to governments, better and more comparable and reliable data and analysis, and in general to deliver much better as one support system at country level to realize the SDGs. That means a UNDS that is more coherent, better coordinated, and more context-specific at the country level, based on a clear understanding of capacities and constraints both in relation to national priorities (the demand side) and UN systemic capacities (the supply side). In this context, the new and expanded role of the resident coordinator (RC)—as representative of the Secretary-General in country, anchored in the Development Operations and Coordination Office (DOCO) of the UN Secretariat—will be crucial.

The most fundamental question, however, must be whether the universality of the SDGs—in contrast with their predecessors, the Millennium Development Goals of 2000, which applied only to developing countries—should translate into an equally universal UNDS. That is, should the services, advice, and supporting efforts of the UNDS be available to all countries, whether "rich" or "poor"? That does not mean that these activities should be funded in the same manner. ODA would still be the backbone of financing UNDS activities in developing countries, while developed and emerging economies should shoulder the costs themselves, as is already the practice in a number of countries, particularly in Latin America. Should the UNDS develop into a global consultancy system, in the same way that the Organisation for Economic Co-operation and Development (OECD), for instance, provides advisory services to its member states, although in a more limited way?

An answer to this question is at the end of this chapter. It proceeds through a review of the present scope of the UN's operational activities for development (OAD); the current funding of these activities; the likely donor support in the future; the legitimacy of the UNDS in the eyes of developing countries; and the strength of the capacity and institution-building dimensions of the UNDS, especially for fragile states.

Complexity, delivery, and funding

Some 50 years ago Robert Jackson—in his report on the *Capacity of the UN Development System*—stated that the UN development system was probably "the most complex organization in the world." Jackson asked who controlled this "machine," and his answer was no one, neither governments nor the machine itself: "it is so organized that managerial direction is impossible. In other words, the machine as a whole has become unmanageable in the strictest use of the word."[2]

Some of Jackson's reforms became policy, but the UNDS has become more and not less complex. Development is a difficult issue for the UN. In terms of international peace and security, the UN Charter places the Security Council at the center of coordinated international action in respect of any threats to, or breach of, international peace and security. The council may have difficulties in delivering, but member states agree to its mandate; it remains unchallenged. There is no alternative international body with a similar mandate. Something similar could be said about the UN and humanitarian action; while it has no monopoly on the delivery of emergency assistance and is often poorly coordinated, the UN's mandate is not questioned. The world organization is also the unquestioned custodian of its human rights treaties, starting with the Universal Declaration.

Development, however, is completely different. The World Bank, regional development banks, and bilateral donor agencies are important players in their own right; they do not necessarily take their cues from the UNDS but follow banking rules. Much depends on the host countries' strategies, institutional preferences, capacities, and degrees of ownership.

Future funding will be a major determinant of the viability of the UNDS. The universality of the United Nations—the image of a system, providing support to all countries and territories, and for all people, including before, during, and after a crisis—is not mirrored by a similar universality when it comes to the funding of its development system. The UNDS is only to a very limited extent funded by assessed contributions from member states. Most of the funding is provided through voluntary donor contributions, mostly as official development assistance (ODA) from the member states of the OECD's Development Assistance Committee (OECD-DAC). Other sources of funding for the UNDS may increase in the future.

Overall, the UN's operational activities for development (OAD), which include humanitarian assistance, amounted to some $34.3 billion in 2017, more than 70 percent of the system-wide UN expenditure of $48.3 billion in 2017, with peacekeeping accounting for another 20 percent. Of the $34.3 billion in OAD, a little more than half was allocated to development activities while a little less than half was allocated for humanitarian assistance.[3]

Putting this into perspective, the UNDS channeled around a quarter of total ODA (23.3 percent) provided by OECD-DAC members in 2017. This represents a significant increase over recent years, primarily driven by a strong increase in humanitarian assistance provided through the UN's humanitarian organizations, but also the ability of the various parts of the UNDS to deliver development assistance in situations of fragility. Comparing 2017 with 2007 figures, the UN operational funding for development and humanitarian activities has doubled. The increase in funding, however, reflects a huge increase in non-core contributions and almost a standstill in core funding. It is not likely that recent reform initiatives like the Funding Compact will significantly change this trend, especially because the OECD-DAC represents 30 (out of 36) OECD member states and the European Union.[4]

A closer look at the figures in many ways challenges the existence of the "S" in the UNDS acronym. The eight UNDS entities with the largest funding—the World Food Programme (WFP), UNICEF, UN Development Programme (UNDP), Office of the UN High Commissioner for Refugees (UNHCR), World Health Organization (WHO), UN Relief Works Agency for Palestinian Refugees (UNRWA), the Food and Agriculture Organization (FAO), and UN Population Fund (UNFPA)—receive 83 percent of all contributions. The same concentration exists on the donor side. The United States, the United Kingdom, and Germany accounted for half of the donor contributions to the UNDS in 2017; the seven largest donors provided more than two-thirds of all government contributions. Although growing, the contributions to the UNDS from non-DAC sources are limited—only $1.5 billion in 2017, again challenging the notion of a global system on the funding side.[5]

A "system" in name only?

Looking at the overall level and growth of developmental and humanitarian activities, the UNDS can be considered successful; it is also a system of choice by donors. As stated, the recent increase has almost entirely been in the form of non-core contributions. This clearly signals that the many key funding partners among bilateral donors, vertical funds, and global initiatives like GAVI, GFATM, and GPE, and the European Commission, see the UNDS not as a system, but as a number of individual entities, some of which may act as solid and effective implementing partners with strong in-country presence and experience. The UNDS is a loose federation of autonomous operational organizations. The absence of a meaningful "system" underlines the discrepancy between discussions in New York on how to improve the collective potential of the UNDS and the relevance of the 2030 Agenda and the SDGs, and many donor countries' funding decisions at the country level. Such allocations reflect the donors' perceptions about the comparative advantages of individual parts of the system in getting things done, based on policies and approaches defined by donor governments and other parts of the multilateral development system.

How will the picture look in 2030 and beyond? How will it look in terms of the "supply" of ODA vs. other sources of external financing? How will it appear in terms of countries' demand for development assistance, especially from the UNDS?

The first question will be whether ODA remains a valid political concept in the donor countries whose taxpayers jointly provide around $140–150 billion annually as ODA—around 0.2 percent of the global economy. It is possible to sound ODA's death knell and to argue coherently that this has always been a kind of moral guilt-trip and compensation for the wrongs of the colonial past of the West. It can be argued that it is modern-day colonialism that exports Western values through technical assistance; or perhaps that ODA in itself is a feature of the late twentieth century that will not stand the test of time and the coming of a new global world order characterized by the "rise of the rest."

However, the opposite argument has validity: ODA will continue, and most probably at the present level or slightly below. If we look back some 10 years to the global economic and financial crisis of 2008–2009, which led to significant budget cuts in many advanced economies (and traditional donor countries), it was a positive surprise that ODA levels withstood the budgetary pressure. The concept of "official development assistance" as a kind of "voluntary global taxation" by donor taxpayers proved to be resilient, even when other government budget priorities were under serious scrutiny. At the same time, the use of ODA also become a more explicit foreign policy tool in many donor countries.

Danish experiences—conveyed through regular polling of citizens through many years—point to the fundamental observation that voters/taxpayers tend to be quite satisfied with disbursements and contributions as they are. Fairly strong support for the present level of ODA is likely to remain, with little mainstream popular pressure to reduce that level. If ODA budgets were reduced, however, popular support would quickly converge around the new and lower level, with little pressure to increase the level again in the future.[6] This clearly indicates that ODA is a non-contentious policy area where people easily adapt to the new normal. It is also worth stating that the element of self-interest in ODA has increased over recent years, both in real life—including in a stronger voice by DAC members in the governance of the organizations—and in relation to the public narrative in donor countries with respect to ODA. As a recent example, ODA was an essential instrument to deal with the European refugee and migration crisis in 2015–2016. In this context, there was a significant increase in European humanitarian assistance toward regions nearby—and a redirection of development funds to regions and countries in Africa and the Middle East, from where refugees and migrants came or transited on their way to the Mediterranean. It is difficult to see these fundamental parameters changing dramatically over the next 10–20 years.

With that caveat—that there will always be a broader political agenda, into which the ODA narrative will have to fit, and for which the 2030 Agenda alone will not suffice—there is no indication that present ODA levels will go down significantly in the years to come. A few countries—primarily the Scandinavians—will most likely keep their assistance level at the official UN target of 0.7 percent of GNI or higher; most other OECD-DAC members are also likely to maintain contributions more or less as they are. Increased versatility of ODA seeking to create better interface with private-sector interventions, primarily in the form of blended finance where ODA is combined with private capital (often from pension funds and the like), has, in fact, provided a stronger political *raison d'être* for ODA. Also, the present increase in voters' concern—and especially among young voters—for the ever more visible climate crisis and the use of ODA to mitigate the effects of, or even prevent, global warming and a potentially disastrous increase in global temperatures by 2100 indicates continued strong support for ODA linked to this issue.

The establishment of a common European development policy and the integration of humanitarian and development activities in the EU budget occur through the regular budget and the particular budget envelope for the EU's cooperation with developing countries through its ACP envelope (African, Caribbean, and Pacific Group of States). New member states are obliged to contribute to these joint EU activities, which account for more than 10 percent of total ODA (in 2018, some $16.4 billion).[7] Effectively, this "ODA-tax" on EU member states constitutes part of the *acquis communautaire* when a country joins the EU. In practice, however, new members from Central and Eastern Europe have not become significant donors of ODA, and a number of them have not joined the OECD-DAC.

The major bilateral donors within the EU (the United Kingdom, the Netherlands, Germany, and the Nordics) have mainly created and sustained its development policy. This group of member states might lose part of their political influence with the withdrawal of the United Kingdom. Budget anxieties of many EU member states reflect a number of new challenges, both in terms of the future relationship with the United Kingdom and in terms of new and emerging policy issues. The result is likely to be a limited budgetary reduction of the EU's external activities in the next long-term budget, the Multiannual Financial Framework (2021–2027).

An increased global buy-in to the concept of ODA is unlikely. ODA will remain a "Western" invention and categorization, conceptually linked to the post-WWII institutional framework, and not least to the OECD-DAC. China, India, Brazil, and others will not embrace traditional ODA or see their own economic relationships with other countries in their region or across the world in that light. Therefore, ODA will remain a valid concept, but only for those that are already members of the club.

The second question is more difficult: will the UNDS be able to maintain or even increase its present level of voluntary donor funding? It is unlikely that there will be global support in the future for establishing a funding mechanism, whereby the UN humanitarian and development activities will be financed through a significant increase in assessed contributions to the UN. Voluntary funding is likely to retain its predominance.

The ongoing reforms of the UNDS seek to reposition the system and to reduce present fragmentation and volatility, in large part because of current funding practices—i.e., the movement toward more non-core funding and the difficulties in getting donors to provide either core contributions to UN funds and programs, or sufficient funding for inter-agency pooled funds. As stated, the financial basis for the UNDS—as a system centered in New York and Geneva and in the future probably also more at regional level—is primarily provided by the Europeans and the EU, including the important voluntary contributions to fund the RC system. Politically the system is based on consensual decisions by the UN General Assembly and the boards of the individual funds and programs, driven by leading developing countries of the Group of 77 (G-77) and EU member states. Important players have so far worked actively and constructively to find common ground and agree on incremental reform and improvement of the system. If the EU's member states become too absorbed in internal issues and challenges in the years to come and less concerned with and involved in global economic and developmental issues, a negative impact on the European engagement with the UNDS could result, especially if some of the major European donors (or the United States) suddenly and significantly reduce their voluntary contributions.

That, however, seems unlikely. Again, there is clear self-interest among European donors to work with and continue to support the UNDS both financially and politically. Other related key questions are whether donors see the UNDS as simply a system for implementation of "their" development assistance; or whether they see the UNDS as a unique player in its own right, bringing the force and the founding values of the UN to the table in a way that has an impact and assists the attainment of the SDGs. Similarly, do developing countries view the UNDS as a trustworthy partner that will stand up for and ensure their substantial interests in the policy dialogue on aid conditionalities, which remain part of any assistance arrangement?

The advantages of the UNDS

There are three strong selling points for the UNDS. First, the UNDS has legitimacy in the eyes of developing countries. The United Nations bases its in-country programs on the priorities and plans of the host countries, which generally have more leverage in respect of the UN system than they do with bilateral country programs. Government officials view UN RCs and UN organizations in general as more responsive to the perceived interests of the government than most donors and other multilateral organizations. UN representatives are also more likely than bilateral donors to understand the internal workings of the governments with which they work.

Most developing countries view the UNDS as "their" system because it is a privileged development partner for the more than 150 countries with a UN country program. Each of these countries is also a proud and equal member of the various organizations that constitute the UNDS and take part in their governance structures. Most also feel more in control and often trust the UN more than other development partners.

Second, the UNDS is part of a normative global organizational network, establishing hard and soft rules for global interaction between countries at different levels of development and with different economic, social, and political systems. The UNDS assists member states in adapting to international norms and standards, helping them to interact better and more effectively with other countries. The key concept here is the provision of much-needed technical assistance in order to build human and other capacities in government. Such capacity is seen as a means to improve key societal institutions, creating a higher degree of economic, social, and political resilience in countries, not least to establish the necessary partnerships to do so. This is what UN development organizations do well.

Technical assistance, capacity-building, and institutional development are also activities and services from which many bilateral donors are withdrawing; they have reduced the number of technical experts and consultants from their traditional bilateral development programs. At the same time, they have increased their support for key institutions of governance, such as tax and revenue offices, electoral commissions, and human rights bodies. Bilateral donors now often have to rely on the capacities of UN organizations to implement programs and projects, and this need is likely to increase given the continued pressure on donor agencies to reduce their own staffing levels and managerial overheads as part of their own ongoing public sector reforms. In many ways this is a bilateralization of multilateral assistance, often seen not least in conflict-prone and fragile states.

The character of international norm-setting may change, with less emphasis on legally binding norms and standards (like formal conventions) and more emphasis on the development of soft norms, often initiated outside the UN system, in forums like the Group of 20 (G-20) or the OECD. These new kinds of instrument do not necessarily rely on formal agreement by all states, but more by a critical mass of major economies like the G-20 members. Other countries most often will then have to adopt, and adapt to, these norms and standards in order to maintain their economic relations with the major economies. The result is a system of carrots as well as sticks, once the major powers have struck the necessary deals. There will, however, still be a need for the kind of technical assistance, which the UNDS can offer member states in order to align with these new norms and standards—even if the standards themselves are not generated by the UN.

Third, the focus on technical assistance, capacity-building, and institutional development also means that the UNDS will never be able to stand alone in a global development context. Other institutions, like the World Bank, other multilateral development banks (MDBs), or bilateral donors, will be needed to provide budget support or financing for major infrastructure projects, either through grants, concessional loans, or blended financing. Such a financial reality will necessarily limit the size of the UNDS. However, it will also emphasize the need for more partnerships among key players.

The present situation in which UN development spending accounts for almost a quarter of all ODA can only be understood in light of the huge increase in humanitarian assistance over recent years, due to the grave deterioration in the humanitarian situation globally and not least in the form of human-made disasters in Africa and the Middle East. That development, of course, is primarily due to the inability of the UN to reach agreement on the conflicts and political problems that provoke the largest humanitarian crises around the world. The biggest UNDS country programs—the 11 amounting to more than $800 million in 2017—almost all have significant humanitarian dimensions. In most cases, they also host peacekeeping or special political missions, thus enabling the UN system to use its full range of tools: in Yemen, Lebanon, South Sudan, Syria, Afghanistan, Iraq, Somalia, Occupied Palestinian Territories, Jordan, Ethiopia, and Nigeria.[8]

The future

Looking to the future of the UNDS, it will continue to confront fragmentation and a lack of cohesion; but efforts are underway to reduce these long-standing shortcomings, not least through the recently empowered RC system. The overall funding basis most likely will be there also in the future. Developing countries have confidence in the system and want to make use of it, so future demand should reflect that. A number of issues remain; but they could, if properly managed, be turned into opportunities rather than threats to the system.

This analysis may, however, underestimate the volatility of the present international political climate. There may be no immediate systemic threats to the UNDS, but the world is seemingly teetering on the edge of uncertainty, and things may change quickly. Thus, it may be argued that the UNDS, and the world at large, would benefit if the UN were able to go back to basics, and to harness once more the key selling points of the UNDS: its strength in respect of institutional development and capacity-building, based on the normative work of the UN system, and its abilities to establish and promote partnerships with others.

This line of argument is especially important in relation to those developing countries that are generally perceived as being in situations of fragility, with weak governance structures and institutions, either in broad terms or in key policy areas, and often also with governments marked by corruption and struggling to control internal conflict, including terrorism. There is no internationally agreed definition of fragility—unlike the situation pertaining to least developed countries (LDCs). The OECD works with five different aspects of fragility (economic, environmental, political, societal, and security); it ties fragility with the lack of resilience in these areas and deficiencies in the mechanisms to cope with negative developments. In 2016, some 1.8 billion people—24 percent of the world's population—lived in fragile contexts, primarily in Sub-Saharan Africa and the Middle East. This number is expected to grow to 2.3 billion in

2030, equal to 28 percent of the world's population. By then, approximately 80 percent of the world's poor people will be living in fragile contexts. The OECD counts 58 countries in fragile contexts, of which 15 are extremely fragile. These are also the developing countries in which earmarked donor funding will most likely increase in the years to come. In 2016, two-thirds of all earmarked ODA was for fragile states.[9]

In such contexts, and especially in the situations of extreme fragility, ODA-funded interventions are often a combination of massive humanitarian assistance and comparatively smaller development assistance programs. Even though it has been difficult to elaborate a satisfactory humanitarian–development nexus and to create an effective and efficient modus operandi between the different informal "protocols" that guide these two distinct forms of external assistance, the UNDS probably has better prospects of doing so than other development actors, not least through the strengthening of the RC system at country level. Only the EU has the scope of activities that may, in some respects, match the UNDS; but it has neither the same trust of developing countries nor the same breadth of technical expertise.

Equally importantly, many bilateral donors will probably expand their reliance on and collaboration with UNDS entities in order to "sub-contract" the implementation and oversight of their planned development activities to UN organizations. The important issue for donors is the existence of a narrative about why assistance is provided at country level and what it accomplishes, not who is actually managing it, or whether this is done bilaterally or multi-bilaterally. In addition, a strong donor commitment to combating corruption and mismanagement will be part of development financing. Further, many donors will have an interest in engaging others, and not least UNDS entities, in the accountability frameworks around bilateral development activities in order to transfer some or all reputational risks to the UNDS.

For the UNDS to act as a "contractor" or in a limited implementation role—assuming most of the risks involved—may also be an opportunity. This would require that the UNDS, in collaboration with the host country, can turn these various donor-funded elements into a legitimate joint UN country program to attain the SDGs while gradually replacing the relevant parts of donors' bilateral programs, to be financed by pooled funds. Increased emphasis on the building of administrative and institutional capacities in fragile states may also lead to increased and more systematic and reliable efforts to help weak governments in question to incorporate non-ODA funding as well (remittances, increased domestic resources/taxation, and foreign direct investment). The objective would be to expand inclusive and sustainable economic growth and link these countries more firmly to the global economy. This framework could enhance the role of the RC and the UN country team (UNCT) in such fragile situations, not only ensuring coordination with the host country government and within the UNDS, but also potentially assuming a coordinating role, together with an often under-capacitated government, in respect of all development stakeholders in the country. At present, however, the approach remains a patchwork, which could benefit greatly from stronger coordination efforts by all relevant partners.

On this basis, it is reasonable to imagine a UNDS moving toward a focus on countries in fragile contexts: its comparative advantage. The needs are considerable from a "leave no one behind" point of view. Countries in fragile situations are high on the list of donor priorities, mostly from a political point of view, so funding is available. They fit well with the capacities and strength of the UNDS and its various individual entities. In severely fragile contexts there is hardly any competition from MDBs, vertical funds, the EU, or bilateral donor agencies. Donors will happily leave responsibility—and risk of failure—to the UNDS.

It is important to recall the normative basis of the UNDS. In situations of fragility, with weak and often dysfunctional rule-of-law institutions, the human rights-based approach and the UN's human rights machinery can be a strong basis for better systemic delivery in relation to SDG goal 16. In three other key cross-cutting policy areas the UNDS has similar potential: on gender equality and women's empowerment, on youth (education, employment), and on climate change. A UNDS that can assist countries in fragile situations and achieve progress in these four policy areas will get much closer to making a real difference in realizing the 2030 Agenda.

This does not mean that the UNDS should limit itself to assisting countries in a more limited number of policy areas. The breadth and strength of the UNDS lies clearly in the competences and capacities which each UN organization or entity has in its area of expertise. For decades, however, the problem has been that each entity has been pushing its own agenda, including fundraising, with scarce regard for overall priority-setting and with limited focus on the cross-cutting policy issues such as the four areas highlighted here. More important, however, will be the way in which the UNDS addresses the issue of a lack of personal security, the non-existence of the rule of law, corruption, fraud, and mismanagement within some governments. Without such issues being addressed and problems rectified, most of the other activities in fragile states will prove to be in vain. This challenge represents a clear opportunity for the UNDS—but also a great risk of failure if the system is not able to deliver in such situations.

The strengthening of the RC and their function at country level must therefore be backed both by funding muscle that can be applied to the individual entities within the UNDS, and by an equally important political muscle that can provide leeway for what undoubtedly will be tension vis-à-vis governments. Otherwise, it will not work. It will also need to be backed up at headquarters level and in the boards of the organizations, with real commitments and buy-in from all senior managers and leaders of the various organizations and entities. Lip service will not suffice.

Conclusion: some final thoughts

Focusing the UNDS's donor-funded activities on countries in situations of fragility does not necessarily mean that the United Nations would do only that. The UNDS is a universal system, encompassing 193 member states, and it should be of service to all member states. A special focus on countries in fragile situations only implies that the major part of future financing by way of ODA funding for operational activities should be earmarked for that purpose. This would result either through decisions by various governing boards to allocate more core funding to these countries or—politically more likely—by donors providing earmarked funding for these situations, de facto mandating the UNDS to focus ODA-funded activities on fragile states.

However, what is in it for the rest, for the majority of countries that are not fragile but not rich either—not least those countries that are middle income or upper-middle income, emerging economies that are generating growth rates at a level above the West? These countries are generally not requesting ODA to help develop their key government institutions and systems, to strengthen their administrative, managerial, or financial capacities, or to build up their legal institutions. They more often request highly specialized analyses and advice within technical areas where they feel short-changed or are in need of a neutral, impartial view or a second opinion, not least in areas where they look to further implementation and adherence to international norms or standards, allowing them to better integrate in the global economy. The future challenges of transitioning to a low- or even zero-carbon economy could be a case in point for advanced economies as well.

Upper-middle-income countries, emerging economies, and some industrialized countries in Europe or North America might also want to draw on advice and services from the UNDS—particularly from the specialized and technical agencies. Moreover, better-off countries can pay for such services themselves, as many countries in Latin America and Eastern and Central Europe already do. Their needs are more ad hoc, often shifting and highly technical. They might go to an international consultancy firm to get what they need, but the UNDS would be highly competitive and with a supportive set of values. The staff of the many UN technical agencies are qualified, knowledgeable, and experienced across national and regional boundaries—they often merit the overused label of "expert." They are presumably more independent, less acquisitive, and represent a high-valued brand of knowledge, which could establish a clear competitive edge.

The UNDS could thus act as a consultancy system, providing advisory services to countries based on their selective and prioritized needs. It will not necessarily call for much in-country presence, but it will call for a managerial system that is highly agile, efficient, and geared to respond quickly to inquiries and requests. In some key areas like climate change, it will be able to draw on the whole system of inter-disciplinary expertise, which will be able to match any other kind of advisory services. The challenge of such a universal, sustainable development consultancy network under the auspices of the United Nations will be the management and transparency of the system, centrally and at country level. That will call for a massive change, emulating all best practices from the field of global consultancy companies.

It is not difficult to see such a universal system with certain financial windows provided by donors, private foundations, or companies in order to assist other countries with the funding for priority tasks, pertaining especially to areas of global importance such as climate change, implementation of renewable energy solutions, and phasing out fossil fuels. Increased collaboration with regional organizations or the OECD on specific projects, both at national and regional levels, would be another advantage.

In short, the UNDS is not doing too badly. Donor funding is available, as is the political support and actual demand from host countries. The UNDS could probably continue for some time on this basis, doing a little bit of everything; but maintaining the status quo would not be without risks. In a highly volatile world, reform—and reform in-depth—is wise, and before politics changes for the worse. A major crisis for the UN in political terms, in the area of international peace and security, could easily also affect negatively the humanitarian and development activities of the organization. The new nationalisms could also have a negative impact on ODA.

Today's UNDS should, therefore, give way to a new UNDS, which will base itself on the fundamental value proposition of the UN: normative foundation; convening power; competence to deliver effective and efficient support for institutional development; capacity-building; and forging partnerships, especially at country level, in order to realize the SDGs. In operational terms, this means a much stronger focus on those countries that are furthest behind, the 50+ fragile states where the UNDS has the potential to become an influential and trusted partner of host governments and of donor countries alike, providing a competitive and strong platform for the UN to exert leverage in New York and Geneva. That would be the logical next step, a "UNDS Version 2.0."

The increased focus on fragile states, however, would not rule out a parallel development of a UNDS Version 3.0, which would take the universality of the SDGs to its logical conclusion: to provide its services on a fully costed and funded basis to all countries that wish to avail themselves of the expertise of the UNDS. The driver would be climate change and the profound transformational processes that all countries will have to go through over the coming years in order to limit their CO2 emissions for the benefit of future generations without damaging the aspirations of present ones.

In the aftermath of the 75th anniversary of the founding of the world organization, there is a risk of an inter-generational revolt, by which young people protest against the lack of serious global action related to such key SDG themes as climate change, social inclusion, and decent work. The increased generational bias toward non-sustainable policies, preferences, and political cultures in countries on every continent could create a strong political push for change, not least among youth across the globe. They could and should be channeled into the United Nations as an essential arena to discuss and foster change. The UNDS Version 3.0 could provide one way.

NOTES

1 UN, *Repositioning the United Nations Development System to Deliver on the 2030 Agenda: Ensuring a Better Future for All: Report of the Secretary-General* (UN documents A/72/124–E/2018/3), 11 July 2017.
2 UN, *A Study of the Capacity of the United Nations Development System* (Geneva: United Nations, 1969), Vol. 1, "Foreword" and iii.
3 UN, *Funding Analysis of Operational Activities for Development—Addendum 2*, UN documents A/74/73–E/2019/4, Add.2, 18 April 2019, Advance unedited version.
4 OECD-DAC, *Development Assistance Committee*, www.oecd.org/dac/development-assistance-committee.
5 UN, *Funding Analysis of Operational Activities for Development.*
6 This observation reflects Danish polling in relation to the reductions of ODA in 2002. I was head of the Danish International Development Agency (DANIDA) at the time.
7 Donor Tracker, *Country*, https://donortracker.org/country/eu.
8 UN, *Funding Analysis of Operational Activities for Development*, Figure 2.2.2.
9 OECD, *States of Fragility 2018* (Paris: OECD, 2018).

ADDITIONAL READING

Max-Otto Baumann, Erik Lundsgaarde, Silke Weinlich, and Peter Wolff, *Earmarking in the Multilateral Development System: Many Shades of Grey* (Bonn, Germany: Deutsches Institut für Entwicklungspolitik, forthcoming).
OECD, *2019 Multilateral Development Finance Report: Recharging Multilateral Development Co-operation to Achieve the 2030 Agenda Together* (Paris: OECD, 2018).
OECD-DAC, *Development Cooperation Reports* (Paris: OECD-DAC, annual).
Carsten Staur, *Shared Responsibility: The United Nations in the Age of Globalization* (Montreal: McGill-Queen's University Press, 2013).
UN Multipartner Trust Fund Office and Dag Hammarskjöld Foundation, *Financing the UN Development System: Time for Hard Choices* (Uppsala: DHF, 2019).

20

REFORMING THE UN AND GOVERNING THE GLOBE

Georgios Kostakos

At the outset of the third decade of the twenty-first century and as the UN celebrates its 75th anniversary in 2020, the global geopolitical, economic, and ideological settings look significantly different from those during the UN's creation at the end of World War II. To its credit, the world body has managed to remain relevant, not least by reinventing itself time and again, and adjusting to changing circumstances. More than that, the UN has contributed to shaping those circumstances, as demonstrated through such innovations as peacekeeping, the various human rights–related instruments, global goals like the Millennium Development Goals (MDGs) and their successor, the Sustainable Development Goals (SDGs), the Paris Agreement on Climate Change, and the Global Compact for Migration. Acting collectively, the UN member states (First UN) have negotiated all this, in one form or another, with the support of and at times following an initiative by the UN Secretariat (Second UN) or civil society (Third UN).[1]

Despite these signs of livelihood and relevance, the UN is currently under significant stress, along with the rest of the global multilateral system. An apparent reason for that is the ascendance to the highest positions of power in several countries around the globe of nationalist leaders, who want to reclaim decision-making as the exclusive prerogative of the sovereign nation-state. Emblematic among them has been US President Donald Trump and his "America First" approach that leaves little room for consensual discussions about the global, common interest. Ironically, while "national populism"[2] is spreading worldwide, the challenges facing humanity could not be greater or more connected.

This chapter starts with an overview of the current state of the world. It then proceeds to review the roles played by the United States and emerging powers such as China, the European Union (EU), and new actors in global governance such as the Group of 20 (G-20). It then traces the reasons for the UN's waning authority in the actions or inactions of those actors and of the UN itself. It concludes with some alternative scenarios and some proposals that could help stabilize the global governance system, restore a normative framework for thought and action, and tackle the major challenges confronting humanity today.

The state of the globe under today's UN-headed governance system

The most prominent global challenge of our times, climate change, is looming larger by the day. Heatwaves are now a commonplace even in previously cool countries of the Northern

Hemisphere, while forest fires rage not only around the Mediterranean or California but as far north as Sweden and Siberia, as well as in tropical Amazon and "down-under" Australia. Melting glaciers put at risk the water resources of millions of people around the world and contribute to already measurable sea-level rise. Efforts at mitigating the causes of climate change in the context of the Kyoto Protocol and the Paris Agreement clash with the need for urgent adaptation measures, some of which entail further greenhouse gas emissions, such as the spreading use of air conditioners, which in turn exacerbates the situation. Human security broadly defined, including food and water security and health, is under increasing strain by the climate change impacts. Despite its pronouncements, there is little that the UN has been able to do to ensure in practice the necessary change of course, which has to do with the way that the economy and society work and interact with each other and with the environment around the world.

The challenges posed by new technologies cannot be underestimated either. From the future of employment to the processes and content of democracy, today's algorithm-powered artificial intelligence systems and the ever-present social media lead to a de facto reinterpretation, to say the least, of the way that we live, relate to each other, organize our societies, and define the meaning of life, in no modest terms. New commons and new possibilities are opening, but the rules of the game and who controls what are not clear, beyond the fact that things are not as they used to be. The governance of cyberspace seems to be out of anybody's hands, at a time when ever larger parts of people's lives, especially of young people, are spent there. Outer space is also increasingly becoming a challenge, with more countries and even private companies announcing ambitious goals of exploration and exploitation from the upper atmosphere all the way to the moon, Mars, and beyond, not always for peaceful purposes. Progress in biotechnology further pushes the limits of who we are and what should be allowed in terms of cloning, organ creation or harvesting, and machine and human merging.[3] All the while more traditional challenges continue to threaten humanity, from violent armed conflicts to weapons proliferation (including nuclear weapons), from migration to human trafficking.

This conjuncture of challenges should require multilateralism, with the world body at its apex, to acquire renewed significance and legitimacy, with additional human and material resources put at its disposal. However, after decades of increasing globalization, especially in terms of industrial production, trade, and finance, it is at this specific moment that multilateralism is challenged by "national populism" that is sweeping the globe. Riding on anxieties, to a large extent caused by such impacts of globalization as cultural homogenization through universal consumerism, switching of production sites to lower-wage countries, widening inequalities in income distribution, and the squeezing of the middle and lower classes in the pursuit of ever greater business profits, national populism has emerged as a major political force. Whether it is acknowledged as such or not, this is the underlying ideology that the leaders of countries as diverse as the United States, Turkey, India, the Philippines, and Brazil share at this moment, manipulating popular concerns to gain and retain power, while taking advantage of people's insecurities and telling them what they want to hear. As so many times in the past, the energy of the masses is not channeled toward understanding and addressing the challenge at hand but toward finding scapegoats, those who are different within and outside each society, masking the leaders' incapacity or unwillingness to address the real issues.[4]

With such leaders at the helm of nations and guiding country representation in multilateral bodies, those of the United Nations system but also international and regional organizations like the European Union, it is proving increasingly arduous to put together collective responses. Thus, the UN Security Council is unable to deal with the perennial taboo of Israeli-Palestinian relations but also with the situations in Syria, Libya, Yemen, Kashmir, and Venezuela—to mention only a few particularly explosive situations. In a state of global climate emergency, which most now accept as a reality (even if some still dispute its human causes), there is minimal international coordination in dealing with its consequences. In addition, human rights seem to be in retreat in many parts of the world—including the rights of free assembly and expression, asylum, and of migrants—in the hands of autocratic governments that often emerge in a broadly democratic setting.[5]

The repercussions may prove much more serious than initially thought for the UN and beyond, as the very foundations of international cooperation are being eroded. The go-it-alone, my-country-first approach undermines multilateralism and international/supranational institutions, which gradually lose their legitimacy and the capacity to have a meaningful impact. Some pundits are sensing reverberations of 1914 and 1939, namely the collapse of orderly state interactions in the political, diplomatic, and economic fields leading to the outbreak of war.[6]

Out goes the creator and in comes the Medea of multilateralism

The geopolitical conditions at the UN's creation were unusual. The end of World War II had left the United States as the undisputed leader among the other war winners. There was a historic moment; a window of opportunity to set new rules. Washington made use of it and helped build the UN, not without resistance from other major powers or coalitions of smaller ones, as well as domestic forces in the United States itself.[7]

Today, the United States has been challenging the UN that it championed. The enlightened self-interest and often calculated magnanimity of Franklin D. Roosevelt and Harry S. Truman have been replaced by threats and demands toward the world body put forward by President Trump and his representatives. There was no hesitation to withdraw from the Paris Agreement on Climate Change (a process set in motion in June 2017),[8] leave the Intermediate-Range Nuclear Forces Treaty (INF) (effective 2 August 2019),[9] or even withdraw from UNESCO (effective 1 January 2019), a whipping boy for multilateralism punished also in the past by US unilateralists.[10] Not to mention the perennial threat, which occasionally materializes, to withhold US contributions to the UN regular and peacekeeping budgets, something that is being used with a vengeance by the current administration. Cuts implemented or sought by Trump and associates endanger targeted UN entities, like the United Nations Population Fund (UNFPA) and the United Nations Relief and Works Agency for Palestine Refugees in the Near East (UNRWA), as well as crucial institutions like peacekeeping.[11]

Such anti-multilateralism is not without precedent. For example, during the administration of Ronald Reagan, the UN was again the target of US ire. A perceived leftist tilt in the world body, carried over from the anti-colonial and economic emancipation struggles of developing countries, clashed with the privatization drive and neoliberalism that was emerging as the victor of the ideological confrontation between capitalism and communism in the Cold War.[12] More recently, the UN had to suffer the consequences of not supporting the 2003 US invasion of Iraq during the administration of George W. Bush.

Indicative of the current US administration's attitude toward the UN and multilateralism was the speech given by Trump at the opening of the 73rd session of the UN General Assembly in September 2018. He began by presenting his administration's domestic achievements in the economic sphere, including tax cuts and increased military spending, causing an outburst of laughter among General Assembly attendees. He went on to justify the US withdrawal from the UN Human Rights Council, reject "the ideology of globalism," and stress that Washington would not pay more than 25 percent of the UN peacekeeping budget, asking other countries to step up and share the burden.[13]

Truth be told, the UN is not the only multilateral institution singled out for criticism and disciplinary measures by the US administration. Trump has consistently attacked even those closest to US interests and influence, such as the North Atlantic Treaty Organization (NATO).[14] Even limited membership bodies, where the United States has more weight compared to the one-state-one-vote 193-member UN General Assembly, are feeling the heat from the negative approach the Trump administration has adopted. Recent Group of 20 (G-20) summit communiqués, for example, break with the established tradition of consensus, because of Trump's dissenting voice, notably regarding issues related to climate change.[15]

Penelope's suitors

While the United States has been abandoning multilateralism in theory and practice, other actors find themselves in a position to play a more central role in the international system. China is the world's most populous country and with the biggest economy, at least in Purchasing Power Parity (PPP) terms;[16] it is also the second contributor to the UN regular budget with 12 percent for the 2019–2021 period (compared to 22 percent by the US). In comparison with Washington, Beijing sounds like a predictable, status-quo-abiding, and constructively engaged major power. In his first address to the General Debate of the UN General Assembly in September 2015, Chinese President Xi Jinping spoke about renewing the commitment to the UN Charter and announced the establishment of a 10-year, US$1 billion China Peace Development Fund for the United Nations, as well as the establishment of an 8,000-troop stand-by peacekeeping force to be ready to contribute to international efforts.[17] Beyond that, we have heard the unthinkable: the Chinese President speaking at the town hall meeting of Western liberalism, the annual World Economic Forum in Davos, Switzerland, as the guardian of multilateralism and defender of "economic globalization," which should "become more invigorated, more inclusive, and more sustainable."[18]

Does all this amount to China's claiming the central role at the UN and, by extension, the global governance system? To do that, China would need to have a coherent vision with forward-looking targets beyond the preservation of the status quo, to rally others around it. Would the "building of a community with a shared future for mankind" promoted in Chinese statements to the UN and beyond amount to that?[19] While this may be a vision and ideology in the making, it does not seem to constitute as yet a complete rallying cry of a new universal leader. In fact, there is the sense that China and other non-Western powers like Russia and India still feel like guests in an organization that has been primarily shaped and mostly dominated by the West, even though the majority has rested for decades now with the Global South—the "G-77" group of developing countries currently including 134 of the UN's 193 member states.[20]

The defensive attitude of non-Western powers often reflects an effort to ensure that they do not lose out to primarily Western-inspired and promoted innovations like "the responsibility to protect" or the Human Rights Council and the Peacebuilding Commission. This perceived Western bias had led during the height of the Cold War to Soviet demands for the replacement of the UN Secretary-General with a "troika" of three Secretaries-General representing the West, the East, and the non-aligned South, respectively.[21] In practice, regional balancing has occurred in a less pronounced way through the "hereditary rights" that countries or groups of countries have established in the leadership of UN departments and offices. Thus, the head of the UN Department of Economic and Social Affairs (DESA) is a Chinese diplomat, guarding closely the development agenda that constitutes the utmost priority for developing countries. At the same time, the Department of Political and Peacebuilding Affairs (DPPA) is headed by a US diplomat, and the Department of Peace Operations (DPO) by a French diplomat, indicating the priorities of the West.

Beyond this "balance of power(s)" within the UN, China may well feel more comfortable pursuing its own initiatives, enhancing its profile, and building its influence outside the UN framework. This is notably the case with the Belt and Road Initiative (BRI), a modern and grandly reconceived Silk Road, which involves some 60 countries, connects East Asia to Europe through Central Asia, but also South and Southeast Asia and even East Africa, and comprises huge infrastructure and investment projects.[22] Furthermore, the major emerging countries and economies collectively known as the BRICS—namely Brazil, Russia, India, China, and South Africa—at the initiative of Russia have established since 2008 their own club analogous to the Western Group of 7 (G-7), with regular summits and working-level sessions. They have taken the extra step of establishing institutions like the New Development Bank and a BRICS Contingent Reserve Arrangement,[23] arguably challenging the role of the Western-dominated Bretton Woods institutions. Nevertheless, the BRICS group is heterogeneous in terms of the interests and political orientations of its members, and its pronouncements do not carry their full collective weight in practice. So it cannot as yet be seen as an alternative system of global leadership.

What about the original Group of 7 (G-7) group of Western democracies? Is it holding the torch of global leadership? The host of the 2019 G-7 Summit, French President Emmanuel Macron, certainly sought to make it seem so. Coinciding with a spike in forest fires in the Amazon, the 2019 G-7 summit in Biarritz, France gave Macron the opportunity to place the issue at the top of the Summit agenda, as part of the global climate emergency.[24] Whether the initiative to speak in the name of the international community and demand action to save "the lungs of the world" was well intended or not, it was rebuffed by the Brazilian President Jair Bolsonaro as a threat to Brazilian sovereignty. Eventually the Brazilian army was brought in to help extinguish the fires, and international offers of assistance were accepted despite the controversy.

While the G-7 and BRICS are clearly alliances of like-minded powers, in recent years we have seen the rise of a more cross-cutting, consensus-building, and action-taking organization of sorts. Even without a permanent support structure like the UN, relying on its annual presiding country to provide secretariat services and leadership, the Group of 20 (G-20) is currently the most obvious competitor to the UN, at least in the economic and development field. A small but powerful body bringing together 19 countries plus the EU that collectively represent two-thirds of the world population and significantly more in terms of global GDP and trade, the G-20 has risen to prominence in the years since the global financial crisis of 2008. It operates outside the UN framework, with the UN Secretary-General usually invited to attend as a guest among several other international organization heads, and briefings provided to UN bodies by the G-20 presiding country each time. The G-20 uses the UN system when it needs specialized input, from bodies like the International Monetary Fund (IMF), the World Bank, and the International Labour Organization (ILO). Nonetheless, it seems to have been losing focus over the years, with an expanding agenda and numerous pronouncements but no clear impact.[25]

And what about the EU, the planet's regional integration organization *par excellence*? It counts several powerful states among its members and collectively constitutes the largest financial contributor to the UN system. It has thus far failed, though, to assert itself as a distinct pole of political influence and an effective guardian of a rules-based multilateral system.[26] Divergent member-state interests, a fragmented and politically weak center, and contradictions between words and deeds are clearly among the reasons that maintain the EU as a political lightweight. This situation prevails despite its economic superpower status and the fact that it counts at present two UN Security Council permanent members within its ranks (soon to be only one,

France, after the United Kingdom leaves the EU via Brexit). Global leadership could not thus be realistically expected from the EU under a business-as-usual scenario. It remains to be seen whether the far-reaching vision of the European Commission president, Ursula von der Leyen, will alter this reality in the coming five years—not only for climate action and sustainability with the "European Green Deal" but also for common foreign and security policy, by "strengthening [Europe's] unique brand of responsible global leadership."[27]

Global governance actors are not limited to states and state groupings. In a situation that could be functionally explained as part of multi-level governance, a system of diverse actors with authority and responsibilities in different physical and thematic areas and vis-à-vis different population groups has been emerging, with varying degrees of global engagement. This changing configuration increasingly includes actors at the subnational level, like governors and mayors, who also act through collective institutions like the Covenant of Mayors, Local Governments for Sustainability (ICLEI), and C-40 Cities. Moreover, large nongovernmental organizations (NGOs) like Oxfam, the World Wildlife Fund (WWF), or Greenpeace, powerful multinational corporations like the Big Five energy companies, car producers, and the social media giants all play their role on the international stage, mobilizing people, influencing decisions, and allocating resources, even if they do not control, explicitly at least, the power of coercion and of waging war that sovereign states still monopolize. Does this constitute a new global governance architecture, and can it really steer the world toward peace and prosperity in a balanced way on its own?[28] For now, what we see is that all these subnational, regional, civil society, and private actors are trying to exert influence in the context of the UN, without replacing the world body but rather having more of a say in its decisions.

The UN's waning authority

Among the many issues of emerging global importance, from conflicts at various stages to critical economic, social, and environmental issues, the UN seems to be successfully engaged in only a handful of cases. What is more prominent, for example, is the inability of the five permanent members (P-5) of the Security Council to agree on how to deal with conflict areas like Syria, Venezuela, Libya, Yemen, and Israel-Palestine. Thus, no substantive decision can be reached by the Council, and no decisive action can be taken by "the UN" as such. For the same conflicts, "the secular Pope" that for some is the UN Secretary-General limits himself to calls for the opponents to negotiate peacefully, often accompanied by special envoys deployed without clear direction or effect, and certainly no bold initiative in sight. The most daring seems to be the increased use of Twitter, à la Trump, but with much smaller impact.

Like his predecessor, Secretary-General António Guterres has been a vocal advocate for climate change, "the defining global challenge of our times," calling for urgent action and convening high-level meetings. His advocacy does not seem to have produced adequately radical results after the 2015 Paris Agreement, despite the now broadly shared recognition that climate change is life-threatening. The US withdrawal from the Paris Agreement has made foot-dragging more acceptable elsewhere. As for issues of inequality, human rights, trade, and finance, again there has not been much beyond platitudes and calls, either from the Secretary-General or from the competent intergovernmental bodies, notably the fractious Human Rights Council, the Economic and Social Council (ECOSOC), and the High-Level Political Forum for Sustainable Development (HLPF).[29]

This apparent lack of conviction and determination for action by the UN in its various incarnations is not missed by governments, other public and private actors, and the broader public, whether they are of bad or good will vis-à-vis the world body. They increasingly feel that it is safe to ignore it and rely on alliances, deterrence, and the principle of "the enemy of my enemy is my friend." The change since the term of Kofi Annan is noticeable: astute navigation of difficult political waters and the good chemistry with the likes of Bill Clinton and Tony Blair allowed the UN to experience a relatively "golden era" in the first half of the 2000s. However, that luster has been tarnished under the stewardship of Ban Ki-moon and António Guterres, who seem too cautious, aware of their weak status, and primarily responding to the demands of those powers that were instrumental in their election. In the meantime, national leaders take it upon themselves to speak for the world, as they see it and as it serves their partial interests, making things worse.

To be fair, the foundations for the decline of the UN's authority had been laid earlier. They were somewhat camouflaged, however, by the charismatic personality of Kofi Annan and the sophisticated national leaders of that time, many of whom shared a third-way-to-socialism, principles-can-be-bent-to-stay-in-power, neoliberalism-with-a-human-face approach. There has been a clear preference for voluntary, "peer-reviewed" arrangements, like the Human Rights Council, a product of the 2005 UN reform process led by Annan, or the HLPF, a product of the Rio+20 Conference led by Ban Ki-moon, or the more recent Paris Agreement on Climate Change, also under Ban, and the Global Compact for Migration, under Guterres. Their common characteristic is that these agreements are not traditional, legally binding treaties, but flexible statements of intent that rely on the goodwill of each participating government for their implementation, with only the embarrassment of peer criticism as a soft stick. We now know what often happens when states change government: they abandon their commitments unilaterally, undermining the purpose that led to their often arduous conclusion in the first place.

Other initiatives of the Annan years and thereafter, often hailed as major reforms, also reflected a similar logic. This was the case with the UN Global Compact that brings closer to the UN thousands of private companies that agree to abide by the compact's 10 principles.[30] Again, the point of departure is basically accepted that powerful actors do not want to be bound by legal obligations and enforceable rules, but they are needed as partners of the UN in global governance. So they are enticed through preferential arrangements that partly renege on previously established legal commitments and enforceable treaties by shrinking them to a few brief and flexible principles. "If you cannot beat them, join them," or "speaking the language of the private sector and showing it is profitable to be nice," has been the prevailing UN approach, an effort to make the private sector co-responsible for the sustainable stewardship of our planet. This situation has resulted in high-level corporate engagement with the UN, along with the concept of corporate social responsibility (CSR) and modest implementation actions. The cost of blurring the roles between the UN, as the guardian of human and labor rights, environmental, and other rules, on the one hand, and the entrepreneurial world, on the other, is only now becoming clear, for those who want to see it. Along with the moral permissiveness that has penetrated, the purported benefits have not materialized, as illustrated by the intensifying climate challenge and ever-increasing inequalities, to mention two key parameters of measuring success in this case.[31]

The UN's reputation and honor are saved on those not-so-frequent occasions when an intergovernmental or expert body or person rises up to the expected moral standards and speaks the language of truth on key issues confronting humanity. The Intergovernmental Panel on Climate Change (IPCC), despite its mixed scientific-political character and past management issues, can be said to be one of them, as it has clearly pointed to the causes of and the required action for addressing climate change. Bold have also been the findings by Olivier de Schutter in his *Final Report: The Transformative Potential of the Right to Food* that concluded his mandate as UN special rapporteur for the right to food,[32] and of Agnes Callamard, UN special rapporteur on extrajudicial, summary, or arbitrary killings, who looked into the murder of Saudi journalist Kemal Khashoggi at the Saudi Consulate in Istanbul in October 2018.[33] However, they are lonely voices, especially the individuals concerned, without follow-up to their reports and without many followers in their footsteps.

A more solid institutional success for the UN has been the establishment of goals, namely the MDGs and the successor SDGs. The former were extracted at Annan's initiative from the Millennium Declaration adopted by world leaders in September 2000. The UN High-Level Panel on Global Sustainability recommended the latter,[34] which small and medium-sized countries, notably Colombia, pushed for, and which were finally included in the 2030 Agenda for Sustainable Development adopted by world leaders in September 2015 in New York. This agreement reflected a protracted negotiation process prescribed by the UN Conference on Sustainable Development (Rio+20). A series of indicators and periodic reports are supposed to keep track of implementation, which is reviewed by the UN's HLPF, an arrangement that will hopefully prove its value in practice over time.

A positive sign is that the SDGs and their representation in the form of a colorful wheel have attracted people's attention and offered public and private bodies and civil society an organizing methodology and rallying cry for action. However, the mobilization of the resources necessary to implement the SDGs is lagging, and the role of the UN itself in financing for development remains very limited in practice, amounting to a few billion dollars compared to the trillions actually needed.[35]

Future options for the UN and global governance

Almost as soon as he took office in January 2017, Secretary-General Guterres embarked on a major reform effort, aiming to construct "a 21st-century United Nations focused more on people and less on process, more on delivery and less on bureaucracy." For the purposes of this Handbook, the most relevant emphasis of his three-pronged reform initiative was a revamping of the UN development system's (UNDS's) country team approach. The two other areas of reform concerned improvements in peace operations and special political missions with a functional merging of the Departments of Political Affairs and Peace Operations, and management reforms.[36] At the same time, he had to deal with an increasingly precarious situation in the finances of the organization, due to arrears in the payment of assessed contributions by member states.[37] The results will take time to show. The overall sense, though, is that some needed rationalization of the UN's operational structures in the field and headquarters has been brought about through these reforms but the much-needed strategic vision that will carry the UN into the future is still missing.[38]

On similar occasions in the past, reform was mostly about putting the house in order and reshuffling the internal cards to favor the position of the newly installed Secretariat leadership team and to please major contributors with a display of the intention to heighten efficiency. At the same time, undermining the Secretariat's independence and autonomy as one of the principal organs of the UN has continued, through high-level political appointments and reduced human and material resources. One cannot expect many things from this process, or from the decades-long and inconclusive reform process for the increasingly dysfunctional Security Council.

The future of the UN, the UNDS, and UN-led global governance seems to be hanging in the balance. If the attacks on multilateralism continue, with more withdrawals from treaties and other legal instruments by the United States and other countries, the future seems ominous. If

UN bodies and the Secretariat continue to prove ineffective, prioritizing political and institutional self-preservation or even playing up expectations that they cannot fulfill—for example, the UN Framework Convention on Climate Change (UNFCCC) vis-à-vis the climate challenge[39]—the UN's status will keep diminishing. In the event of such a "death by a thousand cuts" spiral, it will be difficult to tell when the UN was dealt the fatal blow, but the first withdrawal of a major country would be a clear sign. Alternatively, under leaders such as US President Trump, Turkish President Reccep Tayyip Erdogan, Indian Prime Minister Narendra Modi, Hungarian Prime Minister Viktor Orban, and the Philippines' President Rodrigo Duterte, the UN could gradually be turned into a "Community of Populist Autocracies" or "Community of Illiberal Democracies," to paraphrase "the Community of Democracies," a group of like-minded countries established under US leadership in a previous period of ideological confrontation at the UN.[40]

Could either of the above scenarios seal the fate of the UN and global governance? In both cases the few remaining checks and balances in the conduct of international affairs would be removed, with increasingly volatile alliances and brinkmanship acts taking centerstage, in response to leaders' whims and countries' electoral calendars. Disaster seems the likely outcome in both cases.

Despite the multiplying negative signs, it is wrong to surrender to pessimism; we should instead strive to reverse the situation and come up with a positive (and practical) vision for the future. Recognizing the concerns that lead to national populism and the insecurity caused by globalization gone astray, the need becomes apparent for a new, people-centered narrative of unity-in-diversity and hope. Such a narrative should create the normative base for addressing globally shared challenges such as poverty, disease, inequality, and climate change—essentially the 17 SDGs—rather than attempting to homogenize the world or prop up economic and financial globalization that increases inequalities further.

A more proactive, independent, and modern UN and UNDS, characterized by objectivity but also empathy, guided by considerations of the broadest common good and having the courage to actually express it, could play a key role, both in narrative dissemination and implementation oversight. This UN system would actually serve as the central node in a network of governance structures that permeate human society from the global to the local and everything in between. Clearly a major reorientation of the UN is required, so that it convincingly plays the role of normative center, convener of authorities and people, principal steward, and overseer of the management of the global commons, both traditional and new (including the atmosphere, the oceans, and outer space, but also the global economy and cyberspace). This should be done not only through intergovernmental organs but also the Secretariat, thematic expert groups, and civil society.

Concrete steps to achieve the above could include, in no specific order:

- a coherent, UN system-wide mechanism to monitor and pronounce on human and planetary well-being, with a periodic "State of the Planet Report" issued by the Secretary-General;
- departure from measuring and pursuing growth to measuring and pursuing human well-being in a context of respect for different traditions and individual freedoms (a human development approach), complete with regulation that brings this into the functioning of the global financial sector;
- revamping of the Security Council to include the major "continental size" federal states and regional integration entities;
- integration into the UN structures of limited-participation bodies, notably the G-20, as an Economic Security Council;

- mobilization of additional resources in support of the UN and UNDS's work by allowing citizens around the world to contribute through tax-deductible donations and/or by transferring a small part of globally enforced taxes (e.g., on cross-border financial transactions, social media, and other Internet platforms) to the world body, with reinforced transparency and oversight in their use;
- establishment of consultative assemblies that the Secretary-General and General Assembly President would periodically convene—e.g., parliamentarians, scientists, religious leaders, artists, sportspeople;
- increased use of the UN system's country presence to build capacity and otherwise support the implementation of commitments by governments at regional, national, and local level by sharing knowledge and good practices from around the world;
- worldwide observance of one or more symbolic global holidays (e.g., Universal Day of Peace, Global Thanksgiving, or Earth Day) that go beyond today's numerous international days;
- a symbolic and practical representation of global citizenship and joint ownership of the global commons, something like equal "shares of the planet" for each and every human being.[41]

The UN's 75th anniversary in 2020 is as good an opportunity as any to move in this direction. It remains to be seen where such visionary leadership may come from, if it comes at all.

NOTES

1 Previous attempts at UN reform have been studied in detail, including by this author: Georgios Kostakos, "UN Reform: The Post-Cold War World Organization," in *The United Nations in the New World Order—The World Organization at Fifty*, ed. Dimitris Bourantonis and Jarrod Wiener (London: MacMillan Press Ltd, 1995), 64–80; and "About Form and Function: An Overview and Typology of UN Reforms since the 1990s," *Global Society* 32, no. 2 (2018): 176–197.

2 Roger Eatwell and Matthew Goodwin, *National Populism: The Revolt against Liberal Democracy* (London: Penguin Random House UK, 2018).

3 Yuval Noah Harari, *Homo Deus: A Brief History of Tomorrow* (London: Harvill Secker, 2015).

4 Eatwell and Goodwin, *National Populism*.

5 Kenneth Roth, "World's Autocrats Face Rising Resistance," in *Human Rights Watch: World Repot 2019 (events of 2018)* (New York: Human Rights Watch, 2019), 1–13.

6 See, for example, Ana Swanson, "The World Today Looks a Bit Like It Did before World War I—But What Does That Mean?" *World Economic Forum* in collaboration with *Wonk Blog*, 5 January 2017, www.weforum.org/agenda/2017/01/why-the-world-looks-a-bit-like-it-did-before-world-war-i.

7 Stephen C. Schlesinger, *Act of Creation: The Founding of the United Nations* (Boulder, CO: Westview Press, 2003).

8 Rick Duke, "Leaving the Paris Agreement Is a Bad Deal for the United States," *Foreign Policy*, 19 May 2019, https://foreignpolicy.com/2019/05/19/leaving-the-paris-agreement-is-a-bad-deal-for-the-united-states.

9 "INF Nuclear Treaty: US Pulls Out of Cold War-Era Pact with Russia," *BBC News*, 2 August 2019, www.bbc.com/news/world-us-canada-49198565.

10 Thomas Adamson, "U.S. and Israel Officially Withdraw from UNESCO," *PBS News Hour* and *Associated Press*, 1 January 2019, www.pbs.org/newshour/politics/u-s-and-israel-officially-withdraw-from-unesco.

11 Laura Hillard and Amanda Shendruk, "Funding the United Nations: What Impact Do U.S. Contributions Have on UN Agencies and Programs?" Council on Foreign Relations, New York, 2 April 2019, www.cfr.org/article/funding-united-nations-what-impact-do-us-contributions-have-un-agencies-and-programs; and Mark Leon Goldberg, "The White House Is Trying to Circumvent Congress to Strip Funding for Diplomacy and Development," UN Dispatch, 6 August 2019, www.undispatch.com/the-white-house-is-trying-to-make-and-end-run-around-congress-to-strip-funding-for-diplomacy-and-development.

12 Kostakos, "UN Reform."

13 *Remarks by President Trump to the 73rd Session of the United Nations General Assembly*, New York, 25 September 2018, www.whitehouse.gov/briefings-statements/remarks-president-trump-73rd-session-united-nations-general-assembly-new-york-ny.

14 "Trump: What Does the US Do for NATO in Europe?" *BBC News*, 3 June 2019, www.bbc.com/news/world-44717074.

15 Axel Berger, "G20 Summit in Osaka—The Drought Years of International Cooperation," *Diplomatisches Magazin*, German Development Institute, 11 June 2019, www.diplomatisches-magazin.de/en/article/deutsches-institut-fuer-entwicklungspolitik-der-g20-gipfel-in-osaka-die-duerrejahre-internationaler.

16 Andrea Willige, "The World's Top Economy: The US vs China in Five Charts," *World Economic Forum*, 5 December 2016, www.weforum.org/agenda/2016/12/the-world-s-top-economy-the-us-vs-china-in-five-charts.

17 *Summary of Statement by H.E. Mr. XI Jinping, President of China, at the General Debate of the UN General Assembly*, 28 September 2018, https://gadebate.un.org/en/70/china.

18 *President Xi's Speech at the World Economic Forum*, Davos, Switzerland, 17 January 2017, www.weforum.org/agenda/2017/01/full-text-of-xi-jinping-keynote-at-the-world-economic-forum.

19 *Keynote Speech by H.E. Yang Jiechi, Member of the Political Bureau of the CPC Central Committee and Director of the Office of the Central Commission for Foreign Affairs*, "Working for a Community with a Shared Future for Mankind by Promoting International Cooperation and Multilateralism," 55th Munich Security Conference, 16 February 2019, www.fmprc.gov.cn/mfa_eng/zxxx_662805/t1638512.shtml.

20 Washington also feels defensive and squeezed at the UN, especially in the General Assembly, where it finds itself in the minority, occasionally with very few others, on issues such as Israel and Palestine and the embargo on Cuba.

21 Maurice Bertrand, "The Historical Development of Efforts to Reform the UN," in *United Nations, Divided World*, ed. Adam Roberts and Benedict Kingsbury (New York: Oxford University Press Inc., 1993), 423.

22 Council on Foreign Relations, "China's Massive Belt and Road Initiative," Backgrounder by Andrew Chatzky and James McBride, 21 May 2019, www.cfr.org/backgrounder/chinas-massive-belt-and-road-initiative.

23 BRICS Information Portal, "History of BRICS," http://infobrics.org/page/history-of-brics.

24 Sébastien Treyer and Lola Vallejo, "What Momentum Has the G7 Given to Sustainable Development?" *IDDRI Blogpost*, 4 September 2019, www.iddri.org/en/publications-and-events/blog-post/what-momentum-has-g7-given-sustainable-development.

25 Tom Chodor, "The G-20 since the Global Financial Crisis: Neither Hegemony nor Collectivism," *Global Governance* 23, no. 2 (2017): 205–223.

26 See Alfonso Medinilla, Pauline Veron, and Vera Mazzara, "EU–UN Cooperation: Confronting Change in the Multilateral System," *ECDPM Discussion Paper No. 260*, September 2019, https://ecdpm.org/publications/eu-un-cooperation-confronting-change-in-the-multilateral-system.

27 Ursula von der Leyen, "A Union That Strives for More—My Agenda for Europe," presented to the European Parliament on 16 July 2019, https://ec.europa.eu/commission/sites/beta-political/files/political-guidelines-next-commission_en.pdf.

28 See Thomas G. Weiss and Rorden Wilkinson, *Rethinking Global Governance* (Cambridge: Polity, 2019).

29 See, for example, Matilda Hald, "Hope and Despair at the HLPF 2019—Reflections on the High-Level Political Forum (HLPF) 2019," *Dag Hammarskjöld Foundation Blog*, www.daghammarskjold.se/hope-and-despair-at-hlfp-2019.

30 United Nations Global Compact, "The Ten Principles of the UN Global Compact," www.unglobalcompact.org/what-is-gc/mission/principles.

31 A critical review of the state of global governance for sustainability is found in the Global Civil Society Report on the 2030 Agenda and the SDGs, "Spotlight on Sustainable Development 2019: Reshaping Governance for Sustainability," www.2030spotlight.org.

32 *Report of the Special Rapporteur on the right to food, Olivier De Schutter—Final Report: The Transformative Potential of the Right to Food*, UN document A/HRC/25/57, 24 January 2014.

33 *Annex to the Report of the Special Rapporteur on Extrajudicial, Summary or Arbitrary Executions: Investigation into the Unlawful Death of Mr. Jamal Khashoggi* (UN document A/HRC/41/CRP.1), 19 June 2019.

34 United Nations Secretary-General's High-Level Panel on Global Sustainability, *Resilient People, Resilient Planet: A Future Worth Choosing* (New York: United Nations, 2012), 72–73.

35 See Dag Hammarskjöld Foundation 2019, "Financing the UN Development System: Time for Hard Choices," https://docs.daghammarskjold.se/financing-the-un-development-system-2019; and Fiona Bayat-Renoux, "The United Nations Secretary-General's Strategy for Financing the 2030 Agenda for Sustainable Development," Dag Hammarskjöld Foundation, 2019, www.daghammarskjold.se/wp-content/uploads/2019/08/financial-instr-report-2019-interactive.pdf#page=74.

36 The UN has a website dedicated to reform: UN, "United to Reform," https://reform.un.org.

37 Hong Xiao, "UN Running Out of Funds, *China Daily*, 24 June 2019, http://global.chinadaily.com.cn/a/201906/24/WS5d0fbf53a3103dbf14329bce.html.

38 Bertrand Ramcharan, "António Guterres's Strategy for Modernizing the UN," *Global Governance* 25, no. 1 (2019): 13–21.

39 See Georgios Kostakos, "Barking Up the Wrong Tree: What If the COP Cannot Deliver Us from Climate Change?" *Katoikos*, 10 December 2019, www.katoikos.eu/dialogue/barking-up-the-wrong-tree-what-if-the-cop-cannot-deliver-us-from-climate-change.html.

40 The "Community of Democracies" group still exists, online at least, and has as its mission "to advance and protect democratic freedoms, strengthen democratic institutions, and expand political participation," with the abovementioned leaders' countries as members of its Governing Council; see https://community-democracies.org.

41 Some of these proposals have been analyzed in Foundation for Global Governance and Sustainability (FOGGS), "Proposals for a Modern, Effective, Ethical and People-Centred United Nations," Discussion Paper, 27 January 2019, www.foggs.org/wp-content/uploads/2019/01/FOGGS-UN2100-Discussion-Paper27-Jan-2019.pdf.

ADDITIONAL READING

Roger Eatwell and Matthew Goodwin, *National Populism: The Revolt against Liberal Democracy* (London: Penguin Random House UK, 2018).

Yuval Noah Harari, *Homo Deus: A Brief History of Tomorrow* (London: Harvill Secker, 2015).

Georgios Kostakos, "About Form and Function: An Overview and Typology of UN Reforms since the 1990s," *Global Society* 32, no. 2 (2018): 176–197.

Mark Mazower, *Governing the World: The History of an Idea* (London: Penguin Books, 2012).

Thomas G. Weiss and Rorden Wilkinson, *Rethinking Global Governance* (Cambridge: Polity, 2019).

21

REFLECTIONS

Prospects for the UN development system

Stephen Browne and Thomas G. Weiss

Fundamental questions underlie our project, but that this Handbook has not posed until now: with the rise of new nationalisms and with multilateralism under siege, is the UN development system (UNDS) still required? If it is, for what is it really needed and with what comparative advantage? Which of its functions are still pertinent and important, and which are not? Is it fit for purpose?

While the preceding chapters have provided some answers, they certainly have not rendered these questions redundant. This Handbook suggests that the UNDS must continue to change substantially—even "transform" itself—if it is to remain pertinent, useful, and necessary. This reality has become obvious, all the more so in light of the growing number of alternative sources of development cooperation and the rebalancing of global power and influence.

The world body is in practice a balancing act among "three UNs": the First UN of member states, the Second UN of organizations and their secretariats, and the Third UN of wider civil society embodied in the opening words of the Charter: "WE, THE PEOPLES." The UN's effectiveness is determined largely by the relationship among the three UNs, a balance that has evolved over three-quarters of a century.

This final chapter examines the main five functions of the UNDS and asks whether they continue to be relevant, and if so, how. The four ideational functions are global policy-making; research, dissemination, and advocacy; technical norm generation; and goal-setting. The fifth function is operational and consists of technical assistance, training, and other services.

Global policy: an indispensable forum?

Climate change—in addition to such other pressing global development crises as pandemics, water scarcity, and resource degradation in addition to such security challenges as proliferation and terrorism—emphasizes the UN's recognized incomparable role as the globe's only universal and hence indispensable forum. If global problems require global solutions, there literally is one option: the only convener with universal membership is the United Nations and its family of organizations. However, while the world organization facilitates useful conversations, its predictable and sclerotic processes often hinder progress. The clashes and disharmony among and within the three UNs exemplify the cacophony of voices and variety of interests that are often camouflaged by outdated categories, including continental groupings in addition to the divide between the North and Global South.

Among many governments in the First UN, there is a deficit of genuine multilateral commitment. Some powerful member states are indifferent, or worse, to multilateralism; others are committed, but on their own patronizing terms; still others look to the UN for solutions and support but resist any sacrifice of sovereignty. The Second UN suffers from a deficit of leadership, including the willingness to run the risk of irritating some or even any of its 193 masters. Ruffling diplomatic feathers is required to persuade member states to delegate more responsibility without undue interference in its inner workings, and from a willingness to confront the disingenuous rhetoric so prevalent across the North and Global South. While criticism at audible decibel levels is more likely from the Third UN, in many countries that suffer from a democracy-deficit the messages of civil society are muted.

The Second UN has nevertheless encouraged international NGOs to play a more active role in global debates, helping widen public scrutiny of intergovernmental discussions. Civil society participation has been formalized since the early 1990s through nine "major groups." They are invited to participate in UN consultations, even while member states jealously guard their prerogatives for the final approval of any texts or agreements. Ex post, where it is given the wherewithal to do so, civil society can act as an effective monitor of the First UN—that is, of government compliance with UN decisions. Nonetheless, there is much room to improve the Third UN's inputs into independent monitoring of performance, especially of the Sustainable Development Goals (SDGs). A model of sorts is in the global debate on a political and technical subject such as climate change, for which the clamor from NGOs and the findings of the Intergovernmental Panel on Climate Change (IPCC) have transformed the conversation and transcended national boundaries.

Research, dissemination, and advocacy

In the early days, the United Nations was a central point of departure for pioneering research on economic development; it attracted some of the most original and creative minds to New York, Geneva, and Santiago de Chile. Three-quarters of a century later, this function remains an asset on the UN's balance sheet. Unquestionably, as well as inspiring economic policy thinking, the UN's work also stimulated parallel research activities in numerous academic and research institutions worldwide. The growing aid business—comprising many multilateral, bilateral, and private organizations—drew on these expanding research activities outside the UN as well as stimulating such capacities within the UNDS.

While the widening domain of development became enriched by the growth in research capabilities, a measure of redundancy in the UN was inevitable, particularly as many of the best minds migrated to other centers of excellence, while predictable bureaucratic inertia set in. The continuing rationales for UN research required originality. It thus is important to distinguish between a healthy competition that spawns alternative viewpoints, on the one hand, and a wasteful overlap and redundancy that reflects counterproductive turf-battles, on the other.

One example of the UN's unusual role is its research on demography, which involves the collation of reliable and authoritative sources of data and the calculation of population sizes and projections. Data and research on global warming and its consequences by the IPCC is another example, which provides the global basis for effective policy advocacy. Similarly, the UN specialized agencies also collect and collate data and information in their respective fields—including labor and employment (ILO), industrial production (UNIDO), education (UNESCO), health (WHO), and agriculture (FAO). While these are not the sole sources, they are the basis for much global messaging and advocacy. Other UN organizations produce state-of-the-world reports. One of the best known is UNICEF's annual *State of the World's Children* that serves both for advocacy and as a benchmark for measuring progress on children's rights. Among other authoritative UN reports are the *World Drug Report* of the Office for Drugs and Crime, and the five-yearly *World's Women* reports of the Department of Economic and Social Affairs (DESA).

Arguably, the best example of research originality, with policy and public-relations traction emanating from the UN, is the human development paradigm. It came at the right time but from the wrong place. It proclaimed an alternative path in the 1990s to the then pre-eminent neoliberal doctrine of the Bretton Woods institutions (BWIs). However, coming from an essentially operational arm of the United Nations—the UN Development Programme (UNDP)—the paradigm gained only modest traction in intergovernmental debates, particularly because the analysis unapologetically referred to the development performance of member states. The annual global *Human Development Report* (HDR) was a rare example of the Second UN leading the First UN, with some cheerleading from the Third UN. The reports were influential but led to questions about the independence and objectiveness of secretariats: to what extent could UN research be original? Over time, the independence of the Second UN, the focus of this volume, has diminished, partly as a result of merit yielding to politics in the appointment of senior staff. The influence of member states—or in this instance, of a single country—has grown with the rising prominence of China, whose nationals have headed DESA since 2007.

The absence of a genuine New York consensus, in juxtaposition to the so-called Washington neoliberal consensus, has left the UN without a comprehensive alternative focus for its development thinking. Much research on global trends has consequently tried to retrofit alternative interpretations to reflect available data. The numerous reports published by DESA and the UN Conference on Trade and Development (UNCTAD) question, but do not always fundamentally challenge, economic orthodoxy or conventional wisdom about the winners and losers of globalization.

There is much overlap of research conducted by the UNDS. Both DESA and UNCTAD produce annual reports on global macroeconomic trends. Confusingly, DESA—marketing itself as the "home of sustainable development"—also produced almost simultaneously *The Sustainable Development Goals Report 2019* and the *Global Sustainable Development Report 2019* for the SDG summit (see below). There are numerous other examples of unhelpful duplication and pure redundancy, both across the UN and even within organizational members. In preparing for the Millennium Summit in 2000, the UN Secretariat brought out its *We, the Peoples* report, just one day before UNDP's *Overcoming Human Poverty* report appeared on the other side of Manhattan's First Avenue; both, in fact, covered similar subject matter. In the same year, UNDP produced its newest edition of the HDR, which anchored development firmly in the human rights agenda. These reports were all high quality; but they were launched separately, none even acknowledging the existence of the others. Still less did they put forward a coherent UN development approach.

In only rare cases has the publication of a regular UN report ceased. For instance, the UN Economic Commission for Europe (ECE) stopped publication of its annual economic survey of the region in 2005. This resulted after pressure from the European Union, which considered that the reports duplicated its own research. The comparative advantage of all UN publications should be scrutinized from time to time. It may be argued that the production of multiple UN reports reflects a healthy breadth of research inquiry. If so, such a justification makes sense. However, the reason for producing so much material, which is not always up to date and of varying quality, often has more to do with bureaucratic inertia than a response to felt needs and an objective evaluation of quality. Every publication begins with a mandate, consisting of an official request through an intergovernmental body. However, the UNDS rarely undertakes market surveys of its massive documentary output to explore the continuing value of its publications. Since most output is now online, the UN could and should measure the value of its reports through the number of downloads and questionnaires. Where demand falls below a prescribed threshold, which is set according to some notion of cost-effectiveness, publications should be comprehensively revised or terminated.

The plethora of reports that flow from the UNDS is another manifestation of the disparate nature of the development family and its inability to forge coherent policies. For the UNDS to deliver as one (DaO), it must also think more coherently and act with less duplication. That objective would be facilitated if there were a single, managed portal for its extensive research and information output.

Technical norms

The determination of common technical standards was at the root of the first public international unions in the nineteenth century; they can well be considered the foundations of what eventually became the UN development system. This function remains a strength of the UN system. The International Telegraph Union (now International Telecommunication Union, also ITU) and Universal Postal Union (UPU) were created in the nineteenth century to facilitate international communications; other post-war UN organizations, including the International Maritime Organization (IMO) and the International Civil Aviation Organization (ICAO), subsequently established global standards for international transportation. All these organizations were incorporated into the UN system after 1945 and have remained the principal custodians of technical standards in their respective fields.

At their inception, the intergovernmental composition of the technical organizations would have seemed inevitable. Countries, including their private sectors, were represented by governments and only they could enshrine global standards in national legislation. However, the UN has not retained a monopoly of technical standard-setting. In the variegated and complex area of industrial standards, for example, national bodies came together as the war ended in 1945 to form the International Organization for Standardization (ISO). It is not a UN organization and although most of its membership is composed of national standards bodies, it calls itself an "NGO"; it forms a bridge between public and private sectors. The ISO works by voluntary consensus and exemplifies a hybrid organization in which relevant parties—governments, producers, and consumers—have a say. Its ambitions have stretched beyond its original "nuts-and-bolts" (literally) concerns to encompass work processes and quality management, environmental regulation, and corporate social responsibility.

The lesson of the ISO experience for the UN is that standard-setting is not an exclusive prerogative of governments. To ensure that technical standards are widely accepted, and "consensual," UN organizations should systematically involve relevant non-state parties in their norm-setting deliberations—that is, a job for all three United Nations.

Goal-setting

From the First UN Development Decade onwards (the 1960s), the UN has defined progress and fostered development through goal-setting; this function remains an essential contribution. That initial decade was characterized by goals of growth—5 percent for developing countries— and transfers of resources. Governments agreed a target for official development assistance (ODA) of 0.7 percent of the gross (later national) development product (later income, or GNI) of developed countries, thereby setting up an artificial relationship between growth performance and aid generosity. While it is difficult to establish any straightforward causality, the growth and aid nexus strongly influenced UN debates, in which inadequate ODA was the constant scapegoat for poor performance.

UN global conferences subsequently set goals for education, health, and the environment. Several of these formed the basis of the first comprehensive development agenda of the UN: the Millennium Development Goals (MDGs) that were extracted from the Millennium Declaration of the 2000 World Summit. This was an example of the Second UN helping to build on the precedents of past intergovernmental agreements by the member states of the First UN.

The 2030 Agenda was agreed in 2015 and based on 17 Sustainable Development Goals (SDGs); as noted, it was a point of departure and has provided a focus for this Handbook. The SDGs, in contrast to the MDGs, were the outcome of a protracted process directed substantially by the First UN of member states but reflecting extensive consultations with representations from the Second UN and Third UN. Many have praised the universal aspiration of the SDGs. Ultimately, however, the First UN had the loudest voice; many of the most crucial political dimensions of development thus were toned down—almost to exclusion in the case of such issues as poor governance, religious intolerance, and armed conflict. There were no references to state fragility, forced migration, human rights abuses, and the corrosive consequences of corruption and capital flight; all have undermined development performance and could and should be measured as part of the development agenda. Only one goal (16), promoted mainly by the countries of the North, mentioned the essential political and institutional underpinnings of development. Subsequently, some of the missing items—especially human rights promotion—were referred to in the preamble to the goals, but were not included among the 169 indicators.

The role of the Second UN—and particularly DESA, acting as the SDG secretariat—was largely passive in the formulation of the goals. Officials provided limited original research input, and governments largely ignored attempts to constrain the number of targets and indicators and establish priorities and sequencing. Thus, while agreement among 193 countries can be viewed as a success, the realization of the 2030 Agenda will depend on the effectiveness of the Second UN and of the Third UN in helping to configure the agenda at the national level and in objective monitoring and reporting.

Goal-setting with aspirational yet attainable and specific indicators within a specified period is a legitimate activity for the UNDS; it is much better than an agenda couched in vague outcomes, however well meaning, or one that reflects unrealistic targets mainly with rhetorical appeal. The idea of attaching targets, indicators, and time-frames to goals is closer to a genuine action plan. Many chapters of this Handbook have noted that the SDGs are less than ideal—a view to which the editors subscribe. A group of independent development experts would have fashioned a more coherent agenda around some harder political realities with fewer targets accompanied by specified mechanisms for autonomous monitoring. However, unlike the MDGs, there certainly is a high degree of interest and (at least verbal) commitment to the 2030 Agenda on the part not just of the First UN of member states, but also of the Second UN and— because of the strong sustainability content—global civil society and the private sector. It is important that the Second UN engages more in the implementation of the SDGs than it did in the preceding MDGs; but this higher level of engagement exposes the UN organizations to blame if the goals are not achieved.

UN operations: technical assistance and training

With the support of major donors, the UNDS's organizations have expanded their operations continuously since the 1940s, but especially since the 1990s; while this function is of diminishing pertinence for many developing countries, it nonetheless remains essential for many, for which the growth in resources is essential. Donors earmark by theme or geographic destination the vast majority of these projects. Although nominally responding to the strategic frameworks of each organization, many of these projects are aligned closely with the development priorities in donor countries and their parliaments. This practice effectively gives a bilateral slant to assistance, with the UNDS acting more as an implementing mechanism (or consultancy firm) than an independent source of development cooperation. Supply-driven availability of resources fuels turf-battles and unhealthy competition among UN organizations. With funding coming from for-profit sources, other dangers arise that also threaten the autonomy of the UNDS. Because funders like to maintain their links with their preferred organizations and topics, widespread donor patronage inhibits the objective evaluation of UN technical assistance. Proposals to establish meaningful system-wide evaluations, which would help to determine both the relevance and effectiveness of UN assistance, have never materialized.

The willingness of UNDS organizations to pursue and accept seemingly ever-increasing amounts of earmarked funding has also produced ever-widening mandates, resulting in unnecessary overlap and redundancy in addition to counterproductive competition over resources. As this Handbook has made clear, the UNDS has always lacked a strong center or "brain," which could have attenuated centrifugal forces and pulled the system more tightly together. In 2006, a high-level panel on reform of the UNDS found "policy incoherence, duplication and operational ineffectiveness" across the system—the latest in a long line of such laments about fragmentation in reports that have regularly emanated from commissions, panels, experts, scholars, the media, and practitioners since the landmark 1969 Jackson overview of the development system.

The latest proposed solution was for the UNDS to "deliver as one" (DaO) at the country level, with a single leader, program, office, and funding source. DaO has continued to focus efforts on the reform of UN operations; it has resulted in a degree of convergence in the field. The idea originally stemmed from a panel representing the First UN, but not all program countries have fully embraced the concept because many governments prefer to maintain their relations with individual organizations, rather than a single UN. For donors, multiple patronage through individual UN organizations has its place, and the largest members of the UNDS often can pursue fundraising more effectively by going it alone. The governments of the Global South and their ministries are in turn patronized by different parts of the UNDS, leading to a reluctance to support any reduction or consolidation of the system lest resources be reduced. Thus, reform has not stopped the proliferation of either fundraising efforts or even the numbers of country offices (15 or more in many countries), which have continued to grow. Such proliferation clearly exacerbates the challenge of integration.

The future direction of development cooperation is clear. As a source of technical assistance— its original *raison d'être*—the UNDS has diminishing pertinence for developing countries graduating to middle- and upper-middle-income status. At the same time, it continues to have a comparative advantage in the poorest and most fragile countries (which often are recovering from armed conflict or are conflict-prone). However, the UNDS continues also with a universal appeal as a propagator of global norms and standards, which could justify its (far more limited) presence in more advanced developing countries—and some observers argue as well for an enhanced presence in developed countries if the pursuit of SDGs is genuinely to be universal. UNDS operations should therefore be geared to assisting countries in complying with the norms that they have agreed as UN member states: for instance, with UNICEF supporting the Convention on the Rights of the Child; the World Health Organization on health standards; the International Labour Organization on employment conditions; and the UN Educational, Scientific and Cultural Organization on school curricula.

Logically, therefore, the UNDS's operational activities should increasingly focus on support in fragile and conflict-prone states, where it is required to work in close conjunction with peace operations and humanitarian relief. The UN system as a whole reveals its operational value and comparative advantage when it can successfully combine the full range of its functions—arguably a range of expertise unavailable elsewhere. By the same token, the UNDS should eliminate its operational capacity in at least half of developing countries, using the same logic that it has no operational role in the North.

Final thoughts

This final chapter has sought to draw together the main themes from the preceding analyses in order to provide answers to our existential questions. It has drawn on the wisdom of our contributors from the preceding pages, but it also necessarily reflects our own views. We have organized our reflections around the main ideational and operational functions of the UNDS. Our respective careers have reflected a firm commitment to multilateral approaches to international problem-solving, not unquestioningly in support of all multilateral efforts but of those that make the most normative, operational, and economic sense.

This chapter reflects the simplification of messages from the chapters; no one would dispute the urgency to alter substantially the way that the UNDS does business. Earlier, we referred to the need for "transformation" of the UNDS—indeed, that is a theme song for many contributors. While this book appears on the UN's 75th anniversary and such change is impossible in the short run, it is not an impossible aspiration for the UN's 100th anniversary. If we are wrong and the status quo continues, the world organization may not have disappeared by that time but will be so marginal that it will be of no consequence.

These pages illustrate in various ways and to varying extents the four major constraints on UN reform: pressures from member states, competition from other multilateral sources, the growing complexity of problems, and organizational inertia. The first three are impediments that are beyond the scope of this volume and perhaps beyond political plausibility. However, the fourth is the target of our analysis because it is not an insuperable challenge but subject to alteration—not readily but feasibly, with commitments from the First UN and the Second UN. A useful point of departure is modesty mixed with an informed sense of comparative advantage—to realize that the UN cannot be all things to all 193 member states or to all people all of the time.

Both of us in previous publications have cited Reinhold Niebuhr's "Serenity Prayer." To paraphrase that prominent theologian, UN member states and its civil servants should focus their energies on those aspects of the world organization that they can alter and recognize the ones that they cannot. That is this book's and the editors' bottom line.

INDEX

Page numbers in **bold** denote tables, those in *italics* denote figures.

"2015 Review of the United Nations Peacebuilding Architecture" 109, 111
2030 Agenda for Sustainable Development 81, 91, 96, 100, 112–13, 123, 140, 165, 167, 170, 177–8, 180, 238–9, 249, 263

AAAA *see* Addis Ababa Action Agenda
ACABQ *see* Advisory Committee on Administrative and Budgetary Questions
academics 138–9, 184
accountability 32, 34–5, 61–2, 64, 68, 70, 75, 122–3, 128–9, 132, 157, 170–1, 194, 221–31, 233; corporate 92; government 189; internal 225, 259; mechanisms 62, 194, 258; multilateral 168; organizational 259; public 77; schemes 125; structures 229; system-wide 221, 232
Accra Conference 2008 188
Active Learning Network for Accountability and Performance in Humanitarian Action 122
activists 62, 64
activities 26–9, 110, 112–14, 136–7, 151–9, 165–8, 170–1, 178–80, 210–12, 221–2, 230–1, 238–9, 264–5, 267–8, 270–2; donor-funded 271; economic 216; excluded 179; external 267; legitimate 290; reinforcing 179, 255–6
ad hoc conferences **21**, 22, 71
Addis Ababa Action Agenda 25, 32, 143, 189, 263
Advisory Committee on Administrative and Budgetary Questions 224
Advisory Group of Experts 99, 109
advocacy 3, 5, 17, 19, 34, 59, 68, 74, 78, 115, 117, 128, 159, 279, 286–8; business-led 170; groups 112; roles 39, 193; work 75
affected populations 121–3, 125–6, 129–33

Africa 12, 35, 47–8, 58, 72, 90, 136, 200, 204, 242, 266, 269; economic development of 47; and the emergence of China as the largest investor in 48; and the export of migrants to 47; and the joint African–Chinese–European partnership to develop 48; and the knowledge-sharing networks for planners and statisticians of 242; and Latin America 88, 199–200, 204; and the UN Economic Commission for Africa 12–13, 17, 19, 88, 200, 242
African Union 114
Africans 47–8, 115, 201, 252, 267; boatloads trying to cross the Mediterranean 47; entering Europe legally and illegally 47; and the Lagos Plan of Action 200; planners and statisticians 242
agencies 17, 19, 26–7, 60, 62–3, 129, 131–2, 135, 139–40, 143–4, 172–4, 176, 254, 257, 259; donors 168, 172; executing 27; executive 38; financial 88; global 176; government 188; individual 39, 226; international 126, 131, 199; recruitment 140; semi-autonomous 257; technical 87, 271–2
agenda 23–5, 34–7, 39–41, 81–2, 91–2, 96–7, 100, 102–5, 123–5, 139–40, 184–5, 189–91, 229, 249–60, 290; ambitious 98, 257; broader 36, 116; common 255–6; competing 104; developmental 210; donor 27; economic 200; financial 199; international 37; neoliberal 16, 71; new trade 24, 35–6, 218, 252; transformative 68
Agenda for Humanity 124
agreements 3, 5, 18, 36, 38, 59–61, 63–4, 187, 192, 212, 214, 218, 280–1, 287, 290; and the Addis Ababa Action Agenda 25, 32, 143, 189, 263; binding 61; climate change 18, 21, 35, 37,

agreements *continued*
58–62, 64, 81, 180, 203, 205, 271–2, 274–7,
279–80, 282, 286–7; formal 60, 268; global 28;
and initial relationship between the UN and the
UNF 169; and the Intergovernmental Panel on
Climate Change 18, 60–1, 205, 280, 287;
international 28, 64; and the International Civil
Aviation Organization 10–11, 13, 28, 193, 289;
Kyoto Protocol 18, 61, 275; long-term strategic
160; mutual 229; negotiated 68; non-binding
142; Paris Agreement 25, 32, 60–1, 64–5, 81,
190, 263, 274–6, 279; political 229; provisional
214
agriculture 24, 168, 202, 212, 214, 239, 244, 287
aid 11–13, 15, 22–3, 62, 85, 122, 124, 126–8,
131–2, 138–9, 142, 145, 224; concessional 203;
donor 64; external 25; financial 62;
manipulation 121–2; programming 130; and
trade conditions 23; workers 126, 132
AIIB *see* Asian Infrastructure Investment Bank
ALNAP *see* Active Learning Network for
Accountability and Performance in
Humanitarian Action
Alwaleed Bin Talal Foundation 173
"America First" (Donald Trump) 274
Annan, Kofi (Secretary-General) 63, 90–1, 98,
138, 166, 169–70, 186, 188, 250, 252, 280–1
anti-multilateralism 276
appeals 85, 127–8, 171–3, 184; to individual
giving *172*; persistent 160; rhetorical 290
Arab development assistance 16
architecture 73, 99, 229; changing 4, 109;
contemporary 19; new global governance 143,
279; peacebuilding 96, 98–9, 101, 107, 109–11,
113–14, 116–17
armed conflicts 4, 35, 51–2, 69, 71, 75, 96,
98–101, 105–6, 111, 121–2, 126, 130, 132,
290–1; external 53; and peace 73; resolving 105
Asia 12–13, 50–3, 58, 204, 207
Asian financial crisis 16, 204
Asian Infrastructure Investment Bank 50, 53, 154,
204–5
Asylum Capacity Support Group 144
asylum processes 136
auditors 223, 226
audits 222–5, 229; external 222, 224; functions
222–3, 225; independent 223–4; internal 222;
and oversight committees 224

Bachelet, Michelle 77, 258
Ban Ki-moon 166, 168, 280
Bank of America 169
Bank of Japan 166
banks 12, 15, 116, 154, 198–200, 202–3, 205–7;
expanding programs of technical assistance 15;
multilateral development 155, 269; regional
development 154, 204–5, 264

Barro, Robert J. 201
BCUN *see* Business Council for the United
Nations
Beijing 50, 72, 76, 90
Beijing Conference on Women 1995 20, 71–2,
187
Belt and Road Initiative 48, 50, 278
benefits 15–16, 25, 28, 135–6, 154, 156, 158,
177–8, 233, 237, 240, 242, 244, 269–70, 272;
global 216; intangible 116; knowledge
management 236, 238; potential 174; system-
wide 215
Berg Report 1981 200
Betts, Richard 51
BHP Billiton Foundation 173–4
bilateral donors 26, 89, 265, 267–70
Bill and Melinda Gates Foundation 173
biodiversity 19, 24, 35, 57–9, 63–4, 89; assessment
of 19, 57–9, 63, 89; environmental arguments
to safeguard 64; loss 24, 35
Blair, Tony 44, 187, 280
Blundin, Donald 33
BNP Paribas 173
Board of Auditors *see also* auditors
Bolton, John 43
border guards 137
borders 43, 52, 124, 126, 137, 156, 244
brain drain 138, 140, 143
Bretton Woods Conference 1944 198
Bretton Woods institutions 2, 15, 22, 33–4, 36,
38–40, 88, 187, 199–202, 204–8, 211, 288
Brexit 52, 279
BRI *see* Belt and Road Initiative
BRICS group 50, 278
budgets 18, 25, 44–5, 54, 71, 74, 77, 165–6, 176,
223, 226, 250, 253, 257, 267; assessed 74, 167;
core 45, 159–60; global 39; long-term 62, 267;
peacekeeping 106, 117, 276; regular 81, 111,
114, 167, 257, 267, 277
bureaucracies 2, 243, 252, 281; modulating 243;
separate 210; traditional hierarchical 240
Bush, George W. 276
Business Council for the United Nations 168
Buzan, Barry 52
BWIs *see* Bretton Woods institutions

Cáceres, Berta 192
Callamard, Agnes 281
campaigns 17, 73, 76, 112, 136; concerted 23;
global health 28; "Make Poverty History" 187;
multifaceted communications 242; supporting
UNF 168; well-orchestrated 20
Capital Development Fund 171
capitalism 15, 201, 207, 276; and communism in
the Cold War 276; national state 15; pragmatic
207; soaring unfettered 201
Carayannis, Tatiana 184

care work 72–3, 76–7
catalytic role (in mobilizing funds) 111, 117, 153
CBD *see* Convention on Biological Diversity
CDF *see* Capital Development Fund
CDP *see* Committee for Development Policy
CEDAW *see* Convention on the Elimination of
 All Forms of Discrimination Against Women
Central African Republic 115
Central Emergency Response Fund 106
Central Europe 52, 272
centrist parties 47
CERF *see* Central Emergency Response Fund
CFCs *see* Common Fund for Commodities
CFS *see* Committee on World Food Security
The Challenge of Sustaining Peace 99
change management 255, 259–60
Chenery, Hollis 199
children 11, 17, 21–2, 32, 69, 89, 91, 125, 128,
 141, 173, 194, 200, 227; and the annual *State of
 the World's Children* publication 17; health of
 258; labour of 141; school-aged 125
China 10, 27, 43–5, 48–50, 52–3, 153, 156, 167,
 189, 203, 208, 267, 274, 277–8, 288; Africa's
 biggest economic partner *49*; claiming the
 central role at the UN 277; contributions to the
 World Bank 153–4; economy of 52; and Indian
 economy 204; leadership of 153; resources of
 153
China Peace Development Fund 277
China Petroleum 170
CHR *see* Commission on Human Rights
civil and political rights 85
civil society 39–41, 56, 58, 62–3, 102, 104,
 111–12, 166, 168, 174–5, 184, 187–96, 279,
 281–2, 286–7; actors 91, 193–4, 263; effective
 engagement of *194*; global 36, 39, 290;
 influence in policy and decision-making 190;
 organizations 19, 24, 34, 73, 166, 181, 185,
 187–9, 191, 193, 195, 258; role of 59, 62, 184;
 see also Third UN
climate change 18, 21, 35, 37, 58–62, 64, 81, 180,
 203, 205, 271–2, 274–7, 279–80, 282, 286–7;
 abating 60; action 62; addressing 65, 280;
 agreements 61; combating 24, 205; conventions
 on 56, 59, 65; debates 64; and environmental
 action 205; mitigating 85; negotiations 62;
 obligations 60
climate politics 63
Clinton, Bill 44, 280
co-facilitators 99, 142–3
CO2 emissions 272
Cold War 3, 14, 44, 51–2, 87–8, 97, 276–7
Commission on Global Governance 39
Commission on Human Rights 83, 85
Commission on Population and Development
 137–8, 145
Commission on Sustainable Development 63, 187

Commission on the Status of Women 69, 72, 81,
 115, 195
Committee for Development Policy 36–7, 191
Committee on World Food Security 17
Common Country Analysis 102
Common Fund for Commodities 16, 18
Common Set of Exclusionary Criteria **179**
Comprehensive Refugee Response Framework
 144
Comprehensive Review of Governance and Oversight
 226
conferences 10, 12, 32–4, 36–7, 40–1, 56–8, 60,
 63, 68, 70–1, 89–91, 137, 184–7, 189, 195;
 Accra Conference 2008 188; Beijing
 Conference on Women 1995 20, 71–2, 187;
 Conference on Environment and
 Development, Rio de Janeiro 1992 89;
 Conference on Financing for Development 36;
 Fourth World Conference on Women, Beijing
 1995 71–2, 89; Havana Conference on Trade
 and Employment 1947 214; Conference on the
 Human Environment, Stockholm 1972 2, 18,
 33, 56–9, 61–2, 88, 205; International
 Conference on Population and Development,
 Cairo 1994 89; Rio de Janeiro Earth Summit
 1992 24, 32, 36, 57, 59–60, 63, 187, 192;
 Conference on Sustainable Development 2012
 35, 57, 59, 281; Third Financing for
 Development Conference 2015 25; Conference
 on Trade and Development 1964 11–13,
 15–16, 26, 33–4, 201, 211–12; World
 Conference of the United Nations Decade for
 Women: Equality, Development and Peace
 1980 70; World Conference on Education for
 All 1990 89; World Social Summit,
 Copenhagen 1995 71; World Summit for
 Children in New York and World Conference
 on Education for All 1990 89
conflict 28, 50–2, 64, 70, 72–3, 76, 96–8, 100–1,
 104, 106, 123–4, 139, 175, 177, 279; internal
 269; intra-state 97–8; managing institutional
 177; organizational 177; prevention 72, 96–7,
 100, 105, 112, 136; resolution 105; resolving
 124; root causes of 102–3; violent 72, 100–1,
 105, 110; in the workplace 228
"Conflict Prevention and Sustaining Peace" 113
Congo 27–8, 128
consultants 170, 184, 236, 239, 242, 268
contracting parties 214, 217
contributors 2, 154–5, 161, 173, 194, 292;
 individual 173; major 45, 114, 281; member-
 state 169; non-core 45, 156, 160, 257, 265;
 non-state 153, 174; to UNDS *156*; voluntary
 114; Western 152
Convention concerning Equal Remuneration for
 Men and Women Workers for Work of Equal
 Value 1951 69

Convention on Consent to Marriage, Minimum Age for Marriage and Registration of Marriages 1962 69
Conventions 17–18, 28–9, 33, 58–61, 63, 68–70, 82, 84, 89, 124, 138, 179, 192, 291; UN Convention Against Corruption 2003 29; UN Convention on All Forms of Discrimination Against Women 1985 68; UN Convention of the Law of the Sea 1982 18; UN Convention on Biological Diversity 1992 19; UN Convention Relating to the Status of Refugees 1951 144
cooperation 23, 26, 28, 33–4, 37, 39, 80, 86, 111, 139–40, 166, 170–2, 174–5, 218, 221; digital 180; enhanced 177; impeding 161; policies 91; public-private 180; substantive 130; voluntary 61
Copenhagen 20, 61, 71, 89; agenda 89; and the UN World Social Summit 1995 71; and the World Conference of the United Nations Decade for Women: Equality, Development and Peace 1980 70
core budgets 45, 159–60
core funding 154–5, 160–1, 171, 173, 202, 231–2, 265, 271
corporate social responsibility 170, 280, 289
COVID-19 6, 208
crises 15, 19, 45, 71, 87, 92, 96, 102, 105, 122, 124, 126–30, 162, 208, 265; environmental 18, 56; global 28, 142; major 272; preventing 263
CRRF *see* Comprehensive Refugee Response Framework
CSD *see* Commission on Sustainable Development
CSOs *see* civil society organizations; Third UN
CSR *see* corporate social responsibility
CSW *see* Commission on the Status of Women
culture 17, 50, 52, 242–3; bureaucratic 111, 116; male-dominated 195; multilateral security 53; organizational 229, 245; strategic 53; system-wide KM 244
cyber-security 203

DaO *see* deliver as one
Davos 184, 186, 277
DAW *see* Division for the Advancement of Women
delegations 58, 112, 117, 158, 161, 213; of authority 230; developing 217; official 70–1
deliver as one 250–2, 259, 289, 291; approach codified with the UNDG's adoption of Standard Operating Procedures 251; countries 259; independent evaluation of 250, 259; initiatives 250–1
Department of Operational Support 230, 252
Department of Peace Operations (formerly Department of Peacekeeping Operations) 75, 98, 102, 278
Department of Political and Peacebuilding Affairs (formerly the Department of Political Affairs) 75, 81, 102, 116, 277
Department of Public Information 185
Dervis, Kemal 40
DESA *see* Department of Economic and Social Affairs
Development in the Global Compact for Migration **143**
Development Operations Coordination Office 253, 264
DGC *see* UN Department of Global Communications
diaspora 135–6, 142–4; discussions on engagement and remittances 143, 145; initiatives 138; investments 140, 144; policies 140; voting 144
disasters 122–3, 125, 130, 153, 173, 282; human-made 269; natural 35, 73, 126, 226; nuclear 85
Division for the Advancement of Women 74
Doha Round 212–13, 218
donor agencies 46, 264, 268, 270
donors 23, 27, 83, 88, 122, 124, 130, 137, 153–61, 167–9, 175, 231–2, 265, 267–8, 270–2; bilateral 26, 89, 265, 267–70; binary 91; contributions 106, 265; countries 23, 154, 157, 187, 202, 233, 252, 265–6, 272, 291; funding 105, 202, 253, 267, 270, 272; governmental 160; major 62, 161, 290; non-state 160, 168; preferences 11, 27, 202; private-sector 168–9, 174
DPA *see* Department of Political Affairs
DPI *see* Department of Public Information
DPKO *see* Department of Peacekeeping Operations
DPO *see* Department of Peace Operations
DPPA *see* Department of Political and Peacebuilding Affairs
Draper, William H. 19
drugs 11–13, 81, 288
dual citizenship policy 136
due diligence process 177–8, 242

earmarked funding 152, 154–5, 157–61, 174, 271, 291; *see also* non-core contributions
Earth Day Network 62
"Earth Summit" (also called "Rio+20") 19, 185
Eastern Europe 138, 172, 267
ECA *see* UN Economic Commission for Africa
ECE *see* UN Economic Commission for Europe
ECLAC *see* UN Economic Commission Latin America and the Caribbean
ESCAP *see* UN Economic and Social Commission for Asia and the Pacific
ESCWA *see* UN Economic and Social Commission for Western Asia

Economic and Financial Organization 9
economic development 3, 15, 36, 47–8, 135–7,
    199, 214, 287
economic growth 15–16, 20, 22, 58, 82–3, 85,
    87–90, 137, 199–201, 206; accelerating 87;
    lowering 205; retarding 201; sustainable 24,
    141, 270
EEC *see* European Economic Community
EFO *see* Economic and Financial Organization
electoral reform programs 73
emergencies 123, 130, 132, 144, 159, 275, 278;
    and development crises 40; global climate 275,
    278; humanitarian action addresses 123; and
    humanitarian aid requests 128; rapid reactions
    in 157; victims of 121
emigration 135–7, 142
emissions: CO2, 272; greenhouse gas 18, 61–2,
    85, 275; reductions 19
employment 16, 24, 34, 73, 77, 88–9, 91, 104,
    136, 139, 214, 241, 244, 271, 275; conditions
    291; opportunities 70; productive 34–5, 141;
    wage 91; youth 90
empowerment 103, 229–30; economic 73–4, 105;
    women's 68, 271
Enterprise-Wide Risk Management 226
environment 18, 20, 22–3, 28–9, 56–9, 61–2, 64,
    71, 170, 172, 186, 192, 238–9, 244, 254–6;
    collegial 237; global 50, 58–9; healthy 82, 88;
    international 109, 113; sustainable 85
environment and development 57, 59, 61, 71; and
    post-colonialism 58; tensions between 56–7
environmental 12, 14, 17–19, 23, 32–7, 39–40,
    56–9, 61–5, 76–7, 80, 88–9, 186, 192–3, 205,
    279–80; action framework for the Stockholm
    Action Plan 57; agreements 56–8, 64;
    conventions 57–9, 61, 63; disasters and conflicts
    76; governance 58, 65, 192; institutions 58–9, 63
EOSG *see* Executive Office of the Secretary-
    General
epidemics 46, 226; *see also* pandemics; *see also*
    SARS
EPTA *see* Expanded Programme of Technical
    Assistance
equality 33–6, 68, 70–1, 74, 76, 89–90; gender 34,
    70–1, 74, 76, 89–90; racial 83; substantive 70,
    73–4, 78 for Asia and the Pacific
ERM *see* Enterprise-Wide Risk Management
Escazú agreement: a regional attempt to expand
    civic space *192*
Escazú Convention 192
ethics 177, 222, 225–7
Europe 12–13, 43–5, 47–8, 50–3, 135, 143, 271,
    278–9; countries 12, 44; donors 267; donors
    reducing voluntary contributions 267; and the
    "European Green Deal" 62, 279; humanitarian
    assistance 266; and North America 45; refugee
    and migration crisis 266

European Commission 265, 279
European Economic Co-operation 12
European Economic Community 15
European Union 52, 61–2, 136, 153, 204, 265,
    274–5, 288
evaluations 37, 41, 113, 139, 190, 193, 222–3,
    225–6, 229, 231, 236, 239, 241, 243, 250;
    cross-cutting 232; independent 171, 232, 254;
    objective 288, 291; official 172; strategic 50;
    system-wide 233, 291
evolution 4, 15, 51, 69, 82, 97–8, 135, 210,
    214–15; historical 14; incremental 218;
    institutional 214; positive 91
exclusionary criteria 177–9
Executive Office of the Secretary-General 116
Expanded Programme of Technical Assistance 11,
    26–7
exploitation 140–1, 275; of procedural flaws and
    modalities of participation 195; sexual 259; and
    trafficking 137; of the world's abundant
    resources 219
Extinction Rebellion 62, 64

facilitators, full-time 241
failure 4–5, 12, 22, 52, 73, 77, 82, 86, 98, 122,
    138, 188, 212, 226, 229; egregious 86; market
    213; risk of 270–1; systemic 86, 179
families 1, 9, 11–12, 18–19, 75, 77, 84, 124,
    136–8, 188, 286
Families in a Changing World 2019–2020 75
FAO *see* Food and Agriculture Organization
female genital mutilation 76–7
FENSA *see* Framework for Engagement with
    Non-State Actors
FGM *see* female genital mutilation
field offices 1, 86, 157–8
Figueres, Christiana 65
finance 53, 60–4, 106, 153, 165, 167–71, 173,
    175, 177, 179, 181, 202–3, 266–7, 279, 281;
    and partnerships 5, 167, 169, 171, 173, 175,
    177, 179, 181; peacebuilding activities 106;
    projects 143
financial 9–10, 15–16, 37–9, 43–4, 60–2, 117,
    144, 166–7, 172–3, 176–7, 202–4, 224, 226–8,
    266–7, 282–3; cooperation 9; data 232;
    disclosure processes 222, 224, 226–8;
    globalization 282; institutions 2, 5, 39, 44, 48,
    91, 102, 117, 188; irregularities 227; leverage
    10; resources 20, 81, 103, 126
financing 21, 32, 36, 40, 63, 106, 114, 117,
    166–7, 175–6, 180, 187, 189, 269, 271;
    common 256; external 266; inadequate 38, 166,
    174; joint 255; operational 26; predictable 98,
    111; sustainable 105, 251
First UN 3, 187, 252; and international civil servants
    97; of governments 2, 3, 24; of member states 19,
    26, 78, 185, 189, 207, 228, 232, 286, 290

FOGS *see* Functioning of the GATT System
Fonda, Jane 62
food standards 29
Ford Foundation 166
Foreign Trade Association 180
Foundation Center 232
Foundation Chanel 173
foundations 15, 46, 60, 92, 98, 166, 168–71,
    173–4, 189, 192, 222, 232, 276, 280, 289;
    critical 104; fundraising activities 170; global
    funds and philanthropic 172; normative 272;
    and philanthropies 189
Founex Report 58
Fourth World Conference on Women, Beijing
    1995 71–2, 89
fragmentation 2, 63, 76, 97, 99, 101, 110–12, 153,
    171, 174, 269, 291; exacerbating 73; high 152;
    least mitigating 117; system's 28, 115
Framework for Engagement with Non-State
    Actors 175, 177
framework for environmental action of the
    Stockholm Action Plan *57*
France 47, 53, 83, 167, 224, 278–9
free trade 137
Friedberg, Aaron L. 51
Fuji Xerox Company Ltd 170
Functioning of the GATT System 217
funding 1, 27, 29, 124–9, 136–7, 151–61, 165–7,
    169, 178, 241, 250–1, 255–7, 259, 264–5, 267;
    arrangements 74, 172; centralized 26; current
    75, 264; decisions 157, 172, 265; earmarked
    152, 154–5, 157–61, 174, 271, 291; foreign
    195; inter-agency 232; NGO attracted 188;
    non-core 27, 154, 165, 267; non-state 153,
    174; pooled 156, 158, 160–1, 171, 255–6;
    predictable 114, 117, 151, 253; private-sector
    166, 171, 174, 178; sustainable 160, 260;
    thematic 160, 254; voluntary 12, 18, 253, 267
Funding Compact 230; inter-agency 233; mirrors
    the Grand Humanitarian Bargain 2016 161;
    proposed parameters for a *231*
funding mechanisms 26, 106, 123, 152, 176, 250,
    267; centralized 26, 152; essential 106; new
    123, 176
funding sources 26, 153, 160, 165, 175, 291;
    extra-budgetary 172; main groups of 2017 *175*
funds 11, 26–7, 45, 47, 109–11, 127–9, 131,
    151–3, 155–7, 165, 167–9, 171–2, 174, 221,
    267; global health 171; mobilizing 117; new 11;
    pension 180, 266; pooled 155, 161, 231–2, 250,
    267, 270; private capital market 169, 203; public
    188; risk-tolerant 106; special 11, 13, 26, 160,
    200, 224, 228, 237; startup 143; voluntary 176

G-7 Summit 2019 278
G-20, 16, 37–8, 40, 44, 203, 268, 274, 277–8, 282
Gates, Bill 210

Gates, Melinda 210
Gates Foundation 46, 168, 171–2
GATT *see* General Agreement on Tariffs and
    Trade
gay people 74
GCIM *see* Global Commission on International
    Migration
GCM *see* Global Compact for Migration
GCR *see* Global Compact on Refugees
GDP *see* Gross Domestic Product
GEAR *see* Gender Equality Architecture Reform
gender 2, 4, 17, 29, 36, 71–2, 77, 88, 91, 115,
    129, 139, 141, 205
gender equality 33–6, 68, 70–1, 74, 76, 89–90;
    and empowerment of women 34; goals 77;
    issues 71; programming 128; substantive 77;
    supported 74
Gender Equality Architecture Reform Campaign
    73
gender inequality 35, 68, 73–6; measuring 73;
    multidimensional 74; reductions of 36, 203
General Agreement on Tariffs and Trade 10,
    15–16, 33, 38, 211–12, 214, 216–17, 219;
    contracting parties 214, 217; contribution to
    achieving greater coherence in global economic
    policy-making 217; negotiations 214; and the
    WTO rounds 216
Generalized System of Preferences 15
"Geneva Group" 45
geographic borders 244; *see also* borders
Germany 16, 47, 53, 153, 167, 224, 265, 267
GFMD *see* Global Forum on Migration and
    Development
GHA *see* Global Humanitarian Assistance
GHD *see* Good Humanitarian Donorship
GHO *see* Global Humanitarian Overview
global agenda 5, 23, 32, 45, 76, 135
Global Alliance for Vaccinations and
    Immunization 23, 157, 171–2, 265
Global Business Alliance 189
global challenges 16, 43, 56, 165, 203, 208
global climate emergencies 275, 278
Global Commission on International Migration
    138
Global Compact 5, 128, 135, 142, 145, 167–8,
    170–1, 186; Board 170; Government Group
    170; Local Networks 170; for Migration 142,
    143, 144–5, 274, 280; Office 170; on Refugees
    128, 144–5; Trust Fund 166–7, 170
global conferences 18, 20, 22, 56–7, 59, 177,
    185–6, 205, 290
Global Economic Coordination Council 39–40
global economy 16, 18, 40, 135, 142, 199, 203–5,
    207–8, 266, 270–1, 282
global financial crisis 38, 43, 203, 266, 278
Global Forum on Migration and Development
    139–40, 145

global governance 19, 36, 39, 50, 90, 92, 135, 204, 206, 225, 274, 280–2; institutions of 36, 50; organizations of 43, 54; and political reform 206; strengthening of 5, 198; systems 274, 277; and United Nations 204, 281

global health 28, 45–6, 171, 175; agency 46; campaigns 28; funding 171; institutions 45; priorities 46

Global Health Centre, Geneva 46

global institutions 32, 45–6, 50, 57, 98

global leadership 203, 278–9

Global Migration Governance 140, 143

Global Migration Group 138–40, 145

Global North 135–7

global pandemics *see also* pandemics 45

global partnerships 23–4, 34, 36, 92, 112, 167, 169, 258

Global Refugee Forum 144

Global South 3, 12, 15–17, 50, 53–4, 63–4, 129, 132, 135–6, 139, 153–4, 160–1, 185–6, 207, 286–7

The Global Sustainable Development Report 2019 288

global trade 15, 212, 214; *see also* trade

Global Voice of Business 180

Global War on Terrorism 131

globalization 3, 282

GMG *see* Global Migration Group

GNI *see* Gross National Income

GNP *see* Gross National Product

Good Humanitarian Donorship 122

Goodrich, Leland 9

governance 32, 35, 37, 64, 110, 136, 138–40, 203–4, 212, 214, 224–6, 229, 250–1, 266, 268; mechanisms 63, 175; multilateral 157, 160; national 35–6; structures 32, 37, 40, 170, 213, 221, 268–9, 282; trading system's 212; transparent 169; weak 25

governments 16, 18–20, 24–5, 57–64, 85–6, 89–92, 153–4, 156–9, 186–8, 190–2, 202–3, 224, 250–1, 268–9, 289–91; applicant 26; audit functions 224; autocratic 276; budget priorities 266; donor 266; funding of NGOs 188; host country 103, 111, 159, 270, 272; national 35–6, 62, 86, 105, 125, 127, 129, 192, 199; troop-contributing 227; under-capacitated 270; weak 270

Grand Bargain 124–5, 127, 132, 156, 161

grants 26, 106, 154, 168, 188, 232, 269

greenhouse gas emissions 18, 61–2, 85, 275

Greenpeace 279

Gross Domestic Product 89, 139, 206–7; and economic growth 89; and growth driven by buoyant commodity exports 23; percentage share of world (in PPP terms), 1980–2050 *51*; regional and country shares of global *51*

Gross National Income 87, 89, 266, 289

Gross National Product 89, 199, 201

GSP *see* Generalized System of Preferences

Guterres, Secretary-General António 62, 86, 102, 109, 112, 180, 184, 190, 195, 229, 251–2, 279–81

GWOT *see* Global War on Terrorism

Hammarskjold, Dag

Havana Conference on Trade and Employment 1947 214

hazardous waste 57–9, 64

HDIs *see* Human Development Index

health 17–18, 22–3, 28, 46, 71, 77, 88–9, 92, 136, 168, 172, 199–202, 205–6, 287, 290; care 70, 91, 188; financial 117; global 46, 175; mental 85; policies 177; professionals 138; public 168, 177; reproductive 18, 68, 71–2, 76–7, 89; women's 73

Heritage Foundation 166

High Commissioner for Human Rights 81, 89, 139, 194, 206

High Commissioner for Refugees 11, 73, 252

High-Level Political Forum for Sustainable Development 25, 37, 41, 187, 190, 195, 232–3, 279–81

HLPF *see* High-Level Political Forum for Sustainable Development

Hong Kong 45

HRC *see* Human Rights Council

human development 17, 19–20, 80, 88, 90, 199, 206; measuring by combining income per capita, education, and longevity 20; paradigm 206, 288; sustainable 92

Human Development Index 20, 89

Human Development Report 1990 19, 89

Human Development Report 1992 39

Human Development Report 1994 98

Human Development Report 1995 75

human rights 20–3, 71–4, 80–3, 85–9, 91–2, 97–8, 104, 109–10, 137–40, 142–3, 179–80, 184, 193–5, 206, 258; abuses 86, 92, 121, 179, 290; agenda 87, 180, 184, 258, 288; bodies 91–2, 268; commitments 250, 258, 260; defense of 97, 110; and development 80–1, 83, 85; forums 76; infrastructure 85; initiatives 102; instruments 81, 84; international 91; mechanisms 104, 258; nexus of 101, 104; promotion of 83, 115, 290; realization of 250, 260; standards 181, 194, 258; and sustainable development 4, 80–92; violations 81, 85, 97, 103, 139, 258

Human Rights Council 81, 85–6, 91, 110, 180, 276–7, 279–80

humanitarian agencies 12, 86, 129–31

humanitarian aid 127, 130, 1989–2018 (in $ millions) *127*; and appeals associated with emergencies 128; facilitating greater access to 125; funding 125, 161; localization of 125; relief programs 87

humanitarian assistance 28, 81, 86, 112, 115–16, 125, 128, 142, 152, 165, 265, 269–70
humanitarian crises 25, 73, 121, 125, 269
Humanitarian Investing Initiative 106
humanitarian operations 28, 80
humanitarian principles 122, 129
humanitarian system 121, 123, 125–6, 128, 130, 132
humanitarianism 121–5, 130–2
humanitarians 3–5, 10, 105–6, 121–6, 128–33, 143, 145, 152–5, 158, 254, 259–60, 267, 270, 272
Hungary 47–8
hunger 23–4, 35, 77, 130, 189

IAEA *see* International Atomic Energy Agency
IATI *see* International Aid Transparency Initiative
ICAs *see* International Commodity Agreements
ICC *see* International Chamber of Commerce
ICCPR *see* International Covenant on Civil and Political Rights
ICERD *see* International Convention on the Elimination of All Forms of Racial Discrimination
ICESCR *see* International Covenant on Economic, Social and Cultural Rights
ICMW *see* International Convention on the Protection of the Rights of All Migrant Workers and Members of Their Families
ICPED *see* International Convention for the Protection of All Persons from Enforced Disappearance
IDA *see* International Development Association
IDPs *see* internally displaced persons
IFAD *see* UN International Fund for Agricultural Development
IFIs *see* international financial institutions
IFRC *see* International Federation of Red Cross and Red Crescent Societies
illegal (im)migrants 47
ILO *see* International Labour Organization
IMF *see* International Monetary Fund
IMFC *see* International Monetary and Financial Committee
immigrants 47, 136–7
immigration 135, 137
IMO *see* International Maritime Organization
In Larger Freedom: Towards Development, Security and Human Rights for All 98
In Pursuit of Justice 75
incentives 218, 243, 251, 256, 258–9; of common financing 256; for companies to partner with UNESCO 174; for donors to maintain or improve their funding 161; economic 60; for engagement remain sector-based and project-driven 64; strong 157–8
income 20, 36, 45, 141, 170, 172, 205, 207, 289;

developed country 22; distribution 275; flexible 172; generating 257; national 22, 63, 87; per capita 137, 201; poverty 35, 89, 189
individual giving, appeals, to **172**
Industrial Development Organization 11, 60
industrial states 211–15
industrialized countries 12, 16, 18, 22, 58, 63, 76, 202, 207–8, 213, 271
industry 58, 64–5, 77, 89, 187; agendas 181; global 189; growth 4; tobacco 177
inequalities 35–6, 76, 80–1, 90–1, 97, 105, 135, 137–8, 141, 145, 203, 205, 210, 279, 282; addressing 77, 105; deepening 92; global 135, 142–3, 205; international 36; reducing 32, 205; structural 90–1; unsustainable 205; wage 139; widening 275, 280
information 17–18, 59, 71, 98, 100, 115, 129–30, 155, 192–4, 200, 227, 232, 237, 287; exchange 60; management 237–8; and research on population 18
infrastructure 14, 77, 180, 278; basic 69; major projects 269; resilient 24; sustainable 180; technology of 241
initiatives 86, 88, 96, 98, 124, 166–70, 175–6, 203–4, 237–8, 241, 243, 245, 259–60, 278, 280; environmental 58; global 62, 265; industry-focused 175; joint 172, 259; new 123, 184, 204, 207; regional 138, 204; transformational 237
innovation 24, 37, 64, 77, 104, 218, 254–5, 258–60, 274; approaches 114; approaches for women's and youth empowerment. 114; and approaches to the use of partnerships to realize UN goals and programs 167; High-Level Political Forum for Sustainable Development 25, 37, 41, 187, 190, 195, 232–3, 279–81; prioritizing 258; significant institutional 60; Voluntary National Reviews 25, 37, 41, 91, 190–1, 232
INSTRAW *see* International Research and Training Institute for the Advancement of Women
intellectual property rights 33
Intergovernmental Panel on Climate Change 18, 60–1, 205, 280, 287
Intergovernmental Science-Policy Platform on Biodiversity and Ecosystem Services 19
internally displaced persons 4, 126, 128, 173
International Aid Transparency Initiative 122, 232
International Atomic Energy Agency 11, 44–7, 224, 237
International Campaign to Abolish Nuclear Weapons 193
International Chamber of Commerce 180, 187, 189
International Children's Emergency Fund (now the UN Children's Fund) 11
International Civil Aviation Organization 10–11, 13, 28, 193, 289

international civil service 3, 5, 97, 185, 189, 228;
see also Second UN
International Commodity Agreements 16
International Conference on Population and
Development, Cairo 1994 89
International Covenant of Economic, Social and
Cultural Rights 1966 33
International Covenant on Civil and Political
Rights 83–4
International Covenant on Economic, Social and
Cultural Rights 83–5
International Development Association 15, 33, 38,
106, 199
International Dialogue on Statebuilding and
Peacebuilding 2016 124
International Federation of Red Cross and Red
Crescent Societies 125
international financial institutions 2, 5, 44, 48,
102, 188
international human rights instruments **84**
International Labour Organization 10–11, 13,
16–17, 19, 33, 69, 75–6, 87–8, 135, 139–41,
199–200, 225, 227–8, 238, 278
International Law 97, 192–3
International Maritime Organization 11, 13, 28,
224, 289
International Monetary and Financial Committee
53
International Monetary Fund 2, 10, 22, 26, 43–4,
48, 50, 53, 87, 186, 198–205, 207, 278;
programs 201; Special Drawing Rights 16;
support 206; voting systems 202; and the World
Bank 44, 50, 53, 212
International Organization for Migration 1, 11,
135, 138–40, 142–4, 229
International Public Sector Accounting Standards
224
International Research and Training Institute for
the Advancement of Women 17, 73
International Telecommunication Union 11, 28,
87, 289
International Trade Centre 11–13, 211–12
International Trade Organization 10, 12, 212,
214
IOM *see* International Organization for Migration
IPBES *see* Intergovernmental Science-Policy
Platform on Biodiversity and Ecosystem
Services
IPCC *see* Intergovernmental Panel on Climate
Change
IPRs *see* intellectual property rights
Iraq 50, 52, 269, 276
irregular immigration 137
Islamic states 18
ITC *see* International Trade Centre
ITO *see* International Trade Organization
ITU *see* International Telecommunication Union

Jackson, Robert 2, 11, 26, 264, 291
Japan 153, 166
Jenks, Bruce 34
JIU *see* Joint Inspection Unit
Joint Inspection Unit 159, 170, 174, 177, 221–6,
228–9, 237–40, 244; and the *Lacunae Report*
226; perception survey 245; recommendations
240
Joint Steering Committee 129
JSC *see* Joint Steering Committee
justice 25, 75, 81, 96–7, 121, 153, 189, 192–3,
195; access to 24, 70, 112, 141, 192; research
13; social 64, 83, 195

Kaufmann, Daniel 64
Kaul, Inge 33
Kennedy, John F. 20, 199
Ki-moon, Ban 166, 168, 280
KM *see* knowledge management
knowledge 20, 52, 68, 130, 191, 193, 235–9,
241–2, 244, 272; diaspora transfer 144;
employee's 236; flows 236, 242; global 242;
individual 236, 240; sharing 236, 283; technical
25; transfer of 136, 139
knowledge management 235–40, 242–4;
benchmarking efforts 243; benefits 236, 238;
efforts 238, 242–3; incorporated activities 238;
interpretations and strategies 235, 237–41, 245;
portfolios 244; systems 235, 237, 242, 245; in
the UN system 2007–2020 *238*
knowledge-sharing networks 241–2, 244–5;
corporate 236; global 244; inter-organizational
245; voluntary 240
Kyoto Protocol 18, 61, 275

labor 140, 170, 179, 254, 287; compulsory 179;
migration 135, 140; rights 280; standards 29,
39, 91
Lacunae Report 226
Latin America 12–13, 58, 72, 88, 156, 192,
199–201, 204, 264, 272
law 18, 35, 43, 64, 72, 82, 103, 110, 192, 215,
271; binding 87; international environmental
59; international human rights 180;
international humanitarian 126, 130; and
International Law 97, 192–3; patent 46
LDCs *see* least developed countries
leadership 50, 52–4, 57, 62, 64, 90, 92, 229, 231,
240, 242, 244, 250–1, 255–6, 277–8; enhanced
54; enlightened 107, 242; national 104; political
37, 41, 69; populist 47–8; proactive 203; senior
44, 103, 243; strong 103, 207; visionary 208,
283; women's 105
League of Nations 5, 9–10, 25, 33, 87
learning organizations 235, 245
least developed countries 141, 205, 207, 269

"leaving no one behind" 5, 81, 121–33, 263, 270; embedding 128; ethos 132; humanitarian actors resisting 130; principle of 125–6; results 131; scale 131; transformations 128; vision of cohering humanitarianism and development 123–4

Lee, Kelley 45–6

Lewis, Arthur 199

LGBT (lesbian, gay, bi-sexual, and transgender) 74

LGBT+ people 92

LNOB *see* "leaving no one behind"

Macpherson, Andrew 152

macroeconomic policies 87–8, 200

main groups of funding sources 2017 *175*

"Make Poverty History" campaign 187

malaria 23, 157, 168

management 112, 114, 160, 169, 177, 213, 222–3, 225–6, 229–30, 235–6, 240, 252, 258, 263, 272; economic 204; environmental 18; executive 224–6, 228; hierarchies 230; new 256; reforms 281; responses 223; senior 226–7, 242, 259; social 203; sustainable 24, 136

Mandela, Nelson 219

Marshall Islands 62

mass migration 48

Maternal and Newborn Health Thematic Fund 156

McKeon, Nora 65

McNamara, Robert 199–200

MCOs *see* Multi-Country Offices

MDBs *see* multilateral development banks

MDGs *see* Millennium Development Goals

Measures for Full Employment 199

Measures for International Economic Stability 199

mechanisms 2, 12, 26, 37, 39, 41, 60–2, 64, 83, 104, 125, 162, 177, 211, 216; financial 169; implementation support 60; institutional 71, 194; reporting 229, 233; resources-transfer 154; system-wide 282

Médecins Sans Frontières 131, 188

member states 3, 5, 12, 18, 24, 28–9, 34, 36, 39, 45, 52, 56, 61–2, 70, 85, 87–8, 160, 228–9

MICs *see* middle-income countries

Middle East 47–8, 52, 58, 69, 266, 269

middle-income countries 34, 189, 252, 271

migrants 47, 126, 128, 135–7, 139–40, 142–5, 194, 266, 276; contributions of 142–3; economic 4, 48; human rights of 139–40; illegal 47; irregular 137; rights of 137, 140; sub-Saharan 47; vulnerable 136

migration 11, 47, 81, 91, 96, 124, 130, 135–45, 203, 274–5; causes of 136–7, 139; and development 5, 135–43, 145; economic 37, 144; forced 25, 144, 290; illegal 47; irregular 137, 140, 144; labor 135, 140; mainstreaming 139, 142; management 138; policies 140–1; in the SDGs *141*

Millennium Declaration of the 2000 World Summit (Millennium Summit) 21–3, 34, 36, 90, 98, 186–7, 202, 204, 281, 288, 290

Millennium Development Goals 21–2, *23*, 32, 34–5, 37, 76–7, 81, 90–1, 138, 187, 189, 199, 202, 274, 290

Mitrany, David 9

MOPAN *see* Multilateral Organization Performance Assessment Network

moral standards 243, 280

A More Secure World: Our Shared Responsibility 98

Morgenthau, Henry 198

MPTFO *see* Multi-Partner Trust Fund Office

MSF *see* Médecins Sans Frontières

Multi-Country Offices 254

Multi-Donor Trust Funds 174

Multi-Partner Trust Fund Offices 155

multi-stakeholder partnerships 36, 90, 168, 172, 174, 180

Multiannual Financial Framework (2021–7) 267

multilateral agreements 137, 186

multilateral assets 151, 159, 161

multilateral assistance channels of OECD-DAC countries, core and earmarked 2013 and 2017 (in 2017 constant US *155*

multilateral development banks 155, 269–70

Multilateral Fund 60

multilateral funding 202

multilateral institutions 43–4, 153, 277

multilateral lending agencies 111

Multilateral Organization Performance Assessment Network 243

multilateral organizations 52, 151, 154, 157–8, 223, 263, 268

multilateral system 44, 233, 249; current 54; global 44, 274; rules-based 278; trading 211–15, 218–19; weaker global 44

multilateralism 4–6, 43–7, 49–51, 53, 113, 158, 162, 184, 190, 195–6, 215, 249, 275–7, 281, 286–7; ambitious 10; defending 184; people-centered 92; strengthening 43–4, 50

Myanmar 86, 191

NAM *see* Non-Aligned Movement

national income 22, 63, 87

national ownership 99, 102–3, 111, 190, 250–1

national populism 274–5, 282

nationalism 5–6, 29, 249, 263, 272, 286

NATO *see* North Atlantic Treaty Organization

Naujoks, Daniel 136

negotiations 15, 19, 38, 58, 60–1, 63, 74, 111, 116, 143, 158, 161, 167, 186, 213–18; competitive 215; intensive 251; intergovernmental 56; international 60, 64; piecemeal 216–17; post-war ITO 216

networks 40, 86, 143, 236, 239–44, 255, 282; civil society 193; normative global organizational 268; sustainable development consultancy 272; system-wide gender-equality 244
New Development Bank 278
new global partnerships 36
New Regime for Orderly Movements of People 138
New Way of Working 125, 129
New World Information and Communication Order 17
New York Declaration for Refugees and Migrants 142
New York Times 46
Newell, Peter 62
NGLS *see* Non-Governmental Liaison Service
NGOs *see* non-governmental organizations
NIROMP *see* New Regime for Orderly Movements of People
Nobel Peace Prize 17, 64, 193
Non-Aligned Movement 3, 17
non-core contributions 45, 156, 160, 257, 265; *see also* earmarked funding
Non-Governmental Liaison Service 185, 191
non-governmental organizations 3, 56, 59–60, 64, 71, 127, 129, 174–5, 184–5, 187–8, 191, 193–4, 279, 287, 289; *see also* Third UN
non-state revenue for six UN organizations 2017 176
nongovernmental organizations 3, 56, 89, 153, 185, 210, 221, 241, 279
North Atlantic Treaty Organization 277
nuclear power plants 46–7
NWICO *see* New World Information and Communication Order
NWOW *see* New Way of Working

OBEs *see* other business enterprises
OBEs *see* other business enterprises
OCHA *see* Office for the Coordination of Humanitarian Affairs
ODA *see* Official Development Assistance
OECD *see* Organization for Economic Co-operation and Development
OEEC *see* Organization for European Economic Co-operation
Office for Internal Oversight Services 223, 225, 227–9
Office for the Coordination of Humanitarian Affairs 73, 81, 124, 127–8, 238
Office for the High Commissioner for Human Rights 81, 86, 92, 139, 194
Office of the Special Adviser on Gender Issues 74
official development assistance 22–3, 26, 33–4, 36, 87–8, 106, 152, 188, 191, 230, 233, 264–7, 269, 271–2, 289; community 36; contributions

152; funded activities 271; total 265, 267; use of 266–7
OHCHR *see* Office for the High Commissioner for Human Rights
OIOS *see* Office for Internal Oversight Services
OPEC *see* Organization of Petroleum Exporting Countries
operational activities 26, 28, 153–4, 165, 171, 174, 178, 239, 264–5, 271, 292
Organization for European Economic Co-operation 12
Organization of Petroleum Exporting Countries 16
organizations 12, 17–19, 25–8, 45–8, 73–6, 151–8, 160–1, 171–8, 210–15, 221–3, 225–33, 235–45, 253–6, 270–2, 289–91; activist youth 56; autonomous operational 265; bureaucratic 243; diaspora 140; economic governance 10; grass-roots 193; humanitarian 265; hybrid 289; national 125, 185; post-bureaucratic 243; regional 101–2, 104, 111, 188, 193, 272, 275, 278; self-governing 1; sub-regional 104; women's 68, 70, 74
ORR *see* other resources regular
other business enterprises 180
other resources regular 172
Our Common Future 18
Outcome Document 91
outcomes 4, 37, 88, 98, 116, 121, 201, 207, 211, 213–16, 218, 222, 230, 233, 290; asymmetrical 213; collective 124–5, 128; formal 113; improved trade 216; institutional 142; political 157; qualitative 90; sustainable 159
oversight committees 222–4, 229
ozone-depleting substances 18, 57–61

Palais Royal Initiative 40
pandemics 17, 43, 45, 203, 286
Paris Agreement on Climate Change 25, 32, 60–1, 64–5, 81, 190, 263, 274–6, 279–80
parties 19, 56–7, 60–1, 63, 96, 214–15, 217, 228; centrist 47; contracting 214, 217; mandated 60; national 131; non-state 289; political 38; populist 47
partners 5, 104, 106, 115, 167, 174, 177, 239, 259, 268, 280; co-financing 169; key funding 265; non-governmental 172; privileged development 268
partnerships 3, 5, 64, 104–6, 158, 160, 165, 167, 169, 171–3, 175, 177–9, 203, 259, 268–9; business sector 178; importance of 104, 111, 167; new 219; private 167, 169, 180–1, 189; small-scale 212; strong 32, 105–6
Paul, James 186
PBA *see* Peacebuilding Architecture
PBC *see* Peacebuilding Commission
PBF *see* Peacebuilding Fund

PBSO *see* Peacebuilding Support Office
PDAs *see* Peace and Development Advisors
PEA *see* Political Economic Analysis
peace 28, 35, 50–2, 63–4, 70–5, 80–2, 87–8,
    97–105, 107, 109–16, 121, 193, 203–4, 279,
    283; issues concerning 2, 100; negotiations 69,
    72; operations 2, 75, 86, 98–9, 110, 124, 227,
    252, 257, 281, 292; and security 14, 35–6, 63,
    73–4, 97, 100, 102–5, 109, 112–13, 115, 122,
    252; solidifying 97; sustainable 82, 97, 101,
    104–5, 109–10, 112–14, 117
Peace and Development Advisors 102
peacebuilding 3–4, 28, 97, 99–106, 109–11,
    113–16, 124, 136, 142, 260; activities 105;
    addressing 112; architecture 96, 98–9, 101, 107,
    109–11, 113–14, 116–17; efforts 105, 112, 116;
    gender-responsive 105; global 106; operational
    110; post-conflict 98, 111; strategies 104
Peacebuilding and Sustaining Peace 100
Peacebuilding Commission 98–102, 105–6,
    109–16, 277
Peacebuilding Fund 98–9, 106, 109–11, 114, 117,
    153
Peacebuilding Support Office 75, 98–9, 109–10,
    112, 116, 193
peacekeeping 97–8, 274, 276; accounting 265;
    force 277; missions 97–8; operations 98, 115,
    165, 250, 263
People's Bank of China 53
per capita incomes 137, 201
percentage share of world GDP (PPP terms),
    1980–2050 *51*
Pew Research Center 47
philanthropic foundations 160, 166, 171, 174–5
philanthropies 160, 172, 174, 189
philanthropists 168–9, 174
policies 44–6, 50, 88, 100–1, 136, 138–9, 142,
    177, 189–90, 194–5, 199–203, 227–8, 235–6,
    238–9, 259; budgetary 39; coherent 110, 289;
    common agriculture 15; domestic 191;
    economic 180; enlightened 50; evidence-based
    143; explicit 97, 194; flawed 45; free-market
    88; human resource 239; neoliberal-based fiscal
    46, 76; non-sustainable 273; social protection
    77
policy recommendations 102, 114, 198–9
political agendas 58, 266
political covenants with member states 228–9
Political Economic Analysis 232
political processes 60, 65, 73
political reform 206
political rights 69, 82–5, 88
politics 87, 99, 132, 158, 288; changing 272;
    contested trade 213; domestic 139;
    environmental 59; global 203; resource 151
populations 13, 17–18, 21, 43, 47, 50, 54, 71, 89,
    121–2, 125–7, 129–32, 137, 141, 207; affected

121–3, 125–6, 129–33; displaced 128; forsaken
    124; global 50, 54; growing 35; sizes 18, 125,
    139, 287; vulnerable 86, 145, 192; world's 53,
    210, 269–70
populism 274–5, 282
Post-2015 Business Engagement Architecture
    171
poverty 68, 71, 77, 80, 87, 89–90, 92, 97, 126,
    130, 136, 138–9, 142–3, 199–201, 205;
    elimination 103; eradication 89, 100, 156;
    extreme 23, 35, 90, 92; fighting
    multidimensional 36; global 210; household-
    level 137; reducing 22, 89–90, 137, 199–200
power 16, 19, 37–40, 43–4, 47, 51–3, 85, 87, 102,
    131–2, 195–6, 214–15, 272, 274–5, 279–80;
    balance of 48, 204; colonial 83; dominant 25,
    207; global 286; inequalities 216; major
    economic 3, 41, 48, 87, 269, 276; non-Western
    277; relationships 130, 212; women in 71,
    195
PPP *see* Purchasing Power Parity
principles 5, 10, 12, 24, 26, 33–6, 38, 97, 99, 131,
    170–1, 179, 192, 243, 280; agreed 225;
    developing common 244; distributive 130;
    flexible 280; global 28; shared 219
priorities 2, 4, 17, 63, 68, 70, 109–10, 171–2, 176,
    199, 202, 204–6, 229–30, 259–60, 277–8;
    bilateral 155, 159; donor 270; early 11;
    economic 233; global 205; high-level 240;
    political 159; post-conflict 101; programmatic
    157; social 68; universal 76
private sector 40–1, 56, 58, 102, 104, 143–5, 165,
    167–8, 170–5, 177–8, 180–1, 241, 243, 280,
    289–90; entities 175; exercises 63; partnerships
    104
problems 17, 19, 37–8, 43, 58, 60, 62–4, 129–30,
    132, 143, 145, 210–11, 215–16, 228, 271;
    balance-of-payments 199–200; global 2, 56, 61,
    64, 169, 286; international 10, 14, 153;
    operational 132; political 269
Programme of Action (often called the Cairo
    Programme of Action) 137
programs 11–14, 16–18, 73–5, 78, 80, 137, 144–5,
    167–9, 171–2, 174, 206–8, 223–4, 226, 237–8,
    267–8; anti-poverty 187; austerity 76; bilateral
    270; expanding 15; global 64, 159; joint 155,
    158; medium-term 158; operational 239;
    ·training 228
projects 27, 135–6, 145, 156, 159, 168–9, 171–2,
    192–3, 202, 236, 241–2, 268, 272, 286, 291;
    individual 159, 217; institutional 212;
    integrated 159; major infrastructure 269;
    partnership 174; peace-related 105; political
    130, 133; women's 73
property rights 74
Proposed Parameters for a Funding Compact *231*
protection 18, 34, 59–60, 83–6, 104, 121, 124,

128, 138, 193, 228, 259; environmental 61, 82, 88; maternal 17, 69; ozone layer 59; processes 227; social 92, 115; systems 28
protectionism 15
Purchasing Power Parity 51, 137, 277

QCPR *see* Quadrennial Comprehensive Policy Review
Quadrennial Comprehensive Policy Review 74, 112, 156, 167, 239–40, 251

racial equality 83
Ramsar Convention on Wetlands 63
RBFs *see* regular budgetary funds
RC *see* resident coordinator
RCPs *see* Regional Consultative Processes
RCs *see* resident coordinator
Reagan, Ronald 276
Real change over time of funding for UN-OAD 2002–2017 *152*
recommendations 19, 39–40, 70–1, 84–6, 89, 98–100, 104–6, 109–11, 114–16, 140, 190, 193–4, 214, 223–6, 229; central 111; core development 90; endorsed 86; high-priority 226; report's 239; of the UN High Commissioner on Human Rights for the effective engagement of civil society **194**
reductions of inequality 36, 203
reform agenda 252, 259–60
reform debates 215
reform efforts 231, 240, 249–51, 255, 260, 281
reform initiatives 255, 260, 263, 265
reform processes 115, 161, 214–15, 263, 280–1
reform programs 166, 222, 251, 256
reform proposals 28, 112, 116–17, 213–14
reforms 2, 5, 98, 100–2, 203–4, 206, 208, 210–18, 229–33, 240, 249–52, 254–6, 258–60, 281, 291–2; comprehensive 230, 251; current 245, 252, 255, 257, 259–60; important 229; incremental 267; institutional 201; major 280; organizational 240; public sector 268; resisting 54; technocratic 132; voting 206
refugees 4, 11, 48, 64, 76, 126, 128, 135–9, 142, 144–5, 152, 173, 265–6; communities 145; helping 142; issues concerning 139; registration 144; resettling 87; self-reliance of 144
regional and country shares of global GDP *51*
Regional Consultative Processes 138
regions 12, 52, 115, 138, 192, 204–5, 266–7, 288; conflict-affected 51–2, 98; economic successes 207; and European humanitarian assistance for 266; helping displaced people 138; high-risk operational 226
regular budgetary funds 45
Relationship Agreement 2014 169
relationships 82, 89, 99, 101, 104, 129–30, 137, 166, 168, 170, 178, 213, 218–19, 253, 257;

artificial 289; changing 166; complex 103; economic 267; personal 243; supporter 173
The Report of the Panel on United Nations Peace Operations 2000 98
reports 35–7, 58–9, 97–101, 105–6, 109–11, 113–17, 138, 170–1, 177–80, 193–5, 223–4, 226–9, 231–2, 237–40, 288–9; *Berg Report 1981* 200; *The Challenge of Sustaining Peace* 99; *Founex Report* 58; *The Global Sustainable Development Report 2019* 288; *Human Development Report 1990* 19, 89; *Human Development Report 1992* 39; *Human Development Report 1994* 98; *Human Development Report 1995* 75; *In Larger Freedom: Towards Development, Security and Human Rights for All* 98; *Measures for Economic Development* 199; *Measures for Full Employment* 199; *Measures for the International Economic Stability* 199; *Our Common Future* 18; *The Sustainable Development Goals Report 2019* 288
reproductive health 18, 68, 71–2, 76–7, 89
Republic of the Congo *see* Congo
reputational risks 169, 177, 226, 270
research 12–13, 17–19, 28, 135–6, 138–40, 144, 199, 201, 212, 218, 232, 236, 239, 241, 286–9; activities 287; capabilities 28, 287; centers 143; contributions 6; input 290; institutes 1, 80, 168, 287; organizations 13, 16; pioneering 287; scientific 18
resident coordinators 86, 101, 116, 145, 190, 230, 241, 250, 253, 264; full-time 256; function of 259; and members of UNCTs 253; offices 102
resolutions 17, 60, 64, 72–3, 78, 96–7, 99–101, 104–5, 109–17, 167, 179, 188–9, 202, 205, 252–7; additional parallel 96, 100; adopted 251; assembly's 167; dispute 190; founding 74, 99; joint 105, 111–12, 114; landmark 113; new procedural 101; partnership 167; path-breaking 72; sovereign debt 38; successful 60; umbrella 74
resources 25–6, 45–6, 63–4, 106, 123–4, 128, 130–3, 152–4, 157–60, 169, 171–4, 194–5, 203, 205, 291; additional 106, 111, 145, 158, 205, 257, 283; allocating 279; available 128, 167; donor 27; earmarked 154, 157–60, 171; economic 77; human 75, 86, 152, 177, 199, 228; insufficient 106, 126; leveraging 106; material 275, 281; new 136, 178; non-core 27, 45, 157, 160, 165, 171, 254; providing to local and national parties 131, 205; shifting 131; voluntary 257
responsibilities 22–3, 35, 37, 39–40, 54, 56, 60, 63, 97, 99, 102, 130–1, 225–6, 230, 232; additional development 11; broader 41; collective 160; combined 227; corporate 82, 170, 180, 280, 289; differentiated 36; environmental 40; eroding 63; financial 157; shared 36; special 39; system-wide 101, 111

revenues 158–9, 168; private sector 172; total 153–4, 174, 179
Review of Mechanisms and Policies Addressing Conflict of Interest in the United Nations System 177
reviews 85, 91, 96–9, 101, 107, 109–11, 113, 115, 218, 227, 235, 238–9, 253–4, 264, 274; first formal 109; five-year 117; historical 184; independent external quality 223; knowledge architecture 240; new 110, 117; panel 86, 194; periodic 85, 104; Quadrennial Comprehensive Policy 74, 112, 156, 167, 239–40, 251; statistical 201
rights 17–18, 29, 68–9, 71, 74, 76–8, 80–5, 87–8, 91–2, 136, 138–9, 142, 179, 192–3, 206; based approach 36, 80–1, 87–8, 206, 259, 270; children's 159, 288; collective 82, 88; designated 126; economic 77, 91; environmental 192; hereditary 277; individual 19; labour 141; legal 70, 91; minority 43; negative 82; reproductive 72, 81, 92, 124, 128, 168; second-generation 82–3; social 33; third-generation 82
Rio de Janeiro Earth Summit 1992 24, 32, 36, 57, 59–60, 63, 187, 192
risk management strategies 124, 222, 224, 226–8
risks 97, 100, 103, 123, 125–6, 130–1, 171–2, 174–5, 218, 226, 228, 258–9, 270, 272, 275; addressing 101; global 130; political 137, 232; potential 178; reducing 125; reputational 169, 177, 226, 270; significant 258
Rockefeller, John D. 166
Roosevelt, Franklin D. 10, 276
Rostrup, Morten 188
rules 16, 34–5, 43, 53, 64, 103, 110, 113, 178, 185, 214–15, 217, 271–2, 275, 280; associated 34; banking 264; new 276; soft 268; trade 215; transportation 37
Russia 47, 50, 53, 277–8

San Jose Principles 62
Santo Domingo 17, 73
SARS epidemic 45, 47
SBAAs *see* Standard Basic Assistance Agreements
"Schools for Africa" initiative 172
Schultz, Theodore 199
scientists 18, 58–60, 187, 205, 283
SCN *see* Standing Committee on Nutrition
SDGs *see* Sustainable Development Goals
SDRs *see* Special Drawing Rights
Second UN 3, 19, 185, 187, 252, 286; *see also* international civil service
Segal, Gerald 52
sexual violence 68, 75, 126
SIDS *see* small island developing states
Singapore 27, 45, 52–3
small island developing states 141, 252
social progress 14, 20, 33, 80, 83, 107

sovereign borders 43; *see also* borders
Special Drawing Rights 16
Standard Basic Assistance Agreements 26
standards 28–9, 32, 53, 68, 71, 78, 87, 122, 143, 193, 225, 244, 250, 268–9, 271; and governance for and by the humanitarian sector and donors *122*; high professional 223; industrial 289; international 46, 152, 194, 232; living 188; phytosanitary 212
Standards and Trade Development Faculty 212
Standing Committee on Nutrition 17
State of the World's Children (annual publication) 17
STDF *see* Standards and Trade Development Faculty
Stern, Ernie 199
Stewart, Frances 89
Stockholm Action Plan 57
Strong, Maurice 58
Sustainable Development Goals 3–5, *24*, 25, 34–7, 76–7, 91–2, 103, 123–5, 140–2, 189, 203–6, 229–33, 244–5, 252–6, 263–5, 290–1; and Addis Ababa Action Agenda 143; cross-cutting 231; expanding 92; expenditures 257; framework 258, 263; Fund 106, 256; implementation 112, 190, 258–60; priorities 256; prioritizing data collection 140; secretariat 290
The Sustainable Development Goals Report 2019 288
sustaining peace 4, 68, 72, 75, 96, 99–105, 107, 109, 111, 113–17, 263; agenda 103; calls for the PBC to focus on its three main functions 102; framework 106; resolutions 96–101, 103–5, 107; service of 102–3
Sutherland, Peter 138
Syria 50, 52, 127, 269, 275, 279
system 1–4, 37–41, 44–5, 54, 68–70, 72–5, 97–102, 165–8, 210–16, 221–33, 237–8, 243–5, 249–50, 254, 265–9; capitalist 201; decentralized 257; dual-reporting 256; economic 90, 142; global 265; international 277; managerial 272; organizations 177, 238; partnership 254; political 268; reform 217; statistical 72; universal 271–2; voting 202
systematic abuses of civil and political rights 85

Terms of Reference 99, 117, 139, 224
Third Financing for Development Conference 2015 25
Third UN 290 Thunberg, Greta 62
TNCs *see* trans-national corporations
Tolba, Mostafa 60
ToR *see* Terms of Reference
torture 82, 84, 141
Toye, John 38, 198
Toye, Richard 38, 198
trade 11–12, 15–16, 22, 33–4, 36, 59–60, 85, 91, 201, 211–14, 217, 219, 275, 278–9; agenda 16,

212, 218; agreements 33; disputes 217; free 137; global 15, 212, 214; governance 212, 214, 216; industrial 10; international 15, 211; liberalizing 48, 214; negotiations 190, 211–13, 216–17

trafficking, and exploitation 137

trans-national corporations 169, 180, 187

transaction costs 141–2, 144

Transforming Economies, Realizing Rights 75

transgender 74

treaties 10, 17, 28, 59–60, 83, 138, 179, 280–1

Truman, Harry S. 25, 276

Trump, Donald J. 43, 46, 276–7, 279

Trump administration 43, 46, 212, 215–16, 263, 277

Trust Fund for Partnerships 169

trust funds 27, 153, 155, 158, 166, 168, 253, 257

UDHR *see* Universal Declaration of Human Rights

Ul Haq, Mahbub 19, 89

UK *see* United Kingdom

UN 3–5, 56–7, 60, 63–5, 68, 70, 109, 111, 113–16, 155, 157, 169, 177–80, 271–3, 286–9; accountability framework *222*; agencies 177; Agenda 2030 221; Board of Auditors 222, 224, 229; Charter 3, 5, 20, 29, 32, 40, 80–1, 83, 85, 87, 97, 125, 129, 184–5, 193; Charter Articles 10, 14, 40, 153, 158; country team 74, 86, 101–3, 111, 230, 241, 250–3, 259, 270; Development Programme 80, 152, 253; Development System 167, 190, 210, 229, 252, 263; Environment Programme 56, 58; establishes the Centre on Transnational Corporations 166; *Financing for Development: Progress and Prospects 2018* (New York 2018) *180*; Foundation 166, 168–9; Fund for International Partnerships 166, 168–9; global ad hoc conferences *21*; global commitments 190; and global governance 204, 281; governing bodies 41, 154, 160, 221, 223–6; Office on Drugs and Crime 11–13, 29, 81, 139; Peace Operations 98; and private funders 166; resident coordinators 26, 74, 86, 101, 103, 106, 230–1, 241, 250–1, 253, 256, 259, 264, 268, 270–1; Sustainable Development Group 178, 253–4, 256

UN Children's Fund 1, 11, 13, 17, 19, 22, 26, 74, 87, 152–4, 159–60, 166, 172–4, 200, 258; activities in helping countries 29; Private Fundraising and Partnerships 172; Thematic SDG Funds 167

UN Conference Financing for Development 23, 25, 32, 36, 40, 180, 186–7, 189, 281

UN Conference of the Parties, Paris 2015 and 2018 19

UN Conference on Environment and Development 1992 (Rio Earth Summit) 57, 89

UN Conference on Financing for Development 36

UN Conference on Sustainable Development 2012 35, 57, 59, 281

UN Conference on the Human Environment, Stockholm 1972 2, 18, 33, 56–9, 61–2, 88, 205

UN Conference on Trade and Development 11–13, 15–16, 26, 33–4, 201, 211–12, 214, 288

UN Convention Against Corruption 2003 29

UN Convention of All Forms of Discrimination Against Women 1985 68

UN Convention of the Law of the Sea 1982 18

UN Convention of the Rights of the Child 1989 17

UN Convention on Biological Diversity 1992 19

UN Convention on the Nationality of Married Women 1957 69

UN Convention Relating to the Status of Refugees 1951 144

UN Democracy Fund 169, 188

UN Department of Global Communications 191

UN Development Assistance Framework 250

UN Development Coordination Office 244–5, 260

UN Development Group 35, 249–51, 254

UN Development Operations Coordination Office 253

UN Development Programme 11–13, 19–20, 26–7, 73–4, 86–9, 135, 138–9, 154–5, 172, 174, 229–31, 238, 240–1, 258–9, 288; country programs 190; Independent Evaluation Office 190; Innovations and Development Alliances Group 172; offices 240; partnerships 172; program results 190; staff 20, 240, 260; thematic priorities 240

UN Development System 1–6, 9–17, 19–21, 25–9, 87–8, 151–7, 159–61, 202–8, 210–13, 221–2, 229–33, 243–5, 249–61, 263–72, 286–92; agenda 3; alphabet soup *13*; contributions to *156*; coordination structures 156; country programs 269; engagement at country level 167; entities 151–3, 172, 265, 270; funding contributions 153; organizations 4, 25, 27–8, 74, 171–2, 212, 221, 235, 240, 243–5, 257, 290–1; outlining priorities for its improved functioning 251; priorities of climate change, reducing inequalities, and providing resources for poorer countries 205

UN Economic Commission for Africa 12–13, 17, 19, 88, 200, 242

UN Economic Commission for Europe 12–13, 192, 201

UN Economic Commission for Latin America and the Caribbean 12–13, 192, 201

UN Economic and Social Commission for Asia and the Pacific 12–13

UN Economic and Social Commission for Western Asia 12–13

UN Educational, Scientific and Cultural Organization 10–11, 13, 17, 22, 28, 63, 73, 87, 154, 174, 190, 193, 241, 287, 291

UN Entity for Gender Equality and the Empowerment of Women *see also UN* Women 11

UN Environment Fund 60

UN Environment Programme 2, 11–13, 18, 56–9, 63, 186, 244

UN Ethics Office 226–8

UN Evaluation Group 225

UN Financing for Development meetings 21, 23, 25, 32, 36, 40, 180, 186–7, 189, 281

UN Food and Agriculture Organization 10–11, 13, 17, 28–9, 75, 152, 174, 193, 212, 238, 241, 244, 265, 287

UN Framework Convention on Climate Change 18, 32, 60, 63, 282

UN Funding Compact 151, 153, 156, 160–2, 165, 167, 231, 253–4, 256–7, 265

UN General Assembly 15–17, 38–40, 73, 75, 81, 83, 86–7, 98–9, 101–2, 109–11, 113, 115–17, 167, 251, 276–7; and the Biennial Strategic Framework and Budget for approval by the 74; and civil society 112; and ECOSOC 38, 81, 110, 229; and the Security Council 99

UN Global Compact 5, 135, 166, 170, 179, 280

UN High Commissioner for Human Rights 77, 84, 193, *194*, 206, 258

UN High Commissioner for Refugees 1, 11, 73, 128, 135, 138–9, 144, 152–4, 171, 173–4, 229, 252, 265

UN Human Settlements Programme 11

UN Industrial Development Organization 11–13, 28, 60, 154, 211–12, 227, 287

UN International Convention for the Protection of All Persons from Enforced Disappearance 84

UN International Fund for Agricultural Development 11, 13, 16, 193, 239–40, 244

UN Joint Programme on HIV and AIDS 11–13, 21, 23, 28, 74, 76, 90, 157, 168, 176, 193, 224, 229

UN Monetary and Financial Conference, Bretton Woods 1944 10

UN Office for Partnerships 168–9

UN Office for Project Services 13, 81, 171, 244

UN Population Fund 11–13, 17–18, 74, 76, 87, 152, 154, 174, 223–4, 265, 276

UN Relief and Rehabilitation Agency 10–11

UN Relief and Works Agency for Palestine Refugees in the Near East 1, 11, 152, 154, 265, 276

UN Summit on Climate Change 2019 205

UN Sustainable Development Cooperation Framework 102, 167, 253, 256, 259–60

UN Vienna Convention for the Protection of the Ozone Layer 1985 18, 60

UN Women 2, 11–13, 17, 68–9, 73–7, 154, 171, 173, 178, 240, 244, 250

UN World Tourism Organization 11, 13, 224

UNAIDS *see* UN Joint Programme for Aids

UNCLOS *see* UN Convention of the Law of the Sea

UNCT *see* UN country team

UNCTAD *see* Conference on Trade and Development

UNCTC *see* UN Centre on Transnational Corporations

UNDAF *see* UN Development Assistance Framework

UNDCO *see* UN Development Coordination Office

UNDF *see* UN Democracy Fund

UNDP *see* UN Development Programme

UNDS *see* UN Development System

UNEG *see* UN Evaluation Group

UNEP *see* UN Environment Programme

UNESCO *see* UN Educational, Scientific and Cultural Organization

UNF *see* United Nations Foundation

UNFCCC *see* UN Framework Convention on Climate Change

UNFIP *see* United Nations Fund for International Partnerships

UNFPA *see* UN Population Fund

UNGC *see* UN Global Compact

UNHCHR *see* UN High Commissioner for Human Rights

UNHCR *see* UN High Commissioner for Refugees

UNICEF *see* UN Children's Fund

UNIDO *see* UN Industrial Development Organization

UNIFEM *see* United Nations Fund for Women

UNIHP *see* United Nations Intellectual History Project

United Kingdom 10, 16–17, 53, 63, 83, 113, 153, 167, 204, 214, 224, 232, 265, 267, 279

United Nations *see* UN

United Nations Fund for Women 73

United Nations Intellectual History Project 3

United Nations Peacebuilding Architecture 109

United States 9–10, 12, 43–4, 48, 52–3, 62–3, 70, 72, 152–3, 190–1, 201–2, 204, 214, 216, 275–7; commitment to development in the UN 9; contributions to the new Expanded Programme of Technical Assistance 26; and emerging powers 274; and Europe 44–5, 53; leadership 282; non-profit Foundation for the Global Compact 170, 190; and the North Atlantic Treaty Organization 277; segregated 83; and the United Kingdom 17; withholding

contributions to the UN regular and peacekeeping budgets 276
Universal Periodic Review 85, 104
Universal Postal Union 3, 11, 28, 87, 224, 227, 289
UNODC *see* UN, Office on Drugs and Crime
UNOP *see* UN Office for Partnerships
UNOPS *see* UN Office for Project Services
UNRWA *see* UN Relief and Works Agency for Palestinian Refugees
UNRRA *see* UN Relief and Rehabilitation Agency
UNSDCF *see* UN Sustainable Development Cooperation Framework
UNWTO *see* UN World Tourism Organization
UPR *see* Universal Periodic Review
UPU *see* Universal Postal Union
Urquhart, Brian 92
US see United States
Utstein group 160

VNRs *see* Voluntary National Reviews
Volcker, Paul 166
voluntary contributions 74, 81, 106, 152, 154, 166–8, 175, 253, 267; additional 114, 157; important 267; specified 166; total 166
Voluntary National Reviews 25, 37, 41, 91, 190–1, 232
votes 38–9, 47, 185, 202, 207
voting rights 87, 89, 155, 160, 206
Vreeland, James 201

Waldheim, Kurt 44
wars 10, 12, 47, 50, 52, 69, 75, 98, 100, 107, 110, 276, 289
Washington 10, 17–18, 25, 44–6, 53, 62, 186, 200, 202, 276–7; based international financial institutions 5; conversations on the design of the future UN 10; neoliberal consensus 288
Washington Consensus 16, 23, 88, 200
water 21, 24, 35, 59, 69, 76–7, 85, 91–2, 172; management 172; resources 85, 275; security 275; sources 69
weapons 46, 69, 179
Weapons of Mass Destruction 47
WEF *see* World Economic Forum, Davos
Western donors 45, 153, 165, 186
WFP *see* World Food Programme
whistleblowing 228
WHO *see* World Health Organization
WHS *see* World Humanitarian Summit, Istanbul
WIPO *see* World Intellectual Property Organization
WMD *see* Weapons of Mass Destruction
WMO *see* World Meteorological Organization
Wolfensohn, James 206
women 2, 11–12, 17, 20–1, 68–78, 88–9, 91–2,

105, 122, 124, 171, 173, 187, 190, 244; advancement of 17, 69–71, 73–4; conferences on 2, 68–70; empowerment of 11, 34, 69, 180, 250; and girls 24, 72, 76–8, 124, 128, 141; indigenous 76; integrated 72; led peace movements 72; migrant 136, 143–4; movements of 68, 70–1, 73, 76–8; peace movements of 72; political rights of 69; religions stereotype 71; rights of 17, 72, 76; role of 17, 20, 76; rural 72; status of 13, 69–71, 75, 81, 195; upper-caste 69
women's rights 69–71, 74, 78, 89; attacking 71; married 69; protecting 70; recognizing 72
work 25–7, 63–4, 68–9, 73–4, 76, 82–3, 86–9, 99, 102–7, 111–14, 116–17, 240–2, 244–5, 251–3, 267–8; domestic 77, 140; equal 69; on human rights 73; humanitarian 1, 87, 131; normative 75, 269; organizational 76; pioneering 76; regular 73; and society 275; unpaid 75–6
working groups 35, 56, 139, 180
World Bank 15, 17, 19, 36, 38, 43–4, 46, 48, 50, 53, 105–6, 114, 188–9, 198–208, 212; collaborates with the United Nations 104; financially dominant 257; and the IMF voting systems 202; and the International Development Association 33; and International Monetary Fund 87, 211; provides concessional loans 15; sets up the International Development Authority 199; and the World Trade Organization 225
World Commission on Environment and Development 18, 59
World Conference of the United Nations Decade for Women: Equality, Development and Peace 1980 70
World Conference on Education for All 1990 89
World Conference on Human Rights, Vienna 1993 72, 89
World Conference on Women, Mexico 1975 77
World Conference on Women and Development 1976 88
World Drug Report 288
world economy 16, 34, 38, 199, 203–4, 207
World Food Programme 1, 11, 13, 26, 54, 73–4, 152, 154, 172–4, 224, 229, 265
World Health Assembly, Geneva 2018 46
World Health Organization 3, 10–11, 13, 17, 28, 44–6, 73, 76, 152–4, 159–61, 171, 174–7, 204, 238, 265
World Heritage Convention 63
World Heritage Sites 17
World Humanitarian Summit, Istanbul 123–4, 156
World Intellectual Property Organization 11, 13
World Meteorological Organization 11, 13, 18, 60, 227, 238
World Organization for Animal Health 212

World Social Forum 195
World Summit for Social Development, Copenhagen 1995 71, 89
World Summit on Sustainable Development, Johannesburg 2002 57, 59
World Trade Organization 2, 5, 10, 16, 33, 38–9, 43, 139, 155, 186, 188, 190, 207, 210–19, 225; contribution to global development 217; in global development 211; houses and manages the Standards and Trade Development Faculty 212; model 38; negotiations 211, 213; reform 215, 217–19; system 212, 214, 217
World War I 33

World War II 15, 33, 52, 87, 113, 208, 214, 274, 276
World Wildlife Fund 279
WTO *see* World Trade Organization
WWF *see* World Wildlife Fund
WWI *see* World War I
WWII *see* World War II

Yanguas, Paul 157
Yeo, George 52
youth 65, 72, 89, 105, 122, 124, 129, 187, 271, 273; activities 136; employment 90; empowerment 114; groups 190; workshops 145